T3-BGW-994

THE FLOOD MYTH

THE FLOOD MYTH

EDITED BY *Alan Dundes*

University of California Press *Berkeley · Los Angeles · London*

BL
325
.D4
F55
1988

University of California Press
Berkeley and Los Angeles, California

University of California Press, Ltd.
London, England

© 1988 by
The Regents of the University of California

Library of Congress Cataloging-in-Publication Data
The Flood myth.
Bibliography: p.
Includes index.
1. Deluge—Comparative studies. I. Dundes, Alan.
BL325.D4F55 1988 291.1′3 87-10832
ISBN 0-520-05973-5 (alk. paper)

Printed in the United States of America

1 2 3 4 5 6 7 8 9

I am indebted to anthropological folklorist Lee Davis for a bibliographical survey of flood scholarship she undertook in 1977. I thank all the authors and publishers of the essays selected for their kindness in allowing me to reprint copyrighted materials.

Contents

Introduction

Of all the myths of the world, probably none has attracted more attention through the centuries of recorded time than the flood myth. Literally dozens upon dozens of books, monographic treatises, and essays have been devoted to the consideration of this narrative. Quantitatively speaking, the flood myth must surely be the most studied narrative ever. No other myth or folktale or legend has been subjected to anything like the intensive scrutiny that has been lavished on the story of a cataclysmic deluge.

Modern technology and medicine have succeeded in eliminating many of the dread diseases and in reducing the dire consequences of natural disasters which have plagued mankind over the centuries. Yet they have failed to check the ravages of fire and flood. Every year forest fires and flash floods take their deadly toll in lives and property around the globe. Even the latest advances in water resource management and flood control, for example, seem unable to prevent the almost annual inundations of certain waterways. Navigable rivers have long attracted human settlers to dwell along their banks, and the history of many of the world's greatest cities is in part a history of such settlements. If the absence of water in drought-ridden areas is one extreme, having too much water is also a curse. Floods continue to be a hard fact of life for many riparian communities. In theory, at least, this could be one reason for the widespread distribution and long-standing popularity of the flood myth. (This literal understanding of the flood myth contrasts sharply with my own notion that the myth is a metaphor—a cosmogonic projection of salient details of human birth insofar as every infant is delivered from a "flood" of amniotic fluid.)

In order to place the flood story in context, one must first identify it generically as a myth. In comparison to the large numbers of folktales and especially legends recounted and reported, one finds that there are relatively few myths. A myth may be defined as a sacred narrative explaining how the world or humans came to be in their present form.

Folklorists often refer to myths by motif number in accordance with the system devised by Stith Thompson in his six-volume *Motif-Index of*

Folk-Literature, initially published in 1932–1936 and later revised in 1955–1958. The first volume contains motifs with A through C prefixes. A includes "Mythological Motifs," B is "Animal Motifs," and C is "Tabu Motifs." It is among the A motifs that one can locate nearly all of the principal myths ever told. Major myth types so listed include: A625, World parents: sky-father and earth-mother as parents of the universe; A641, Cosmic egg: the universe brought forth from an egg; A1010, Deluge: Inundation of whole world or section; A1200, Creation of man; and A1335, Origin of death.

The *Motif-Index* includes both categories and subcategories of motifs. Accordingly, the deluge actually falls within A1000–A1099: world calamities and renewals. In this section, for example, are A1000, World catastrophe: the world is destroyed, and A1030, World-fire: a conflagration destroys the earth. These categories are in addition to A1010, Deluge. Under Deluge, one can discover A1018, Flood as punishment, as well as the more particular A1018.3, Flood brought as revenge for injury. Similarly, under the more general A1020, Escape from deluge, we note A1021, Deluge: escape in boat (ark); A1022, Escape from deluge on mountain; and A1023, Escape from deluge on tree.

The motif system is only a classification scheme and is not intended as a substitute for analysis. Nevertheless, someone seriously interested in the flood or deluge myth might wish to consult such other related motifs as A810, Primeval water: in the beginning everything is covered with water, or A812, Earth Diver. From a raft in the primeval sea, the creator sends down animals to try to bring up earth. After a number of animals have failed, one (often the muskrat) succeeds. The earth is made from the soil brought up.

After each motif heading are bibliographical references to published versions of the narrative in which such motifs appear, and these references serve as a useful preliminary guide to an approximation of the geographical distribution of a particular motif. No motif has worldwide distribution, and most motifs are limited to just one or two continents. While scholars specializing in myth should in theory refer to the *Motif-Index* to obtain references to earlier studies of a given narrative and to gain some idea of that motif's dispersion, in practice few students of myth outside the folklore field utilize it.

There are several obvious reasons for the long-standing and apparently unending fascination with the flood myth. First of all, the flood myth is one of the most widely diffused narratives known. Only in Africa is it relatively rare. It is therefore a narrative of interest to most peoples of the world. Yet surely the primary stimulus for the veritable "flood" of scholarship on the subject is the occurrence of the story in the Old

Testament. The adventure of Noah and the Ark is known throughout the Judeo-Christian world and beyond through the ceaseless efforts of missionaries. As Genesis is part of the sacred history of Western civilization, the flood myth is not just another interesting oral narrative told by tribal peoples in remote corners of the globe. While one might imagine that the recognition that non-Western peoples also had a flood myth could be used to challenge the sacral quality of the Genesis story of Noah, quite the opposite occurred. The comparative study of flood myths was invoked as documentary "proof" that the flood had indeed been a worldwide historical event. Why would so many peoples around the world tell a story about a flood, it was argued, if it were not an actual catastrophic happening, so awful that it remained permanently etched in the folk memory preserved by oral tradition?

Many Bible scholars have felt compelled to take a stand on the question of whether Genesis (and other parts of the Bible as well) are to be understood literally—as essentially a historical record. While some argued that the flood might have been only a local phenomenon (in the Near East), others insisted that the deluge was universal. Either way, the flood was perceived as history, not fiction or metaphor. Thus the debate on the flood in theological circles often turned not on the historicity issue but rather on whether the Noachian deluge was local or global.

It was in the nineteenth century that the flood myth took on new meaning. The development of geology in particular seemed to challenge the postulated historical nature of the account of the world's creation in Genesis. Darwinian evolutionary theory, which proposed a gradual creation of Homo sapiens from earlier primate ancestors, was also an obvious threat to those believing in the instantaneous creation of man by God. There were numerous attempts to reconcile "science" with the Bible, and a good many of these efforts concentrated on the flood. It was almost as though the integrity of the Bible rested on one's attitude toward the flood. If the historicity of the flood could be maintained in the face of scientific knowledge, then the Bible itself as a bastion of Christian faith could remain safe and intact. But it was not science alone which challenged the special status accorded to the flood myth in Genesis. It was the developing field of comparative mythology as well.

In 1872, a young Assyriologist, George Smith, working in the British Museum, came upon a cuneiform tablet which had been found earlier by archaeologists excavating at Nineveh, and on this table was an account of the flood "earlier" than the biblical account. Before 1872, it had been possible to assume that all the other, various, flood myths reported from different areas of the globe were simply derivative from the biblical narrative. With the discovery of earlier Near Eastern flood myths—from Babylonia, for example—which seemed to be cognate with the Genesis version, a new tack had to be taken by the literalists. Even if the biblical account were derived from a Sumerian version, it was maintained that the Sumerian text—as well as the biblical one—was still a bona fide indication that an actual flood had occurred. Thus neither geological evidence nor comparative mythology has daunted Fundamentalists in their unswerving faith and belief in the literal truth of the flood as told in Genesis.

The question of the historical authenticity of the biblical flood myth is still being hotly debated in the twentieth century. For this reason, the narrative continues to be studied by theologians as well as by anthropologists, classicists, folklorists, and geologists. This casebook is designed to bring together some of the highlights of the massive scholarship inspired by the flood myth. Although folklorists do not like to give priority to any one version of a narrative they investigate, in this instance it would be foolish to deny the very special position held by the version of the flood myth in Genesis. That is why we shall begin with that text, followed by a discussion of its composite nature.

The bombshell lecture given by George Smith in December 1872, announcing his startling discovery, is the first of several essays concerned with other versions of the flood myth which circulated in the ancient Near East. The comparative treatments by Frymer-Kensky and Follansbee demonstrate how other Near Eastern versions can stimulate new and intriguing interpretations of the Genesis flood account. Archaeologist Woolley's essay and classicist Calder's discussion of a Greek version of the deluge illustrate the literal-historical approach to the flood. A wider comparative outlook is represented by a brief selection from James George Frazer's extensive consideration of "The Great Flood" as well as by considerations by Kelsen and Róheim, who respectively seek underlying moral and psychological elements in the narratives. The psychological perspective is continued in my own short study of the flood as a male fantasy.

Then, to gain insight into the nature of specific flood traditions in particular areas of the world, the book presents analyses of the flood myth in Mesoamerica (Horcasitas), South America (Lammel), aboriginal Australia (Kolig), Africa (Kähler-Meyer), the Philippines (Demetrio), Thailand (Lindell, Swahn, and Tayanin), and India (Koppers, Shulman). These diverse essays provide not only a generous sampling of flood myths outside the biblical and Near Eastern orbit, but they also suggest an array of different methods of interpreting myth.

After a substantial look at the New World, Africa, and Asia, we return to Europe and the Near East by examining Jewish apocryphal versions of the flood (Ginzberg) and a widespread folktale clearly inspired by the biblical plot, "The Devil in the Ark" (Utley), which concludes the comparative section of this book.

The final portion of the coverage of the flood myth consists of samples of the struggle to reconcile the findings of science with the literal approach to the biblical flood. These essays cover the seventeenth (Allen), eighteenth (Rappaport), nineteenth (Moore), and twentieth (Gould) centuries. They show just how important the flood myth has been in theology and the history of science. A selected bibliography of further readings on the flood myth is designed to guide readers desiring more information on the subject.

The essays chosen for this volume come from a wide variety of sources ranging from scientific and religious periodicals to unpublished master's theses. Many are admittedly esoteric, but all add something to our understanding of this intriguing narrative which continues to have impact on our lives. The olive branch as a symbol of peace comes from the flood myth, and even those who do not accept the flood as history are obliged to recognize the importance of such symbols in the contemporary world.

The Flood (Genesis 6–9)

Most readers are already familiar with the account of the flood in Genesis, but since it has been the direct or indirect stimulus for so much of the research devoted to the flood myth, it was thought best to remind everyone of the details of this narrative. Although Noah is first introduced at the end of Genesis 5, we begin the story with Genesis 6 and continue until the conclusion of Genesis 9 with his death. There are several excellent English translations of Genesis available, among them the Jerusalem Bible, *the* New English Bible, *and the* Anchor Bible. *The* Revised Standard Version *probably has the wording known to the majority of readers, however, so it was decided to use this translation. The newer translations differ only slightly with respect to occasional individual words or phrases.*

6 When men began to multiply on the face of the ground, and
daughters were born to them, 2 the sons of God saw that the daughters of men were fair; and they took to wife such of them as they chose.
3 Then the Lord said, "My spirit shall not abide in man for ever, for he
is flesh, but his days shall be a hundred and twenty years." 4 The
Nephilim were on the earth in those days, and also afterward, when
the sons of God came in to the daughters of men, and they bore children to them. These were the mighty men that were of old, the men of
renown.

5 The Lord saw that the wickedness of man was great in the earth,
and that every imagination of the thoughts of his heart was only evil
continually. 6 And the Lord was sorry that he had made man on the
earth, and it grieved him to his heart. 7 So the Lord said, "I will blot
out man whom I have created from the face of the ground, man and
beast and creeping things and birds of the air, for I am sorry that I have
made them." 8 But Noah found favor in the eyes of the Lord.

9 These are the generations of Noah. Noah was a righteous man,
blameless in his generation; Noah walked with God. 10 And Noah had
three sons, Shem, Ham, and Japheth.

The Scripture quotations contained herein are from the Revised Standard Version of the Bible, copyrighted 1946, 1952, 1971 by the Division of Christian Education of the National Council of the Churches of Christ in the USA, and are used by permission. All rights reserved.

11 Now the earth was corrupt in God's sight, and the earth was
filled with violence. 12 And God saw the earth, and behold, it was corrupt; for all flesh had corrupted their way upon the earth. 13 And God
said to Noah, "I have determined to make an end of all flesh; for the
earth is filled with violence through them; behold, I will destroy them
with the earth. 14 Make yourself an ark of gopher wood; make rooms
in the ark, and cover it inside and out with pitch. 15 This is how you
are to make it: the length of the ark three hundred cubits, its breadth
fifty cubits, and its height thirty cubits. 16 Make a roof for the ark, and
finish it to a cubit above; and set the door of the ark in its side; make it
with lower, second, and third decks. 17 For behold, I will bring a flood
of waters upon the earth, to destroy all flesh in which is the breath
of life from under heaven; everything that is on the earth shall die.
18 But I will establish my covenant with you; and you shall come into
the ark, you, your sons, your wife, and your sons' wives with you.
19 And of every living thing of all flesh, you shall bring two of every
sort into the ark, to keep them alive with you; they shall be male and
female. 20 Of the birds according to their kinds, and of the animals
according to their kinds, of every creeping thing of the ground according to its kind, two of every sort shall come in to you, to keep them
alive. 21 Also take with you every sort of food that is eaten, and store it
up; and it shall serve as food for you and for them." 22 Noah did this;
he did all that God commanded him.

7 Then the Lord said to Noah, "Go into the ark, you and all your
household, for I have seen that you are righteous before me in this
generation. 2 Take with you seven pairs of all clean animals, the male
and his mate; and a pair of the animals that are not clean, the male
and his mate; 3 and seven pairs of the birds of the air also, male and
female, to keep their kind alive upon the face of all the earth. 4 For in
seven days I will send rain upon the earth forty days and forty nights;
and every living thing that I have made I will blot out from the face of
the ground." 5 And Noah did all that the Lord had commanded him.

6 Noah was six hundred years old when the flood of waters came
upon the earth. 7 And Noah and his sons and his wife and his sons'
wives with him went into the ark, to escape the waters of the flood.
8 Of clean animals, and of animals that are not clean, and of birds, and
of everything that creeps on the ground, 9 two and two, male and female, went into the ark with Noah, as God had commanded Noah.
10 And after seven days the waters of the flood came upon the earth.

11 In the six hundredth year of Noah's life, in the second month, on
the seventeenth day of the month, on that day all the fountains of the

great deep burst forth, and the windows of the heavens were opened.
12 And rain fell upon the earth forty days and forty nights. 13 On the
very same day Noah and his sons, Shem and Ham and Japheth, and
Noah's wife and the three wives of his sons with them entered the ark,
14 they and every beast according to its kind, and all the cattle according to their kinds, and every creeping thing that creeps on the
earth according to its kind, and every bird according to its kind, every
bird of every sort. 15 They went into the ark with Noah, two and two of
all flesh in which there was the breath of life. 16 And they that entered,
male and female of all flesh, went in as God had commanded him; and
the Lord shut him in.

17 The flood continued forty days upon the earth; and the waters
increased, and bore up the ark, and it rose high above the earth. 18 The
waters prevailed and increased greatly upon the earth; and the ark
floated on the face of the waters. 19 And the waters prevailed so might-
ily upon the earth that all the high mountains under the whole heaven
were covered; 20 the waters prevailed above the mountains, covering
them fifteen cubits deep. 21 And all flesh died that moved upon the
earth, birds, cattle, beasts, all swarming creatures that swarm upon
the earth, and every man; 22 everything on the dry land in whose
nostrils was the breath of life died. 23 He blotted out every living thing
that was upon the face of the ground, man and animals and creeping
things and birds of the air; they were blotted out from the earth. Only
Noah was left, and those that were with him in the ark. 24 And the
waters prevailed upon the earth a hundred and fifty days.

8 But God remembered Noah and all the beasts and all the cattle
that were with him in the ark. And God made a wind blow over the
earth, and the waters subsided; 2 the fountains of the deep and the
windows of the heavens were closed, the rain from the heavens was
restrained, 3 and the waters receded from the earth continually. At the
end of a hundred and fifty days the waters had abated; 4 and in the
seventh month, on the seventeenth day of the month, the ark came to
rest upon the mountains of Ar'arat. 5 And the waters continued to
abate until the tenth month; in the tenth month, on the first day of the
month, the tops of the mountains were seen.

6 At the end of forty days Noah opened the window of the ark
which he had made, 7 and sent forth a raven; and it went to and fro
until the waters were dried up from the earth. 8 Then he sent forth a
dove from him, to see if the waters had subsided from the face of the
ground; 9 but the dove found no place to set her foot, and she returned to him to the ark, for the waters were still on the face of the

whole earth. So he put forth his hand and took her and brought her into the ark with him. 10 He waited another seven days, and again he sent forth the dove out of the ark; 11 and the dove came back to him in the evening, and lo, in her mouth a freshly plucked olive leaf; so Noah knew that the waters had subsided from the earth. 12 Then he waited another seven days, and sent forth the dove; and she did not return to him any more.

13 In the six hundred and first year, in the first month, the first day of the month, the waters were dried from off the earth; and Noah removed the covering of the ark, and looked, and behold, the face of the ground was dry. 14 In the second month, on the twenty-seventh day of the month, the earth was dry. 15 Then God said to Noah, 16 "Go forth from the ark, you and your wife, and your sons and your sons' wives with you. 17 Bring forth with you every living thing that is with you of all flesh—birds and animals and every creeping thing that creeps on the earth—that they may breed abundantly on the earth, and be fruitful and multiply upon the earth." 18 So Noah went forth, and his sons and his wife and his sons' wives with him. 19 And every beast, every creeping thing, and every bird, everything that moves upon the earth, went forth by families out of the ark.

20 Then Noah built an altar to the Lord, and took of every clean animal and of every clean bird, and offered burnt offerings on the altar. 21 And when the Lord smelled the pleasing odor, the Lord said in his heart, "I will never again curse the ground because of man, for the imagination of man's heart is evil from his youth; neither will I ever again destroy every living creature as I have done. 22 While the earth remains, seedtime and harvest, cold and heat, summer and winter, day and night, shall not cease."

9 And God blessed Noah and his sons, and said to them, "Be fruitful and multiply, and fill the earth. 2 The fear of you and the dread of you shall be upon every beast of the earth, and upon every bird of the air, upon everything that creeps on the ground and all the fish of the sea; into your hand they are delivered. 3 Every moving thing that lives shall be food for you; and as I gave you the green plants, I give you everything. 4 Only you shall not eat flesh with its life, that is, its blood. 5 For your lifeblood I will surely require a reckoning; of every beast I will require it and of man; of every man's brother I will require the life of man. 6 Whoever sheds the blood of man, by man shall his blood be shed; for God made man in his own image. 7 And you, be fruitful and multiply, bring forth abundantly on the earth and multiply in it."

8 Then God said to Noah and to his sons with him, 9 "Behold,
I establish my covenant with you and your descendants after you,
10 and with every living creature that is with you, the birds, the cattle,
and every beast of the earth with you, as many as came out of the ark.
11 I establish my covenant with you, that never again shall all flesh be
cut off by the waters of a flood, and never again shall there be a flood to
destroy the earth." 12 And God said, "This is the sign of the covenant
which I make between me and you and every living creature that is
with you, for all future generations: 13 I set my bow in the cloud, and
it shall be a sign of the covenant between me and the earth. 14 When I
bring clouds over the earth and the bow is seen in the clouds, 15 I will
remember my covenant which is between me and you and every living
creature of all flesh; and the waters shall never again become a flood to
destroy all flesh. 16 When the bow is in the clouds, I will look upon it
and remember the everlasting covenant between God and every living
creature of all flesh that is upon the earth." 17 God said to Noah, "This
is the sign of the covenant which I have established between me and
all flesh that is upon the earth."

18 The sons of Noah who went forth from the ark were Shem, Ham,
and Japheth. Ham was the father of Canaan. 19 These three were the
sons of Noah; and from these the whole earth was peopled.

20 Noah was the first tiller of the soil. He planted a vineyard; 21 and
he drank of the wine, and became drunk, and lay uncovered in his
tent. 22 And Ham, the father of Canaan, saw the nakedness of his father, and told his two brothers outside. 23 Then Shem and Japheth
took a garment, laid it upon both their shoulders, and walked backward and covered the nakedness of their father; their faces were turned
away, and they did not see their father's nakedness. 24 When Noah
awoke from his wine and knew what his youngest son had done to
him, 25 he said,

"Cursed be Canaan;
a slave of slaves shall he be to his brothers."
26 He also said,
"Blessed by the Lord my God be Shem;
and let Canaan be his slave.
27 God enlarge Japheth,
and let him dwell in the tents of Shem;
and let Canaan be his slave."

28 After the flood Noah lived three hundred and fifty years. 29 All
the days of Noah were nine hundred and fifty years; and he died.

The Two Flood Stories in Genesis

NORMAN C. HABEL

Scholars specializing in Bible study have suspected for some centuries that the Pentateuch (first five books of the Old Testament) in general and Genesis (the first book of the Old Testament) in particular was a composite consisting of different elements contributed by different authors and editors. While there has been a long-standing reluctance to apply any form of "literary" criticism to the Bible—its sacred status in Western civilization has discouraged such secular academic efforts—the evidence assembled by these scholars has proved difficult to dispute.

One reason why different versions of the "same" story have been joined or conflated in the Old Testament is the oral nature of the basic source material. Folklorists are familiar with the principles of "multiple existence" and "variation" which are characteristic of all *folkloristic phenomena. There can be no single version of any item of folklore. All folklore must exist in more than one place or time or both. One of the inevitable results of multiple existence and oral transmission is variation. No two versions of an item of folklore are absolutely identical.*

When an item in oral tradition is written down, the collector of the folklore often records more than one version of that item, sometimes even from the same informant. The diligent folklorist keeps the versions separate so that each version can be studied independently in its entirety. However, scientific folkloristics has existed only since the late nineteenth century. Before that time, recorders of oral tradition were often tempted to combine different versions, taking one element from one version and another element from another version. Even the famous Grimm brothers, although they claimed that they were recording folktales exactly as they were related by peasant informants, actually combined four or five versions of the same tale in the composite text they presented in various editions of their Kinder- und Hausmärchen, *which first appeared in 1812 and 1815.*

In earlier times, redactors of manuscripts would commonly add details from different versions of the same story, details which apparently contradicted each other. We find this to be the case in the Old Testament. For example, there are

Reprinted from Norman C. Habel, *Literary Criticism of the Old Testament* (Philadelphia: Fortress Press, 1971), pp. 29–42.

two separate and distinct creations of man. In one account, God creates man in his own image and he creates male and female at the same time (Genesis 1:27). In the other, God creates man first and later creates Eve from the rib of the sleeping Adam (Genesis 2:7, 21–22). Now presumably these two accounts cannot both be accurate. Either man and woman were created at the same instant or one was created first and the second later. There are many such discrepancies. Admittedly some of them are relatively minor. For example, the name of Moses' father-in-law is variously reported as Jethro (Exodus 3:1, 4:17, 18:1), as Reuel (Exodus 2:18), and as Hobab (Judges 4:11). Presumably Moses did not have three fathers-in-law and the one he had did not have three distinct names.

The same type of "literary" criticism can be applied to the New Testament. From the folklorist's perspective, the four gospels are four versions of the same legendary narrative. For instance, what were Christ's final words? In Matthew (27:46) and Mark (15:34), Jesus cried "My God, my God, why has thou forsaken me?" In Luke and John, these words do not appear. Instead (Luke 23:46), Jesus cried "Father, into thy hands I commit my spirit!" And having said this he breathed his last. According to John (19:28), Jesus said "It is finished"; and he bowed his head and gave up his spirit. Now it is possible that Jesus said all of the above, but it is reasonable to assume that only one of the three expressions was the very last thing he said. Bible scholars searching for the correct version are more concerned with such variation than folklorists who quite frankly expect such variation as an inevitable result of oral transmission.

The flood narrative in Genesis has been subjected to the same kind of textual examination. As early as 1753, a French physician, Jean Astruc, noticed that some narratives in Genesis referred to God using the name Yahweh (Jehovah) while others used Elohim, the Hebrew word for "divine being." Through the later attempts to disentangle the "documentary" sources of Genesis, scholars claimed to have discerned a "priestly" source, typically indicated in discussions by the initial letter "P"; an "E" source (from the initial letter of Elohim); and a "J" (from Jehovah) or Yahwist source among others. The diversity of sources helps to explain some of the internal inconsistencies in the biblical flood account. For example, God instructs Noah (7:2–3) to take "seven pairs of all clean animals" onto the ark and also (6:19) to bring "two of every sort into the ark." Similarly, the flood was said to have lasted "forty days" (7:17) and "one hundred and fifty days" (7:24).

While this casebook is not primarily concerned with the Bible per se, it seems appropriate in view of the undeniable centrality of the flood version in Genesis with respect to flood myth scholarship to give a sample of biblical literary criticism. The following discussion by Norman C. Habel, Professor of Old Testament at Concordia Seminary, is surely representative of the interests of Bible scholars in identifying the various narrative strands contained in Genesis. For additional discussion of the documentary sources of the Old Testament, see such works as E. A. Speiser, Genesis, 3rd ed. (Garden City, 1964), pp. lxi–lxiii. Other references include M. Noth, History of Pentateuchal Traditions (Englewood Cliffs, N.J., 1972); David L. Petersen, "The Yahwist on the

Flood," Vetus Testamentum *26 (1976): 438–446; and Victor P. Hamilton,* Handbook on the Pentateuch *(Grand Rapids, Mich., 1982), pp. 72–76. For useful comparisons of the J and P accounts, see the first part of G. Lambert, "Il n'y aura plus jamais de déluge (Genèse IX, 11),"* Nouvelle revue théologique *77 (1955): 581–601, 693–724; and the second part of W. J. Dalton, "The Background and Meaning of the Biblical Flood Narrative,"* Australasian Catholic Record *34 (1957): 292–304; 35 (1958): 23–39.*

It should be noted that there is one school of Bible scholars who, although they recognize the different strands of the flood narrative, feel strongly that the flood story as recounted in Genesis should be considered as a whole—that is, as the work of a redactor who simply combined different versions of a narrative into a composite text. See Bernhard W. Anderson, "From Analysis to Synthesis: The Interpretation of Genesis 1–11," Journal of Biblical Literature *97 (1978): 23–39; Eduard Nielsen,* Oral Tradition *(London, 1954), pp. 102–103. See also Susan Niditch,* Chaos to Cosmos: Studies in Biblical Patterns of Creation *(Chico, Calif., 1985), pp. 22–24, 59–60.*

TWO INTRODUCTIONS TO THE FLOOD STORIES

One of the conclusions to which many readers come as they study Genesis 6–9 is that there seem to be two different stories about the flood which are intertwined in these chapters. Even if we grant that a harmonizing process would naturally occur as these chapters were retold over the years, or that an editor organized these materials into an artistic unit, is there sufficient evidence remaining in the text to substantiate this frequent impression of two story lines? And if there are two such strands, are they related to the two groupings of material in Genesis 1–5?

We note that major structural divisions in Genesis are introduced by the expression, "These are the generations of. . . ." This formula normally marks a new phase in the divine plan of salvation history throughout Genesis. Genesis 6:9 begins with the same introductory formula. An appropriate introduction to the flood account appears in the following verses (Gen. 6:9–11). However, a parallel introduction had already preceded in Genesis 6:5–8 where the same basic points were made, but from a different orientation. The contrasting elements of these two introductions offer some of the most cogent arguments in favor of two distinct authors of the flood narrative.

In verses 5–8 the problem which God faces is the evil of man. This evil exists because of the "evil" in the "heart" of man. Employing rather a bold anthropomorphism the writer maintains that Yahweh "changed his mind" (*naḥam*) about the creation of man. Yahweh then deliberates with himself about "blotting out" (*maḥah*) man from "the face of the ground." The resolution of man's fate lies solely in the grace of God. Noah "found grace!" Noah is not yet depicted as a hero of superior character. Thus the basic perspective of these verses seems to be consistent with that of the so-called Yahwist text in Genesis 2–4.

In Genesis 6:9–11 the introductory formula announcing the generations of Noah leads the reader directly to Noah as a great example of faithfulness, a hero who is both righteous and "perfect" (*tamim*). He, like his grandfather Enoch (Gen. 5:24), "walked with God." The situation which God must rectify in Genesis 6:9–11, however, is not primarily the evil of man as such, but the universal corruption at large in the earth. The earth is said to be "corrupt" (*shaḥaṭ*) and filled with "violence" (*ḥamas*). Both of these Hebrew expressions suggest a chaotic force of destruction at work in the order of creation. The perspective seems to be cosmic. Man as such is not the primary concern here as he is in Genesis 6:5–8. The blame is not laid directly on man as it is in the first introduction. Rather, the viewpoint of this introduction is in harmony with that expressed by the so-called Priestly Writer of Genesis 1.

The contrast between the two introductions to the flood narrative (A. Gen. 6:5–8; B. Gen. 6:9–13) can be seen by tabulating the major features as follows:

Introductory formula:	A.
	B. These are the *generations* of . . .
Divine recognition of the situation:	A. And *Yahweh* saw that . . .
	B. And *Elohim* saw . . . and behold . . .
Nature of the problem:	A. The *evil* in *man's* heart
	B. The *corruption* of the *earth*
Extent of the problem:	A. *Man's heart* and thoughts are evil continuously and totally
	B. Violence in the *earth* Corruption of *all flesh*
The reaction of God:	A. His heart is *grieved* *Changes his mind* about man
	B. God issues a decree to Noah
The verdict of God:	A. To obliterate *life* from the *ground*
	B. To destroy *all flesh* and *the earth*
Noah's role:	A. The chosen son of *grace* (cf. Gen. 7:1)
	B. The hero who is *perfect* in his day

Distinctive terms:	A. evil, obliterate, find grace, change one's mind, grieve in the heart, from the face of the ground B. violence, corrupt, destroy, his generation, the generations of . . . , perfect
Style:	A. Presented as an episode in which Yahweh sees, suffers, changes his mind, makes a decision, and gives grace. Colorful and dramatic. B. A formal introduction to Noah, his family, and the situation. God observes the scene and decrees. Repetitious and stiff. The action and decree of God (v. 13) repeats the wording of the previously described situation (in vv. 11–12).

TWO VERSIONS OF THE FLOOD STORY

In Genesis 6:13–22 the divine instructions to Noah are formally delineated in great detail. "Two animals" from "all flesh" must be led into the ark. These must be "male and female" each "after its kind." God's intention to "destroy" all flesh is repeated (Gen. 6:13, 17) in the same formal terms as in the introduction of Genesis 6:9–12. God's relationship to Noah is defined in terms of a covenant. "I will *establish* my covenant with you" (Gen. 6:18) reappears as a central theological idiom later in Genesis. Noah executes God's demands "precisely as God commands" and thereby exhibits his character as a heroic example of unquestioning obedience.

In Genesis 7, however, God's instructions on how to load the ark are repeated. This set of directions seems to ignore the commands already given in Genesis 6:13–22. Noah is again introduced as a righteous man, that is, a man living in the right relationship with his God. He is thereupon commanded to take *seven* of each kind of animal into the ark. This time the animals are designated "man and woman" (or "a male and his mate"). God reiterates the purpose which he announced in the first introduction (Gen. 6:5–8), namely, to "obliterate" life "from the face of the ground." This devastation is to be achieved by sending rain on the land for forty days and forty nights. It seems, therefore, that Genesis 7:1–5 presents a continuation of the first introduction in Genesis 6:5–8 and reflects the same perspective, while Genesis 6:14–

22 perpetuates the features and thought of the second introduction in Genesis 6:9–13.

After Genesis 7:5 the two strands of the narrative are not as readily divided, or rather, the divergent materials do not fall into the neat blocks typical of the texts we have studied thus far. However, a reading of the two proposed sources as they have been translated in the following pages suggests the presence of two sets of materials, each of which presents a generally consistent portrait. This translation and division is given here for didactic purposes. We recognize that this kind of neat isolation of sources is not possible with the degree of accuracy which might be assumed by this translation. The retelling of the story, the transmission of the text, and the process of harmonization all argue against demanding the kind of precision in literary analysis which was presumed possible in the last century.[1] In short, the text of the following translation is designed to be illustrative rather than definitive. The distinctive and characteristic terms and expressions of each literary strand have been italicized so that the reader can observe some of the evidence for identifying one source or the other on literary grounds. This identification process also demands a consideration of the total perspective of the author involved in each case, a factor which can only be isolated by even closer scrutiny of each text in its context.

The Yahwist Version
(Gen. 6:5–8, 7:1–5, 7–8, 10, 12, 16b–17, 22–23; 8:2b–3, 6–12, 13b, 20–22)

Introduction (6:5–8)

5 And *Yahweh* saw that the *wickedness* of man was great in the earth, and that every imagination of the *thoughts of his heart* was only *wicked continually.* 6 And *Yahweh was sorry* that he had made man on the earth, and *his heart grieved.* 7 So *Yahweh* said, "I will *blot out* man whom I have created from upon *the face of the ground,* man and beast, creeping

The Priestly Writer's Version
(Gen. 6:9–13, 14–22; 7:6, 9, 11, 13–16a, 18–21, 24; 8:1–2a, 4–5, 13a, 14–17; 9:1–19)

Introduction (6:9–13)

9 *These are the generations of Noah.* Noah was a righteous man, *perfect* among his contemporaries. And Noah *walked with God.* 10 And Noah had three sons, Shem, Ham, and Japheth. 11 And the earth grew *corrupt* before *God.* And the earth was full of *violence.* 12 And *God* saw the earth and behold it was *corrupt,* for all flesh had *corrupted* its way on the earth.

[1]One of the important efforts to modify the source analysis of the flood narrative on the principles of oral tradition studies is found in E. Nielsen's work, *Oral Tradition* (Naperville, Ill.: Allenson, 1954), pp. 93–103.

things and birds of the air, because *I am sorry* that I made them." 8 But Noah *found grace in the eyes of Yahweh.*

Concerning the Ark (7:1–5)

1 So *Yahweh* said to Noah, "Go aboard the ark, you and all your household, for I have seen that you are righteous before me in this generation. 2 Take with you *seven* pairs of all *clean* animals, *the male and his mate,* and one pair of the animals that are not clean, *the male and his mate.* 3 (Also from the birds of the heaven seven pair, male and female), to keep their seed alive upon *the face of* the earth. 4 For in seven days time I will *cause it to rain* upon the earth *40 days and 40 nights,* and I will *blot out* everything *animated* which I made, from *the face of the ground.* 5 So Noah did just as *Yahweh* had commanded him.

The Advent of the Flood (7:7–8, 10, 12, 16b)

7 Then Noah and his sons and his wife boarded the ark to escape the waters of the flood. 8 From the *clean*

13 And *God* said to Noah, "I have determined to make an end of *all flesh,* for the earth is filled with *violence* through them and behold I will annihilate (*corrupt*) them *with* the earth."

Concerning the Ark (6:14–22)

14 "Make yourself an ark of resinous wood. Make it with reeds and cover it with pitch inside and out. 15 This is how you are to make it: the length of the ark 300 cubits, its breadth 50 cubits and its height 30 cubits. 16 Make a roof for the ark and finish it to a cubit above, and set the door of the ark in its side; make it with the first, second and third decks. 17 For my part, behold I am bringing the flood of waters upon the earth to annihilate (*corrupt*) *all flesh* in which is the breath of life under heaven. 18 But *I will establish my covenant* with you, and you shall go on board the ark, you, your sons, your wife, and your sons' wives along with you. 19 And from every living thing of *all flesh, two of each sort,* you shall bring aboard the ark, to save their lives with yours; they must be *male and female.* 20 From the birds according to their kind, from every creeping thing of the ground *according to its kind,* two of every sort shall come in to you to keep them alive. 21 And take with you every sort of food which is eaten and store it up, and it shall serve *for food* for you and them. 22 So Noah did just as *God* had commanded him. *So he did.*

The Advent of the Flood (7:6, 9, 11, 13–16a)

6 And Noah was *600 years old* when the flood of waters came upon the earth. (9 Two of each kind boarded

animals and animals that are *not clean,* and from the birds, and from everything that creeps on the ground (they boarded).
10 After *seven* days the waters of the flood came upon the earth. 12 And *rain* fell upon the earth *40 days and 40 nights.* 16b and *Yahweh* shut him (Noah) in.

the ark with Noah, *male and female,* as *God* had commanded Noah.)

11 In the *600th year* of Noah's life, in the 2nd month, on the *17th* day of the month, *on the very day,* all the fountains of the *great deep* burst forth and the windows of heaven were opened. . . . 13 *On the very same day* Noah and his sons, Shem, Ham and Japheth, and Noah's wife and the three wives of his sons with them, boarded the ark, 14 they and every beast *according to its kind* and all the cattle *according to their kinds,* and everything that creeps on the earth *according to its kind,* and every bird *according to its kind,* every bird of every sort. 15 They boarded the ark with Noah, *two and two of all flesh* in which there was the breath of life. 16 And those who boarded, *male and female* from *all flesh,* entered as *God* had commanded him.

The Flood (7:17, 22–23)

17 And there was a flood on the earth for *40 days.* And the waters increased and lifted the ark and it rose above the earth. 22 Everything on the dry land in whose nostrils were the *breath of life* died. 23 He *blotted out* everything *animated* which was on the *face of the ground,* both man and beast, creeping things and birds of the heaven. They were *blotted out* from the earth. Only Noah was left and those that were with him in the ark.

The Flood (7:18–21, 24)

18 The waters *prevailed* and increased *greatly,* and the ark went upon the face of the waters. 19 And the waters *prevailed exceedingly* upon the earth and covered *all* the high mountains which are under *all* the heavens. 20 The waters *prevailed* above the mountains, covering them fifteen cubits deep. 21 And *all flesh expired* that moved on the earth, birds, cattle, beasts, all *swarming creatures who swarm* on the earth, and every man. 24 And the waters *prevailed* upon the earth *150 days.*

The End of the Flood
(8:2b–3, 6–12, 13b)

2b Then the rain was restrained from heaven. 3a And the waters receded

The End of the Flood
(8:1–2a, 4–5, 13a, 14–19)

1 Then God *remembered* Noah and all the beasts and all the cattle that

from the earth continually. 6a And at the end of *40 days* Noah opened the window of the ark which he had made. 7 And he sent forth a raven; and it went to and fro until the waters were dried up from the earth. 8 Then he sent forth a dove from him, to see if the waters had *subsided* from the face of the ground. 9 But the dove found no *resting place* for her foot, so she returned to him into the ark, for the waters were still upon *the face of* all the earth. And he stretched forth his hand and took her and brought her into the ark with him. 10 He waited another *seven days* and again he sent forth the dove out of the ark. 11 And the dove came back to him in the evening, and lo, in her mouth a freshly plucked olive branch. So Noah knew the waters had subsided from the earth. 12 Then he waited another *seven days* and sent forth the dove and she did not return to him any more. 13b So Noah removed the covering of the ark, and looked and behold *the face of the ground* was dry.

were with him in the ark. And *God* made a wind blow on the earth, and the waters *subsided.* 2a And *the fountains of the deep* and the windows of heaven were closed. 3b At the end of *150 days* the waters had *abated.* 4 And in the 7th month, on the *17th day* of the month the ark came to rest on the mountains of Ararat. 5 And the waters continued to abate until the *10th month;* and in the *10th month,* the *1st day* of the month, the tops of the mountains were seen. 13a In the *601st year,* in the *1st month,* on the *1st day* of the month, the waters were dried up from the earth. 14 In the *2nd month,* on the *27th day* of the month, the earth was dry. 15 *And God* ordered Noah: 16 "Go out from the ark, you and your wife, and your sons and your sons' wives with you. 17 Bring forth with you every living thing that is with you of *all flesh*—birds and animals and *every creeping thing that creeps* on the earth—that they may *breed abundantly* and be *fruitful and multiply* on the earth." 18 So Noah went forth, and his sons and his wife and his sons' wives with him. 19 And every beast, every creeping thing, and every bird, everything that moves upon the earth, went forth by families out of the ark.

Conclusion (8:20–22)

20 Then Noah built an altar to *Yahweh* and took from every *clean animal* and every *clean bird* and offered burnt offerings on the altar. 21 When *Yahweh smelled* the pleasing odor *Yahweh said in his heart,* "I will never again *curse the ground* because of man for the *imagination of man's heart* is *wicked* from his youth. And I will never again smite all living creatures. 22 While the earth endures,

Conclusion (9:1–17)

1 And *God blessed Noah* and his sons, and said to them, "*Be fruitful and multiply,* and fill the earth. 2 The fear of you and the dread of you shall be upon every bird of the air, upon everything that creeps on the ground and all the flesh of the sea; into your hand they are delivered. 3 Every moving thing that lives shall be food for you; and as I gave you the green plants, I give you everything. 4 Only you shall

seedtime and harvest, cold and heat,
summer and winter, day and night,
shall not cease."

not eat flesh with its life, that is, its
blood. 5 For your lifeblood I will
surely require a reckoning; of every
beast I will require it and of man;
of every man's brother I will require
the life of man. 6 Whoever sheds the
blood of man, by man shall his blood
be shed; for *God* made man *in his*
own image. 7 And you *be fruitful and*
multiply, bring forth abundantly on
the earth and multiply in it."
8 Then *God* said to Noah and to his
sons with him, 9 "Behold, *I establish*
my covenant, with you and your *de-*
scendants after you, 10 and with
every living creature that is with you,
the birds, the cattle, and every beast
of the earth with you, as many as
came out of the ark. 11 *I establish my*
covenant with you, that never again
shall *all flesh* be cut off by the waters
of a flood, and never again shall there
be a flood to destroy the earth."
12 And God said, "This is *the sign of*
the covenant which I make between
you and me and every living creature
that is with you, for all future generations: 13 I set my bow in the cloud,
and it shall be a *sign of the covenant*
between me and the earth. 14 When
I bring clouds over the earth and the
bow is seen in the clouds, 15 *I will re-*
member my covenant which is between you and me and every living
creature of all flesh; and the waters
shall never again become a flood to
destroy all flesh. 16 When the bow is
in the clouds, I will look upon it and
remember the everlasting covenant
between *God* and every living creature of all flesh that is upon the earth."
17 God said to Noah, *"This is the sign*
of the covenant which I have estab-
lished between me and all flesh that is
upon the earth."

A careful scrutiny of the two proposed versions of the flood narrative above reveals an almost unbroken story line for both versions, despite the fact that these sources have been combined into one account. Each story has a theological introduction and conclusion giving divine reasons for the flood and divine reactions to it. Each version has its own rendering of the major elements of the story. And each rendering has its own consistent set of terms to describe the details of the flood story. This literary contrast is coupled with a theological contrast. The same conflicting theological approach discussed above in the introduction to the flood account persists throughout the narrative versions. Rather than discussing each of the literary and theological characteristics of each of these versions in detail, we have summarized the evidence in the following table. This evidence suggests that the two proposed literary sources or complexes isolated in Genesis 1–5 are continued in the two flood versions given above.

The Yahwist Version	**The Priestly Writer's Version**
Introduction:	
As in Genesis 2–4, *Yahweh* is portrayed in human terms. He suffers because of man. Man is his central concern. Man is to be removed from the ground. One man finds undeserved favor.	As in Genesis 1 *Elohim* stands at a distance and speaks decrees about the earth. Cosmic destruction is decreed upon the cosmic corruption. One man is found perfect.
The Divine Instructions:	
Noah is to take 7 of each of the clean animals into an ark and 2 each of the unclean.	Noah is to build an ark and take 2 of each kind of animal into the ark.
The Nature of the Flood:	
Yahweh sends rain (showers) which produce a flood capable of lifting the ark off the ground.	A cosmic upheaval occurs in which the cosmic waters above the heavens and the waters of the cosmic deep below the earth effect a return to chaos (as in Gen. 1:2). The mountains disappear.
The Duration of the Flood:	
Rain and flooding for 40 days and 40 nights. Noah waits three weeks before disembarking.	A full cycle of 12 months (or 1 year and 10 days) passes before creation is restored to order.

Conclusion:

Yahweh is again viewed in human terms, smelling the sacrifice, talking to himself and expressing a promise never to smite life with a similar curse.

Genesis 9:1–17 offers a twofold conclusion, the first part reaffirming man's role as God's ruler on earth (vv. 1–7) and the second establishing a covenant between Himself and all Life.

Distinctive Expressions:

wicked, blot out, face of the ground, find grace, subside, clean, be sorry, male and his mate, Yahweh, etc.

generations, corrupt, all flesh, expire, the deep, establish a covenant, the very same day, prevailed, according to its kind, swarming creatures who swarm, etc.

In addition to recognizing these literary features of the two flood versions, we can discern evidence of the literary structure of the Priestly Writer. We noted above how the Priestly Writer organized both the creation account of Genesis 1 and the genealogy of Genesis 5. His organization of the flood materials is calendric.

Genealogical Introduction:
6:9–10 "These are the generations of. . . ."

Calendric and chronological superstructure to the events of the flood:
7:6 "Noah was 600 years old when. . . ."
7:11 "In the 600th year in the 2nd month. . . ."
7:24 "The waters prevailed 150 days. . . ."
8:3 "At the end of 150 days. . . ."
8:4 "In the 7th month. . . ."
8:5 "In the 10th month. . . ."
8:13 "In the 601st year. . . ."
8:14 "In the second month. . . ."

Genealogical Conclusion:
9:28–29 "After the flood Noah lived 350 years . . . and he died."

It is important to note that the events of the flood take twelve months[2] according to this pattern and that the whole episode is viewed as a restoration of the order of creation. In the ancient Near Eastern world the conflict between the forces of creation and chaos was thought to involve an annual battle, the victory of the God of creation being cele-

[2]The Hebrew text has 12 months and 10 days, allowing for the 10 day intercalation adjustment between solar and lunar calendar, while the Greek translation (in the Septuagint) has precisely 12 months.

brated at the New Year festival. In this flood account dry land also appears on New Year's Day (Gen. 8:13) as a sign of new life and of God's control. However, the covenant by God in Genesis 9:8–17 asserts that there is no annual battle to be feared, but that God has the authority never to let the chaos waters return.

TWO CONCLUSIONS TO THE FLOOD NARRATIVE

The stylistic and theological similarities between the two flood accounts and their respective counterparts in the text of Genesis 1–5 suggest the likelihood of two authors or organizers of material. The accumulated evidence seems to point specifically to the work of two men or schools of men who have arranged and colored the materials they have received for a specific purpose. The narratives are told, introduced, and presented to speak a pertinent message with a definite theological emphasis. This point can be argued, not only on the basis of how the events of the narrative are told, but also because of the structural organization of the materials in one complex (the Priestly Writer). These arguments are supported by the distinctive theological introductions and conclusions to the accounts of the flood. The introductions were discussed in some detail above. If our theory of two literary authors is plausible, the same kind of evidence for a distinctive perspective and purpose on the part of the respective writers should also be evident in their conclusions to the flood story.

The first conclusion in Genesis 8:20–22 incorporates a number of the same idioms and expressions found in the Yahwist version of the flood. The portrait of Yahweh, moreover, is totally consistent with the human way he is depicted in Genesis 2–4 and 6:5–8. Yahweh "smells" the odor of the sacrifice of Noah and "talks to himself" as he reacts to the changed situation after the flood. The problem of man's evil heart is the same as that presented in Genesis 6:5–8. Man remains the primary concern of this writer. The flood is described as a "cursing" of the "ground" (*'aḏamah*) because of man (*'aḏam*). The same terminology and motifs are found in Genesis 3:17, an earlier Yahwist section. The basis for Yahweh's decision never again to smite man or life on earth is the perpetual evil of man's heart. That reason is identical with the one given for sending the flood in Genesis 6:5–8. In short, the conclusion of the flood account by this author is a necessary complement to the introduction of Genesis 6:5–8 and consistent with the suggested Yahwist materials in Genesis 1–8.

The conclusion of the second author is somewhat longer (Gen.

9:1–17). Some of the typical expressions which suggest the hand of the Priestly Writer in this text include, "And God blessed . . . and said . . . ," "be fruitful and multiply," "fill the earth," "for food," "image," "establish my covenant," "all flesh," "eternal covenant," and the like. Genesis 9:1–6 continues the theme of man as God's vice-regent, operating in God's image, and controlling the earth. This perpetuates the motif and language of the Priestly Writer in Genesis 1:26–28 and 5:1–3. The new features introduced include an element of fear which makes man's task of controlling earth more difficult, and the right of man to kill animals provided their blood is not consumed. In Genesis 9:7–17 Elohim issues his decree and promise that no more floods will appear on earth. No ground for his decree is given (as it is in Gen. 8:21). His promise, moreover, is not made only with man, but with all of nature, and a cosmic sign is set in the heavens to remind Elohim of his own promise. The concept of the covenant as "eternal," as "established," and as a promise "with you and your descendants after you," is found many times throughout Genesis in later materials of the Priestly Writer.

CONCLUSIONS

Our preceding analysis of Genesis 1–9 suggests that certain kinds of literary evidence can be isolated. In some sections this evidence is more obvious than in others. The evidence was sought both in generally parallel accounts of a common subject and also in the combined account of one tradition. We have proposed that where the evidence for a given style occurs, a specific set of literary idioms and terms is consistently present. Each combination of style and terminology is supported by a corresponding literary or theological outlook. The combined "constants" of style, terminology, and perspective provide the primary evidence for maintaining that two literary sources are present in Genesis 1–9. To this evidence we would add the above indications of structural organization and arrangement of the literary materials.

We recognize that each of the two literary sources or complexes involved are dependent upon earlier materials, whether literary or oral. The two literary sources under consideration in Genesis 1–9 are not so much sources as interpretations and formulations of earlier traditions. It is our contention that literary evidence can isolate two such formulations of past traditions available to the ancient Israelite writer. In some cases the smaller units incorporated by the writer may be modified very little, if at all. Examples of this may be seen in the cry of

Lamech at the end of the Yahwist genealogy (Gen. 4:23–24), or the blessings and curses at the end of the flood narrative (Gen. 9:25–27). The presence of such relatively independent units within the total complex does not nullify the literary evidence cited above. These units do, however, force us to recognize the limited nature and extent of the literary process involved.[3]

Nor is it possible to be dogmatic about the precise division of literary sources in many combined accounts. Our division of source materials in the flood narrative was illustrative rather than definitive. We must grant the possibility of conflated stories being combined in an oral stage as well as the probability of later literary editors removing inconsistencies or difficulties in the text. The repeated copying and use of literary materials would also tend to soften the differences between one original literary hand and another. Examples of this may perhaps be found in the flood narrative. The unexpected use of the Priestly Writer's favorite term "create" in the Yahwist introduction to the flood in Genesis 6:7 may be explained on these grounds. A similar difficulty is presented by the appearance of the Priestly Writer's terminology in Genesis 7:3a and 9, verses which appear within larger blocks of Yahwist material. More important, however, is the fact that so much evidence of distinct literary sources or writers has been preserved and has not been obliterated by later redactors.

We must also view this literary evidence in terms of the writer who compiled Genesis 1–9. Whoever this writer was, he did not attempt to unify style, terminology, and perspective so as to remove the tensions and differences that existed. It is quite possible that the writer in question was the Priestly Writer. His tendency to provide structures and frameworks for his materials support his candidacy for literary organizer of the materials of Genesis 1–9. The significant fact remains, however, that he did not attempt to eliminate duplicate features. Two introductions and two conclusions, stand as testimonies to two differing approaches to the flood narrative. He apparently honored the theology of his sources. If he is the organizer and final interpreter of Gene-

[3]Space does not permit an answer to past criticisms of the source hypothesis of the Pentateuch. Many of these are directed against a form of literary critical analysis which does not take into account form criticism or tradition studies, or against that kind of literary critical process which claims to be able to divide verses with an unwarranted degree of finality. In other cases the attack is directed against the evolutionary approach to religion which Wellhausen supposedly espoused and reflected in his interpretation of the literary sources of the Pentateuch. The current understanding of the literary critical process is not linked to this approach, but takes into account all the recognized techniques of historical critical research. Typical negative analysis of the source hypothesis of the Pentateuch includes U. Cassuto, *The Documentary Hypothesis* (Jerusalem: The Magnes Press, 1961), and E. Young, *An Introduction to the Old Testament* (Grand Rapids: Eerdmans, 1958).

sis 1–9, we may have a clue as to why he did not include in his own hand anything about the fall of man or the death of Abel.

The preceding analysis does enable us to assert some kind of major literary continuity within two different groups of material traditionally identified with the work of the Yahwist and the Priestly Writer. Many elements of these two literary sequences gain special significance in the light of literary and theological connections after Genesis 9. The Sabbath and the covenant concepts are features of the broader superstructure of the Priestly Writer. For the Yahwist the struggle between Yahweh and Cain has significance in the light of subsequent Yahwist encounters between man and God. For the Yahwist and the Priestly Writer are more than literary artists or organizers of accumulated traditions. They are theological interpreters of their people's history.

In summary, we can assert that the preceding literary evidence apparent in Genesis 1–9 suggests the probability of two literary complexes or writers. The dependency of these complexes on prior traditions, oral forms, or literary units is in no way challenged by this conclusion.

The Chaldean Account of the Deluge

GEORGE SMITH

One of the landmarks in the study of the flood myth occurred on December 3, 1872, when a young Assyriologist named George Smith (1840–1876) read a paper to the Society of Biblical Archaeology in London. The story of Smith's research reads like a novel.

At the age of fourteen, George Smith was apprenticed to a firm to learn banknote engraving, a skill which would later prove invaluable in copying cuneiform tablets. He was fascinated by the Bible and read avidly in Near Eastern archaeology of that era. Much of his free time was spent in the British Museum, and he learned a great deal from studying the exhibits of antiquities from Nineveh and Babylon. Around 1861, his passion and zeal came to the attention of the staff at the museum, and on the basis of his considerable knowledge he was employed as a "repairer"—that is, he was assigned the arduous and somewhat tedious task of looking through hundreds of inscribed fragments from Nineveh to find those which belonged to the same original tablet and hence might be rejoined. He soon developed a remarkable knack for identifying bits and pieces and he was able to make many "joins."

By 1866, when he had been appointed Assistant, he had begun to publish some of the results of his painstaking research, and in 1871 he demonstrated his mastery of the subject by publishing a twenty-three-page pamphlet, The Phonetic Values of the Cuneiform Characters *(London, 1871), which was a considerable aid to the growing number of students of Assyrian. But it was in 1872 that Smith's work came to the attention of the world.*

In searching for tablet pieces containing portions of the flood story, Smith found a large fragment which appeared to have to do with the narrative. However, only one side was legible. The other side was covered with a thick whitish deposit which he was unable to remove. Unfortunately, Robert Ready, the top expert on cleaning fragments, happened to be away from the museum at that time for a period of several weeks. Moreover, Samuel Birth, then Keeper of Oriental Antiquities at the British Museum, refused to allow anyone else to work on removing the deposit. Smith, who was evidently a very nervous, high-strung individual, could not bear the delay. As the days passed, he became more and more impatient and agitated. Finally, when Ready returned and agreed to

Reprinted from the *Transactions of the Society of Biblical Archaeology* 2 (1873): 213–234.

do his best to clean the fragment side in question, Smith's excitement grew even more. Ready's best was good enough. When he brought the tablet to Smith, the latter eagerly read the lines revealed and found that they contained the portion of the flood narrative he had hoped might be there. Supposedly he cried, "I am the first man to read that after more than two thousand years of oblivion," and placing the tablet on a table, he jumped up and ran around the room in a state of great exhilaration and to the astonishment of those present actually began to undress himself. For this and other details of Smith's life, see Sir E. A. Wallis Budge, The Rise and Progress of Assyriology *(London, 1925), pp. 106–119, R. Campbell Thompson,* A Century of Exploration at Nineveh *(London, 1929), pp. 48–54, or Smith's own account in* Assyrian Discoveries *(New York, 1875), pp. 9–14.*

Smith's tablet fragment told the story of a great flood. The story bore striking resemblances to the account in Genesis, but it was evidently a good deal older than the biblical version. Later research has revealed various errors in Smith's initial translation of what was eventually identified as the eleventh tablet of the Gilgamesh epic. Some of the names of the principal characters, for example, have been amended by scholars who followed. But rather than burden Smith's original lecture with a host of bracketed glosses and corrections, I have elected to present it as he gave it and published it. Actually, Smith himself revised his initial translation of the "Chaldean" flood myth on the basis of later discoveries. See "The Eleventh Tablet of the Izdubar Legends: The Chaldean Account of the Deluge," Transactions of the Society of Biblical Archaeology *3 (1874): 530–596; or Chapter XI, "The Izdubar or Flood Series of Legends," in George Smith,* Assyrian Discoveries *(New York, 1875), pp. 165–222; and* The Chaldean Account of Genesis *(New York, 1876).*

The consequences of Smith's discovery and his 1872 paper were enormous. The next month, January 1873, the Daily Telegraph, *a London newspaper, arranged with Smith that he should go to Nineveh to carry out excavations in order to find the missing fragments of the deluge story. The paper's owners offered the sum of one thousand guineas to subsidize the expedition, and the British Museum's trustees granted Smith a six-month leave of absence. Incredibly, Smith did turn up additional fragments (although subsequent research revealed that they belonged to yet another version of the flood myth) and he returned to England in triumph. In 1874, he undertook another expedition, this time at the behest of the British Museum. But alas a final expedition in 1876 for the museum ended in tragedy. Brilliant though Smith had been in deciphering cuneiform texts, he was simply not temperamentally or physically suited for the rigors of archaeological fieldwork and he proved incapable of dealing effectively with the native rulers of the sites he wished to excavate. Against advice, Smith attempted to travel to Aleppo, Syria, during the hottest part of the summer and fell seriously ill of dysentery, dying finally in Aleppo on August 19, 1876. So a meteoric career came to a sad close.*

Smith's 1872 paper is now primarily of historical interest. Still, one can with a bit of imagination place oneself back in that time period and try to sense the excitement both in the speaker and the audience as the paper was being delivered. Few papers presented to small scholarly societies have attracted as much worldwide interest as Smith's unveiling of an Assyrian flood story which had been "lost" so to speak to mankind for hundreds and hundreds of years. It is fair to say that Smith's discovery had an immediate and permanent effect on the future course of flood scholarship. For one of the first favorable responses to his paper, see A. H. Sayce, "The Chaldean Account of the Deluge and Its Relation to the Old Testament," Theological Review *10 (1872): 364–377.*

A short time back I discovered among the Assyrian tablets in the British Museum, an account of the flood; which, under the advice of our President, I now bring before the Society.

For convenience of working, I had divided the collection of Assyrian tablets in the British Museum into sections, according to the subject-matter of the inscriptions.

I have recently been examining the division comprising the Mythological and Mythical tablets, and from this section I obtained a number of tablets, giving a curious series of legends and including a copy of the story of the Flood. On discovering these documents, which were much mutilated, I searched over all the collections of fragments of inscriptions, consisting of several thousands of smaller pieces, and ultimately recovered 80 fragments of these legends; by the aid of which I was enabled to restore nearly all the text of the description of the Flood, and considerable portions of the other legends. These tablets were originally at least twelve in number, forming one story or set of legends, the account of the Flood being on the eleventh tablet.

Of the inscription describing the Flood, there are fragments of three copies containing the same texts; these copies belong to the time of Assurbanipal, or about 660 years before the Christian era, and they were found in the library of that monarch in the palace at Nineveh.

The original text, according to the statements on the tablets, must have belonged to the city of Erech, and it appears to have been either written in, or translated into the Semitic Babylonian, at a very early period. The date when this document was first written or translated is at present very difficult to decide, but the following are some of the evidences of its antiquity:

1st. The three Assyrian copies present a number of variant readings, which had crept into the text since the original documents were written.

2nd. The forms of the characters in the original documents were of an ancient type, and the Assyrian copyist did not always know their modern representatives, so he has left some of them in their original hieratic form.

3rd. There are a number of sentences which were originally glosses explanatory of the subjects; before the Assyrian copies were made these glosses had been already incorporated in the text and their original use lost.

It must here be noted that the Assyrian scribe has recorded for us the divisions of the lines on the original documents.

On examining the composition of the text, some marked peculiarities are apparent, which likewise show its high antiquity. One of these is the constant use of the personal pronoun nominative. In later times this was usually indicated by the verbal form, but not expressed. On comparing the Deluge text with dated texts from the time of Sargon I, it appears to be older than these, and its original composition cannot be placed later than the seventeenth century before the Christian era; while it may be much older. The text itself professes to belong to the time of a monarch whose name, written in monograms, I am unable to read phonetically; I therefore provisionally call him by the ordinary values of the signs of his name, Izdubar.

Izdubar, from the description of his reign, evidently belonged to the Mythical period; the legends given in these tablets, the offer of marriage made to him by the goddess Ishtar, the monsters living at the time, Izdubar's vision of the gods, his journey to the translated Sisit, with a curious account of a mythical conquest of Erech when the gods and spirits inhabiting that city changed themselves into animals to escape the fury of the conqueror: all these things and many others show the unhistorical nature of the epoch. From the heading of the tablets giving his history, I suppose that Izdubar lived in the epoch immediately following the Flood, and I think, likewise, that he may have been the founder of the Babylonian monarchy, perhaps the Nimrod of Scripture. This, however, is pure conjecture; so many fabulous stories were current in Babylonia respecting Izdubar that his existence may even be doubted. The fragments of the history of Izdubar, so far as I have at present examined them, remind me of the exploits and labors of Hercules, and, on the supposition that our present version of Berosus is correct as to dates, Izdubar may have been placed about 30,000 years before the Christian era. No document can belong to so remote an age. The legends of Izdubar and the account of the Flood must however belong to a very early period, for there are references to the story in the bilingual lists which were composed in Babylonia during the early Chaldean empires.

The question might here be asked, "How is it that we find an early

Chaldean document from Erech transported to Nineveh, copied, and placed in the royal library there?" On this point we can show that it was a common custom for the Assyrians to obtain and copy Babylonian works, and a considerable portion of Assyrian literature consists of these copies of older standard writings.

Assurbanipal, the Assyrian monarch in whose reign the Deluge Tablets were copied, had intimate relations with the city of Erech. Erech remained faithful to him when the rest of Babylonia revolted, and to this city Assurbanipal restored the famous image of the goddess Nana, which had been carried away by the Elamites one thousand six hundred and thirty-five years before.

In order properly to understand the reason why the narrative of the Flood is introduced into the story, it will be necessary to give a short account of the tablets which precede it before giving the translation of the Deluge inscription itself.

It appears that Izdubar, the hero of these legends, flourished as before stated, in the mythical period soon after the Flood, and the center of most of his exploits was the city of Erech, now called Warka, which must have been one of the most ancient cities in the world. Four cities only are mentioned in these inscriptions, Babel, Erech, Surippak, and Nipur. Two of these, Babel and Erech, are the first two capitals of Nimrod, and the last one, Nipur, according to the Talmud, is the same as Calneh the fourth city of Nimrod. Of the first five tablets of the history of Izdubar I have not recognized any fragments, but in the mass of material which I have collected it is possible that some portions may belong to this part of the story.

The following passage forms the opening of the sixth tablet and shows the style of the writing.

Before giving the translation I must notice that in various places the tablets are broken and the texts defective: as I cannot point out each of these defective passages, I will endeavor to indicate them by pausing in my reading.

1. . . . . . Belesu, he despised Belesu
2. like a bull his country he ascended after him
3. he destroyed him, and his memorial perished
4. the country was subdued, and after he took the crown
5. Izdubar put on his crown, and after he took the crown
6. for the favor of Izdubar, the princess Ishtar lifted her eyes.
7. And she spake thus, "Izdubar thou shalt be husband
8. thy word me shall bind in bonds,
9. thou shalt be husband and I will be thy wife,

10. thou shalt drive in a chariot of Ukni stone and gold,
11. of which its body is gold and splendid its pole
12. thou shalt ride in days of great glory
13. to Bitani, in which is the country where the pine trees grow.
14. Bitani at thy entrance
15. to the Euphrates shall kiss thy feet.
16. There shall be in subjection under thee, kings, lords, and princes.
17. The tribute of the mountains and plains they shall bring to thee, taxes
18. they shall give thee, thy herds and flocks shall bring forth twins
19. . . . . the mule shall be swift
20. . . . . in the chariot shall be strong and not weak
21. . . . . in the yoke. A rival shall not be permitted."

Ishtar, who was the same as Venus, was queen of beauty, but somewhat inconstant, for she had already a husband, a deity, called the "Son of Life"; she however led her husband a poor life, and of this Izdubar reminds her in his answer to her offer.

One of the next exploits of Izdubar and Heabani his servant was the conquest of the winged bull, a monster supposed to have existed in those days; but I must pass over this and other matters, to approach the subject of the Flood.

In course of time Izdubar, the conqueror of kings and monsters, the ruler of peoples, fell into some illness and came to fear death, man's last great enemy. Now, the Babylonians believed in the existence of a patriarch named Sisit, the Xisuthrus of the Greeks, who was supposed to have been translated and to have attained to immortality without death. Izdubar, according to the notions of the time, resolved to seek Sisit, to ascertain how he became immortal, that he might attain to a similar honor. The passage reads as follows:

1. Izdubar to Heabani his servant
2. bitterly lamented and lay down on the ground
3. I the account took from Heabani and
4. weakness entered into my soul
5. death I feared and I lay down on the ground
6. to find Sisit son of Ubaratutu
7. the road I was taking and joyfully I went
8. to the shadows of the mountains I took at night
9. the gods I saw and I feared
10. . . . . to Sin I prayed
11. and before the gods my supplication came
12. peace they gave unto me
13. and they sent unto me a dream.

The dream of Izdubar is unfortunately very mutilated, few fragments of it remaining, and his subsequent journey is not in much better condition. It appears that he went through a number of adventures, and three men are represented, in one place, to be telling each other the story of these adventures.

After long wanderings, Izdubar falls into company with a seaman named Urhamsi, a name similar to the Orchamus of the Greeks. Izdubar and Urhamsi fit out a vessel to continue the search for Sisit, and they sail along for a month and fifteen days, and arrive at some region near the mouth of the Euphrates, where Sisit was supposed to dwell. In this journey by water there are fresh adventures and, in their course, Urhamsi tells Izdubar of the waters of death, of which he states, "The waters of death thy hands will not cleanse."

At the time when Izdubar and Urhamsi are approaching him, Sisit is sleeping. The tablet here is too mutilated to inform us how they came to see each other, but it appears probable from the context that Sisit was seen in company with his wife, a long distance off, separated from Izdubar by a stream.

Unable to cross this water which divided the mortal from the immortal, Izdubar appears to have called to Sisit and asked his momentous question on life and death. The question asked by Izdubar and the first part of the answer of Sisit are lost by the mutilation of the tablet. The latter part of the speech of Sisit, which is preserved, relates to the danger of death, its universality, &c. It winds up as follows: "The goddess Mamitu the maker of fate to them their fate has appointed, she has fixed death and life, but of death the day is not known."

These words, which close the first speech of Sisit, bring us to the end of the tenth tablet; the next one, the eleventh, is the most important of the series, as it contains the history of the Flood.

The eleventh tablet opens with a speech of Izdubar, who now asks Sisit how he became immortal, and Sisit, in answering, relates the story of the Flood and his own piety as the reason why he was translated. The following is the translation of this tablet:

1. Izdubar after this manner said to Sisit afar off,
2. ". . . . . . Sisit
3. The account do thou tell to me,
4. The account do thou tell to me,
5. . . . . to the midst to make war
6. . . . . I come up after thee.
7. say how thou hast done it, and in the circle of the gods life thou hast gained."
8. Sisit after this manner said to Izdubar,

9. "I will reveal to thee, Izdubar, the concealed story,
10. and the wisdom of the gods I will relate to thee.
11. The city Surippak the city which thou hast established . . . . placed
12. was ancient, and the gods within it
13. dwelt, a tempest . . . . . their god, the great gods
14. . . . . Anu
15. . . . . Bel
16. . . . . Ninip
17. . . . . lord of Hades
18. their will revealed in the midst of . . . . .
19. . . . . . . hearing and he spoke to me thus
20. Surippakite son of Ubaratutu
21. make a great ship for thee . . . .
22. I will destroy the sinners and life . . . . .
23. cause to go in the seed of life all of it, to preserve them
24. the ship which thou shalt make
25. . . . cubits shall be the measure of its length, and
26. . . . cubits the amount of its breadth and its height.
27. Into the deep launch it."
28. I perceived and said to Hea my lord,
29. "Hea my lord this that thou commandest me
30. I will perform, it shall be done.
31. . . . . army and host
32. Hea opened his mouth and spake, and said to me his servant,
33. . . . . thou shalt say unto them,
34. . . . . he has turned from me and
35. . . . . fixed . . . .

Here there are about fifteen lines entirely lost. The absent passage probably described part of the building of the ark.

51. it . . . .
52. which in . . . .
53. strong . . . . I brought
54. on the fifth day . . . . . . it
55. in its circuit 14 measures . . . . its sides
56. 14 measures it measured . . . . over it
57. I placed its roof on it . . . . . I enclosed it
58. I rode in it, for the sixth time I . . . . . . for the seventh time
59. into the restless deep . . . . . for the . . . . time
60. its planks the waters within it admitted,
61. I saw breaks and holes . . . . . . my hand placed

62. three measures of bitumen I poured over the outside,
63. three measures of bitumen I poured over the inside
64. three measures the men carrying its baskets took . . . . . . they fixed an altar
65. I enclosed the altar . . . . . . the altar for an offering
66. two measures the altar . . . . . Pazziru the pilot
67. for . . . . slaughtered oxen
68. of . . . . in that day also
69. . . . . altar and grapes
70. . . . . like the waters of a river and
71. . . . . like the day I covered and
72. . . . . when . . . . covering my hand placed,
73. . . . . and Shamas . . . . the material of the ship completed,
74. . . . . strong and
75. reeds I spread above and below.
76. . . . . . . went in two thirds of it.
77. All I possessed I collected it, all I possessed I collected of silver,
78. all I possessed I collected of gold,
79. all I possessed I collected of the seed of life, the whole
80. I caused to go up into the ship, all my male and female servants,
81. the beasts of the field, the animals of the field, and the sons of the army all of them, I caused to go up.
82. A flood Shamas made, and
83. he spake saying in the night, 'I will cause it to rain from heaven heavily;
84. enter to the midst of the ship, and shut thy door,'
85. A flood he raised, and
86. he spake saying in the night, 'I will cause it to rain from heaven heavily.'
87. In the day that I celebrated his festival
88. the day which he had appointed; fear I had,
89. I entered to the midst of the ship, and shut my door;
90. to guide the ship, to Buzursadirabi the pilot,
91. the palace I gave to his hand.
92. The raging of a storm in the morning
93. arose, from the horizon of heaven extending and wide
94. Vul in the midst of it thundered, and
95. Nebo and Saru went in front;
96. the throne bearers went over mountains and plains;
97. the destroyer Nergal overturned;
98. Ninip went in front, and cast down;
99. the spirits carried destruction;

100. in their glory they swept the earth;
101. of Vul the flood, reached to heaven;
102. the bright earth to a waste was turned;
103. the surface of the earth, like . . . . it swept;
104. it destroyed all life, from the face of the earth . . . . .
105. the strong tempest over the people, reached to heaven.
106. Brother saw not his brother, it did not spare the people. In heaven
107. the gods feared the tempest, and
108. Sought refuge; they ascended to the heaven of Anu.
109. The gods, like dogs with tails hidden, couched down.
110. Spake Ishtar a discourse,
111. uttered the great goddess her speech
112. 'The world to sin has turned, and
113. then I in the presence of the gods prophesied evil;
114. when I prophesied in the presence of the gods evil,
115. to evil were devoted all my people, and I prophesied
116. thus, 'I have begotten man and let him not
117. like the sons of the fishes fill the sea.'
118. The gods concerning the spirits, were weeping with her:
119. the gods in seats, seated in lamentation;
120. covered were their lips for the coming evil.
121. Six days and nights
122. passed, the wind tempest and storm overwhelmed,
123. on the seventh day in its course, was calmed the storm, and all the tempest
124. which had destroyed like an earthquake,
125. quieted. The sea he caused to dry, and the wind and tempest ended.
126. I was carried through the sea. The doer of evil,
127. and the whole of mankind who turned to sin,
128. like reeds their corpses floated.
129. I opened the window and the light broke in, over my refuge
130. it passed, I sat still and
131. over my refuge came peace.
132. I was carried over the shore, at the boundary of the sea.
133. For twelve measures it ascended over the land.
134. To the country of Nizir, went the ship;
135. the mountain of Nizir stopped the ship, and to pass over it, it was not able.
136. The first day and the second day, the mountain of Nizir the same.
137. The third day and the fourth day, the mountain of Nizir the same.
138. The fifth and sixth, the mountain of Nizir the same.

139. On the seventh day in the course of it
140. I sent forth a dove, and it left. The dove went and searched and
141. a resting place it did not find, and it returned.
142. I sent forth a swallow, and it left. The swallow went and searched and
143. a resting place it did not find, and it returned.
144. I sent forth a raven, and it left.
145. The raven went, and the corpses on the waters it saw, and
146. it did eat, it swam, and wandered away, and did not return.
147. I sent the animals forth to the four winds I poured out a libation
148. I built an altar on the peak of the mountain,
149. by sevens herbs I cut,
150. at the bottom of them, I placed reeds, pines, and simgar.
151. The gods collected at its burning, the gods collected at its good burning.
152. the gods like flies over the sacrifice gathered,
153. From of old also, the great God in his course,
154. the great brightness of Anu had created; when the glory
155. of these gods, as of Ukni stone, on my countenance I could not endure;
156. in those days I prayed that for ever I might not endure.
157. May the gods come to my altar;
158. may Bel not come to my altar
159. for he did not consider and had made a tempest
160. and my people he had consigned to the deep
161. from of old, also Bel in his course
162. saw the ship, and went Bel with anger filled to the gods and spirits;
163. let not any one come out alive, let not a man be saved from the deep.
164. Ninip his mouth opened and spake, and said to the warrior Bel,
165. 'who then will be saved,' Hea the words understood,
166. and Hea knew all things,
167. Hea his mouth opened and spake, and said to the warrior Bel,
168. 'Thou prince of the gods, warrior,
169. when thou art angry a tempest thou makest,
170. the doer of sin did his sin, the doer of evil did his evil,
171. may the exalted not be broken, may the captive not be delivered;
172. instead of thee making a tempest, may lions increase and men be reduced;
173. instead of thee making a tempest, may leopards increase, and men be reduced;

174. instead of thee making a tempest, may a famine happen, and the country be destroyed;
175. instead of thee making a tempest, may pestilence increase, and men be destroyed.'
176. I did not peer into the wisdom of the gods,
177. reverent and attentive a dream they sent, and the wisdom of the gods he heard.
178. When his judgment was accomplished, Bel went up to the midst of the ship,
179. he took my hand and brought me out, me
180. he brought out, he caused to bring my wife to my side,
181. he purified the country, he established in a covenant and took the people
182. in the presence of Sisit and the people.
183. When Sisit and his wife and the people to be like the gods were carried away,
184. then dwelt Sisit in a remote place at the mouth of the rivers.
185. They took me and in a remote place at the mouth of the rivers they seated me.
186. When to thee whom the gods have chosen thee, and
187. the life which thou has sought after, thou shalt gain
188. this do, for six days and seven nights
189. like I say also, in bonds bind him
190. the way like a storm shall be laid upon him."
191. Sisit after this manner, said to his wife
192. "I announce that the chief who grasps at life
193. the way like a storm shall be laid upon him."
194. His wife after this manner, said to Sisit afar off,
195. "Purify him and let the man be sent away,
196. the road that he came, may he return in peace,
197. the great gate open, and may he return to his country."
198. Sisit after this manner, said to his wife,
199. "The cry of a man alarms thee,
200. this do, his scarlet cloth place on his head."
201. And the day when he ascended the side of the ship
202. she did, his scarlet cloth she placed on his head,
203. and the day when he ascended on the side of the ship,

The next four lines describe seven things done to Izdubar before he was purified. The passage is obscure and does not concern the Flood, so I have not translated it.

208. Izdubar after this manner, said to Sisit afar off,
209. "This way, she has done, I come up
210. joyfully, my strength thou givest me."
211. Sisit after this manner said to Izdubar
212. . . . . thy scarlet cloth
213. . . . . I have lodged thee
214. . . . .

The five following lines, which are mutilated, refer again to the seven matters for purifying Izdubar; this passage, like the former one, I do not translate.

219. Izdubar after this manner said to Sisit afar off
220. . . . . Sisit to thee may we not come.

From here the text is much mutilated, and it will be better to give a general account of its contents than to attempt a strict translation, especially as this part is not so interesting as the former part of the tablet.

Lines 221 and 223 mention some one who was taken and dwelt with Death. Lines 224 to 235 gives a speech of Sisit to the seaman Urhamsi, directing him how to cure Izdubar, who, from the broken passages, appears to have been suffering from some form of skin disease. Izdubar was to be dipped in the sea, when beauty was to spread over his skin once more. In lines 236 to 241 the carrying out of these directions and the cure of Izdubar are recorded.

The tablet then reads as follows:

242. Izdubar and Urhamsi rode in the boat
243. where they placed them they rode
244. His wife after this manner said to Sisit afar off,
245. "Izdubar goes away, he is satisfied, he performs
246. that which thou hast given him and returns to his country."
247. And he heard, and after Izdubar
248. he went to the shore
249. Sisit after this manner said to Izdubar,
250. "Izdubar thou goest away thou art satisfied, thou performest
251. That which I have given thee and thou returnest to thy country
252. I have revealed to thee Izdubar the concealed story."

Lines 253 to 262, which are very mutilated, give the conclusion of the speech of Sisit, and then state that after hearing it, Izdubar took great stones and piled them up as a memorial of these events.

Lines 263 to 289 give in a very mutilated condition subsequent speeches and doings of Izdubar and Urhamsi. In this part journeys are mentioned of 10 and 20 kaspu, or 70 and 140 miles; a lion is also spoken of, but there is no further allusion to the Flood. These lines close the inscription, and are followed by a colophon which gives the heading of the next tablet, and the statement that this (the Flood Tablet) is the 11th tablet in the series giving the history of Izdubar, and that it is a copy of the ancient inscription.

Before entering into the details of the tablet, I must first refer to the accounts of the Deluge given in the Bible, and by Berosus, the Chaldean historian, as I shall have to compare these with the Cuneiform record.

The Biblical account of the Deluge, contained in the sixth to the ninth chapters of Genesis, is of course familiar to us all, so I will only give the outline of the narrative.

According to the Book of Genesis, as man mutiplied on the earth, the whole race turned to evil, except the family of Noah. On account of the wickedness of man, the Lord determined to destroy the world by a flood, and gave command to Noah to build an ark, 300 cubits long, 50 cubits broad, and 30 cubits high. Into this ark Noah entered according to the command of the Lord, taking with him his family, and pairs of each animal. After seven days the Flood commenced in the 600th year of Noah, the seventeenth day of the second month, and after 150 days the ark rested upon the mountains of Ararat, on the seventeenth day of the seventh month. We are then told that after 40 days Noah opened the window of the ark and sent forth a raven which did not return. He then sent forth a dove, which finding no rest for the sole of her foot, returned to him. Seven days after he sent forth the dove a second time, she returned to him with an olive leaf in her mouth. Again, after seven days, he sent forth the dove which returned to him no more. The Flood was dried up in the 601st year, on the first day of the first month, and on the twenty-seventh day of the second month, Noah removed from the ark and afterwards built an altar and offered sacrifices.

The Chaldean account of the Flood, as given by Berosus, I have taken from Cory's Ancient Fragments, pages 26 to 29, as follows:

"After the death of Ardates, his son Xisuthrus reigned eighteen sari. In his time happened a great Deluge, the history of which is thus described: The Deity, Cronos, appeared to him in a vision, and warned him that upon the fifteenth day of the month Daesius, there would be a flood, by which mankind would be destroyed. He, therefore, enjoined him to write a history of the beginning, procedure, and conclusion of all things; and to bury it in the City of the Sun at Sippara; and to build a vessel, and take with him into it his friends and relations; and to convey on board everything necessary to sustain life, together with all the different animals, both birds and quadrupeds, and trust himself fearlessly to the deep. Having asked the Deity whither he was to sail? he was answered, 'To the Gods'; upon which he offered up a prayer for the good of mankind. He then obeyed the Divine admonition, and built a vessel five stadia in length, and two in breadth. Into this he put everything which he had prepared: and last of all conveyed into it his wife, his children, and his friends.

"After the Flood had been upon the earth, and was in time abated, Xisuthrus sent out birds from the vessel, which not finding any food, nor any place whereupon they might rest their feet, returned to him again. After an interval of some days he sent them forth a second time, and they now returned with their feet tinged with mud. He made a trial a third time with these birds, but they returned to him no more: from whence he judged that the surface of the earth had appeared above the waters. He, therefore, made an opening in the vessel, and upon looking out found that it was stranded upon the side of some mountain, upon which he immediately quitted it with his wife, his daughter, and the pilot. Xisuthrus then paid his adoration to the earth, and having constructed an altar, offered sacrifices to the gods, and, with those who had come out of the vessel with him, disappeared.

"They, who remained within, finding that their companions did not return, quitted the vessel with many lamentations, and called continually on the name of Xisuthrus. Him they saw no more; but they could distinguish his voice in the air, and could hear him admonish them to pay due regard to religion; and likewise informed them that it was upon account of his piety that he was translated to live with the gods, that his wife, and daughter, and the pilot, had obtained the same honor. To this he added that they should return to Babylonia, and as it was ordained, search for the writings at Sippara, which they were to make known to all mankind; moreover, that the place wherein they were was the land of Armenia.

"The rest having heard these words, offered sacrifices to the gods, and taking a circuit, journeyed towards Babylonia.

"The vessel being thus stranded in Armenia, some part of it yet remains in the Corcyraean mountains."

In pages 33 and 34 of Cory's Fragments there is a second version, as follows:

"And then Sisithrus. To him the deity of Cronos foretold that on the fifteenth day of the month Daesius there would be a deluge of rain:

and he commanded him to deposit all the writings whatever which were in his possession, in the City of the Sun at Sippara. Sisithrus, when he had complied with these commands, sailed immediately to Armenia, and was presently inspired by God. Upon the third day after the cessation of the rain Sisithrus sent out birds, by way of experiment, that he might judge whether the Flood had subsided. But the birds passing over an unbounded sea, without finding any place of rest, returned again to Sisithrus. This he repeated with other birds. And when upon the third trial he succeeded, for the birds then returned with their feet stained with mud, the gods translated him from among men. With respect to the vessel, which yet remains in Armenia, it is a custom of the inhabitants to form bracelets and amulets of its wood."

There are several other accounts of the Flood in the traditions of different ancient nations; these, however, are neither so full nor so precise as the account of Berosus, and their details so far as they are given differ more from the Biblical narrative, so I shall not notice them now, but pass at once to the examination of the text.

In comparing the text of the Deluge Tablet with the accounts in the Bible and Berosus, the first point that meets us is the consideration of the proper names. This is the least satisfactory part of the subject, for, while the Greek forms show variant readings and have evidently been corrupted, the Cuneiform names on the other hand, being written mostly in monograms, are difficult to render phonetically. The father of the hero of the Flood bears in the inscriptions the name Ubara-tutu which ought to correspond to one of the Greek forms, Otiártes or Ardátes; the resemblance however cannot be called a close one. The hero of the Flood I have provisionally called Sisit; he corresponds, of course, to the Greek Xisuthrus, but no comparison of the two names can be made until we know the phonetic reading of the Cuneiform name. Neither the Cuneiform nor the Greek names appear to have any connection with the Biblical Lamech and Noah. In the opening of the account of the Flood there is a noticeable difference between the Cuneiform and Biblical narratives, for while in the Jewish account one God only is mentioned, the Cuneiform inscription mentions all the principal gods of the early Babylonian Pantheon as engaged in bringing about the Flood.

The Cuneiform account agrees with the Biblical narrative in making the Deluge a divine punishment for the wickedness of the world; this point is omitted in the Greek accounts of Berosus.

The gods having resolved on the Deluge, the deity whom we have hitherto provisionally called Hea announces the coming event to Sisit. Now, in the account of Berosus, the god who announces the Deluge is stated to be Cronos; so this passage gives us the Cuneiform name of the deity identified by the Greeks with Cronos. The Greek account states that the communication of the coming Deluge was made in a dream. From the context it is probable that the Cuneiform account stated the same, but the text is here mutilated so that the point cannot be decided.

The dimensions of the vessel in the inscription are unfortunately lost by a fracture which has broken off both numbers; the passage, which is otherwise complete, shows that the dimensions were expressed in cubits as in the Biblical account, but while Genesis makes the ark 50 cubits broad and 30 cubits high, the inscription states that the height and breadth were the same.

The greater part of the description of the building of the ark is lost. In the latter part of the account which is preserved, there is mention of the trial of the vessel by launching it into the sea, when defects being found which admitted the water, the outside and inside were coated with bitumen. These details have no parallel either in the Bible or Berosus. The description of the filling of the ark agrees in general with the two other accounts, but it differs from Genesis in not mentioning the sevens of clean animals and in including others beside the family of the builder.

The month and day when the Deluge commenced, which are given in the Bible and Berosus, are not mentioned in the text, unless the fifth day, mentioned in a mutilated passage, is part of this date.

The description of the Flood in this inscription is very vivid; it is said to have been so terrible that the gods, fearing it, ascended to the heaven of Anu, that it is the highest and furthest heaven, the destruction of the human race is recorded, and the corpses of the wicked are said to have floated on the surface of the Flood.

With regard to the duration of the Deluge, there appears to be a serious difference between the Bible and the inscription. According to the account in the Book of Genesis, the Flood commenced on the seventeenth day of the second month, the ark rested on Ararat after one hundred and fifty days on the seventeenth day of the seventh month, and the complete drying up of the Flood was not until the twenty-seventh day of the second month in the following year. The inscription, on the other hand, states that the Flood abated on the seventh day, and that the ship remained seven days on the mountain before the sending out of the birds.

On this point it must be remarked that some Biblical critics consider that there are two versions of the Flood story in Genesis itself, and that these two differ as to the duration of the Flood.

The Greek account of Berosus is silent as to the duration of the Deluge.

With regard to the mountain on which the ark rested there is a difference between the Bible and the inscription, which is more apparent than real. The Book of Genesis states that the ark rested on the mountains of Ararat. According to the popular notion this refers to the mountain of Ararat, in Armenia; but these mountains may have been anywhere within the ancient territory of Ararat, and some Commentators looking at the passage in Berosus, where the ark is stated to have rested in the Gordiaean mountains, have inclined to place the mountain referred to in the Kurdish mountains, east of Assyria. In accordance with this indication the inscription states that the ship rested on the mountain of Nizir.

Now, the position of Nizir can be determined from the inscription of Assur-nazir-pal, king of Assyria. He made an expedition to this region, and starting from an Assyrian city, near Arbela, crossed the Lower Zab, and marching eastward between latitudes 35 and 36, arrived at the mountains of Nizir. These mountains of Nizir thus lay east of Assyria, but they form part of a series of mountain chains extending to the north-west into Armenia.

The vessel being stranded on the mountain, the Bible, Berosus, and the inscription all agree that trial was made by birds in order to ascertain if the Flood had subsided; but in the details of these trials there are curious differences in all three narratives. According to the Book of Genesis, a raven was sent out first, which did not return; a dove was sent next, which finding no resting place returned to Noah. Seven days later the dove was sent out again, and returned with an olive leaf; and seven days after, on the dove being sent out again, it returned no more.

The account of Berosus mentions the sending out of the birds, but does not mention what kinds were tried. On the first trial the birds are said to have returned, and on the second trial likewise, this time with mud on their feet. On the third occasion they did not return.

The inscription states that, first, a dove was sent out, which finding no resting place returned. On the second occasion a swallow was sent, which also returned. The third time a raven was sent out, which feeding on the corpses floating on the water, wandered away and did not return. Thus, the inscription agrees with the Bible as to the sending out of the raven and dove, but adds to these the trial of the swallow, which is not in Genesis. In the number of the trials it agrees with Berosus, who has three, while Genesis has four. On the other hand there is no mention of the dove returning with an olive leaf, as in Genesis, and of the birds having their feet stained with mud, as in Berosus.

In the statement of the building of the altar, and offering sacrifice after leaving the ark, all three accounts agree; but in the subsequent matter there is an important difference between the Bible and the inscription, for while the Bible represents Noah as living for many years after the Flood, the inscription on the other hand agrees with Berosus in making Sisit to be translated like the gods. This translation is in the Bible recorded of Enoch, the ancestor of Noah.

On reviewing the evidence it is apparent that the events of the Flood narrated in the Bible and the inscription are the same, and occur in the same order; but the minor differences in the details show that the inscription embodies a distinct and independent tradition.

In spite of a striking similarity in style, which shows itself in several places, the two narratives belong to totally distinct peoples. The Biblical account is the version of an inland people, the name of the ark in Genesis means a chest or box, and not a ship; there is no notice of the sea, or of launching, no pilots are spoken of, no navigation is mentioned. The inscription on the other hand belongs to a maritime people, the ark is called a ship, the ship is launched into the sea, trial is made of it, and it is given in charge of a pilot.

The Cuneiform inscription, after giving the history of the Flood down to the sacrifice of Sisit, when he came out of the ark, goes back to the former part of the story, and mentions the god Bel in particular as the maker of the tempest or deluge; there appears to be a slight inconsistency between this and the former part of the inscription which suggests the question whether the Chaldean narrative itself may not have been compiled from two distinct and older accounts.

It is remarkable that the oldest traditions of the early Babylonians seem to center round the Persian Gulf. From this sea, Oannes the fish god is supposed to have arisen, and the composite monsters who followed him in the antediluvian period came from the same region. Into this sea the ark was launched, and after the subsiding of the Deluge when Sisit was translated, he dwelt in this neighborhood. To this sea also came the great hero Izdubar, and was cured, and here he heard the story of the Flood.

In conclusion I would remark that this account of the Deluge opens to us a new field of inquiry in the early part of the Bible history. The question has often been asked, "What is the origin of the accounts of the antediluvians, with their long lives so many times greater than the longest span of human life? Where was Paradise, the abode of the first parents of mankind? From whence comes the story of the flood, the ark, of the birds?" Various conflicting answers have been given to these important questions, while evidence on these subjects before the Greek period has been entirely wanting. The Cuneiform inscriptions are now shedding a new light on these questions, and supplying material which future scholars will have to work out. Following this inscription, we may expect many other discoveries throwing light on these ancient periods, until we are able to form a decisive opinion on the many great questions involved. It would be a mistake to suppose that with the translation and commentary on an inscription like this the matter is ended. The origin, age, and history of the legend have to be traced, and it has to be compared with the many similar stories current among various nations.

All these accounts, together with considerable portions of the ancient mythologies have, I believe, a common origin in the Plains of Chaldea. This country, the cradle of civilization, the birthplace of the arts and sciences, for 2,000 years has been in ruins; its literature, containing the most precious records of antiquity, is scarcely known to us, except from the texts the Assyrians copied, but beneath its mounds and ruined cities, now awaiting exploration, lay, together with older copies of this Deluge text, other legends and histories of the earliest civilization in the world.

Some Observations on the Assyro-Babylonian and Sumerian Flood Stories

DANIEL HÄMMERLY-DUPUY

George Smith's 1872 discovery was only the first of a number of successes in unearthing ancient Near Eastern versions of the flood myth. These various Assyrian, Babylonian, and Sumerian flood texts have inspired a myriad of essays by specialists in these cultures. The majority are highly technical papers largely concerned with the finer points of translation or dating the texts more accurately. These texts have also encouraged the undertaking of comparative studies focusing upon the names of the protagonists and such details as the onset of the flood and the subsequent escape of the survivors.

The following succinct survey of some of the principal ancient flood myth texts from the Near East by Daniel Hämmerly-Dupuy of the Colegio Unión of Lima, Peru, should give the reader some idea of their content although full texts are not included. It is difficult to convey the fragmentary nature of these texts. There are many lacunae and it is rather like a cryptographic puzzle to decipher them. Nevertheless, sufficient sense has been made of them to demonstrate conclusively that the flood myth has been known in the Near East from 2000 B.C. *or earlier. It is thus one of the oldest myths in recorded history.*

A sample of the abundant scholarship on flood myths from the ancient Near East includes: E. Babelon, "La tradition phrygienne du Déluge," Revue de l'histoire des religions *23 (1891): 174–183; P. Dhorme, "Le Déluge babylonien,"* Revue biblique *39 (1930): 481–502; H. V. Hilprecht,* The Earliest Version of the Babylonian Deluge Story and the Temple Library of Nippur *(Philadelphia, 1910); A. T. Clay,* A Hebrew Deluge Story in Cuneiform *(New Haven, 1922); E. A. Wallis Budge,* The Babylonian Story of the Deluge and the Epic of Gilgamesh *(London, 1920); Alexander Heidel, "The Story of the Flood," in his* The Gilgamesh Epic and Old Testament Parallels *(Chicago, 1946), pp. 224–269; Georges Contenau,* Le Déluge babylonien *(Paris, 1952), pp. 11–129; Jørgen Laessøe,*

Reprinted from *Andrews University Seminary Studies* 6 (1968): 1–18. [A section treating "Latest Discoveries of Fragments of the Gilgamesh Epic," pp. 11–17, has not been included in this reprinting—Ed. Note]

"The Ātraḫasīs Epic: A Babylonian History of Mankind," Bibliotheca Orientalis 13 (1956): 90–102; Edmond Sollberger, The Babylonian Legend of the Flood (London, 1962); W. G. Lambert, "A New Look at the Babylonian Background of Genesis," Journal of Theological Studies 16 (1965): 287–300; Samuel Noah Kramer, "Reflections on the Mesopotamian Flood: The Cuneiform Data New and Old," Expedition 9(4) (Summer 1967): 12–18; A. R. Millard, "A New Babylonian 'Genesis' Story," Tyndale Bulletin 18 (1967): 3–18; W. G. Lambert and A. R. Millard, Atra-Ḫasīs: The Babylonian Story of the Flood (Oxford, 1969); Giovanni Pettinato, "La Tradizione del Diluvio Universale nella Letteratura Cuneiforme," Biblia e Oriente 11 (1969): 159–174; Eugene Fisher, "Gilgamesh and Genesis: The Flood Story in Context," Catholic Biblical Quarterly 32 (1970): 392–403; William L. Moran, "Atrahasis: The Babylonian Story of the Flood," Biblica 52 (1971): 51–61; Jeffrey H. Tigay, "The Flood Story," in The Evolution of the Gilgamesh Epic (Philadelphia, 1982), pp. 214–240. For detailed comparisons of the Babylonian, Sumerian, and other versions of the flood with that of Genesis, see the second part of G. Lambert, "Il n'y aura plus jamais de Déluge (Genèse IX, 11)," Nouvelle revue théologique 77 (1955): 581–601, 693–724; and the first part of W. J. Dalton, "The Background and Meaning of the Biblical Flood Narrative," Australasian Catholic Record 34 (1957): 292–304; 35 (1958): 23–39.

The topic of the Flood has interested Assyriologists for almost a century.[1] In fact, only a few years after the birth of Assyriology the first cuneiform text alluding to the Flood was deciphered. That discovery brought attention to the Biblical Flood story of Genesis and to the story of the Flood according to Berossus, who had written a history of Babylonia in Greek a generation after Alexander the Great.

In the sequence of archaeological discoveries in Mesopotamia the Assyro-Babylonian texts came to light first; later the Sumerian. The decipherment, study and analysis of texts mentioning the Flood awakened much interest because of their obvious relationship with the Bible records of the Flood. On the one hand, topical studies were of value, because they established points of agreement and differences among the texts as they became known. On the other hand, a study of the texts establishing their relative dates of origin and their chronological order also proved helpful. These two aspects of the investigation are of importance in order to establish the priorities of composition with regard to texts and to ascertain the parentage of the Flood traditions as presented in the Assyro-Babylonian and Sumerian recensions.

[1] Translated from Spanish by Leona G. Running.

CHARACTERISTICS OF THE ASSYRIAN FLOOD TEXTS

The First Assyrian Tradition of the Flood

The first discovered cuneiform text of the Flood in Accadian was identified by George Smith, a minor official of the Assyrian Department of the British Museum, when he encountered the fragment of a text containing the Assyrian story of the Flood among the tablets coming from the ruins of Nineveh. Smith gave an account of his discovery in a lecture which he delivered before a select audience of the Society of Biblical Archaeology on December 3, 1872.[2]

The mutilated text was part of Tablet XI of a composition known as the Gilgamesh Epic consisting of twelve tablets, of which the ancient title corresponded to the first three words of the text, *Ša nagba imura,* "He who saw everything." It is supposed that the tablets containing the Gilgamesh Epic, to which Tablet XI belonged, were discovered by Hormuzd Rassam in 1853 during the excavations at Kuyunjik, one of the ruin-hills of ancient Nineveh, carried out by Henry Layard and Rassam from 1848 to 1854. During those years some 25,000 cuneiform tablets, many of them in a fragmentary condition, were brought to light. The majority of them belonged to the library of King Ashurbanipal (668–626 B.C.).

In the first seven lines of Tablet XI[3] of the poem *Ša nagba imura,* Gilgamesh is presented asking Utnapishtim, whose name means "long of life,"[4] how he had attained to immortality. The answer of Utnapishtim extends from line 8 to line 196. He relates how the god Ea spoke to him while he was living in Shuruppak in a reed hut similar to the *mudhif* which is still used in lower Mesopotamia. According to the message received, he was to build a ship to save himself from the coming disaster. Having done this he gave a great banquet. Without letting his fellow countrymen in on the secret that had been revealed to him by Ea, he loaded the ship with his wealth, his family, and domestic and wild animals. After closing the door and windows he entrusted the ship to the boatman Puzur-Amurri.

[2] George Smith, "The Chaldean Account of the Deluge," *Transactions of the Society of Biblical Archaeology,* II (1873), 213–234.

[3] All references with regard to Tablet XI of the Gilgamesh Epic are from the translation of E. A. Speiser in *Ancient Near Eastern Texts,* pp. 93–97.

[4] Speiser (*ANET,* p. 90, n. 164) suggests that the Assyrian name Utnapishtim means "I have found life," though he admits that the grammar is "somewhat anomalous," in contrast to the warning *balāṭam lā tuttā* (i. 8; iii. 2), "life thou shalt not find," with which Gilgamesh was confronted.

In the Assyrian Flood tablet, the tempest is described in eloquent terms from lines 96–130, after which lines 131–143 relate how the storm was calmed and the ship came to rest on Mount Nisir. Next Utnapishtim enumerates the birds that were set free, from lines 145–155. The description of the sacrifice that he offered on the mountain, which pleased the gods so much that they "crowded like flies about the sacrificer," occupies lines 156–161.

Lines 162–169 of the narrative say that the goddess Ishtar admonished the gods not to permit the god Enlil to meet Utnapishtim since he, Enlil, had been guilty of bringing on the Deluge. But Enlil came anyway, and after having listened to the reproaches of Ea, recorded in lines 178–188, went aboard the ship and blessed Utnapishtim and his wife. Their apotheosis was the result of Enlil's touching their foreheads, through which they became gods and received, according to lines 189–196, an eternal dwelling place at the mouth of the rivers.

The Second Assyrian Tradition of the Flood

A deluge tablet representing a second Assyrian tradition was found by George Smith at Kuyunjik. After having discovered the first fragmentary Flood tablet in the British Museum, public opinion was aroused to such an extent by his lecture on the subject that the owners of the "Daily Telegraph" of London sent him to Mesopotamia in order to find the missing parts of the text.

When Smith began his excavations at Kuyunjik in 1875, he almost immediately unearthed a fragment of a tablet that described the Flood.[5] Unfortunately, it was not one of the missing pieces of Tablet XI that he had translated in London, nor was it even a part of the same story or tradition. Nevertheless the new lines discovered were concerned with the Flood. But they differed from the Gilgamesh Epic. In the former text deciphered by Smith the hero Utnapishtim was the leading character in the Flood story, while in the new fragment the heroic figure was Atrahasis, or the "Exceeding Wise."

The new fragment discovered by Smith at Kuyunjik consists of about 17 lines of cuneiform text that deal with the subject of the Deluge. In spite of the brevity of the text, it was apparent that it was part of another poem concerning the Flood.[6] However, both texts, each repre-

[5] Smith, *The Chaldean Account of Genesis* (New York, 1876), p. 7.

[6] L. W. King, *Cuneiform Texts from Babylonian Tablets, etc., in the British Museum,* XV (London, 1902), 49; E. Ebeling, in *Altorientalische Texte zum Alten Testament,* ed. H. Gressmann (2d ed.; Berlin, 1926), p. 200; A. Boisier, *Revue d'assyriologie et d'archéologie orientale,* XXVIII (1931), 92–95.

senting a separate tradition of the Deluge, belonged to the library of Ashurbanipal.

The contrast between these two Assyrian epics was not limited to the differences in the names of the actors. Although André Parrot thinks that Utnapishtim and Atrahasis represented two different legendary cycles,[7] E. A. Speiser has expressed the opinion that the appearance of the name Atrahasis in line 187 of the first Assyrian tradition of the Deluge, i.e., in Tablet XI of the Gilgamesh poem, is an epithet given by the god Enlil to Utnapishtim. He therefore believes that reference is being made to the same hero in two forms.[8] The fundamental contrast between the two Assyrian texts that meant so much for George Smith resides in a singular detail: Utnapishtim of the Gilgamesh Epic appears as an experienced ship-builder, as lines 54 to 79 present him, referring in detail to the construction of the refuge-ship and to its builder. On the other hand, in the second Assyrian tradition Atrahasis declares emphatically, in lines 11 to 17, that he never had built a ship, hence he begs the god Ea to make a design of the ship upon the ground so that he will be able to build it.[9]

The Third Assyrian Tradition of the Flood

The third Assyrian tradition of the Flood is represented by a somewhat mutilated tablet with four columns of text, three of them having 61 lines devoted to the catastrophe. This tablet likewise comes from the library of King Ashurbanipal. Its first translation was made by L. W. King. Later it was the object of the investigations of A. T. Clay and E. Ebeling.[10] This recension is characterized by a different focus. Human beings, in a state of depravity, appear punished first by famine. Then, after they repented, the famine ceased; but as they returned to sinful life a pestilence was sent upon them. On relapsing, they were punished with sterility of fields as well as of people and flocks. Finally, because of their disorderly lives, they were swept away by the Flood.[11]

[7] André Parrot, *Déluge et arche de Noé* (Neuchâtel, 1955), pp. 24, 25.

[8] Speiser, *op. cit.*, p. 95, n. 218.

[9] Speiser, *op. cit.*, p. 105, Fragment C; R. Largement, "Le thème de l'arche dans les traditions suméro-sémitiques," *Mélanges bibliques redigées en l'honneur d'André Robert* (Paris, 1957), pp. 60–65.

[10] King, *op. cit.*, p. 49; Ebeling, *op. cit.*, pp. 203–206.

[11] Sidney Smith, *Revue d'assyriologie et d'archéologie orientale*, XXII (1925), 63, 64; G. Contenau, *L'Epopée de Gilgamesh, poème babylonien* (Paris, 1939); Alexander Heidel, *The Gilgamesh Epic and the Old Testament Parallels* (Chicago, 1946), pp. 111–116; Speiser, *op. cit.*, pp. 105, 106, Fragment D.

CHARACTERISTICS OF THE BABYLONIAN TRADITIONS REFERRING TO THE FLOOD

First Babylonian Tradition of the Flood

The first tradition is represented by a tablet discovered in the ruins of Nippur, and published by H. V. Hilprecht.[12] The tablet was found in such a poor state of preservation that only 11 lines could be deciphered. They refer to the command to build the ark, into which the larger animals and birds to be saved were to be brought.

The antiquity of this tablet goes back to the First Dynasty of Babylon, which, according to the long chronology, would correspond to the period between the years 1844 and 1505 B.C.[13] One of the characteristics of this Babylonian version of the Flood is that the hero of the Flood is ordered to name the ship that would save him, "Preserver of Life."[14]

Second Babylonian Tradition of the Flood

The second Babylonian tradition of the Flood appears in a tablet discovered in the ruins of Sippar. It contains eight columns with a total of 46 lines of the 439 that were in the complete text.[15] A chronological detail given by this second tradition consists of the information contained in the colophon. There the copyist, Ellit-Aya, the junior scribe, declares that this was Tablet II of the series *Enūma ilu awēlum.*[16] Besides, he indicates that he copied it in the year when King Ammiṣaduqa rebuilt Dur-Ammi-ṣaduqa, near the lower Euphrates, in the 11th year of his reign. Modern chronologists differ with regard to the dates for Ammiṣaduqa. Those who follow the "long" chronology date his reign to

[12] H. V. Hilprecht, *The Earliest Version of the Babylonian Deluge Story and the Temple Library of Nippur,* "Babylonian Expedition of the University of Pennsylvania; The Babylonian Expedition," Ser. D, Vol. V, Part I (Philadelphia, 1910), pp. 1–65; Speiser, *op. cit.,* p. 105, Fragment X; A. Deimel, "Diluvium in traditione babylonica," *Verbum Domini,* VII (1927), 186–191; Deimel, "Biblica diluvii traditio cum traditione babylonica comparata," *Verbum Domini,* VII (1927), 248–251.

[13] Parrot, *Sumer* (Madrid, 1960), p. 310.

[14] Speiser, *op. cit.,* p. 105, Fragment X, line 8; A. Salonen, *Die Wasserfahrzeuge in Babylonien* (Helsinki, 1939), p. 51, under *eleppu qurqurru.*

[15] A. T. Clay, *Babylonian Records in the J. Pierpont Morgan Library,* IV (New Haven, Conn., 1923), Pl. I; Heidel, *op. cit.,* pp. 109, 110; Speiser, *op. cit.,* pp. 104, 105, Fragments A and B.

[16] Speiser, *op. cit.,* pp. 104, 105, Fragment A, col. viii.

1702–1682,[17] while those adhering to the "short" chronology date his reign to 1582–1562.[18]

The individual saved from the Deluge, according to this story, is named Atramhasis and not Atrahasis.[19] Another dissimilarity of this tradition is the reference to the growing number of human beings and to their oppressive spirit, for which the gods decided to send the Flood. This is described in the form of a great flood-storm with many clouds accumulated by the wind. The god Enki accuses the god Enlil of having sent the Flood.

Probably belonging to the second Babylonian tradition is a fragment of a tablet with only 15 legible lines, not counting the colophon. The latter gives the following information: ". . . Total 1245 [lines] of three tablets. By the hand of Ellit-Aya, the junior scribe. . . ."[20] That statement gives evidence that the tablet comes from the same hand as the previous one and that, consequently, it belongs to the same perod.[21] The few lines remaining refer to the command to destroy the house of the main actor, probably Atramhasis—whose name does not appear in those few lines—in order to build a ship in which he could be saved, leaving behind his earthly possessions.[22]

CHARACTERISTICS OF THE SUMERIAN TEXTS REFERRING TO THE FLOOD

First Sumerian Tradition of the Flood

The first is a fragmentary tablet discovered by A. Poebel among the tablets of the University Museum, Philadelphia, which had been found in the ruins of Nippur. Its condition permits the reading of only about

[17] F. Thureau-Dangin, "La chronologie de la première dynastie babylonienne," *Mémoires de l'Académie,* Tome 43, Part 2 (1942), pp. 229–258.

[18] W. F. Albright, *Bulletin of the American Schools of Oriental Research,* No. 88 (Dec. 1942), p. 32.

[19] Boisier, *op. cit.,* pp. 91–97. Obviously Atramhasis was simply the Old Babylonian form for the later Assyrian Atrahasis.

[20] Speiser, *op. cit.,* p. 105, Fragment B.

[21] Boisier, *op. cit.,* pp. 92–95.

[22] The Babylonian traditions of the Flood have some resemblance with the Gilgamesh Epic. But the tablets from Ashurbanipal's library originated at a much later date. E. A. Wallis Budge and C. J. Gadd, *The Babylonian Story of the Deluge and the Epic of Gilgamesh* (London, 1929); A. Schott and W. von Soden, *Das Gilgamesch-Epos* (Stuttgart, 1958); cf. von Soden, *Zeitschrift für Assyriologie und verwandte Gebiete,* LIII (1959), 228.

90 lines, distributed over six columns, and it is calculated that some 230 lines of cuneiform text have been lost.[23] This singular text has also engaged other Sumerologists.[24]

As 37 lines are missing from the beginning of the tablet, it is not known which god began the dialogue. Kramer says: "The name of the speaker (or speakers) is destroyed; probably it is either Enki or Anu and Enlil (perhaps better Anu Enlil, . . .)."[25]

This Flood tradition presents the king and priest Ziusudra ("Long of Life") in the moment when he is carving a god of wood to worship and consult as an oracle. The text claims that in this way Ziusudra was informed of the grave decision of the gods: "By our hand a Deluge . . . will be [sent]; to destroy the seed of mankind. . . ."[26] The hero was saved in a ship during the cataclysm, which lasted seven days. When he opened the covering, the sun god Utu appeared. After sacrificing an ox and a sheep and bowing before Anu and Enlil, Ziusudra received the gift of immortality in the land of Dilmun.

The Sumerian text of the Flood, after mentioning the creation of the animals and man, refers to the founding of five antediluvian cities. Lacking are the lines that could have referred to the causes that determined the cataclysm of the Flood. The hero Ziusudra is presented as a pious king who was informed of the decision taken by the gods to destroy mankind. The section of the text that could have mentioned the building of the saving ship also is broken. On the other hand, the violence of the Flood during seven days and seven nights is described. After the disaster the sun god Utu appears and "brought his rays into the giant boat." And Ziusudra, in order to live as the gods, is translated to the land of Dilmun, "the place where the sun rises."[27] Dilmun, according to the preamble of the myth of Enki and Ninḫursag, represented a pure, clean, and brilliant place where, probably, there was neither sickness nor death.

[23]Arno Poebel, *Historical Texts*, "The University Museum, Publications of the Babylonian Section," Vol. IV, No. 1 (Philadelphia, 1914), pp. 9–70; S. N. Kramer, *Ancient Near Eastern Texts*, pp. 42–44; A. Pacios, "Diluvio," *Enciclopedia de la Biblia*, II (Barcelona, 1964), col. 930.

[24]Thorkild Jacobsen, *The Sumerian King List* (Chicago, 1939), pp. 58, 59; Kramer, *Sumerian Mythology* (Philadelphia, 1944), pp. 97, 98; Heidel, *op. cit.*, 102–105.

[25]Kramer, *Ancient Near Eastern Texts*, p. 42, n. 1, but see also n. 4.

[26]Heidel, *op. cit.*, p. 103.

[27]Kramer, "Dilmun the Land of the Living," *Bulletin of the American Schools of Oriental Research*, No. 96 (Dec. 1944), pp. 18–28; Kramer, *L'histoire commence à Sumer* (Paris, 1957), pp. 206, 207.

Reference to the Flood in the Sumerian King List

The Sumerian King List involves texts of a completely different character from all the preceding ones. These appear as poems or epics that recur in the common tradition of the Flood cataclysm, while the Sumerian King List constitutes documents of a historiographic character. Such documents containing a list of the kings of Sumer were published for chronological and historical purposes, and divided Sumer's history into two periods: *lam abubi,* "before the Flood," and *arki abubi,* "after the Flood."[28]

The texts of this kind are scarce. They consist, first of all, of two documents acquired by H. Weld-Blundell and, in addition, of a tablet published by V. Scheil,[29] furthermore of a list of the first kings of Mesopotamia. The critical examination of that material by Thorkild Jacobsen, studying textual, stylistic and historical problems, has shown that the original was written in the days when Utuhegal, king of Uruk, liberated Sumer from the Guti domination.[30] Scholars are still divided with regard to dates for the end of the Guti Dynasty and for Utuhegal of Uruk, which lie between *ca.* 2120 and *ca.* 2065 B.C.[31]

The two documents obtained by Weld-Blundell are complementary to each other. The first consists of a prism that mentions five antediluvian cities and enumerates eight kings who reigned before the Flood.[32] The second document has only 18 lines, but is also of interest because it again mentions the names of the antediluvian kings and the Flood itself.[33]

The study of all Sumerian King Lists has been undertaken by Jacobsen in order to establish a "standard version," by a combination of different texts. The reference to the Flood appears after the mention of eight kings and five antediluvian cities (Eridu, Badtibira, Larak, Sippar and Shuruppak). The text alluding to the Flood is brief: "These are five cities,

[28] Contenau, *Le déluge babylonien* (Paris, 1952), p. 55.

[29] V. Scheil, "Liste susienne des dynasties de Sumer-Accad," in *Memoires de l'Institute français d'archéologie orientale,* LXII (Cairo, 1934), (=*Mélanges Maspéro,* I), 393–400.

[30] Jacobsen, *op. cit.,* pp. 140, 141.

[31] For the earlier date see Gadd, "The Dynasty of Agade and the Gutian Invasion," *The Cambridge Ancient History,* 2d ed., Vol. I, Fasc. 19 (Cambridge, 1966), p. 56. For the late date see Albright, *loc. cit.*

[32] W.B. 444 was published by S. Langdon, *Oxford Editions of Cuneiform Texts,* II (Oxford, 1923), 8–21, Pls. I–IV. See also Edouard Dhorme, "L'aurore de l'histoire babylonienne," *Recueil Edouard Dhorme* (Paris, 1951), pp. 3–79.

[33] For the document W.B. 62 see Langdon, *Journal of the Royal Asiatic Society of Great Britain and Ireland,* XC (1923), 251 ff.; Ebeling, *op. cit.,* pp. 148, 149.

eight kings ruled them for 241,000 years. (Then) the Flood swept over (the earth). After the Flood had swept over (the earth) (and) when kingship was lowered (again) from heaven, kingship was (first) in Kish."[34]

The Sumerian Tradition Reflected in the Flood Account of Berossus

Berossus, priest of the cult of Marduk in the city of Babylon, a contemporary of the king Antiochus I Soter (281–260), wrote in Greek a history of his country entitled *Babyloniaca*. That work, written on the Aegean island of Cos about the year 275 B.C., has been lost. Nevertheless many of its principal paragraphs are known through quotations of the following historians: Apollodorus of Athens (*ca.* 144 B.C.), Alexander Polyhistor (*ca.* 88 B.C.), Abydenus (*ca.* 60 B.C.), King Juba of Mauretania (*ca.* 50 B.C.–*ca.* A.D. 23), Flavius Josephus (A.D. 37–103), Eusebius of Caesarea (A.D. 265–340), and Georgius Syncellus (*ca.* A.D. 792).[35]

The Flood story of Berossus was the only Mesopotamian tradition of that cataclysm that was known before the discovery of cuneiform texts containing Flood stories. The account of Berossus, which begins with the creation of the world, points out ten antediluvian kings of long life, indicating Xisuthros as the tenth, who appears as the hero of the Flood. According to Berossus, Xisuthros was warned by one of the gods of the imminence of the Flood, being ordered to prepare a ship to save his family and his friends, and also the animals. Saved in this manner, he disembarked on a mountain in Armenia. After having worshipped the gods, he and his wife, his daughter, and the pilot disappeared from among mortals to be with the gods.

It is interesting to note, as Parrot has pointed out, that the account of Berossus has great affinities with the Sumerian text of the Flood and with the Sumerian King Lists. It can be observed that in the tablet W.B. 62 the names of the kings of Shuruppak are indicated: Su-kur-lam, son of Ubar-Tutu, and Ziusudra, son of Su-kur-lam. Ziusudra appears both in the Sumerian tablet of the Flood and, with the name Xisuthros, in the account of Berossus, who must have selected the Sumerian text as the most ancient.[36]

[34] Oppenheim, *Ancient Near Eastern Texts*, p. 265.

[35] Ebeling, *op. cit.*, pp. 200, 201; Heidel, *op. cit.*, pp. 116–119; Paul Schnabel, *Berossos und die babylonisch-hellenistische Literatur* (Leipzig, 1923), pp. 264 ff.; F. Lenormant, *Essai de commentaire des fragments cosmogéniques de Bérose* (Paris, 1872).

[36] Parrot, *Déluge et arche de Noé*, pp. 28–32.

GENERAL CONCLUSIONS

A study of the available Flood texts considered in this paper leads to the following conclusions:

1. The Accadian—Assyrian and Babylonian—texts of the Flood have a similar theme, but show secondary differences with reference to the names of gods and in expressions due to regional coloring.
2. The names Utnaphistim, Atrahasis, Atramhasis, Ziusudra, Xisuthros given to the hero of the Flood are different, because preferential epithets were adopted in different regions of Mesopotamia. However, this does not constitute sufficient reason to assume that more than one person was actually meant.
3. The Assyrian texts, coming from the library of Ashurbanipal, as the most recent compositions, are regarded by scholars to be dependent upon the Babylonian traditions, from which local adaptations of the Deluge theme were made.
4. The Babylonian texts of the Flood, although following the lines of two parallel recensions, point to a common origin, which chronologically goes back to the tradition that had circulated in Sumer.
5. It is evident that some of those who used the Accadian language were familiar with the classical Sumerian literature, by which they attained a direct acquaintance with the traditions of Sumer, as evidenced much later by Berossus.
6. The Mesopotamian texts of the Flood—Assyrian, Babylonian, and Sumerian—contain the same old tradition of a great cataclysm, and show that the Deluge was considered to mark a clear break between two periods: the prediluvian and the postdiluvian world.

The Atrahasis Epic and Its Significance for Our Understanding of Genesis 1–9

TIKVA FRYMER-KENSKY

No small part of the excitement arising from the study of Near Eastern texts of the flood myth had to do with the illumination it might shed on the biblical account. The texts, of course, are interesting in their own right, but it is hard not to think of comparisons with the Noachian deluge when one reads Assyrian and Babylonian flood texts. The critical question is: what precisely can the comparative method tell us with respect to the flood narrative in Genesis? Often comparisons can demonstrate just what is unique about a given text. For the comparative method can reveal not only how texts are alike but how they are dissimilar.

In the following essay by Professor Tikva Frymer-Kensky of the Near Eastern Studies Department at Wayne State University, we find an ingenious interpretation of the biblical account stimulated by a comparative study. For another comparative-interpretative essay, see Ruth E. Simoons-Vermeer, "The Mesopotamian Floodstories: A Comparison and Interpretation," Numen *21 (1974): 17–34.*

THE BABYLONIAN FLOOD STORIES

Three different Babylonian stories of the flood have survived: the Sumerian Flood Story, the eleventh tablet of the Gilgamesh Epic, and the Atrahasis Epic. Details in these stories, such as the placing of animals in the ark, the landing of the ark on a mountain, and the sending forth of birds to see whether the waters had receded, indicate clearly that

Reprinted by permission of the publisher, the Biblical Archaeology Society, from the November/December 1978 issue of *Biblical Archaeology Review.* For further information write to Biblical Archaeology Society, 3000 Connecticut Ave., NW, Washington, D.C. 20008.

these stories are intimately related to the biblical flood story and, indeed, that the Babylonian and biblical accounts of the flood represent different retellings of an essentially identical flood tradition. Until the recovery of the Atrahasis Epic, however, the usefulness of these tales toward an understanding of Genesis was limited by the lack of a cohesive context for the flood story comparable to that of Genesis. The Sumerian Flood Story has survived in a very fragmentary state, and even its most recent edition (by Miguel Civil in Lambert and Millard, *Atrahasis: The Babylonian Story of the Flood,* Oxford, 1969) can only be understood with the aid of the other known flood stories. The Gilgamesh Epic presents a different problem for comparative analysis. Here the flood story is clearly in a secondary context, and, more importantly, this context is so different from the biblical as to cause serious differences in content. In the Gilgamesh Epic the story of the flood is related as part of the tale of Gilgamesh's quest for immortality. Utnapishtim tells his descendant Gilgamesh the story of the flood in order to tell him why he became immortal and, in so doing, to show Gilgamesh that he cannot become immortal in the same way. This purpose is explicitly stated, for the story is introduced by Gilgamesh's question, "As I look upon you, Utnapishtim, your features are not strange; you are just as I . . . how did you join the Assembly of the gods in your quest for life?" (Gilgamesh XI:2–7). Utnapishtim concludes his recitation with the admonition. "But now who will call the gods to Assembly for your sake so that you may find the life that you are seeking?" (Gilgamesh XI:197–98).

The nature of the story as "Utnapishtim's tale" colors the recitation of the flood episode and makes it fundamentally different from the biblical flood story. The "first person narrative" format means that Utnapishtim can only tell those parts of the story that he knows, and that he may leave out those aspects that do not concern him or fit his purpose. For example, even though Babylonian gods are not portrayed as capricious and are considered as having reasons for their actions, Utnapishtim tells us nothing about the reasons that the gods brought the flood. This lapse is dictated by the literary format: Utnapishtim may not know the reason for the flood, or he may not record it because it is irrelevant to his purpose, which is to recount how he became immortal. Similarly, the only event after the flood that Utnapishtim relates to Gilgamesh is the subsequent convocation of the gods that granted him immortality. The result of the "personalization" of the flood story in the Gilgamesh Epic is that the scope of the story is restricted to the adventures of one individual and its significance to its effects upon him, with the flood itself emptied of any cosmic or anthropological significance. The flood stories in Genesis and in Gilgamesh are so far removed from each other in focus and intent that one cannot compare the ideas in the two versions of the flood without setting up spurious dichotomies.

THE ATRAHASIS EPIC

The recovery of the Atrahasis Epic provides new perspectives on Genesis because, unlike the other two Babylonian versions of the flood, the Atrahasis Epic presents the flood story in a context comparable to that of Genesis, that of a Primeval History. The flood episode of the Atrahasis Epic has been known for a long time, but the literary structure of the epic, and therefore the context of the flood story, was not understood until Laessøe reconstructed the work (J. Laessøe, "The Atrahasis Epic: A Babylonian History of Mankind," *Biblioteca Orientalis* 13 [1956] 90–102). In 1965, Lambert and Millard (*Cuneiform Texts from Babylonian Tablets in the British Museum,* London) published many additional texts from the epic, including an Old Babylonian copy (written around 1650 B.C.E.) which is our most complete surviving recension of the tale. These new texts greatly increased our knowledge of the epic and served as the foundation for the English edition of the epic by Lambert and Millard (*Atrahasis: The Babylonian Story of the Flood,* Oxford, 1969).

The Atrahasis Epic starts with a depiction of the world as it existed before man was created: "When the gods worked like Man" (the first line and ancient title of the composition). At this time the universe was divided among the great gods, with An taking the heavens, Enlil the earth and Enki the great deep. Seven gods (called the Anunnaki in this text) established themselves as the ruling class, while the rest of the gods provided the work force. These gods, whose "work was heavy, (whose) distress was much," dug the Tigris and Euphrates rivers and then rebelled, refusing to continue their labors. On the advice of Enki, the gods decided to create a substitute to do the work of the gods, and Enki and the mother goddess created man from clay and from the flesh and blood of a slain god, "We-ilu, a god who has sense," from whom man was to gain rationality. The various themes and motifs out of which this part of the epic is composed can all be documented elsewhere and do not seem to have originated with this text.

This epic, ancient though it is, is already the product of considerable development, and the author of the composition has utilized old motifs and has united them into a coherent account of man's beginnings in which he presents a picture of the purpose of man's creation, his *raison d'être,* as doing the work of the gods and thus relieving them of the need to labor. In the same way, he seems to have taken the previously known story of the flood and juxtaposed it to his creation story to continue the tale of primeval man and indicate the prerequisites of human life upon earth.

In the Atrahasis Epic the creation of man causes new problems. In the words of the epic (I 352f. restored from II 1–8):

> Twelve hundred years [had not yet passed]
> [when the land extended] and the peoples multiplied.
> The [land] was bellowing [like a bull].
> The gods were disturbed with [their uproar].
> [Enlil heard] their noise
> [and addressed] the great gods.
> "The noise of mankind [has become too intense for me]
> [with their uproar] I am deprived of sleep.

To solve this problem, the gods decided to bring a plague, which ends when Enki advises man to bring offerings to Namtar, god of the plague, and thus induce him to lift the plague. This plague does not solve the problem permanently, for twelve hundred years later the same problem arises again (Tablet II 1–8) and the gods bring a drought, which ends when men (upon Enki's advice) bribe Adad to bring rain. Despite the fragmentary state of Tablet II, it is easy to see that the same problem recurs, and the gods bring famine (and saline soil), which again do not end the difficulties. At last Enlil persuades the gods to adopt a "final solution" (II viii 34) to the human problem, and they resolve to bring a flood to destroy mankind. Their plan is thwarted by Enki, who has Atrahasis build an ark and so escape the flood. After the rest of mankind have been destroyed, and after the gods have had occasion to regret their actions and to realize (by their thirst and hunger) that they need man, Atrahasis brings a sacrifice and the gods come to eat. Enki then presents a permanent solution to the problem. The new world after the flood is to be different from the old, for Enki summons Nintu, the birth goddess, and has her create new creatures, who will ensure that the old problem does not arise again. In the words of the epic (III viii 1):

> In addition, let there be a third category among the peoples,
> Among the peoples women who bear and women who do not bear.
> Let there be among the peoples the *Pašittu*-demon to snatch the baby from the lap of her who bore it.
> Establish *Ugbabtu*-women, *Entu*-women, and *Igiṣitu*-women
> and let them be taboo and so stop childbirth.

Other post-flood provisions may have followed, but the text now becomes too fragmentary to read.

Despite the lacunae, the structure presented by the Atrahasis Epic is clear. Man is created . . . there is a problem in creation . . . remedies are attempted but the problem remains . . . the decision is made to destroy man . . . this attempt is thwarted by the wisdom of Enki . . . a new remedy is instituted to ensure that the problem does not arise again. Several years ago Anne Kilmer ("The Mesopotamian Concept of Overpopulation and Its Solution as Represented in the Mythology," *Orientalia* 41 [1972] 160–77) and William J. Moran ("The Babylonian Story of the Flood [review article]," *Biblica* 40 [1971] 51–61), working independently, demonstrated that the problem that arose and that necessitated these various remedies was that of overpopulation. Mankind increased uncontrollably, and the methods of population control that were first attempted (drought, pestilence, famine) only solved the problem temporarily. This overpopulation led to destruction (the flood), and permanent countermeasures were introduced by Enki to keep the size of the population down. The myth tells us that such social phenomena as non-marrying women, and such personal tragedies as barrenness and stillbirth (and perhaps miscarriage and infant mortality) are in fact essential to the very continuation of man's existence, for humanity was almost destroyed once when the population got out of control.

GENESIS AND ATRAHASIS

This Babylonian tale, composed no later than 1700 B.C.E., is very attractive to us today and can almost be called a "myth for our times," for we share with the Babylonians a consciousness of a limited ecology and a concern about controlling the human population. In addition to this inherent relevance, however, it is very important for biblical studies, for it points out what (by the clear logic of hindsight) should have been obvious to us all along: there is an organic unity to the first section of Genesis. The importance of the Atrahasis Epic is that it focuses our attention away from the deluge itself and onto the events immediately after the rains subside. In Genesis, as in Atrahasis, the flood came in response to a serious problem in creation, a problem which was rectified immediately after the flood. A study of the changes that God made in the world after the flood gives a clearer picture of the conditions prevailing in the world before the flood, of the ultimate reason that necessitated the flood which almost caused the destruction of man, of the essential differences between the world before the flood and the world after it, and thus of the essential prerequisites for the continued existence of man on the earth.

Unlike Atrahasis, the flood story in Genesis is emphatically not about overpopulation. On the contrary, God's first action after the flood was to command Noah and his sons to "be fruitful and multiply and fill the earth" (Gen 9:1). This echoes the original command to Adam (1:28) and seems to be an explicit rejection of the idea that the flood came as a result of attempts to decrease man's population. The repetition of this commandment in emphatic terms in Gen 9:7, "and you be fruitful and multiply, swarm over the earth and multiply in it," makes it probable that the Bible consciously rejected the underlying theme of the Atrahasis Epic, that the fertility of man before the flood was the reason for his near destruction.

It is not surprising that Genesis rejects the idea of overpopulation as the reason for the flood, for the Bible does not share the belief of Atrahasis and some other ancient texts that overpopulation is a serious issue. Barrenness and stillbirth (or miscarriage) are not considered social necessities, nor are they justified as important for population control. On the contrary, when God promises the land to Israel he promises that "in your land women will neither miscarry nor be barren" (Exod 23:26). The continuation of this verse, "I will fill the number of your days," seems to be a repudiation of yet another of the "natural" methods of population control, that of premature death. In the ideal world which is to be established in the land of Israel there will be no need for such methods, for overpopulation is not a major concern.

Genesis states explicity that God decided to destroy the world because of the wickedness of man (Gen 6:5). Although this traditionally has been understood to mean that God destroyed the world as a punishment for man's sins, this understanding of the passage entails serious theological problems, such as the propriety of God's destroying all life on earth because of the sins of man. Such an interpretation also causes great problems in understanding the text of Genesis itself and creates what seems to be a paradox, for the "wickedness of man" is also given as the reason that God decides never again to bring a flood (Gen 8:21). Since the evil nature of man is presented after the flood as the reason for God's vow never again to bring a flood, we should not infer that God brought the flood as a punishment because man was evil. Genesis also states that God brought the flood because the world was full of *ḥāmās*. The term *ḥāmās* is very complex, and a semantic analysis is presented below. The wide range of meanings for the term *ḥāmās* means that a lexical analysis of the word is not sufficient to allow us to determine what particular evil is here called *ḥāmās* and what it was about this particular evil that necessitated a flood. The nature of the evil and the cause of the flood must be found in the story of Genesis.

The Atrahasis Epic is so important to biblical studies because it enables us to determine the cause of the flood by focusing our attention away from the deluge itself and onto the events immediately after the flood, i.e., to Genesis 9. In this chapter God offers Noah and his sons a covenant, in which he promises never again to bring a flood to destroy the world, and gives the rainbow as the token of this promise. At this time God gives Noah and his sons several laws, and the difference between the ante- and the post-diluvium worlds can be found in these laws. These laws are thus the structural equivalent of the new solutions proposed by Enki in the Atrahasis Epic. In Atrahasis the problem in man's creation was overpopulation, and the solutions proposed by Enki are designed to rectify this problem by controlling and limiting the population. In the Bible the problem is not overpopulation, but "since the devisings of man's heart are evil from his youth" (Gen 8:21), God must do something if he does not want to destroy the earth repeatedly. This something is to create laws for mankind, laws to ensure that matters do not again reach such a state that the world must be destroyed.

The idea that man's nature is basically evil and that laws are therefore necessary to control his evil is a rather Hobbesian view of mankind, and it should be mentioned that this was not always the philosophy of Israel. The Bible also affords support for the idea that man is intrinsically good, and even Gen 8:21 can be reinterpreted to agree with this philosophy, as in the Midrash Tanhuma, where this verse is interpreted to mean that the evil inclination does not come to a man until he becomes a youth, i.e., 10 years old, and that it is man who raises himself to be evil (Midrash Tanhuma Bereshit 1.7). The simple meaning of the statement in Gen 8:21, "the imagination of man's heart is evil from his youth," however, indicates clearly that Genesis comes down on the *Leviathan* side of what is obviously a very old controversy about the nature of man. Such perceptions of an inherently evil aspect of man's nature, one which is naturally prone to violent and unrighteous acts, logically entails a recognition that man cannot be allowed to live by his instincts alone, that he must be directed and controlled by laws, that in fact laws are the *sine qua non* of human existence. It is for this reason that God's first act after the flood is to give man laws.

THE FLOOD IN GENESIS

The realization that the granting of laws after the flood was a direct response by God to the problem posed by man's evil nature resolves the apparent paradox between the statement that the wickedness of man somehow caused the flood and the statement that the wickedness of man caused God to take steps to ensure that he will never again have to bring a flood. However, it does not answer the question of why the flood was necessary, why God could not simply have announced a new order and introduced laws to mankind without first destroying almost all of humanity. This problem does not arise in the Babylonian flood stories, where there is a clear distinction between the gods who decide to bring a flood (Enlil and the council of the gods) and the god who realized the error of this decision, saved man and introduced the new order (Enki). The problem, however, is quite serious in the monotheistic conception of the flood in which the same God decides to bring the flood, saves man, and resolves never to bring a flood again. If God is rational and consistent in his actions, there must have been a compelling reason that necessitated the flood. "Punishment" is not enough of a reason, for it not only raises the question of God's right to punish all the animals for the sins of man, but also raises the serious issue of God's right to punish man in this instance at all: if man has evil tendencies, and if he has not been checked and directed by laws, how can he be punished for simply following his own instincts? The flood cannot simply have been brought as a punishment, and its necessitating cause must lie in the particular nature of the evil which filled the world before the flood. Our best way to find out the nature of evil is to look at the solution given to control the evil, i.e., to the laws given immediately after the flood.

The oral tradition of Israel (as reflected in the rabbinic writings) has developed and expanded the laws given to Noah and his sons after the flood into a somewhat elaborate system of "the seven Noahide commandments." The traditional enumeration of these is the prohibition of idolatry, blasphemy, bloodshed, sexual sins, theft, eating from a living animal, and the commandment to establish legal systems. Additional laws are sometimes included among the commandments to Noah and his sons, and the system of Noahide commandments can best be understood as a system of universal ethics, a "Natural Law" system in which the laws are given by God. Genesis itself, however, does not contain a list of all seven of these commandments. According to Genesis 9, God issued three commandments to Noah and his sons immediately after the flood: (1) he commanded man to be fruitful, to increase, multiply and swarm over the earth; (2) he announced that although man may eat meat he must not eat animals alive (or eat the blood, which is tantamount to the same thing—Gen 9:4); and (3) he declared that no one, neither beast nor man, can kill a human being without forfeiting his own life, providing for the execution of all killers, "whoever sheds the blood of man, by man shall his blood be shed."

The significance of the first commandment (that of fertility) has already been mentioned: it is an explicit and probably conscious rejection of the idea that the cause of the flood was overpopulation and that overpopulation is a serious problem. Together the other two commandments introduce a very clear differentiation between man and the animal kingdom: man may kill animals for food (while observing certain restrictions in so doing), but no one, whether man or beast, can kill man. The reason for this "Absolute Sanctity of Human Life" (as it is usually called) is given in the text: "for man is created in God's image" (Gen 9:6). Taken independently, these two commandments—the prohibition against eating blood (and the living animal), and the declaration of the principle of the inviolability of human life with the provision of capital punishment for murder—embody two of the basic principles of Israelite law.

The Bible views blood as a very special substance. Israel is seriously enjoined against eating the blood of animals, and this prohibition is repeated six times in the Pentateuch (Gen 9:4; Lev 3:17; 7:26; 17:10–14; Deut 12:16 and 12:23–24). This prohibition is called an eternal ordinance (Lev 3:17), and the penalty for eating blood (at least in the Priestly tradition) is *kārēt,* which is some form of outlawry, whether banishment or ostracism (Lev 7:27; 17:10, 14). The reason for this strict prohibition is explicit: the spirit (*nepeš*) of the animal is in the blood (Lev 17:11, 14; Deut 12:23). The greatest care must be exercised in the eating of meat. According to the Priestly tradition, slaughtering of animals (other than creatures of the hunt) can only be done at an altar. Failure to bring the animal to the altar was considered tantamount to the shedding of blood (Lev 17:4). The sprinkling of the animal's blood upon the altar served as a redemption (Lev 17:11). In Deuteronomy, where the cult is centralized and it is no longer feasible to bring the animals to an altar, permission is given to eat and slaughter animals anywhere. However (as with the animals of the hunt in Leviticus), care must be taken not to eat the blood, which should be poured upon the ground and covered (Deut 12:24).

The idea expressed in the third commandment, that of the incomparability and inviolability of human life, is one of the fundamental axioms of Israelite philosophy, and the ramifications of this principle pervade every aspect of Israelite law and distinguish it dramatically from the other Near Eastern legal systems with which it otherwise has so much in common. In Israel, capital punishment is reserved for the direct offense against God and is never invoked for offenses against property. The inverse of this is also true; the prime offense in Israel is homicide, which can never be compensated by the payment of a monetary fine and can only be rectified by the execution of the murderer.

Despite the importance of this principle, if we look at the world before the flood, it is immediately apparent that this demand for the execution of murderers is new. Only three stories are preserved in Genesis from the ten generations between the expulsion from the Garden and the bringing of the flood. Two of these, the Cain and Abel story (Gen 4:1–15) and the tale of Lemech (Gen 4:19–24), concern the shedding of human blood. In the first tale Cain, having murdered his brother Abel, becomes an outcast and must lose his home. However, he is not killed. In fact, he becomes one of "God's protected" and is marked with a special sign on his forehead to indicate that Cain's punishment (if any) is the Lord's and that whoever kills him will be subject to sevenfold retribution. The next story preserved—that of Lemech five generations later—also concerns murder, for Lemech kills "a man because of my wounding, a young man because of my hurt" (Gen 4:23). Lemech, too, is not killed and claims the same protection that Cain had, declaring that as Cain was protected with sevenfold retribution he, Lemech, will be avenged with seventy-sevenfold (Gen 4:24). The main difference between the world before the flood and the new order established immediately after it is the different treatment of murderers, and the cause of the flood should therefore be sought in this crucial difference.

Murder has catastrophic consequences, not only for the individuals involved, but for the earth itself, which has the blood of innocent victims spilled upon it. As God says to Cain after Abel's murder (Gen 4:10–12):

> Your brother's blood cries out to me from the soil. And now you are cursed by the earth which opened her mouth to receive the blood of your brother from your hand. When you till the ground it shall no longer yield its strength to you; a wanderer and a vagabond you will be on the earth.

The innocent blood which was spilled on it has made the ground barren for Cain, who must therefore leave his land and become a wanderer. This process of the cursing and concomitant barrenness of the ground had become widespread. The explanation of the name given to Noah makes this point. The Masoretic Text reads: "This one will comfort us from our acts and the toil of our hands." Alternatively, if we follow the Septuagint (old Greek translation), the text would read: "This one will give us rest from our acts and the toil of our hands." Either way, the latter part of the verse, "because of the ground which God has cursed" is clear: Noah's name is explained by Genesis as related to the conditions which caused the flood, the "cursing" of the ground, and Noah's role somehow alleviates the condition.

By the generation of the flood the whole earth has become polluted (KJV "the earth also was corrupt") and is filled with *ḥāmās* (Gen 6:11). The wide range of meanings of the word *ḥāmās* in the Bible encompasses almost the entire spectrum of evil. The term can stand for evil of any sort (Ps 11:5; Prov 13:2); it may simply stand for falsehood, as in *ʿēd ḥāmās* "false witness" (Exod 23:1; Deut 19:15; Ps 35:1) and its occurrence with *mirmâ* (Isa 60:18; Jer 6:7, 20:8), with the two together meaning something like "plunder and pillage." *Ḥāmās* has a very close connection to *dāmîm* "bloodshed," as can be seen from Ezek 9:9. Like *dāmîm*, the term *ḥāmās* can be used in a physical way, for *ḥāmās* (or the pollution from it) can cover clothes (Mal 2:16) and hands (Job 16:17; 1 Chron 12:17). In Genesis, the earth is filled with *ḥāmās* and has itself become polluted because all flesh had polluted its way upon the earth (Gen 6:11–12). It is the filling of the earth with *ḥāmās* and its resultant pollution that prompts God to bring a flood to physically erase everything from the earth and start anew. The flood is not primarily an agency of punishment (although to be drowned is hardly a pleasant reward), but a means of getting rid of a thoroughly polluted world and starting again with a clean, well-washed one. Then, when everything has been washed away, God resolves (Gen 8:21):

> I will no longer curse the ground because of man, for the devisings of man's heart are evil from his youth, and I will no longer strike all the living creatures that I have created;

and goes on to give Noah and his sons the basic laws, specifically the strict instructions about the shedding of blood, to prevent the earth's becoming so polluted again.

POLLUTION IN THE BIBLE

The idea of the pollution of the earth is not a vague metaphor to indicate moral wrongdoing. On the contrary, in the biblical worldview, the murders before the flood contaminated the land and created a state of physical pollution which had to be eradicated by physical means (the flood). Although this concept may seem strange to us, it is not surprising to find it here in the cosmology of Israel, for Israel clearly believed that moral wrongdoings defile physically. This is explicitly stated with three sins—murder, idolatry, and sexual abominations—and it is interesting to note that these are the three cardinal sins for which a Jew must suffer martyrdom rather than commit them (*b. Sanhedrin* 74a). These are mentioned in Acts as offenses from which all the nations must refrain (Acts 15:20); these three offenses are given as the explanation of *ḥāmās* in the flood story by Rabbi Levy in Genesis Rabbah (31:16); and these (together with the non-observance of the sabbatical year) are given in the Mishna as the reasons that exile enters the world (Nezigin 5:8). According to the biblical tradition, the pre-Israelite inhabitants of Canaan had defiled the land with the sexual abominations enumerated in Leviticus 18. As a result God had punished the land (Lev 18:25), and the land had therefore vomited up the inhabitants which had defiled it. For this reason, Israel is admonished not to commit these abominations and defile the land lest it vomit them out in the same way (Lev 18:24–28). Later, Israel was told that it has defiled the land (Jer 2:7) and that because Israel defiled the land with their idols and because of the blood which they spilled upon the land, God poured his fury upon them (Ezek 36:18).

The most serious contaminant of the land is the blood of those who have been murdered; the concept of "bloodguilt" is well known in Israelite law. Because of the seriousness of the crime of murder, and perhaps also because of the mystical conception of blood in Israelite thought, the blood of the slain physically pollutes the land. For this reason, the discovery of a corpse posed a real problem for the people. When such an unsolved murder occurred, recourse was had to the procedure of the *ʿeglā ʿărūpā* ("the breaking of the heifer's neck") a ritual meant to cleanse the land of the pollution of the murder: the elders of the nearest town were to bring a heifer to an uninhabited wadi, strike off its head, wash their hands over it and offer the following prayer:

> Our hands have not shed this blood, nor have our eyes seen (the deed). Be merciful O Lord, to your people Israel whom you have redeemed and lay not innocent blood into the midst of the people (Deut 21:7–8).

The shedding of human blood was of concern to the whole nation, for it involved an actual pollution of the land. Israel was enjoined against this bloodguilt pollution and was admonished neither to allow compensation for murder, nor even to allow an accidental murderer to leave a city of refuge, for by so doing they would cause the land of Israel to become contaminated:

> You shall take no ransom for the life of a murderer who is deserving of death. He shall be executed. You shall take no ransom to (allow someone to) flee a city of refuge or to (allow someone to) return to live in the land before the priest's death. You shall not pollute the land that you are in, for the blood will pollute the land, and the land may not be redeemed for blood spilled on it except by the blood of the spiller. You shall not contaminate the land in which you are living, in which I the Lord am dwelling among the children of Israel (Num 35:31–34).

The idea of the pollution of the earth by murder, of the physical pollution caused by "moral" wrongs such as sexual abominations and idolatry, underlies much of Israelite law. The composer of Genesis 1–9 had reinterpreted the cosmology and the early history of man in the light of these very strong concepts. He has used a framework that is at least as old as the Epic of Atrahasis, the framework of the Primeval History of Creation-Problem-Flood-Solution, and has retold the story in such a way as to reinterpret an ancient tradition to illuminate fundamental Israelite ideas, i.e., the biblical ideals that law and the "sanctity of human life" are the prerequisites of human existence upon the earth.

The Story of the Flood in the Light of Comparative Semitic Mythology

ELEANOR FOLLANSBEE

The application of a form of the comparative method to the flood myth can yield more than one interpretive result. When the comparative method is combined with the so-called myth-ritual theory—in which it is argued either that a given myth derives from an initial ritual or that a particular ritual reenacts a significant myth—we shall almost certainly find an analysis predicated upon principles of magic and fertility. Typically, the ritual is performed and the myth is narrated—with both actions designed to ensure that crops grow well and harvests will be bountiful.

In the following highly speculative essay, we have a novel reading of the flood myth. Although the author elects to analyze a composite text (consisting of a combination of elements from diverse flood myths from different cultures) rather than considering a single text from one culture, she does succeed in suggesting a rather unique theory of the original flood hero as a vegetation deity. Insofar as she recognizes the theoretical difficulties arising from her analysis, it is a fairly well argued thesis. However, she, like many scholars specializing in Near Eastern studies, tends to accept as absolute dogma the validity of the myth-ritual approach.

For a representative sample of the enormous literature devoted to myth-ritual theory, see Theodor H. Gaster, "Myth and Story," Numen *1 (1954): 184–212 (reprinted in Alan Dundes, ed.,* Sacred Narrative: Readings in the Theory of Myth *[Berkeley and Los Angeles, 1984], pp. 110–136), Joseph Fontenrose,* The Ritual Theory of Myth *(Berkeley and Los Angeles, 1966), and Robert A. Segal, "The Myth-Ritualist Theory of Religion,"* Journal for the Scientific Study of Religion *19 (1980): 173–185.*

In the several Semitic stories of the Flood, Hebrew and Babylonian alike, there occur a number of curious elements which have so far de-

Reprinted from *Religions* 29 (1939): 11–21.

fied adequate explanation. Using the evidence now provided by the mythological poems recently discovered at Ras Shamra (Ugarit) on the north coast of Syria, and dating approximately from the middle of the second millennium B.C., an attempt will here be made to reconstruct a primitive and original version of the story of which those elements were an integral and essential feature, and from which our extant forms may well have been derived. In this version the hero of the Flood will be seen to be identical with the Genius of Vegetation, and it will be shown that this original identity explains those elements of the extant narratives which now appear so perplexing and so seemingly irrelevant. The suggestion will be offered that in the original Hebrew Flood Story, of which our Biblical text is a later redaction, the hero Noah (or originally Nakhom), playing the part of Aleyan-Baal, the Ras Shamra counterpart of Tammuz-Adonis, was castrated by Ham, and that in consequence of this act a drought ensued. Only when Noah, the genius of vegetation, had miraculously recovered from this unmanning, did the drought give way to rain, and the Flood follow. This primitive myth, it may be supposed, was connected, in the first place, with the seasonal rituals of Canaan, being, in fact, the mystagogic explanation of a ritual ceremony—an opinion suggested by T. H. Gaster's view that "some of the early legends of Genesis, are in reality, the disintegrated *mythoi* of the Canaanite festival rituals."[1]

In order to provide a convenient framework for succeeding arguments, the following reconstruction is presented at the beginning of the article. The story is supported chiefly from the cuneiform sources of Nineveh, Nippur and Ras Shamra; passages from the Old Testament will also be recognized.

ALEYAN-BAAL AND ANAT

Aleyan-Baal reigned with his sister, Anat, over the land by the sea. His palace was built of cedar on the slope of the sacred mountain of the North; beneath it, the great river Orontes flowed into the sea. He was "the first husbandman and planted the first vineyard." In him the corn had its being, the cedar, the vine and all that grew.[2] He presided over husbandry and brought rain for the increase and prosperity of the land.

[1] I am deeply indebted to Mr. T. H. Gaster who generously placed his wide knowledge and profound learning at my disposal and whose corrections and suggestions are almost too numerous to mention.

[2] Cf. *SYRIA*, 1937, p. 259, l. 15: In my power is thy verdure, thy trees, thy herbage.

MOT, THE GOD OF DEATH

There was also in the land, reigning over the dark and desert places, Mot, the god of death and the unwatered soil. He challenged the power of Aleyan-Baal and contended for his throne. One day in the fourth month, when his rival had drunk some wine and fallen asleep, Mot entered his chamber and beheld his nakedness. Having thus gained power over him, he lured him into the desert and sent wild beasts against him. There Aleyan-Baal was found wounded in the thigh by a boar; he was carried to his palace and laid on his couch, but he stirred not and was like a dead man.

Anat, his sister, saw the grass wither in the fields and knew that it had gone ill with her brother. She entered his chamber and saw that his power was gone. She said, "Mot has overcome him, he has taken him to the lower world, leaving only his image behind." She raised her voice in mourning and the women at the palace gate cried, "Alas, the Lord of Life." They wailed "for the plants that they grew no more, for the perishing of the wedded ones, for the dark headed people who multiply no more": they lamented for "the great river that it brought floods no more."[3]

When the rainy tenth month came again there was no rain. Aleyan-Baal had withdrawn "his clouds and winds and rain from the upper world." On the surface of the parched earth salt appeared along the jagged cracks "so that by night it seemed that the ground was covered with snow." No animals were born and the womb of the women was closed. "The land's life breath had vanished"; the earth was no longer "bedewed by the heavens, it was a waste prairie."[4] There was famine and a space of time went by.

Then Anat descended into the country of Mot, the land of no return. She spread a net and caught the god and held him tight. When he cried for mercy, she said, "find my brother and bring him back to the upper world."[5] A dream came to the god El d-Ped and was told to Anat. "The heavens shall rain fatness, honey shall flow in streams."[6] And by this she knew that Aleyan-Baal still lived.

In his palace Aleyan-Baal awoke. He laughed and said, "It will rain for our abundance, the sea and the rain will fight over the land but the

[3] Cf. the Babylonian version of the threnody in Langdon, *Tammuz and Ishtar*, p. 11.

[4] Cf. Ras Shamra Poem I AB 11. 17–18.

[5] Ibid., II 9–12.

[6] Ibid., col. iii.

rain will triumph and restore fruitfulness. Make haste, bring your families and your cattle and seeds of all kinds into the mountain, into my palace for refuge. Bring gold and silver, or the deluge will wash away all that remains in the valley." Some of the people would not come for there was no cloud in the sky, but the others came up into the mountain, into the palace of Aleyan-Baal, for refuge against the storm.

THE DELUGE

At last the watchers at the window saw a black cloud. It came nearer, the rain began to fall. The wind rose and the sea was driven upon the land, the river widened at its mouth, "until the land and sea were one." The rain came down like a torrent, it swept through the mountain "like a broom": the water of the sea and the water of the rain "fought together like armies." For six days and six nights the people huddled together fearing the onslaught. On the seventh day the rains ceased. Slowly the people raised their eyes from the ground and looked down into the valley. A layer of clay covered the fields, the river bubbled muddy water. As far as the eye could see there was no living thing. But the people rejoiced for they saw in the waters a promise of future fertility. They crowned Aleyan-Baal with vine leaves and strewed his palace with cedar branches. A festival was proclaimed to celebrate the fact that drought and flood would overwhelm the land no more.

THE RAS SHAMRA TABLETS

Arranging the above mentioned sources in order of the probable antiquity of the originals, we may begin with the Ras Shamra tablets, which, though dated 1500 B.C., point to a long established cult and retain those features which we know reflect a primitive society. Here we have the story of a king-god, closely identified with vegetation, whose death or injury causes a long drought. His sister-consort wins from Death the promise of his return. The king fights for his throne against the usurper, the battle symbolizing not only the combat between life and death but also the conflict between the sea and the rain. The triumph of the latter, typified by Aleyan-Baal, signifies that it is his sway which shall prevail upon earth.[7] In Poem II there is an account of the building of a temple for this king, Aleyan-Baal, by a divine architect called

[7] Gaster, "The Battle of the Rain and the Sea."

Kashir-w-Khasis: a window is finally inserted, presumably in the roof, and opened in sympathetic magic to bring about the opening of the window of heaven with its consequent rainfall.[8] It will be shown below how the actual erection of the temple may be associated with the renewal of fertility.

OTHER VERSIONS

The Morgan Library tablet, found at Sippar and dated 1966 B.C., has an earlier original as proved by the word "broken" at the end of line 11, showing clearly that it was copied from an ancient archetype. The late Professor Clay of the University of Pennsylvania finds evidence[9] in its account of prolonged drought and famine, followed by a flood, of an origin in Amurru on the Syrian coast. According to this scholar the language of the text is Amoritic, rather than Assyrian, as is generally thought, and he finds further evidence for this provenance in the fact that the poem alludes to heavy rains (the annual rainfall in Lebanon is fifty inches) subterranean waters, mountains, fig-trees and other features missing in alluvial regions such as the Tigris-Euphrates valley. There is little doubt that this is an early redaction of the Nineveh tablet (dated seventh century) called *Ea and Atra-Khasis* which recounts a similar famine ending in cannibalism. The name Atra-Khasis appears also on the Morgan Library tablet. The Sumerian version (from Nippur, dated 2100 B.C.) relates the story of Ziusudda (the Sumerian counterpart of Atra-Khasis), who for his piety is warned of an approaching flood. The famine has here disappeared but the other elements remain to prove the direct descent from earlier accounts. This version is in many ways the closest to that in the Bible. The eleventh tablet of the *Epic of Gilgamesh* is also the history of a flood in which Ut Napishtim, called also Atra-Khasis, is the hero.[10] After the flood he is made immortal, and in the "far away land," at the source of the rivers, he institutes viticulture. The version of Berossus (300 B.C.) shows its affinity with the Sumerian version, by the fact that the hero is there called Xisothros, a transliteration of Atra-Khasis. The account of the flood in Genesis lies in the midst of enigmatic verses, referring apparently to the role previ-

[8]Williams, Ras Shamra Inscriptions, *American Journal of Semitic Languages and Literatures,* vol. 50, p. 236.

[9]Clay, *A Hebrew Deluge Story,* Chap. 1.

[10]T. H. Gaster says "this version also exists in a Hittite recension and there are even fragments of one in Hurrian in which the hero is called Nahmolel—a name which has been compared to the Biblical Noah."

ously played by Noah. In the earliest layer, called J[1], there is no mention of a flood, although there is Babylonian influence as shown by the mention of the name Nimrod (Gen. 9:8). Noah belongs to the line of benefactors of the human race such as Tubal Cain the smith and Jubal the musician. Noah's contribution is husbandry and viticulture.[11]

THE MONTH OF RAINS

It is the theory of Professor Zimmern[12] that the flood story was attached to Noah, as it was to Ut Napishtim, because as the tenth in the line of patriarchs, both represented the tenth month in the world year and thus the month of rains and floods. Clay suggests that the following lines

> Upon you will he (Enlil) then rain abundance
> In the evening will send you heavy rain.

belong to a lost account of famine in the story of Gilgamesh;[13] in any case they show the association of thought between rain and abundant harvest.

TOTEMS AND TABOOS

In all the accounts except that of Ras Shamra both famine and flood are represented as part of a series of punishments designed to diminish the number and clamour of mankind. We know from the evidence of the first ten commandments, for instance, that even after the age in which these stories were conceived, there was only a non-moral magic relationship between cause and effect. The laws, "Thou shalt not seethe a kid in its mother's milk" and "Thou shalt not offer the blood of my sacrifice with leavened bread," are taboos against harming magically flocks and harvest. By analogy there must have existed in the story of Noah a transgression of the magic rather than of the moral law which was the cause of famine and flood. Seeking a taboo in the story of the vegetation deity we find prominent the motif of castration. It is usually euphemized as "wounded in the thigh by a wild boar." Although the *nature* rather than the *agent* of the wound is the significant point, an elucidation of the role of the boar will further emphasize this

[11] Gunkel, *Schöpfung und Chaos,* p. 515.

[12] *Babylonian and Hebrew Genesis,* p. 28.

[13] Clay, *A Hebrew Deluge Story,* p. 14.

fact. As other divinities were associated with other animals so this Tammuz-Aleyan Baal. Adonis was the Swine-god. (His counterpart, Adad, god of the rains, is actually described as the Boar).[14] At the feast of the god his totem animal was evidently killed and eaten; the skin of the sacrifice, having magic properties, being apparently placed on the shoulders of the officiating priest.[15] As the priests increased in number they were each covered by a skin and in the ritual play which developed subsequently, they became theriomorphic mummers.[16] Now, since as Frazer points out,[17] the totem animal frequently becomes the enemy of the god, a combat probably took place between the vegetation-deity and the boar-priests, in which the god was wounded.

This wounding, or castrating, as Albright points out, symbolized the reaping of the grain which was cut just below the ear. As the women reaped, they wept, although they know that from the severed member vegetation would yet spring again.[18] Tears, as Canney maintains, may indeed be fertilizing but this is not their main role in the present ritual.

HARVEST SYMBOLISM

The women wept not so much out of sorrow as out of a desire to disclaim responsibility for the death of the god. In the Sumerian vintage harvest festival, so we are told, they cut Uncud, the divine grape-cluster, saying, "Excuse us, we knew it not," for "all harvest is seen as a violent extinction of the divine particle of life."[19] The castration of Osiris, a hero closely related to Aleyan-Baal, plays a large part in his story; the birth of Horus after his resurrection is given as proof of the survival of his dismembered body. The pieces were cast into the water, like the image of Tammuz, and the act of fishing, known also in the Orphic mysteries, symbolizes the retrieving of the life principle from the water.[20] We have here what is undoubtedly a form of vegetation myth concerned with the rebirth of the grain after the harvest.

Although our evidence for connecting with the Tammuz ritual the

[14] C. T. 23, 19. (T. H. Gaster, *Orientalische Literaturzeitung*, 1936).

[15] W. Robertson, *Religion of the Semites*, p. 475.

[16] Mr. Gaster calls my attention to articles by him on this point in *Folklore*, 1938, p. 355, and in the *Journal of the Royal Asiatic Society of Great Britain and Ireland*, 1935, p. 39 n. I regret they are not available to me.

[17] *Golden Bough*, Vol. II, p. 50.

[18] Albright, "Goddess of Life and Wisdom," p. 236.

[19] *Religion of the Semites*, p. 413.

[20] Nitze, "Review of Jessie L. Weston, *From Ritual to Romance*," p. 388.

story of the fisher king as preserved in Parsifal is wholly circumstantial, the fact that both contain the otherwise rare motifs of weeping women and of a king with whose virility the health of the land is bound up is sufficient excuse for introducing the tale at this point. The fisher king, attended by weeping women, lies upon a bier as if dead. His kingdom suffers from drought, the river beds are dry, the animals bring forth no young. The spell is broken and the waters freed as soon as an innocent knight, having gone through an initiation, asks ritual questions. The king and his kingdom revive. Eisler and Zimmern both identify Tammuz, lord of the nets, with the fisher god portrayed on Babylonian seals,[21] and there are other facts pointing to the probability that an Adonis initiation ritual has survived.[22]

The descent to the underworld is performed not only by the sister of the god, but, when his chief place of worship was Erech, also the home of Gilgamesh, Ishtar, the mother goddess, descends for his release. In the Gilgamesh epic, the hero descends to seek the plant of immortality for his friend Enkidu. Miss Weston believes that the vigil of Parsifal in the Chapel Perilous is a ritual initiation to death which precedes the life ceremony.[23] I see no objection to finding in it a parallel to the descent to the underworld. Confirmatory material is provided in Firmicus Maternus, *De Errore Religionum* (c.18), where the initiate in the analogous Attis mysteries is described as entering *the interiores partes* as a *homo moriturus.*[24]

In the light of these legends let us examine the story of Noah. Is it possible to recognize in him not only Ut Napishtim but Tammuz? Why was Noah the first husbandman instead of Cain, unless some special emphasis was placed upon this role? If the ground was cursed it was not with the curse of Adam since after the flood this curse was removed.[25] Why did Noah awake aware that his son had seen his nakedness unless this had an effect!

THE FERTILITY KING-GOD

If we accept the association of Noah with the type of king-god who is bound up with the principle of growth, we can answer these ques-

[21] Eisler, "Diktys von Byblos und die Zwiebeln," p. 722.

[22] Weston, *From Ritual to Romance,* passim; see also Nitze, op. cit.

[23] Weston, ibid.

[24] In a private letter from T. H. Gaster.

[25] Cf. Prince, *Hymn to Tammuz:* "The land with a curse is destroyed."

tions. His son, as his potential sexual rival,[26] broke a taboo which resulted in the cursing of the land by drought. The still surviving Jewish law against the sons seeing the nakedness of their father was designed to abolish the primitive temptation of castrating the older rival. Noah built according to divine instruction and was warned of a flood which restored fertility of the land. The promise of no more flood, of summer and winter, of seedtime and harvest, is the restoration of the normal balance between the seasons after the frightful years without rain. A passage in the Koran,[27] portrays Noah as bringing "plenteous rains, children, gardens and watercourses."

The chief difficulties with this explanation are, *one,* the flood in a beneficent light, *two,* the absence of the ship, *three,* the lack of the taboo in the Tammuz ritual drama and in intervening legends.

The flood appears in a beneficent light in countries where a drought means famine. In 1931 the excavators of Nuzi witnessed a flood[28] in a little village near Kirkuk in northern Iraq, which was in no way considered a disaster by the inhabitants. The story of this modern flood tells of rain pouring for almost a week, and of waters racing down from nearby mountains until the village was waist deep in water and the narrow streets became small torrents. Mud walls were undermined and houses crumbled so that when the sun shone again little of the village was to be seen. The inhabitants were disturbed at losing their small possessions but cheerfully set about rebuilding, joyful in the knowledge that the rain from heaven assured a particularly abundant harvest. Tammuz is called "bringer of beneficent floods." Like Indra he is worshipped for the freeing of the waters. Corn cakes eaten in his honor are baked in the shape of fish.[29] In Lebanon with its heavy rainfall we expect a different attitude toward a flood from that in Babylonia where a swollen river may wipe out a village overnight. If the drought-rain story travelled to the Tigris valley and back to Canaan, we should not be surprised that the famine had been minimized and the flood become a punishment.

[26] Mr. F. L. Utley calls my attention to rabbinical legends to this effect. See L. Ginzberg, *Legends of the Jews* (Phila., 1912), vol. I, pp. 168–9, vol. V, p. 191, and August Wünsche, *Der Midrasch Bereschit Rabba* (Leipzig, 1881), pp. 161–3.

[27] Koran Sura 71, Everyman's ed., p. 85.

[28] Described to me by Dr. R. F. S. Starr, Field Director.

[29] The fish was sacred to gods leading men from death to life.

BABYLONIAN ARKS

Although the ship appears first in the story of Ea and Atra-Khasis, there are ships closely associated with Tammuz and Osiris which bear a resemblance to the ark. Those who make every god a sun-god have no difficulty in explaining these ships, but Osiris, originally a water-spirit, and later, through his control of the Nile, the bringer of fertility, uses his crescent-hulled houseboat not only as a moon god, but in his voyage to the lower world.[30] When Tammuz dies he is laid upon a boat in a river to be conducted to the lower world. Noah's forty days in the ark may correspond to Tammuz' imprisonment; after riding out the storm they both return to bring life back to earth.[31]

Professor Jensen believes that the original ark was a building, both the house of the god and a place of refuge.[32] He compares it with the Ark of the Covenant. It is impossible to prove the identity of Atra-Khasis with Khashir-w-Khasis[33] but it is interesting to speculate on the window in the temple reminding us of the window in all the more complete flood stories. I believe that the building of the temple is an alternate solution for the restoration of fertility. When Gudea was king (2500 B.C.) there was a dearth of water in the rivers and a resulting famine. In a dream the god commanded the king to build a sumptuous temple and when it was complete, the rivers ran once more.[34] Apropos of the building of Zuisudda, L. W. King says, "referring possibly to a temple or other structure of sacred character, its foundation may have been regarded as striking evidence of his devotion.[35] Compare the line in the Gilgamesh epic, "To the master of the ship I entrusted the great house and all its possessions." The ark has always been criticized by ship designers. In the Avesta a great Vara or park is built in which to save from destruction by frost all seed and the best specimens of human beings and animals. The Vara is divided in nine parts like the interior of Ut Napishtim's ship. Summing up the foregoing, it would seem that the act of building under divine instruction is at least equally important with the ship itself.[36]

[30] Budge, p. 122.

[31] Suggestion of H. Glidden of the Institute for the Advancement of Study, Princeton.

[32] "Der babylonische Sintflutheld," p. 983.

[33] Mr. Glidden's opinion after comparing related etymologies.

[34] *Legends of Babylon and Egypt*, p. 67.

[35] Ibid.

[36] Cf. the Josephus version; the tower of Babel was built to escape the second flood.

CONCLUDING SUGGESTIONS

If the magic cause of the famine was the breaking of a taboo why was this omitted from other accounts? It is well known to students of ritual that there exist two forms, one for the public observance and one reserved for priests and initiates. Langdon suggests a secret chamber for the Tammuz mysteries to account for the absence of their representation in art.[37] Such a motif in the mysteries would have had no place in the public version until its meaning had become obscured. This would explain the act of Ham and its displacement in the Genesis narrative after the flood; it was felt that the account belonged to the story of Noah, but since its meaning had been lost, it was given a new one, however implausible, and tacked on at the end.

We have thus a sequence in the Tammuz ritual play, repeated in the story of the fisher king, of castration, famine and flood, with the triumph of the fertile waters, the subduing of the king's enemies, and the renewal of life. The Ras Shamra account of the warring waters, pointing to September squalls and rain characteristic of Syria, bear out Clay's contention that the original flood story was coastal. We have shown the close parallels between the building of temples and arks and the mutations of the theme of warning from the god.

If it can be proved that the original flood hero was also a vegetation deity, it would not be difficult to explain the identification of Noah first with the latter and then with the former. We may hope that further excavations will bring more data in a case presented here only tentatively.

BIBLIOGRAPHY

Albright, W. F.

"The Goddess of Life and Wisdom." *American Journal of Semitic Languages and Literatures* 36 (1919–1920): 258–294.

"The North Canaanite Epic of Al Eyan Baal and Mot." *Journal of the Palestine Oriental Society* 12 (1932): 185–208.

"More Light on the Canaanite Epic of Aleyan Baal and Mot." *Bulletin of the American Schools of Oriental Research* 50 (1933): 13–20.

Barton, G. A.

"The Second Liturgical Poem from Ras Shamra." *Journal of the American Oriental Society* 55 (1935): 31–58.

[37] *Tammuz and Ishtar,* p. 7.

Budge, Sir E. A. T. W.

Osiris and the Egyptian Resurrection. New York, 1911.

Clay, A. T.

A Hebrew Deluge Story in Cuneiform. New Haven, 1922.

The Origin of Biblical Traditions. New Haven, 1923.

Eisler, R.

"Nachleben Dionysischer Mysterienriten?" *Archiv für Religionswissenschaft* 27 (1929): 171–183.

"Diktys von Byblos und die Zwiebeln." *Orientalistische Literaturzeitung* 39 (1936): 721–726.

Gaster, T. H.

"The Combat of Death and the Most High: A Proto Hebrew Epic from Ras-Samra." *Journal of the Royal Asiatic Society of Great Britain and Ireland* (1932): 857–896.

"The Combat of Aleyan-Baal and Mot." *Journal of the Royal Asiatic Society of Great Britain and Ireland* (1934): 677–714, (1935): 1–44.

"The Battle of the Rain and the Sea: An Ancient Semitic Nature-Myth." *Iraq* 4 (1937): 21–32.

"The Harrowing of Baal." *Acta Orientalia* 16 (1937): 41–48.

Gunkel, H.

Schöpfung und Chaos in Urzeit und Endzeit. Göttingen, 1895.

Hepding, H.

Attis. Giessen, 1903.

Jensen, P.

"Der Babylonische Sintflutheld und sein Schiff in der israelitischen Gilgamesch-Sage." In *Orientalische Studien Theodor Nöldeke,* 983–996. Giessen, 1906.

Khvol'son, D. A.

Die Ssabier und der Ssabismus. St. Petersburg, 1856.

King, L. W.

Legends of Babylon and Egypt. Oxford, 1918.

Langdon, S. H.

Babylonian Liturgies. Paris, 1913.

Tammuz and Ishtar. Oxford, 1914.

Nitze, W. A.

"Review of Jessie L. Weston, *From Ritual to Romance.*" *Modern Language Notes* 35 (1920): 352–360.

Prince, J. D.

"A Hymn to Tammuz." *Journal of the American Oriental Society* 30 (1910): 94–100.

Smith, W. R.
Lectures on the Religion of the Semites. Edinburgh, 1889.

Weston, J. L.
Quest of the Holy Grail. London, 1913.

From Ritual to Romance. Cambridge, 1920.

Williams, W. G.
"The Ras Shamra Inscriptions and their Significance for the History of Hebrew Religion." *American Journal of Semitic Languages and Literatures* 51 (1935): 233–246.

Zimmern, H.
The Babylonian and the Hebrew Genesis. London, 1901.

Stories of the Creation and the Flood

LEONARD WOOLLEY

Archaeologists too have been deeply involved in investigating the flood narrative. Clearly, if the Bible is understood as literal history, there ought to be archaeological traces of the events described in the Old and New Testaments. The field of biblical archaeology has in fact documented many of the sites referred to in the Bible. In this context, it was only natural that some archaeologists would seek to find "evidence" of the flood.

Not one but several eminent archaeologists claimed to have found traces and material proof of the flood. Leonard Woolley (1880–1960) had been digging at Ur for several years. The son of a parson, Woolley had once been trained as a theologian and had been destined to enter the church. By digging at Ur, Woolley hoped to find vestiges of the Old Testament. He was specifically interested in finding traces of Abraham who, according to Genesis 11:31, had come from Ur of the Chaldees. In 1929, Woolley's crew consisted of general assistant Max Mallowan (who was later to marry Agatha Christie) and Father Eric Burrows, who served as epigrapher. In his report "Excavations at Ur, 1928–9," Antiquaries Journal *9 (1929): 305–339, Woolley devoted a section to "The Flood" (pp. 323–330) which included the following unequivocal statement: "That this flood is identical with that of the Sumerian annals, and so with that of Sumerian legend, can scarcely be doubted: its connection with the affiliated Flood story of Genesis follows" (p. 330). For further details of Woolley's claims, see his* Excavations at Ur *(London, 1954).*

Woolley's discovery produced a flurry of excited essays by scholars who either agreed with him or criticized his findings. Soon thereafter, another archaeologist, Stephen Langdon, maintained just as adamantly that he had found comparable evidence at Kish. Woolley disputed Langdon's rival claim. See C. Leonard Woolley, "Excavations at Ur, 1929–30," Antiquaries Journal *10 (1930): 315–343 (esp. 340–341).*

Woolley's original crew was somewhat divided in evaluating the discovery. Father Burrows seems to have concurred with Woolley—for example, in his "The Discovery of the Deluge," Dublin Review *186 (1930): 1–20—but Max Mallowan had second thoughts. See his "Noah's Flood Reconsidered,"* Iraq *26 (1964): 62–82. Mallowan later in his memoirs spoke affectionately but*

Reprinted from the *Palestine Exploration Quarterly* 88 (1956): 14–21.

dispassionately about Woolley's penchant for showmanship, noting that he was "a man of knowledge endowed with a vivid imagination which sometimes got the better of him." See Max Mallowan, Mallowan's Memoirs *(New York, 1977), p. 56.*

For other considerations of the archaeological "evidence" for the flood, see John Bright, "Has Archaeology Found Evidence of the Flood?" Biblical Archaeologist *5 (1942): 55–62; André Parrot,* The Flood and Noah's Ark, *Studies in Biblical Archaeology (New York, 1955), pp. 45–53; Heinrich Jakob Lenzen, "Zur Flutschicht in Ur,"* Baghdader Mitteilungen *3 (1964): 52–64; and R. L. Raikes, "The Physical Evidence for Noah's Flood,"* Iraq *28 (1966): 52–63.*

Sometimes archaeology becomes "arkeology" and the search for physical remains of Noah's actual ark is the principal focus of interest. There have been a surprisingly large number of expeditions to Mount Ararat in quest of Noah's Ark. Most of these have been instigated by dedicated amateurs possessing genuine religious faith. While we need not accept Mario Lopes Pegna's estimate of some eighty thousand works in seventy-two languages devoted to the vicissitudes of Noah and his ark, it is true that there are too many books and essays to list. For a representative sampling of the innumerable, mostly popular, publications devoted to such expeditions, see Mario Lopes Pegna, "L'Arca di Noè et la Torre di Babele; Miti e Realtà nella Tradizione Biblica," L'Universo *(Firenze) 34 (1954): 701–710; Fernand Navarra,* Noah's Ark: I Touched It *(Plainfield, N.J., 1974); John Warwick Montgomery,* The Quest for Noah's Ark, *2nd ed. (Minneapolis, 1974), where the term "arkeology" is dated 1971; Dave Balsiger and Charles E. Sellier, Jr.,* In Search of Noah's Ark *(Los Angeles, 1976); Tim LaHaye and John Morris,* The Ark on Ararat *(Nashville, 1976); and Lloyd R. Bailey,* Where Is Noah's Ark? *(Nashville, 1978); Violet Cummings,* Has Anybody Really Seen Noah's Ark? *(San Diego, 1983); Charles Berlitz,* The Lost Ship of Noah: In Search of the Ark at Ararat *(New York, 1987). Among the attempts to debunk these arkeological quest reports is Howard M. Teeple,* The Noah's Ark Nonsense *(Evanston, 1978).*

In addition, there is a vast scholarly literature devoted to the ark. Typical are Eugene S. McCartney, "Noah's Ark and the Flood: A Study in Patristic Literature and Modern Folklore," Papers of the Michigan Academy of Science, Arts and Letters *18 (1932): 71–100; Lutz Röhrich, "Noah und die Arche in der Volkskunst," in Klaus Beitl, ed.,* Volkskunde: Fakten und Analysen: Festgabe für Leopold Schmidt zum 60. Geburtstag *(Vienna, 1972), pp. 433–442; and Walter E. Rex, "'Arche de Noé' and Other Religious Articles by Abbé Mallet in the* Encyclopédie," Eighteenth Century Studies *9 (1975–1976): 333–352.*

In the year 1872 George Smith published the tablets from Kouyunjik, which contained what he called "the Chaldean account of Genesis."

It is unnecessary to recall today the sensation which this publication aroused as something which seemed to invalidate the inspiration of the Old Testament. That there was some connection between the Hebrew and the Akkadian versions could not be denied, but did this mean that the Hebrew was copied from the Akkadian? The Assyrian Royal Library, from which the tablets came, was dated no earlier than the seventh century B.C.; surely, then, it could be assumed that the Assyrian scribes had borrowed their stories from the Hebrews. George Smith, however, was able to prove that the Assyrian tablets were copied from very much older Babylonian tablets and in due course actual documents were forthcoming which showed that the Babylonian versions in their turn depended upon Sumerian originals written before the birth of Abraham. Some diehards were found to argue that, this being so, the Mesopotamian and the Hebrew accounts were independent traditions going back to a common source; this would explain resemblances but the Hebrew version was the purer of the two and therefore was free of the gross polytheism with which revealed truth had been overlaid by Mesopotamian paganism. In various distant parts of the world there were races whose folklore included a Flood story, conclusive evidence that the universal deluge of Genesis had impressed itself upon the minds and memories of all alike, and if in two neighbouring lands the stories took similar forms that was only natural. A few entrench themselves behind some such arguments as these, but for most the evidence of the tablets is convincing; the fact that the Genesis stories are based upon the ancient Sumerian is generally accepted, although to some even of those who accept it it remains somewhat of a stumbling-block.

If that be so, it is because they make the fundamental mistake of classing together in the same category two things which are essentially different. Even the title given to my lecture today to some extent perpetuates the error—"Stories of the Creation and the Flood"—it seems to put them upon the same footing, whereas they could scarcely be more diametrically opposed. Let me explain this. The Flood story purports to be history. It deals with a definite incident in man's experience, with the adventures of an individual human being whose name and genealogy are on record, and it recounts the facts of that experience as they were remembered and handed down by tradition through subsequent generations. On the other hand, the Creation story deals with times and events prior to the appearance of man upon the earth, prior indeed to the very existence of the earth. It cannot therefore be based on human memory. If it be claimed to be a record of facts, then it can only result from divine revelation, since nobody but God could know the facts—and I certainly cannot imagine anyone attributing to divine inspiration the very unpleasant theogony of the Sumerian tablets from which the Genesis account is derived. Otherwise it is necessarily an invention, but a serious one; an essay in cosmological speculation whereby man attempts to explain the universe. Here, then, we have two things, tradition and myth, which are absolutely different; we have tended to confuse the two, but, as I hope to show later, the Hebrews did not; they recognized the difference and treated the two things differently. Let me take the Creation myth first.

The cuneiform tablets which contain the Creation story are terribly fragmentary, so that the text is very far from complete. Moreover, they contain not one legend but several, and these cover a very wide field. The main subject is not the creation of the universe but something much more important, the creation or genesis of the gods who rule the universe. It is an extraordinarily barbarous tale and utterly unmoral; these monstrous gods fight amongst themselves, cheat and kill each other, supplant one another, so that the original gods disappear or are degraded and a pantheon of younger gods usurps their powers, and it is only late in time and almost incidentally that the world is made and man created to minister to the comfort of the gods. From the scanty remains of the tablets giving the story of the creation of the universe it would appear that this took seven days and that the order was similar to that in the Hebrew version; but if this latter be compared with the whole cycle of the Sumerian cosmogony they seem to have so little in common that even the dependence of the Hebrew on the Sumerian might be called in question. But the Mesopotamian origin is, I think, unmistakable. Quite apart from the parallelism with the Sumerian version implicit in the Six Days of creation and the seven-day week, there is the occurrence in the Hebrew text of the (I think I am right in saying) non-Hebrew word *tehom* to describe the waters that covered the unformed earth, a word derived from *tiamat,* the name of the goddess of chaos who appears similarly in the Sumerian story "before the waters were collected in one place"; most scholars—though there are, I admit, exceptions to the rule—regard this as in itself proof of the derivative character of the Hebrew version. But the point on which I should insist is this, that the account given of the creation is applicable to Lower Mesopotamia alone. "And God said, Let the waters under the heaven be gathered together into one place, and let the dry land appear: and it was so." Now no people living in central Arabia, or in the Caucasus, or in the hills of Judea or on the Syrian plateau would ever have imagined that their country had once been underneath the sea; the gathering-together of the waters and the appearance of dry land as the result would have been meaningless to them. But to the inhabitant of Lower Mesopotamia that was the obvious course of nature; not only had it happened but it was happening all the time before his eyes. There the whole valley had once been marsh, quite a lot of it was marshland still; but by degrees the water-level had sunk, the streams had cut channels for themselves and man by digging canals had helped the natural process, and as the waters were thus gathered together the dry land forthwith appeared. Nor was this all. The order of creation as given in Genesis is a very logical one—it has often been pointed out how close it comes to that postulated by modern science—but there is one curious departure from logic. Immediately after the creation of dry land, on the same day, in obedience to God's word "the earth brought forth grass, and herb yielding seed after his kind, and the tree yielding fruit, whose seed was in itself, after his kind" and all this on the third day before ever the sun and moon and the stars were made. Now the whole of Lower Mesopotamia is formed by the silt deposited by the rivers Tigris and Euphrates, and that river silt is the richest soil imaginable. As the old marshes dried up the new land would be covered at once with vegetation of every sort; it was the amazing fertility of the soil recovered from the waters that had attracted the first settlers into the river valley and made possible the development of the Sumerian city-states. For the Sumerian, the earth was made for man, and when he spoke of "the earth" he thought of the earth as the place on and by which man could live. The waste stretches of the upper desert lying to the west meant nothing to him; the Elamite mountains to the east meant nothing; what concerned him was the fruitful land that supported human life. So when he attempted to describe the creation of the world it was the creation of the river valley that he described, and the picture that he drew was realistically true; the waters that had once prevailed everywhere were gathered together into one place and the dry land appeared and at once brought forth all that was needed for man; there was your world. It was as simple as that. The Genesis account is precisely what a Sumerian would have written, and it could not have been written by an inhabitant of any other country where the physical conditions were different. The Hebrews therefore borrowed it from Sumer.

In the case of the Flood legend there can be no doubt whatsoever. Here we have to deal not with similarity but with identity; not only is the story in the Old Testament the same, but the details of it and even the language, the turns of expression, reproduce exactly the cuneiform version. The fact is too obvious and too familiar to call for any discussion here. Now in the tablets the Flood story is almost incidental; it is narrated to the hero Gilgamesh by Uta-Napishtim, the Sumerian Noah, himself, and is told therefore in the first person, which makes it very vivid but scarcely more credible; it is true that Uta-Napishtim is represented as a man and as a citizen of Suruppak, a well-known city, but that might be merely a literary artifice; in itself it would not justify us in regarding this interpolated poem as anything more than a folk tale put into poetical form. But that is not at all how the ancient Sumerians regarded it; for them the story dealt with a historical fact.

We possess, on various tablets, the list of kings which the Sumerian scribe drew up as the framework of their country's history. It begins—in Mesopotamia—with eight fabulous semi-divine rulers whose combined reigns total nearly a quarter of a million years. Then, they say, "the Flood came. After the Flood came, kingship was again sent down from on high." Then are enumerated the kings who ruled after the Flood. First comes a dynasty whose capital city was Kish; then, the First Dynasty of Erech; then, the First Dynasty of Ur. The kings of Kish and of Erech are still, some of them, the gods and heroes of legend, and they enjoy an incredible longevity; but with the kings of Ur we come down to earth and not only are they credited with lives of normal span but we have actually discovered at Ur their written monuments, proving that they at least are genuine historical characters. Undoubtedly to the Sumerian all alike were equally genuine (mere length of life presented to the Sumerian no greater difficulty than the Hebrew writer felt about Methuselah—and in any case the figures as we have them are corrupt) and into the middle of this schematized historical framework they insert the simple and unadorned reference to the Flood. There is no story about it here, any more than there are accounts of the lives of the several kings; they just state a fact. It was necessary to state it because the Flood had caused a breach in the continuous history of the country—not an absolute break, because some of the antediluvian cities continued in existence after the disaster; but it had so upset the economy of the land that for a time the whole social system had broken down, there was no longer any rule or government, and kingship had to be sent down again from on high before the ordered sequence of society could be resumed. It was a real event which they could date, at least as well as they could date the kings who ruled before and after it; we cannot accept their nonsensical chronology, but it may well be that they put it in its right place in relation to their history as a whole.

What has archaeology to say about it?

At Ur we excavated a number of deep pits on the north—i.e., on the up-river flank of the mound formed by the remains of the earliest settlement, all the pits being in or close to the area containing the old

Royal tombs. The evidence given by the pits was absolutely consistent. In the upper levels we dug through as many as eight building-strata, the first two or three belonging to the Early Dynastic Period which culminated in and by the Sumerian historians was identified with the First Dynasty of Ur, and the rest belonging to the preceding era, which in the archaeological jargon of today is called the Jamdat Nasr Period. Then there came a stratum some eighteen feet thick composed entirely of broken potsherds, at intervals in which we found the brick kilns in which the pots had been fired—they were the "wasters" of a factory which had been active literally for centuries. In the upper part of the stratum the pots were of the Jamdat Nasr type; then these stopped and we had the plain red or gray ware of an earlier time, the Uruk Period, and at the bottom was a relatively thin layer of fragments showing a debased form of the decoration characteristic of al 'Ubaid pottery, which is the pottery of the oldest inhabitants of southern Mesopotamia. Below this there was a stratum (with a maximum thickness of eleven feet) of perfectly clean water-borne silt, obviously deposited against the mound's flank by a great inundation—the silt was of the type brought by the Euphrates from northern Mesopotamia—and underneath that there were again house ruins rich in the fine painted pottery of the early al 'Ubaid culture; these were the antediluvian houses.

We have at Ur definite evidence of a very great flood whose waters, upwards of twenty-five feet deep,[1] must have destroyed everything in the Delta except for a few of the greater towns which had grown up into mounds high enough to be out of the Flood's reach; thus Ur itself, we know, escaped, but the houses at the foot of the mound perished, and in the open plain we have found the ruins of not one but several villages of the same date which were overthrown and never again inhabited. The disaster came at the close of what we call the al 'Ubaid Period. The al 'Ubaid culture is that of the earliest settlers in Lower Mesopotamia, and it lasted for a very long time; at Eridu, regarded by the Sumerians as the most ancient of their cities, the Iraq Government excavators discovered the remains of sixteen temples built one above the other and all belonging to the al 'Ubaid Period. After the Flood the al 'Ubaid culture lingered on for a short while in a degenerate form and then gave place to a quite different culture brought in by immigrants from the North. This Uruk (or Erech) culture was in its turn supplanted by that of another immigrant race which dominated the country during what we call the Jamdat Nasr Period; after that again comes

[1] In the Genesis account the depth of the flood is given as twenty-six feet.

the Early Dynastic Period which culminated in the First Dynasty of Ur. The First Dynasty of Ur is, as I have said, named in the Sumerian King Lists; the period of the Kings before the Flood in those lists must correspond to the al 'Ubaid Period for the simple reason that the latter does come before the Flood and is the earliest in the land's history; if we venture to go farther and to correlate the two archaeological periods of Uruk and Jamdat Nasr with the two dynasties of Kish and Erech recorded in the Lists, the equation is complete and the "date" of the Flood given by the Sumerian scribes tallies exactly with its position in the archaeological sequence. Naturally there is no archaeological support for the details of the Uta-Napishtim story; but that the story is founded on a basis of historical fact cannot well be denied.

The Creation myth and the Flood legend therefore were taken over by the Hebrews from Mesopotamian originals. When did that happen?

Some scholars have maintained that the early chapters of Genesis were based upon the Babylonian legends by the Hebrew scribes who, during the Captivity, drew up the Canon of Jewish scriptures. That seems to me to be, in any case, psychologically impossible. The scribes were pious men whose concern it was to preserve in all their purity the religious books and the religious beliefs which had been handed down to them and had—not without difficulty—survived in spite of the apostasy of kings and priests in Jerusalem. It is inconceivable that they should have taken the opportunity to delve into the pagan mythology of their conquerors and extract therefrom new material to be incorporated in their sacred writings as part of the divine revelation. But the psychological argument does not stand alone. If the scribes had wanted to use the Babylonian legends in order to make a novel addition to the Canon they would have consulted the standard version of those legends which was preserved in the libraries of the Palace and of the temples; they would therefore have been dealing with a single text and we should not have had in the Old Testament that intricate and sometimes not very successful welding together of variant versions which actually we do find there. If they were translating from the Babylonian, how did the scribes arrive at the name of Noah, which could not possibly be derived from the Uta-Napishtim of the tablets? Why did they make the Ark ground on Mt. Ararat, not mentioned in the tablets? It is indeed far more likely that the stories of the Creation and the Flood were part of the cultural heritage which Abraham took with him from Ur, and that they had been familiar to the Hebrew people ever since that time. There is archaeological evidence to support this. A fragmentary inscription shows that in the Haran district there was current a "northern version" of the Flood legend in which the name of the hero is not Uta-Napishtim but something very like the Noah of Genesis; and seeing that Abraham lived at Haran and the patriarchs took their wives thence, the adoption of the name "Noah" is easily explained; whether the name "Ararat" also occurs in the "northern version" we have no means of knowing but it is at least quite possible that a northern people would conceive of the Ark's coming to ground on the highest mountain of which they had ever heard—a mountain, be it remarked, quite outside the knowledge of the people of southern Mesopotamia. If, from that early date, the stories borrowed from Ur continued to be handed down by oral transmission through the successive generations of the Hebrew people, then the existence in late times of two variant versions equally sanctioned by the traditions of the different tribes need not cause any surprise. The redactors of the Genesis account had to reconcile the two versions without sacrificing either simply because both alike were part of the spiritual inheritance of the nation.

Actually it is difficult to say to what extent these stories influenced the early Hebrews; they play virtually no part in the subsequent books of the Old Testament. There is, of course, in the Decalogue the detailed reference to the six days of creation, but this is generally taken to be an addition to the original text and to be not earlier than the Captivity. But even if we grant this, there remains the commandment itself, establishing, or confirming, the seven-day week with its six working days, which we cannot but associate with the six days of creation; if the second clause containing the explicit parallel is of late date it does not introduce a novelty but simply puts into words what everybody had always known. That the Decalogue in its oldest form implies a knowledge of the Creation story can be confidently assumed. If, with this important exception, the books of the Old Testament do not directly refer to the early chapters of Genesis, we need not be surprised; why should they? The Psalmist may well be recalling the old story when, for instance, he sings the praises of the Creator who has set for the sea "its bounds which it may not pass neither turn again to cover the earth"; but the historical books obviously would not quote the legends and the prophets have no occasion to do so. This silence is no argument at all against the legends being current throughout the Old Testament period.

We can reasonably assume that they were current as folklore. During the greater part of the time at least they would not be written down but would be transmitted orally; and because they were not in the same category as the records of the peculiar religion of the Hebrew nation which were guarded and promulgated by the religious orders, but were the common property of the multitude, always ignorant and often unorthodox, they would surely retain a good deal of the original polytheistic coloring. The redactors of the Canonical books in the time of the Captivity had a difficult task in making the legends conform to the orthodox views which they wanted to inculcate; such curious survivals as we have in the verse about "the sons of God 'seeing' the daughters of men, that they were fair . . . and there were giants in the land in those days" show how difficult. But if they felt that the stories had none the less to be included in the Scriptures and that where there were variants the versions had to be combined in such a way that the traditional wording of both should be preserved, then we have the strongest possible testimony to the important place that the stories held in the popular belief.

But the treatment accorded to the two stories, the myth and the legend, was very different.

The Sumerian Creation-story was an elaborate cosmology giving the basis of the whole Sumerian religion. Since that religion was false, the entire theogony had to be scrapped; as religious leaders the redactors had a free hand in the matter and were obliged to cut away everything that was opposed to their own faith. Only the relatively small part dealing with the creation of the world as we know it had to be kept because it was intrinsic to Jewish religious practice, to the observance of the Sabbath.[2] But it was reduced to the simplest and most essential form, purged of all monstrous elements that might have survived in the oral tradition; but it reconciled to the reformed religion what had always been the popular belief. But the Flood story was history. The flood had taken place in Mesopotamia, the written Mesopotamian accounts of it went back farther than any Hebrew tradition, and so the closer you kept to the Babylonian version the closer you would be to the truth. Of course, the references to false gods had to be eliminated, but so far as the facts of the history went, the original source should be followed, if possible verbatim. This is why the history of Noah reproduces so exactly the cuneiform version, whereas the Creation myth has relatively little in common with the cosmogony of the tablets.

Let me sum up the whole matter as I have tried to deal with it. The story of the Creation and the story of the Flood both originate in

[2] I venture to suggest that if the second clause of the fourth commandment of the Decalogue "For in six days the Lord made heaven and earth, the sea and all that in them is . . ." was really a gloss added at this time, it was put there to excuse, or rather to explain, the addition to the beginning of Genesis of what had not hitherto been any part of the sacred books.

southern Mesopotamia, and we have texts of them that go back in date to before the time of the patriarch Abraham. The first is a piece of pagan mythology, the second is a saga about human beings which was regarded as historical; the first is necessarily pure invention, the second is based upon an actual event of which we possess the proof, though, of course, there can be no proof of the saga's details. Both stories would have been known to Abraham if he lived (as he certainly did) at Ur, and one at least, probably both, would have been current at Haran in the patriarchal period. Both were adopted by the patriarchal family and were handed down as oral tradition, becoming part of the popular belief of the Hebrew people and influencing them to the extent shown by the institution of the seven-day week and the ritual observance of the Sabbath. When, in the time of the Captivity, the sacred books were edited, these stories were incorporated although they were not found in either of the two more ancient sources on which the redactors drew. The old Sumerian (Babylonian) Creation myth was radically cut down so as to leave only that philosophical speculation which recognizes in God the Prime Cause; the Flood saga was preserved in its traditional form but moralized in agreement with the religious ideas of the later Jews. To compare the Genesis version with that of the cuneiform tablets from which it is derived is to realize the astonishing development of those religious ideas since the days when "your fathers worshipped strange gods beyond the River."

New Light on Ovid's Story of Philemon and Baucis

W. M. CALDER

The flood myth was also reported in Greek and Roman versions, although it does not seem to have had the philosophical import in these contexts as in the earlier Babylonian and Sumerian settings. Nevertheless, it is of interest that the narrative was part of classical literary antiquity. In the following essay by W. M. Calder, Hulme Professor of Greek at the University of Manchester, we find an excellent illustration of the literal/historical approach to deluge accounts. The flood in this instance is understood to be local, not universal, and a serious attempt is made to locate the possible site of that flood.

For other considerations of Greek and Roman flood narratives, see Carlo Pascal, "La leggenda del diluvio nelle tradizioni greche," Atti della R. Accademia delle Scienze di Torino *30 (1894–1895): 785–798; "Ancient Greek Stories of a Great Flood," in James George Frazer,* Folk-Lore in the Old Testament, *vol. 1 (London, 1918), pp. 146–174; Ludolf Malten, "Motivgeschichtliche Untersuchungen zur Sagenforschung: I. Philemon und Baukis,"* Hermes *74 (1939): 176–206; Joseph Fontenrose, "Philemon, Lot, and Lycaon,"* University of California Publications in Classical Philology *13(4) (1945): 93–119; and Emil G. Kraeling, "Xisouthros, Deucalion, and the Flood Traditions,"* Journal of the American Oriental Society *67 (1947): 177–183.*

One of the best-known stories in classical literature is Ovid's charming tale of Philemon and Baucis. It is the story of an aged couple who dwelt among the hills of Phrygia—as the Roman poets were wont to call the interior of Asia Minor. One day two strangers appeared in the district, and begged for food and shelter. After "a thousand doors" had been closed against them, they were taken in by Philemon and Baucis, who set before them a plain but abundant rustic meal, with a treasured chine of pork to crown the fare. Fearful lest this should not be enough, the aged couple decided to offer the guests their gander, the only living creature they possessed. The bird fled, and took refuge with

Reprinted from *Discovery* 3 (1922): 207–211.

the strangers, whereupon the latter declared themselves to be Jupiter and Mercury. The neighborhood, said they, must suffer for its sin of inhospitality, and Philemon and Baucis were directed to accompany the gods up the long slope which led to the mountains. When near the top they turned round, and saw the whole valley flooded, except their own dwelling. While they gazed in wonder, their dwelling changed before their eyes into a temple with marble foundations and gilded roof. They were given a wish, and chose to be priest and priestess in the gods' temple, and, even as they had lived in oneness of heart, to die in one and the same hour. In extreme old age they suffered change into an oak and a lime, which are still shown to the visitor, holy trees, surrounded by a low wall and covered with garlands. The teller of the story vouched for its truth; he had himself been to the spot, and had hung fresh garlands on the trees, with a prayer.

This story is told in the eighth book of Ovid's *Metamorphoses.* The work is a collection of stories, loosely strung together, the feature common to them being that they all describe transformations of mythical personages into animals, trees, flowers, rocks, and so forth. In common with the *Fasti,* it illustrates Ovid's interest, and the interest of his readers, in what modern writers call the aetiology of ritual—the search for an explanation of the religious practices which they saw around them, or in which they took part. This interest was one effect of the religious revival fostered by Augustus, which has left such a deep impress on the literature and monuments of the period. Just as every city had its sacred foundation-legend, so the explanation of every ritual practice was sought in a story which served as a sort of running commentary on the religious act. The cult was usually traced back to the experiences of some mythical personage; for example the association of Apollo with the laurel was traced back to his love for a maiden called Daphne (Laurel), who fled from his embrace, and was changed into the tree which bore her name.

Ovid was born in the year of Cicero's death, 43 B.C. Between the age of 40 in 3 B.C., and his exile to Tomi in A.D. 9, he was at work on the *Metamorphoses* and the *Fasti.* When he left Rome, the *Metamorphoses* was apparently complete—at least in a first edition; the *Fasti* was certainly not. It would be straining the evidence to argue from this that the *Metamorphoses,* in its totality, was the earlier work of the two, but the balance of probability is that the story with which alone we are concerned was composed about the turn of the centuries. It is not necessary for our purpose to fix an exact date; about 3 B.C. to A.D. 3 is near enough. Ovid must, of course, have been collecting material for the book for some time before he set about its formal composition.

The aetiological myth, or foundation-legend, is a universal feature in ancient Mediterranean religion, and the establishment of a city, temple, or cult had always a religious sanction. The foundation of Rome is told, after their respective manners, by Livy and by Vergil; by the historian as well as by the poet it is given a religious setting. Greek literature is full of such legends; the scene which is impressed on the audience before they leave the theatre at the end of Aeschylus' *Oresteia* is the foundation of the cult of the Eumenides under the Athenian acropolis; the *Oedipus Coloneus* of Sophocles is a dramatized version of the weird story which was told to explain the cult of Oedipus at Colonus; the *Bacchae* of Euripides turns on the establishment of the worship of Dionysus at Thebes.

Let us look at Ovid's story of Philemon and Baucis from this point of view. It is professedly a foundation-story, and relates how a particular shrine beside a lake in Asia Minor, in which Jupiter and Mercury were worshipped together, came to be established. Such is the essence of the story, as he who runs reads it. But the story is one of a series which was addressed not only to those who were interested in religious origins, but to a fashionable and flippant public. Add that Ovid was the prince of Roman story-tellers, and that all good story-tellers have a habit of touching up and amplifying their material. The student of ancient religion must accordingly use Ovid's stories with caution; such caution is necessary even in the case of the *Fasti*, which is a more severely technical book than the *Metamorphoses*.

I hope to be able to prove that the story of Philemon and Baucis is a genuine Anatolian legend, to conduct the reader to the very spot where the legend was originally told, and to indicate the channel through which it reached Ovid in Rome. We shall find that the story contains features derived directly from its Anatolian source. Other features, while germane to Ovid's purpose as a *raconteur*, are without value for the student of ancient religion. Still other features—there are two of them in the story—are of doubtful import. I shall refer to them, but do not found any part of my argument on them.

We may pass over what may be described as mere picturesque detail—the simple, uncomplaining poverty of the old couple, the rustic meal with course after course of country fare, all the details which go to the telling of a good tale—and pass at once to the kernel of religious truth underlying the story. First, there are the sacred trees, covered with garlands, and (do not miss this detail) surrounded by a low wall. How is the sacredness of the trees to be accounted for? For the Anatolian peasant, ancient and modern, such sanctity can only be explained in one way—the spirit of some dead holy man or woman dwells in the trees. Manifestly the sacredness of this oak and lime, standing together, is best explained on the theory that a man and a woman—say, the original priest and priestess of the neighboring temple—were changed into these trees. The temple itself is of an unusual sort—it is the shrine of two gods, worshipped in common. It stands near a lake, covering what was once habitable land—a sort of Dead Sea, covering the abodes of the wicked. Obviously the two gods were the authors of this local deluge, and we at once, with many analogies in our minds, recognize in Philemon and Baucis the Noah and his wife of a local legend of the flood, the only righteous survivors of a race of sinners overwhelmed in a deluge, meet and acceptable as the priest and priestess in the gods' temple. Next we examine the deluge itself, and we find that it was caused not by rain from heaven, but by water issuing out of the earth. This distinguishes our deluge, which we shall presently find to be of the normal Anatolian type, from the Semitic flood which is described in Genesis, in which the chief stress is laid on the rain from heaven. But surely Ovid will mention an ark? Nothing of the sort—in this version of the deluge the righteous are saved by walking up a hill. All these points are of significance to the student of Anatolian religion. There are two other points, referred to above, on which it would be rash to lay stress—the incident of the gander, and the production by the gods' hosts of a chine of pork. The gander reminds us that the Noah and his wife in many flood legends are associated with birds—in Genesis it is the raven and the dove, in the Chaldaean version it is a variety of birds—and we wonder whether the gander had not his place in the original legend. But then we reflect that Ovid required a motive for the self-revelation of the gods, and that the gander was a sacred bird at Rome (had he not saved the Capitol in an old cult legend?), and we feel disinclined to press this point. And when we read of the pork, we are reminded that Asia Minor lay as a debatable land between the "pig-eaters of Europe and the pig-haters of the Semitic East," and that tales of old feuds centering round the use of swine flesh were told in the temple-legends of the country. But here again we feel that we cannot press the argument, and we prefer to assume that Ovid regarded a gammon of bacon as an essential course in such a meal as a rustic would offer to an honored guest.

Having thus cleared the ground, we pass on to consider these features in the story which we have provisionally marked as of Anatolian origin. But before doing so, we must glance at another feature in the story, a feature which it shares, I think, with only one other story in the *Metamorphoses*. The tale of Philemon and Baucis is connected with the preceding story by the flimsiest of devices; as Pichon says, Ovid's transitions from story to story in this work often depend on an accidental turn of phrase, sometimes even on a connecting or adversative particle. In this case, a speaker expresses scepticism regarding the preceding story, who poses as an eyewitness of the trees, temple, and lake. "I saw the place myself," "Truthful elders, with no motive for deceiving me, told me the tale, and I saw the garlands hanging on the trees," etc. He would be a blind critic who would miss the significance of this feature in the story, shared, I repeat, by only one other story in the *Metamorphoses,* and that story also from the interior of Asia Minor. Ovid is at pains to tell us that his story of Philemon and Baucis is derived from someone who had been to the scene of the legend, and heard it from the lips of the peasants. I may add incidentally that the caution "they had no motive for deception" will be found *passim* in the writings of all moderns whose business it has been to elicit information from the peasants of Anatolia, who can never understand why they are asked for such information by inquisitive strangers from Europe. This trait is as genuinely Anatolian as any in the story.

We see then that Ovid, writing about the turn of the centuries, is telling us the foundation-story of a temple of Jupiter and Mercury beside a lake in Asia Minor, reported by an eyewitness of the locality. The lake occupies ground formerly inhabited: the language used in the poem would suit either a marsh or a lake, but for Asia Minor the distinction is immaterial. In this land of seasonal rainfall, many of the lakes, and even some large ones, are seasonal, and may be called lake or marsh according to the time of year.

Now let us consider the details of religious significance which we have detected in the story. First let us take the sacred trees. On this constant feature of the Anatolian landscape much might be written; I will content myself with a quotation from a book[1] by a modern traveller which is full of acute observation of the social custom of Asia Minor. My friend Mr. W. J. Childs, describing a tree in the Cilician Gates Pass which was covered over with pious rags and surrounded by a rampart of small stones placed there one by one by Moslem travellers, writes: "These sacred trees . . . are found wherever trees and bushes grow, are decorated always with rags, and surrounded by an accumulation of stones." "The best explanation I got was that these bushes mark the haunt of some dead holy man . . . at which, as at a shrine, offerings might produce lesser miracles, or at least be acccounted as good works." Ovid's trees were covered with fillets and surrounded by a low wall. The fundamental things in the old Anatolian religion live on

[1] *Across Asia Minor on Foot* (London, 1918), p. 321.

still, and the sacred bushes which every traveller sees in modern Anatolia are good evidence of the Anatolian character of the details recorded by Ovid.

Next let us take the story of the flood. We have noted that the flood in the Philemon and Baucis legend was caused by subterranean water, and that this feature distinguishes it from the Semitic version, in which the principal source of the flood was rain from heaven. The Anatolian versions of the flood legend regularly imply a deluge caused by water issuing out of the earth, as is natural in a volcanic land, where similar phenomena on a smaller scale are of common occurrence. In his story Ovid follows this Anatolian version, and follows it strictly; and this is a point of some importance, for Ovid was first and foremost a story-teller, with an eye for good copy, and he has a habit of accumulating picturesque detail without much regard to its consistency. This tendency may be observed in another flood story told in the *Metamorphoses,* the Greek version, with Deucalion and Pyrrha playing the part of Noah and his wife. In that story Ovid is manifestly drawing partly on literary sources and partly on his imagination, and here he actually derives his deluge both from heaven and from under the earth. Jupiter first sets the storm-clouds in motion, producing torrents of rain, and then calls on Poseidon to shake the earth and flood the rivers with subterranean waters. The contrast is significant. In the Deucalion story, drawn from literary sources, the Semitic and Phrygian methods are combined to produce a deluge worthy of the occasion. In the Philemon and Baucis story, derived from the truthful old men who lived near the lake, only the Phrygian method is used.

The Phrygian or Anatolian story of the flood is known chiefly from the legends which two Phrygian cities, Apamea and Iconium, told regarding their origin and early history. Both these cities lie on that somewhat unstable portion of the earth's crust which lines the northern slope of the Taurus range. Here extinct volcanoes, numerous hot springs, and frequent earthquakes reminded the ancient population that they lived in a land where Zeus or Poseidon, if strong to save, was also strong to smite. Of the rivers of Apamea, bursting full-grown from the earth, many strange old tales were told; it was here that the Sibylline Books located Mount Ararat, identifying it with the mountain overhanging the Marsyas, a river famous in story.

Here an abyss opened in the earth, to close again only when the king's son plunged into it, in panoply, on his steed. And here, in later days, we find a legend on the coins of the city which is unexampled in the whole Roman world. Coins struck in the earlier part of the third century of our era represent an ark with a man and a woman in it, and

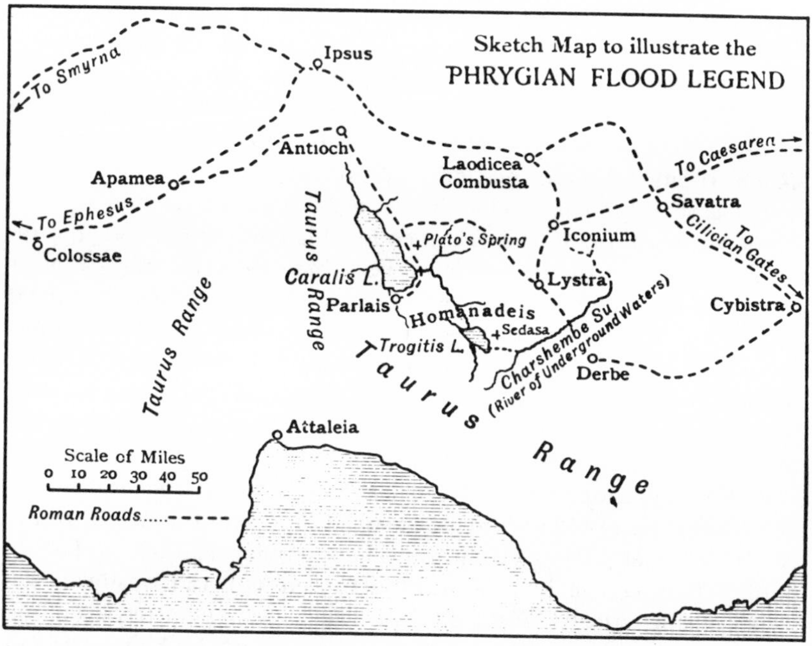

with the name of Noah written on it. Now it is well known that there was a large body of Jews among the citizens of Apamea; but the same was true of many cities in Asia Minor; yet it was only at Apamea that the legend of Noah was represented on the coins. The problem was thoroughly investigated by a young Jewish scholar, one of the first French officers to fall in the war, in a book published in 1913,[2] and he was able to supply convincing proof that the legend of the flood had been located at Apamea from remote antiquity, and that the Jewish version was simply superimposed on the old Anatolian story. The flood-story lasted on in this district till Byzantine times, when, according to the local tradition, a deluge threatened to overwhelm Colossae. The city which had been specially warned by the Apostle Paul against the worship of angels was on that occasion saved by the archangel Michael, who hacked out the gorge west of the city, and allowed the water to escape. The gorge is there for all to see; for the Christians it represented the beneficent act of Michael, just as by the pagans it had no doubt been attributed to the trident of Poseidon or the *harpe* of Perseus.

[2] *Noé Sangariou*, by Adolphe Reinach (Paris, 1913).

It is, however, with the Iconian version of the flood legend that we are mainly concerned. The Byzantine chroniclers preserve the story of a King Nannakos who ruled at Iconium for 300 years, and foretold a flood which was to overwhelm his people. The flood took place, and the new race was created by Prometheus and Athena out of mud—the *eikones* of mud thus formed giving its name to the city (Eikonion in the Greek version). This is a familiar type of foundation-legend, turning on the name of a city. The evidence for this story is late; but the recently discovered mimes of Herondas[3] show that the story of Nannakos had become proverbial on the coast of Asia Minor in the third century B.C., and the story in itself has all the marks of great antiquity.

But we are not dependent on the Byzantine chroniclers, or even on Herondas, for proof that the story of the flood had an Iconian version. The myth of a local deluge lingers on in the folklore of Iconium till the present day. The Moslems relate that the city was once threatened by a flood from a mountain valley lying to the west, but that Plato (the Arabian counterpart of Virgil the magician) stopped up the hole through which the water passed. And if you visit this valley, you will find a fine fountain issuing from beneath a Hittite monument, and locally known as the "spring of Plato." Plato is simply the Moslem counterpart of the Christian Michael and of the older Perseus, a god who looms large in the early history of this neighborhood, and who is known elsewhere as a drainer of marshes and a reclaimer of agricultural land.

Iconium lies on the western edge of an arid desert, formed of one of the richest tracts of soil in the Mediterranean area. All the elements of fertility are present in this Lycaonian plain, except water. The district immediately around Iconium is a belt of surpassing fertility—which it owes mainly to a river running down from the Isaurian hills and losing itself in many channels in the plain. An old Arab geographer calls this the River of Underground Waters, and with this description in mind we may ascend the river valley to its source. Here we are confronted by a strange situation.

The water which feeds this river comes mainly from the Taurus range, far to the south. But it is said to be fed at times also from a lake of peculiar behavior. This lake, called in ancient times Lake Trogitis, lies at the bottom of a large catchment area, and is separated by a low rim from a canyon which runs down to the River of Underground Waters. Sometimes Lake Trogitis, which is continuously fed by a large stream coming from the larger Lake Caralis, rises sufficiently in height to run over this rim and discharge into the plain of Iconium; normally

[3] Mime III, l. 10 (Nairn's or Headlam's edition). See also Ramsay, *Cities of St. Paul*, p. 319.

it runs off through an underground passage to the south, and occasionally, at long intervals, say the natives, it dries up completely. The engineers of the Baghdad Railway Company diverted the stream which feeds Lake Trogitis into the plain of Iconium, and had actually contracted to drain the greater part of the area covered by the lake. But the lake refused to be drained, and remained obstinately at its old level. Such a body of water as this, behaving capriciously, draining off at will into the plain of Iconium or into the southern sea, rising in level and disappearing as if at the bidding of some unseen power, naturally becomes the focus of strange tales. The few archaeologists and other travellers who have visited this lake all record the story told by the natives on its shores, that when at rare intervals the lake dries up completely, an ancient town appears at the bottom.

Here indeed is a lake which might well give rise to such a legend as that told by Ovid—a lake lying in a region from which Iconium folklore brought the Iconian flood, appearing and disappearing mysteriously, covering rich agricultural land, and, according to the local myth, with an ancient town lying in its depths. But is it only a fancy of mine that Ovid's story came from this lake? It lies in a remote nook in the mountains, far from the great routes of trade and administration which crossed Asia Minor in Ovid's day. Can we claim it is even probable that Ovid had so much as heard of it?

I have already described in *Discovery*[4] what was happening in this region a few years before Ovid wrote the *Metamorphoses,* and while he was collecting the material for his book. Quirinius, the Governor of Syria mentioned by Luke in the passage in which he dates the birth of Christ, was engaged between 11 and 6 B.C. in a war for the pacification of Pisidia, which, from the name of the tribe which was the principal enemy and gave most trouble to the Roman army, was called the Homanadensian War. The war was a success for the Roman arms. Only two facts concerning it need be repeated here. It was over in 6 B.C., and the principal scene of operations was the country round Lake Trogitis, the home of the Homanadeis. Quirinius, as Strabo and Pliny inform us, reduced their fastnesses one by one, took 6,000 men alive, and planted them in the neighboring cities. Clearly his army got to know the valley of Lake Trogitis very thoroughly. About 6 B.C. Quirinius returned to Rome, where he was honored as a conqueror, and no doubt many of his officers accompanied him. Ovid, who moved in the best society, would have ample opportunity of hearing the story of Lake Trogitis.

Strangely enough, we can prove a good knowledge of the topogra-

[4] April 1920, pp. 100 ff. [The essay is entitled "The Date of the Nativity"—Ed. Note.]

phy of Lake Trogitis in the case of at least one Roman officer. It has always puzzled those students of Strabo who know the country he is describing that he twice makes reference to Lake Trogitis, without being aware that on both occasions he is referring to the same lake. Strabo travelled widely in Asia Minor, and in the first of the two passages he lets fall a hint which shows us the route by which he crossed Lycaonia. He mentions the city Savatra, where the wells are so deep that you buy water at so much a bucket, and the sheep are fat and fleecy—obviously an eyewitness account, proving that he had passed by Savatra, and therefore along the northern branch of the Syrian Highway, which does not touch Iconium. But he is quite explicit on the point himself. He goes on to say, "and in that region lie Lakes Caralis and Trogitis, and somewhere hereabouts Iconium"—evidently he had not been to Iconium or the lakes. Now this is strange, for a few pages farther on he gives us an admirably exact description of the military topography of the valley of Trogitis. He is now describing the Homanadensian War, and says that it was fought in a region of crags and precipices surrounding a fertile plain, divided into several canyons, and defended on all sides by mountains. This is obviously the description of a military eyewitness, and Ramsay acutely discerned that Strabo got it from one of Quirinius' officers, and used it without being aware that it referred to Lake Trogitis which he had already mentioned.

If information regarding Lake Trogitis was accessible to Strabo (wherever he wrote; there is doubt on the point), it was accessible to Ovid in Rome when he was collecting materials for his *Metamorphoses*. We have now seen that Lake Trogitis—that mysterious lake which accords so well with Ovid's story—was *the one lake* in Asia Minor which is certain to have been much talked of in Rome after the year 6 B.C. And we have seen that Ovid's story of Philemon and Baucis—an eyewitness story—is a genuine Anatolian legend, answering to every test of local veracity that we can apply to it. I venture to think that few cases which have been made out for an ancient literary origin are more substantial.

But this is not all. So far I have set out the case for the location of Ovid's legend at Lake Trogitis as it can be established by independent witnesses. One day in 1909 our party visited the lake, and in the evening (to avoid the mosquitoes) we rode up the long slope to the high ledge which overlooks the lake on the east. By such trivial considerations is discovery often guided. We passed the night in a village which had already been visited by the American Sterrett, who found evidence that it was one of the villages of the Homanadeis, called Sedasa. Near Sedasa we were fortunate enough to find an inscription which told us that on this ledge, in the Greek and Roman periods, there had stood a temple of Jupiter and Mercury.[5]

The writer's realization of the bearing of this discovery on Ovid's story has followed from Ramsay's[6] brilliant reconstruction of the topography of the Homanadensian War, recently published. Its bearing on another story told of this neighborhood was plain to us at once. One of the series of garrison cities founded by Quirinius to control the Pisidians, and the nearest of the whole series to Lake Trogitis, was Lystra. Lystra was visited some fifty years later by Paul and Barnabas, and there Paul healed a lame man. "And when the people saw what Paul had done, they lifted up their voices, saying in the speech of Lycaonia, The gods are come down to us in the likeness of men. And they called Barnabas Jupiter, and Paul Mercurius."

[5]Published by the writer in *Classical Review,* 1910, pp. 76 ff., and *Expositor,* July 1910, pp. 1 ff.

[6]*Journal of Roman Studies,* vii, pp. 229 ff.

For the story of Philemon and Baucis see Ovid's *Metamorphoses,* viii, ll. 611–724; trans. by F. J. Miller in the Loeb Classics (Heinemann).

The Great Flood

JAMES GEORGE FRAZER

While much of the scholarly attention devoted to the flood myth tended to center on the account in Genesis and on other versions from the Near East, for several centuries scholars assiduously compiled lists of flood narratives from other areas of the world. The roster of articles and monographs in which these flood myths are cited is impressive. For the most part, these early comparative studies consisted entirely of retelling flood stories from many cultures.

In Alexander Catcott's Treatise on the Deluge, *first published in 1761, we find, for example, that Part II comprises "A Collection of the Principal Heathen Accounts of the Flood" and includes Roman, Greek, Babylonian, Persian, Chinese, and American Indian texts. See the second edition (London, 1768), pp. 100–123. Another instructive example is provided by Jacob Bryant, who sought a key to mythology in general. In the third edition of his six-volume* A New System; or, An Analysis of Ancient Mythology *(London, 1807), he devoted all of Volume III to the flood myth. In this work, first published in 1774, Bryant assumes that pagan myths are but degraded or degenerate forms of the Bible, but he also argues that these gentile traditions of the flood constituted bona fide memory traces of the historical event. Other mythologists concentrated even more upon the flood. G. S. Faber, in* A Dissertation on the Mysteries of the Cabiri *(Oxford, 1803) and a three-volume work,* The Origin of Pagan Idolatry *(London, 1816), went so far as to claim that all myth derives from the biblical flood. Faber contended that all great father gods were versions of Noah, great mother goddesses derived from the Ark, and the various triads of gods stemmed from the three sons of Noah. For details about Bryant and Faber, see Burton Feldman and Robert D. Richardson,* The Rise of Modern Mythology 1680–1860 *(Bloomington, 1972).*

Throughout the nineteenth century, we find various comparative essays on the flood myth. Among the more prominent ones are: Philipp Buttmann, "Über den Mythos der Sündflut," in Mythologus, *vol. I (Berlin, 1828), pp. 180–214; Julius Braun, "Über die ältesten biblischen Sagen, ihren Verbreitungskreis und ihre Herkunst: Die Fluthsage,"* Das Ausland *34 (1861): 517–520, 537–541; Otto Böckler, "Die Sintfluth-Sagen des Alterthums, nach ihrem Verhältnis zur biblischen Sintfluthgeschichte: Ein Vortrag,"* Jahrbücher für deutsche Theologie

Reprinted from *Folk-Lore in the Old Testament,* vol. 1 (London: Macmillan, 1918), pp. 104–107, 332–338, by permission of A. P. Watt Ltd. on behalf of Trinity College, Cambridge.

2 (1870): 319–343; Ludwig Diestel, Die Sintflut und die Flutsagan des Altertums *(Berlin, 1871); Francois Lenormant, "The Deluge: Its Traditions in Ancient Nations,"* Contemporary Review *36 (1879): 465–500, or his "The Deluge," in* The Beginnings of History According to the Bible and the Traditions of Oriental Peoples: From the Creation of Man to the Deluge *(New York, 1883), pp. 382–488; Richard Andree,* Die Flutsagen *(Braunschweig, 1891); Anton Herrmann, "Die Flutsagen der finnisch-ugrischen Völker,"* Globus *63 (1893): 333–338; Auguste Gittée, "Les légendes du Déluge devant l'ethnographie et l'histoire,"* Revue de Belgique *27 (1899): 250–265, 350–362; and Hermann Usener,* Die Sintfluthsagen *(Bonn, 1899).*

The penchant for comparative treatments of the flood myth continued into the twentieth century: M. Winternitz, "Die Flutsagen des Alterthums und der Naturvölker," Mitteilungen der Anthropologischen Gesellschaft in Wien *31 (1901): 305–333; Ernst Böklen, "Die Sintflutsage: Versuch einer neuen Erklärung,"* Archiv für Religionswissenschaft *6 (1903): 1–61, 97–150; G. Gerland,* Der Mythus von der Sündflut *(Bonn, 1912); H. F. Feilberg,* Skabelsessagn og Flodsagn *(Copenhagen, 1915), pp. 133–178; Walter Anderson,* Nordasiatische Flutsagen, *Acta et Commentationes Universitatis Dorpatensis B. Humaniora 4(3) (Dorpat, 1923); and Johannes Riem,* Die Sintflut in Sage und Wissenschaft *(Hamburg, 1925). See also R. H. Lowie, "Zur Verbreitung der Flutsagen,"* Anthropos *21 (1926): 615–616.*

Of all the extensive comparative studies of the flood myth ever undertaken, probably none is better known than that assembled by James George Frazer (1854–1941), master of the art of retrieving materials from arcane and fugitive sources ranging from obscure government reports to accounts written by missionaries. Frazer was fascinated by the possibility of finding parallels to details contained in the Old Testament, and he compiled no fewer than three ample volumes of such parallels in his Folk-Lore in the Old Testament, *published in 1918. Several years earlier, in 1916, Frazer chose the flood myth as the subject of the Huxley lecture which he had been invited to give by the Council of the Royal Anthropological Institute. This lecture was to form the basis of his elaborate treatment of the flood myth in the latter three-volume work. Frazer's essay is far too long to be included in this volume, as it runs to more than two hundred pages, but to give the reader an idea of Frazer's style as well as some of his more important conclusions, I am presenting the introduction to the essay and his summary of "The Geographical Diffusion of Flood Stories" which follows his endless retelling of hundreds of flood myths. Readers who wish to consider the myths themselves rather than relying upon Frazer's overview should consult Frazer's full essay or, better yet, his sources where the accounts are closer to the original, native wording of the stories.*

The vast materials assembled by the comparativists were utilized in diverse fashion by theologians. On the one hand, the wide diffusion of the flood myth was held to constitute prima facie evidence for the existence of a universal (as opposed to a merely local) flood. On the other hand, since some peoples apparently lacked flood myths—many peoples in Africa, for example—this was construed to be data suggesting that the flood was not universal. For the argument that "races existed on the earth at the time of the Flood who lived outside the area affected by it and were consequently not involved in the catastrophe," see Edmund F. Sutcliffe, S.J., "The Ethnographical Restriction of the Flood," Clergy Review *22 (1942): 442–454, or J. A. Zahm, "The Noachian Deluge,"* American Ecclesiastical Review *8 (1893): 14–34, 84–99. (For sources on the earlier discussions of the theory of the nonuniversality of the deluge, see Zahm, p. 92, n. 2; for an interesting analysis of three "schools"—the school of absolute universality, the school of restricted universality, and the school of nonuniversality—see Jean d'Estienne, "Le Déluge biblique et les races antédiluviennes,"* Revue des questions scientifiques *18 (1885): 468–551.)*

To better understand Frazer's approach to the flood myth, one needs to be aware of the two principal competing theories proposed to explain apparent parallel phenomena in different cultures. If the "same" myth was reported in widely separated geographical-cultural areas, this parallel was attributed either to monogenesis (one birth) plus diffusion or *to polygenesis (many births). In the first instance, it was typically assumed that any given cultural item, including a myth, originated only once in one particular place and at one particular time. After monogenesis had occurred, the myth might diffuse from one people to another. Often the avowed goal of advocates of a monogenetic approach to myth was to determine just where and when a myth first came into existence. The chief difficulty was that if a myth were found among people A and among people B, it was not always easy to ascertain whether B learned it from A or A learned it from B. The polygenetic theory, predicated upon the notion of so-called psychic unity (of all peoples), argued that the "same" myth among different peoples developed independently in each instance. So if A and B both possessed the same myth, there was no need to postulate that A transmitted it to B or vice versa. Rather, both A and B came up with the myth as an inevitable product of a common unilinear evolutionary intellectual sequence. Frazer, like most of his Victorian British anthropological colleagues, generally subscribed to the second alternative, believing that all peoples on the face of the earth evolved from initial "savagery" and passed through "barbarism" to eventual "civilization." Myth was considered to have developed during savagery, which explained why so many "savage" peoples possessed the same myths. Myths still found among civilized peoples were understood to be survivals from their savage ancestors.*

It was, of course, possible to employ both theories. Thus some versions of the flood myth were obviously cognate, that is, genetically and historically related. Thus Frazer deemed the Babylonian and Genesis flood myths. On the other hand, the idea of a flood was sufficiently simple to have occurred independently among diverse peoples, and so there was a case for polygenesis as well, according to Frazer.

Despite Frazer's impressive amassing of flood myths from all corners of the earth, his conclusions concerning the geographical spread of flood myths must be accepted only with reservations. His claims that the flood myth is absent in Africa and China are debatable at the very least.

For surveys of the flood myth later than Frazer, one may profitably consult the excellent discussion of flood myth theories and interpretations in Leopold Walk, "Die Sintfluttradition der Völker," Österreichische Leo-Gesellschaft Jahrbuch *(1931): 60–81, and the superb essay by François Berge, "Les légendes de Déluge," in* Histoire generale des religions, *vol. 5 (Paris, 1951), pp. 59–101.*

When the Council of the Royal Anthropological Institute invited me to deliver the annual Huxley lecture, I gratefully accepted the invitation, esteeming it a high honor to be thus associated with one for whom, both as a thinker and as a man, I entertain a deep respect, and with whose attitude towards the great problems of life I am in cordial sympathy.[1] His own works will long keep his memory green; but it is fitting that our science should lay, year by year, a wreath on the grave of one of the most honored of its exponents.

Casting about for a suitable subject, I remembered that in his later life Huxley devoted some of his well-earned leisure to examining those traditions as to the early ages of the world which are recorded in the Book of Genesis; and accordingly I thought that I might appropriately take one of them for the theme of my discourse. The one which I have chosen is the familiar story of the Great Flood. Huxley himself discussed it in an instructive essay written with all the charm of his lucid and incisive style.[2] His aim was to show that, treated as a record of a deluge which overwhelmed the whole world, drowning almost all men and animals, the story conflicts with the plain teaching of geology and must be rejected as a fable. I shall not attempt either to reinforce or to criticize his arguments and his conclusions, for the simple reason that I am no geologist, and that for me to express an opinion on such a matter would be a mere impertinence. I have approached the subject from a different side, namely, from that of tradition. It has long been known that legends of a great flood, in which almost all men perished, are widely diffused over the world; and accordingly what I have tried to do is to collect and compare these legends, and to inquire what conclusions are to be deduced from the comparison. In short, my discussion of the stories is a study in comparative folk-lore. My purpose is to discover how the narratives arose, and how they came to be so widespread over the earth; with the question of their truth or false-

[1]The part of this chapter that deals with the ancient flood stories of Babylonia, Palestine, and Greece was delivered as the annual Huxley lecture before the Royal Anthropological Institute of Great Britain and Ireland, November 1916.

[2]"Hasisadra's Adventure," *Collected Essays,* vol. 4 (London, 1911), pp. 239–286.

hood I am not primarily concerned, though of course it cannot be ignored in considering the problem of their origin. The inquiry thus defined is not a novel one. It has often been attempted, especially in recent years, and in pursuing it I have made ample use of the labors of my predecessors, some of whom have discussed the subject with great learning and ability. In particular, I would acknowledge my debt to the eminent German geographer and anthropologist, the late Dr. Richard Andree, whose monograph on diluvial traditions, like all his writings, is a model of sound learning and good sense, set forth with the utmost clearness and conciseness.[3]

Apart from the intrinsic interest of such legends as professed records of a catastrophe which destroyed at a blow almost the whole human race, they deserve to be studied for the sake of their bearing on a general question which is at present warmly debated among anthropologists. That question is, How are we to explain the numerous and striking similarities which obtain between the beliefs and customs of races inhabiting distant parts of the world? Are such resemblances due to the transmission of the customs and beliefs from one race to another, either by immediate contact or through the medium of intervening peoples? Or have they arisen independently in many different races through the similar working of the human mind under similar circumstances? Now, if I may presume to offer an opinion on this much-debated problem, I would say at once that, put in the form of an antithesis between mutually exclusive views, the question seems to me absurd. So far as I can judge, all experience and all probability are in favor of the conclusion that both causes have operated extensively and powerfully to produce the observed similarities of custom and belief

[3] R. Andree, *Die Flutsagen* (Brunswick, 1891). Other notable discussions of the same theme in recent years are the following: H. Usener, *Die Sintflutsagen* (Bonn, 1899); idem, "Zu den Sintfluthsagen," *Kleine Schriften* 4 (Berlin, 1913): 382–396; M. Winternitz, *Die Flutsagen des Alterthums und der Naturvölker* (Vienna, 1901) (reprinted from *Mitteilungen der Anthropologischen Gesellschaft in Wien,* vol. 31); E. Böklen, "Die Sintflutsage, Versuch einer neuen Erklärung," *Archiv für Religionswissenschaft* 6 (1903): 1–61, 97–150; G. Gerland, *Der Mythus von der Sintflut* (Bonn, 1912). Of these works, that of Winternitz contains a useful list of flood legends, with references to the authorities and a full analysis of the principal incidents in the legends. Like the treatise of Andree, it is characterized by the union of accurate learning and good sense. On the other hand, the works of Usener, Böklen, and Gerland are vitiated by their fanciful and improbable theories as to the origin of the legends in solar or lunar myths. But in spite of this defect Gerland's treatise is valuable for the number of parallel legends which the author's ethnological learning has collected from many races. Among earlier discussions of the same theme may be mentioned Philipp Buttmann, "Über den Mythos der Sündflut," *Mythologus,* vol. 1 (Berlin, 1828–1829), pp. 180–214; François Lenormant, *Les Origines de l'Histoire d'après la Bible, de la Création de l'Homme au Déluge* (Paris, 1880), pp. 382–491; (Sir) Henry H. Howorth, *The Mammoth and the Flood* (London, 1887).

among the various races of mankind: in other words, many of these resemblances are to be explained by simple transmission, with more or less of modification, from people to people, and many are to be explained as having originated independently through the similar action of the human mind in response to similar environment. If that is so—and I confess to thinking that this is the only reasonable and probable view—it will follow that in attempting to account for any particular case of resemblance which may be traced between the customs and beliefs of different races, it would be futile to appeal to the general principle either of transmission or of independent origin; each case must be judged on its own merits after an impartial scrutiny of the facts and referred to the one or the other principle, or possibly to a combination of the two, according as the balance of evidence inclines to the one side or to the other, or hangs evenly between them.

This general conclusion, which accepts the two principles of transmission and independent origin as both of them true and valid within certain limits, is confirmed by the particular investigation of diluvial traditions. For it is certain that legends of a great flood are found dispersed among many diverse peoples in distant regions of the earth, and so far as demonstration in such matters is possible, it can be demonstrated that the similarities which undoubtedly exist between many of these legends are due partly to direct transmission from one people to another, and partly to similar, but quite independent, experiences either of great floods or of phenomena which suggested the occurrence of great floods, in many different parts of the world. Thus the study of these traditions, quite apart from any conclusions to which it may lead us concerning their historical credibility, may serve a useful purpose if it mitigates the heat with which the controversy has sometimes been carried on, by convincing the extreme partisans of both principles that in this as in so many other disputes the truth lies wholly neither on the one side nor on the other, but somewhere between the two.

THE GEOGRAPHICAL DIFFUSION OF FLOOD STORIES

The foregoing survey of diluvial traditions suffices to prove that this type of story, whether we call it legendary or mythical, has been widely diffused throughout the world. Before we inquire into the relation in which the traditions stand to each other, and the cause or causes which have given rise to them, it may be well to recapitulate briefly the regions in which they have been found. To begin with Asia, we have found examples of them in Babylonia, Palestine, Syria, Phrygia, ancient and modern India, Burma, Cochin China, the Malay Peninsula, and Kamtchatka. Roughly speaking, therefore, the traditions prevail in Southern Asia, and are conspicuously absent from Eastern, Central, and Northern Asia. It is particularly remarkable that neither of the great civilized peoples of Eastern Asia, the Chinese and the Japanese, should, so far as I know, have preserved in their voluminous and ancient literatures any native legends of a great flood of the sort we are here considering, that is, of a universal inundation in which the whole or the greater part of the human race is said to have perished.

In Europe native diluvial traditions are much rarer than in Asia, but they occurred in ancient Greece, and have been reported in Wales, and among the Lithuanians, the gipsies of Transylvania, and the Voguls of Eastern Russia. The Icelandic story of an inundation of giant's blood hardly conforms to the general type.

In Africa, including Egypt, native legends of a great flood are conspicuously absent; indeed no single clear case of one has yet been reported.

In the Indian Archipelago we find legends of a great flood in the large islands of Sumatra, Borneo, and Celebes, and among the lesser islands in Nias, Engano, Ceram, Rotti, and Flores. Stories of the same sort are told by the native tribes of the Philippine Islands and Formosa, and by the isolated Andaman Islanders in the Bay of Bengal.

In the vast islands, or continents, of New Guinea and Australia we meet with some stories of a great flood, and legends of the same sort occur in the fringe of smaller islands known as Melanesia, which sweeps in a great arc of a circle round New Guinea and Australia on the north and east.

Passing still eastward out into the Pacific, we discover diluvial traditions widely spread among the Polynesians who occupy the scattered and for the most part small islands of that great ocean, from Hawaii on the north to New Zealand on the south. Among the Micronesians a flood legend has been recorded in the Pelew Islands.

In America, South, Central, and North, diluvial traditions are very widespread. They have been found from Tierra del Fuego in the south to Alaska in the north, and in both continents from east to west. Nor do they occur only among the Indian tribes; examples of them have been reported among the Eskimo from Alaska on the west to Greenland on the east.

Such being in general the geographical diffusion of the traditions we have next to ask, how are they related to each other? Are they all genetically connected with each other, or are they distinct and independent? In other words, are they all descended from one common original, or have they originated independently in different parts of the world? Formerly, under the influence of the Biblical tradition, inquirers were disposed to identify legends of a great flood, wherever found, with the familiar Noachian deluge, and to suppose that in them we had more or less corrupt and apocryphal versions of that great catastrophe, of which the only true and authentic record is preserved in the Book of Genesis. Such a view can hardly be maintained any longer. Even when we have allowed for the numerous corruptions and changes of all kinds which oral tradition necessarily suffers in passing from generation to generation and from land to land through countless ages, we shall still find it difficult to recognize in the diverse, often quaint, childish, or grotesque stories of a great flood, the human copies of a single divine original. And the difficulty has been greatly increased since modern research has proved the supposed divine original in Genesis to be not an original at all, but a comparatively late copy of a much older Babylonian or rather Sumerian version. No Christian apologist is likely to treat the Babylonian story, with its strongly polytheistic coloring, as a primitive revelation of God to man; and if the theory of inspiration is inapplicable to the original, it can hardly be invoked to account for the copy.

Dismissing, therefore, the theory of revelation or inspiration as irreconcilable with the known facts, we have still to inquire whether the Babylonian or Sumerian legend, which is certainly by far the oldest of all diluvial traditions, may not be the one from which all the rest have been derived. The question is one to which a positive answer can hardly be given, since demonstration in such matters is impossible, and our conclusion must be formed from the consideration of a variety of probabilities which different minds will estimate differently. It is no doubt possible to analyze all the stories into their elements, to classify these elements, to count up the number of them which the various versions have in common, and from the sum of the common elements found in any one narrative to calculate the probability of its being a derivative or original version. This, in fact, has been done by one of my predecessors in this department of research,[4] but I do not propose to repeat his calculations: readers with a statistical and mathematical turn of mind may either consult them in his work or repeat them for themselves from the data submitted to them in the foregoing pages. Here I shall content myself with stating my general conclusion, leaving

[4]Winternitz, *Die Flutsagen*, pp. 312–333.

the reader to verify, correct, or reject it by reference to the evidence with which I have furnished him. Apart, then, from the Hebrew legend, which is unquestionably derived from the Babylonian, and from modern instances which exhibit clear traces of late missionary or at all events Christian influence, I do not think that we have decisive grounds for tracing any of the diluvial traditions to the Babylonian as their original. Scholars of repute have, indeed, maintained that both the ancient Greek and the ancient Indian legends are derived from the Babylonian; they may be right, but to me it does not seem that the resemblances between the three are sufficient to justify us in assuming identity of origin. No doubt in the later ages of antiquity the Greeks were acquainted both with the Babylonian and the Hebrew versions of the deluge legend, but their own traditions of a great flood are much older than the conquests of Alexander, which first unlocked the treasuries of Oriental learning to western scholars; and in their earliest forms the Greek traditions exhibit no clear marks of borrowing from Asiatic sources. In the Deucalion legend, for example, which comes nearest to the Babylonian, only Deucalion and his wife are saved from the flood, and after it has subsided they are reduced to the necessity of miraculously creating mankind afresh out of stones, while nothing at all is said about the restoration of animals, which must presumably have perished in the waters. This is very different from the Babylonian and Hebrew legend, which provides for the regular propagation both of the human and the animal species after the flood by taking a sufficient number of passengers of both sorts on board the ark.

Similarly a comparison of the ancient Indian with the Babylonian version of the legend brings out serious discrepancies between them. The miraculous fish which figures so prominently in all the ancient Indian versions has no obvious parallel in the Babylonian; though some scholars have ingeniously argued that the deity, incarnate in a fish, who warns Manu of the coming deluge in the Indian legend is a duplicate of Ea, the god who similarly warns Ut-napishtim in the Babylonian legend, for there seems to be no doubt that Ea was a water deity, conceived and represented partly in human and partly in fish form.[5] If this suggested parallel between the two legends could be

[5] Lenormant, *Les Origines de l'Histoire d'après la Bible*, pp. 424 ff.; Winternitz, *Die Flutsagen*, p. 328. As to the aqueous and fishy nature of Ea in Babylonian mythology, see M. Jastrow, *Religion of Babylonia and Assyria*, pp. 136 f.; P. Dhorme, *La Religion Assyro-Babylonienne* (Paris, 1910), pp. 73 f.; and especially Alfred Jeremias, "Oannes-Ea," in W. H. Roscher's *Ausführliches Lexikon der Griechischen und Römischen Mythologie*, vol. 3, pp. 577 ff., where the half-human, half-fish character of the god is illustrated from Babylonian monuments. Berosus speaks of this deity under the name of Oannes, and describes his amphibious form nearly as it is figured in Babylonian art; he tells us that Oannes

made out, it would certainly forge a strong link between them. On the other hand, in the oldest Indian form of the story, that in the *Satapatha Brahmana,* Manu is represented as the solitary survivor of the great flood, and after the catastrophe a woman has to be miraculously created out of the butter, sour milk, whey and curds of his sacrifice, in order to enable him to continue the species. It is only in the later versions of the story that Manu takes a large assortment of animals and plants with him into the ship; and even in them, though the sage appears on shipboard surrounded by a band of brother sages whom he had rescued from a watery grave, nothing whatever is said about rescuing his wife and children. The omission betrays a lack not only of domestic affection but of common prudence on the part of the philosopher, and contrasts forcibly with the practical foresight of his Babylonian counterpart, who under the like distressing circumstances has at least the consolation of being surrounded by the family circle on the stormy waters, and of knowing that as soon as the flood has subsided he will be able, with their assistance, to provide for the continuance of the human race by the ordinary processes of nature. In this curious difference between the two tales is it fanciful to detect the contrast between the worldly prudence of the Semitic mind and the dreamy asceticism of the Indian?[6]

On the whole, then, there is little evidence to prove that the ancient Indian and Greek legends of a flood are derived from the corresponding Babylonian tradition. When we remember that the Babylonians, so far as we know, never succeeded in handing on their story of a deluge to the Egyptians, with whom they were in direct communication for centuries, we need not wonder if they failed to transmit it to the more distant Greeks and Indians, with whom down to the days of Alexander the Great they had but little intercourse. In later ages, through the medium of Christian literature, the Babylonian legend has indeed gone the round of the world and been echoed in tales told under the palms of coral islands, in Indian wigwams, and amid the Arctic ice and

appeared from the Red Sea, that is, from the Persian Gulf, and after passing the day in conversation with men, whom he taught the elements of civilization, retired at sunset to the sea. See Berosus, in *Fragmenta Historicorum Graecorum,* ed. C. Müller, vol. 2, pp. 496 f.; Eusebius, *Chronic.,* ed. A. Schoene, vol. 1, col. 14.

[6]The theory of the dependence of the Indian on the Babylonian legend was maintained by Eugène Bournouf and François Lenormant (*Les Origines de l'Histoire d'après la Bible,* 1880, pp. 423 ff.) and more recently by M. Winternitz (*Die Flutsagen,* pp. 327 f.). Professor H. Oldenberg also inclines to it (*Die Literatur des Alten Indien* [Stuttgart and Berlin, 1903], p. 47). On the other hand the theory was rejected by F. Max Müller (*India: What Can It Teach Us?* [London, 1892], pp. 133 ff.) and more hesitatingly by Andree (*Die Flutsagen,* pp. 17 ff.).

snow;[7] but in itself, apart from Christian or Mohammedan agencies, it would seem to have travelled little beyond the limits of its native land and the adjoining Semitic regions.

If, among the many other diluvial traditions which we have passed in review, we look about for evidence of derivation from a common source, and therefore of diffusion from a single center, we cannot fail to be struck by the manifest tokens of such derivation and diffusion in the Algonquin stories of North America.[8] The many flood legends recorded among different tribes of that widely spread stock resemble each other so closely that we cannot but regard them as mere variations of one and the same tradition. Whether in the original story the incident of the various animals diving into the water to fetch up earth is native or based on a reminiscence of the birds in the Noachian story, which has reached the Indians through white men, may be open to question.

Further, we have seen that according to Humboldt a general resemblance may be traced between the diluvial traditions among the Indians of the Orinoco,[9] and that according to William Ellis a like resemblance prevails among the Polynesian legends.[10] It may be that in both these regions the traditions have spread from local centers, in other words, that they are variations of a common original.

But when we have made allowance for all such cases of diffusion from local centers, it seems probable that there still remain deluge legends which have originated independently.

[7] For traces of the legend, in its Christian form, among barbarous and savage tribes, see *Folk-Lore in the Old Testament,* vol. I, p. 195 (Kamars), p. 223 (Minahassans), pp. 245 f. (Hawaiians), pp. 265 f. (Macusis), pp. 275 f. (Michoacan Indians), p. 280 (Cora Indians), p. 297 (Cree Indians), p. 312 (Tinneh Indians), pp. 328 f. (Eskimo), pp. 330 f. (Masai).

[8] *Folk-Lore in the Old Testament,* vol. I, pp. 295 ff.

[9] *Folk-Lore in the Old Testament,* vol. I, p. 266.

[10] *Folk-Lore in the Old Testament,* vol. I, pp. 241 f.

The Principle of Retribution in the Flood and Catastrophe Myths

HANS KELSEN

Not all the comparative studies of the flood myth were concerned solely with establishing the range of geographical diffusion of the narrative, or even of the possible or probable historicity of the flood. Scholars from different intellectual disciplines had different reasons for exploring the content of flood myths. Hans Kelsen (1881–1973), an authority on international law and jurisprudence, for example, tried to discern or extrapolate general moral principles from the myths. He was especially interested in what he termed "the principle of retribution." In the following essay, he looks at a wide variety of flood myth texts to see the extent to which retribution figures in the plot.

Kelsen's style of presentation is somewhat reminiscent of Frazer inasmuch as he retells snippets of stories taken out of their ethnographic contexts. He is also like Frazer in that he repeats the long-standing ethnocentric distinction between "civilized" and primitive" peoples, a distinction which stems from a colonialist-inspired evolutionary view from the nineteenth century which assumed that all peoples evolved from savagery to civilization in fixed fashion. The epitome of such a condescending attitude in which writers from "civilized" societies described the thought processes or values of "primitive" peoples is perhaps Lucien Lévy-Bruhl's (1857–1939) controversial book Primitive Mentality, *in which he spoke of what he labeled the "prelogical" mind of primitives. The racist implications of Lévy-Bruhl's view was that primitive peoples were incapable of thinking logically (the way civilized writers like Lévy-Bruhl did!). Although he did recant to some extent in his posthumously published* Notebooks, *claiming that he had been misunderstood, a close reading reveals that Lévy-Bruhl never did abandon his conviction that primitive people could not conceptualize or think in terms of causality.*

In fairness, it should be observed that Kelsen is arguing that there is a similarity in the thinking of primitive and civilized peoples, but the point is that the very distinction between primitive and civilized peoples reflects an unfortunate bias, based on a traditional historical framework which must be understood as part of the context of Kelsen's inquiry.

Reprinted from *Society and Nature: A Sociological Inquiry* (Chicago: University of Chicago Press, 1943), pp. 169–185.

For a sample of Lévy-Bruhl's reasoning, see Primitive Mentality *(Boston, 1966) and* The Notebooks on Primitive Mentality *(New York, 1975). For other considerations of the possible underlying motivations for the flood, see A. W. Nieuwenhuis, "Die Sintflutsagen als kausal-logische Natur-Schöpfungsmythen,"* Festschrift Publication d'Hommage Offerte au P. W. Schmidt *(Vienna, 1928), pp. 515–526; Donat Poulet, "The Moral Causes of the Flood,"* Catholic Biblical Quarterly *4 (1942):293–303; G. Pettinato, "Die Bestrafung des Menschengeschlechts durch die Sintflut,"* Orientalia *37 (1968):165–200; and David Clines, "Noah's Flood: The Theology of the Flood Narrative,"* Faith and Thought *100 (1972–1973): 128–142.*

More than any others, the flood myths clearly illustrate the similarity between the mental beginnings of different peoples and show how even the most civilized groups in the infancy of their thinking betray the same characteristics as the most primitive societies. Among the common elements of flood and catastrophe tales the principle of retribution is so manifest that one must consider it, if only for that reason, as one of the oldest ideas of humanity.

That retribution is the chief motive in the biblical account of the Flood, as well as in the story of the sulphur and fire rain over Sodom and Gomorrah, are not conclusive proofs, since these stories may be later versions. But, also, the Babylonian record of a great flood handed down in the *Gilgamesh Epic,* to which the biblical story can be traced, contains the idea of retribution. The gods—foremost among them, Bel—agree to inflict punishment upon men for their sins; this punishment will assume the form of an immense flood to destroy all human beings. One god, Ea, however, chooses a certain man whom he wishes to save, Utnapishtim (the meaning of the name is "he found life"), of the town of Shurippak.[1] He had the nickname Atrachasis, which means "the very intelligent."[2] His devoutness is stressed in the poem. Ea tells Utnapishtim of the decision of the gods and commands him to build a boat and take into it living beings of all kinds. Thus the pious Utnapishtim is saved. Bel, the real author of the flood, is furious at first when he sees Utnapishtim and his people saved. But at Ea's suggestion that in the future he should punish the sins of men with famine, pestilence, and wild beasts, rather than by floods causing general destruction, Bel is finally reconciled to the rescue of Utnapishtim. He even grants the man and his wife divine nature and removes them far

[1] Cf. Heinrich Zimmern, *Biblische und babylonische Urgeschichte* ("Der alte Orient," 2. Jahrg., Heft 3 [3d ed., 1903]), p. 32.

[2] H. Gunkel, *Schöpfung und Chaos in Urzeit und Endzeit* (1895), p. 428.

away, to the mouth of the rivers, to lead a life of immortality.[3] Piety receives its greatest reward. The words spoken by Ea to Bel to calm his wrath at the saving of Utnapishtim are important for the significance which the poems give to the flood:

> Thou mighty among the gods, warrior,
> Thus, thus rashly hast thou caused the deluge.
> May the sinner bear his sin's reward, and the wicked his wickedness.
> Be lenient, let not (all) be crushed; be merciful, let not (everything) be destroyed.
> Instead of causing a flood, lions might have come and diminished mankind.[4]

The idea of retribution is obvious.[5] The Babylonian flood fable is probably of Sumerian origin. Even in its oldest form the motive of retribution is apparent: Ziugiddu, or rather Ziudsuddu, at once king and a priest of the god Enki, the Sumerian deity who was the equivalent of the Semitic Ea, is warned by Enki, as reward for his piety, of the coming flood and thus escapes certain death in a boat.[6]

The destruction of sinful mankind, executed at the order of the highest god, Ra, by the vengeance-goddess, Hathor, is the content of inscriptions which decorate the tomb of Pharaoh Seti I (about 1350 B.C.).[7] Zeus destroyed the bronze race, as punishment for its crimes, by

[3] Cf. Zimmern, p. 33.

[4] The Chaldean account of the Deluge (*Gilgamesh Epic*), translated by W. Muss-Arnolt in the *Biblical World*, III (1894), 109 ff.

[5] According to Hugo Gressmann (*Das Gilgamesch Epos*, neu übersetzt von Arthur Ungnad und gemeinverständlich erklärt von Hugo Gressmann [1911], p. 202), the ethical motivation already appeared very early, "if it did not exist from the very beginning." See also Friedrich Jeremias in Bertholet und Lehmann, *Lehrbuch der Religionsgeschichte*, I (1925), 598.

[6] Cf. Frazer, *Folk-Lore in the Old Testament*, I (1919) 122.

[7] Heinrich Brugsch, *Die neue Weltordnung nach Vernichtung des sündigen Menschengeschlechtes* (1881), pp. 35 ff., represents the tale as follows: In the first period after the creation, the gods lived with human beings in Egypt as in paradise; the god Ra ruled as their first king. "Men were already divided into good and evil beings. The former dwelt near their god and king, Ra, and travelled with him up the Nile. The latter, afraid of the light of his eyes, fled to the mountainous parts of the desert in order to plot a conspiracy against him." Ra consequently decided to destroy these human beings. He "lets a goddess Hatter (the cosmic order) proceed from his eye, and accept the office of a goddess of vengeance. She killed the human beings whose blood covered the earth. But since there were also good men, God showed mercy, applying a peculiar way to stop the rage of the goddess. She drank a secretly prepared drink . . . got intoxicated and was therefore unable to recognize men. Despite the judgment which had destroyed the sinful part of mankind, the god of light no longer liked to stay on earth. He feared the human race like a contagious disease and became tired of living with them. He wanted to go where no one could reach him. With the fulfillment of his wish, a new world order began. . . .

means of a flood which overflowed the whole of Greece. Only the two just people, Deucalion and Pyrrha, were spared. Because Zeus and Hermes were denied hospitality by all human beings except two old people, Philemon and Baucis, the gods transformed the inhospitable country into a lake; only the friendly old couple were allowed to survive in their little cottage.[8] In the *Mahabharata* the flood appears as the expiatory washing of the earth.[9] The "Brahmana of the hundred paths" (*Satapatha-Brahmana*) reports that once, when Manu, the first human being, was washing himself, he suddenly found a small fish which asked to be spared and requested protection from the big fishes which devour the smaller ones. In return the fish promised Manu to save him from an imminent flood. And, indeed, events happened as the fish had predicted they would.[10] Here, too, the principle of retribution serves as justification not so much of the catastrophe as of the rescue; the element of reward, and not that of punishment, is in the foreground.

In the *Bundahis* of the Persians there is a story of the angel Tistar,

---

The good men themselves took revenge on the enemies of the god of light by resorting to war against them. Ra promised to forgive them their sins for as he added in his own words: The sacrifices (the enemies of sun-god killed by other human beings) abolished and made superfluous the further killing of bad men through divine intervention."

[8] Hermann Usener, *Die Sintflutsagen* (1899), pp. 33, 47.

[9] Richard Andree, *Die Flutsagen* (1891), p. 19.

[10] Usener, p. 25. In the *Satapatha-Brâhmana*, translated by Julius Eggeling, I Kânda, 8 Adhyâya, I Brâhmana, 1–3 (*The Sacred Books of the East*, ed. Max Mueller, XII [1882], 216), it is said: "(1) In the morning they brought to Manu water for washing, just as now also they (are wont to) bring (water) for washing the hands. When he was washing himself, a fish came into his hands. (2) It spake to him the word, 'Rear me, I will save thee!' 'Wherefrom wilt thou save me?' 'A flood will carry away all these creatures: from that I will save thee!' 'How am I to rear thee?' (3) It said, 'As long as we are small, there is great destruction for us: fish devours fish. Thou wilt first keep me in a jar. When I outgrow that, thou wilt dig a pit and keep me in it. When I outgrow that, thou wilt take me down to the sea, for then I shall be beyond destruction.'"

In *The Mahabharata* the motive of retribution becomes even more apparent. There it is said (Book III: *Vana Parva*, translated into English by P. Ch. Roy [2d.; Calcutta, 1889], pp. 552 f.): "He [Manu] was the son of Vivaswan and was equal unto Brahma in glory. And he far excelled his father and grand-father in strength, in power, in fortune, as also in religious austerities. And standing on one leg and with uplifted hand, that lord of men did severe penance in the jujube forest called Visala. And there with head downwards, and with steadfast eye, he practised this rigid and severe penance for ten thousand years. And one day, whilst he was practising austerities there with wet clothes on, and matted hair on head, a fish approaching the banks of the Chirini addressed him thus: Worshipful sir, I am a helpless little fish, I am afraid of the large ones; therefore, do thou, O great devotee, think it worth thy while to protect me from them; especially, as this fixed custom is well established amongst us, that the strong fish always prey upon the weak ones. Therefore, do thou think it fit to save me from being drowned in this sea of terrors! I shall requite thee for thy good offices." Out of gratitude the fish saved him from the deluge.

who in his fight against the Evil Spirit produced rain until "all noxious creatures, the breed of the Evil Spirit, were drowned." This is the reason why the sea is salty today.[11] The catastrophe employed as a factor in the victorious contest of the good principle against the evil is only a more abstract treatment of the principle of retribution as it appears in the ordinary flood fables. In the *Younger Edda* the giants—obvious representatives of evil—who are hostile to the gods, drown in a sea of blood which springs up from the killing of the giant Ymir by the sons of the god Bör.[12]

The Australian natives have a legend which tells how Bahlu, the moon, let it rain until everything was inundated by the water and Murego was drowned in the flood as a penalty for not having lent one of his boomerangs and opossum bags to Bahlu.[13]

The aborigines of Victoria have the following myth:

> There was a time when men and women were numerous. In some parts of the earth they were very numerous, and they were wicked; and Pund-Jel became angry. Pund-Jel became very sulky (*Nar-eit*), when he saw that men and women were many and very bad. He caused storms to arise, and fierce winds to blow often. In the flat lands there arose suddenly whirlwinds of great force, and on the mountains the big trees were shaken with strong winds. Pund-Jel came down to see the men and women. He spoke to no one. He carried with him his big knife. With his knife he went into the encampments, and he cut with his knife. He cut this way and that way, and men, women, and children he cut into very small pieces. But the pieces into which he had cut the men, women, and children did not die. Each piece moved as the worm (*Turror*) moves. *Bullito, bullito, koor-reen, pit-ker-reen* (great, great storms and whirlwinds) came and carried away the pieces that moved like worms, and the pieces became like flakes of snow (*Kabbing*). They were carried into the clouds. The clouds carried the pieces hither and thither over all the

[11] Frazer, I, 180. The *Zend-Avesta* contains the following story: As there was, in early times, neither disease nor death, mankind and animals increased at such an alarming rate that at intervals they had to be destroyed by hard winters. In order to secure future generations, Yima, the ruler of the world—at Ahura Mazda's command—conveyed into a square enclosure the best seeds of all living beings—men, animals, plants—so that only the best and finest might survive. "There shall be no hump-backed, none bulged forward there; no impotent, no lunatic, no poverty, no lying, no meanness, no jealousy, no decayed tooth, no leprous to be confined, nor any of the brands wherewith Angra Mainyu stamps the bodies of mortals." (*The Zend-Avesta,* Part I: *The Vendidad,* Fargard II, 29 [80], translated by J. Darmesteter, in *The Sacred Books of the East,* ed. Max Mueller, Vol. IV [1880], p. 17.) Bodily and moral deficiencies are placed on a par. Only the best deserves to be preserved. Such is the meaning of this selection. And here, too, the principle of retribution is—though not clearly—expressed.

[12] Andree, p. 43.

[13] A. van Gennep, *Mythes et légendes d'Australie* (1905), p. 45.

> earth; and Pund-Jel caused the pieces to drop in such places as he pleased. Thus were men and women scattered over the earth. Of the good men and good women Pund-Jel made stars. The stars are still in the heavens, and the sorcerers can tell which amongst the stars were once good men and good women.[14]

Another version tells how Bundjel became angry at the blacks because they had behaved evilly. He punished them by urinating until all were drowned in the urine except the good ones, whom he fished out and placed as stars in the firmament.[15]

A kind of flood myth is this tale of the Aranda reported by Strehlow.[16] Originally the earth was covered with water; only a few mountains emerged. In heaven a godly being, Altjira, reigned. On the mountains lived other godly beings, the *altjirangamitjina* (or *inkara*), who were the totem gods of men. Since they were unable to find any food on earth, they repeatedly had recourse to heaven, where they hunted in Altjira's realm and returned with booty. Later on, Altjira forbade the *altjirangamitjina* to hunt in his realm. Then one of these totem gods grasped a stick and beat the water, commanding it to go away. Thereupon the sea withdrew to the north, and the continent appeared. Disobeying Altjira's order, several *inkara*, the *wetoppetoppa* (the slender ones), went up to heaven to hunt. Whereupon, at the command of Altjira, the tall mountain Eralera submerged, cutting off the retreat of the *wetoppetoppa*. They were forced to remain in heaven, where they now live as stars.

The Narrinyeri (South Australia) relate that a man whose two wives deserted him brought about by magic a great flood in which both women were drowned.[17]

In the Kabadi district of New Guinea the natives have a tradition that

> once upon a time a certain man Lohero and his younger brother were angry with the people about them, and they put a human bone into a small stream. Soon the great waters came forth, forming a sea, flooding all the low land, and driving the people back to the mountains, till step by step they had to escape to the tops of the highest peaks. There they lived till the sea receded, when some of them descended to the low-

[14] R. B. Smyth, *The Aborigines of Victoria*, I (1878), 427 ff.

[15] Gennep, p. 88; cf. also W. Schmidt, *Der Ursprung der Gottesidee*, III, 685.

[16] C. Strehlow, *Die Arandja- und Loritja-Staemme en Zentral-Australien* (1907–20), I, 3.

[17] George Taplin, *The Narrinyeri*, in J. D. Woods, *The Native Tribes of South Australia* (1879), p. 57.

lands, while others remained on the ridges and there built houses and formed plantations.[18]

The Valmans on the northern coast of New Guinea have a myth about a flood sent as punishment for the fact that the people, despite the warnings of a good man, killed and ate a certain large fish. Everyone was drowned except the good man and his family.[19]

The Fijians

> speak of a deluge which, according to some of their accounts, was partial, but in others is stated to have been universal. The cause of this great flood was the killing of Turukawa—a favorite bird belonging to Ndengei—by two mischievous lads, the grandsons of the god. These, instead of apologizing for their offense, added insolent language to the outrage, and, fortifying, with the assistance of their friends, the town in which they lived, defied Ndengei to do his worst. It is said that, although the angry god took three months to collect his forces, he was unable to subdue the rebels, and, disbanding his army, resolved on more efficient revenge. At his command the dark clouds gathered and burst, pouring streams on the devoted earth. Towns, hills, mountains were successively submerged; but the rebels, secure in the superior height of their own dwelling-place, looked on without concern. But when, at last, the terrible surges invaded their fortress, they cried for direction to a god, who, according to one account, instructed them to form a float of the fruit of the shaddock; according to another, sent two canoes for their use; or, says a third, taught them how to build a canoe, and thus secure their own safety. All agree that the highest places were covered, and the remnant of the human race saved in some kind of vessel, which was at last left by the subsiding waters on Mbengga: hence the Mbenggans draw their claim to stand first in Fijian rank. The number saved—eight—exactly accords with the "few" of the Scripture record. By this flood, it is said, two tribes of the human family became extinct. One consisted entirely of women, and the other were distinguished by the appendage of a tail like that of a dog.[20]

An interesting "nature" myth of the Palau Islands is reported by Kubary.[21] The story refers to a god, Obakad. The name hints a relation

[18] Frazer, I, 237, following J. Chalmers and W. Wyatt Gill, *Work and Adventure in New Guinea* (1885), p. 154.

[19] P. Chr. Schleiermacher, "Religiöse Anschauungen und Gebräuche der Bewohner von Berlinhafen (Deutsch-Neuguinea)," *Globus,* LXXVIII (1900), 6.

[20] Thomas Williams and James Calvert, *Fiji and the Fijians* (1859), pp. 197 ff.

[21] J. Kubary, "Die Religion der Pelauer," in A. Bastian, *Allerlei aus Volks- und Menschenkunde* (1888), I, 53 ff. This myth is interesting because Kubary represents the religion of the Palauans as though the principle of retribution did not play any role whatsoever in it.

to man; for *oba* means "possess" and *kad* means "man." Therefore the name of the deity in question seems to imply a lord or creator of man. And this is borne out by the contents of the fable which Kubary calls "the most important of all the tales dealing with Obakad."

> In times of yore before the present race of human beings existed, the inhabitants of the Palau Islands were all Kaliths (deities); they were strong and achieved wonders. One of these Kaliths, whose name was Athndokl, who was one of the Obakads [this implies that there were several Obakads, perhaps a family of gods of that name], came to Ngarekobukl, which today is in Eyrray, and was killed by the inhabitants there. Seven friendly gods went out to search for him and came to the same village, the residents of which were known as malicious and presumptuous. The gods were received everywhere unkindly with the exception of one woman, Milathk, who welcomed them to her house and told them of the death of Athndokl. Grieved and infuriated, the gods resolved on vengeance. In order to repay the woman's kindness, however, they agreed to spare her and suggested to her that she prepare a raft and fasten it to a tree by a rope. At the time of the full moon a terrific flood came upon Palau which covered the whole village.

Milathk also perished but was recalled to life by the oldest Obakad, who even wanted to make her immortal. This, however, was prevented by another god, Tariit, who was in turn punished by the angry Obakad. Milathk became the mother of mankind. Anyone reading this nature myth without prejudice must be impressed by the fact that its essential content is the idea of retribution, especially the punishment for the murder. The Kaliths, who apparently are the ancestors elevated to gods, are regarded as the authors and guarantors of this fundamental principle of human society.

Of the flood fables of Polynesia, W. Ellis writes:

> Traditions of the deluge . . . have been found to exist among the natives of the South Sea Islands, from the earliest periods of their history. . . . The principal facts are the same in the traditions prevailing among the inhabitants of the different groups, although they differ in several minor particulars. In one group the accounts state that in ancient times Taaroa, the principal god (according to their mythology, the creator of the world) being angry with men on account of their disobedience to his will, overturned the world into the sea, when the earth sank in the waters, excepting a few *aurus* or projecting points.[22]

The natives of the Leeward Islands tell the following: A fisherman angled in a prohibited place; his line became entangled in the hair of a

[22]William Ellis, *Polynesian Researches*, I (1836), 386 f.

resting deity. The god, infuriated at the violation of the taboo, wanted to destroy the whole sinful country but was placated by the pleas of the penitent fisherman and gave him a chance to save himself from the great flood which he nevertheless loosened upon the land.[23] On the Hervey Islands there is the following legend of a deluge: "A king named Taoiau (peace-bearer) was on one occasion greatly incensed against his people for not bringing him the sacred turtle. The irate chief 'awakened' all the mighty seagods . . . who . . . rose up in anger . . . and the ocean swept over the entire island."[24]

In a tale of the Maoris of New Zealand the deluge came upon men because "the worship of Tane was neglected and his doctrines openly denied." Two teachers, cursed by men, called for the deluge by prayers so that it "would convince men of the power of Tane."[25] Another Maori fable reports that the hero Tawhaki, having been murdered by his brother-in-law but revived by his wife, asked the gods to avenge him. Thereupon they sent a flood called "the overwhelming of the Mataaho," by which all human beings perished.[26]

A legend of the Batak of Sumatra connects the great flood with the fight of the good principle against the bad. According to the idea of these people, the earth rests on the head of a giant snake, Naga-Padoha. One day the reptile became weary of supporting its burden; so it shook off the earth into the water. But the god, Batara-Guru, caused a mountain to fall into the water in order that he might provide a place of residence for his daughter, Puti-orla-bulan. She had three sons and daughters from whom the new human race was derived. Later the earth was replaced on the head of the snake. From that time there has been a continual struggle between the evil reptile which wishes to rid itself of the burden and the deity who wants to avoid that disaster.[27]

The natives of Nias, an island to the west of Sumatra, say that

> in days of old there was a strife between the mountains of their country as to which of them was the highest. The strife vexed their great ancestor Baluga Luomewona, and in his vexation he . . . said: "Ye mountains, I will cover you all." . . . The ocean rose higher and higher till only the tops of two or three mountains in Nias still stood above the heaving billows . . . and the strife is proverbial among his descendants to the present day.

[23] Andree, p. 64.

[24] William Wyatt Gill, *Life in the Southern Isles* (n.d.), pp. 83 f.

[25] John White, *The Ancient History of the Maori,* I (1887), 172 ff.

[26] G. Grey, *Polynesian Mythology* (1855), pp. 42 f.

[27] Wilhelm von Humboldt, *Über die Kawi-Sprache auf der Insel Java* (1836), I, 239 ff.

They interpret the catastrophe as punishment for arrogance and disunion.[28]

A myth of the Dayak of Borneo intimates that the flood was sent as punishment for the killing of a snake.[29] In a story of the Toradja of Central Celebes the principle of retribution, as in other flood myths, becomes apparent after the catastrophe. "Nobody escaped the flood except a pregnant woman and a pregnant mouse." The mouse procured a little rice for the woman. "But . . . the mouse stipulated that as a recompense for her services mice should henceforth have the right to eat up part of the harvest."[30] The Andamanesian tale of a flood inflicted upon men by Puluga, the Creator, as punishment for their disobedience has been mentioned in another connection.[31]

The Bahnars, a primitive tribe in Cochin China, tell how "once on a time the kite quarrelled with the crab, and pecked the crab's skull so hard that he made a hole in it, which may be seen down to this very day. To avenge this injury to his skull, the crab caused the sea and the rivers to swell."[32] The Lolos (in the mountains of Yunnan) have a legend of the deluge which says "that people were wicked and Tse-gu-dzih to try them sent a messenger to earth, asking for some blood and flesh from a mortal. All refused but Du-mu. Tse-gu-dzih then locked the rain-gates and the waters mounted to the sky. Du-mu was saved with his four sons."[33] A tale of the Hos or Lurka Kolse in southwestern Bengal relates that god once destroyed mankind "because people became incestuous (some say he destroyed it with water, some say with fire)."[34] The flood which appears in the tales of the Singphos[35] and the Ahoms of Assam[36] is mentioned as punishment for the omission of prescribed sacrifices.

[28] Frazer, I, 219, following L. N. H. A. Chatelin, "Godsdienst en bijgeloof der Niassers," *Tijdschrift voor Indische Taal-, Land- en Volkenkunde,* XXVI (1881), 115.

[29] Andree, p. 32.

[30] Frazer, I, 222, following N. Adriani en Alb. C. Kruijt, *De Bare'e-sprekende Toradja's van Midden-Celebes* (1912), I, 20.

[31] Cf. above, pp. 124–25; further, W. Schmidt, *Der Ursprung der Gottesidee,* III, 71 ff., and Nieuwenhuis, *Die Sintflutsagen als kausallogische Natur- und Schöpfungsmythen,* p. 519.

[32] Frazer, I, 209, following Guerlach, "Moeurs et superstitions des sauvages Bahnars," *Les Missions catholiques,* XIX (1887), 479.

[33] A. Henry, "The Lolos and Other Tribes of Western China," *Journal of the Anthropological Institute of Great Britain and Ireland,* XXXIII (1903), 105.

[34] Tickell, "Memoir on the Hodésum (Improperly Called Kolehan)," in *Journal of the Asiatic Society of Bengal,* IX (1840), Part II, 798. See also the tale of the Mundari, a tribe of the Koles, reported by Andree, pp. 25f.

[35] Frazer, I, 198.

[36] *Ibid.,* pp. 199 f.

In Africa flood fables are comparatively scarce. In those which do exist, however, the principle of retribution appears prominently. So when the natives of Unyoro say that "God, infuriated at the arrogance of human beings, threw the firmament to earth and thus completely destroyed the first human race,"[37] they have in mind the idea of retribution—and of a flood. To describe a heavy rain, the Herero say "heaven breaks down," since they believe rain clouds (heaven as a substance) fall to earth.[38] Hence the expression "God threw heaven to earth" in the fable of the Unyoros probably also means rain.

In the myths of the Edo or Bini there is a story according to which the god Ogiwu intended to punish men for the death of his son by letting heaven fall down on earth. But the Edo had a great king, the hero Ewuare, who frustrated Ogiwu's intention.[39]

The Yoruba tell of a god Ifa who

> became tired of living in the world, and accordingly went to dwell in the firmament, with Obatala. After his departure, mankind, deprived of his assistant, was unable to properly interpret the desires of the gods, most of whom became in consequence annoyed. Olokun was the most angry, and in a fit of rage he destroyed nearly all the inhabitants of the world in a great flood.[40]

A tale of the Basonge relates how the leopard, buffalo, elephant, and zebra woo Ngolle Kakesse, the granddaughter of God. Only the zebra, whose name is also Ngolle, is accepted as a son-in-law. The zebra, however, breaks its promise not to allow Ngolle Kakesse to work. From her stretched-out legs runs water which floods the whole land. And Ngolle herself drowns.[41]

The Mandingo and Mossi (hinterland of the Ivory Coast) have a story of a charitable man who distributed all his possessions among the animals. As a consequence his wife and children deserted him. But he nevertheless gave Ouende, a celestial god who wandered unrecognized on earth, the last meal he had. Since he had no more grain, Ouende gave him three handfuls of flour in a basket. When he sowed the three handfuls of flour, they perpetually renewed themselves in the basket; finally they became gourds, which God asked him to cut.

[37] H. Baumann, *Schöpfung und Urzeit des Menschen im Mythus der afrikanischen Völker* (1936), p. 307, following Emin Pascha, *Sammlung von Reisebriefen,* herausg. von Schweinfurth und Ratzel (1888), p. 469.

[38] *Ibid.,* p. 307.

[39] P. Amaury Talbot, *The Peoples of Southern Nigeria* (1926), III, 961 f.

[40] A. B. Ellis, *The Yoruba-speaking Peoples of the Slave Coast of West Africa* (1894), p. 64.

[41] L. Frobenius, *Atlantis, Volksmärchen, und Volksdichtungen Afrikus,* XII: *Dichtkunst der Kassaiden* (1928), 88 f.

From the sliced fruits great quantities of cowry, millet, gold, and even girls, etc., emerged. Then Ouende suggested to the man that he should depart from that place with all his goods, inasmuch as the god desired to punish the selfish relatives of the man. Thereupon Ouende caused it to rain for six months. Everything perished. But the new descendants of the rich man spread and formed the present human race.[42]

The formation of Lake Dilolo is the subject matter of the following account: "A female chief, called Moéne Monenga . . . asked for a supply of food . . . and was refused. . . . In order to show what she could do, she began a song in slow time, and uttered her own name, Monenga-woo. As she prolonged the last note, the village, people, fowls, and dogs sank into the space now called Dilolo."[43] Myths of this kind, according to Baumann,[44] are frequently found in Africa.

[42] L. Tauxier, *Le Noir du Yatenga* (1917), pp. 498 f.

[43] David Livingstone, *Missionary Travels and Researches in South Africa* (1858), p. 353.

[44] Baumann, pp. 316 f. Baumann says, p. 322: "As far as Africa is concerned, two kinds of myths have to be distinguished, those which contain the motive of 'sin' and 'retribution' and those which lack it." But if the nine myths in his opinion lack the retribution motive, at least six appear to contain it, even according to his own accounts.

1. Among the Bushmen (p. 307, following J. M. Orpen in "A Glimpse into the Mythology of the Maluti Bushmen," originally published in the *Cape Monthly Magazine*, Vol. IX [1874], reprinted in *Folk-Lore*, XXX [1919], 145 ff.): The flood is caused by snakes "out of revenge."
2. Among the Vili of Loango (p. 309; cf. John H. Weeks, *Among the Primitive Bakongo* [1914], p. 286): "The sun and moon once met together and the sun plastered some mud over a part of the moon, and thus covered up some of the light, and that is why a portion of the moon is often in shadow. When this meeting took place, there was a flood." It is highly probable that the motive behind the sun's hostile behavior was, as in many analogous tales, vengeance.
3. Among the Ababua (p. 311, following De Calonne in *Le Mouvement sociologique international* [1909], X, 119): "An old woman who hoarded water kills the men who search for the liquid. The hero Mba kills the old woman. Thereupon the water flows in such quantities that it floods everything. Mba is washed away and lands on the summit of a tree." The principle of retribution appears here twice. The water woman is killed by the hero because she had retained the water and had killed those who looked for it. The flood is obviously retribution for the killing of the woman. That the avenging deed is thus avenged in turn is in accordance with the primitive idea of retribution. (A myth of a bad woman who hoards water—with a clearly pronounced motive of retribution—can also be found among the Fuegian Indians; see M. Gusinde, *Die Feuerland-Indianer*, I [1931], 613.)
4. Among the Bena-Lulua (p. 311; cf. Frobenius in *Atlantis*, XII, 157): The old water woman gives water only to him who sucks out her sores. One man does it. "Water flows in such floods that almost everyone is drowned. But the man goes on with his disgusting work and thereupon the water stops flowing." Here, too, the motive of retribution appears twice; first, when the needed water is granted as a return gift for the carrying-out of the disgusting performance; second, when the water stops flowing again as a reward for a good deed. The same motive also appears in the following tale of the Fiote (p. 311; cf. R. E. Dennett, *Notes on the Folklore of the Fjort* [1898], p. 122): "An old lady (Nzambi), after some days' journey, arrived at a town called Sinauzenzi, footsore and weary, and covered with those terrible sores

which afflict a great number of negroes in the Congo district. The old woman asked for hospitality from each householder as she passed through the town but they all refused to receive her saying she was unclean. When she finally arrived at the very last house, the kind folks there took her in, nursed and cured her. . . . When she was quite well and about to depart, she told her kind friends to pack up their trays and leave the town with her, as assuredly it was accursed and would be destroyed by Nzambi. And the night after they left, heavy rains fell, the town was submerged, and all the people drowned."

5. Among the Komililo Nandi (p. 312; cf. C. W. Hobley, "British East Africa: Anthropological Studies in Kavirondo and Nandi," *Journal of the Anthropological Institute of Great Britain and Ireland,* XXXIII [1903], 359): "About thirty miles east of Kisumu in Nandi country, there is a forest-clad extinct volcano named Tinderet. The Kamililo Nandi who inhabit its southern and western flanks tell a legend that high up on the mountain there is a cave in which Ilet, the spirit of the lightning, who descended there in the form of a man, took up his abode. After his descent it rained incessantly for many days, and the Oggiek or Wandorobbo hunters who lived in the forest were nearly all killed by the terrible downpour. Some of them, while searching for the cause of the rain, found Ilet in the cave and wounded him with their poisoned arrows. Thereupon he fled, and died in Arab Kibosone's country; directly he was dead, the rain ceased." Here the motive of retribution is reversed: God does not punish men with evil but men punish God because of the evil.
6. Among the Ndorobo (p. 313, following Kannenberg in *Zeitschrift für afrikanische und ozeanische Sprachen,* V [1900], 161) they tell that originally men lived with God in heaven; then they climbed down with him on a rope to earth. On earth god let a heavy rain fall so that the Ndorobo could no longer shoot game and had to go hungry. But a Ndorobo cut the rope and it immediately stopped raining. Since then god has lived in heaven with the human beings who remained with him. Men pay for the cessation of rain by suffering a final separation from God. This, too, is retribution.
7. Among the Ashanti (p. 313, following Edmond Perregaux, "Chez les Ashanti," *Bulletin de la Société Neuchâteloise de Géographie,* XVII [1906], 198): When the first seven human beings created by God climbed on a chain down to earth and brought fire with them, their downward climb was preceded by heavy rain which ceased only when the chain was lowered. When their descendants increased during the following years, they returned on the chain amidst heavy rain to heaven. The original identity of chain and rain appears clearly, according to Perregaux's representation, especially when the first seven human beings returned to heaven. "When the number of men continued to increase, the first seven men said to their children: 'As far as we are concerned, we shall return thither whence we came (to God), but you remain on earth; you will also have children and you will scatter over the earth.' As soon as they had said this, a heavy rain fell and the same chain, on which they had climbed down, took them. . . ." The rain signifies the road from heaven to earth and back. But the myth contains still another detail (Perregaux, p. 198): "One day, unfortunately, the women while stamping their *foufou* felt embarrassed at the presence of God; they told him to go away and when he did not retire quickly enough, they hit him with their stampers. Then God, angered, retired from this world and left its direction to the spirits (fetishes). A proverb reads: Without the old woman, we would be happy." The motive of retribution appears here, too; but the myth does not belong to the flood tales.

The reason why Baumann does not always discover the motive of retribution lies in the fact that his concept of retribution is too narrow. He perceives retribution, as he says on p. 314, only where a "violation of norms" occurs. But revenge, too, is included, as well as reward for a good deed, and exchange, especially renunciation of a good as compensation for liberation from an evil. Baumann rightly asserts, p. 314, that a separation of tales interpreting the deluge as punishment from mere flood tales is impossible; "the momentum of sin is so indeterminate that in primitive stages it can hide itself in an unobtrusive way and appear as quite

As in the case of the other continents, the Americas also produced flood tales in which the motive of retribution appears more or less decidedly. A myth of the Yamana relates[45] that

> once upon a time at the approach of spring a man looked up and saw a Bandurria (female ibis) fly over his hut. He was extremely happy about this and called out to his neighrbors: "A Bandurria is flying over my hut. Look there!" When the others heard this news, they ran out of their houses and cried: "Spring is here. The ibis are already flying!" They leaped with joy and noisily amused themselves. The Lexuwa [the ibis woman], however, is very sensitive and needs to be treated gently. When these men, women, and children shrieked so loudly and for such a long time, she heard the noise and became excited. In her annoyance and anger, she loosened a thick snow storm accompanied by cold and much ice.

The whole earth was covered with snow and ice; and many people died. When the snowfall ceased,

> a hot sun burned down so fiercely that all the snow and ice, which covered the earth up to the mountain tops, melted. Great quantities of water flowed into the rivers and the sea. Indeed the sun shone so strongly that the mountain tops burned and have consequently remained treeless until today. The ice which covered both the broad and narrow streams also dissolved so that people were able to get to the coasts and to enter their canoes in order to look for food. On the mountain slopes and in the deep valleys the thick ice has remained until today. . . . Since then the Yamana treat every Bandurria with great respect. When the bird approaches their huts people remain silent and calm the children so they do not cry.

In one of the myths of the Uitoto, Nofuyeni causes an earthquake and a flood because Meni has stolen the ax-shaped parrot.[46] In another story Dyaere lets it rain incessantly because Nadyerekudu mutilated a red parrot.[47] According to a legend of the Carayas (Brazil), the great flood was caused by a demoniacal being called Anatiua, who became furious because men did not understand him and wanted to run away.[48] In a myth of the Tupinamba, Monan, in order to punish men

---

unimportant guilt." But punishment for sin is only one of the typical cases in which the principle of retribution is applied.

[45] Gusinde, II, 1232.

[46] Preuss, *Religion und Mythologie der Uitoto,* I (1921), 60.

[47] *Ibid.,* p. 61.

[48] Frazer, I, 257, following P. Ehrenreich, *Beiträge zur Völkerkunde Brasiliens* (1891), pp. 40 f.

for ingratitude, effects a natural catastrophe.[49] Ehrenreich[50] points out that generally the crimes of men against the culture-hero are the causes of cataclysms in the myths of South American aborigines.

The Ipurina (on the Purus River, an affluent of the Upper Amazon) regard the sloth as their ancestor. They have a myth in which Mayuruberu, the chief of the storks and the creator of all birds, produced a great flood by making a kettle of water boiling in the sun overflow.

> Mankind indeed survived, but of the vegetable world nothing escaped but the cassia. . . . Next the sloth begged Mayuruberu to give him seeds of useful fruits. So Mayuruberu appeared with a great basket full of plants, and the Ipurina began to till their fields. He who would not work was eaten by Mayuruberu. Every day Mayuruberu received a man to devour.[51]

Punishment for laziness is the chief theme of this story. But the connection between this motive and the flood itself is not clear.

In a tale of the Murato Indians (a branch of the Jibaros in Ecuador) the deluge appears as the vengeance of a crocodile—the mother of crocodiles in general—for the murder of her child.[52]

According to the fable of the Acawoios (British Guiana), the flood was caused by the lazy and mischievous monkey who opened a basket in which the swelling water was enclosed. He, "whose dishonest propensities caused the flood, remained uncured of his idleness, love of mischief and pilfering, and transmitted those qualities unimpaired to his children."[53]

The Arawaks in British Guiana "believe that since the Creation the world has been twice destroyed; first, by a flame of fire sent to sweep over it, and afterwards by a flood of water. Each of those destructions was on account of the evil doings of men and specially threatened by Aiomun Kondi, the great 'Dweller on High.'"[54] The motive of retribution is varied in a peculiar way in a myth of the Muyscas, natives of the plateau of Cundinamarca (Colombia).[55] Here the flood is not punish-

[49] A. Métraux, *La Religion des Tupinamba et ses rapports avec celle des autres tribus Tupi-Guarani* (1928), p. 44.

[50] Ehrenreich, *Die Mythen und Legenden der südamerikanischen Urvölker* (1905), p. 31.

[51] Frazer, I, 259 f., following P. Ehrenreich, *Beiträge zur Völkerkunde Brasiliens*, pp. 71 f.

[52] Frazer, I, 261, following Rivet, "Les Indiens Jibaros," *L'Anthropologie*, XIX (1908), 236.

[53] Brett, *The Indian Tribes of Guiana* (1868), pp. 378 ff., 384.

[54] *Ibid.*, p. 398.

[55] Andree, p. 114, following L. F. Piedrahita, *Historia general de las conquistas del Nuevo Reyno de Granada*, p. 17, and A. v. Humboldt, *Sites des Cordillères et monuments des peuples indigènes de l'Amérique* (1869), pp. 42 f.

ment but itself a wrong which must be avenged; this idea is similar to the primitive concept of death as either punishment or a crime, caused by magic:

> In olden times before the moon existed, the tableland of Cundinamarca was shut off and the pass of Tequendama was not yet open. The Muyscas still lived as savages without government or agriculture when there came to them a bearded old man who had the following names: Botschika, Nemquetheba, Zuhe. He taught them to cultivate the land, manufacture clothes, venerate the gods, and form states. His wife also had three names: Huythaca, Chia, and Yubecayguya. She was beautiful but malicious and wanted to destroy all the good works of her husband. And indeed by means of magic she caused the river Funza, now the Rio Bogota, to swell so that the whole plateau was flooded. Only a few of the inhabitants could flee to the mountain tops. Botschika became furious and banished the wicked woman from the earth, changing her into the moon. In order to redress the disaster on earth Botschika opened the pass and the water poured down in the majestic waterfall of Tequendama. The country dried out and was cultivated by the remaining human beings.

According to another tale of these Indians, the flood was sent by the god Chibchachum as punishment for the insults heaped upon him by their ancestors. But the great god Bochica saved mankind and punished Chibchachum by condemning him "to bear on his shoulders the whole weight of the earth. . . . When the weary giant tries to get a little ease by shifting his burden from one shoulder to another, he causes an earthquake."[56]

Farabee reports the following myth of the Jivaran Indians, an Arawakan tribe.

> A great feast was to be held, and two boys were sent away into the forest to get game. They made a camp under a tree, and went out to hunt. They secured much game, dressed it, and hung it up at the camp. The second day when they returned heavily laden with game, they were surprised to find that their first day's catch had been stolen. When they returned on the third day, they again found the meat had been stolen. On the next day, one remained in hiding to discover the thief. He found it was a great snake that lived in the hollow of the tree under which they had camped. To destroy the snake they built a fire in the tree, and the snake fell into the fire. The boys were hungry, and one of them ate some of the roasted flesh of the snake. He soon became thirsty, drank all of the water they had at the camp, then went to the spring, and from there to the lake. He

[56] Frazer, I, 267, following H. Ternaux-Compans, *Essai sur l'ancien Cundinamarca* (Paris, n.d.), pp. 7 f.

was soon transformed into a frog, next into a lizard, and finally into a snake, which began to grow very rapidly. His brother was frightened, and tried to pull him out of the water, but the lake began to overflow. The snake then told his brother that the lake would continue to grow until the whole world would be covered, and that the people would perish unless he returned and told them to make their escape. He told his brother to put a calabash in his pocket, to go on top of the highest mountain, and when the water came, to climb the highest palm tree. The brother returned, and told his people what had happened, but they refused to believe him, accusing him of destroying his brother; so he fled to the top of the mountain, and when the water came, climbed the palm tree. After many days the water began to subside, and he came down to the ground. From the top of the mountain he could see the vultures eating the dead people in the valley, so he went back to the lake where he found his brother, and carried him away in his calabash.[57]

The motive of retribution appears several times here. First, the killing of the snake is vengeance for the theft. The transformation of the one of the brothers into a frog, lizard, and a snake is punishment for the fact that the snake was killed and that its flesh was eaten. The flood, too, is punishment for this delict. Finally, men drown as punishment for not having believed in the warning and for having falsely accused the other brother.

A tale of the Quiché Indians (Guatemala) recorded in the *Popol Vuh* (popular book), which was discovered at the beginning of the eighteenth century, justifies the catastrophe by pointing out the inadequacy of the first beings created by the gods.[58] The fact that they are not guilty, according to modern concepts of justice, should not be a hindrance to our seeing here, too, an application of the principle of retribution which in the sense of primitive thinking also comprises absolute liability.

According to the Popol Vuh the gods, having created animals, were dissatisfied with them because the beasts could neither talk nor venerate the deities. Therefore the gods created men out of clay; but these were also imperfect. They could not move their heads and although they could speak they were unable to hear. Thereupon the gods destroyed these defective creations by a flood. A second creation of men followed; this time man was composed of wood and woman of resin. This second race of humans was better than its predecessor but the people still had an animal demeanor. They could speak only indistinctly and they were

[57] William Curtis Farabee, *Indian Tribes of Eastern Peru* ("Harvard University, Papers of the Peabody Museum of American Archeology and Ethnology," Vol. X [1922]), p. 124.

[58] Andree, p. 109.

> not at all grateful to the gods. Hurakan, the "Heart of Heaven," let burning resin fall to earth and then sent an earthquake in which nearly all the human beings perished. Those who survived, however, became monkeys.[59] At last the gods formed human beings out of yellow and white maize. They were so perfect that the gods were frightened; therefore they took some of the qualities away. Thus they became men to whom the Quiche trace their descent.

An interesting shift of the motive of retribution may be found in a tale of the Papagos:[60] The godly king Montezuma saved himself from the flood, the cause of which is not divulged. When the world was again repeopled, the care and government of the new race had been allotted to Montezuma;

> but puffed up with pride and self-importance, he neglected the most important duties of his onerous position, and suffered the most disgraceful wickedness to pass unnoticed among the people. In vain the Great Spirit came down to earth and remonstrated with his vicegerent, who only scorned his laws and advice, and ended at last by breaking out into open rebellion. Then indeed the Great Spirit was filled with anger, and he returned to heaven, pushing back the Sun on his way, to that remote part of the sky he now occupies. But Montezuma . . . set about building a house that should reach up to heaven itself. Already it had attained a great height . . . when the Great Spirit launched his thunder and laid its glory in ruins. Still Montezuma hardened himself . . . he

[59] Brinton, *The Myths of the New World* (1868), p. 208, reproduces this part of the tale as follows: "Because they had not thought of their Mother and Father, the Heart of Heaven, whose name is Hurakan, therefore the face of the earth grew dark and a pouring rain commenced, raining by day, raining by night. Then all sorts of beings, little and great, gathered together to abuse the men to their faces; and all spoke, their mill-stones, their plates, their cups, their dogs, their hens. Said the dogs and hens, 'Very badly have you treated us, and you have bitten us. Now we bite you in turn.' Said the mill-stones, 'Very much were we tormented by you, and daily, daily, night and day, it was squeak, squeak, screech, screech, for your sake. Now yourselves shall feel our strength, and we will grind your flesh, and make meal of your bodies,' said the mill-stones. And this is what the dogs said, 'Why did you not give us our food? No sooner did we come near than you drove us away, and the stick was always within reach when you were eating, because, forsooth, we were not able to talk. Now we will use our teeth and eat you,' said the dogs, tearing their faces. And the cups and dishes said, 'Pain and misery you gave us, smoking our tops and sides, cooking us over the fire, burning and hurting us as if we had no feeling. Now it is your turn, and you shall burn,' said the cups insultingly. Then ran the men hither and thither in despair. They climbed to the roofs of the houses, but the houses crumbled under their feet; they tried to mount to the tops of the trees, but the trees hurled them far from them; they sought refuge in the caverns, but the caverns shut before them. Thus was accomplished the ruin of this race, destined to be destroyed and overthrown; thus were they given over to destruction and contempt. And it is said that their posterity are those little monkeys who live in the woods."

[60] Bancroft, *The Native Races of the Pacific States of North America*, III, 76 f.

> ordered the temple-houses to be desecrated. . . . Then the Great Spirit prepared his supreme punishment. He sent an insect flying away towards the east, towards an unknown land, to bring the Spaniards. When these came, they made war upon Montezuma and destroyed him, and utterly dissipated the idea of his divinity.

Presumably the motive of retribution was transferred from the flood tale itself to the fate of the survivor, since his downfall had to be explained. The biblical-Christian influence on Montezuma's tower is obvious.

The retribution theme appears among the Maya (Yucatan) in the form of a prophecy relative to the end of the world. Brinton[61] records this document as follows:

> At the close of the ages, it hath been decreed,
> Shall perish and vanish each weak god of men,
> And the world shall be purged with a ravening fire.
> Happy the man in that terrible day,
> Who bewails with contrition the sins of his life,
> And meets without flinching the fiery ordeal.

The Caribs (Antilles) report "that the Master of Spirits, being angry with their forefathers for not presenting to him the offerings which were his due, caused such a heavy rain to fall . . . that nearly all the people were drowned."[62] In a tale of the Tarahumares (Mexico) the deluge is interpreted as punishment for internal dissension.[63]

Of the flood myths of the North American Indians the following may be mentioned: A tale of the Wiyot (central California) tells of a deity who sent a flood which destroyed everything because men were wicked.[64] The existence of the motive of retribution can be deduced indirectly from a tale of the Zuñi Indians (western New Mexico). Here the flood is removed by a human sacrifice: "A youth and a maiden, son and daughter of two priests, were thrown into this ocean."[65] Through

[61] Brinton, p. 221.

[62] Frazer, I, 281, following De la Borde, "Relation de l'origine, moeurs, coustumes, religion, guerres et voyages des Caraibes sauvages des Isles Antilles de l'Amérique," in *Recueil de divers voyages faits en Afrique et en l'Amerique qui n'ont point esté encore publiez* (Paris, 1684), p. 7.

[63] Carl Lumholtz, *Unknown Mexico* (1902), I, 298 f.

[64] W. Schmidt, *Der Ursprung der Gottesidee*, II, 40.

[65] Mrs. Tilly E. Stevenson, "The Religious Life of the Zuñi Child," *5th Annual Report of the Bureau of Ethnology* (1887), p. 539; Stevenson, "The Zuñi Indians," *23rd Annual Report of the Bureau of American Ethnology* (1904), p. 61.

the sacrifice it is intended that the ire of the water-god be allayed. The wrath of the deity, however, generally means that a norm proclaimed by it, issued in its interest, or guaranteed by it, has been violated. The idea that in return for the offering the deity takes the flood away is a direct application of the principle of retribution. This concept is clearly expressed by the Mandan Indians in their tale of a great flood. Here the story of the deluge is the basis of certain yearly rites which include sacrifices to the water spirit. The Mandan believe "that the omission of this annual ceremony, with its sacrifices made to the waters, would bring upon them a repetition of the calamity which their traditions say once befell them, destroying the whole human race."[66] In a story of the Acagchemem Indians (California) the deluge is an act of vengeance.[67]

A myth of the Potawatomi is reminiscent of the tale of the Quiché Indians.

> Kčemnito first created the world and filled it with a race of beings that did not look like men. They were perverse, ungrateful, and malicious dogs which never raised their eyes to heaven to beg for the assistance of the great spirit. Such ingratitude aroused his anger and so he submerged the whole world in a great lake.[68]

The Navajo Indians have the following myth:

> The world in which we now live is the fifth world. Our fathers dwelt in four worlds before reaching this. In the first world there dwelt three; the first man, the first woman and the coyote. It was dark there and the world was small, so they ascended to the second world. On the second world they found two other men; the Sun and the Moon. There was then no sun or moon in the firmament; but these people are so called because they afterwards became the sun and the moon (or the sun and the moon gods). Yet there was light in the second world. In the east there was a great darkness; it was not a cloud, but it was like a cloud. In the south there was blue light; in the west a yellow light and in the north a white light. At times the darkness would rise in the east until it overspread the whole sky and made the night. Then the darkness would sink down, the blue light would rise gradually in the south, the yellow light in the west and the white light in the north, until they met in the zenith, and made the day. . . .

[66] George Catlin, *O Kee-Pa: A Religious Ceremony; and Other Customs of the Mandans* (1867), pp. 1 ff.

[67] Frazer, I, 288, following Father Friar Geronimo Boscana, "Chinigchinich, a Historical Account, etc., of the Acagchemem Nation," annexed to A. Robinson's *Life in California* (New York, 1846), pp. 300 f.

[68] W. Schmidt, II, 510.

But the land into which they came was not empty; another race of people dwelt in the mountains, and they called the people of the mountains into council and said to them: "We have come to this land to stay a long time and we desire to live at peace with you." And they of the mountains said: "It is well; the land is wide enough for us all, and we seek not war; but there lives in the great water beyond the eastern mountains a monster named Tïèholtsòdi (he who seizes you in the sea), whom we warn you not to approach or harm." The Navajos promised to heed this warning and the council broke up. But the coyote listened to no one, and he went where he chose, none controlled him. So, in time he strayed to the great water beyond the eastern mountain, stole two of the children of the ocean monster, brought them back into camp unperceived and hid them in his blankets. When Tïèholtsòdi missed his young he went in search of them. He sought in the great waters at the four corners of the earth, but found them not, so he, at length, came to the conclusion that they must be in the possession of the strangers who had recently come from the lower world. Then he caused the waters that were in the east, the south, the west, and the north to rise and flow over the land; so that at the end of the second day there was but little dry land left for the people to stand on. They all became greatly alarmed and held a council. They knew they must have done some wrong; but what the crime or who the culprit, they could not discover. Then they took soil from all of the four corner mountains of the world, and placed it on top of the mountain that stood in the north, and thither they all went including the people of the mountains, the salt-woman, and such animals as then dwelt on the third world. When the soil was laid on the mountain the latter began to grow higher and higher, but the waters continued to rise and the people climbed upwards to escape the flood. At length the mountain ceased to grow and they planted on the summit a great reed, into the hollow of which they all entered. The reed grew every night but it did not grow in the daytime; and this is the reason why the reed grows in joints to this day—the hollow internodes show where it grew by night, and the solid nodes show where it rested by day. Thus the waters gained on them in the daytime. The turkey was the last to take refuge in the reed and, therefore, he was at the bottom. When the waters rose high enough to wet the turkey they all knew that danger was near. Often did the waves wash the end of his tail; and it is for this reason that the tips of the turkey's tail-feathers are, to this day, lighter than the rest of his plumage. At the end of the fourth night from the time it was planted, the reed had grown up to the floor of the fourth world, and here they found a hole through which they passed to the surface. . . .

But all this time the coyote had still kept hidden the young of the sea-monster, Tïèholtsòdi, and the latter, having searched for them in vain in all the seas of the fourth world, caused the waters to rise as before. Again was the council held, again was soil taken from the four mountains; . . .

once more the reed sheltered the fugitives and bore them upwards out of danger. In short all the circumstances that attended their flight from the third world were repeated until they reached the floor of the present world, when an appalling difference was observed. Instead of finding a hole through which they could pass, as on the former occasion, all above them, as far as they could see, was solid earth, like the roof of a great cavern. . . .

On the fifth day the sun arose, climbed as usual to the zenith and stopped. The day grew hot and all longed for the night to come, but the sun moved not. Then the wise coyote said: "The sun stops because he has not been paid for his work; he demands a human life for every day that he labors; he will not move again till some one dies." At length a woman, the wife of a great chief, ceased to breathe and grew cold, and while they all drew around in wonder, the sun was observed to move again, and he travelled down the sky and passed behind the western mountain. As we now never see him stop on his way we know that every day some one must die. . . .

That night the moon stopped in the zenith, as the sun had done during the day; and the coyote told the people that the moon also demanded pay and would not move until it was given. He had scarcely spoken, when the man who had seen the departed woman in the nether world died, and the moon, satisfied, journeyed to the west. Thus it is that some one must die every night, or the moon would not move across the sky.[69]

In the biblical story of the fall of man the first human beings, with their moral inadequacy, are created by an omnipotent authority who, angered at his own creatures, punishes them. Consequently, those primitive religions in which the punishing deity is at the same time the author of the moral evil for which men are punished are not so very remote from the Jewish-Christian myth which considers the justice of God as compatible with his omnipotence, because it still maintains the primitive idea of absolute liability. In this connection a flood tale of the Algonquin Indians is significant. A serpent (one may not be wrong in suspecting in it an ancestral soul) is the "foe" and "great evil" which brings sin to men and then punishes them cruelly. This is the form in which the myth has been handed down to us:

Long ago came the powerful serpent (*Maskanako*) when men had become evil. The strong serpent was the foe of the beings, and they became embroiled, hating each other. Then they fought and despoiled each other, and were not peaceful. And the small men (*Mattapewi*) fought with the keeper of the dead (*Nihanlowit*). Then the Strong Serpent re-

[69] W. Matthews, "A Part of the Navajo's Mythology," *American Antiquarian*, V, No. 3 (1883), 207–13.

> solved all men and beings to destroy immediately. The Black Serpent, monster, brought the snake-water rushing, the wide waters rushing, wide to the hills, everywhere spreading, everywhere destroying. . . . Then the waters ran off, it was dry on mountain and plain, and the great evil went elsewhere by the path of the cave.[70]

The genuine old Algonquin legend of the flood seems, according to Frazer,[71] to be the following, which was found among the Chippeway Indians.[72] The medicine man Wis-kay-tchach, while hunting, loses a young wolf, his "nephew," who is then killed by some water lynxes. In order to avenge the wolf, Wis tries to kill one of these beasts but succeeds only in wounding it. The creatures rush to a river, which overflows its banks and floods the whole country. This same tale can be found in various versions among other tribes. All show the same motives: vengeance for the killing of the wolf and countervengeance in the form of a flood.

According to a fable of the Tinneh Indians, the flood was foreseen by an old man who warned his fellows, but all in vain. They were all drowned.[73] In another fable of the same tribe the flood comes as an act of vengeance.[74] The Loucheux Indians explain the flood as punishment for the killing of a raven.[75] A tale of the Tlingit Indians also describes the flood as punishment for the attempted murder of Jelch, the raven.[76] In a tale of the Tsimshian Indians the flood is said to have been sent by heaven as a punishment for the ill-behavior of man.[77] According to a fable of the Kootenay Indians,[78] the flood was produced because a small gray bird, despite the prohibition of her husband, the

[70] E. G. Squier, *Historical and Mythological Traditions of the Algonquins,* pp. 12 ff. (paper read before the New York Historical Society).

[71] Frazer, I, 297.

[72] W. H. Hooper, *Ten Months among the Tents of the Tuski* (1853), pp. 286 ff.; cf. also the tale of the Ojibway, reported by Andree, pp. 75 ff.

[73] Frazer, I, 312, following E. Petitot, *Monographie des Dènè-Dindjié* (1876), p. 74.

[74] J. Jetté, "On Ten'a Folk-Lore," *Journal of the Royal Anthropological Institute of Great Britain and Ireland,* XXXVIII (1908), 312 f.

[75] Frazer, I, 315 f., following Petitot, *Traditions Indiennes du Canada Nord-ouest,* pp. 22–26.

[76] A. Krause, *Die Tlinkit-Indianer* (1885), p. 257.

[77] Frazer, I, 319, following F. Boas, in "Fourth Report of the Committee on the Northwestern Tribes of the Dominion of Canada," *Report of the Fifty-eighth Meeting of the British Association for the Advancement of Science, held at Bath in September, 1888* (London, 1889), p. 239.

[78] A. F. Chamberlain, "Report on the Kootenay Indians of South-Eastern British Columbia," in *Eighth Report of the Committee on the North-Western Tribes of Canada (Report of the Sixty-second Meeting of the British Association for the Advancement of Science, held at Edinburgh, 1892),* pp. 575 f.

chicken hawk, bathed in a certain lake. "Suddenly the water rises, and a giant . . . comes forth, who seizes the woman[79] and ravishes her." Her husband is very angry when he learns of this, and, going to the lake, shoots the monster, who swallows up all the water, so there is none for the Indians to drink. The woman "pulls the arrow out of the giant's breast, whereupon the water rushes forth in torrents, and a flood is the result. . . . In a variant of this legend the 'giant' is a 'big fish' . . . it is the blood of the fish that causes the deluge. . . . In another variant the 'giant' is a 'lake animal.'" The Twanas, an Indian tribe of the state of Washington, have a tradition of a deluge, from which only good Indians were saved.[80] In another tribe the flood is supposed to have been caused by the fact that a beaver, whose wife left him to marry a panther, cried for five days until the whole country was flooded with his tears.[81] Obviously, this is to be interpreted not only as an expression of pain but also as an act of vengeance.

It cannot be denied that many flood tales do not contain any trace of a motive of retribution.[82] This may be partly accounted for because

[79] Frazer, I, 323, referring to the fact that bird and woman is used alternatively, says: "In these Indian tales no sharp line of distinction is drawn between the animal and the human personages."

[80] M. Eells, "Traditions of the 'Deluge' among the Tribes of the North-West," *American Antiquarian,* I (1878–79), 70.

[81] Franz Boas, *Kathlamet Texts* (Bureau of American Ethnology Bull. 26 [1901]), pp. 20 ff.

[82] Andree, p. 131, finds that out of the eighty-eight tales collected by him only eight interpret the flood as a judgment proceeding from a superior being and inflicted because of sins committed by men. But the decisive element is comprehended too narrowly. What matters is whether and how far the principle of retribution plays a decisive role. From this point of view a much greater number of those tales reported by Andree are involved here. Thus, for instance, the tale of the Dajak, the *Edda* tale, the tale of the creation of the Dilolo-lake, the Montezuma tale of the Papagos, the tale of Jelch of the Tlingit, the tale of the Quiché Indians, especially the tale of the Mayscas and some other myths, reported by Andree but not counted among the retribution myths, fit into this class.

Johannes Riem, *Die Sinflut in Sage und Wissenschaft* (1925), also sets up some statistics for flood tales. Of two hundred and sixty-eight reports, the motive of retribution is only traceable, according to his opinion, in seventy-five cases. But he comprehends only those where the flood is based "on a guilt of mankind or an individual" or "on the revenge of an annoyed god." But the cases where the wrong is committed by an animal or is an act of private revenge of an individual must also be included. Further, there must be counted those cases where reward and not punishment is involved, or where the delict seems to be negligible, or where not the flood as such but rather the death it brings appears as punishment and the rescue from it as reward. That the flood is not punishment but a crime does not mean that the principle of retribution is missing, for this crime demands punishment. If one examines these reports collected by Riem from this point of view, the principle of retribution becomes manifest in more than one hundred tales. Yet Riem assumes that only eighty reports indicate any reason for the flood. In several tales reported by him the principle of retribution does not become apparent, although it exists in the reproductions of other authors. This is so in the Babylonian in the texts handed down to us no reasons for the floods are given; this, in turn, is quite often due to the fact that the problem under consideration concerns the violation of a religious taboo. And primitive man, who is restrained on this point, may be inclined, when questioned by an explorer, to omit those parts of the tale which violate his self-consciousness because they reflect discredit on his ancestors. Another reason for the incompleteness of the material may be that explorers have not paid much attention to finding out the causes of the flood. This may be particularly true if some act which modern morality would not consider a "sin" seems to have been the cause. It must also be borne in mind that a motive of retribution which existed originally may have faded into insignificance or even have disappeared altogether. Considering the decisive importance which the principle of retribution has in the interpretation of nature of even the least civilized peoples and considering that primitive man is inclined to interpret those facts which directly affect him and which arouse his fear, such as illness, death, lightning, and earthquake, according to the principle of retribution, one may assume that, originally at least, this principle also appeared in many of those flood tales where it is no longer apparent today.[83]

---

flood tale; here Riem says, p. 21, that the gods decided upon the flood "obviously out of mere caprice."

[83]Wundt, *Mythus und Religion,* Part III (1915), pp. 298 f., says that the older form of flood tales lacks the ethical motives, the elements of revenge, punishment, and reward. This cannot be true, at least not for the motive of revenge, since this is one of the oldest elements of mythical thinking.

The Flood Myth as Vesical Dream

GÉZA RÓHEIM

Quite a different use of the comparative method is evident in Géza Róheim's (1891–1953) psychoanalytic consideration of flood myth content. Róheim believed that dreams are the primary source of myths and folktales, and in his book-length The Gates of the Dream *he discusses the application of his theory to the flood myth in particular.*

In arguing a dream origin of the flood myth, Róheim was following in the path of an earlier Freudian student of myth, Otto Rank. In an essay first published in 1912, Rank suggested that the need to urinate was transformed during the night into the sleeper's dream. Rank felt there was a parallel between such individual dream responses to a basic need to urinate and myths of floods. He confined his mythological discussions, however, to classical and Near Eastern texts.

In contrast, Géza Róheim, who was perhaps the first psychoanalytic anthropologist and folklorist, carried out ethnographic fieldwork in Australia and among American Indians in the Southwest. Moreover, he was widely read in comparative folklore, unlike the majority of psychoanalytic writers who invariably tend to limit their analyses to biblical, classical, or strictly European data.

In the following essay, Róheim tries to document his psychoanalytic readings of flood myths by citing a number of texts from a variety of cultures, including American Indian. Róheim is sometimes his own worst enemy, however, insofar as his choppy and disjointed writing style often proves distracting. Moreover, his extremely dogmatic manner in pronouncing psychoanalytic views tends to put off even the most favorably disposed reader. Still, the flood myth texts he has amassed do contain some curious details which certainly require explanation, and his interpretations are nothing if not provocative.

For other psychological approaches to the flood, see Otto Rank, "Die Symbolschichtung im Wecktraum und ihre Wiederkehr im mythischen Denken," Jahrbuch für psychoanalytische und psychopathologische

Reprinted from *The Gates of the Dream* (New York: International Universities Press, 1952), pp. 439, 448–460, 465.

Forschungen *4 (1912); 51–115, reprinted under the title "Zur Deutung der Sintflutsage: Ein Beitrag zur Symbolschichtung im mythischen Denken," in* Psychoanalytische Beiträge zur Mythenforschung *(Leipzig, 1922), pp. 82–106; see also Donald F. Tuzin, "Reflections of Being in Arapesh Water Symbolism,"* Ethos *5 (1977): 195–223.*

The basic dream is certainly not the only dream that has become a myth. We know that the desire to urinate, the bladder pressure and also the excremental pressure cause dreams of a certain type. In these the urine is projected into space as a lake or river or ocean and an element of anxiety is bound to occur. In dreams that combine fire and water, the urethral significance is quite certain. The dreamer is in conflict; by projecting these images into space he is trying to prolong the dream and delay awakening. These dreams evidently occur in light sleep, just before awakening. Moreover, they usually try to transform bladder pressure into an erotic scene (morning erections in men) or into birth or delivery. Both techniques are frequently combined. They are also another instance in which environment is formed out of the dreamer's own body.

. . .

Flood myths frequently represent the flood as urine, thereby revealing their dream origin.

In the New Hebrides we have the following myth:

Tabui Kor was a woman, Tilik and Tarai were her two sons. They lived near a sacred spring where they were making the land. While the men worked, she cooked their cabbage. Their food tasted nasty, so one of them decided to hide and watch the cooking. He saw that she urinated into their food, and put sea water into her own food. Then they exchanged the food and ate hers. She got angry and rolled away the stone which had hitherto kept the sea confined and the sea poured out in a great flood, and this was the origin of the sea.[1]

Buin tells a similar story. Atoto was the primeval woman. She had children but no husband. She had a son Kugui and a daughter. The son married the daughter and they had many children. Before that time there was no water. People roasted taro but could not boil it. But Atoto cooked the food by urinating into a pot and this was the food she gave her son. Then she changed this and had the urine ready all the time in a hole under her bed. One day he came home unexpectedly. He beat his mother when he saw what she was doing. He broke

[1] Brown, G., *Melanesians and Polynesians,* London, 1910, p. 357.

all the pots that contained the urine, the water poured out and flooded the land. This is how the ocean originated.[2]

The Narrinyeri told the story of Nurundere and his wives. The two women run away when he chases them. At a place called urine he urinates. Then he orders the Sea to rise and drown his two wives.[3]

In a Heiltsuk story two brothers lived with their sister. They made a small weir and caught a small fish and put it in the weir. They kept chasing bigger and bigger fish, and making bigger weirs. Every night the fish disappear from the weir. One of the brothers says, "Go to sleep" (meaning the other brother and the sister), "*I shall stay awake* and see what happens." A big headless man with eyes on his chest takes the salmon. He shoots at him four times seemingly without hitting it. He follows the cannibal to his home, cures him of his wounds (made by his arrows) and marries the cannibal's daughter. He wants to take his wife home. She urinates and they go home in a boat on the river made by her urine.[4]

In a Pomo myth, this is how the deluge came about.

Coyote *dreamed* that water was about to cover up the world but nobody believed him. He said, "There is going to be water all over the world." It was raining and presently the water began to rise. The people climbed trees because there were no mountains on which they could escape. Coyote with a number of people was on a log. With the aid of Mole, Coyote creates mountains and then the world was new and he created people.[5]

Thunder People lived in a village. They used to go to a spring. But one day a very large trout appeared in the spring. First they were afraid to eat these miraculous fish, but finally as there was nothing else to eat they did eat them. An old woman told her three grandchildren not to eat the miraculous fish.

Presently everyone went to bed as usual, but when the children awoke next morning there was nobody in the camp. They had all been transformed into deer. The children went to a very high mountain. The rain began to pour down. It rained very hard. The world was flooded and there was only a little bit of ground left. They asked an old man

[2]Thurnwald, R., *Forschungen auf den Salomo Inseln und dem Bismarck Archipel*, Berlin, 1912, II, pp. 347, 348.

[3]Meyer, H. E. A., "Manners and Customs of the Aborigines of the Encounter Bay Tribe," in Words, J. D., *The Native Tribes of South Australia*, Adelaide, 1879, pp. 202–204.

[4]Boas, F., *Indianische Sagen von der Nord Pazifischen Küste Amerikas*, Berlin, 1895, pp. 237, 238.

[5]Barrett, S. A., *Pomo Myths*, Bulletin of the Public Museum of the City of Milwaukee, XV, 1933, p. 130.

what he could do about the water. He said he did not know. But when night came the children went to sleep. The old man dug in the ground all night. In the morning he woke the children. The flood had disappeared and the world was a beautiful place.[6]

I emphasize the fact that sleeping occurs twice in this story. If we take it as the dream of Coyote (who is identical with the old man), the flood is the urethral flood. The fish in the water would be an attempt to transform the danger into the fantasy of being born. But only when he digs a deep hole (phallic) does the water disappear—that is, he awakes with an erection.

The next myth is about Gopher, a character in many ways similar to Coyote.[7]

"During the Deluge everyone except Gopher was killed. He saved himself by climbing on the top of Mt. Kanaktai. As the water rose, he saved himself by climbing to the top of Mt. Kanaktai. He climbed higher and higher, and just as the water was about to wash him off the top of the mountain it receded. Now he had no fire so he dug down into the mountain till he found fire inside. In this way he got fire again for the world."[8]

Fire and water as destroyers of the world frequently appear in the same myth or as sequels or substitutes. Coyote who destroys the world by a deluge also destroys it by fire.

Coyote lived with his two little boys whom he had got by deceit from one of the Wood-duck sisters. Everybody abuses his children so he decides to set the world on fire. He digs a tunnel at the *east end of the world,* fills it with fir bark and then lights it. He puts his two children into his hunting sack, ascends the roof of the dance house and expects the conflagration. Coyote calls for rescue from the sky. Spider descends from the sky with his web and Coyote jumps on Spider's belly. He is pulled up through the gates of the sky. He comes back again and finds everything roasted. He drinks too much water and gets sick. Kuksu as medicine man jumps on his belly, the water flows out and covers the land.[9]

Leaving out numerous variants of the same theme found in Pomo mythology, we quote the following version.

The young men of the village had killed Coyote's mother, they had choked her with a hot rock. When Coyote saw what had happened he

[6] *Ibid.,* pp. 131–133.

[7] I mean in the phallic significance.

[8] Barrett, *op. cit.,* p. 135.

[9] *Ibid.,* p. 9.

cut open the breast of his mother and took out her heart. He took a stick and removed the bark and with the blood of his mother's heart he made four red bands around it. Just below each band he tied some down. Then he put a topknot of falcon feathers at the upper end of this wand. . . . At the lower end he suspended the heart of his mother. "Thus Coyote made a sleep-producing wand." He ties the wand to the center pole of the dance house. Everybody is asleep inside. He sets fire to the house and burns all the people. Then he becomes thirsty again (as above). He goes to Frog Woman. By pointing his arrows at her he compels her to show him the water she is sitting on. Then he returns to his mother's grave and revives her. She becomes a young and beautiful woman and Coyote acquires Falcon for his grandson[10]—which probably indicates incest with his mother.

If we take this as a waking dream of Coyote with the vesical pressure symbolized by fire and water and his "mother's heart" as representing sleep, we must regard Frog and Turtle who retain the water as symbols of his mother (retaining the water—preventing him from micturating and awakening) and the incest with mother as the erotic stimulation caused by the bladder pressure.

While Frog denies that she has water, she keeps making baskets. One of these baskets she threw into the Blue Lake. "When a menstruating woman passes by these lakes she is very likely to see one of these baskets and to be made ill by it."[11]

The following story I quote is not a flood story, yet I think I should insert it here because of its connection with water and sleeping.

Tsuntia, the culture hero of the Lillooet, threw his mother into a lake because she would not tell him who his father was. She begat people by her intercourse with the lake. Her descendants were beautiful, especially the young women. The young men of the village would have liked to marry them, but on entering the houses of the "frog people" they were overcome by the smell of frog and *fell into a sleep in which they invariably died.* A young man went into the mountains and prepared his "medicine" for five years because he wanted to overcome the difficulty. He gained the desired knowledge of escaping death while having intercourse with the frog-eaters.[12]

When he went in, an elderly person said to him, "You are a young man and I would not like to see you die, therefore do not enter." He did not eat their food and they were astonished that he did not fall into a

[10] *Ibid.,* p. 124.

[11] *Ibid.,* p. 201; cf. Index under *Frog.*

[12] The people in the lake ate only frogs, and frog skins were their blankets.

death sleep. He took to wife two of the prettiest maidens. He then persuaded some of them to eat deer and these became human beings.[13]

In another group of flood myths we find a different situation. The water is first in the inside of a living being.

According to the aboriginals of Lake Tyers all the water was contained in a huge frog and they did not know how to get water. They agreed that the way to do it was to make the frog laugh. Many animals danced without success. Finally the remarkable contortions of the eel produced the desired effect. The frog laughed and many were drowned in the flood.[14] In an Andamanese myth quoted by Andrew Lang the toad that contains the waters dances with the same result.[15]

I have shown the genital significance of this dancing and this, of course, is in context of the urethral meaning of these myths.[16] The Andamanese myths combine fire, water and the origin of animals. The Aka Jeru version is this, *the people were all asleep.* Sir Sea Eagle came and threw fire among them. They awoke in a fright and all ran in different directions. Some ran into the sea and became fishes and turtles, others ran into the jungle and became birds.[17]

In a Jivaro story we have two young men who were companions. One of them tastes the flesh of a giant serpent. He is very thirsty and he starts to drink. "I shall burst from the water I drink," he said, "and be changed into a lake because I have eaten serpent flesh." He first became a frog, then a small alligator and finally a water serpent which kept growing. At the same time the water in the pool increased more and more and became a lake and then a very big lake which threatened to engulf the earth. All the people drowned except the friend of the youth who was turned into a serpent. He appeared to his friend *in a dream* and said, "Do not come near me or I am bound to swallow you."[18]

The Tahtlan relate how Raven wanted to make lakes but a man swallowed all the water and the whole lake was in his belly. *When the man sleeps* Snipe pushes his bill through the belly and the water runs out.[19]

The water in the belly of a living being condenses two dream mo-

[13] Teit, J., "Traditions of the Thompson River Indians of British Columbia," *Memoirs of the American Folklore Society,* VI, 1898, pp. 96, 97.

[14] Brough Smyth, R., *The Aborigines of Victoria,* Melbourne, 1878.

[15] Lang, A., *Myth, Ritual and Religion,* London, 1906, I, p. 44.

[16] Cf. Róheim, *Australian Totemism,* London, 1925, p. 432.

[17] Brown, A. R., *The Andaman Islander,* Cambridge, 1922, p. 207.

[18] Karsten, R., "The Head Hunters of Western Amazonas," *Societas Scientiarum Fennicae Commentationes Humaniarum Litterarum,* VII. I, Helsingfors, 1935, p. 534.

[19] Teit, J. E., "Tahtlan Tales," *Journal of American Folk-Lore,* XXXII, 1919, p. 219; cf. *idem,* "Kaska Tales," *ibid.,* XXX, 1917, p. 439.

tives, (a) the hero of the flood inside of something (inverted), (b) the urine in the bladder.

In the following Chippewayan myth the hero named Wis represents his dream by displacing the sleeping situation to his antagonist. A wolf man who is also a medicine man wants to be revenged on the water lynxes who have killed his nephew. He must first turn himself into a stump at the edge of the lake. *Frogs and snakes are sent to pull the stump down. Wis had a severe struggle to keep himself upright* (i.e., not asleep). The lynx, his suspicions now lulled to rest, lay down to sleep on the sand. Wis resumed his natural shape and although he had been warned to strike at the *shadow* of the lynx he forgot this and shot at the body. The second arrow, however, was aimed at the shadow and the wounded animal ran into the water. The river began to boil and rise and Wis escaped in his canoe. The water continued flowing until land, trees and hills were all covered (follows the Earth Diver myth).[20]

The stump myth is also told about Nanibozhu. When transformed into a stump the serpent coiled himself round him till he nearly screamed with pain. Then the sea spirit came forth and soon all the monsters were *sleeping* on the beach. Nanibozhu shot the sea spirit in the heart and then he fled, pursued by all the monsters and the waters. When he could no longer find dry land a canoe appeared and he was saved.[21] Another Wisaka myth reads exactly like a dream.

The people hurled fire into all the places where they thought Wisaka might be hiding. After the fire came the rain. Rivers rose, lakes overflowed, water ran over the land. The water followed him wherever he fled even to the top of the mountain. It pursued him up a lofty pine to the very topmost branch. He called on the pine to help him. A canoe slid off the top and he floated on the water with a paddle in his hand.[22]

The disturbed sleep of the sea is responsible for the flood in Tahiti. A fisherman let his hooks down and they became entangled *in the hair of the sleeping god.* The angry god came bubbling to the surface. When the sun set the waters of the ocean began to rise and the next morning only the tops of the mountains appeared above the sea.[23]

The Loucheux or Dene tell the story of a man who was the first per-

[20] Frazer, J. G., *Folklore in the Old Testament,* London, 1919, I, pp. 229, 230; Hooper, W. H., *Ten Months among the Tents of the Tuski,* London, 1853, pp. 285–292. Other versions of the same myth are quoted by Frazer.

[21] Chamberlain, A. F., "Nanibozhu amongst the Otchibwe, Missisagas and other Algonkian Tribes," *Journal of American Folk-Lore,* IX, 1891, p. 205.

[22] Jones, W., "The Culture Hero Myth of the Sauks and Foxes," *Journal of American Folk-Lore,* XIV, 1896, p. 234.

[23] Frazer, *op. cit.,* I, p. 234; Ellis, W., *Polynesian Researches,* I, pp. 389–391.

son to build a canoe. He rocked the boat and this caused a flood. *He got into a gigantic hollow straw and caulked up the ends.* Finally he landed on a hill. The only living thing inside was a raven, who gorged with food *was fast asleep. He thrust the raven into a bag and dropped him in the bag,* so that he was dashed to pieces at the foot of the mountain.

The only living beings he found were a loach and a pike. He revived the raven and they went together to the beach *where the loach and the pike were still sleeping in the sun.* They bore holes into them and out of the pike came a crowd of men, out of the loach a crowd of women.[24]

The hero caulked in the straw, the sleeping animals, all characterize sleep as such. The falling raven is the moment of falling asleep. The people coming out of the animal's inside—awakening.

We quote the story here because of the connection of motives: going into the mother, sleep and death. And the reverse side of the picture, water = mother, triumph of the libido.

In some of the flood myths the *duration is from evening to morning.*

Once upon a time the whole world was flooded. All were drowned except one man and one woman who ran to the highest peak of a hill where they climbed up a tree and hid themselves among its branches. They intended to pass the night there. However, in the morning they found that they had become a tiger and a tigress. Pathiany (the supreme god) sent a man and a woman from a cave to repeople the earth.[25] From evening to morning the threat of flood is over.

In the Guiana version, the myth starts with cutting the world tree that contains the waters. The culture hero covers the stump with a closely woven basket. The monkey was sent by the culture hero to fetch water in an open basket—to keep him out of mischief. But he came back and out of curiosity lifted the basket from the tree trunk and the water poured forth.

The culture hero assembles all his people on the highest palm tree to rescue them from the rising waters. Those who could not climb he sealed up in a cave. He and his followers spent the night on the tree till finally the birds hailed the approach of the day.

One episode of this myth is the dismal cry of the monkey—the sleeper awakening from a nightmare.[26]

The flood ends with the approach of day—it is a dream. It begins with the *unfinished task* (like water in a sieve)[27] and continues with the

[24] Petitot, E., *Traditions Indiennes du Canada Nord Ouest,* 1886, 13, 34–38.

[25] Shakespear, J., *The Lushei Kuki Clans,* London, 1912, p. 177.

[26] Brett, W. H., *The Indian Tribes of Guiana,* London, 1868, pp. 378–382.

[27] Cf. below, *The Danaids, Work and Punishment.*

voyeur element (tree trunk like Pandora's box, mother's vagina). Then the flood (urethral), the cave (uterine) and the climbing (genital).

One version of the Pima myth again contains the "sleep" motive. The sleeping prophet is warned three times by an eagle of the flood approaching but he pays no attention.[28]

The myths of world destruction by water and those of destruction by fire merge into each other.

In a Toba myth of the Great Fire, we are told that the *people were all sound asleep.* They awoke to see that the moon was being eaten by the jaguars—and the jaguars were the spirits of the dead. Fragments of the moon began to fall down on earth and started a big fire. The entire earth was on fire. They all ran to the lagoons covered with bull rushes.[29]

A typical urethral awakening dream projected into cosmic proportions.

In a Yokuts myth on the origin of fire the animals who are stealing the fire come to a place *where everybody is asleep.* Coyote took and covered the fire. Then he saw a baby asleep. He picked it up, put it in the hot ground where the fire had been and ran. The baby screamed and woke all the people. The chief picked the fastest runners and started them after Coyote. Coyote dodged on one side, then the other, and as he ran the water followed his trail, and that is why the river is so crooked.[30]

If we *condense the personnel* of this story, we have the sleeper who dreams that he is a baby (rebirth) and owing to the bladder pressure he keeps running. Water and fire are the same thing. It is interesting to note that among the Lipan Apache, Coyote stories are bedtime stories.[31]

The dream origin of the flood myth is quite clear in the following Tsetsaut story.

A man and his wife went up the hills to hunt marmots. When they reached the top of the hill they saw that the water was still rising. They climbed higher and higher but the water rose steadily. Finally when the water was about to reach them they resolved to enclose their children in hollow trees. They supplied them with food and closed the cavities up with wooden covers.

But the water continued to rise and all the people were drowned.

[28] Bancroft, H. H., *The Native Races of the Pacific States,* New York, 1875, III, p. 78.

[29] Metraux, A., *Myths of the Toba and Pilaga Indians of the Gran Chaco, Memoirs of the American Folklore Society,* XL, Philadelphia, 1946, p. 33.

[30] Stewart, G. W., "Two Yokuts Traditions," *Journal of American Folk-Lore,* XXI, 1908, pp. 237, 238.

[31] Opler, M. E., "Myths and Legends of the Lipan Apache Indians," *Memoirs of the American Folklore Society,* XXXVI, 1940, p. 107.

Then the water began to retreat. *The children went to sleep and when they awoke one of the boys opened a hole and came out.*[32]

The Tsimshian relate the deluge as follows:

The waters of the Lake of the Beginning arose and a great whale came to the surface. When the whale went down the water subsided. One man went down to the bottom of the Lake of the Beginning to get supernatural power. Then the water rose again and the great whale came out. At the bottom of the lake there was a large house. The door opened suddenly, he entered.[33] (We omit the rest of the story.) The rising waters are here combined with the basic dream of falling asleep.

Boas gives a condensed version of all the Northwestern stories of *how Raven obtained water.*

Raven causes the owner of the water to go to sleep, makes him believe that he has soiled his bed, and by means of the threat that he will tell on him, Raven obtains permission to drink.

(The soiling in this case is excremental, but in many cases these two pressures go together.)

After he has thus obtained water, he creates the rivers. He spits them out, or he *makes the rivers by urinating.*

In one version, obtaining water and obtaining the sun are the same thing.

Raven becomes the lover of the daughter of the Sun-owner who also owns the water. He asks for a drink and *when the girl is asleep he flies away with the water basket.*[34]

The flood myth is frequently combined with others such as the fire or conflagration, the theft of the *sun and especially the Earth-Diver motive of the creation myth.*

In the Iroquoian myth (Onondaga version) quoted above, when the pregnant woman thrown down from the sky is floating toward the earth, there seemed to be a lake at the spot where she was falling. There she saw many ducks and other water fowl falling. The Loon shouted, "A woman is coming to the depths of the water, her body is floating hither." So recognizing that she needs earth to live on, they dive for the earth. After several failures, the Turtle gets the earth and he is also the one who carries it on his back.[35]

In a Kathlamet myth, Beaver floods the world with his tears. Bluejay

[32] Boas, F., "Traditions of the Tsetsaut," *Journal of American Folk-Lore,* IX, 1896, p. 262.

[33] Boas, F., "Tsimshian Mythology," *Bureau of American Ethnology,* XXXI, Report, 1916, pp. 346, 347.

[34] Boas, F., *op. cit.,* XXXI, 1916, pp. 651--652.

[35] Hewitt, J. N. B., "Iroquoian Cosmology," *Annual Report of the Bureau of American Ethnology,* XXI, 1903, pp. 181, 182.

dives, but his tail remains above the water. Then Otter tries in vain. Finally the muskrat dives and remains under the water a long time.

In a myth of the Potawatomi, after the world has been inundated, Messon sends a raven to build up another world. Everything was covered with water. The raven could not find any earth. The otter also returned without achieving anything. At last, the muskrat descended and brought back some earth.

In the Menominee version the same happens with Manabush. The animals are the Otter, the Beaver, the Mink, and finally the Muskrat. In another version, when the Muskrat reappears on the surface he is nearly dead and he has one single grain of sand in his paws. From this the world is remade by Great Hare who courses around it.[36]

Boas comes to the conclusion that the opening of the Raven and the Mink myths in Northwest American mythology is a deluge myth "which has been elaborated in different directions but presents in all these tales the beginning of the world. The loss of the deluge element in the Raven tales of the Tsimshian and Newettee may be due to the occurrence of other deluge legends in these tribes. Among the Newetee the Mink tale not only contains the element of destruction of the world by fire, but refers also to the start of all vegetation which is brought up by diving animals the same way the new earth is created after the deluge by the eastern tribes.[37]

From the point of view of the dream nucleus of these myths, we have here a rather interesting situation. The flying, diving bird element is the basic dream, the transition from waking to sleeping. The deluge and world fire myth is the awakening urethral dream, the transition from sleeping to waking. The dream, in so far as it is "historical," i.e., personal, is left out, and the beginning of the world is the awakening of the sleeper. We quote Campbell who writes, "Dream is the personalized myth, myth is the depersonalized dream."[38]

The second half of this view is right or nearly right, but the first half can only be accepted if we believe in inherited symbols or "the collective unconscious."

To return, however, to our flood and creation myths. The diving dream is both regressive and libidinal. The moment of falling asleep is also awakening or rather in this case the resistance to awakening. The water as the origin of things is both the uterus and the pressure exerted by the bladder. Sin, guilt and anxiety are components of the

[36] Alexander, H. B., *The Mythology of All Races, North American,* X, Boston, 1916, pp. 42, 43, with references.

[37] Boas, F., *op. cit.,* pp. 640, 641.

[38] Campbell, J., *The Hero with a Thousand Faces,* New York, 1949, p. 19.

flood myth; they are also found in all urethral waking dreams on a superficial level because by urinating the dreamer will mess the bed, and on a deeper level because of the magic aggressive elements implied in the dream of urine.

In some North American myths the flood is followed by the birds flying up to the sky.

In a Papago myth a baby deserted by its father and mother starts to cry. First the earth around the baby is moist, then there is a stream and then it is evident that a flood is coming that will destroy the world.

Older Brother made a pot out of greasewood to save himself in. Coyote did the same. Older Brother told the birds to hang on to the sky.[39]

We must substitute urine for tears and then the myth with its urethral, intrauterine (box) and genital symbolism becomes quite clear.

If we look at the biblical narrative closely we find the same equivalence of the creation and the deluge myth.

The Spirit of God soaring over the water (Genesis I, 1) is evidently a bird and when God says, Let there be light! that might well be the moment of awakening. As for the biblical narrative of the Flood, the ark of Noah with the male and female couples in it already indicates the tendency to re-create (as in the dream) and the birds emitted one after the other from the ark (Genesis VI, 6–8) are obviously identical with the diving birds of our creation and deluge myths.[40] The Spirit of God above the waters usually appears in the shape of a dove.[41]

Offshoots of the biblical myth indicate the reaction of the unconscious to the meaning of the ark as symbolizing the womb.[42]

Numi Tarem (Sky God) wishes to kill Xulater, the prince of the underworld, by destroying the universe in a cataclysm of fire. Xulater is having an affair with the wife of the Vogul sky god and he gets into the ark by crawling into her stomach. In various other versions the devil abetted by Noah's wife crawls into the ark or bores a hole in the ark, in the shape of a serpent or a mouse.[43]

Greek myths of the hero rescued by the dolphin are parallel versions of the flood myth. The dolphin is δελφις, the womb. Usener con-

[39] Kroeber, H. R., "Traditions of the Papago Indians," *Journal of American Folk-Lore*, XXV, 1912, p. 98.

[40] I am not discussing primitive beliefs that are due to missionary influence.

[41] Eisler, R., "Kuba-Kybele," *Philologus*, LXVIII, p. 180.

[42] By offshoots, I do not mean modern missionary influence but archaic cultural traditions.

[43] Dähnhardt, O., *Natursagen*, I, Leipzig, 1907, pp. 257–290.

cludes that Phalantos, that is, the phallos, must have been one of the hero gods rescued by the dolphin.[44] Eros is actually represented on the back of the dolphin.[45]

Flood myths in which the "closed in" aspect of the rescuing boat is especially emphasized are probably derived from urethral awakening dreams combined with the intrauterine situation.

The people of Banks Island tell the flood myth about their culture hero Qat.

He made himself a large canoe and when he finished he collected all living creatures and shut himself in the canoe with them. A deluge of rain came and the canoe tore a channel for itself and disappeared.[46]

It is perhaps of interest that Qat is also the hero who brings Night and Daylight. Qat travels to Night who shows him how to sleep. He returns to his brothers with a knowledge of sleep and with birds that would awaken them in the morning.

"What is this coming out of the sea—they cried—that is night, sit down on both sides of the house and when you feel something in your eyes lie down and be quiet." When their eyes began to blink they said What is this? Shall we die? Shut your eyes and go to sleep, he said. When night had lasted long enough the cock began to crow and the birds to twitter. Qat took a piece of red obsidian and cut the night with it, the light shone forth again and Qat's brothers awoke.[47]

In dreams of menstruating women we also find the same structure as in vesical dreams. The volume of the fluid increases, it is a flood.

Once upon a time (Toba myth) a woman was menstruating. Her mother and sister forgot to leave drinking water for her. So she went down to the lagoon to drink. It rained until all the people were drowned. All the corpses turned into birds and flew up (the flying dream). This is because Rainbow is angry when a menstruating woman goes near a lagoon.[48] A parallel version of this myth from the same tribe is interesting. The cataclysm is due to fire instead of water. Menstruation is not mentioned—but the moon has something to do with the cataclysm.

The people were all sound asleep. One of them awoke, the others slept. The moon is about to be eaten by an animal. The jaguars were eating the moon, they were really the spirits of the dead. Fragments of

[44] Usener, H., *Die Sintflutsagen,* Bonn, 1899, p. 159.

[45] *Ibid.,* p. 223; cf. on the fish symbolism also Eisler, R., *Orpheus—the Fisher,* London, 1921.

[46] Codrington, R. H., *The Melanesians,* Oxford, 1891, p. 166.

[47] *Ibid.,* p. 157.

[48] Metraux, *Myths of the Toba and Pilaga Indians of the Gran Chaco,* p. 29.

the moon fell on the earth and started a great fire. Everything was burned, even the lagoon of water. Birds flew up out of the corpses.[49]

The Wemale relate a flood story. Human beings were under the rule of a woman called Bouwa. She was the daughter of the sun god Tuwale. Tuwale floods the world and she ascends higher and higher escaping from the water. She reminds her father that he still owes mankind the purchase money for Rabie, his wife. In order to do so she covers her genitalia with a silver girdle. She wore this girdle for three days and since then women menstruate for three days. That ended the flood and mankind was rescued by the morning star[50] (awakening).

We find another flood myth based on menstruation in Arnhem Land.

According to Elkin and Berndt, the Wauwelak were two sisters who came from the interior of Arnhem Land. Following incest with a man belonging to their own moiety the elder sister gave birth to a child. The journey was continued while the afterbirth blood was still flowing and they approach a water hole belonging to a large, female, rock python, Julunggul. She smelled the blood and came out and made lightning and rain. The rain gradually washed some of the afterbirth blood into the pool. The female python gradually came nearer the "shade" in which the sisters sat. The dancing of the elder sister which caused her blood to flow attracted the snake while that of the younger sister stopped it. Finally the python pushed her head in through the door and swallowed the two sisters and the child. The python returned to the well and standing upright talked to the other pythons. Then the country was flooded.[51]

In the Murngin version of this myth Yurlunggur is a male, the Big Father. When the menstrual blood dropped into the pool Yurlunggur smelled the odor of the blood. He raised his head and smelled again and again. He advanced slowly in snake form and as the snake advanced so also the flood. The sisters sang to prevent the flood (snake) from swallowing them. *But he crawled into the camp and they fell into a deep sleep from his magic.* He then swallowed them and finally he regurgitated them.[52]

If we take these two myths together we must come to the conclusion that they are really based on two different dreams, one male, one female. The male dream must be that the dreamer—the snake—has intercourse with the woman, goes into her (i.e., is asleep) and his se-

[49] *Ibid.,* p. 33.

[50] Jensen, A. R., *Hainuwele,* Frankfurt am Main, 1933, pp. 54–56.

[51] Elkin, A. P., and Berndt, C. and R., *Art in Arnhem Land,* Chicago, 1939, p. 32.

[52] Warner, W. Lloyd, *A Black Civilization,* New York, 1937, pp. 250–257.

men is the flood. In the female version the woman is excited when her blood flows, i.e., she is in her own vagina and in her mother's uterus in her dream. The flood is here the menstrual blood.[53]

We should also compare the Sumerian version of the flood myth.

Ea tells Enlil how he caused Utnapishtim, "the exceedingly wise one," to have a dream by which he learned the plan of the gods to send a flood.[54]

Fire and water and the sun and the culture hero all merge into each other in these myths. . . .

The symbolism of the vesical dream is so typical that there is little chance of being mistaken in the interpretation. The increasing volume of water (or the growing fish), the running or escaping of the hero (heroine) or dreamer, the womb symbolism, phallic traits, moreover a combination of fire and water are the characteristics of the vesical dream. The fact that our stories frequently mention one or more of the *dramatis personae* as sleeping, or relate the whole thing as a dream, makes it quite clear that what we have here is not a parallelism of unconscious symbolism in dreaming and in inventing a story, but a type of narrative or several types of narratives that were actually retellings of vesical awakening dreams.

[53]The proofs for this interpretation are derived from an unpublished manuscript of R. and C. Berndt.

[54]Langdon, S. H., *The Mythology of All Races, Semitic*, V, Boston, 1931, p. 222.

The Flood as Male Myth of Creation

ALAN DUNDES

Questions of meaning are often eschewed in myth scholarship. A large number of the essays treating the flood myth consist of retellings of diverse versions of the narrative. A good many merely rehash the results of previous treatises, with little or no effort to interpret the possible significance of flood myth texts. Frazer, for example, after citing two hundred and fifty pages of flood myths, concludes: "On the whole, then, there seems to be good reason for thinking that some and probably many diluvial traditions are merely exaggerated reports of floods which actually occurred, whether as the result of heavy rain, earthquake-waves, or other causes. All such traditions, therefore, are partly legendary and partly mythical: so far as they preserve reminiscences of floods which really happened, they are legendary; so far as they describe universal deluges which never happened, they are mythical." The critical question is, or ought to be, why are flood myths told at all? Whether they are historical events or fictional figments of the human imagination, that difficult question of why *they occupy such an important part of our reconstruction of the beginnings of the world remains unanswered. Any answer would be speculative, but if an answer were plausible and consonant with the specific details of flood myths, it might prove a welcome addition to flood myth scholarship. The following essay is an effort to grapple with one possible meaning of the flood myth. For a fuller statement of Frazer's meager conclusions, see* Folk-Lore in the Old Testament, *vol. I (London, 1918), p. 359.*

Theories of myth interpretation may be roughly divided into two major groupings: literal and symbolic. Literalists tend to seek factual or historical bases for a given mythical narrative while advocates of one of the many symbolic approaches prefer to regard the narrative as a code requiring some mode of decipherment. It is important to realize that the literal and symbolic exegeses of myths are not necessarily mutually exclusive. In the specific case of the flood, there could in theory

Reprinted from the *Journal of Psychoanalytic Anthropology* 9 (1986): 359–372.

have been an actual deluge, either local or global, but at the same time one of the reasons why the flood narrative might have diffused as widely as it undoubtedly has—even to peoples who live far inland away from natural floods—could be attributable to its symbolic content. For example, inasmuch as all human neonates are so to speak delivered from an initial flood (of amniotic fluid) when the sac breaks, it is not impossible that the creation of the world was thought to have occurred in a parallel fashion. As the individual is born, so was the earth born. From the *Motif-Index of Folk Literature,* we can easily establish that very often the same techniques used to create humanity were used to create the world; or perhaps in terms of logic or chronologic the analogy should be stated the other way round: the identical techniques used to create the world are used to create the first man. Compare, for instance, motif A641, Universe brought forth from an egg, and motif A1222, Mankind originates from eggs, or the Earth Diver motif (A812) in which the earth is formed from a bit of mud, and the Creation of man from earth, clay, mud, or dust (A1241).

To be sure, both literal and symbolic interpretations may be in error—that is, perhaps there was no historical universal deluge, and perhaps early peoples did not imagine any similarity between the nature of human birth and the beginning of the world. Or one interpretation may be correct and the other incorrect. What is crucial is the ability to distinguish between literal and symbolic approaches to myth in general, and in this instance to the flood myth in particular.

Because the flood myth is part of the sacred charter of much of Western (Judeo-Christian) civilization, there has been noticeable reluctance to interpret it symbolically. By far the majority of the huge spate of books and essays devoted to elucidating the flood myth have treated it as a literal phenomenon. Those discussing the issue of whether the biblical flood was a local or universal deluge did not question the historicity of the biblical account. It was simply assumed that there had been a flood to which Noah had been a participating eyewitness. This was deemed true regardless of whether the flood was local or universal.

Although in general the comparative method was employed to denigrate the truth value of biblical materials—if other peoples had the same story, then it became much more difficult to maintain the uniqueness of the biblical narratives as the divine word of God—it was employed in the case of the flood in quite another way. The argument was in part that the occurrence of flood narratives among so many diverse peoples of the world, past and present, civilized and primitive, was prima facie "evidence" that there had indeed been a universal flood, the echoes of which survived in flood myths recounted up to modern times. Accordingly, religious enthusiasts were not in the least put off by the large number of flood myths recorded around the world. On the contrary, they welcomed each new instance of a flood myth as further corroboration of the truth of the Genesis narrative. Thus the application of the comparative method proved nothing with respect to the historicity question. Those who believed in the literal truth of the flood myth regarded comparative data as confirmatory; those who rejected the literal reading of the biblical flood narrative pointed to the hundreds of flood myths as evidence of its noncanonical status. Probably there are only a few contemporary theologians who would contend that the widespread distribution of the flood myth was a marker of "primitive revelation"—according to which doctrine, all mankind had originally been given the divine word from God (see Schmidt, 1939). In this theoretical framework, it was presumed that primitive peoples had "lost" most of the original revelation, retaining only a few isolated vestigial fragments such as the flood myth.

The indisputable wide diffusion of the flood story proved also to be of interest to those espousing a symbolic approach to myth. For whatever the flood myth might signify in symbolic terms, it was pretty clearly something which must be relevant to a great variety of peoples and cultures. Of course, it need not be assumed that the flood myth must mean the same thing in every culture in which it appears. Still the nagging question remains: what then does the flood myth *mean?*

Previous attempts by symbolically inclined interpreters to decode the flood myth have generally fallen along the conventional lines of standard folklore theories. The flood story has been variously interpreted as a lunar myth (Böklen, 1903), a solar myth (Frazer, 1918:342, nn. 1–3; Berge, 1951), or as a vegetation or fertility ritual (Follansbee, 1939). The floodwaters have also been regarded as a celestial cleansing agent to punish mankind for a blood-spilling transgression which "polluted" the antediluvial earth (Frymer-Kensky, 1978). Both Freudians (Rank, 1912) and Jungians (Kluger, 1968; Williams, 1974) see a dreamlike aspect of flood stories. Róheim expanded Rank's notion that the origin of the flood myth might be sought in vesical dreams in which the urge to urinate during the night was expressed in dream format. According to Róheim, "Flood myths frequently represent the flood as urine, thereby revealing their dream origin" (1952:448). For Rank and Róheim, therefore, flood myths are derivatives of dreams expressing a need to urinate. If that is all there is to flood myths, how can we account for all the details of various flood myths? Why is the flood so often used as a means of punishing mankind for various sins? How is the flood myth to be explained as a re-creation myth, that is, a secondary creation following the destruction of the world produced by the first creation? How can urination as a primal cause satisfactorily account for the explicitly punitive and creative aspects of flood myths?

In order to interpret the symbolic content of flood myths, we need to establish several axioms. First of all, I would contend that the relationship of god to man is essentially that of parent to child. This is Freud's astute insight in *The Future of an Illusion* as modified by Kardiner's revision of Freudian theory (1939, 1945). Kardiner's revision consists of culturally relativizing the Freudian notion. To the extent that parent–child relationships differ from culture to culture, so the god–man relationship will vary accordingly. It should be remarked that the hypothetical isomorphism or congruence of infantile training with adult projective systems (which include myths) can be empirically tested in diverse cultures. It is by no means a matter of accepting the Kardinerian–Freudian formulation on faith. Either there is a parallelism of structure and content or there is not.

Secondly, I maintain that males envy female parturition. The principle of male pregnancy is well documented—there are numerous instances in the patriarchal Old Testament. The creation of Eve from Adam's rib is an obvious reversal of biological reality insofar as man creates woman from *his* body. Moreover, it is quite likely that the crucial male bone in question is not the rib at all but the phallus, which lacks the *os baculum* found in some other animals. As woman gives birth to males from *her* genital area, it is (psycho)logically reasonable for man to fantasize giving birth to females from *his* genital area (Dundes, 1983).

Now what has all this to do with the symbolic content of flood myths? For one thing, most flood myths involve *male* gods destroying the world but saving a *male* survivor to repopulate the earth. It is, in sum, a male creation myth with little if any mention of females. Noah's wife does not even have a first name (see Utley, 1941)—just as Lot's wife is nameless. (The Lot story is typologically and structurally similar to the Noah story.) But why does a male create or re-create the world by means of a flood? I would argue that it is because a flood constitutes a cosmogonic projection of the standard means by which every childbearing female creates (see Bertine, 1944:48; Pratt, 1955:68). It is the bursting of the sac releasing the amniotic fluids which announces the birth of each newborn baby. As the anthropologist Donald F. Tuzin put it in his study of Arapesh water symbolism in New Guinea (1977:220): "Anyone witnessing a childbirth cannot fail to notice that the event is accompanied by a forcible discharge of an impressive volume of water." This is the primordial flood which is repeated anew with every generation. But in male-produced myths, the male must use whatever means he has to create a flood. As the female flood seemingly emerges from her genital area, so it makes (psycho)logical sense for the male flood to come from his genital area. So here we have a rationale for a urinal flood. When Róheim observed that flood myths frequently represent the flood as urine, he was on the right (urinary) track. But he erred in assuming that these urinary flood myths must have stemmed from a dream source. It is far more likely that *both* dreams and myths are reflections of unconscious wishes. There is no need to asume that dreams are necessarily antecedent to myths. For that matter, one could just as well argue that individual dreams in a given culture reflect the myths that the dreamer has heard. In any case, the proposition is that flood myths are an example of males seeking to imitate female creativity.

Is there any evidence to support this interpretation? Certainly the connection postulated between pregnancy envy on the part of males and urinary flood is explicitly articulated in myth texts. A striking instance is afforded by a Chukchee creation myth reported by Bogoras (1910:151–154). The culture hero Raven and his wife live alone on a small plot of ground. Raven's wife tells him, "Better go and try to create the earth!" He replies, "I cannot, truly!" Shortly thereafter, Raven observes his wife asleep. "Again he looks at his wife. Her abdomen has enlarged. In her sleep she creates without any effort. He is frightened and turns his face away." His wife then delivers twins. Raven's response is interesting. "There, you have created men! Now I shall go and try to create the earth. . . . Raven flies and defecates. Every piece of excrement falls upon water, grows quickly, and becomes land." But the creation is insufficient, for there is no fresh water. "Oh," says Raven, "shall I try again?" He begins to pass water. "Where one drop falls, it becomes a lake; where a jet falls, it becomes a river. . . . Oh, Raven, the good fellow, flew farther on. He strains himself to the utmost, creates ground, exhausts himself, and creates water for the rivers and lakes." This creation myth demonstrates how men compete with procreative women. By anal means, the earth is created (see Dundes, 1962); by urinary means, the waters of the earth are created. In this Chukchee myth, the male's actions are specifically precipitated by observing the "natural" creativity of females. Now one can better understand the existence of motifs A923.1, Ocean from urine, and A1012.2, Flood from urine, and the urinary flood myths assembled by Róheim (1952:439–465). By the same token, it is now possible to appreciate such curious flood myth details as the fact that the water in question is *hot!* Motif A1016.2, Deluge produced by hot liquid which burns as it floods, is intelligible, as is the common motif in Islamic (and Jewish) tradition of the "hot water" which flows over the earth (Rooth, 1962:67). Even more fascinating is the additional facet of the popular Islamic tradition which reports that "the sign of the beginning of the flood was that *water began to flow out of the oven*" (Rooth, 1962:88). The oven is a standard womb symbol (Freud, 1953:170). When the folk claim that the beginning of the flood is marked by hot water coming out of an oven, they offer confirmation of the basic symbolism hypothesized here.

We may now better comprehend a flood myth from the Jivaro Indians of the Amazon, a myth which puzzled Frazer. He spoke of a tradition,

> more or less confused, of a great deluge which happened long ago. They say that a great cloud fell from heaven, which turned into rain and caused the death of all the inhabitants of the earth; only an old man and his two sons were saved, and it was they who repeopled the earth after the deluge, though how they contrived to do so without the assistance of a woman is a detail about which our authority does not deign to enlighten us. However that may be, one of the two sons who survived was cursed by his father, and the Jibaros are descended from him. The curse may be a reminiscence of the story of Noah and his sons recorded in Genesis, of which the Jibaros may have heard through missionaries. The difficulty of propagating the human species without the help of the female sex would seem to have struck the acuter minds among the Jibaros, for according to some of them the survivors of the deluge were a man and a woman. (Frazer, 1918:260–261)

What Frazer failed to realize is that if the myth were designed to demonstrate male procreative abilities, then it makes perfect sense for the action to take place without the help of a female. It is always risky to call a tradition "more or less confused." More often, it is the analyst of myth who is more or less confused!

It has often been suggested that flood myths "are closely linked with creation myths; the flood wipes out the old creation and a new creation begins" (Barnard, 1966:153). However, it might be more apt to say that the flood is not so much a creation myth as a re-creation myth. (The original creation, biologically speaking, is obviously from women and so men, to repudiate women's natural procreative superiority, must "destroy" the *first* creation and substitute a second creation of their own. For a discussion of the flood as "uncreation" see Clines, 1972:136–138.) In the myths, man is first created and then nearly destroyed before surviving a flood. This pattern is seemingly analogous to the details of human birth. The flood of amniotic fluids released at birth does not create the fetus-infant. The creation took place nine months before the flood of birth. Birth releases an already fully formed neonate who has been floating around the womb for approximately nine months. (It is noteworthy that many cosmologies, including our own Judeo-Christian one, begin with "And the earth was without form, and void; and darkness was upon the face of the deep." The common notions of darkness and floating could derive from the prenatal intrauterine experience that all men and women share. Even so-called modern theories of the "expanding universe" could reflect that same intrauterine experience.) Thus in Genesis it is a male Noah who builds an ark-womb. Similarly, in the widespread Earth Diver myth (see Mitra, 1929; Walk, 1933; Schmidt, 1937; Count, 1952; Köngäs, 1960; Eliade, 1961; Dundes, 1962) it is an already created *male* who dives into the deluge to seek a bit of mud with which to re-create the earth.

Those who might consider a male urinal flood as a farfetched theory will have to find some alternative way of explaining the existence of myths in which floods are produced through micturition (see motif A1012.2, Flood from urine). The very existence of such myths—myths, incidentally, composed and transmitted by individuals who have never heard of Freud or psychoanalytic theory—would at least suggest that the connection between urination and flooding is not a Freudian invention. In retrospect, we can see that Rank and Róheim were correct as far as they went, but the flood myth is not simply a dream translation of a basic bodily need to urinate. Rather it is a male creation myth modeled after the female flood, the release of amniotic fluids. As the individual is created or brought forth by females, so the world is created or "re-created" by males. If Eliade (1958:212) is correct in equating baptism with a ritual enactment of the deluge, then it is surely significant that baptisms are traditionally performed by *men*.

The use of urine in a punitive context is also plausible, although admittedly more difficult to document. In American folk speech, the idiom "to piss on it" is undeniably a metaphor of repudiation. The lack of extensive ethnographic data on urination practices makes it problematic to assert that there may be some cross-cultural agreement on the technique of urinating on someone to show disgust or contempt. It is, though, at the very least possible and certainly tenable.

"To make water" is another idiom referring to urination which may be relevant. It would seem to constitute another bit of linguistic data supporting the idea that urinating can be perceived as a creative flood-producing act. Urine and semen may be equivalent in the folk mind. The Hebrew word for water can also mean semen, for example, just as "*maiyeh,* water, in colloquial Arabic is used also as the name of male semen, the life medium" (Canaan, 1929:58; see also Walker, 1976:52). In Isaiah 48:1, the people of the house of Jacob "are come forth out of the waters of Judah." Moreover, the association between the male organ which produces posterity and the same organ's ability to urinate is signaled by the standard threat in the Bible (1 Kings 21:21): "Behold, I will bring evil upon thee and will take away thy posterity and will cut off from Ahab him that pisseth against the wall" (see also 1 Kings 14:10 and 16:11). The urinary cast of so many flood myths might also help explain why in some myths the primeval floodwaters are initially contained in a (chamber) pot. In such texts, breaking the pot releases the urinary flood. If urine = semen = water, then a male *procreative* myth might well have a male culture hero or deity producing a urinary flood.

This new perspective on flood myths allows us to understand for the first time some of the other, more puzzling, aspects of such myths. Consider what is perhaps one of the oldest known versions of the flood myth, a Babylonian account which states that the gods are annoyed by "the clamor of mankind. By their uproar they prevent sleep" (Pritchard, 1950:104). As one scholar puts it, "In the Babylonian myth of the flood, the gods decided to destroy mankind for the rather absurd reason that they had become so noisy that they prevented the gods from sleeping at nights" (Hooke, 1963:131). It has been argued that "noise" and "wickedness" are paradigmatic equivalents (Casalis, 1976:50), but this doesn't explain the apparent absurdity. If, however, god is to man as adult is to child, then the reason is not absurd at all. For the crying of infants at night does disturb the sleep of adults, making them angry enough to wish to "destroy" the noisy children in question. Just as young children can express anger through nocturnal enuresis, thereby creating a flood through bedwetting, so adults, especially males, may express anger in a similar way.

There is yet one other piece of data which supports the idea that the male organ may be intimately connected to the flood myth, and that is the widespread occurrence of incest, especially sibling incest, as a precipitating factor or consequence (see Walk, 1949; Hwei, 1955). This is an extremely common pattern in Southeast Asian myths. Often the pattern includes violation of a sexual prohibition, such as incest, which leads to a punitive flood. Frazer (1918:195) reports a flood myth from southwestern Bengal in which the flood was sent to destroy the first people who had grown incestuous.

If we examine all the "re-creation" myths in Genesis, we find precisely this pattern. A sexual taboo is ignored, which angers God, who punishes the sinners by destroying their homes. The story of Adam and Eve could be perceived in this light. If Eve is born from Adam's body, then she in some sense might be considered Adam's daughter. In that case, it would be father–daughter incest. If Adam and Eve were created simultaneously as in one of the two creation myths in the first part of Genesis, then they could be considered brother and sister. In the Garden of Eden, initial paradise, Eve yields to the temptation of the serpent to eat from the forbidden tree. Although the fruit is not specified, tradition makes it an apple (see Heisig, 1952–1953; Leder, 1961; Brazda, 1977 :121–129), a fruit which has symbolic overtones of the breast (Freud, 1953 :163; Levy, 1917–1919 :19). In any event, the result of the sin is an awareness of *nakedness* which suggests a discovery of the sexual parts of the anatomy. God's response is to banish Adam and Eve from Eden, whereupon *immediately* after leaving the garden, "Adam knew Eve his wife; and she conceived." The point is that sexual activity takes place as the very first thing following the departure from Eden, and the peopling of the earth begins through an incestuous act.

In the Genesis flood myth, there is a curious episode (6 :2–4) in which the "sons of God saw the daughters of men . . . and they took them wives." It is apparently this sexuality (see Poulet, 1942; Delcor, 1976 :4) which offends God once again because there is no other explanation of "And God saw that the wickedness of man was great in the earth." Noah and his family survive the flood which God sends as a punishment. After the flood, Noah discovers wine and drinks to excess. Ham sees his father's nakedness—here too nakedness is apparently a sin, as it was in the Garden of Eden account. "To see the nakedness of someone" has been construed as a metaphor for sexual intercourse (Bassett, 1971 :233) in biblical rhetoric. God is displeased and curses Canaan, the son of Ham. Apocryphal versions of the story hint at a possible homosexual adventure (Bassett, 1971).

The themes of the Noah story are repeated in the account of Lot. God is disturbed by homosexual activity in the cities of Sodom and Gomorrah. Abraham manages to bargain so that if God finds as many as ten righteous men in these cities, God will not destroy them. Two angels come to Sodom as investigators for God. The Sodomites find the angels attractive and ask Lot to "bring them out unto us, that we may know them" (19 :5). Lot offers his two virgin daughters to the homosexual crowd as a substitute for his angel guests, an offer that is scorned. Those in the crowd are struck blind. Lot is then instructed by the angels to leave the city with his family and is told, "Look not behind thee." Lot's wife disobeys (just as Eve disobeyed) and is turned into a pillar of salt. Looking was a sin for Adam and Eve when their "eyes were opened" and they saw one another's nakedness; looking was a sin for Ham when he saw his father Noah's exposed body. Lot in a cave with his two daughters is made drunk—a clear parallel with Noah's drunkenness. The daughters seduce their father: "Thus were both the daughters of Lot with child by their father" (19:36). In this Electral plot, the mother is conveniently out of the way, leaving the father to the daughters' sexual advances, a point seemingly missed by folkloristic and anthropological studies of the story (see, for example, Cocchiara, 1949; Aycock, 1983). But more strikingly we have a destruction of the world, or a part thereof, followed by an incestuous union to repopulate the earth. While father–daughter incest is more rare—the typical incestous couple is brother and sister—incest is a common aftermath of a world destruction myth. The clear-cut connection between destruction of the world (for example, through flood) and the incest motif in Genesis seems directly parallel, if not cognate, with flood myths in Southeast Asia and China. It is noteworthy that right after Lot's daughters seduce their father, we have an episode when Abraham pretends that his wife Sarah is his sister so that Abimelech will not harm them—once more a play upon the ubiquitous incest theme. It has been established that the wife–sister motif is a recurring element in Genesis (Speiser, 1967).

There is a great dispute over the meaning and significance of the introduction to the Noachian flood with respect to the "sons of God" mating with the "daughters of men." Were the "sons of God" fallen angels (Poulet, 1942)? Whoever they were, it is clear that it was essentially a sexual act which precipitated the flood—in this sense, an action similar to the one which led to God to expel Adam and Eve from the Garden of Eden and, in a roughly analogous way, parallel to the sexual excesses which motivated God to destroy Sodom and Gomorrah. In all three "uncreations," it is sexuality or lust which constituted the "original" sin.

This sexuality, and especially its incestuous aspects, is directly related to the idea of creation myths as expressions of male fantasy. Of course, as has been observed (Moore, 1964:1309): "Any myth about the creation of man which postulates a single first family is bound to give rise to some incestuous riddles. Who married the children of the first couple?" After observing the incidence of incest motifs in Genesis, Leach suggests that the logical basis of incest categories "must occur in all mythologies" (1969:15). He contends further that "the original first parents engage in sex relations . . . in a union that is contaminated with the sin of abnormality. The function of Flood stories is to destroy this first Creation and its ambiguities and to start again" (1983:14–15). But what Leach neglects to point out is that *after* the flood or destruction (in Lot's case), sexual activity, often incestuous, takes place.

It is true that unless a creator has exceptional foresight, the creation of one original man or even an original human couple cannot avoid the incest issue. How can the original man or couple possibly populate the earth without incest? The rationale for the incest taboo has never been satisfactorily explained despite a host of theoretical attempts to do so. Although incest may be defined differently in various cultures, it does seem to be universal. In some cultures, first-cousin marriage is not only permitted but is the preferred means of spouse selection. Cross-cousin marriage (when the children of opposite-sex siblings marry) is in fact a form of symbolic sibling incest one step removed (see Moore, 1964). One thing is certain, though: the existence of any kind of incest taboo attests to the fact that there is a desire for incest. No prohibition would come into existence if there were no human tendency to indulge in the proscribed behavior.

From the point of view that the flood is a male myth of creation, it is not at all unreasonable to understand incest as part of male fantasy. In terms of that fantasy, male creators can engage in sexual intercourse with mothers, sisters, and daughters—in addition to destroying previous female procreativity through a urinary flood and re-creating the world and man through anal means (manipulating mud or a more desiccated version: dust). In this light, we can better appreciate the details of a myth from the Toradjas of Central Celebes recounted by Frazer (1918:222) in which a pregnant woman survives the flood. "She in due time gave birth to a son, whom she took for want of another to be her husband. By him she had a son and a daughter, who became the ancestors of the present race of mankind." Here we have mother–son incest followed by brother–sister incest. The father's absence encourages the mother to take her own son as husband (just as the loss of Lot's wife encourages father–daughter incest).

If we consider patriarchal myths, including the flood myth, in the context of male psychology, we find consistent themes. The first is Oedipal insofar as a father figure forbids sexuality, a son figure violates the interdiction, and the son is punished for his sexual transgression. Despite the punishment, some fantasy is still possible: Noah goes on to get drunk and Lot commits incest with his daughters. Although in theory it is the righteous who are spared, in practice it is these same individuals who go on sinning! The second theme involves a male versus female opposition (rather than male versus older male). In this second theme, which has not been adequately recognized by psychoanalytically informed critics, we typically have males attempting to usurp female procreativity. It is male gods who create the earth; it is females who are born from males' bodies (Athena being a perfect "brainchild" of Zeus); it is males who produce (urinary) floods in place of the amniotic ones produced by females. The pain of parturition becomes transformed into a male fantasy of inflicting wholesale destruction on the world.

Finally, if flood myths are truly male myths of creation, we can better understand why male scholars, including theologians, have been so concerned with studying them. Just as a male-dominated society created the myths in the first place, so modern males, increasingly threatened by what they perceive as angry females dissatisfied with ancient myths which give priority to males, cling desperately to these traditional expressions of mythopoeic magic. The flood myth in Genesis belongs to a patriarchal period of human history and as such constitutes a sacred charter for man's privileged position in the world. The vehemence and vigor with which defenders of the faith insist that the flood myth represents historical (and not psychological) reality may well involve much more than a test of Judeo-Christian dogma and belief. It may represent instead or in addition a last bastion of male self-delusion.

REFERENCES

Aycock, D. Alan
1983 "The Fate of Lot's Wife: Structural Mediation in Biblical Mythology." In Edmund Leach and D. Alan Aycock, eds., *Sructuralist Interpretations of Biblical Myth.* Cambridge: Cambridge University Press. Pp. 113–119.

Barnard, Mary
1966 "Space, Time and the Flood Myths." In *The Mythmakers.* Athens: Ohio University Press. Pp. 147–161.

Bassett, Frederick W.
1971 "Noah's Nakedness and the Curse of Canaan: A Case of Incest?" *Vetus Testamentum* 21:232–237.

Berge, François
1951 Les légendes de Déluge." In *Histoire generale des religions,* vol. 5. Paris: Librairie Aristide Quillet. Pp. 59–101.

Bertine, Eleanor
1944 "The Great Flood." *Spring,* 33–53. Reprinted in *Jung's Contribution to Our Time: The Collected Papers of Eleanor Bertine.* New York: G. P. Putnam, 1967. Pp. 182–208.

Bogoras, Waldemar

1910 *Chukchee Mythology.* Memoirs of the American Museum of Natural History, vol. XII, pt. I. New York: G. E. Stechert.

Böklen, Ernst

1903 "Die Sintflutsage: Versuch einer neuen Erklärung." *Archiv für Religionswissenschaft* 6:1–61, 97–150.

Brazda, Monika Karola

1977 *Zur Bedeutung des Apfels in der antiken Kultur.* Bonn: Rheinische Friedrich-Wilhelms-Universität.

Canaan, T.

1929 "Water and 'The Water of Life' in Palestinian Superstition." *Journal of the Palestine Oriental Society* 9:57–69.

Casalis, Matthieu

1976 "The Dry and the Wet: A Semiological Analysis of Creation and Flood Myths." *Semiotica* 17:35–67.

Clines, David

1972 "Noah's Flood: The Theology of the Flood Narrative," *Faith and Thought* 100:128–142.

Cocchiara, Giuseppe

1949 "La 'storia' delle moglie di Lot." In *Genesi di Leggende.* 3rd ed. Palermo: G. P. Palumbo. Pp. 43–61.

Count, Earl W.

1952 "The Earth-Diver and the Rival Twins: A Clue to Time Correlation in North-Eurasiatic and North American Mythology." In Sol Tax, ed., *Indian Tribes of Aboriginal America.* Chicago: University of Chicago Press. Pp. 55–62.

Delcor, M.

1976 "Le mythe de la chute des anges et de l'origine des géants comme explication du mal dans le monde dans l'apocalyptique juive: Histoire des traditions." *Revue de l'histoire des religions* 190:3–53.

Dundes, Alan

1962 "Earth-Diver: Creation of the Mythopoeic Male." *American Anthropologist* 64:1032–1050.

1983 "Couvade in Genesis." *Studies in Aggadah and Jewish Folklore.* Folklore Research Center Studies VII. Jerusalem: Magnes Press. Pp. 35–53.

Eliade, Mircea

1958 *Patterns in Comparative Religion.* New York: Meridian Books.

1961 "Mythologies asiatiques et folklore sud-est européen. I. Le Plongeon cosmogonique." *Revue de l'histoire des religions* 160:157–212.

Follansbee, Eleanor

1939 "The Story of the Flood in the Light of Comparative Semitic Mythology." *Religions* 29:11–21.

Frazer, James George

1918 *Folk-Lore in the Old Testament.* Vol. 1. London: Macmillan.

Freud, Sigmund

1953 *A General Introduction to Psychoanalysis.* Garden City: Permabooks.

1957 *The Future of an Illusion.* Garden City: Doubleday Anchor.

Frymer-Kensky, Tikva

1978 "The Atrahasis Epic and Its Significance for Our Understanding of Genesis 1–9." *Biblical Archaeology Review* 4(4):32–41.

Heisig, Karl

1952–1953 "Woher stammt die Vorstellung vom Paradiesapfel?" *Zeitschrift für die neutestamentliche Wissenschaft* 44:111–118.

Hooke, S. H.

1963 *Middle Eastern Mythology.* Baltimore: Penguin Books.

Hwei, Li

1955 "The Deluge Legend of the Sibling-Mating Type in Aboriginal Formosa and Southeast Asia." *Bulletin of the Ethnological Society of China* 1:171–206. [In Chinese with English summary, pp. 205–206.]

Kardiner, Abram

1939 *The Individual and His Society.* New York: Columbia University Press.

1945 *The Psychological Frontiers of Society.* New York: Columbia University Press.

Kluger, Rivkah S.

1968 "Flood Dreams." In J. B. Wheelwright, ed., *The Reality of the Psyche.* New York: Putnam. Pp. 42–53.

Köngäs, Elli Kaija

1960 "The Earth-Diver (Th. A 812)." *Ethnohistory* 7:151–180.

Leach, Edmund

1969 *Genesis as Myth and Other Essays.* London: Jonathan Cape.

1983 "Anthropological Approaches to the Study of the Bible during the Twentieth Century." In Edmund Leach and D. Alan Aycock, eds., *Structuralist Interpretations of Biblical Myth.* Cambridge: Cambridge University Press. Pp. 7–32.

Leder, Hans-Günter

1961 "Arbor Scientiae: Die Tradition vom paradiesischen Apfelbaum." *Zeitschrift für die neutestamentliche Wissenschaft* 52:156–189.

Levy, Ludwig

1917–1919 "Sexualsymbolik in der Paradiesgeschichte." *Imago* 5:16–30.

Mitra, Sarat Chandra

1929 "On the Cosmological Myth of the Birhors and Its Santali and American Indian Parallels." *Journal of the Anthropological Society of Bombay* 14:468–478.

Moore, Sally Falk

1964 "Descent and Symbolic Filiation." *American Anthropologist* 66:1308–1320.

Poulet, Donat

1942 "The Moral Causes of the Flood." *Catholic Biblical Quarterly* 4:293–303.

Pratt, Jane Abbott

1955 "The Symbolism of the Mountain in Time of Flood." *Spring* 64–82.

Pritchard, James B., ed.

1950 *Ancient Near Eastern Texts Relating to the Old Testament.* Princeton: Princeton University Press.

Rank, Otto

1912 "Die Symbolschichtung im Wecktraum und ihre Wiederkehr im mythischen Denken." *Jahrbuch für psychoanalytische und psychopathologische Forschungen* 4:51–115.

Róheim, Géza

1952 *The Gates of the Dream.* New York: International Universities Press.

Rooth, Anna Birgitta

1962 *The Raven and the Carcass: An Investigation of a Motif in the Deluge Myth in Europe, Asia and North America.* FF Communications No. 186. Helsinki: Academia Scientiarum Fennica.

Schmidt, Wilhelm

1937 "Das Tauchmotif in der Erdschöpfungsmythen Nordamerikas, Asiens und Europas." In *Mélanges de linguistique et philologie.* Paris: C. Klincksieck. Pp. 111–122.

1939 *Primitive Revelation.* London: B. Herder.

Speiser, E. A.

1967 "The Wife-Sister Motif in the Patriarchal Narratives." In *Oriental and Biblical Studies: Collected Writings of E. A. Speiser.* Philadelphia: University of Pennsylvania Press. Pp. 62–82.

Tuzin, Donald F.

1977 "Reflections of Being in Arapesh Water Symbolism." *Ethos* 5:195–223.

Utley, Francis Lee

1941 "The One Hundred and Three Names of Noah's Wife." *Speculum* 16:426–452.

Walk, Leopold

1933 "Die Verbreitung der Tauchmotifs in den Urmeerschöpfungs (und Sintflut-) Sagen." *Mitteilungen der Anthropologischen Gesellschaft in Wien* 63:60–76.

1949 "Das Flut-Geschwisterpaar als Ur- und Stammelternpaar der Menschheit: Ein Beitrag zur Mythengeschichte Süd- und Südostasiens." *Mit-*

teilungen der Österreichischen Gesellschaft für Anthropologie, Ethnologie, und Prähistorie 78/79:60–115.

Walker, Gerald Bromhead
1976 "Sources of the Great Flood and Its Diffusion." In *Diffusion: Five Studies in Early History.* London: Research Publishing Co. Pp. 43–63.

Williams, Mary
1974 "Before and After the Flood." *Journal of Analytical Psychology* 19: 54–70.

An Analysis of the Deluge Myth in Mesoamerica

FERNANDO HORCASITAS

Most studies of the flood myth confine themselves to a specific cultural or geographical area. One area where the flood narrative has been amply documented is Mesoamerica. Mexican anthropologist Fernando Horcasitas undertook a detailed consideration of the range of texts reported there. This excellent review has had little impact upon flood myth scholarship, however, for it was submitted as an M.A. thesis in Mexico City in December 1953 and was never published. Horcasitas skillfully surveys sixty-three versions of the flood myth, taking care to note possible relationships with biblical sources and indigenous American Indian narrative elements.

For other considerations of the flood myth in the New World, see H. de Charencey, "Le Déluge d'après les traditions indiennes de l'Amerique du Nord," Revue americaine, *2nd series, 2 (1865): 88–98, 310–320; Werner Müller,* Die ältesten amerikanischen Sintfluterzählungen *(Bonn, 1930); Johannes Gille,* Der Manabozho-Flutzyklus der Nord-, Nordost-, und Zentralalgonkin: Ein Beitrag zur indianischen Mythologie *(Göttingen, 1939); and Marialice Moura Pessoa, "The Deluge Myth in the Americas,"* Revista do Museu Paulista, *N.S. 4 (1950): 7–48.*

METHOD OF CLASSIFICATION

The texts are classified or separated according to the system traditionally used by ethnologists. Should we encounter stories containing the same elements combined in the same manner, it will be justifiable to consider them the same type and therefore to include them in the same classification. As Franz Boas observes, the more complex the plot or combination of motifs, the more certain we can be that two tales containing them are essentially one story and can be classified as

Reprinted from "An Analysis of the Deluge Myth in Mesoamerica," unpublished M.A. thesis, Centro de Estudios Universitarios of Mexico City College, December 1953, pp. 7–67.

such.[1] In the case of two very simple plots it is more difficult to decide whether the stories are of one origin or whether they developed independently.

Let us compare two complex versions: one is an Aztec flood myth recorded in 1558[2] and the other a modern Totonac story.[3] The outlines follow:

Aztec (1558)	*Totonac* (1953)
1. A man and a woman are warned by Tezcatlipoca that a flood is coming.	1. A man is warned by God that a flood is coming.
2. The man and woman are saved in a hollow tree.	2. The man is saved in a hollow tree.
3. After the flood they are hungry and begin to cook fish.	3. After the flood he is hungry and begins to cook fish.
4. The gods smell the smoke and send Tezcatlipoca down to punish the survivors.	4. God smells the smoke and sends Saint Michael down to punish the survivor.
5. Tezcatlipoca turns the people into dogs by reversing their faces and hind parts.	5. Saint Michael turns the man into a monkey by reversing his face and hind parts.

After a careful comparison of the elements of the two original texts we must conclude that both myths have a common origin or that one is derived from the other. As can be seen, the discrepancies are few and the causes of some of them can be explained easily. (For instance, on the Aztec plateau the survivors are changed into dogs, while in the jungle land of the Totonacs the survivor becomes a monkey. The reasons for the variation are obvious.) The almost identical motifs and their fairly complicated combination justify our considering them as basically the same story.

Let us now consider another case, that of two stories with very simple motifs. One is a sixteenth-century Otomí version,[4] and the other is a modern account originating in Yucatán.[5]

[1] Franz Boas, "Dissemination of Tales Among the Natives of North America," *Race, Language and Culture* (New York: Macmillan, 1949), p. 438.

[2] "Leyenda de los Soles," *Códice Chimalpopoca* (Mexico City: Universidad Nacional Autónoma, 1945), p. 120.

[3] Fernando Horcasitas, unpublished text dictated by a Totonac informant in Papantla, Veracruz.

[4] Fray Gerónomio de Mendieta, *Historia eclesiástica indiana* (Mexico City: Chávez Hayhoe, 1945), vol. III, pp. 199–200.

[5] Alfred M. Tozzer, *A Comparative Study of the Mayas and the Lacandones* (New York: Archaeological Institute of America, 1907), pp. 153–154.

Otomí	*Yucatán*
1. A great flood destroys the world.	1. A great flood destroys the world after the third creation.
2. Seven people are saved in an ark.	2. Three people are saved in an ark.

It is obvious that we have gained nothing by this comparison except to establish the not very helpful fact that flood myths have existed at certain times among both the Otomí and the Maya. The stories may be of independent origin or, on the other hand, they may have a common source. The motifs and the way in which they are combined are far too simple to enable us to reach any definite conclusions. (Incidentally, this does not mean that the original myths themselves were simple; the apparent simplicity is due to the rather sketchy way in which they were recorded.)

Even more difficult than the previous cases is the problem of two versions that resemble one another to a certain degree only—not similar enough to establish their common origin and yet not different enough to exclude that possibility. This case may be exemplified by a comparison of the following myths: one recorded in Quito during the sixteenth century[6] and the other recently among the Tlapanecs of southern Mexico.[7]

Quito	*Tlapanecs*
1. Two brothers are saved after the flood.	1. A man is saved after the flood.
2. The two brothers realize that someone is preparing food for them while they are at work.	2. The man realizes that someone is preparing food for him while he is at work.
3. The elder brother spies to see who the cook is.	3. The man spies to see who the cook is.
4. He sees two macaws enter the house, take off their mantles, and begin to work.	4. He sees a bitch, who takes off her skin and begins to work.
5. The man comes out of his hiding place.	5. The man comes out of his hiding place.
6. The birds fly away.	6.

[6] Cristóbal de Molina, *Ritos y fábulas de los Incas* (Buenos Aires: Editoria Futuro, 1947), pp. 30–33.

[7] H. V. Lemley, "Three Tlapaneco Stories," *Tlalocan* (Mexico City) III (1949): 76–81.

7. Three days later the younger brother hides himself in the house to spy on the birds.	7.
8. He is able to catch one of the macaws.	8.
9.	9. The man burns the bitch's skin, whereupon she becomes a woman.
10. The man and the bird-woman repopulate the earth.	10. The man and the dog-woman repopulate the earth.

As can be seen by this comparison the Mesoamerican and the South American stories are strikingly similar. Six of the ten elements listed are practically identical. Yet I believe that most folklorists would be reluctant to declare that they are the same story, even though many of their characteristics point to a common origin.

In such cases (and many are far more complicated than the comparison between the Quito and Tlapanec flood myths) I believe that anthropologists must restrict themselves to indicating the similarities and differences, and hope that in the future, when more texts are available, they may be able to reach truly definitive conclusions.

GENERAL COMMENTS ON THE FLOOD MYTH

Causes of the Flood

Though Mexican flood myths follow a certain pattern in describing man's destruction or his dramatic escape from the waters, none of them emphasize the causes of the cataclysm. Those which mention any causes at all vary greatly. In fact, only eighteen percent of the myths I have collected offer any explanation whatsoever for the deluge itself. Eighty-two percent of the informants apparently did not consider it an important part of the story. It is also probable that many of the myths which do contain explanations are strongly influenced by European ideas. Indeed, in a few of them such a European background is quite obvious. In a Tarascan story,[8] for instance, it is mentioned that humanity was destroyed because Cain killed Abel.

Let us review the few sources that deal with the motives for the flood:

[8] Pedro Carrasco, four unpublished texts in Spanish from Jarácuaro, Michoacán, 1945.

1. Five sources[9] state that the flood occurred because of sin. None of them sheds more light on the point, however. It is quite probable that these stories were strongly influenced by the biblical account.

2. A Tzeltal version[10] states that mankind was punished because of cannibalism. A man told his wife to cook the "tender one" for lunch. He was referring to beans, but she misunderstood him and killed and cooked their child. They enjoyed eating it and soon the entire world was cooking and eating children. God became angry and sent down the waters to punish mankind.

The preceding story is a common one in Mesoamerica and is generally told as a joke—not necessarily as part of the flood myth. One other version of the deluge[11] also contains this motif, though the incident takes place after the catastrophe, not before. Perhaps this element crept into the Tzeltal story in the same manner that so many completely foreign traits have entered modern Mexican fairy tales. It can be suspected also that the teachings of the early missionaries against cannibalism gave rise to this motif.

3. God annihilated mankind because Cain killed Abel.[12] This information is obviously of biblical origin.

4. The flood came because man forgot God, who had created him. This motif is undoubtedly an ancient one. A highly reliable source, the *Popol Vuh*,[13] and a modern text[14] mention it.

5. The flood came "because the world was very old."[15] This explanation of the deluge seems to fit perfectly into the Mesoamerican concept of world history. It was believed that the story of mankind was not a continuous course from the beginning to the present time, but that humanity had lived in *cycles*, each world succeeding a previous one.

After examining this scant evidence of interest in the causes for the

[9] Arturo Monzón, "Teogonía trique," *Tlalocan* (Mexico City) II (1945): 8; Alfonso Caso, "Cultura mixteca," *México prehispánico* (Mexico City: Emma Hurtado, 1946), p. 522; "Histoyre du Mechique," *Journal de la Société des Américanistes* II (Paris, 1905), chap. 6; J. de la Fuente, *Yalálag: una villa zapoteca serrana* (Mexico City: Museo Nacional de Antropología, 1949), p. 347; Robert M. Zingg, *The Huichols: Primitive Artists* (New York: G. E. Stechert, 1938), p. 539.

[10] Marianna Slocum, unpublished texts from Ococingo, Chiapas, 1947.

[11] Manuel Oropeza Castro, "El diluvio totonaco," *Tlalocan* (Mexico City) II (1947): 275.

[12] Carrasco, op. cit.

[13] *Popol Vuh: las antiguas historias del Quiché*, trans. Adrián Recinos (Mexico City: Fondo de Cultura Económica, 1947), p. 99.

[14] Arabelle Anderson, unpublished text in Chol from the Chol tribe of Chiapas, ca. 1948.

[15] George M. Foster, "Sierra Popoluca Folklore and Beliefs," University of California Publications in American Archaeology and Ethnology 42 (1945): 235.

deluge, it is my conclusion that the average pre-European myth teller was not especially concerned with them. Less than four percent of the sixteenth-century flood chroniclers even mention the causes: the flood came, like an earthquake, a thunderstorm, or sudden death, and there was little that mankind could do about it.

Position of the Flood in Mesoamerican Cosmogony

A striking characteristic of Mesoamerican cosmogony is the story of the creation and destruction of successive worlds. The early colonial chroniclers recount how the gods created the universe and mankind and how, dissatisfied with the results of their labor, they destroyed and re-created them again and again. The cataclysms vary in number. In Mexico we generally find a list of four destructions and one final creation, the beginning of our present world.

On examining the early accounts it immediately becomes obvious that there are discrepancies: most authors describe cataclysms caused by water, tigers, fire, and wind, yet many of them disagree on the consecutive order in which they occurred. It is an extremely complex subject which we need not examine here. Essentially, the only question that we must answer in this study is: after which of the creations did the deluge occur?

Two schools of thought are found among the Spanish and Indian writers of the colonial period: some describe the flood as the first cataclysm and others as the last. Let us examine the accounts which describe the deluge as the *first* destruction. Without a doubt they are writings of great significance and authenticity and are by far the most numerous: the *Codex Vaticanus A,* the "Anales of Cuauhtitlán," the "Histoyre du Mechique," Gómara, Motolinía, and Ixtlilxóchitl. A more recent author, Boturini, in the eighteenth century, studied the subject with a wealth of material no longer available to us and considered the deluge to be first in chronological order.[16] Veytia,[17] who analyzed the order from a completely critical point of view, agreed with Boturini.[18]

Many scholars are tempted to agree with these eight authoritative writings. Yet there are tremendous difficulties to be overcome before one can accept the order they propose. These difficulties may be seen

[16] Lorenzo Boturini Benaduci, *Idea de una nueva historia general de la América Septentrional* (Madrid: Juan de Zúñiga, 1746), p. 47.

[17] Mariano Veytia, *Historia antigua de México* (Mexico City: Editorial Leyenda, 1944), pp. 23–27.

[18] Veytia agrees with Boturini in placing the flood first, though he disagrees on the order of the other creations and destructions.

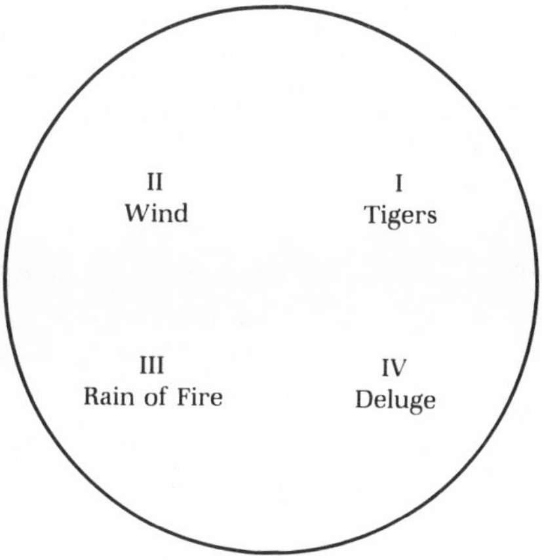

THE AZTEC CALENDAR STONE

in the "Historia de los mexicanos por sus pinturas"[19] and in the "Leyenda de los Soles."[20] The anonymous authors of both these documents state that the deluge was the *last,* not the first, of the four destructions.

The "Historia de los mexicanos por sus pinturas" is a short, badly copied account originating around 1540. Judging by its title and contents, some scholars have considered it a *glosa* or interpretation of indigenous pictographic material and have attributed it to either Olmos or Sahagún.[21]

The second source, the "Leyenda de los Soles," is, in my opinion, probably the only sixteenth-century deluge myth (excepting the *Popol Vuh*) which can be considered, to a certain extent, a truly indigenous text. The certainty that it is an interpretation of native picture writing, its style, the rather lively conversation that takes place between the gods and mankind, its early date (1558)—all mark it as the most authentic and complete flood myth of the sixteenth century.

Another source of conflict is the Aztec Calendar Stone at the National Museum of Mexico City. This monument, authentic beyond any doubt, gives the order of world cataclysms as shown in the accom-

[19] "Historia de los mexicanos por sus pinturas," *Pomar, Zurita, relaciones antiguas* (Mexico City: Chávez Hayhoe, n.d.).

[20] "Leyenda de los Soles," *Códice Chimalpopoca* (Mexico City: Universidad Nacional Autónoma, 1945).

[21] Angel María Garibay K., *Historia de la literatura Náhuatl* (Mexico City: Porrúa, 1953), p. 51.

panying figure. The Aztec Calendar, therefore, agrees with the "Historia de los mexicanos por sus pinturas" and with the "Leyenda de los Soles" in placing the flood *last*. These three sources, then, represent a formidable opposition to the previous eight sources.

The following solutions to this difficult question of correct order can be considered:

1. The "Historia de los mexicanos por sus pinturas," the "Leyenda de los Soles," and the Aztec Calendar are correct; that is, the original pre-Hispanic order placed the deluge as the first of the world cataclysms. Such a simple answer is not acceptable. If it were correct, Motolinía, Ixtlilxóchitl, and the other independent and semi-independent writers and their informants would not have made such obvious blunders.

2. The eight sources mentioned first are correct and the "Historia de los mexicanos por sus pinturas," the "Leyenda de los Soles," and the Aztec Calendar are wrong. This is even less acceptable than the first. The characteristics of the two documents and the calender stone, as indicated, preclude any possibility of their falsity.

3. *None* of the sources is to be considered "correct" since the native informants themselves, shortly after the Conquest, did not agree on the order of the successive worlds and destructions.

We are forced to conclude that the third answer is the acceptable one. It is to be suspected that the order of the cataclysms was never very clear in the minds of the native informants themselves. (It is quite possible that even before the Conquest there already existed discrepancies.) The indigenous informants of the missionaries may have come from different parts of the Aztec Empire; the missionaries probably recorded them in different places. The story was probably never consistent in pre-European days, much less by the time the sixteenth-century missionaries wrote their chronicles.

DIVISIONS OF THE FLOOD MYTH

Introduction

After studying the sixty-three versions gathered for this essay, it seems advisable to group them into five separate divisions, which will be called A, B, C, D, and E. The process to be followed for each of the divisions or types will consist of:

1. A brief résumé of the plot of the myth
2. Résumés of all the versions that seem to fall within the division
3. A discussion of the problems connected with each division or type

Division A

The world was destroyed by water. A number of human beings were able to escape. Fourteen of the sixty-three versions fall into this category. The following are outlines of the fourteen myths.

1. *Nahua I* (*Codex Vaticanus A*). The human race had been propagated by the two primogenitors, but the world was destroyed by a great flood which occurred at the end of the first age. One man and one woman escaped in an *ahuehuetl* (cypress) tree and later repopulated the earth.[22]

2. *Nahua II* (*Codex Vaticanus A*). When the great deluge came, a number of persons managed to hide in a cave. Later they emerged from their refuge and repopulated the earth.[23]

3. *Nahua III* (Ixtlilxóchitl—*Primera relación*). The first world ended in a great flood which destroyed mankind through rainstorms and lightning. Even the highest mountains were submerged fifteen cubits beneath the waters. A few human beings were able to escape in an ark. They repopulated the world.[24]

4. *Nahua IV* (Clavijero). The deluge destroyed the mass of mankind; however, a man named Cóxcox (or Teocipactli) and a woman called Xochiquétzal were saved in a canoe. When the waters subsided they found themselves on a mountain called Colhuacan. They had many children, all of them born dumb. Later a dove taught them to speak.[25]

5. *Maya I* (Landa). The world was destroyed by a flood. The four Bacab gods were able to escape. They now hold up the four corners of the sky to prevent its falling upon the earth.[26]

6. *Maya II* (*Chilam Balam de Chumayel*). After man was created the sky fell upon the earth and the waters descended in its wake. The four Bacabs then took their places (at the four corners of the earth).[27]

7. *Maya III* (Tozzer). After two floods had destroyed humanity, a third and final one occurred. Only three people were able to escape in a canoe.[28]

[22] *Il Manoscritto Messicano Vaticano 3738 detto il Códice Ríos* (Rome: Stabilimento Danesi, 1900), p. 24.

[23] Ibid.

[24] Fernando de Alva Ixtlilxóchitl, *Obras históricas* (Mexico City: Secretaría de Fomento, 1891–1892), vol. I, p. 17.

[25] Francisco J. Clavijero, *Historia antigua de México* (Mexico City: Editorial Delfín, 1944), vol. I, p. 273.

[26] Fray Diego de Landa, *Relación de las cosas de Yucatán* (Mexico City: Robredo, 1938), p. 144.

[27] *Chilam Balam de Chumayel* (Mexico City: Universidad Nacional Autónoma, 1941), p. 63.

[28] Tozzer, *A Comparative Study of the Mayas and the Lacandones*, p. 154.

8. *Otomí* (Mendieta). The earth and all living things were once destroyed by a flood. Seven persons were able to escape in an ark.[29]

9. *Zapotec I* (*Relación de Ocelotepeque*). There was once a great deluge. A number of persons were able to escape in a boat. They found themselves on top of a hill when the waters subsided. A great Zapotec chieftain of Ocelotepeque, Petela (Dog), was descended from the survivors of the deluge.[30]

10. *Quiché I* (Torquemada). The people of Guatemala adored the Great Father and the Great Mother. A deluge flooded their world. A number of persons were able to survive and repopulate the world.[31]

11. *Quiché II* (Mendieta). A great deluge flooded the world. The Achies (?) of Guatemala had records of it in their codices.[32]

12. *Trique* (Monzón). Since the ways of the world were very wicked, Nexquiriac sent down a great flood to punish mankind. He called one good man and instructed him to make a large box to preserve many animals and the seeds of certain plants. The man shut himself up in the box. When the flood was almost over, Nexquiriac warned the man not to come out of the box but to bury himself, box and all, until the face of the earth had been burned. Once this was done, the man emerged and repopulated the earth.[33]

13. *Mixtec* (Caso). When the earth was well populated, mankind committed a magical fault which was punished by the great deluge. Only a few men were saved. The Mixtec people descended from the survivors.[34]

14. *Tarascan I* (Herrera). When the great flood was coming a priest named Tespi made an ark, took aboard his wife and children together with different animals and seeds, and in this way was able to survive.[35]

Though I have grouped the preceding versions under one heading, their basic unity is disputable. They agree only in the bare essentials—that there was a deluge and that a few persons were saved. The sparsely worded, vague manner in which they were recorded prevents us from arriving at any conclusive judgments.

[29] Mendieta, *Historia eclesiástica indiana,* vol. III, pp. 199–200.

[30] Francisco del Paso y Troncoso, ed., *Papeles de Nueva España* (Madrid: Ribadeneyra, 1905), vol. IV, p. 139.

[31] Fray Juan de Torquemada, *Monarquía indiana* (Mexico City: Chávez Hayhoe, 1943), vol. II, p. 53.

[32] Mendieta, *Historia eclesiástica indiana,* vol. III, pp. 199–200.

[33] Monzón, "Teogonía trique," vol. II, p. 8.

[34] Caso, "Cultura mixteca," p. 522.

[35] Antonio de Herrera, *Décadas,* Década tercera, quoted in Alfredo Chavero, "La piedra del sol: segundo estudio," *Anales del Museo Nacional de México* I (1877): 366–367.

As twelve of these fourteen versions date back several hundred years, it is now impossible to amplify them: we cannot go to the living descendants of the groups originating these myths in order to verify them or to obtain more information. Even if we recorded extensive indigenous texts, we would have no certainty that the original story was being told.

It is quite possible that a number of these versions, if they had been recorded in a more ample manner, would reveal themselves to be Type C—that is, the story of the survivors who were converted into animals for having lighted a fire.

Division B

When the world was destroyed by water, no one managed to escape. All mankind was drowned. The following twelve versions fall into this division.

1. *Nahua V* ("Anales de Cuauhtitlán"). A great flood ended the first world. All human beings became fish.[36]

2. *Nahua VI* ("Histoyre du Mechique"). Because of sins committed against the gods, a great flood annihilated all men except a few, who became fish.[37]

3. *Nahua VII* (Motolinía). At the end of the first age, under the sign *nahui atl*, a great flood destroyed mankind.[38]

4. *Nahua VIII* ("Historia de los mexicanos por sus pinturas"). On the last year of the age in which Chalchiuhtlicue was sun, the sky fell upon the earth. The waters drowned all the inhabitants, who thereupon became fish.[39]

5. *Nahua IX* (Mendieta). A great flood occurred. All men perished.[40]

6. *Nahua X* (Muñoz Camargo). When the giants inhabited the earth, the earth was turned upside down and a great deluge destroyed humanity.[41]

7. *Nahua XI* (Gómara). At the end of the first sun a great deluge destroyed humanity.[42]

[36] "Anales de Cuauhtitlán," *Códice Chimalpopoca* (Mexico City: Universidad Nacional Autónoma, 1945), p. 5.

[37] "Histoyre du Mechique," vol. II, chap. 6.

[38] Motolinía, *Memoriales* (Mexico City: García Pimentel, 1903), pp. 346–347.

[39] "Historia de los mexicanos por sus pinturas," p. 214.

[40] Mendieta, *Historia eclesiástica indiana*, vol. I, p. 84.

[41] Diego Muñoz Camargo, *Historia de Tlaxcala* (Mexico City: Ateneo Nacional de Ciencias y Artes, 1948), p. 165.

[42] Francisco López de Gómara, *Conquista de Méjico*, vol. 22 of *Biblioteca de autores españoles* (Madrid: Ribadeneyra, 1852), p. 431.

8. *Nahua XII* (Hernández). At the end of the first sun all human beings were drowned.[43]

9. *Nahua XIII* (Ixtlilxóchitl—*Historia chichimeca*). At the end of Atonatiuh, the first sun, a great flood destroyed humanity and all living beings.[44]

10. *Nahua XIV* (Herrera). The end of the world of the giants was brought about by a great deluge. The earth was turned upside down.[45]

11. *Maya IV* (Redfield). The dwarfs, inhabitants of the earth, heard that there was to be a terrible storm. So they put some stones in a pond and sat on them. But the waters came and destroyed the dwarfs. Then Jesucristo sent down four angels to see what was happening upon the earth. They took off their clothes and began to bathe, whereupon they became doves. Some other angels were sent down but they began to eat the dead and were turned into buzzards.[46]

12. *Maya V* (Villa Rojas). The first inhabitants of the earth were the industrious Puzob, a dwarf people. They were careless in their observation of custom; therefore God sent down a flood and they all perished.[47]

My observations regarding the inconclusiveness inherent in Type A are also applicable to Type B. The twelve versions of the latter are rudimentary in the extreme.

The concept of a world populated by giants who perished in the flood is a fairly common one and is mentioned by several chroniclers of the colonial period. Some of the later versions may be influenced by European ideas. Probably owing to biblical references they had read, many of the Spaniards showed a lively interest in investigating the large fossil bones which were often found in New Spain during the sixteenth century and which were said to have belonged to giants. This interest may have been the cause of some later versions of tales about giants spreading among the native population.

Division C

When the world was destroyed by water, a number of human beings managed to escape, but they lighted a fire without divine permission

[43] Francisco Hernández, *Antigüedades de la Nueva España* (Mexico City: Robredo, 1946), p. 129.

[44] Alva Ixtlilxóchitl, *Obras históricas*, vol. II, p. 22.

[45] Chavero quoting Herrera, "La piedra del sol: segundo estudio," p. 366.

[46] Margaret Park Redfield, *The Folk Literature of a Yucatecan Town*, vol. 13 of *Contributions to American Archaeology* (Washington, D.C.: Carnegie Institution, 1937), p. 74.

[47] Alfonso Villa Rojas, *The Mayas of East Central Quintana Roo* (Washington, D.C.: Carnegie Institution, 1945), p. 153.

and were turned into animals. No fewer than twenty versions of Type C are available for analysis. The résumés follow.

1. *Nahua XI* ("Leyenda de los Soles"). At the end of the fourth age, under the sun called *nahui atl,* Tezcatlipoca called a man and a woman to him and told them to work no more since a great deluge was coming. He instructed them to hollow out a large *ahuehuetl* tree and to get into it, taking with them two ears of corn. Each was to eat one ear, no more. They entered the improvised bark. Then the sky collapsed upon the earth and the whole world was destroyed, but the man and woman were saved. When the waters abated they noticed that the tree was no longer moving. They emerged and lighted a fire to cook fish (which had been the previous inhabitants of the world). But the gods Citlallinicue and Citlallatónac looked toward the earth and exclaimed, "Gods! Who has lighted a fire? Who has smoked the sky?" Tezcatlipoca appeared, reproached the man and woman, and turned them into dogs by reversing their faces and hind parts.[48]

2. *Tarascan II* (Carrasco). When the great flood began, God built a house. Everyone tried to crowd into it and those who succeeded were saved. The house floated upon the waters for twenty days. It struck the sky three times. When the waters subsided, some of the survivors were very hungry. Even though God had told them not to eat anything they began to cook tortillas inside the house. God sent down an angel who said to them, "My father told me to see that no fire be lighted yet." But the smoke was going up into the sky and God was seeing it. He sent the angel down again with the same message. The people answered that they were very hungry. "Do as you wish," said the angel, "but my father told me to tell you not to do it." The angel went up again and God said to him, "If they don't understand you this time, let Me know!" The angel went up again to tell God that the people did not understand. God said, "Very well, go give them all a good kick!" And all this time the smoke was going up into the sky. All these people became dogs and buzzards. They cleaned up the earth.[49]

3. *Tarascan III* (Carrasco). When the world was destroyed by water, a boy was very hungry. He got out of the canoe to heat a *gorda.* The Eternal Father said, "It is not time to light the fire yet. You, Saint Bartholomew, go down to the world and see who is making a fire." Saint Bartholomew came down and spoke to the boy: "Why are you making smoke? Don't you see that no orders have been given yet to build a fire?" The boy answered, "But I was very hungry and that is why I built

[48] "Leyenda de los Soles," pp. 119–120.

[49] Pedro Carrasco, unpublished texts from Jarácuaro, Michoacán, 1945.

the fire." Saint Bartholomew went up into Heaven again and told the Eternal Father. The Eternal Father sent him down again, saying, "If he doesn't understand, kick him so he won't be so ignorant." So Saint Bartholomew came down once more and kicked the boy. His voice changed and he became a dog.[50]

4. *Tarascan IV* (Carrasco). The angel came down a third time. He kicked the man and said, "This is so that you may understand; you haven't obeyed me." And the man began to whine like a dog and became a dog. That is why dogs exist.[51]

5. *Tarascan V* (Carrasco). While the *k'uanari* (idolatrous giants) inhabited the world, Cain killed Abel and the Lord sent down a message that an ark was to be built since a flood was to destroy humanity. A pair of every kind of animal was put into the ark. The survivors were changed into dogs.[52]

6. *Tarascan VI* (Carrasco). God ordered a man to make a large house and to put animals and food in it. When the man had finished, it began to rain. It rained six months. The house floated on the waters and all those who had helped build it were saved in it. When the world was beginning to dry, the man sent forth a raven to see if the earth was solid, but the raven did not return. It remained behind to eat dead bodies. Then the man sent forth a dove, which came back to report that the raven was eating the dead. The raven was condemned to eat corpses thereafter. God had ordered that no fire be kindled, but one man disobeyed and was turned into a dog.[53]

7. *Tarascan VII* (Carrasco). When the great flood was over, God saw smoke. He sent down an angel, who found a survivor. God, who was very angry, turned him into a Huaxtecan monkey.[54]

8. *Popoluca I* (Foster). Christ ordered a man to build an ark and to take along in it pairs of all useful animals. Then the world was flooded. When the waters subsided, the survivors began to cook fish, into which all the other inhabitants of the world had been converted. Christ sent down the buzzard to see what was happening, but the buzzard remained to get his share of fish. Then Christ send down the hawk and the hummingbird. Christ himself finally came down and turned the people upside down, whereupon they became monkeys.

[50] Ibid.

[51] Ibid.

[52] Ibid.

[53] Pedro Carrasco, unpublished text from Cocucho, Michoacán, 1945.

[54] Pedro Carrasco, unpublished text from Ocumicho, Michoacán, 1945.

The buzzard was condemned to eat only dead animals thereafter. Then Christ repopulated the world by turning the dead fish back into human beings.[55]

9. *Popoluca II* (Foster). A man was surprised to find that all the trees he cut down were growing again overnight. Jesucristo appeared and warned him of the coming of the flood. The man made an ark, taking with him pairs of each kind of animal. When the waters subsided the man and his family began to eat fish, which were scattered all over the ground. Jesucristo smelled the smoke and sent down a vulture to see where the fire was. The vulture remained behind to eat dead animals. Then Jesucristo sent the hummingbird to see, and the hummingbird returned to Heaven with the news. Then Jesucristo came down and turned the people into monkeys by reversing their faces and hind parts. He condemned the vulture to eat henceforth only of dead animals.[56]

10. *Popoluca III* (Lehmann). God told a man to stop working since a flood was to destroy the world. The man was instructed to build a canoe for himself and his family. The deluge came, but the man and his family were saved. After the waters subsided the man began to cook the bodies of dead animals. Saint Peter smelled the smoke and came down to see what was happening. He turned the man into a buzzard and his children into monkeys.[57]

11. *Popoluca IV* (Lehmann). God, *El Viejito*, asked where fire was burning and upon finding that the first man, against his orders, had built a fire to cook fish, transformed him into a monkey by reversing his face and hind parts.[58]

12. *Totonac I* (Horcasitas). A man was warned by God that the deluge was coming. He hollowed out a tree and was saved in it. After the deluge the man was very hungry and he built a fire. God smelled the smoke and told the buzzard to go down to see what was happening. The buzzard stayed to eat dead animals, and God condemned him to eat only rotten flesh from that day on. Then God told Saint Michael the Archangel to go down. Saint Michael the Archangel reversed the man's face and hind parts and turned him into a monkey.[59]

[55] George M. Foster, "Sierra Popoluca Folklore and Beliefs," p. 239.

[56] Ibid., pp. 235–238.

[57] W. Lehmann, "Ergebnisse einer mit Unterstützung der Notgemeinschaft der Deutschen Wissenschaft in den Jahren 1925/1926 ausgeführten Forschungsreise nach Mexico und Guatemala," *Anthropos* 23 (1928): 749–791, quoted in Foster, "Sierra Popoluca Folklore and Beliefs," p. 238.

[58] Ibid.

[59] Fernando Horcasitas, unpublished texts from Papantla, Veracruz, 1953.

13. *Tepehua* (Gessain). After clearing his fields a man was surprised to find that the vegetation grew again overnight. He spied and found that a monkey was responsible for this harm. The monkey told him that God did not want him to work any more, since a great flood was coming. Following the instructions of the monkey the man built a coffinlike craft and got into it. When the deluge began, the monkey sat on top of the coffin. When the waters subsided the man climbed out, picked up some fish he found on the ground, and built a small fire to cook them. But out of the sky appeared the Almighty, who, irritated with the man for having built the fire, turned him into a monkey.[60]

14. *Tzeltal I* (Slocum). One day, through a misunderstanding, a wife killed and cooked her child. She and her husband ate it and enjoyed it very much. Soon everyone was killing and cooking children. God became very angry and sent down the deluge. One intelligent man was saved in a canoe. After the waters subsided he lighted a fire. God smelled the smoke. He sent down the buzzard, the turkey buzzard, and a churn-owl to see what was happening upon the earth, but they all remained behind to eat dead bodies. God condemned them to eat only dead bodies thereafter. Then God sent down the hawk, which fulfilled his mission. The man was turned into a monkey.[61]

15. *Tzeltal II* (Slocum). The Padre Santo warned two brothers that the flood was coming. Together with many animals they were able to survive in an ark. When the waters were beginning to subside, the younger brother fell out of the ark and landed on a tree, whereupon he became a monkey. The elder brother was saved.[62]

16. *Chol I* (Anderson). God was tired of seeing men. He decided to kill them and exchange them for new men. Therefore God created darkness to destroy them. One man sealed his house well with thick boards. At night he went up onto the roof of the house. When God came down to see who had died, he found this man still alive. God reversed his face and hind parts and turned him into a monkey.[63]

17. *Chol II* (Beekman). When the deluge came a few people climbed to the top of the highest trees and were saved. But Ahau became angry with them and, reversing their faces and their hind parts, turned them into monkeys.[64]

[60] Robert Gessain, unpublished texts from the Tepehuas, 1953.

[61] Marianna Slocum, unpublished texts in Tzeltal and Spanish from Ococingo, Chiapas, ca. 1947.

[62] Ibid.

[63] Arabelle Anderson, unpublished text from the Chol of Chiapas, ca. 1949.

[64] John Beekman, unpublished text from the Chol of Yajalón, Chiapas, ca. 1949.

18. *Quiché III* (*Popol Vuh*). The Heart of Heaven desired to populate the world with men who would adore him. He created animals, men of clay, and men of wood, who all successively refused to worship him in the correct way. To destroy the wooden men the Heart of Heaven sent down a flood. During the flood four animals were sent down to fight against man. Man was also attacked by the animals of the earth, and by the implements he had been using. At the end of the deluge all the wooden men were turned into monkeys.[65]

19. *Quiché IV* (Tax). When the deluge occurred some men tried to save themselves by making boxes and going under the ground in them. But God, not approving of this, turned the people into bees.[66]

20. *Zapotec II* (de la Fuente). When the earth was dark and cold, the only inhabitants were the giants. God was angry with them because of their idolatry. A number of giants, feeling that the deluge was coming, carved great slabs of rock to make houses for themselves under the earth. Some escaped destruction in this way and are still to be found hidden in certain caverns under the ground. Other giants hid themselves in the forests and became monkeys.[67]

On examining the preceding versions (which I have classified as Type C) one immediately becomes aware of the abundance and quality of the material. No fewer than twenty versions of the same story have been recorded and outlined for this study. Furthermore, in contrast to the texts assembled under Types A and B, this group of twenty contains at least thirteen texts which are dependable and full of detail.[68] (Nine of the thirteen versions, in their turn, may be considered almost as reliable as if they had come directly from the indigenous informants.)

Another advantage is the fact that, aside from the modern texts, we have an excellent sixteenth-century version: the "Leyenda de los Soles." Of all the ancient versions of the deluge the "Leyenda de los Soles" and the *Popol Vuh* are the only truly detailed texts I have encountered. We are therefore working with a wealth of material, both ancient and modern.

Having examined the motifs and their combination in the ancient

[65] *Popol Vuh: las antiguas historias del Quiché,* pp. 98–103.

[66] Sol Tax, "Folktales in Chichicastenango: An Unsolved Puzzle," *Journal of American Folklore* 62 (1949).

[67] J. de la Fuente, *Yalálag: una villa zapoteca serrana* (Mexico City: Museo Nacional de Antropología, 1949), p. 237.

[68] Tarascan I, Tarascan III, Tarascan VI, Popoluca I, Popoluca II, Popoluca III, Totonac I, Tepehua, Tzeltal I, Tzeltal II, Chol I, Quiché III, and Zapotec II.

and more recent texts, I concluded that they are basically the same story. The two Quiché and the Zapotec versions are perhaps the only doubtful cases: they are similar enough to warrant their classification under Type C but different enough to cause doubt.

The story itself is unquestionably indigenous and pre-European. This is an inevitable conclusion as we consider the following points:

1. The "Leyenda de los Soles" is a native source. All of its characteristics indicate this fact, and no serious scholar has doubted the authenticity of the document.

2. The *Popol Vuh,* which contains a version similar to that of the "Leyenda de los Soles," is also of unquestionable pre-European origin (if not in all its parts, at least in the section containing the flood myth).

3. The version is not to be found in European or African folklore.

The plot, as given in the "Leyenda de los Soles" and supported by the modern versions, may be outlined as follows: A human couple is told by a supernatural being that a great flood is coming. They are saved in a wooden craft. After the flood is over they emerge and light a fire to cook food. The deity smells the smoke and becomes angry. He sends down a messenger, who punishes them and turns them into animals.

Having described the qualities of the source material and the story itself we can now proceed to the following observations.

1. The idea of wrongdoing seems to be prominent in the myth. In the "Leyenda de los Soles" it appears that the wrongdoing consists in disobedience. The survivors are warned not to eat more than one ear of corn; because they disobey and begin to cook fish they are punished. It is necessary to consider that the fish had once been human beings—the inhabitants of the previous world.

This last concept introduces an idea akin to cannibalism, prominent in several of the versions. Cannibalism is the cause of the flood in one version,[69] and in another it occurs immediately after the deluge.[70] In many of the stories the buzzard is punished for having eaten dead bodies.[71] In yet another myth it is angels who eat human flesh and are punished for it.[72] In any event, whether it is basically pre-Hispanic or not, the idea of cannibalism is one that must be taken seriously into consideration in discussing the flood myth in Mesoamerica.

[69] Tzeltal I.

[70] Norman McQuown, Totonac text from Coatepec, Puebla, 1940 (mimeographed); Oropeza Castro, "El diluvio totonaco," vol. II, pp. 269–275.

[71] Popoluca I, Popoluca II, Totonac I, Tzeltal I, Zapotec III, Zapotec IV, and Zapotec V.

[72] Maya V.

Another possible cause for the punishment of the survivors for wrongdoing is the fact that they offended the deity by smoking the sky. The words of the "Leyenda de los Soles" seem to suggest this: "The gods Citlallinicue and Citlallatónac looked down and said, 'Gods! Who is burning something? Who is smoking the sky?'"[73] Later the text reads: "Therefore, the heavens were smoked in the year Two Reed."[74]

Another possibility exists: perhaps mankind's only sin was survival. Some of the versions imply that mankind was doomed to perish, that no one was to be allowed to escape. One even receives the impression that the supernatural being who warned the chosen ones of the coming of the waters was acting against the wishes of the supreme deity, or at least that it was through his special intervention that they were saved. In any case, the gods are not pleased to see man survive:

> When the deluge ended, God saw smoke. He sent down an angel, who saw that there was a survivor who had not perished in the flood. God was angry and turned him into a Huaxtecan monkey.[75]

Another text reads:

> It is said that God sent his servant down from Heaven. "Go ask him how he managed to survive," God said. The servant came down. "How were you saved, sir?" he said to the man. "I was saved in a boat, boss," the man answered. [God said to the man in Heaven], "Well, you aren't going to stay like you are now; you are going to be changed." "All right, boss; whatever you say," he answered. God said, "I am going to give you a tail." So he gave him a tail and he became hairy. The man asked, "Where am I going to live, boss?" "You are going to live in the forests," God answered. That is how the monkey went to live in the forests.[76]

In another text we read:

> When the god came down to see who had died, he arrived to find a man still alive. . . . He broke off his neck. When he broke off his neck, he put his head on at the end of his spine. . . . Thus the man was changed into a white stomach monkey.[77]

More cases could be cited of God's displeasure at the survival of mankind, but the texts cited here illustrate the idea clearly enough.

[73] "Leyenda de los Soles," p. 120.

[74] Ibid.

[75] Tarascan VII.

[76] Tzeltal I.

[77] Chol I.

The fact that the deity had never intended man to survive fits in well with the Mesoamerican pattern of world history: humanity was destroyed again and again and no one was allowed to escape. In view of these observations it is necessary to reconsider the motif of the smoking of the sky. Perhaps the important aspect of this element is not the fact that the sky was smoked (dirtied), but that the smoke was an innocent signal of man's survival. Viewed in this light, the fire was a great blunder, since it revealed to the unsuspecting gods that their plans had been frustrated.

2. Another interesting motif of the Type C versions is the personality of the messenger who warns man not to light a fire and who eventually punishes him. In the Aztec text, the "Leyenda de los Soles," he is called Titlacahuan (Tezcatlipoca). The name in itself, in my opinion, is not a basic part of the myth: "Tezcatlipoca" can simply be considered the name given to the messenger by the Aztecs. In previous times and in other cultures the name was probably totally different.

Though the last statement cannot be verified, the substitution of names for the same personage may be illustrated perfectly by examining the post-Conquest versions. The myth is basically the same, but the name of the messenger varies. In one story, for instance, he is called Saint Michael the Archangel, in another Saint Peter, in yet another Saint Bartholomew. Others speak of Jesucristo, or of a simple angel, or of an unnamed "servant of God." Others place a buzzard in the role of the messenger. But the personality remains unchanged: he is always the intermediary between God and the survivors. Just as the story is now told in several languages in modern Mexico (each with its own name for the messenger), so it may have been told in multicultural and multilingual Mesoamerica in pre-European times.

3. A map of the distribution of Type C according to linguistic groups may be seen in the accompanying figure. Following Jiménez Moreno's classification of languages we become aware of the fact that the version is known to at least five totally different linguistic groups: Taño Aztecan, Zapotecan, Totonac, Zoque-Mayan, and Tarascan.

4. It is interesting to speculate on the period in which the story spread over southern Mexico. Was the myth the common heritage of many linguistic groups since very ancient times? Did its diffusion take place during the Aztec expansion? Or did it occur after the Spanish Conquest? At present it is impossible to give categorical answers to these questions. The diffusion of folktales in Mexico has been imperfectly studied and there is a lack of colonial material. It is possible that the story spread considerably after the Conquest. Many of the versions are too similar to warrant many hundreds of years of independent exis-

TYPE C IN MESOAMERICA

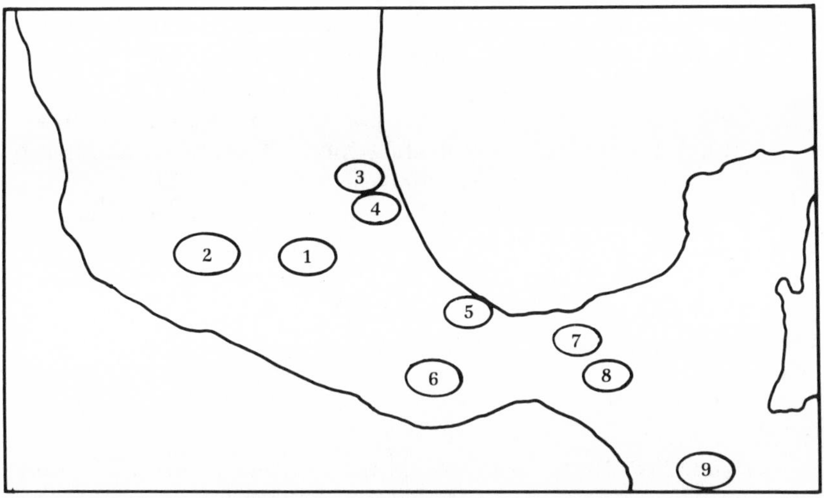

1. Nahuatl
2. Tarascan
3. Tepehua
4. Totonac
5. Popoluca
6. Zapotec
7. Chol
8. Tzeltal
9. Quiché

tence. Many Indian cultures which may have been totally isolated before the Conquest found themselves suddenly connected by religious and political ties to alien institutions. Communications improved. Part of the diffusion of the story may have taken place as late as the nineteenth century. At present we can do little more than to point out these possibilities.

Division D

When the world was destroyed by water one man and a bitch were able to escape. The man discovered that the bitch was cooking food for him, whereupon he spied on her. He burned her skin and she turned into a woman. They repopulated the world. The following twelve versions may be termed "the story of the Dog-Wife."

1. *Huichol I* (Lumholtz). A man felling trees found that the trees he had cut down grew again overnight. He spied and found that it was the grandmother Nakawé who was doing this mischief. She told him that he was working in vain, since a great deluge was soon to destroy the world. She also instructed him to make a box out of a tree and to put in it grains of corn, beans, a fire, five squash stems to feed the fire,

and a black bitch. For five years the box floated on the waters. After the waters subsided the box settled upon a hill. The man went back to work as before the flood. Every day, when he came back to the cave in which he lived, he found that someone had prepared tortillas for him. He spied and discovered that it was the bitch. She had taken off her skin, had become a woman, and was grinding corn for him. He threw her skin into the fire, whereupon she whined. Then he bathed her in *ni̮xtamal* water. They repopulated the earth.[78]

2. *Huichol II* (Preuss). Timušáve, the Sower of Corn, was surprised to find that all the trees he cut down were rising up again. He found that Tahutsi Nakawé was doing this. She told him not to work, as a great flood was coming. He hollowed out a tree in the form of a hut and put a cover on it. He took along all kinds of corn, beans, and animals with him. He also took fire and a bitch. When the flood was over, the children of Timušáve and the bitch were the founders of the new mankind.[79]

3. *Huichol III* (Zingg). Kauymáli went out to clear his fields every day and found that the bushes had grown back to where they had been before he had started his task. He spied and found that it was the old woman Nakawé who was making the bushes rise. She told him that a great deluge was coming. Under her instructions he made a canoe and put in it fire, a bitch, and the seeds of corn and other useful plants. During the deluge the boat floated upon the waters. Finally it came down to rest upon a mountain top. After Kauymáli came out of the boat, he built a new house. Every day, on returning home from his daily work, he found that someone had cooked tortillas for him. Nakawé told him to return early from his work in order to spy out the mysterious housekeeper. He found the bitch, absorbed in washing at the river. He took her skin and burned it. The bitch howled, but he bathed her in *ni̮xtamal* water and she changed into a woman. Thereafter they lived as man and wife.[80]

4. *Huichol IV* (McIntosh). A man, on going to clear the fields, was surprised to find that all the trees he had cut the night before had risen again. He decided to watch and discovered that it was an old woman who was responsible for this mischief. The woman told him that a great flood was coming. She advised him to make a canoe and to

[78] Carl Lumholtz, *El Mé̮xico desconocido* (Mexico City: Publicaciones Herrerías, 1945), vol. II, pp. 189–191.

[79] K. Th. Preuss, "Au sujet du caractére des mythes et des chants huichols que j'ai recueillis," *Revista del Instituto de Etnología* (Tucumán: Universidad Nacional de Tucumán, 1932), vol. II, pp. 452–453.

[80] Zingg, *The Huichols: Primitive Artists*, p. 539.

take along with him a bitch and pumpkin seeds. When the waters started to flood the earth, he rode on top of the canoe. When the waters subsided, he went back to work. On returning home every day, he saw that someone had prepared food for him. He spied and found that the bitch was the mysterious housekeeper. While the dog-woman went down to fetch water, he took her skin and burned it. The woman whined like a dog until he bathed her in *nixtamal* water. The couple thereafter lived together and had many children.[81]

5. *Tepecano* (Mason). A man who went to cut down trees every morning was surprised to find that the same had grown again overnight. He spied and found that it was an old man who had been causing this state of affairs. The old man told him not to work anymore since a great flood was coming. He was also instructed to build an ark and to fill it with pairs of each existing animal, some corn, and some water. The deluge began. For forty days the ark wandered over the waters which covered the face of the earth. When the waters subsided, the man abandoned the ark and went back to work. He began to notice that someone had prepared food for him when he returned from work. He spied and discovered that it was his black bitch who was the mysterious housekeeper. He burned her skin and then proceeded to soothe her by sprinkling *nixtamal* water on her. Thence they lived together and had twenty-four children. One day the man took twelve of them to visit God, who gave them clothes. The other twelve were left at home and remained naked. This explains why there are rich and poor in the world.[82]

6. *Totonac II* (Barlow). A deluge destroyed mankind. The children jumped up to where the star is and became flowers. A man was sent a large dog. The man used to go out every day to clear the fields. When he came home, he found that someone had prepared food for him. He determined to learn the identity of the mysterious cook.[83]

7. *Totonac III* (McQuown/Oropeza). Before the deluge occurred a man was instructed by God to make an ark. When the waters subsided, the man sent forth a dove to see if the earth was dry. The dove came back. Later, he sent the dove forth again and it returned with its feet covered with mud. The man emerged from the ark. He happened upon an old house and decided to make it his home. The ants brought him corn. Every day he used to return to his home to find that some-

[81] John McIntosh, "Cosmogonía Huichol," *Tlalocan* (Mexico City) II (1945): 14–21.

[82] J. Alden Mason, "Folktales of the Tepecanos," *Journal of American Folklore* 27: 164–165.

[83] Robert H. Barlow, fragment of an unpublished text in the Barlow Archive, Mexico City College, ca. 1948.

one had prepared food for him. He began to watch his dog. He found that it was the dog herself who was preparing food for him. One day he spied and found her, skinless, grinding corn. He threw her skin into the fire, whereupon she began to weep. The couple then lived together and had a pretty baby. One day the man told his wife to make some tamales out of the "tender one." The woman, misunderstanding him, killed and cooked their child. When the man realized what had happened he scolded his wife and ate the tamales anyway.[84]

8. *Totonac IV* (Horcasitas). When the deluge was over, no one was saved except a man and a bitch. Every day, when the man came home from work, he found that someone had prepared beans and tortillas for him. One day he hid himself and discovered that the dog took off her skin in a *temazcal* and then prepared food for him. He followed her and caught her. The bitch said, "God wants it this way. Now we will be married and have children." They repopulated the world.[85]

9. *Tlapanec I* (Lemley). A buzzard appeared to a man working in the fields. The bird told him not to work anymore, and then made all the trees that had been cut down rise again. Then the buzzard advised the man to make a box and to enter it, taking along a dog and a chicken. The flood came but the man was saved. When the waters subsided, the chicken turned into a buzzard and the dog went to live with the man. The man noticed that someone was preparing tortillas for him while he was away at work. One day he remained home and saw the bitch removing her skin and proceeding to grind corn. He thereupon burned her skin. The dog complained, but she remained a woman and they repopulated the earth.[86]

10. *Tlapanec II* (Lemley). A man went to work in his fields every day. He realized that during the night someone was raising the trees he had cut down. A man appeared and told him not to work anymore, since a great flood was coming. He added that the man should make a box and get into it, taking with him a black chicken and a black dog. The deluge came but the man was saved. Every night, when the man came home, he found that someone had prepared tortillas for him. He spied and discovered that the dog had taken off her skin and was working. Though the dog complained, he threw her skin into the fire.[87]

[84] McQuown, Totonac text from Coatepec, Puebla, 1940; Oropeza Castro, "El diluvio totonaco," vol. II, pp. 269–275.

[85] Horcasitas, unpublished texts from Papantla, Veracruz, 1953.

[86] H. V. Lemley, "Three Tlapaneco Stories," *Tlalocan* (Mexico City) III (1949): 76–81.

[87] Ibid.

11. *Popoluca V* (Foster). When a certain man's wife died, he became very sad and lonely. His dog also looked downcast. One day his dog disappeared. Yet from that day forward the man would return home to find fresh tortillas and other types of food prepared and ready for him. One day the man returned home early and found a beautiful woman baking his tortillas. The dog's skin was hanging near the table. The man married the dog-woman.[88]

12. *Chol III* (Beekman). A woman died and went to Hell. Her husband was left alone upon the earth. The wife took pity on the man and sent a bitch to cook for him. Every day, on coming home, the man discovered that someone had baked tortillas for him. He spied and found the bitch grinding corn. The man cried, "This is not my wife!" And, knife in hand, he chased the dog out of the house.[89]

Type D (in my opinion the most thought-provoking of all the Mesoamerican flood myths) can rightly be identified as "The Dog-Wife Tale" or "The Story of the Mysterious Housekeeper." Here again the source material is excellent: eleven of the twelve versions I have quoted may be considered first-class texts. The fundamental question which must be answered can be reduced to the following words: is the story pre-Hispanic? The question does not find a ready answer, as will be seen by the following observations.

1. *To my knowledge, no pre-Hispanic indigenous version has been recorded.* The earliest text we actually possess is that transcribed by Lumholtz, dating around the year 1900. However, the fact that no version of this story was set down by any chronicler of the sixteenth century is probably less significant than it might seem at first glance. It should be remembered that the bulk of the colonial texts originated in the Nahua linguistic group. It is therefore possible that, while the Nahua group did not know the story, other pre-Europeans may have shared it as part of their heritage. It is also possible that a concept so alien to European minds as that of a union between a man and a dog was repugnant to them, and like so many other aspects of native life, they preferred to ignore it in their writings.

2. *The story itself is not European.* It is difficult to believe that the Spaniards, in their efforts to convert the natives to Christianity, should have brought such a myth to Mexico. The story itself is unknown in European folktale collections and is completely foreign to any Christian concepts of the origin of mankind.

3. *There does seem to be a reference to the myth in a description of*

[88] Foster, "Sierra Popoluca Folklore and Beliefs," p. 211.

[89] Beekman, unpublished text from the Chol of Yajalón, Chiapas, ca. 1949

an incident in pre-Hispanic Mexico. Jiménez Moreno has pointed out[90] a passage in the *Historia Tolteca-Chichimeca* which seems to contain an allusion to it.[91] The text speaks of the sufferings of the Toltec-Chichimecs at the hands of the Olmec-Xicalanca. One of their greatest tribulations was the fact that *nixtamal* water was often thrown on them. This is mentioned three times: "And the Olmec-Xicalanca made great fun of the Toltecs; they threw *nixtamal* water in their faces; they scratched their legs and their backs with quills of feathers; they made them swallow bitter things." The Toltec-Chichimecs complain: "Now they treat us in such a way that they are ruining us, sometimes throwing their women's *nixtamal* water in our faces, sometimes scratching our legs and our backs with quills. Are we dogs, perchance, that they should deal with us so while we live with them?" Later the oppressors ask if the Toltecs want some new weapons and the latter answer: "No, my dear friends. All we want are your old weapons, lest your new ones be spoiled with the *nixtamal* water."[92]

The apparent connection between this episode and the Dog-Wife myth, as conceived by Jiménez Moreno, can be summed up in the following manner. The Toltecs (originally Chichimecs) probably derived their name from a totemic animal, a dog, considered the common ancestor of the group. This dog ancestor is to be considered in connection or identified with the bitch of the deluge myth. In the myth it is said that when the dog's skin was burned, the man bathed her in *nixtamal* water to soothe her. Interpreting the text from the *Historia Tolteca-Chichimeca,* it appears that the Toltec-Chichimecs were being taunted by their enemies regarding their rather curious origin by having *nixtamal* water poured on them.

Another suggestive reference is to be found in the works of Sahagún.[93] In describing the end of the feast of Tlacaxipehualiztli, the Franciscan ethnographer states that those who had been wearing human skins during the feast had to go through a ritual bath to clean themselves of the impurities caused by the skins. This bath took place within the temple, where the individuals were washed in *water mixed with corn flour or corn dough.* After this ceremonial washing, they went to bathe in ordinary water.

[90] Wigberto Jiménez Moreno, *Historia antigua de México* (Mexico City: Escuela Nacional de Antropología, 1949), p. 41 (mimeographed).

[91] *Historia Tolteca-Chichimeca* (Mexico City: Robredo, 1947), pp. 81–85.

[92] The text was written originally in Náhuatl, translated into German, and from the German into Spanish. The present translation, into English, is my own.

[93] Bernardino de Sahagún, *Historia general de las cosas de Nueva España* (Mexico City: Editorial Nueva España, 1946), vol. I, p. 144.

The connection between the removal of the skin and the relief obtained by bathing in water mixed with corn dough certainly seems to be indigenous. This concept strengthens the probability of the native origin of the Dog-Wife story considerably.

Another text which is possibly connected with the myth of the Dog-Wife is the *Relación de Ocelotepeque.*[94] We are told in this source that a famous Zapotecan chieftain, a descendant of the survivors of the deluge, was named Petela (Dog). No further explanation is given, and it is quite likely that the name is simply a calendrical one, totally disconnected with the Dog-Wife story. I simply point it out as a remote possibility.

4. *The motif of the mysterious housekeeper is found in other parts of America.* Cristóbal de Molina, a South American mestizo, recorded a deluge myth in Quito around the year 1580.[95] The following is a résumé of the story: The flood destroyed all mankind with the exception of two brothers, who remained alone upon the earth. At first they only ate roots and herbs but after some time, on returning home from work every day, they noticed that someone had prepared food for them. The elder brother spied to see who the mysterious housekeeper was and found that two macaws entered the house, took off their mantles (feathers?), and undertook the duties of the house. The man came out of his hiding place, whereupon the birds flew away. He was able to catch one of the birds, while the other one flew away. He and the bird-woman married, had six children, and repopulated the world.

Basically, the South American story seems to be identical to the Dog-Wife myth of Mesoamerica. If the former can be proved indigenous to Ecuador or Peru, I am inclined to believe that theory in support of the native origin of the Mexican Dog-Wife story will be greatly strengthened.

Another version of the "Mysterious Housekeeper" is found in Arctic America and on Vancouver Island. Boas, quoting Petitot, outlines the arctic tale as follows:

> A woman was married to a dog and bore six pups. She was deserted by her tribe, and went out daily procuring food for her family. When she returned she found tracks of children around her lodge, but did not see anyone besides her pups. Finally she discovered from a hiding place that the dogs threw off their skins as soon as she left them. She surprised them, took away the skins and the dogs became children—a

[94] Del Paso y Troncoso, ed., *Papeles de Nueva España,* vol. IV, p. 139.

[95] Cristóbal de Molina, *Ritos y fábulas de los incas* (Buenos Aires: Futuro, 1947), pp. 31–33.

number of boys and a girl. These became the ancestors of the Dog-Rib Indians.[96]

In regard to the preceding version it is better not to exaggerate its importance: it is simply a motif, not a fully detailed deluge myth. Isolated motifs have been suspected of developing independently on occasion.

An even more similar version is to be found in Surinam, though it is not clear from the text whether it belongs to the Arawak or to the Carib Indians:

> [An anchorite] had a wonderfully faithful dog. Wandering in the forest, the hermit discovered a finely cultivated field, with cassava and other food plants, and thinking "Who has prepared all this for me?" he concealed himself in order to discover who might be his benefactor, when behold! his faithful dog appeared, transformed herself into a human being, laid aside her dog's skin, busied herself with the toil of cultivating, and, the task accomplished, again resumed her canine form. The native, carefully preparing, concealed himself anew, and when the dog came once more, he slyly stole the skin, carried it away in a *courou-courou* (a woman's harvesting basket) and burned it, after which the cultivator, compelled to retain woman's form, became his faithful wife and the mother of a large family.[97]

A similar story is found in Haiti among the Caribs:

> There was once a widower who lived with his bitch in a little house. Every day when he returned he found that someone had prepared food, grated manioc, baked cassava, washed, swept the house and fetched firewood and water. A talebearer called Uànuhí came and told the man that it was really his dog who was responsible for all of this. He added that if the man wanted the dog to remain a woman he should take her to the river, put her in the water and cause a fish to pass between her legs. He did so and the bitch turned into a woman. Yet, sometime later, the man grew tired of his dog-wife, took her down to the river again and turned her into a male dog. She never became a woman again.[98]

The preceding tale is not told as a deluge myth; it is simply a folktale popular among the descendants of the Carib aborigines. The Haitian version does not strengthen the probability of the myth being peculiar

[96] E. Petitot, *Traditions indiennes du Canada nord-ouest,* quoted in Boas, "Dissemination of Tales Among the Natives of North America," p. 438.

[97] H. B. Alexander, *Latin American Mythology,* in vol. 11 of *Mythology of All Races* (Boston: Marshall Jones Company, 1920), p. 274.

[98] Douglas Taylor, "Tales and Legends of the Dominica Caribs," *Journal of American Folklore* 65 (1952):267–279.

THE DISTRIBUTION OF THE "DOG-WIFE" IN MESOAMERICA

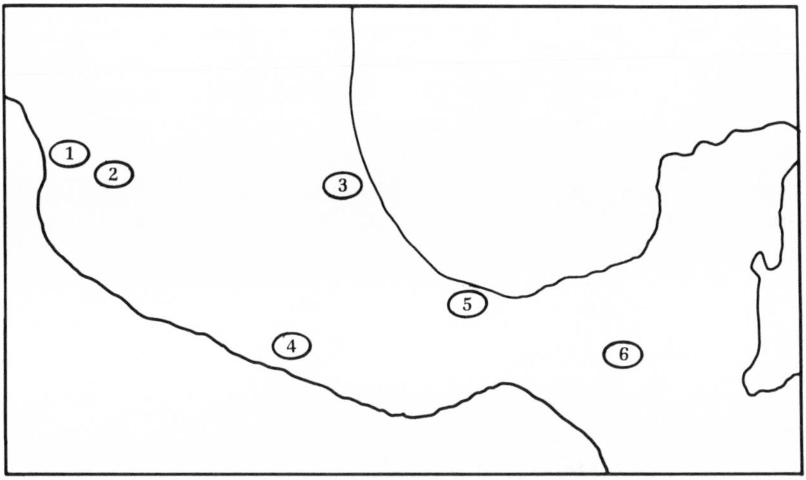

1. Huichol
2. Tepecano
3. Totonac
4. Tlapanec
5. Popoluca
6. Chol

to America, since it is a well-known fact that Haitian folklore is impregnated with African concepts and stories. Though I have not encountered other versions of the story of the Mysterious Housekeeper, I am inclined to believe that it is widely extended in contemporary America. This extensive diffusion does not necessarily prove the indigenous origin of the myth, however. The story of Noah's messenger-birds is perhaps even more widespread in America, and yet it finds its origin in the Old World.

5. *The idea of the transformation of an animal into a human being is a common Mesoamerican concept.* In his "Sierra Popoluca Folklore and Beliefs,"[99] Foster states that

> the belief that many humans are able at will to assume animal form, and many supernatural and animal beings to assume human form and live with humans, is so basic in Mexico that the story of the "Dog Wife" seems to me to integrate perfectly with the autochthonous folk belief.[100]

Foster's statement is undoubtedly true. Yet is can hardly be considered a solution to the problem. The same basic concept is common to other parts of America and is also to be found in Africa.

[99] Foster, "Sierra Popoluca Folklore and Beliefs," p. 211.

[100] Ibid., p. 212.

6. *The geographical distribution of the story reveals little.* The Dog-Wife story's geographical distribution in Mesoamerica is shown in the accompanying figure. The myth seems to be concentrated on or near the coast of Mexico, and to my knowledge no version has been recorded on the Central Plateau. Of course, this does not mean that the story is not to be found there. It is possible that the myth spread in very early times—perhaps since the time that Teotihuacán was a great religious center. Connections between the coasts and the highlands were then very strong. The existence of the story in Ecuador and along the coast of South America is also suggestive of early diffusion; ancient Mesoamerican culture is known to have affected this region.

Division E

A man (Noah) was warned by God that a flood was coming. He made an ark and placed all kinds of animals in it. As the waters were subsiding, he sent out several birds to see if the world was dry. Some birds came back, having succeeded in their missions; others did not. This last division, frankly biblical, finds representatives in most of the preceding versions in that its motifs are included, in one way or another, in the indigenous stories. The following five biblical versions may be added to the previous accounts.

1. *Cora* (Lumholtz). When the flood came a man was ordered to take a woodpecker, a woodcock, and a parrot along with him in the boat. When the waters began to subside, he sent forth the woodcock to see if the earth was dry. The bird came back. Five days later the man sent forth the woodpecker, but it too returned to the boat. He finally sent forth the parrot which returned to announce that the earth was dry.[101]

2. *Zapotec III* (Radin). Two men were in the ark when the great flood subsided. They decided to send out a buzzard to see if the world was dry. But the buzzard abandoned the boat, staying to eat the dead. Therefore he was condemned to become the scavenger of the earth. A heron was sent forth and it accomplished its mission. It was therefore permitted to eat fish as a reward. A raven was sent forth. It too fulfilled its task and was permitted to eat fruit and corn. Finally the dove was sent. It came back to report that the earth was almost dry. As a reward, the dove was granted its freedom.[102]

[101] Lumholtz, *El México desconocido,* vol. II, pp. 191–192.

[102] Paul Radin, *El Folklore de Oaxaca* (New York: Escuela Internacional de Arqueologíay Etnología Americanas, 1917), pp. 7–9.

3. *Zapotec IV* (Parsons). Noéh was warned by the Angel Gabriel that a deluge was in prospect because of the sins of mankind. Noéh warned his people but they did not believe him. Then he constructed a boat and took a pair of each animal along with him. The waters came; Saint Michael the Archangel came forth and blew his trumpet. When the waters subsided, Noéh sent forth the buzzard to see if the world was dry but the buzzard stayed behind to eat dead animals. When the crow was sent forth, it came back to report that the earth was drying. Then the turtledove and the parroquet were sent forth, and they returned to say that the world was dry. The animals were then freed and Noéh descended from the ark.[103]

4. *Zapotec V* (López Chiñas). When the great flood came Noéh put a pair of each animal in the ark. The ark struck the door of Heaven. Then God sent down a beautiful buzzard to see if the earth was dry. But the bird remained eating dead animals, whereupon he became ugly. Then the dove was sent down. In Juchitán the trip of a person unmindful of his mission is called a "buzzard's trip."[104]

5. *Tarascan VIII* (Carrasco). Adam and Eve were the only people saved in the deluge. They made an ark and took food with them. The waters came and the rest of humanity was destroyed. God sent down a bird to see if the waters had subsided and the bird flew back to say that the earth was dry.[105]

At first glance it might seem that the previous texts were inspired directly by the Bible; still, let us compare them with the original biblical elements. The following is a condensation of Genesis 6–9: Men were very wicked. For this reason God decided to destroy them. Only one man, Noah, and his family were found worthy of being saved. Therefore, God instructed him to build a large ark and to put in it a pair of each existing animal. When the waters covered the face of the earth, Noah and his family were saved. As the waters diminished, Noah opened the window of the ark and sent forth a raven to see if the world was dry. Seven days later he sent forth a dove, but it returned. Again he waited seven days and again he sent forth the dove. This time it returned with an olive branch in its beak. Seven days later he sent the dove forth, but it did not return. Then God told Noah to emerge from the ark. In gratitude, Noah built an altar for the Divine Being and

[103] Elsie Clews Parsons, *Mitla, Town of Souls* (Chicago: University of Chicago Press, 1936), pp. 350–352.

[104] Gabriel López Chiñas, *Vinni Gulasa: Cuentos de Juchitán* (Mexico City: Neza, 1940), pp. 34–35.

[105] Pedro Carrasco, unpublished text from Paracho, Michoacán, 1945.

offered a number of animals and birds upon it. God smelled the pleasant odor and promised never to destroy the world again.[106]

On comparing this account with the modern Mexican Bible-influenced stories, one becomes aware of certain added elements in the latter: the buzzard (or the raven) is sent forth but he stays to eat corpses and is condemned to eat only rotten flesh thereafter.[107] This element is possibly of Spanish origin; it may be one of the many apocryphal stories that grew up around authentic Bible passages during the Middle Ages. The earliest reference to it that I have encountered is found in the *Monarquía Indiana* of Torquemada.[108] This writer presents a Cuban deluge account (and though he states that it is pre-Hispanic, it is undoubtedly of European origin). The story is as follows. A certain man, knowing that the deluge was to come, built a great boat. He entered it, together with his family and many animals. Later he sent forth a raven, which did not return, as it stayed behind to eat dead animals. Then he sent forth a dove, which returned singing, bringing back a leafy branch. According to Torquemada, this story was told in Cuba about 1510–1520. This fact leads us to suspect that the motif of the raven eating dead bodies is an ancient theme, probably known to the Spaniards long before the discovery of America.

In the New World the motif of the birds sent forth from the ark found ready acceptance. Themes similar to it were already prominent in native stories. Boas mentions a creation myth from the United States which has a similar motif:

> The Yokut in California say that at a time when the earth was covered with water there existed a hawk, a crow and a duck. The latter, after diving to the bottom and bringing up a beakful of mud, died. Whereupon the crow and the hawk took each one half of the mud, and set to work to make the mountains.[109]

Another pre-Hispanic element which prepared the ground for the motif of the raven (or buzzard) was that of the messenger (Tezcatlipoca in one version) sent down to see who had lighted a fire. In one Totonac story,[110] the European and native elements are so combined as to make it difficult to separate them:

[106] Condensed from *Biblia sacra iuxta vulgatam Clementinam* (Madrid: La Editorial Católica, 1946), pp. 9–12.

[107] Maya IV, Tarascan II, Tarascan VI, Popoluca I, Popoluca II, Popoluca III, Totonac I, Tzeltal.

[108] Torquemada, *Monarquía indiana,* vol. II, p. 572.

[109] Boas, "Dissemination of Tales Among the Natives of North America," p. 440.

[110] Horcasitas, unpublished text from Papantla, Veracruz, 1953.

> The Lord God was up above and He began to smell the smoke going up. He says to the buzzard, "Go down and tell him to put out the fire so that the sky won't be smoked up." The buzzard came down but it remained, eating with the man. Then God said to the buzzard, "From now on you are going to stay there, eating rotten flesh."

Another element not included in the original biblical account is that of the dove's return with its feet covered with mud. Two Zapotec versions state that when the dove was sent forth, its feet became muddy.[111] This was a sign that the world was already drying. A curious counterpart of the story is found in a pre-European Peruvian story:

> They also say that it rained so much once that all the lowlands and all men were submerged, except a few who managed to take refuge on the high mountain ranges. They covered the small entrances of the caves so that water would not enter and put within them provisions and animals. When they heard that the rain had stopped they sent forth two dogs. As the dogs returned, clean but wet, they knew that the waters had not subsided yet. Later they sent forth more dogs, and when the latter returned, muddy but dry, they realized that the deluge was over.[112]

The Peruvian story may strengthen the possibility of the indigenous origin of the motif.

GENERAL CONCLUSIONS

1. Although there undoubtedly existed a number of independent and semi-independent versions of the flood myth in ancient Mesoamerica, in modern times our knowledge of them is limited to Type C (the story of the survivors who lighted a fire and were changed into animals) and (if we accept the story of the dog-wife as pre-Hispanic) to Type D.

2. The Dog-Wife story is not known through any actual text from the pre-Hispanic epoch. Nevertheless, there are strong reasons which lead us to believe that it was known among the ancient indigenous groups. Its wide extension outside the borders of Mesoamerica may indicate a great diffusion of Mesoamerican culture in the southern part of the continent.

3. It is difficult to reconstruct the versions which were not ade-

[111] Zapotec III, Zapotec V.

[112] Francisco López de Gómara, *Historia de las Indias,* in vol. 22 of *Biblioteca de autores españoles* (Madrid: Ribadeneyra, 1852), p. 233.

quately recorded in early colonial times. The fragmentary descriptions of the missionaries and other chroniclers are not sufficient to warrant a reconstruction. Modern texts, no matter how cautiously used, will probably never reveal the original pre-European stories with any degree of certainty.

4. The biblical account has exerted an overwhelming influence on indigenous deluge stories, no matter how remote the native cultures have been from European groups. On the other hand, native influence on the Old World account, as told in Mesoamerica, has been weaker.

5. A number of important questions regarding the function of the modern stories remain unanswered. Are they to be considered myths in the full sense of the word? Or have they lost their sacred character? Do those who tell and hear them believe them to be true? If so, how do they influence indigenous life and thought?

Evidence which might produce solutions to these doubtful points is scant. Still, it will be necessary to ask these questions—and to answer them—if the significance of the Mesoamerican deluge myth is ever to be grasped by the anthropologist.

BIBLIOGRAPHY

Printed Matter

Acosta, José de. *Historia natural y moral de las Indias.* Mexico City: Fondo de Cultura Económica, 1940.

Alexander, H. B. *Latin-American Mythology.* Vol. 11 of *The Mythology of All Races.* Boston: Marshall Jones, 1920.

Alva Ixtlilxóchitl, Fernando. *Obras históricas.* 2 vols. Mexico City: Secretaría de Fomento, 1891–1892.

"Anales de Cuauhtitlán." *Códice Chimalpopoca.* Translated by Primo Feliciano Velásquez. Mexico City: Universidad Nacional Autónoma, 1945.

Biblia Sacra iuxta vulgatam Clementinam. Madrid: La Editorial Católica, 1946.

Boas, Franz. *Race, Language and Culture.* New York: Macmillan, 1949.

Boturini Benaduci, Lorenzo. *Idea de una nueva historia general de la América Septentrional.* Madrid: Juan de Zúñiga, 1746.

Caso, Alfonso. *La religión de los aztecas.* Mexico City: Imprenta Mundial, 1936.

———. "Cultura mixteca." *México Prehispánico.* Mexico City: Editorial Emma Hurtado, 1946.

Chavero, Alfredo. "La Piedra del Sol." *Anales del Museo Nacional de México* I (1877).

Clavijero, Francisco J. *Historia antigua de México.* Translated by J. Joaquín de Mora. 2 vols. Mexico City: Delfín, 1944.

Foster, George M. "Sierra Popoluca Folklore and Beliefs." University of California Publications in American Archaeology and Ethnology 42 (1945).

Fuente, J. de la. *Yalálag: una villa zapoteca serrana.* Mexico City: Museo Nacional de Antropología, 1949.

García Icazbalceta, Joaquín, ed. "Historia de los mexicanos por sus pinturas." *Nueva colección de documentos para la historia de México: Pomar, Zurita, relaciones antiguas.* Mexico City: Chávez Hayhoe, n.d.

Garibay K., Angel María. *Épica nahuatl: divulgación literaria.* Mexico City: Universidad Nacional Autónoma, 1945.

———. *Historia de la literatura náhuatl.* Mexico City: Porrúa, 1953.

Hernández, Francisco. *Antigüedades de la Nueva España.* Mexico City: Robredo, 1946.

Historia tolteca-chichimeca. Mexico City: Robredo, 1947.

"Histoyre du Mechique." *Journal de la Société des Américanistes* II (1905).

Jiménez Moreno, Wigberto. *Mapa lingüístico de Norte- y Centro-América.* Mexico City: Museo Nacional, 1936.

Keller, John Esten. *Motif Index of Mediaeval Spanish Exempla.* Knoxville: University of Tennessee Press, 1949.

Landa, Diego de. *Relación de las cosas de Yucatán.* Mexico City: Robredo, 1938.

Lemley, H. V. "Three Tlapaneco Stories." *Tlalocan* (Mexico City) III (1949).

León y Gama, Antonio. *Descripción histórica y cronológica de las dos piedras.* Mexico City: Alejandro Valdéz, 1832.

"Leyenda de los Soles." *Códice Chimalpopoca.* Mexico City: Universidad Nacional Autonóma, 1945.

Libro de Chilam Balam de Chumayel. Translated by Antonio Mediz Bolio. Mexico City: Universidad Nacional Autónoma, 1941.

López Chiñas, Gabriel. *Vinni Gulasa: cuentos de Juchitán.* Mexico City: Ediciones "Neza," 1940.

López de Gómara, Francisco. *Conquista de Méjico.* In vol. 22 of *Biblioteca de autores españoles.* Madrid: Ribadeneyra, 1852.

———. *Historia de las Indias.* In vol. 22 of *Biblioteca de autores españoles.* Madrid: Ribadeneyra, 1852.

Lumholtz, Carl. *El México desconocido.* Translated by Balbino Dávalos. 2 vols. Mexico City: Publicaciones Herrerías, 1945.

McIntosh, John. "Cosmogonía huichol." *Tlalocan* (Mexico City) III (1949).

Malinowski, Bronislaw. "Myth in Primitive Psychology." *Magic, Science and Religion and Other Studies.* Glencoe, Ill.: Free Press, 1948.

Il Manoscritto Messicano Vaticano 3738 detto il Códice Ríos. Rome: Stabilimento Danesi, 1900.

Mason, J. Alden. "Folktales of the Tepecanos." *Journal of American Folklore* 27 (1914).

Mendieta, Gerónimo de. *Historia eclesiástica indiana.* 4 vols. Mexico City: Chávez Hayhoe, 1945.

Molina, Cristóbal de. *Ritos y fábulas de los Incas.* Buenos Aires: Editoria Futuro, 1947.

Montagu, M. F. Ashley. *An Introduction to Physical Anthropology.* Springfield, Ill.: Charles C. Thomas, 1951.

Monzón, Arturo. "Teogonía trique." *Tlalocan* (Mexico City) II (1945).

Motolinía, Toribio. *Memoriales.* Mexico City: García Pimentel, 1903.

Muñoz Camargo, Diego. *Historia de Tlaxcala.* Mexico City: Ateneo Nacional de Ciencias y Artes, 1947.

Oropeza Castro, Manuel. "El diluvio totonaco." *Tlalocan* (Mexico City) II (1945).

Parsons, Elsie Clews. *Mitla, Town of Souls.* Chicago: University of Chicago Press, 1936.

Paso y Troncoso, Francisco del, ed. "Relación de Ocelotepeque." *Papeles de Nueva España.* Vol. IV. Madrid: Ribadeneyra, 1905.

Popol Vuh: las antiguas historias del Quiché. Translated by Adrián Recinos. Mexico City: Fondo de Cultura Económica, 1947.

Preuss, K. Th. "Au sujet du caractére des mythes et des chants huichols que j'ai recueillis." *Revista del Instituto de Etnología.* Vol. II. Tucumán: Universidad Nacional de Tucumán, 1932.

Radin, Paul. *El Folklore de Oaxaca.* New York: Escuela Internacional de Arqueología y Etnología Americanas, 1917.

Redfield, Margaret Park. *The Folk Literature of a Yucatecan Town.* In *Contributions to American Archaeology,* vol. 13. Washington, D.C.: Carnegie Institution, 1937.

Sahagún, Bernardino de. *Historia general de las cosas de Nueva España.* 3 vols. Mexico City: Editorial Nueva España, 1946.

Tax, Sol. "Folktales in Chichicastenango: An Unsolved Puzzle." *Journal of American Folklore* 62 (1949).

Taylor, Douglas. "Tales and Legends of the Dominica Caribs." *Journal of American Folklore* 65 (1952).

Thompson, Stith. *The Folktale.* New York: Dryden Press, 1946.

Torquemada, Juan de. *Monarquía indiana.* 3 vols. Mexico City: Chávez Hayhoe, 1943.

Tozzer, Alfred M. *A Comparative Study of the Mayas and the Lacandones.* New York: Archaeological Institute of America, 1907.

———. "Landa's *Relación de las cosas de Yucatán.*" In *Papers of the Peabody Museum of American Archaeology and Ethnology.* Cambridge: Harvard University, 1941.

Veytia, Mariano. *Historia antigua de México.* 2 vols. Mexico City: Editorial Leyenda, 1944.

Villa Rojas, Alfonso. *The Mayas of East Central Quintana Roo.* Washington, D.C.: Carnegie Institution, 1945.

Zingg, Robert Mowry. *The Huichols: Primitive Artists.* New York: G. E. Stechert, 1938.

Unpublished Material

Anderson, Arabelle. Unpublished text in Chol and English from the Chol group of Chiapas, ca. 1949.

Barlow, Robert H. Unpublished text in Spanish dictated by a Totonac informant from Coatepec, Puebla, ca. 1948. Barlow Archive, Mexico City College.

Beekman, John. Unpublished texts from Yajalón, Chiapas, in Chol and English, ca. 1949.

Carrasco, Pedro. Unpublished texts in Spanish from Jarácuaro, Michoacán, 1945.

———. Unpublished text in Spanish from Cocucho, Michoacán, 1945.

———. Unpublished text in Spanish from Ocumicho, Michoacán, 1945.

———. Unpublished text in Spanish from Paracho, Michoacán, 1945.

Gessain, Robert. Unpublished text from the Tepehua group, 1953.

Horcasitas, Fernando. Unpublished texts in Spanish dictated by a Totonac informant in Papantla, Veracruz, 1953.

Jiménez Moreno, Wigberto. Notes taken by Miss Leticia Peniche in the course "Historia Antigua de Mexico," 1949. (Mimeographed)

McQuown, Norman. Texts in Totonac recorded at Coatepec, Puebla, 1940. (Mimeographed)

Slocum, Marianna. Unpublished texts in Tzeltal and Spanish gathered at Oxchuc, Ococingo, Chiapas, ca. 1947. Barlow Archive, Mexico City College.

Historical Changes as Reflected in South American Indian Myths

ANNAMÁRIA LAMMEL

We have seen that the flood myth is widely reported in native North America and in Mesoamerica. It is also found in South America. In this stimulating essay by a Hungarian ethnographer, we learn what happens when a "foreign" myth of the flood (from the Bible) introduced by Spanish explorers is juxtaposed with an indigenous flood myth—among the Inca of Peru, for example. The contrasting worldviews implicit in the two traditions of the flood myth are part of the overall acculturation context which inevitably occurs when two diverse cultures come into contact.

For other treatments of South American Indian flood myths, see Robert Lehmann-Nitsche, "Mitología sudamericana I: El diluvio según los araucanos de la pampa," Revista del Museo de La Plata *24(2) (1919): 28–62; Martin Gusinde, "Otro mito del diluvio que cuentan los araucanos,"* Publicaciones del Museo de Etnologia y Anthropologia *2 (1920): 183–200; Konrad Theodor Preuss, "Flutmythen der Uitoto und ihre Erklärung," in Walter Lehmann, ed.,* Festschrift Eduard Seler *(Stuttgart, 1922), pp. 385–400; Rudolfo M. Casamiquela, "The Deluge Myth in Patagonia,"* Latin American Indian Literatures *6 (1982): 91–101; and the entries under "Flood" in Susan Niles,* South American Indian Narrative: An Annotated Bibliography *(New York, 1981), p. 178.*

> Primera generación de indios multiplicó de aquellos españoles que trajo Dios a este reino de los Incas los que salieron de arca de Noe despues del diluvio.[1]

The above quotation is a surprising genesis (i.e., Noah → the Spaniards → Indians) all the more so since it was written by an Indian who in all

Reprinted from *Acta Ethnographica* 30 (1981):143–158.

[1]Guaman Poma de Ayala, 1944, p. 49.

probability had been born in the Inca Empire. The Indian chronicler aims at writing the history of his own people placing it against the chronology reflected in the Bible. In his attempts the two world views and two kinds of knowledge given by the two opposing sources of information bring about an anachronistic situation. *The myth of the conqueror* (which must be true) opposes *the myth of the conquered* (which must be a lie).

It is obvious that such a clear-cut acceptance or rejection is impossible. As the short quotation above shows, the confrontation of the two mythological worlds results in the emergence of a new myth even if temporarily (but in some cases still surviving) which preserves the elements of both mythologies while eliminating some of them. Here we aim at touching upon this moment, the adaptation of myth to the new society.

What is the relationship of myth to historical changes? It is true without doubt that the process of this change cannot be traced among a people who have had no historiography. Although it could be examined—perhaps with the help of archaeology—in what way myths reflect the differentiation of property status that accompanies historical development, it is also obvious, however, that myth is not historiography. There is no sense in searching for a historical myth. As Raglan mentioned those who believe in historical myth talk a lot about how easily these emerge but present nothing to verify this statement: "If a process cannot actually be proved to occur, it is surely the duty of those who postulated it to give some reason for believing in its occurrence. It seems to be regarded as the privilege of a professor of classics or literature to guess the origin of a particular story, and then elevate his guess to the status of an universal rule. What is needed is a comparative study of history and myth, and this, so far as I have been able to carry it, seems to show clearly that the 'historic myth' is a fiction."[2]

We are not trying to find a historical myth, either, but rather the process through which myth adjusts itself to the necessities created by historical changes. We are not aiming at following how myths are created artificially—though partly this is a problem in question, too—but the process in which the *main message systems* of the myth (including the motif of the Deluge) are "equipped" with *sub-message-systems* and with new *armature* that enables them to perform the function of myths while working their way into the system of myths of a new historical period.

[2] Raglan, 1936, p. 124.

THE MYTHS

Myths analyzed and described here have been taken from chronicles written after the Spanish Conquest. Myths were preserved in Spanish, though, with the exception of myth 8, all of them had been created before the Conquest. Among the chroniclers we can find soldiers, adventurers, clerks, priests, baptized Indians. Their view of the Inca Empire is rather ambiguous and the latter tried to defend it and give a more favorable picture of it while most of the Spanish writers despising their uncivilized nature did not make too much effort to understand a historical period which they considered as "the Realm of Satan." Let us introduce here three of the chroniclers from whose works the bulk of myths analyzed here have been taken.

Guaman Poma de Ayala wrote his work *Nueva Crónica y buen gobierno* comprising several thousand folios between 1580–1615. He was a baptized Indian who in his wonderful descriptions preserved pictures of source value of the religious life, feasts and everyday life of the Inca times.

Garcilaso de la Vega was born in 1540 in Cuzco. His father was a member of the Spanish aristocracy; his mother, the niece of Inca 11, had come from the Inca aristocracy. He wrote his most important work *Comentarios reales* as an old man in Cordoba, Spain. This work consists of two parts; the first part deals with Inca history, the second with the history of the Conquest. When writing it he relied on the memories of his youth on what he had experienced and had heard during the time he spent among the surviving members of the Inca royal family. But later he changed his opinion concerning things he had heard there, for instance, in the case of the myth of the Deluge:

"Dicen que pasado el diluvio, del cual no saben dar más razón de decir que lo hubo, ni se entiende si fue el general de tiempo de Noé o de algun otro particular (por lo cual dejarémos de decir lo que cuentan de él y de otras cosas semejantos, que de la manera que las dicen más paracen suenos y fábulas mal ordenadas que susesos historiales)."[3]

Pedro Sarmiento de Gamboa was a typical Spanish adventurer. He wrote his book *Historia de los Incas* upon the request of the Peruvian viceroy where he pieces "facts" together to confirm how tyrannical and despotic and repressive the Inca rule was, as a quasicounter-propaganda against Father Las Casas who tried to defend the Indians in his works.

[3]Garcilaso de la Vega, 1943, vol. III, p. 26.

We consider and describe these texts as myths despite the fact that they were written by literate authors though we lack all data about their future life. Here we refer to Lévi-Strauss who when analyzing the Oedipus myth wrote: "Our method thus eliminates a problem which has, so far, been one of the main obstacles to the progress of mythological studies, namely, the quest for the *true* version, or the *earlier* one. On the contrary, we define the myth as consisting of all its versions; or to put it otherwise, a myth remains the same as long as it is felt as such. A striking example is offered by the fact that our interpretation may take into account the Freudian use of the Oedipus myth and is certainly applicable to it. . . . Not only Sophocles, but Freud, himself, should be included among the recorded versions of the Oedipus myth on a par with earlier or seemingly more 'authentic versions'."[4]

Hereafter we are giving eight rewritten versions of the Deluge. From among these myths 5, 6, 7, 8, which later on are going to be analyzed in detail, were grouped according to the following system: "*actant*"—"*action*"—"*complementary information.*" It might be surprising that we regard the Deluge not an "armature" but a "message" which we think seems reasonable since the Deluge to our mind in myths 1, 4, 8 is identified as the *punishment* and in other myths is referred to as the *message justifying the new creation.*

Myth I

The sons of Pancha the first man (or god?) commit a sin by shooting arrows at a big snake. As a punishment the snake spits so much water that it floods the whole earth. The Deluge. Pancha and his three sons together with their wives survive in their house built on top of Pinchoncha mountain where they had taken animals and food. As soon as the Deluge had retreated they came down from the mountain and settled on a high plateau—where Quito can be found today—and built houses, but they did not understand each other's tongues so they moved away to different parts of the country where their descendants can still be found.[5]

Myth 2

A llama warns his master of the coming Deluge. They run to a high mountain to find shelter there on top of Uillcacoto. The shepherd and

[4]Lévi-Strauss, 1963, p. 217.

[5]Velazco, 1884, vol. I, p. 142.

the animals survive. The shepherd is the ancestor and all the people are his descendants.[6]

Myth 3

The Deluge. Two brothers survive by finding shelter on top of a high mountain in the province of Huaca Yñan. As the water rose, so did the mountain. As soon as the water had stopped flowing they came forth to find some food. They were fed by two mysterious beings. The brothers spied upon them and they turned out to be two guacamayos or torito birds with a woman's face. They caught the younger one and one of the brothers made the bird his wife. They had six sons and six daughters; they lived on seeds which they later on planted and lived on the crop. They are the ancestors of the Canari Indians who worshipped the Huaca Yñan mountain as a place of cult and highly adored the guacamayo bird.[7]

Myth 4

Viracocha for the first time creates giants on the earth but they prove to be too big and so he kills them. For the second time he creates people after his own image. Viracocha makes laws but people sink into sin; they are greedy, self-interested, conceited. Viracocha flies into a temper and turns the people into stone or other objects; they are swallowed by the earth or by the sea. Deluge. It lasts 60 days and 60 nights. Three men survive who are the servants of Viracocha and help to create the second period of the world. Viracocha creates the heavenly bodies. His servants expel Taupacaco, the rebelling servant. He recreates mankind. First he draws and forms on a relief the people he means to create with the help of his two servants on the seaside, and the new tribes come forth wandering in the Andes shouting their name from rivers, trees, rocks, cliffs. Viracocha wandered along. He was almost killed in Cacha as a foreigner. Viracocha punished them by fiery rain but forgave them when they beseeched him. People worshipped Viracocha and erected a huaca for him. Viracocha was wandering around in the country, taught people a lot of things, talked about their future that there would come people who call themselves Viracocha but they should not believe them. Viracocha disappeared in the waves of the sea.[8]

[6] Avila, 1873, p. 133.

[7] Molina de Cuzco, 1916, pp. 123–124.

[8] Sarmiento de Gamboa, 1942, pp. 23–24, 24–28.

Myth 5

After the Deluge

The sun	came out	on the Titicaca island of lake Titicaca—sooner than anywhere else

(Garcilaso's comment: "Finding out that the Indians believe in the ancient myth and respect the island as a sacred place, the first Inca Manco Capac with his ingenuity and shrewdness made an advantage of this and made up the second story.")[9]

Myth 6

Including myth 5 it continues the following way:

The sun	placed its children	Manco Capac and Mama Ocllo on the island of lake Titicaca so that setting out from there
the Incas	should teach and enlighten	the peoples of the earth and release them of all the bestiality they used to live in[10]

Myth 7

Viracocha	after the Deluge creates	the second mankind
people	are ordered	to breed
people	obey,	settle down, build a village, cultivate land, but they have no rule, their lords and masters live without the feeling of indepen-

[9] Garcilaso de la Vega, 1943, vol. III, p. 25.

[10] Ibid.

		dence and in ignorance
Viracocha	creates	their lords, the Ayar brothers
Manco Capac Inca and Mama Ocllo Coya	go to war	Inti (the sun) is the name of their falcon-like bird, people thought that Manco had got the Inca leadership from them
the Incas	subjugated people	and established the town of Cuzco[11]

Myth 8

The Deluge

God	sends the Spaniards	the descendants of Noah to this kingdom of the Indies
following God's order	the first generation of Indian breeds	which lasts 800 years
these are the Huari Viracocha people (an ancient white people)	who were the descendants of the Spaniards	that is why they are called viracocha which means "white" or "lord"
The other Indians	were the descendants of this generation	later this first generation was called Gods; they did not die and did not kill each other and gave birth to a man and a woman at the same time
the first Indians	could not	make clothes from leaves, nor build houses and lived in caves; all their work

[11] Sarmiento de Gamboa, 1906, pp. 29–30, 33–34.

		was the worship of God
people	worshipped God	but not the demons, the huacas
Indians	begin to work	to plough like their father Adam and they were wandering around on the earth like lost people
snakes, lions, pumas and other animals	lived	on the earth
Indians	killed them and subjugated the earth	
God	ordered them	to come to this kingdom of the Indies
The first people	lost their belief and hope in God	and therefore they were also lost, though they had some knowledge of the Creator of the heavens, the earth and people, so he was called runa camac viracocha
the first people	did not know their ancestors	therefore they worshipped neither idols nor the moon nor the demons. They did not remember that they were the descendants of Noah, though they knew about the flood which is called "una yaco pachacuti" (God's punishment)
The first people	worshipped and served	God, like Isaiah the prophet
the first Indians	were taught to plough the land	by Eve and Adam the first people
The first Indians	worshipped	Pachacamamac (the creator of the world)

runa camac (the creator of mankind) ticze viracocha (the Lord of the Beginning), cuylla viracocha (the Lord of the End) kneeling in front of them and crying: "My Lord, my Lord, why did you leave me?"[12]

Analysis

Though the above myths have been selected on the basis of their common motif of the Deluge, which is in itself a natural phenomenon, it is already obvious from the transcriptions themselves that we are faced here not merely with the description of a natural phenomenon. Henry Murray is wrong in placing myths about the Deluge among myths describing natural phenomena which give the description of events thought to be true in the past.[13]

In the following we are giving the main message system of the myths arranged in chronological order and inserted in a table:

Main message	1	2	3	4	5	6	7	8
1 Creation				+				+
2 Committing sin	+			+				+
3 The Deluge	+	+	+	+	+	+	+	+
4/a Survivors remain	+	+	+	+		+	+	+
4/b New creation				+		+	+	
5 The fate of survivors	+		+	+		+	+	+

The five marked messages are inserted in two myth models (myths 4 and 8) created among completely different messages. This is the main message system in our myths which in itself—even without the sub-message systems—is capable of giving the topic of myths.

[12] Guaman Poma de Ayala, 1944, pp. 49–51.

[13] Murray, 1960, p. 306.

Before defining the theme of the myths let us examine for a minute the logical relationship that lies behind the surface of the messages. Now again, myths 4 and 8 that contain all messages are chosen as the basis of our model.

Creator ← → created
(a sinless ruler) (sinful subject)
devastation
↓
new, chosen mankind
sinless and sinful; ruler and subject

Opposition is the confrontation of homogeneous qualities which in this case means that homogeneous *humanity* is in hierarchical opposition to divinity of homogeneous quality. This opposition is resolved by the creation of the hierarchy of qualities (which refers to social and ethnic hierarchy). Opposing qualities presuppose each other. The surviving sinless or sinful (creature) presupposes an opposing quality which is either inferior or superior to it. High social status and sinlessness are correlating pairs, just like low social status with sinfulness. Supposed qualities can appear not only together but also in sequence. (For instance, the surviving but sinful human creature presupposes a sinless superior who has created him, which in case of myth 7 happens later.)

It is the 5th component of the main message that provides most information about the time of the creation of the myth. This is the component which most strictly defines the possible ways of interpreting the above logical system.

There is no hierarchy of qualities in the second myth, since in general no hierarchical relation is reflected in myth. Thus causality—so important in our system of logic—does not become a necessary ingredient of the event. Thus it can be stated that the difference in the dominance of the elements of the logical relationship is explained by the less differentiated nature of the above mentioned social situation. The 5th component reveals this differentiation most explicitly.

The topic of the myths is determined by the messages that give the resolution of the oppositions. This topic now can easily be seen; myths are about the origin of the culture in which they evolve, their function is to maintain the system of rules of this culture, the positive character and the absolute necessity of their institutions; thus in fact we are faced with aetiological myths.

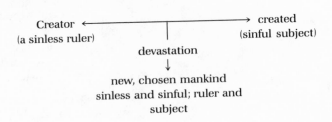

For brevity here we only examine myths where the historical background is verifiable.

Myths 5 and 6

On the basis of archaeological finds modern history maintains the view that the Inca state once was a local kingdom restricted to the area around Cuzco until as late as the rule of Inca Pachacuti. He was 9th Inca of the dynasty and ruled between 1440–1470. It was his and his son Topa Inca's conquest that established the Inca Empire from Quito to the southern Nazca. (It was at this time that they intruded upon the territory of Lake Titicaca. Thus, the Peruvian megalithic architecture was for the most part accomplished before the Incas, since it is unimaginable that the short period of 100 years between the conquering of the land and the Spanish invasion could have been enough to establish such a developed state which would have been necessary for carrying out these vast building operations.) Tiahuanaco culture which created the most outstanding works undoubtedly shows the signs of a highly developed society. In this culture the Sun cult must have had a central role as it is shown by the archaeological finds, such as the Tiahuanaco Sun Gate. From our myths of the Deluge traces of this cult are preserved in myth 5, which according to Garcilaso is the myth of the Indians of Lake Titicaca, and he thinks that it emerged before Inca times. Incas, after they had conquered the territory and had realized the importance of the Sun cult, made it the basis of the verification of their own superiority and power so forming myth 6. *This way the myth of the conquered people became part of the myth of the conquerors,* since myth 5 built into myth 6 appears as a prophecy of the coming rulers. From the very beginning of his coming to power Pachacuti Inca laid a special emphasis on transmitting the history of the Empire which was meant to be the history of the dynasty according to central principles.

Let us examine what happens to the mobile message system of the myth and together with this its armature in a case when a part of a new myth is incorporated from outside.

message:	the prophecy of the Sun about the coming of the rulers of the world
armature:	after the Deluge the sun first shines at Titicaca Island of Lake Titicaca
message:	the Sun creates the rulers of the world
armature:	the sun places Manco Capac and Ocllo on Titicaca Island

message: they are the bearers of civilization

armature: the sun orders them to teach and enlighten the people of the earth so that they can purge out their sins the bestialities they used to live in.

Only one sub-message system is incorporated into the main message system taken as a model. The theme of this one is the interpretation of the origin of the Inca Empire, its function is to verify the positive character of the Inca Empire. This claim makes it obvious why myth 5 is incorporated by which they can prove that they are the descendants of the Sun—through the father-son relationship they are unequivocally of divine origin—and that they are altogether superior in power to all. The original message of myth 5 becomes an armature in the new myth and attains a new meaning, adjusting itself thus to the myth that explains the divine origin of the Incas. At the same time its new meaning enters the group of sub-message systems and becomes an indispensable element of this system. Even when these two myths merge into one the principle of "retaining while terminating" still prevails. The inner logic of the myth that was formed this way follows the pattern of the above logical model.

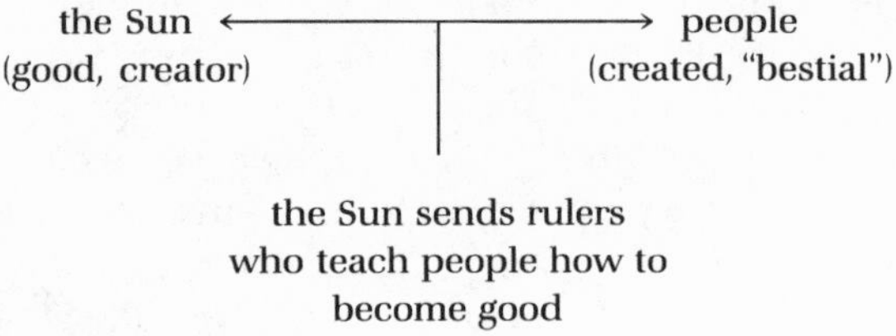

The relationship of opposition and resolution is only formally equivalent to that of the model described above; that resolves oppositions for the entire myth whereas here it only resolves the 5th main-message component. The same hierarchical relationship (ruler and subject) can be found between the Incas and the "common" people that is characteristic of the relationship of the Sun and the people. Good as a moral category is unequivocally superior to the negative category of bestiality. Such a hierarchical relationship of qualities reflects and at the same time justifies the given state of affairs.

Myth 7

Another version of the origins of the Inca dynasty can be read in the myth of the Ayar brothers. Pacaritambo (The House of Procreation) or

Tamputtacao (The House of Windows) is the name of the place in the myth where Viracocha summoned the Ayar brothers (the number of the brothers varies but they are at least six). Its similarity with the second creation described in myth 4 is conspicuous at first sight. This topological myth may have been incorporated into the story of the Ayar brothers. There is a mountain at Pacaritambo in the side of which three window-like holes are to be found. The ancestors of the Incas came to the world through the "Royal Window" which is in the middle; the Mara Indians and the Tambo Indians, who were the allies of the Incas and at the same time formed the non-royal (i.e., non-Inca) section of the ruling class, came through the other two openings. Unlike in myth 6 the story is not about a couple but about a group (perhaps a tribe) from which Manco Capac and Mama Ocllo separated themselves probably through inner strife and they assumed power. The description of the struggle for power contains a motif which makes it worthwhile to summarize the whole myth; one of the brothers, Ayar Achi, with his cruelties intimidates not only his enemies but also his allies so they decide to get rid of him by putting him into a cave. However, once he returns in the shape of a winged flying man and prophesies the future success of the Incas then he turns into a stone (huaca) with his last words ordering them to offer sacrifice for him.

The worship of idols is in opposition with the monotheistic Sun cult. In times before the Incas, worship of idols had been widespread. We can hypothetically state that in the person of the Ayar brother who turned into a stone (huaca) Incas wanted to connect the worship of the huaca with their own myth of origin and thus build it into their own system to use it for the promotion of their efforts towards hegemony.

In spite of all this we can state that we are not analyzing artificially created myths. Their tendency is obvious but it can be accounted for by the special feature of myths since a new ruling class requires new myths. This change cannot take place within a short time. The new that is aimed at, and that meets new requirements, is brought to life by building it into already existing myths.

The myth of the Ayar brothers has a more complex sub-message system than the myth of the Sun (myth 6). The first sub-message system and the system of armature connected with it includes the fate and life of second mankind created by Viracocha after the Deluge but with whom he was completely dissatisfied.

message:	a new mankind comes to life after the Deluge
armature:	Viracocha creates a second mankind after the Deluge
message:	people multiply and occupy the land
armature:	they settle down, build villages and cultivate land

message: they join the Ayar brothers as their henchmen or they are subjugated

armature: Manco Capac and Ocllo fight each other so as to establish the empire where people are kept together and taught

The second sub-message system and system of armature follow the life and fate of the Ayar brothers who were created at Pacaritambo.

message: Viracocha creates rulers for the second mankind who live in a state of anarchy

armature: he calls forth the Ayar brothers at Pacaritambo

message: Manco Capac and Mama Ocllo become rulers

armature: their brothers are sent away by different means

message: the empire is established

armature: they defeat their enemies in war with their followers and build Cuzco

The third sub-message and armature system is structurally separate from the two above lines, but has an important role in the inner logic of the myth.

message: the Inca's power might originate from the Sun

armature: Manco Capac has a falcon-like bird called Inti Sun from which he—as people think—got his leadership

message: the bird ensures the continuity of the Inca's power

armature: Manco Capac leaves Inti to his son and it used to descend from father to son till the rule of Inca Yupanqui

The three message systems are arranged into the following logical relationship:

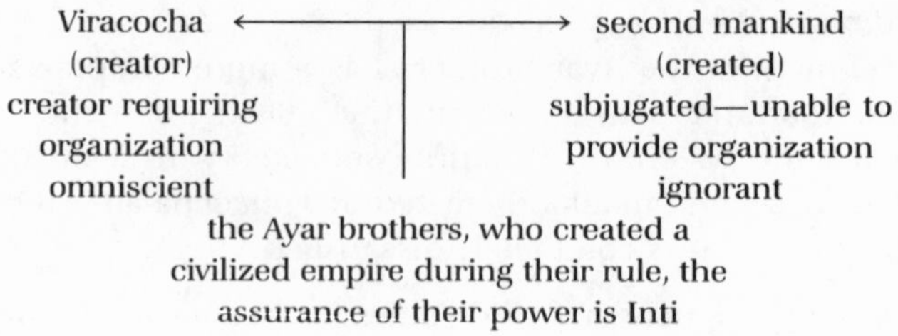

As it is obvious from the above figure the logical relationship of the resolution of oppositions can only be observed in the main message

component. It can be clearly stated from all this that this logical organizing principle of the myth is not an aim in itself but makes the realistic reflection of these hierarchical relations possible. By this all the elements of the myth are logically related to each other irrespective of the number of sub-systems.

Myth 8

Before analyzing this myth it is important to give an outline of the historical period in which it emerged. Guama Poma de Ayala must have written it between 1584–1600. This period is half a century after the Conquest.

On 16 November 1532 the Spaniards captured Atahualpa Inca, the weakened ruler of the empire who lost his power in fratricidal war. He was forcefully baptized, then he was killed. The Spanish conquerors verified their right for the conquest with the spreading of "true" faith. This justified the devastating campaign in which temples and huacas were destroyed. (Even as late as 1616 people were given financial reward for giving information to the authorities about hidden idols.)

The Pope ordered the Spanish king to send an "adequate" number of properly educated missionaries to the subjugated district. Missionaries—having adapted themselves to the special circumstances—and having realized the hierarchy of the Inca society considered the most important to baptize the leaders of the Incas, the ruling class and the *Ayllus* (a clan-community, extended family, sub-tribe). After the christening of Paullu Inca, brother to the rebel Manco-Inca, they achieved great success. After a lot of debates it was accepted that the mission would be more effective if they used those elements and rites of the ancient religion which were reconcilable with Christian dogmas.

Contemporary chroniclers write about serious resistance. The uprising of Manco Inca and his success forced a temporary halt upon both the soldiers and the missionaries (500 missionaries were killed). Because of the Indian resistance and inner struggle among the Spanish conquerors the situation became consolidated only in the first half of the 18th century.

Before analyzing myth 8 we have to refer to the fact that Poma de Ayala presents the Deluge of the Bible on the 25th folio. This is considered to be the beginning of this myth.

One of the basic elements of the logical model is presented by the basic conflict between sinful mankind and God and the resolution (of the conflict), i.e., the rescue of Noah. We have arrived at the conclusion that the 5 components of the main message-system which coincide with the present state of the society that has created the myth verifies the former communications through causal relationships. *The present of the myth,* though it tells about the first generation of the Indians, *is the time of the Spanish Conquest.* This justifies the descent from Spanish conquerors. The Spaniards just like Noah are the descendants of the "good" man and they release the conflict of creator = good ↔ created = evil. As we can see so far it entirely agrees with the above analyzed two myths, fulfils its function in the same way by justifying the rule of the conqueror. This myth—after the story of the Deluge—describes the life and fate of the first generation of the Indians. Let us examine the message system and armature *connected with the Bible:*

message:	God populates the New World with believers
armature:	God sends the Spaniards—the descendants of Noah—to the Inca kingdom
message:	they were monotheistic
armature:	they worshipped God and did not worship the demons and the huaca
message:	all of their deeds praised God
armature:	they did not know how to build houses and lived only for God
message:	they worshipped and served God
armature:	with such enthusiasm like the prophet Isaiah
message:	they cultivated land
armature:	they learnt how to plough from Adam and Eve

Connected with the Indian belief system:

message:	the first generation of Indians become dignified in the eyes of their descendants
armature:	the runa people of Huari viracocha did not die, they did not kill each other, they gave birth to a man and a woman at the same time
message:	the first Indians conquered the land
armature:	they killed beasts living on the earth
message:	they knew the creator of the heavens, the sky and the earth
armature:	he was called runa camac viracocha but no one knew him perfectly
message:	the first Indians did not know where they had come from

armature: they did not worship the idols, the sun, the moon, the demons, they did not remember the role of the Deluge though they had heard about it and they call it God's punishment

message: they worshipped gods

armature: (they worshipped) the creator of the world, the creator of mankind, the lord of the beginning and the lord of the end (these four marks can characterize one God, as well)

The analysis of the myths of the first generation of Indians resulted in an opposing message system and armature system that exclude each other. Nor can we set up an acceptable chronological order which could show a possible causality. At the same time, however, we can state that it is not an incoherent mass. The functional power of myth can overcome this anarchy, too, even if not without contradictions. The sub-message system connected with the Bible refers unanimously to the Spanish conquerors. They are believers of God (which is the only true faith), they taught people to cultivate land (culture heroes), and by this they represent the positive side of the first generation. The second sub-message system and armature system preserved the elements of the Indian belief system if we consider elements taken as "unknown" "unworshipped" with positive mark. Poma de Ayala considers the Spanish belief to be true; nevertheless he does not ignore the Indian belief system either; he would like to unite two opposing religious systems and two opposing kinds of knowledge. However, these are superstructures built upon two different systems of production and this way cannot be united. His aim is to describe without conflict the otherwise conflict-ridden relationship of Spaniards and Indians; by doing this he dissolves the inner logical system of the sub-message system.

With the above analysis of the three myths we proved that our original hypothesis, i.e., *the main message system of the myths is actualized by sub-message systems,* holds true. It has turned out that the different character of the myths is explained by the different life and fate of the human characters in them. The function of the myth to fulfil a social need alters the sub-message systems in accordance with the present of the myth. For the myth to fulfil this function completely it is necessary that there should be certain *continuity* in the socioeconomic development. This is verified by myths 6–7 and on the opposite pole by myth 8. The others could retain their autochthonous character, either because they reflect other economic relationships (e.g., myth 2) which were bypassed by history or there is no reference to social relations (e.g., myth 1) or it is only peripheral and has only local relevance as in myth 3.

Within such a cycle of myths describing a seemingly neutral natural phenomenon like the Deluge society is reflected. So Durkheim and Cassirer are right in saying that the origin of myth must be searched for not in the material but in social reality.

BIBLIOGRAPHY

Armas, Medina, F. 1953. *Cristianización del Peru (1532–1600).* Sevilla.

Avila, F. de. 1873. "A Narrative . . ." In C. R. Markham, ed., *Narratives of the Rites and Laws of the Yncas.* London.

Beidelman, T. O., ed. 1973. *The Translation of Culture.* London.

Boglár, L. 1967. *Eldorádó.* Budapest.

Campbell, J. 1959. *The Masks of God: Primitive Mythology.* New York.

Cassirer, E. 1944. *An Essay on Man.* New York.

Cieza de León, P. 1974. *La crónica del Peru.* Madrid.

Durkheim, E. 1912. *Les formes élémentaires de la vie religieuse.* Paris.

Eliade, M. 1960. *Myths, Dreams and Mysteries.* New York.

Garcilaso de la Vega. 1943. *Comentarios reales de los Incas.* Buenos Aires.

Guaman Poma de Ayala. 1944. *Primer nueva crónica y buen gobierno.* La Paz.

Harris, M. 1973. *The Highland Heritage.* New York.

Hewett, E. 1939. *Ancient Andean Life.* New York.

Hocart, A. 1975. *Mito, ritual y costumbre: Ensayos heterodoxos.* Madrid.

Hoppál, M. 1975. *A mitológia mint jelrendszer* (Mythology as a System of Signs). Szemiotikai Tanulmányok 17. Budapest.

Hoppál, M.—Vándor, Á. (szerk.) 1977. *Jel—kommunikáció—kultúra* (Sign—Communication—Culture). Budapest.

Józsa, P. 1976. *Claude Lévi-Strauss és a "homológ-metaforikus" kód* (Claude Lévi-Strauss and the "Homologous-metaphoric" Code). Ethnographia LXXXVII:3.

Kirk, G. S. 1970. *Myth. Its Meaning and Functions in Ancient and Other Cultures.* Los Angeles.

Krickeberg, W., ed. 1928. *Märchen der Azteken und Inkaperuaner, Maya und Muisca.* Jéna.

Lévi-Strauss, C. 1970. *Antropológia estructural.* La Habana. 1974. *El origen de las maneras de mesa. Mitológicas 3.* Madrid. 1975. *El hombre desnudo. Mitológicas 4.* Madrid.

Molina de C. 1913. *Relación de las fábulos y ritos de los Incas.* Lima.

Osborne, H. 1925. *Indians of the Andes.* Cambridge, Mass. 1968. *South American Mythology.* London.

Paredes, A. C. 1953. *Literatura folklórica.* La Paz.

Murray, A. H. 1960. *Myth and Mythmaking.* New York.

Penuelas, M. 1965. *Mito, literatura y realidad.* Madrid.

Polo de Ondegardo. 1977. *Información acerca de la religión y gobierno de los Incas.* Lima.

Raglan, L. 1936. *The Hero.* London.

Reichenbach, H. 1943. *Elements of Symbolic Logic.* London.

Sarmiento de Gamboa. 1942. *Historia de los Incas.* Buenos Aires.

Uganiza Araoz, M. 1958. *En el escenario de un mito.* La Plata.

Villanar, G. 1942. *Gramática del kechua y del ayamara seguido del diccionario kechua, ayamara, mitos y supersticiones.* La Paz.

Noah's Ark Revisited: On the Myth–Land Connection in Traditional Australian Aboriginal Thought

ERICH KOLIG

The acculturation situation in which two diverse and distinct peoples come into prolonged contact often results in some curious syncretistic forms of religious and mythological expression. Most anthropological studies of acculturation tend to treat what are essentially colonial contexts—that is, a so-called native culture invaded and dominated by a European culture. In one virtually predictable type of nativistic movement arising from the contact, a native religion, containing both old traditional elements and new ones from Christianity, comes into being.

The religious amalgam commonly reflects the native wish that the dominant ruling Europeans be eliminated, leaving the desirable foreign materials—say, manufactured trade goods—solely in the natives' possession. In what have been termed "cargo cults," the natives await ships bearing cargo not for the oppressive Europeans but for them. *Typically native prophets or self-proclaimed messiahs in these "messianic movements" command the native peoples to kill Europeans, destroy European money, and return to the old customs and ways which had been prohibited by the missionaries. These commands were supposedly preconditions for the arrival of goods for the natives. (Natives, having no knowledge of factories, simply assumed that ships themselves were the origin of coveted manufactured goods.)*

In the following account from aboriginal Australia by Erich Kolig, Senior Lecturer in Anthropology, Otago University, in New Zealand, we find an unusual version of the Judeo-Christian flood narrative in a nativistic movement setting. This discussion of Noah's Ark in Australia is part of a longer theoretical essay in which the general relationship between myth and landscape is considered.

For one of the earliest attempts to define nativistic movements, see Ralph

Reprinted from *Oceania* 51 (1980):118–132. (Only pp. 122–126, 128, 129 are reprinted here.)

Linton, "Nativistic Movements," American Anthropologist *45 (1943): 230–240. See also Peter Worsley,* The Trumpet Shall Sound: A Study of "Cargo" Cults in Melanesia *(London, 1957), or Ida Leeson,* Bibliography of Cargo Cults and Other Nativistic Movements in the South Pacific, *South Pacific Commission, Technical Paper No. 30 (Sydney, 1952).*

Anthropologists studying Aboriginal myth usually experience its land-connectedness as a fait-accompli. Such a static, *post hoc* rationalizing perspective necessarily is less revealing than a processual one, i.e., one based on empirical observation of how myth becomes attached to land. This may not only reveal the "how," but may go some way toward explaining the "why" of the connection. The ethnographic case by which I attempt to reconstruct the process of a myth's attachment to land is centered around Noah's Ark. This particular myth version and its site of manifestation combine to form a discrete syndrome, replete with millennial and redemptive features, and also are distinctly set apart from the well-known Christian belief element Aborigines are commonly familiar with. Although the myth has originally been known only locally in a small area south of the Fitzroy River (in the Kimberleys of Western Australia), owing to a far-flung religious communication network it is now well diffused throughout Aboriginal communities in La Grange (where the Petris have made brief reference to it; see Petri and Petri-Odermann 1964:465 and 1968:440), Broome, Derby, on stations along the middle and lower Fitzroy River, Fitzroy Crossing and even as far away as Balgo Mission. The particular myth version centers on a site on the Desert periphery—about 70 km south of Noonkanbah Station, just south of the Barbwire Range and east of the Worral Range—where the Ark is supposed to have come to rest after the deluge. There the Ark can still be seen today. But owing to the site's inaccessibility and remoteness it has not been visited by Aborigines for many years, possibly decades. The myth, however, has been thriving all the while, developing many a colorful offshoot. Over a period of nine years I made four attempts, all unsuccessful, to reach the site by vehicle, but finally succeeded in spotting it from the air in a single-engine aircraft. Unfortunately, while the site was positively identified by a guide, no detail could be made out. Nonetheless, I think this case permits significant insight into the process by which a myth becomes *arbitrarily* superimposed on a geographic site and embellished over the years. Admittedly, the relevant myth does not belong to the traditional Aboriginal repertory, but I can see no intrinsic reason that would disqualify it from being used for certain extrapolations. The Ark myth conforms to the common type of travel myth which relates how a myth being, or beings, appear coming from a distant "country"—the exact origin often being unknown—cover a large distance and finally enter the ground whereby the hero, or heroes, become manifested in the form of usually a rock, hill or water-hole on the surface.

Over the years and through countless hours of often painstaking discussion, I have gradually come to what I trust is a fairly accurate reconstruction of the myth-land connection. Soon after I had commenced research in the Fitzroy River area, in 1970, I came across the belief in a "boat left behind by Noah" somewhere south of the Fitzroy River. Later I chanced across an entry in Native Welfare files about an officer having received information on a "metal boat" on the Desert fringe near the Worral Range. It was speculated that the "boat" may in actual fact be the fuselage of a crashed airplane which on account of their unfamiliarity with planes, Aborigines might have misinterpreted. This seemed not too far-fetched a conjecture, as there had been an Air Force installation on Noonkanbah Station during World War II; and there was also the possibility that a Japanese war plane may have been hit during the raid on Broome and having veered off toward the Desert crashed there. Various Aborigines I discussed the matter with provided fanciful descriptions of the Ark's manifestation from which no unambiguous, clear picture could be inferred. The problem was compounded insofar as those I spoke to had seen the "boat" many years previously, some of them while they were adolescents. Their fading memory was counterpoised by extravagant fabrications, and some, I suspect, may only have known of the site from hearsay while claiming to have actually seen it. The vague image that gradually emerged was of a strange structure of sorts which Aborigines variously described as a metal contraption, a heavily rusted brittle matter, or a glass-like or crystalline substance. Several additional features emerged, forming an integral part of the entrenched belief: a variety of tools and equipment such as anchor, mast, railing, hatch, spade, crow bar and sledge hammer were said to lie about on the site—with further details varying according to a person's imagination, experience with boats and vocabulary. The Ark was said to be laden with gold and precious stone or mineral, and I was cautioned not to remove anything, presumably in view of the apparent greed of whites for mineral wealth. Not one Aboriginal I discussed the matter with had any doubt that it was really Noah's Ark. As one said, the white man's claim that the Ark had landed somewhere in Egypt (*sic*) was a lie consistent with the attempt to keep Aborigines in subservience, for Noah had actually come to Australia. I believe this to be a significant statement. The Ark being manifested in Australia, an important cosmic event through benevolent divine intent has been revealed for the benefit of Aborigines. Whites who have claimed a monopoly of this belief, by falsely associating it with a site and event far away in their own "country," have not only deliberately misled Aborigines, but also have tried to exclude them from obtaining a major revelatory truth.

The mythical story commonly agreed upon by Aborigines goes as follows. During the Dreamtime flood, *woramba,* the Ark Gumana carrying Noah, Aborigines and animals, had circumnavigated the St. George Ranges, having probably approached them from the north or northwest. It then had drifted south and finally as the waters receded had come to rest in its present position in the "flood plain" of Djilinbadu. The Biblical deluge corresponds with a traditional flood motif in this region, according to which the lizard woman Luma fleeing the rising waters traversed the region and eventually drowned at what is today the settlement of Looma (see Kolig 1973/4). Some Aborigines embellished the story of the primordial deluge with the opinion that all "wicked" people, both black and white who had been living in Australia, were drowned and only "good" Aborigines were spared by having been permitted aboard the Ark. Characteristically, all whites perished then and this is why until Captain Cook's arrival, Australia belonged only to Aborigines. (Others, however, maintained whites also travelled in the Ark and one even suggested that God himself had come along for the ride.) The obvious nativistic and mildly xenophobic overtones of this version were further heightened in another one which predicted a deluge to happen when somebody will pull, accidentally or not, the Ark's anchor from the ground and water will be gushing forth from the hole. The millennial augury of this version was that while all whites will subsequently be drowned in a *Götterdämmerung*-like catastrophe Aborigines would be rescued by the Ark and enter a new blissful era. Tying in with this is the belief that the Ark would sometimes be visible and sometimes invisible, in particular whites being most unlikely to see it. Special techniques were claimed to be required in the approach such as clutching a Bible, or praying, or receiving a dream about the Ark beforehand, or simply arriving accompanied by the present "boss" of the boat, an elder living in Looma.

By employing my own preconception about the nature of truth and fiction, I teased out a series of hard facts on the site, which were later verified—as much as this is possible from the air. The main manifestation of the Ark appears to be a whitish, soft or brittle stone monolith rising no more than approximately one meter above the ground and situated in a shallow claypan that fills with water after heavy rain. In the immediate vicinity some veins of similar material appear to run along the surface of the ground, branching out in a radius of probably less than thirty meters. These features are interpreted to be the mast and ribs, or railings, of the boat. The consistency of the monolith seems to be surprisingly soft as one man claimed he could stick a knife in it and reported that somebody else has split it easily with a tomahawk. (According to a personal communication from Dr. P. Playford, a geologist who has worked in the area, it probably is a lense of siltstone.) It is not unimportant to note that several persons had seen the site without noticing the boat, apparently prior to the myth-connection becoming more widely known. One man who had seen, unsuspectingly, the monolith several years ago while mustering cattle in the area—previously there had been a station in the relative vicinity—realized only during our discussion that what he had seen was the famed Ark of Noah. This indicates that there is nothing particularly striking or even faintly suggestive of a boat, of any size or description, about this place. While some claimed that most of the Ark now lies submerged under sand and soil, with only the "mast" protruding, it remains highly doubtful whether there really is some kind of petrographic structure attached to the "mast" underground, which earlier when still visible may have resembled a boat hull. The evidence suggests that the conception of a boat lying half-buried under the sand, more likely than anything else, is the result of a dream vision with no substantiation in either empirical fact or morphological similarity.

How did the superimposition of the myth on the site occur? The original "finder" of the Ark was the father of the present "boss" who lives in Looma and is well known among the Aborigines for synthesizing traditional Aboriginal belief with fundamentalist Protestant tenets. His father, known as "the Gagural"—a title of high honor with mythological connotations—was apparently also versed in Biblical mythology, besides having been an eminent expert of traditional lore and belief, a healer and clairvoyant. Roaming about in the area, he chanced across the site—it is not clear whether he saw it then for the first time or had been already familiar with it for some time. He subsequently received a dream vision in which it was revealed to him that he had found Noah's Ark. Unfortunately, there is little to go on concerning when exactly this had happened, but by inference from other data a time about 40 to 50 years ago seems most likely. Early promulgators of the myth and associated site were in close contact with Gagural, initially spreading the word only among Aborigines living on pastoral stations along the lower Fitzroy River. Only much later, owing to a now rapidly expanding communication network among Aborigines, was the message carried much farther afield.

Over the years, as the myth gradually spread, the initial revelation was elaborated upon not only producing several local and numerous individual variants, but adding to the myth's standard corpus. For instance, the well-entrenched idea of considerable treasures laid up in the boat appears to have been added much later and to have developed from several roots simultaneously. According to one man who provided restrained and reasoned information on the subject, it had occurred to him years after he had seen the Ark that there must be riches heaped up in it. This happened when he worked in the Halls Creek area and saw veins of white stone—some of which, by the way, are quite spectacular and are tourist attractions. These are quartzitic intrusions and in the Halls Creek area they occur in conjunction with gold. Seeing these veins the man felt reminded of the whitish stuff on the site of the Ark and soon made the logical, though geologically improbable and empirically unfounded, connection between gold and the light-colored stone of the Ark. Another contributory factor was the rumor reaching Aborigines about Dutch shipwrecks found in shallow waters off the Western Australian coastline, and some of which were literally laden with gold coins and other valuable objects. It seems plausible that this information, exaggerated and distorted as it may have been when reaching Aborigines, built up the idea that just about every wrecked ship, or Ark for that matter, must contain treasures. Perhaps not to a small extent the experience Aborigines have with mineral prospecting has had some influence too. Aborigines widely believe that most, if not all, stone and mineral, whether of peculiar appearance or not, must be precious since whites seem to search for them so eagerly. And when Aborigines speak of gold stored away in the Ark they may not mean it literally, but use "gold" as the common synonym for all kinds of valuable stone. No wonder Aborigines are reluctant to lead whites to the site, fearing of course their relentless avarice for minerals which may usher in the destruction of the Ark. Then there are less well entrenched variations on the basic theme, such as the belief in the end-time deluge and rescue of true-believing Aborigines. The myth element of the wicked having been drowned presumably is an adjunct of fundamentalist missionary provenance, as that brand of Protestantism habitually stresses atonement for sins. Another one about a left-hander having stopped the flood by dripping off blood from the small finger of his left hand seems to be of traditional origin. Variations range from widely known ones to way-out, idiosyncratic ones that are hardly shared by more than one or two. An example of the latter kind is the belief that a goat—of all possible guardians—is now "looking after" the boat.

By probing underneath the complex trappings of what this myth may have come to mean to individual persons, some fundamental aspects of the myth-land connection, its meaning and process of attachment can be extrapolated. Above all, the case demonstrates how a mytheme becomes suddenly, arbitrarily and one might say whimsically superimposed on a topographical feature that has been known for a long time. The actual physical appearance of the feature is of no account, as has been shown by the fact that Aborigines gave so many divergent descriptions of the site. They were not deliberately trying to obscure the picture; but to them it was a boat regardless of how it might present itself to the nonbeliever's eye. All this and more adds weight to the contention that myths do not convincingly present themselves as explanations of the landscape, or as aetiological theories. . . .

As said before, some physiographic features have an "explanation" and some do not. Selection is random as well as completely arbitrary and apparently depends on chance revelation. As the Ark syndrome shows, the process of myth attachment does not appear to be guided by whether a natural feature is suggestive of the mythic shapes subsequently superimposed on it. This speaks clearly against myth having been developed from the land feature so as to explain it. It might be claimed that Aborigines could not interpret the Ark manifestation as such before their stock of knowledge was expanded so as to include boats. Equipped as they are in post-contact time with enhanced experience (knowledge of western technology and technical things for instance) and new conceptual tools, Aborigines might be able to detect new meaning in familiar shapes and to provide interpretations of land features that had hitherto eluded their mythopoetic efforts since they were not suggestive of anything known. But as it turns out a monolith may be a Dreamtime being, a phallus, a ship's mast or simply a stone. And a tree may come to be seen as a camp marker, a spear, a boomerang, a man's soul or just a tree. There is no outward correlation between the physical manifestation and the manifested. . . .

The history of the Ark myth shows that an initially individual and private revelation becomes gradually more widely accepted and incorporated in a population's standard belief system. Much depends probably on the status and prestige of the recipient of the vision or intuition. Some revelations received by minor men may never become commonly accepted and may soon be dropped as unconvincing. The Ark myth also demonstrates that over the years as a myth becomes embraced by ever more people, it becomes embellished. Additional mythemes are incorporated, pieces of information, actual experiences and the like are tacked on, thus gradually building up a highly complex end result of accumulated sedimentation.[1] Part of this phase—after the connection between myth and land has been established—is that the myth becomes adapted to local geographic or geomorphological peculiarites. In this constricted sense the landscape does serve as a minor source of inspiration; a kind of mythopoetic supplement. So did some Aborigines come to see tools, anchor, etc., manifested in rocks randomly strewn about on the site of the Ark—an addendum of which others are less convinced.

REFERENCES

Kolig, E. (1973/4). Glaube als Rechtsmittel: Anatomie eines Landanspruchs moderner Schwarzaustralier. *Wiener Völkerkundliche Mitteilungen* 20/21 N.F. 15/16:69–93.

Leach, E. (1974). Review of Munz, P., *When the Golden Bough Breaks. Man* 9/2:320–2.

Munz, P. (1973). *When the Golden Bough Breaks: Structuralism or Typology?* Routledge, London.

Petri, H., and Petri-Odermann, G. (1964). Nativismus und Millenarismus im gegenwärtigen Australien. In: *Festschrift für A. E. Jensen,* Teil 2, Klaus Renner, Munich.

Petri, H., and Petri-Odermann, G. (1968). Stabilität und Wandel: historische Gegenwartssituationen unter farbigen Völkern Australiens. *Ethnologica* N.F. 4:420–54.

[1] I do not wish to imply that this process results in increasing specification that would allow arranging myths serially (see Munz 1973 and Leach 1974). As often as myths increase in complexity and detail, they are probably dismantled and broken down into their components which in turn may serve as mythopoetic starting points.

Myth Motifs in Flood Stories from the Grassland of Cameroon

EMMI KÄHLER-MEYER

It is a commonplace among flood myth scholars that the flood story is absent or at any rate rarely reported in Africa. Frazer, one recalls, went so far as to claim that "indeed no single clear case of one [version] has yet been reported." The alleged African flood myth lacuna has been challenged by a specialist in African mythology, Hermann Baumann. In his discussion of "Die Grosse Flut" (pp. 307–319) in his comprehensive Schöpfung und Urzeit des Menschen im Mythus der afrikanischen Völker *(Berlin, 1936), he maps some two dozen occurrences in Africa, although he admits that several of them were undoubtedly introduced by Christian missionaries. In view of the hundreds of distinct cultures in Africa, it remains true that relatively few native flood myth texts have been elicited in this part of the globe.*

Given the paucity of authentic flood myth texts from Africa, the following essay, which includes several oral versions from West Africa, is of special interest. Moreover, its specific details, such as sibling incest, are reminiscent of similar flood myths reported in Southeast Asia, while the pot containing the flood is also found in South Asia. Certainly these few versions must give pause to those comparativists who continue to maintain that the flood myth is not to be found in sub-Sarahan Africa. For additional discussion of possible African texts, see A. J. Wagener, Afrikanische Parallelen zur biblischen Urgeschichte *(Bonn, 1927), pp. 13, 18–19, 30.*

In his "Die Sintflutsagen als kausal-logische Naturschöpfungsmythen," a contribution to *Festschrift P. W. Schmidt* (1928:515–526), A. W. Nieu-

Reprinted in translation from Emmi Kähler-Meyer, "Mythenmotive in Flutsagen aus dem Grasland von Kamerun," in Veronika Six et al., eds., *Afrikanische Sprachen und Kulturen—Ein Querschnitt,* Hamburger Beiträge zur Afrika-Kunde, Band 14 (Hamburg: Deutsches Institut für Afrika-Forschung, 1971), pp. 279–287. I am indebted to anthropologist Uli Linke for translating this essay into English. [The German spellings of tribal and place names have been Anglicized wherever possible. Information given in brackets was supplied by the translator.—Translator's Note] wenhuis strives for a psychologically based explanation of the following facts: that flood legends in general are common throughout the world; that they exist among peoples at all stages of cultural development; and that almost always *one* single flood or some other devastation is involved—even in areas where floods, droughts, and so forth are frequently occurring phenomena. He ascertains the following: "If one abstracts from the local peculiarities, however, then all great-flood legends have in common (1) the destruction of the existing, usually supernatural world, (2) the rise of a new world, frequently the present one, (3) in the course of which, insofar as these myths were transmitted in full length, a deity or another being endowed with superior powers appears on the scene as actor" (1928:517). He substantiates the idea of an initially supernatural world and the emergence of a new world from a catastrophe by means of the assumption that "primitive" peoples had only limited knowledge of the biology of plants and animals and no conception of a gradual, evolutionary development, but they made very exact observations and searched for an *explanation* for everything which attracted their attention. The explanation of the genesis of the present world, their own creation, and their tribal territory can only lie "outside the activities of daily life, thus outside of everything that is natural for them." The "supernatural origin" is conceived, among other things, as the result of a "supernatural act" whose author may be "a supernatural, powerful being, spirit, deity, ancestor, or perhaps even a shaman" (Nieuwenhuis, 1928:524). Even animals appear as super-powerful beings.

In essence, this is Nieuwenhuis's theory. He developed his thesis clearly on the basis of the relevant literature. Apart from the psychological explanation of the legends about the destruction of all that exists, in each case there always remains the respective "local mythical fabric." "Its explanation must be a local, regional, or mixed one, and it may well be dependent on completely different psychological factors" (Nieuwenhuis, 1928:526). With Nieuwenhuis's analysis in front of us, it is unnecessary to enter into a discussion of the basic considerations in the older literature (Andree, 1891; Riem, 1906; Gerland, 1912; Müller, 1930). Only the question about individual mythical traits which surface in recently recorded great-flood and other legends of destruction remains to be explored.

Earlier scholars of the great-flood theme have emphasized that in contrast to other parts of the world, there exist only a few representative versions of the flood legend in Africa. Some have pointed to its occurrence there in Egypt, among the Masai, in South and Southwest Africa, as well as on the Gold Coast (Andree, 1891). Moreover, Gerland (1912:34–35) briefly mentions Oldendorp and his flood legend report.

Since C.G.A. Oldendorp's *Geschichte der Mission der evangelischen Brüder auf den caraibischen Inseln S. Thomas, S. Croix and S. Jan* (1777) can be obtained only with difficulty, I shall here quote from the seventh section of his chapter "Von den Kenntnissen der Neger, ihrem Tode und Begrabnis" (1777:309 [as cited by Gerland, 1912:34–51]), which contains a passage of the flood legend as it was brought by the slaves from their African homeland to the West Indies:

> About the history of creation I have found no trace among them; but I have here and there noted a vague and distorted knowledge about the destruction of the human race as the result of the great flood. Several Watje[1] told me that at home they had heard about a general flood across the earth in which all human beings would have perished had they not immediately sought rescue on the highest mountain. Among the Kassenti is a tradition that God shall once again afflict humanity with such a flood as punishment. . . . The Kanga and Loango[2] also have a tradition about a general extermination of the human race, which however was not caused by water, but by the collapse of the sky,[3] and after all human beings had been crushed beneath its rubble, God produced a new human race.

When drawing on Baumann's *Schöpfung und Urzeit des Menschen im Mythus der afrikanischen Völker* (1936), one not only finds numerous examples of myth motifs in narratives about human catastrophes, but it also becomes apparent that legends concerning the destruction of the human race and the formation of a new world are much more widespread even in Africa than was assumed in the old sources. In 1938, I myself was told a very simple version of the great-flood legend among the local Kaka people at Mbem in the northern Baumenda district of Cameroon. In 1966 a Kaka student at Yaoundé wrote down a more complete version for me which he had also recorded on tape. Since the Kaka text in both cases would require an extensive commentary, I will here omit it and quote only the English translation, beginning with the one by Joseph Ngachí Mekwí, the student at Yaoundé:

> One afternoon, in a certain village, a small girl and her brother were in their home after everybody had gone away to their farms. The girl was grinding on a stone outside their house. A he-goat came and started to

[1] According to Oldendorp (1777:283), they belong to the tribes of the Slave Coast. Is Watje = Watyi, who, according to Westermann (*Wörterbuch der Ewe-Sprache*, Berlin, 1954:x), form the central group of the Ewe dialects together with the Gẽ [or Gā] and Adya peoples?

[2] Linguistically belong to the Congo group.

[3] To this compare the destruction of the first human race as a result of the collapse of the sky in Unyoro [= Bunyoro] (Baumann, 1936:307).

lick the flour she was making. She drove it away, but soon it returned again. The girl allowed it to lick as much of the flour as it could. After it had eaten enough of it, it said to the girl: "I have something very important to tell you. Today there will be a great flood, and because of your kindness to me I advise you and your brother to run away right away to another place."

They gathered up a few things which they could carry and fled away from the village. As they were going away they saw behind them a sheet of water submerging their village.

They found a certain place where they lived on their own for many years without any human beings around them. So they thought of what to do in order to reproduce. Then the he-goat reappeared and told them that they could marry themselves even though they were brother and sister. But, he told them, they must burst the bottom of a clay pot and fix it on to the pointed part of the roof. In addition they had to attach to it an empty hoe-handle. This signified that they were relatives.

That's why up till today when someone marries a very close relative, the couple must have a broken pot and a hoe-handle hung on their roof.

Here is the version by Peter Gṳyʾ in Pidgin-English, which he gave to me in Mbem with his text and which I have modified slightly in accordance with the Kaka text:

The goat be come, small pickin then they grind fufu for some time.[4] The goat lick the boy fufu. The boy drove'm (= him). He go for another boy [the other child], then begin for chop. The pickin say: "Drove'm!" He brother say: "No drove'm, he be my father goat." The goat chop the fufu, he belly full up, he take road for go.

When the goat he go, he talk for the pickin: "When something come, you look the place the mouse[5] go. When the mouse pass, you and your sister must follow him." He talk finish he go. Small time they look water day come. They look now, the mouse pass. He follow him with his sister.

The water come, cover all people, kill them all. He get save with his sister too. He run go for another country.[6] One day he dream, say[7] God[8] give medicine, say he shall broke bottom of pot.[9] He marry sister as his wife, he take the pot, he go cover him for the head house.[10]

[4] In the Kaka text *máraŋ* "afternoon" also means "one afternoon."

[5] In the Kaka text *má-lu´úntɔŋ* is "a lizard."

[6] In the Kaka text *láx̧* "city, village" is inclusive of the nearby vicinity which is identical to the tribal territory.

[7] Kaka *dé* "say" corresponds to the conjunction "that, which."

[8] In the Kaka text *ŋwi,* compare to Bali *ŋikɔb* "divine creator," which is probably a compound construction with *kɔb* "forest, brush."

[9] That is, God has given the pot as medicine.

[10] Kaka *tú-ńdáb* "head of the house" = "roof," here "the tip of the roof"; *tú* "head" is also used for "tip."

While Joseph's rendition of the great-flood legend is the narrative of a young, modern African who tells the legend correctly and matter-of-factly, Peter's short and unclear rendering nevertheless contains authentic mythological traits.

Both tales correspond in that *a brother and a sister* are saved and marry and thereby begins a new era of human history. We encounter this motif also in a great-flood legend from southern China (Riem, 1906:40–44; following Nieuwenhuis, 1928:519). Also among the Mundari, a tribe of the Kolh south of the central Ganges, only a brother and his sister are saved in the legend about the fiery water which God lets pour down from the sky as punishment for those human beings who have grown evil (Andree, 1891:25–26; Gerland, 1912:71–72). But we find similar versions in Africa. Among the Baule (or Baoule) on the Ivory Coast the descendants of the man saved from the flood married each other, even when they were brother and sister (Baumann, 1936: 372). Among the Chagga at Mount Kilimanjaro and elsewhere, brothers and sisters married each other in the beginning, and Baumann (1936: 370) determines generally that according to the creation myths, the beginning was always marked by a *marriage between siblings.* Since the children of the primal couple married each other, and "with the wide distribution of the idea of a primordial couple in African myth, it compels one to presuppose a marriage between brother and sister as a necessity of primeval times" (Baumann, 1936:383). In our Kaka legend as well as in the legends from southern China and eastern India cited above, the primal couple of the new world already consisted of a brother and a sister! Consequently, a brother and a sister had to be the only ones saved from the flood catastrophe. The rescue of the siblings from the world preceding the great flood is here the logical prerequisite for the marriage between brother and sister.

The motif of the pot with the broken bottom which is placed over the tip of the cone-shaped roof as a sign of marriage between relatives seems strange, and I have found no explicit reference to it in other flood legends. However, Huber's essay "Die unheilbringende Schwiegertochter" (1967:789–801), in the subsection on "the creation of lakes and oceans," contains a flood myth from the Kwaya [Kwa-Yao?] peoples of the Musoma district on the east bank of Lake Victoria, according to which the ocean was formerly enclosed in a small pot, which was kept under the roof (!) in the old round hut (!) of an old man and his wife. This pot filled, in a magical way, the larger water pots of the household. On a special occasion, the old man explained to the daughter-in-law who did not know the secret: "There in that pot are our ancestors (the ancestors are sacred to us). Our ancestors are in there; do not let anyone touch it. Even you must not touch it!" But the daughter-in-law could not contain her curiosity and touched the pot. It shattered into pieces, and the water poured forth. Everything drowned in the flood. Huber contends that the daughter-in-law should hardly have believed the improbable story which the old man told her about the ancestors in the pot (1967:799). Our Kaka legend, however, in my opinion, shows that Huber was mistaken, for even according to Peter's simple narrative a supernatural power was actively associated with the pot: it is a gift from God. Furthermore, the fastening of the pot to the top of the roof is supposed to ward off evil (see below).

The motif of the hoe-handle, which, according to the student's narrative, had to be attached to the pot, also suggests a comparison with the Kwaya legend, according to which the ancestors gave their descendants the valuable gift of water by means of the pot. As a symbol of tillage, the hoe-handle may perhaps represent the link to the ancestors. I have not encountered the hoe-handle in connection with the flood legend elsewhere in the literature.

As to the breaking of the bottom of the pot, one wonders whether it may perhaps be interpreted as a sign of the flood which poured forth from the pot. This would presuppose, however, that also among the Kaka there once existed the notion that water was originally enclosed in a pot. In this context reference may be made to a flood legend among the Babua at the upper Ubangi River (in Zaire), according to which an old woman hid all the water in her pots. Baumann (1936:193, 311) includes it in the category of myth concerned with the origin of water. Furthermore, it should be mentioned that among the Ukelle in the Cross River region, the water pot stands as a symbol for their three gods (Baumann, 1936:129–30).

Following the previous discussion, I think that a connection between the pot motif in the East African Kwaya legend and the Kaka legend from the grassland of Cameroon cannot be dismissed out of hand, even if it has been formulated differently in another tribal environment. Some might feel that I am not justified in comparing such details of the Kaka narrative as a pot and a hoe-handle on the roof with similar features mentioned by Huber with respect to the tribes at Lake Victoria on the grounds of the great distance between these peoples. In response, I would mention the fact that in former times the Sahara was fertile and habitable. This means that peoples with these old myths might have lived in other parts of the Sahara than in present-day West and East Africa.

Marriages between relatives are, by the way, common among the Kaka, and without this phenomenon it would likewise be unthinkable that a custom of this kind should be preserved, whereby a couple up to this day attaches a pot with a broken bottom to the tip of the roof of their house. With regard to this, I was told the following at Mbem (Cameroon): "If a man marries a girl who is from the same farmstead as his own mother, then he breaks the bottom of a pot and places it on the rooftop of their house. If, for instance, my mother belongs to the principal farmstead and so does the mother of the bride, then I do this in order that nothing evil will happen to me. Such marriages are permitted. If I marry a girl from my father's family, I do the same. It is done in the case of every marriage between kin. Here it happens frequently."

Let us now turn to the animal motif in our Kaka legend. The goat appears in both versions. It may eat from the porridge which the girl has mashed, and out of gratitude for this kindness it warns the siblings about the coming of the great flood. In the student's narrative, the billy goat reappears after the flood and gives them permission to marry each other, under the condition that they fasten a clay pot with a broken bottom and a hoe-handle to the tip of their house. The billy goat is here the magical agent, while in Peter's narrative God himself gives the "medicine." In his narrative still another animal appears, namely the lizard, which according to the goat's instruction shows the siblings the way to their rescue.

The motif of the animal as helper and savior of human beings has been documented frequently (Baumann, 1936:375). In connection with the great flood, it is for instance known in Peru where a shepherd is warned of the flood by his llamas (Andree, 1891:115–116). That in our legend the goat is capable of a supernatural act need not surprise us. As the traditional African domestic animal, it is very common in the grassland of Cameroon and also serves as a sacrificial offering, as for example at the great Lela festival among the Bali. (The Bali are of the Chamba tribe in Cameroon.)

The fact that the lizard is introduced as a second animal does not really come as a surprise. Since time is of the essence in saving the siblings from the flood, it must be a swift animal. Among the Pangwe and some other Bantu tribes in Cameroon, the lizard also appears as the speedy animal in myths about the origin of death (Baumann, 1936:269ff). The degree to which it is interwoven with myth and ritual is also expressed in the lizard motif which is commonly affixed to products of the arts and crafts from the grassland. In its connection with a flood legend, the lizard is otherwise known only among the Vili of Loango where, during the great flood, men turned into monkeys and women into lizards (Baumann, 1936:309, 329).

The destruction of the first (supernatural) world and the creation of the second (present) world are, according to Nieuwenhuis, the essential building blocks of flood legends. Most of the time such a catastrophe is concerned with a great flood, but sometimes a great fire, the collapse of the sky, snowfall, earthquakes, jet-black rain, and the like are depicted as the triggering element. The concept of the myth of a great flood is thus understood in a very broad sense. In my opinion one can also include the following legend in the same complex even if it makes no mention of the rescue of one or two human beings from destruction, but rather reports the transformation of humans into monkeys. To begin with, the narrative corresponds to the flood legends, and in particular to a segment of those legends of the Vineta type (following Baumann, 1936), which is found more frequently in Africa. Human beings became guilty of a crime by denying someone a request and they were cursed by the old woman who had begged for food at their doorsteps. In our case, however, there does not follow the usual destruction of the village in question nor a great flood (Baumann, 1936:316–317, 318–319, 326–327), but rather the *transformation of human beings into monkeys.* The narrative in which humans are transformed into monkeys because of some sort of offense is, according to Baumann (1936:329), "an especially popular legend in Africa." Monkeys are also reputed to be degraded human beings (Baumann, 1936:349). That people became animals in a flood legend is also documented among the Vili of Loango (Baumann, 1936:329, 309): "The aged human beings took their porridge spoons, attached them to their backs as tails and became monkeys (probably to be able to escape more swiftly). Others say the men became monkeys and the women, lizards" (see above).

Now to our legend, which was dictated to me in the Bali language in 1937 by Johannes **Ndandzə̯́m Fɔ́ŋgɔn,** a born **Mu̯ta,** the headmaster of the school in Bali (Bamenda district, Cameroon):[11]

1. bimɔ̌' bun ní ŋ́gâ, Bǎmu̯ntu̯ŋ bô̤ bimɔ̌' ŋgo̤d bun bi bó ka bó̤ má ṁbȧd Mú̯ndáŋkwe', má lṳ̌' olé yi, bó kúd Baménda station ɣwú' ȧ. 2. bó ɣâ, bo bun ka bó̤ má tsú'kɔb sísi lé, yi á má tsṳŋní ntán Sunday má Baménda. 3. bo bun ka vó̤ lɔ' kwǎm, ḿbṳ̌d ńti' bambitsɔ'.

4. bó ɣâ, a ka bó̤ ni mɔ̌' ḿfú̯ɲum, mɔ̌' ndɛn mu̯ŋgwí la má ŋgɔŋ ntsǔńdâ Bǎmu̯ntú̯ŋ bė mé' ní ńdón ńtsi, bó tí fá i bó̤. 5. álė í ku' ŋgó̤ kú̯ntɛd Fɔ-Mû̯ntú̯ŋ ma lón ntsi lé ɣwú'; ɣwí mfon lé ɲṳ' í ɲṳ̌'. 6. álė ndɛn mu̯ŋgwí lė yô̤ ŋgó̤' a tsǎ mbo mí ȧ má ŋgɔŋ lé ńtsú' lė, mbí' ntṳ í ka dzúm, bun tí bím ḿfá í ntsi bó̤. 7. ndzə̯́m ṡɛn i kú̯mvi, bun tí bím ńnú̯ŋ í má ndáb bó̤. 8. álė a bí tsě ni ɣó̤'ŋgɔŋ ni ndib yi bun bɛ̌d mú̯ ni ńnɔŋkɛ́d ni ṅdi bȧb ȧ, ndɛn mu̯ŋgwí lė kɔ́' kṳ́tṳ mɔ̌' ḿbȧd ńdzɔ̌m yáb ŋ́gâ, a bɔ̌ŋ ɲikɔb bṳd yáb, bó tí' baɲam, mbí' ńdzô̤ ndzení-nu báb fṳní bô̤ i bamvṳ́ á. 9. í ka súŋ yí', mbí'

[11] Because of the spelling, see my "Märchen in der Balisprache," *Zeitschrift für Eingeborenen-Sprachen* 32 (1941/42):135–160, 224–236, and "Spiele bei den Bali in Kamerun," *Afrika und Übersee* 39 (1954/55):179–190. In the following text, as in the Kaka words above, the lower tone has remained unmarked.

ńdzô̤ mvṳ́ ma ní mbím ŋ́gâ, mɔ̌' ḿfɛ́li mvṳ́ kɔ̂d kědzṳ bí ni ndib yi ndzi dzáŋ yáb bó̤. 10. álė ɲikəb ka yú' ndzi ndɛn mṳ̭ŋgwí lė ńnṳ́ŋ ŋ́gó̤' ndû Bămṳ̭ntṳŋ bé; bó bṳd ntí' bambitsɔ'.

11. a ka bǒ̤ ni mbá'ḿbȧ' ntsú' lė ŋgɔŋ ndáb mé' bṳd ńtí ntsúŋńtsu̇ŋ; bun bó ka nɔnkɛ́d mádzǐ á tí' ńtúm bô̤ ni sáŋ ni tsṳŋni yáb, ḿbô̤ bṳ̌d mṳ̭́ ńtí' bambitsɔ'. 12. lɔ' ntsú' lė bambitsɔ' kô̤ túmbȧd Bămbṳ́luɣwi mé' ní ńtí' ńnɔ́ŋ báb bô̤ má kɔb kṳ̭ kṹ' ḿbó̤ bun bó̤. 13. yǒ ńdzô̤ ŋgɔ̌ŋ Bămṳ̭ntṳŋ ka vó̤ ȧ, bambitsɔ' sě saŋ kṳ̭́mvi ȧ.

(1) Some people say that the inhabitants of Muntüng were one human race who lived on the mountain of Mundankwe at just that place where (later) the Bamenda station was built. (2) They say that these human beings congregated in the small dark forest which lies below the (present-day) Sunday market of Bamenda. (3) These humans disappeared a long time ago and turned into monkeys.

(4) It is said that one night an old woman passed by all the doors of the Muntüng people and asked for water without anyone giving her any. (5) Then she went to the farmstead of the chief of Muntüng in order to request some water there, but the wives of the chief drove her away. (6) Then the old woman on that day fell into unbearable distress in the city because her heart (here = her body) was dried up and the people did not want to give her any water. (7) Darkness came upon her outside without anyone having offered to take her into their home. (8) Then when it was midnight, after the people had turned her away and had gone to bed and were asleep, the old woman climbed to the top of a hill and cursed them so that God should transform them into animals because their actions were like those of dogs. (9) She said that because a dog does not allow a brother-dog to touch his food when it is hungry. (10) God heard the voice of the old woman and afflicted the people of Muntüng with misfortune; they became monkeys.

(11) By the next morning all the houses had turned upside down and stood on their heads (with the pointed tip of the roof toward the ground). The human beings who had slept inside came out with tails on their behinds and were transformed and had become monkeys. (12) From that day on the monkeys have taken possession of all the mountains of Bambuluwi and have slept in the forest and are no longer human beings. (13) So it happened that the city of the Muntüng people disappeared and the monkeys spread throughout the world.

Baumann (1936:101) quotes a myth of the Fiote that was mentioned by Bastian, "according to which Nzambi-Mpungu, the divine creator in the sky, transformed the first human beings who had rebelled against him into monkeys and then created a new human race." The narrative of the headmaster at Bali discusses only the destruction of a single village. The creation of a totally new human race was therefore not necessary. But if one presumes that the local legend is based on an older, global myth, then the transformation of human beings into monkeys solely for reasons of punishment would be insufficient. As in the myth of the Fiote, the new world would need a new humanity. In my opinion this seems to be an additional point which allows us to interpret the legend about the destruction of Muntüng as a degenerate flood myth.

What are the results of the analysis of the myth motifs in the two legends from the Bamenda district of Cameroon? Let us summarize them as follows.

The marriage between brother and sister in flood legends is found not only in Africa but is also attested in Asia, yet a direct connection does not necessarily exist. The marriage of siblings who were rescued from the old world and went into the new is rather to be understood in connection with the concept of a primeval couple and the marriage of its children, that is, in the larger context of creation myths.

The motif of the water pot in association with the great flood has also been found among the Kwaya at Lake Victoria and among the Babua of the upper Ubangi River. Here I see a very plausible connection so that the pot is not to be conceived of as a purely local motif, but as one belonging to a larger regional area. It is noteworthy that the pot of the Kaka legend assumes importance only after the great flood while the touching of the pot triggers the flood among the Kwaya. Under these circumstances, it is the breaking of the bottom of the pot and the attachment of the pot to the rooftop which assumes meaning in the Kaka legend. It could be the second phase of a mythological event while the first phase, namely the enclosure of water in a pot hidden under the rooftop before the great flood, was lost. In this case, the broken bottom may perhaps be suggestive of the bursting forth of a flood of water. I consider the hoe-handle, which, among the Kaka, is added to the pot, as a local phenomenon. It symbolizes in all likelihood the effective power of the ancestors with respect to the rescue before the great flood and their shielding hand in the case of marriage between brother and sister.

Animals assume completely different functions in the two legends. Among the Kaka, the goat is a predominantly powerful being who is responsible for the rescue and, later, the marriage of the siblings. The lizard shows them the route of flight at the goat's bidding. Both animals, as well as the dog, which was mentioned in the legend about the destruction of Muntüng, belong to the "local mythical fabric."

A completely different situation pertains with the monkeys in the second legend. They are a rarely attested motif in flood myths and through them the narrative suffers a break. The first part in which the old woman revenges herself by cursing the village inhabitants for their refusal of her plea for water belongs to the Vineta type. But now the human population does not drown; it is degraded to the status of monkeys. The legend thereby links up with the more frequently occurring motif of the transformation of human beings into monkeys, and with the apparent and close relation between humans and monkeys. No mention is made of a flood. Only the inversion of the houses on the morning after the curse so that they stood on their heads points, in my opinion, to a destruction of the village, as in the Vineta legend. There can hardly be another explanation of this curious motif. If one were to detach the legend from its local boundaries and place it in a global framework, however, the transformation of human beings into monkeys should be followed by the creation of a new human race. Only such an interpretation gives us the right to classify this certainly younger and repeatedly modified legend with the old flood myths—myths that tell of the destruction of an originally supernatural world as well as the formation of the present-day world.

REFERENCES

Andree, Richard. *Die Flutsagen: Ethnographisch betrachtet.* Braunschweig, 1891.

Baumann, Hermann. *Schöpfung und Urzeit des Menschen im Mythus der afrikanischen Völker.* 2nd ed. Berlin, 1936.

Gerland, Georg. *Der Mythus von der Sintflut.* Bonn, 1912.

Huber, Hugo. "Die unheilbringende Schwiegertochter: Ätiologische Motive im Mythengut der Kwaya (Ostafrika)." *Anthropos* 62 (1967): 789–801.

Müller, Werner. "Die ältesten amerikanischen Sintfluterzählungen." Dissertation, Bonn, 1930.

Nieuwenhuis, A. W. "Die Sintflutsagen als kausal-logische Naturschöpfungsmythen." In *Festschrift P. W. Schmidt.* Vienna, 1928. Pp. 515–526.

Oldendorp, C.G.A. *Geschichte der Mission der evangelischen Brüder auf den caraibischen Inseln S. Thomas, S. Croix und S. Jan.* Edited by Johann Jakob Bossart. Vol. 1. Barby: Christian Friedrich Laux; Leipzig: in commission of Weidmann's Erben and Reich, 1777.

Riem, Johannes. *Die Sintflut: Eine ethnographisch-naturwissenschaftliche Untersuchung.* Christentum und Zeitgeist: Hefte zu "Glauben und Wissen," No. 9. Stuttgart, 1906.

Thompson, Stith. *Motif-Index of Folk-Literature.* Rev. and enlarged edition. Copenhagen, 1955–1958. (I have not found any references to the subject in this source.)

Westermann, Diedrich. *Wörterbuch der Ewe-Sprache.* Berlin, 1954.

The Flood Motif and the Symbolism of Rebirth in Filipino Mythology

FRANCISCO DEMETRIO

The flood myth has been collected among peoples of the Pacific. In the Philippines, according to Francisco Demetrio, S.J., a long-time student of the folklore of this area, there are a number of versions. Demetrio was greatly influenced by the writings of Mircea Eliade, who in Patterns in Comparative Religion *(New York, 1958), p. 212, argued that "ritual lustrations and purifications with water are performed with the purpose of bringing into the present for a fleeting instant 'that time,'* illud tempus, *when the creation took place; they are a symbolic reenactment of the birth of the world or of the 'new man.'" This is Demetrio's point of departure in his discussion of flood myths in the Philippines. It should be noted that his remarks are part of a general consideration of "creation myths" including that of the cosmic egg (see motif A641, Cosmic egg: The universe brought forth from an egg, or motif A1222, Mankind originates from eggs). For further information on the cosmic egg myth, see Franz Lukas, "Das Ei als kosmogonische Vorstellung,"* Zeitschrift des Vereins für Volkskunde *4 (1894): 227–243; Anna-Britta Hellbom, "The Creation Egg,"* Ethnos *28 (1963): 63–105.*

The egg motif the world over is generally linked with the symbolism not of birth, but of rebirth, or the repetition of the birth of the world at the moment of creation. The egg motif, in both myth and ritual, has definite connections with the symbols of the renovation either of nature or of vegetation as well as with the cult of the dead. Now Spring and the New Year themselves, in mythic thinking, are symbols of the first emergence of the world from chaos and unformed existence or the great round, before it became fragmented. In other words, the coming of Spring and the New Year themselves are symbolic of the eternal return to the state of chaos and the state of latencies or of

Reprinted from "Creation Myths Among the Early Filipinos," *Asian Folklore Studies* 27 (1968):41–79. (Only pp. 70–73 have been included here.)

seeds in the beginning. This return (according to archaic theory) can be effected either by an *ekpyrosis,* general conflagration, or by a cataclysm in the form of a universal deluge. This return to the original state is necessary in order to renew the exhausted forces and energies of the entire universe, and thus secure its continual existence.[1] In this way the eternal round of existence in cycles is secured. In this connection, the egg motif, whether on the cosmic or the human level, is a symbol not so much of birth, but of rebirth. Like the tree, the egg is also a symbol of nature and its continual renewal through death unto new life.[2]

We mentioned that this renewal could be effected by a universal flood. Now we have flood myths among the Ifugaos and other pagan tribes of the Philippines.

The Ifugaos tell of a great drought which dried up all the rivers. The old men suggested that they dig up the river which had sunk into its grave in order to find the soul of the river. For 3 days they dug when suddenly a great spring gushed forth. It came so fast that many died before they could get out of the pit. In their joy over the waters, the Ifugaos celebrated a feast. But while they were rejoicing it grew dark; the rains fell, the rivers rose up so that the old men finally advised the people to run to the mountains for the river gods were angry. The people were all overtaken by the waters except two, a brother and a sister: Wigan and Bugan. Wigan was safely settled on top of Mt. Amuyao and Bugan, on the summit of Mt. Kalawitan. The waters continued to rise until the entire earth was covered except the tops of the mountains. For 6 months the flood covered the earth. There was plenty of fruits and nuts on the mountain tops for the survivors. But only Bugan had fire. Wigan was cold because he had no fire.

The story goes on to tell how after the waters had receded, Wigan journeyed to Mt. Kalawitan and was reunited with his sister. They settled down the valley where the Banaual clan now live. Bugan realized one day that she was with child. In her shame she left her home and followed the course of the river. Exhausted and faint after the long journey and consumed with grief, she sank to the ground only to be comforted by the appearance of the god Maknongan who came to her in the guise of a benign old man with white beard. He assured her that her shame had no foundation. What she and Wigan had done was right because it was through them that the world would be repeopled.[3]

[1]Mircea Eliade, *Patterns in Comparative Religion* (New York, 1963), pp. 212, 254.

[2]Eliade, pp. 324–326, 414–416.

[3]H. Otley Beyer, "Origin Myths Among the Mountain Peoples of the Philippines," *Philippine Journal of Science* 8 (Section D) (April 1913) :212–213.

In this synopsis it is clear that there was a belief among the Ifugaos of the successive existence of races of mankind; that the old race was wiped away by a flood, and that a new generation came into existence through the survivors of the flood. Rebirth is implicit in this flood myth.

Among the Ata we have this report from Cole:

> Long after this (the creation of the first male and female), the water covered the whole earth and all the Ata were drowned except two men and a woman. The waters carried them far away and they would have perished had not a large eagle come to their aid. This bird offered to carry them to their homes on its back. One man refused, but the other two accepted its help and returned to Mapula.[4]

Here again we see presupposed a new generation of Ata sprung from the two remnants of the flood who were flown to their home by the bird. This tale also presupposes the existence of a previous race of men who perished during the cataclysm. The notion of the rebirth of mankind through the survivors helped by the bird is quite clear.

Among the Mandaya we have it reported that many generations ago a great flood occurred which killed all the inhabitants of the world except one pregnant woman. She prayed that her child might be a boy. This was granted and the son who was born of her she called Uacatan. When full grown, he took his own mother to wife, and from their union came all the Mandaya. (Shades of the Oedipus complex.)[5]

Again in this tale there are two things presupposed: the previous existence of a race of men now extinct on account of the flood, and the existence of a new race from the two survivors.

As for the Bisayan, one may not agree with Alzina when he says "concerning the flood which they now call in their tongue *ang paglunup sa calibutan* (lit. 'the inundation of the world') that they knew nothing about it."[6] Fansler at least has a Bisayan story of a flood, supplied by Vicente L. Neri of Cagayan, Misamis, which he had heard from his grandmother. A flood took place on account of the quarrel between Bathala and the god of the sea, Dumagat. It seems that Bathala's sub-

[4] Fay Cooper Cole, *The Wild Tribes of Davao District, Mindanao,* Field Museum of Natural History, Anthropological Series 12 (Chicago, 1913), p. 164.

[5] Cole, p. 173. Generally the survivors of the flood are a brother and a sister. There is another instance of a mother–son partnership. This was brought to my attention by Dr. Juan Francisco of the University of the Philippines after I had written these pages. He says that the flood myth of the Higaunons of Magsaysay in northern Misamis Oriental tells of a mother and a son who survived the great flood.

[6] Francisco Alzina, S.J., *Historia de las Islas Bisayas,* Part I, Book 3, a preliminary translation of the Munoz Text of Alzina, Part I, Books 1–4, by Paul S. Lietz (Chicago, 1961), pp. 191–192.

jects the crow and the dove were stealing fish which were the subjects of Dumagat. He asked for retribution from Bathala and he got nothing. In return he opened the big pipe through which the water of the world passes and flooded the dominion of Bathala until nearly all the people were drowned.[7]

And Pavon tells a story of how the crow got its black color. The story in short goes this way: In very remote times, God thought it good to send a great punishment to men. There followed a great internal war which took away the lives of many. Then a river overflowed its banks and took the lives of many more. The judge of the dead Aropayang, alarmed over the misfortune that had happened, sent out the crow and the dove to examine and count the dead. The dove came back and gave a faithful account of the disaster. The crow who came much later could not do so because it forgot to count the dead in its eagerness to peck at the eyes of the dead. Furious, Aropayang hurled a bottle of ink at the bird and thus stained the feather of the crow forever, and he cursed it to be lame on one foot where it was hit by the inkwell.[8]

In these two tales, we have the motif of a flood if not of a universal deluge. The passing away of one generation of men who perished in the flood waters and the coming of another generation after the flood are at least hinted at. The followers of Bathala and the people in the Pavon tale were not altogether extinguished. So we can suppose that at least two or more survivors remained to repeople the world. And so, too, we can say that the notion of rebirth is implicit. In both stories again, there figure two birds: the crow and the dove. In these tales which are more folktale than myths, the birds do not lay eggs. But it is interesting how they are sent to count the dead. So it seems that the many motifs common to earlier myths of cosmic rebirth reappear in these tales: the flood, the survival of some people, the birds, the dead. The rebirth is not for the individual dead, however, but for the new race of men who will be born to repeople the world from the survivors.

[7] Dean S. Fansler, *Filipino Popular Tales* (New York, 1921), pp. 420–421.

[8] Jose Maria Pavon y Anguro, "The Robertson Translations of the Pavon Manuscripts of 1838–1939," Philippine Studies Program, Department of Anthropology, University of Chicago, 1957, Transcript no. 5-C, pp. 27–28.

The Flood: Three Northern Kammu Versions of the Story of Creation

KRISTINA LINDELL,
JAN-OJVIND SWAHN, AND
DAMRONG TAYANIN

The flood myth is also common in Southeast Asia and China. Characteristic of the narrative in this area is an incestuous sibling marriage following the waning of the floodwaters. The Kammu tradition in northern Thailand is quite similar to Chinese texts. This study of Kammu flood myths is part of a lengthy continuing field study of Kammu language and folklore by a Swedish team of researchers. The essay by Swedish folklorists differs from others presented in this volume insofar as oral texts of the flood myth are included. Oral texts, with all their false starts and stops, differ markedly from the smooth texture of literary, rewritten, or summarized versions. For more ethnographic detail about the Kammu, see Kristina Lindell, Håkan Lundström, Jan-Olof Svantesson, and Damrong Tayanin, The Kammu Year: Its Lore and Music, *Studies on Asian Topics No. 4 (London and Malmö, 1982). For earlier discussions of Chinese versions of the flood, see Terrien de Lacouperie, "The Deluge-Tradition and Its Remains in Ancient China,"* The Babylonian and Oriental Record *4 (1889–1890): 15–24, 49–56, 102–111; Julius Grill, "Zur chinesischen Flutsage," in* Festgruss an Rudolf von Roth *(Stuttgart, 1893), pp. 9–14; and J. F. Rock, "The Story of the Flood in the Literature of the Mo-So (Na-Khi) Tribe,"* Journal of the West China Border Research Society *7 (1935): 64–80. For a detailed consideration of the sibling-incest element of the flood myth, see Leopold Walk, "Das Flut-Geschwisterpaar als Ur- und Stammelternpaar der Menschheit: Ein Beitrag zur Mythengeschichte Süd- und Südostasiens,"* Mitteilungen der Österreichischen Gesellschaft für Anthropologie, Ethnologie und Prähistorie *78/79 (1949): 60–115. For another comprehensive survey of some fifty-one*

Reprinted from *Acta Orientalia* 37 (1976):183–200.

texts, see Li Hwei, "The Deluge Legend of the Sibling-mating Type in Aboriginal Formosa and Southeast Asia" [in Chinese with a two-page English summary], Bulletin of the Ethnological Society of China *1 (1955): 171–206.*

That the world as we know it today emerged after a gigantic flood[1] is an idea shared by many peoples in Southeast Asia.[2]

Often the new world is repopulated through an incestuous marriage of the only two survivors, who are related to each other in a tabooed bloodline. The young couple is unwilling to have sexual relations, and not until some powerful portent has convinced them of the necessity do they finally get married.[3]

In the case of the Kammu story of the Flood[4] it is the malcoha cuckoo[5] which persuades the primeval couple to sleep together. This incident is extremely well known among the Kammu of northern Laos and Thailand. Without exaggeration it may be said that every Kammu speaker in the whole area knows the words the malcoha cooed:

> Tok kɔɔk kɔɔk,
> tok kɔɔk,
> pree kap mɔɔk
> sərkɔɔk yɔ tee.
> 'Tok kɔɔk kɔɔk,
> tok kɔɔk,

[1]The stories presented here were recorded in Lampang in northern Thailand at the field station of the Scandinavian Institute of Asian Studies in the years 1972–1974.

[2]Cf. Alfred Kühn: *Berichte über den Weltanfang bei den Indochinesen und ihren Nachbarvölkern* (Leipzig, 1939), especially pp. 93–109 "Sintflutberichte."

For other Kammu versions from different areas of Laos (Phongsali, Luang Prabang, and Vientiane provinces) see Michel Ferlus: "La cosmogonie selon la tradition khmou" in *Langues et techniques. Nature et société. Approche linguistique,* Vol. I, pp. 277–82, Paris, 1972.

In this interesting article Dr. Ferlus compares the Kammu and Lao stories of the Creation. He points out the remarkable consistency in the structure and the themes of the various Kammu versions. The three versions treated here can only further underline this point. As the storytellers speak Yuan and Rɔɔk dialects their ultimate origin would be in the province of Namtha and the northernmost part of the province of Luang Prabang.

[3]Cf. also David Crockett Graham: *Songs and Stories of the Ch'uan Miao,* Smithsonian Miscellaneous Collections, Vol. 136, No. 1 (Washington, 1954), p. 179f.

[4]In Kammu the name of the story is Om pɛk om ŋɛɛn. Om pɛk means "flood, deluge," and om pɛk om ŋɛɛn is a reduplicated form meaning the same. The latter half of the reduplication, om ŋɛɛn, is meaningless in isolation.

[5]The bird, in Kammu called tokkɔɔk or təkɔɔk, is the greater Greenbilled Malcoha, *Phoenicophaeus tristis.*

Cf. Bertram E. Smythies: *The Birds of Burma* (London, 1953).

brother and sister[6]
embrace one another.'

Despite the fact that at least the first part of the story is so extremely well known, only one out of twenty-seven storytellers told the story spontaneously (version A below). The reason for this is that the story is considered very difficult to tell because of its many intricate details and its profusion of loosely connected themes.

To an outsider it would seem as if the story could, or even should, end after the section dealing with the repopulation of the world. The Kammu, however, hold a different opinion. In the course of the work the storytellers were often invited to come together and discuss the recorded stories at a kind of improvised seminar.[7] They were all agreed that the story should explain not only how the world was repopulated after the deluge but also explain the present world order in greatest possible detail. As a consequence the story is considered better told the longer it becomes and the more phenomena it explains.

It took quite some persuasion to make the second storyteller tell what he remembered of the story (version B below). Many attempts have been made to persuade storytellers to allow recording of fragments of stories. These attempts have hardly ever been successful. The Kammu are keenly aware that most of their stories will be forgotten within a decade or two. This is in fact the main reason why so many stories could be recorded on tape. The Kammu we met regard the stories as their foremost cultural heritage and they are anxious to have them preserved. Most of the storytellers are agreed that fragments should be recorded. Yet hardly anybody is willing to tell a fragment, for although there are no professional storytellers, there is considerable prestige attached to good telling. To press too hard on this point might even hurt the storyteller's feelings, because, being proud of his art, he might loathe the idea of hearing himself tell a story haltingly.

The third storyteller (version C below) had heard the others tell their versions. He remarked that he remembered several incidents which he thought ought not to be left out and declared that there were

[6]The words pree and mɔɔk cannot be adequately translated into English. Pree means "brother or paternal male cousin in relation to sister or paternal female cousin" and mɔɔk "sister or paternal female cousin in relation to brother or paternal male cousin." The meaning is here that the two young people were related in a way which made sexual relations between them incestuous. (The explanations of the kinship terms given in these notes are by no means exhaustive. A separate article dealing with the Kammu family system will, however, soon be published.)

[7]The discussions at these seminars were recorded. Several of the explanations to the stories presented in the footnotes were given by the storytellers.

many others which he could not recollect clearly. Thus his story was told as a kind of amendment to the two other versions.

The three storytellers who have told the present story are all living in or near the city of Lampang in northern Thailand. Mr. Pong and Mr. Kam are speakers of the Yuan dialect while Mr. Nuan speaks the Rɔɔk dialect.[8]

Mr. Pong is in his middle forties. As a storyteller he is lively and entertaining, and he prefers to tell humorous stories. He always took part in the discussions of the tales, and he proved to be well acquainted with the lore of his people. When asked, he gladly tells a story or two, but he does not actively seek an opportunity either to tell or to hear a story.

Mr. Nuan is in his middle seventies. He has a small repertoire, but tells it rather well, although he says that he has not told any stories for over 30 years. The present story is not representative of his ability. He was persuaded to make an attempt, although he protested that he had forgotten the major part of the story.

Mr. Kam is in his middle thirties. He prefers to tell explanatory tales, and in telling he is careful to get all the details right. As a consequence he is usually unwilling to tell a story unless he knows it very well and is given ample time to think. He speaks slowly and thoughtfully and he hardly ever corrects himself. Thus the present story suits his way of telling very well. The reason why he did not tell it spontaneously is that he is not quite satisfied with his own knowledge. There are still some sections which he is unable to recall. Mr. Kam has been interested in stories as long as he can remember, and he seeks his friends among storytellers. Of the three storytellers represented here Mr. Kam is the most active bearer of the tradition, although in actual fact he prefers listening to telling.

A. Mr. Pong:

(I) I will tell the beginning of the story first. Now, at the beginning of it there were two brothers, you see, they . . . no, it was a brother and a sister[9] who went to dig out a bamboo rat, you see. They dug on and on, dug on and on. The bamboo rat went deeper and deeper down, and then it turned around and said to the two young people: "Eh, why do you dig me out? (Now other people will . . .)[10] The water will rise and flood our villages and our land. We must dig a deep, deep hole, dig

[8] Cf. note 2 above.

[9] Mr. Pong uses the words taay hɛɛm "elder and younger sibling in relation to the same sex" but corrects himself saying pree kap mɔɔk. Cf. note 6 above.

[10] Mistakes in the telling are always included but are put in parentheses.

deep, deep down. You ought to go and make a very good house for yourselves you see." "Well, how should we do it?" they asked. The bamboo rat answered: "Cut wood, well cut a round, round piece of wood, hollow it out till you get a hole in it and stay inside the hole, inside it."

(II) The two young people went back and made a drum for themselves, crawled in and stayed inside the hollow and caulked it with wax along the rim.

Some time passed and then the water came and flooded the land, rose higher and higher. Those who had bronze and silver, they were sitting on rafts and in boats which rose higher and higher with the water, but when it receded again these vessels came down flop and they all died.

(But those that, the man . . .) The two people, that brother and sister, they stayed in the drum. They looked outside, and as the water was still there they closed the hole again. They looked again and as the water had dried up they went outside.

Because the water had flooded all the villages and the whole land there was nobody left, just the brother and sister alone. ("Well, brother, go seek for a . . .") "You, sister, go seek for a husband for yourself, go down south! I will go seek a wife for me up north." They went and went, back and forth, but oh! However much they sought there was nobody. They only caught sight of each other. "Oh, I will marry her up there and make her my wife," the young man thought, and went there, but it was his own sister.

(III) There still remained a single bird, one bird, it was a malcoha cuckoo. The malcoha began cooing: "Tok kɔɔk kɔɔk, tok kɔɔk, brother and sister should embrace one another." Finally, in the end they slept with each other, had each other and got a child, after seven years they had a child, but lo and behold it did not come out, it stayed inside the womb and died there, and it was born as a dry shell of a gourd, it was a gourd. They kept it behind their house and went about their work.

(IV) After a long time there was the sound of speaking "ɨŋ, ɨŋ, ɨŋ, ɨŋ" and they said: "Eh, what is this here?" They went to have a look, and it was the gourd, and they moved it further away. Then there was the sound of speaking and chatting. "Eh, what is this here?" They went to look and it was the gourd. The man heated a long, long iron rod and burnt a hole, burnt a hole and out came, out came the Rəmeet.[11] The

[11] The Rəmeet live close to the Kammu in northern Laos. In Western literature they are often called Lamet. They speak a language related to Kammu, but the languages are not mutually intelligible.

The idea is that the Rəmeet got a darker skin than the other ethnic groups because

Rəmeet began, the first time it was they, they were the first to come out. Further on came the Kammu, the Thai, the Westerners, and the Chinese. When they came out they did not know any language, they did not know anything. They just lived like that. When they wanted to say something they could not, and if they wanted to speak they were not able to.

(V) Later there was a professor,[12] and he said: "Shall we discuss the question of words, try to learn words?" There was a long tree trunk across a dry valley, there was a trunk of a red cotton tree, the one we call a "kwaay." They sat down together in a row like that, more and more people came. The trunk broke, it broke and that moment they all laughed. They laughed and were thus able to speak human words. The Kammu said: "Haan lɛ!" The Rəmeet said: "Yam pəʔɔh!" The Lao said: "Taay lɛɛw!" The Chinese said: "Sii ŋɛɛ lɛ!"[13] It came out as words. The Westerner said something, too, but I do not know their language.

(VI) Then they went to study letters, to study letters.[14] They ripped off a rəkpak leaf and made it float with the water, on and on. They looked at it and said: "Well, if we prepare a boat like this, it will be all right." The Kammu, however, said: "No, we won't have it. We will get a buffalo hide instead." They slaughtered a water buffalo, made a big boat for themselves, and put it into the water. In the course of time it rotted away bit by bit, and the Kammu cut pieces out of it to cook soup from, while they punted their boat down the river. The Lao and the

---

they wiped off most of the soot left at the rim of the hole burnt by the hot iron rod. Much social prestige is attached to fair skin, and in having the Rəmeet come out first the storytellers place them one rung below the Kammu on the social scale.

Dr. Ferlus' remark (op. cit., p. 280) that the Kammu always are the ones to exit first is not valid for any of the recordings presented here.

[12] Mr. Pong says aacaan and not khuu, which is the usual word for "teacher."

[13] The imitative phrases here are cries of astonishment, and according to the storytellers are meant as a mild swear word "oh golly!" To get closer to the actual meaning of the several phrases, which all mean the same, they could perhaps be translated as "dead and out!"

[14] This and the following paragraphs would be difficult to understand without the explanations given by the storytellers.

In the recording Mr. Pong uses nɔɔ "they" sometimes referring to the Lao and the Thai, sometimes to the Kammu, and sometimes to all the different ethnic groups. According to the explanations, letters could not be studied in the area where the peoples were. Therefore they had to make boats to go abroad and learn letters there. To build a boat the Lao and the Thai observed the rəkpak fruit floating on the water (Mr. Pong says mistakenly "leaf" but this unidentified plant has long, slender fruits somewhat like a canoe), while the Kammu thought of food only. When the teacher began to teach and the other peoples repeated their lessons, the Kammu munched their buffalo hide so noisily that they were unable to hear what was said.

Thai, however, made their rəkpak leaf float down the river and observed it and then cut a wooden boat like it and sailed down the river.

Their teacher came and said to them: "Go and study letters then. Each one of you should learn his own letters, the letters that will be his, each one should wait for his proper books and documents." We Kammu, however, we don't know any letters, because we ate that buffalo hide. We took that hide and munched it: CRUNCH, CRUNCH, CRUNCH! The Lao, the Thai, the Westerners and the Chinese fried eggs for food, and they were listening while eating, they ate and listened. Then the others said: "Well, who knows what? Let us read and see." Well, the Kammu were unable to read and said: "Oh, we don't know!"

Oh, the Chinese came now, he arrived after the others. When he arrived he looked at the prints of the hens, regarded the hens. The tracks went this direction and that direction, and he began to write like that and said: "Good, I might keep this!" The Chinese write like this to this day. The Thai write Thai letters, the Lao write Lao letters, the Westerners have Western letters. We Kammu, however, do not know letters, because we did not hear anything, did not hear what the others said.

(VII) Then they[15] said: "Well, let us return!" They returned. "Now, as for you, who will be the elder brother, and who will be the younger?"[16] We are Kammu, and in the beginning we were their elder brothers, you see, to begin with we were their elder brothers.[17] The Westerners, the Chinese, the Lao were the younger brothers, while we were the elder brothers, for we were the eldest. They all went and sat down together: "Well, shall we divide up the things between us?" "Oh yes, let us divide them up then and see who will get what." They were the younger ones. They had banana plants, and they set about to divide up the bananas first. "Yes, divide up the banana plants!" They did, and the others got the root and stem while we got the top. We were the elder, therefore we got the top. When we planted our part, however, it did not grow.

"Let us divide up the sugar-cane now!" the Lao said. "You are the elder, and this time you will get the root and stem. We are the younger

[15] In this and the following paragraph the word i "we" stands for the Kammu. (Probably also the Rəmeet are meant, for they are regarded as a brother people. Thus the word pru used by the Kammu speakers in Thailand designates Kammu and Rəmeet. The word seems to be unknown in Laos.) Nɔɔ "they" are the socially more fortunate peoples.

[16] It is impossible to say who the speaker is here, but probably all the peoples discuss this.

[17] Seniority seems to be of far less importance among the Kammu than it is among the Chinese and the Thai, although the eldest brother should be shown some respect. Here the Kammu claim seniority over the Lao because they were the first to leave the gourd. They are not aware of the fact that the Lao are fairly recent settlers in Laos.

and will have the top." They were the younger and got the top, while we got the root and stem. They planted their part of the sugar-cane and it grew, we got the root and stem and it did not grow. We got the top of the banana plant, while they got the top of the sugar-cane, and thus only the parts they got grew at all.

This went on and on, and at last they were to divide up the elephants. Regarding the elephants, as they were the younger, because they were the younger they got the baby elephant, you see. Because we were the elders we were bigger and we got the mother elephant. We got the mother elephant and tied it up. The Lao said: "Let us write a contract and keep it: If the mother elephant goes to find her child, then the younger brothers will get her, too. If the baby elephant goes to find its mother the elder brothers will have both." "Yes," we agreed. We had tied our elephant but not very tightly and now she began to pull forwards and backwards, did the mother elephant. The mother elephant was strong, and she pulled and pushed until the rope broke. Then she went to join her baby, and thus they got both of them, as for us we got nothing, for she went to join her child.

(VIII) At last they (took) made us go—they came to see us, you know, earlier they had come to see us, you know—because they were the younger. We said: "Younger brothers, you will have to come to see your seniors!" "Yes," they agreed. As a matter of fact, they came to see us every day, every day. However, now they said, "No, we won't go, we are too lazy. The elder brothers will have to come to see their juniors. We are the younger brothers, why should we go to see our seniors? If you want to get material and clothes then come to see us who are your juniors. You are the elder brothers, we are your juniors and we will make them for you. As you are the elder brothers and we the younger, we will not go to see you any more."

They did not come to see us any more. Now it is we who go to see them every day, every day. We do not have any material and do not have any clothes. We have to go and get it from them, because they know how to make it. We are the elder brothers, only just the elder brothers, and we are unable to make anything at all. Our younger brothers make everything for us, make everything for us.

In the summer of 1974 the story was recorded anew with the same storyteller. The story is repeated almost word for word, which is enough to prove that in his case it is a repetition of a story he has learnt by heart and not a free rendering.[18] As the two recordings are practically

[18]This is certainly not true of all the storytellers, and the section Mr. Pong adds here seems doubtful in this respect.

identical, the second one has not been included in full in this article. At the very end of the story, however, the teller adds a new motif, which is presented here. It seems to be of special interest, because it is so strikingly modern. Concrete is still not used as building material in the Kammu villages, and one wonders when and how it found its way into Kammu folklore. However, as long as the stories are capable of incorporating new phenomena they are most decidedly alive.

A. (continued)

(IX) They[19] were casting cement, using cement mortar to lay the foundation for their houses. Our lord[20] went to see it and said: "Oh, they can make foundations of stone, then we can make foundations of stone, too. You should make foundations of stone for us, too." He made one of his underlings go to cut stone. He hit the stone but a splinter hurt his body. Then another one hit the stone and a splinter hurt him, too. They then killed the lord, killed their own lord. When he was dead we had no lord, we had no master at all. Thus we have the same lord as the Lao, the same lord as our younger brothers.

B. Mr. Nuan:

(II) Now I will tell the story of the Flood. Long ago, it is said, the great flood was going to come. There were those two brothers, no, I mean that brother and his sister, and they helped each other to make a wooden drum. When they had finished the drum, someone said: "Today, you see, the flood will come." They had already finished the drum, and now they crept into the drum and stayed inside the drum. Together they brought along wax to caulk it with and a needle to keep, and then they crept into the drum. The flood did come, indeed, and then, oh, how many years, how many months went by, I don't know. How many mountains and how many ridges the drum floated past, I don't know, nor how many villages or how many towns. It just floated along like that. The two of them inside took the needle and pricked a hole in the wax to look, but as the water trickled in they closed the hole again. The drum just floated along like that.

Again they pricked a hole to look, and as there was no water at all they crept out. They looked around, and oh! they did not know at all where they were, they looked around and did not see a single person, there was not even a single leaf.

"Well, what are we to do now? A woman wants to get a husband, and a man wants to get a wife. Let us go and make a search!"

[19] Again "they" means the Lao.

[20] The implication is that in ancient times the Kammu had a ruler of their own and that it was the Kammu themselves who killed him.

One of them went south and the other one went north. They searched and looked but there was nobody, looked and looked and the fact remained, however much they looked there were only they themselves, there was no one else but the brother and sister. They set out again, sought here and sought there and sought everywhere, but there was no one at all.

There was a bird, a malcoha cuckoo there was, and it was cooing: "Tok kɔɔk kɔɔk, tok keey keey, brother and sister, embrace one another."

(III) "Oh, that bird will make us marry each other," they thought, and thus they got married, they married each other.

The wife was pregnant for three years, and when she gave birth it was to a gourd, it was but a gourd.

(IV) "What are we to do?" they said. Every day, every day, when the two went to work in the field, there was the sound of speaking "thɨɨt, thɨɨt" inside the gourd, and they could do nothing to it. "What are we to do? Well, let us heat up an iron rod, and when it is hot let us press it in and see what will happen."

They heated up an iron rod and when it was hot they pressed it in to see, and wruuum! before the others the Rəmeet came out, first the Rəmeet, and then the Indians came out, out came the Indians and out came the Kammu, and then came the Chinese, the Shan, the Mon and the Westerners "thɨɨt, thɨɨt", out they came.

Now they were out already, but they did not know any words as yet. "What are we to do about it?" they thought. "If we got to study words, some people will go to learn from the water, others will study all sorts of things."

There was an old man, who said: "Well . . . !" . . . They made a bridge and went to sit down together on it. They sat down for a while and "crɨat" the bridge broke in two. "Oh, what are we to do?" and thus they learnt some words there . . . Then . . . oh well, I will stop here.

C. Mr. Kam:

This is the story of the Flood.

(I) There was a young boy, who went to dig out a bamboo rat. As he dug for the bamboo rat, the rat was burrowing a hole for itself. As the boy dug further in, the bamboo rat burrowed further in, and this went on for quite some time, until the rat came up and said to the boy: "Why are you digging me out? Don't you understand that I am burrowing a hole for myself and a good one at that?"

The young boy said: "Oh, I am going to kill you now, for I dig because I want to eat you."

The bamboo rat said: "Well, I will tell you something very carefully. The water will rise and overflow, it will flood the villages, flood the houses. I am burrowing a deep, deep hole for myself, for I fear the flood to come. If you want to survive then go home and make you a drum, and then crawl into it and stay inside the drum!"

The boy: "Is that true?"

The bamboo rat said: "Yes, that is true."

(II) Now the boy returned and came to the village. He returned and made a drum for himself, and when it was finished he took a tinderbox and took rice and meat and anything he needed with him. He took his sister, a pig and a dog along and crawled into the drum and stayed inside it.

Then the water flooded the villages, flooded the houses, the mountain fields and the paddy fields. The two young people were inside the drum. They took a needle and pricked a hole in the drumskin. The water still poured in and they plugged it up.

The drum floated back and forth with the water, and there was no knowing where it went. The two young people took the needle and pricked a hole again. The water had subsided, there was no water at all. They went out together. They went outside and oh, there was nothing left but the naked earth. All the trees had toppled and all the people were dead.

The two of them looked around, and they did not know at all in what direction they should go. The boy said: "You go and seek a husband for yourself, sister. I will go and seek a wife for myself." Thus she went to seek a husband, and he went to seek a wife.

They walked and walked, walked back and forth. In the end they met one another. He looked into the distance and saw someone walking on a mountain over there. He thought: "Oh I will go and get married to her over there." He went there and saw that it was only his sister. She looked and saw someone walking on the mountain over there and she thought: "Oh, I will go and get married to him over there."

She went there and saw that it was only her brother.

(III) They walked together, and there was a malcoha cuckoo cooing: "Tok kɔɔk kɔɔk, tok kɔɔk, brother and sister, embrace one another!"

The two young people heard the bird coo like that, and they thought: "Well, all the others are dead and gone, we will marry each other," and thus they slept together.

Time passed. They worked a field but had no rice to sow. The young man took some string, made a snare and went to set it. It snared a pigeon. He went to check his snare, and found the pigeon in it. When he came home with it, the bird said: "If you don't kill me, I will give you some rice seed." He said: "Well, where would you get any rice from to give me?" The bird said: "Oh, I have some here." Then the bird spat up rice from its gizzard and gave it to the man. The man took the rice seed and went to sow it in their field, and then they worked their field.

The woman was pregnant for three years, but when she gave birth, that which came out was a round bottle gourd. They took the gourd and kept it at the bathing place. They went to their mountain field, and when they returned they heard people talking "ɨŋ, ɨŋ." They sent the dog down to have a look. The dog went down to look and barked continuously. They went down to look, but there was nothing, and they took the dog and the pig with them and went home.

(IV) The following day they went to their mountain field again, and when they returned they heard the sound of talking again. This was repeated every day, every single day.

During that time they worked their mountain field but did not eat rice as yet. They did not eat its grain as yet, they were eating only its leaves. The two young people tore off the tips of the paddy leaves, nipping the leaves between thumb and little finger. And that is why when today we look at the paddy leaves we see that they have a notch near the tip. That is where they nipped the leaves in the olden days. Thus in working their field they got more and more rice as time went by.

She did not allow anyone to look at the paddy leaves while she cooked them. She put the leaves over the fire and went to fetch water. She said to her husband: "You are at home, but don't look at the leaves I am cooking. I will go to fetch water." When she had left, the husband uncovered the leaves to have a look.

It was only paddy leaves and they were not cooked yet.

The wife returned and when she came home and looked at the leaves, they were still not cooked. She said to her husband: "I told you that I didn't want you to look at the leaves I was cooking. Now they are still not cooked, what are we to eat now?" Her husband answered: "Let us eat the rice now instead of the paddy leaves. Let us thrash the rice and cook it." And that is why people now eat rice.

One day they thought: "Well, what is it that is inside the gourd talking all the time, every day, every day?"

The man took an iron rod, heated it up in the fire and burnt a hole in the gourd. The Rəmeet came out first and following after them, other peoples came out. The Rəmeet thus rubbed off the charcoal left by the red-hot iron rod as they came out and that is why to this very day the Rəmeet are blacker than others. From that day there were people, but they still had no knowledge.

They brought the pig and the dog along when they went to work the mountain field. The pig rooted up the grass and ate it. The dog, however, on coming to the field just slept in the shade. When it was time to return home, the pig called the dog and said: "Dog, let us go home!" The dog: "All right, let us go home then!" The dog rose from its sleeping place and rushed back and forth, back and forth tramping on the work the pig had done. Then they returned home. And when they got home, the pig said: "The dog went to the field and slept, I worked the field alone." The dog answered: "It was the pig that went to sleep, I worked alone. If you don't believe it, just go there and have a look." They went to look, and they saw only the traces of the dog. They could see no traces of the pig. Thus they thought: "Yes, it is indeed the pig, who is lazy. Looking at the field there are no traces of the pig, there are only traces of the dog." When they returned home they slaughtered and ate the pig, but kept the dog as a pet. Today people slaughter pigs and eat pork, but they do not slaughter dogs and do not eat dog's meat.[21]

(IV) At that time the people stayed together but they still could not speak. Once the people were out walking and came to a place where there was a tree trunk lying across a valley like that. They sat down on the tree trunk. More and more and more people came, and in the end the trunk broke and fell to the bottom of the valley. All the people fell off and then they got up and called out: "Ho, hey!" Anyone could say anything, but they still had no writing.

(VI) "Well, those of us who shall go and study writing for us should go now," the people said. Four people went in different directions to study writing. One of them said: "It would be good if we wrote like this, you know." Another one said: "It will be nice, if we write like this." Still another one said: "If we wrote this way it would be nice." The fourth one said: "If we do like this, it will be nice." They said like this and like that and each took his own production, took his own and returned home. When they came home people quarrelled with each other and then broke up in groups. The groups of people went to stay in different areas from then on, because everybody who wanted to learn to read and write went to study with one of these four. Of these four people who taught others to read and write, one was a Westerner, one was a Thai, one was a Chinese and one was an Indian. Thus there were people in all different parts of the world, for they studied writing with these four. The Japanese went to study with the Chinese, the Burmese

[21] Sometimes dog's meat is in fact eaten by the Kammu although they seem to be against the habit.

went to study with the Indian, and the people of the West went to study with the Westerner.

The Lao went to study with the Thai. When he had finished his studies, however, he drank rice wine and got drunk. The Lao returned to his village and taught them his knowledge, but he was drunk. The Thai write the letter ŋɔɔ ŋuu short (ງ), but now when the Lao taught in his drunkenness he wrote the letter ŋɔɔ ŋuu long like this (ງ).

Regarding the people of this earth, in the olden days people said that they were the children of only one father and one mother. But then the four people went to study writing and people quarrelled with each other and went away, and that is why there are people in all different parts of the world.

SOME FOLKLORE NOTES

Remarks on the Contents of the Texts

The epic core of the three texts is the same, although version B is fragmentary. In the other versions some interesting additions are found.

In version A Mr. Pong has added a rather modern variation of the theme "Kammu inferiority" in the section dealing with the acquisition of the art of casting cement. This passage may in fact be of his own making.[22] The second addition, "Deceptive crop division," on the other hand is known in several parts of Eurasia as an independent tale having no connection with the present cogmogonic myth. In the index of folktale types[23] it is listed both as an animal-fable[24] and under the heading "Tales of the stupid ogre."[25] In a form pertaining to man it is known from Assam and Ceylon[26] as well as from Indonesia.[27]

In version C Mr. Kam has also told two sections which are not found in the other versions. One section is the tale of "How man learnt to eat rice." There seems to be no direct parallel to this one, although Wolfram Eberhard[28] reports some similar variations of the theme. Epically

[22] As the passage was recorded on one of the very last days of the stay in Lampang it was never discussed at the seminars.

[23] Antti Aarne and Stith Thompson: *The Types of the Folktale* (Helsinki, 1961).

[24] Type 9B.

[25] Type 1030.

[26] Stith Thompson and Jonas Balys: *The Oral Tales of India* (Bloomington, Ind., 1958), p. 294.

[27] Waldemar Liungman: *Varifrån kommer våra sagor?* (Djursholm, 1952), p. 312 ff.

[28] Wolfram Eberhard: *Typen chinesischer Volksmärchen* (Helsinki, 1937).

these differ strongly from the one found here, however. The other section is the tale of how the dog cheated the pig when they worked the mountain field. According to available motif indexes[29] this story is found as a separate folktale in the Assam Hills. As it has not been recorded by folklorists until recent years, the number of known records is very small indeed.[30]

List of Motifs according to Stith Thompson, *Motif-Index of Folk-Literature*, Vol. 1–6, Copenhagen and Bloomington, Ind., 1955–58

References marked with an asterisk are new numbers suggested by the authors. References preceded by "Cf." only imply superficial correspondence to Thompson's numbers. Differences from the numbers given in Graham (see note 3) depend on the fact that Thompson altered these numbers in his second edition, which we have used. After each motif we have indicated its presence by numbers marking the sections in the text (I–IX) and by capital letters marking the different story-tellers (A–C).

A 1006.2	New race from incest after world calamity. (III:A,B,C)
Cf. A 1016.1	Flood from animals' boring into the ground. (I:A,C)
A 1021.0.2	Escape from deluge in wooden cask (drum). (II: A,B,C)
*A 1029.2.1	Only brother and sister survive flood. (II:A,B,C)
A 1101.2.3	Formerly men dumb. (IV:A,B,C)
*A 1236.3	Tribes emerge from gourd after brother-sister incest. (IV:A,B,C)
A 1273.1	Incestuous first parents. (III:A,B,C)
A 1422	Assignment of edible animals. (V:C)
A 1423.2	Acquisition of rice. (IV:C)
A 1441	Acquisition of agriculture. (IV:C)
*A 1445.2.3	Acquisition of cement mortar for building houses. (IX:A)

[29] Stith Thompson and Jonas Balys: op. cit., p. 292.

[30] "Acquisition of fire," a motif found in one of the versions treated by Dr. Ferlus (op. cit., p. 280), is not found here. It is however recorded in the material as part of another tale dealing with the origins of the slash-and-burn technique of agriculture and of the death rites. Either one of these themes could easily be fitted into the present context.

*A 1482.2	Origin of language: formerly dumb men brought to laughter, after which they start to speak. (IV:A,B,C)
A 1484	Origin of reading and writing. (VI:A,C)
A 1484.2	Origin of alphabet. (VI:A,C)
*A 1484.2.1	Origin of Chinese letters from hens' tracks. (VI:A)
A 1614.6	Origin of light and dark skin color (IV:A,B,C)
A 1616	Origin of particular languages. (V:A,C)
A 1618	Origin of inequalities among men. (VI:A,C)
Cf. A 1650	Origin of different classes. (VII,VIII:A)
*A 1650.3.3	Why the Kammu must go to the Lao for clothes etc. (VIII:A)
*A 1689.14	Why the Kammu do not know letters. (VI:A)
A 2685	Origin of cereals. (IV:C)
B 122.1	Bird as adviser. (III:A,B,C)
*B 437.1.2	Helpful bamboo rat. (I:A,C)
*B 521.7	Animal warns of flood (I:A,C)
B 531	Animals provide food for men. (IV:C)
Cf. C 221.1.1.4	Tabu: eating dog. (V:C)
C 324	Tabu: looking into jug. (IV:C)
K 41.2	Pig and dog as plowmen. (V:C)
K 171.1	Deceptive crop division. (VII:A)
*K 171.3.2	Deceptive division of banana plants. (VII:A)
*K 171.3.3	Deceptive division of sugar cane. (VII:A)
*K 171.7.3	Deceptive division of elephants: will mother elephant join her baby or will baby elephant join its mother? (VII:A)
M 359.8	Deluge prophesied. (I:A,C)
*P 16.10	Why the Kammu have no "Lord." (IX:A)
T 415	Brother-sister incest. (III:A,B,C)
T 415.5	Brother-sister marriage. (III:A,B,C)
T 555.1.1	Woman gives birth to pumpkin (gourd). (III:A,B,C)
T 574.2	Long pregnancy: seven years. (III:A,B,C—B and C three years)

The Deluge Myth of the Bhils of Central India

WILHELM KOPPERS

In 1938–1939, Wilhelm Koppers (1886–1961) carried out fieldwork among the Bhils located in the northwestern part of Central India. Koppers was a devoted student of the anthropologist Father Wilhelm Schmidt (1868–1954), and as such he was particularly interested in studying the religion and mythology of so-called primitive peoples. Schmidt believed in the concept of Kulturkreis, *or "cultural circle," by which he meant a series of interrelated traits common to peoples at a given cultural level or stage. The concept was not original with Schmidt but had been formulated around the turn of the century by Leo Frobenius (1873–1938) and Fritz Graebner (1877–1934).*

According to this theory, individual peoples are presumed to have a whole set of layers belonging to different "circles," and the ethnologist's task is to unravel these various layers and establish their original chronological sequence. Schmidt, a Catholic anthropologist, was convinced that even the most primitive peoples did have a conception of a supreme being, and he and his disciples argued strongly in favor of so-called primitive monotheism. Schmidt even went so far as to champion a view termed "primitive revelation," which maintained that all the peoples of the earth had initially had the same divine message from God.

What is relevant in the present context is that the widespread diffusion of the flood myth was perceived as documentary evidence for the doctrine of primitive revelation. In any event, Schmidt made a point of dispatching his favorite pupils to what he regarded as the most primitive peoples on earth to test his hypotheses. (Such primitive peoples were thought to possess more of the archaic traits.) Accordingly, anthropologists like Koppers spent time with the natives of Tierra del Fuego at the southernmost tip of South America while colleagues worked among the Pygmies in Africa.

To learn more about Father Schmidt, founder of the journal Anthropos, *see his formidable* Der Ursprung der Gottesidee, *12 vols. (Münster, 1926–1955);* The Culture Historical Method of Ethnology *(New York, 1939);* Primitive Revelation *(St. Louis, 1939). For additional discussion of the* Kulturkreislehre,

Reprinted from W. Koppers, "Bhagwan, the Supreme Deity of the Bhils: A Contribution to the History of Indian and Indo-European Religions," *Anthropos* 35/36 (1940–1941): 265–325. (Only pp. 265–267 and 282–288 have been reprinted here.)

see Robert Heine-Geldern, "One Hundred Years of Ethnological Theory in the German-Speaking Countries: Some Milestones," Current Anthropology *5 (1964): 407–418.*

Several scholars, both European and Indian, have in the past made more or less valuable ethnological and anthropological investigations in the regions of Central India (taken here in the geographical and not in the political sense of the term); but there has been an evident lack of systematic research.[1] For this reason I decided in the summer of 1938 to devote at least a year to research work among the primitive races of Central India. My investigations began at the end of October 1938 and continued till the beginning of December 1939. Apart from the civil authorities, I am indebted to both Catholic and Protestant missionaries for help given. As this is not the place for an extensive description of my travels and research work there can be no question of mentioning all these names. One exception however must be made with regard to the Dutch missionary, Father Leonhard Jungblut, S.V.D., to whom I owe a special debt of gratitude, of which more later. The Rockefeller Institute and the Missionary Society of the Divine Word generously undertook to finance the enterprise.

From the great mass of subject matter one task had to be selected and the choice fell upon the problem of the Bhils. The Bhils, as is known, inhabit the north-western part of Central India, to be accurate, the western spurs of the Vindhya and Satpura mountains which divide Northern India from the Deccan. The tribe numbers a million or a million and a half. The Bhils are certainly pre-Aryan in origin although they speak today an Indo-Aryan language, a variety of Gujarati. In the Bhil language there is still a residuum which cannot be traced to any Indo-Aryan source. Whether this residuum may eventually be related to the Munda (= austro-asiatic) or to the Dravidian stock is a question which still remains unanswered.

· · ·

I had my "headquarters" at Rambhapur in the native state of Jhabua and spent the greater part of my time there, in the heart of the Bhil

[1] Among notable exceptions, which however in almost every case relate to the eastern parts of Central India, the following recent publications may be specially mentioned: Sarat Chanra Roy (numerous studies of the different tribes of Chota-Nagpur); P. O. Bodding: *Santal Folk Tales* (Oslo), I (1925), II (1927), III (1929); J. Hoffmann S.J. and A. van Emelen S.J.: *Encyclopaedia Mundarica* (Patna) 1930ff. (volumes I–XII have appeared); W. V. Grigson: *The Maria Gonds of Bastar* (London) 1938; Verrier Elwin: *The Baiga* (London) 1939.

country. But even when I was away, among the other tribes I have mentioned, Missionary Jungblut carried on the research among these Bhils on my behalf. I should also mention that just at the beginning of my sojourn among the Bhils, Jungblut had published a new grammar of the Bhil language, the best we have up to the present time.[2]

• • •

A DELUGE MYTH

There is of course no intrinsic connection between creation myths and deluge myths. But, as is often the case, so also with the Bhils, the thought of creation keeps breaking through the story of the deluge. This seems to justify its introduction at this point.

The Bhil myth of the deluge was published by Konrad[3] in two variants. For text and literal translation we must refer the reader to this study. But a fuller version of the story, embracing both variants, is also sometimes recited by adepts. The contents of this fuller version are as follows.

Bhagwān had created out of earth two washermen: male and female. From this brother and sister the human race had its birth. They lived happily and were very charitable. It fell to the girl's lot to draw water and when going to the river she would take rice with her to feed the fish. This went on for a long time.

Then one day the fish Ro asked her: "Maiden, what reward do you desire? Have you thought of any definite thing?" She answered: "I know of nothing." Then the fish said: "Through water the earth will be turned upside down. Take pumpkin seeds with you and make a cage. Then do you and your brother step into the cage, taking seed and water with you. And do not forget to bring a cock also."

The rains began to fall, slowly at first, then in ever greater torrents. It was as if earth and heaven had merged into one. Then God spoke: "Thus have I turned the world upside down. But has not someone survived? The crowing of the cock informs me of it."

Then Bhagwān himself went to find out more about the matter. He

[2] L. Jungblut: "A Short Bhili Grammar of Jhabua State and Adjoining Territories" (Mhow, C. I.) 1938. In the same year Jungblut had collaborated with Paul Konrad S.V.D., who was then in Central India. This collaboration gave rise to Konrad's article: "Zur Ethnographie der Bhils" (*Anthropos* XXXIV, 1939, 23–117). Considering that Konrad writes without having specialized in ethnography, his work deserves full praise. Nevertheless the more systematic research, which has since been made possible, necessarily entails certain additions to and corrections of his exposition.

[3] Loc. cit., pp. 93ff.

came to where the cage was and asked: "Is anyone inside?" Then the girl answered: "We are two inside, my brother and I." And Bhagwān found within the cage two young people in the full prime and strength of life. Then God spoke: "I have destroyed the whole world. Who warned you and gave you the advice to make such a cage? You must explain this mystery to me. For my plan was hidden from men." Then the girl replied: "It was the fish who instructed me." Bhagwān then called the fish and asked: "Was it you who brought this knowledge to these two?" The fish answered: "Oh no, Lord Father, it was not I who did so." Then God beat the fish and it became disposed to confess: "Yes, Lord Father, I did really do it." Then God spoke: "Had you at once told the truth, nothing would have happened to you." And God cut out the fish's tongue and threw it away. From this tongue leeches took their origin. But the fish has remained without tongue from that time till now.

God turned the girl with her face to the west and the young man with his face to the east. When he had made them turn again so as to face each other, he asked the man: "Who is this?" and he answered: "She is my wife." Then Bhagwān asked the girl: "Who is this?" and she answered: "He is my husband." Then God made them man and wife. In this way they became the progenitors of the human race. Generation followed generation and the different languages came into being.

In this story of the deluge the following points are worthy of note.

1. Bhagwān is the great God, whose activity forms the background of all that happens.

2. Bhagwān created the washermen: brother and sister. The fact that the occupation of the two is expressly stated in all the different versions presupposes that other human beings besides these two must already have existed; but they are never actually mentioned. Why should these two be distinctly designated as washermen? The Bhils no longer know of any explanation. Washermen (*dhobi*) belong to the outcasts (untouchables) and stand pretty well on the lowest rung of the social ladder. Shall we gather that because of their "primitiveness" they were chosen as the first representatives of the human race? Or is there not another, more probable explanation? The Bhils borrowed the story of the fish from the Hindu version of the myth of the deluge but they left out the figure of the First Brahman and First Ascetic, Manu, keeping to the human couple peculiar to their own version. Did they not perhaps transform this couple into washermen because such would necessarily live near water and so have a natural connection with the fish living in this element? Might we not even say that, mutatis mutandis, washermen were introduced as a counterpart to the Brahman as-

cetic, whose obligation to wash himself brings him into contact with the fish? This would be another example of how the Bhils, while succumbing to the Hinduizing process, yet often succeed in adhering to the essential part of their own conception—in this case the original human couple.

3. Bhagwān sends the great flood. The motive of this act is not indicated.

4. The fish draws the attention of the girl to the coming catastrophe.

5. The rescue is brought about with the help of a hollowed-out pumpkin.

6. The brother and sister are instructed by the fish to take seed, water and a cock with them in the hollow pumpkin.

7. Bhagwān discovers them (thanks to the crowing of the cock!) and is astonished to find any human beings still alive. Here again the previous existence of other human beings is tacitly implied.

8. Bhagwān punishes the fish; apparently not for having warned the girl but only for having lied.

9. According to the second variant given by Konrad the couple are also beaten by Bhagwān because the girl in answer to the question "Who are you?" says: "We are brother and sister." It is only when she answers Bhagwān's repeated question with the words: "We are human beings," that he is satisfied and so to speak blesses their union, making them the first parents of the (new) race of men which was to increase and multiply. In another variant the fact that the couple are brother and sister is tacitly ignored towards the end of the legend which speaks only of two human beings, man and woman, who begin to people the earth. We are probably justified in assuming that at this point of the legend the question of incest raised difficulties and so an attempt was made to avoid the pitfall as much as possible.

10. The legend we have been dealing with is a characteristic myth of the deluge. Two features however were probably taken from the domain of creation myths: first, the stress laid on the special creation by Bhagwān of the (washermen) brother and sister; secondly the fraternal relationship of the new first parents saved from the flood. It was unavoidable that the children of the original parents of the human race should intermarry, but that only a brother and sister should have survived the flood appears somewhat illogical. To say the least of it, it is a very unpractical arrangement.

THE STORY OF THE DELUGE AS TOLD IN OTHER BHIL CENTERS

Barwani

From the Bhilalas of this district we heard of a story of the deluge as recited during the marriage ceremonies in connection with the rite of "cutting short speech." When this occurs the marriage has already been solemnized. The go-between rises and all listen attentively while he speaks:

"Once, long ago the world was entirely under water. Only two hills could be seen above the flood, the one called *pāwaṇ ḍuṅgar* (this hill is in the neighborhood of Dohad) and the other *Mata pheṇ* (which means Mata, hood of a snake). These two hills were man and wife. Whenever (at the time of the deluge) the water rose a glass (half a hand) higher, *pāwaṇ ḍuṅgar* rose the span of a hand while *Mata pheṇ* rose *a ḥāth* (an ell). On this higher hill there was a bamboo basket which had not been reached by the water. God saw this basket and, drawing near, looked into it and asked: "Who are you?" He received the answer: "We are Balahis, brother and sister." While speaking to God the two had their backs turned to each other. God said: "Look at each other and say (once more) who you are." Then they looked at each other and said: "We are man and wife."

From this point on we find a double version. One tells us that they both spat upon the earth and that from their spittle another man came into being. According to the other they rolled together a little lump of sweat-moistened dirt and from this formed another man.

When the go-between (using one or other of these versions) has come to this point, he turns to the newly married couple and says: "You also have been married this day. The tie formed by spliced bamboo is not strong. Therefore we use brass to unite you. If the wife breaks this tie, the Panch (council) will decide what is to be her punishment." Or he uses the words: "If the man break the tie he will lose his money. If the bride break the alliance she will be brought before the court, she will have to pay fifty-one rupees and to spend six months in jail."

In front of Hindu shops pictures of the *Mata pheṇ* shaped as a many-folded hood and rising above the water may still be seen on the walls.

There is a further legend that *pāwaṇ ḍuṅgar,* the man, was full of anger when he saw how shamelessly *Mata pheṇ* had raised herself above the water. Lifting his foot, he stamped upon her so that today Lady Hill is considerably lower than *pāwaṇ ḍuṅgar*, her male partner.

That the two Balahis are made to speak of themselves not as brother and sister but as man and woman is clearly connected with the corresponding passage of the Bhil flood myth as treated above.

It is quite possible that by reason of the shortness of our stay (as described in the Introduction) we were not able to gather the whole myth as known to the Bhilalas. Neither did we succeed in definitely ascertaining whether the Tarwis of this district (genuine Bhils) share this myth with the Bhilalas.

Nundarbar

Here also to our regret it was not possible to get clear information with regard to the story of the flood. One of our informants, a Pawrya Bhil, living in Crani District in the Satpura Mountains, knew of the fact that the present, post-flood human race could be traced back to a washerman and washerwoman. Of the punishment of the fish and the loss of its tongue he knew nothing. But he told us that it was the goddess Dhanakokre (not Bhagwān) who formed the two out of loam. The name Dhanakokre signifies: "Maker of Many." Unfortunately the five men that we consulted as authorities knew no more of the matter.

The most noteworthy fact about this fragment of a myth is that a female deity appears as the creator of man. It may be pointed out here that the Bhils of the Western Khandesh, in this as in other important points, go their own way; but we cannot enter into this question for the moment.

Udaipur-Kherwara

Our informants knew of no myths of the deluge current among the Bhils of these parts. It would however be inadmissible to draw definite conclusions from this fact. The need for caution has already been emphasized.

THE HINDU DELUGE MYTH

It is naturally interesting to examine in what ways the Bhil legends of the flood are related to the well-known Hindu story of the deluge. We shall begin by quoting Franz Bopp's short exposé of the Hindu myth.

"The Lord of all creatures, Brahmā, the Supreme Being [he says of himself in the course of this episode: "higher than me there is none"] appeared to a pious king called Manu and announced to him the approaching flood which was to destroy all things. He advised him to build a ship and, in the hour of danger, to embark in it taking with him, well separated from each other, the various seeds of every sort. Manu obeyed the order of the deity, brought into the ship all the different kinds of seeds and then embarked in it himself. The ship, guided by the deity, floated for many years on the waters and finally landed on the highest peak of Mount Himawān, to which, according to the order of the deity, it was made fast. The peak bears to this day the name of Nau-Bandhanam (ship's binding) and Manu, through whom the human race was preserved, became the father of future generations."[4]

Besides this exposé we find in Bopp certain supplementary details of which some are of importance.

(*a*) The deity appears to Manu in the form of a (horned) fish.[5]

(*b*) It is the older version that shows us Brahmā in the form of the fish; only in a later version does Vishnu take his place.[6]

(*c*) Punishment as the motive of the deluge would appear to be indicated by the use of the expression "time of cleansing."[7]

(*d*) Manu becomes the (new) first parent although there is no question of wife or children. Nor does the Hindu mentality seem to be troubled by the fact that seven holy Ṛṣis embark with Manu on his rescue ship. We are even told that Manu afterwards generates in a preternatural manner through *tapas* (asceticism, magic) not only the lesser deities and Asuras but all living and lifeless, all moving and motionless things.

(*e*) In memory of Manu, the first parent, human beings are often called Manujās, i.e., "born of Manu."

(*f*) Floating upon the waters (of the ocean) Manu is said to await the reappearance and help of the deity, who once came to him in the form of the horned fish.

[4]Franz Bopp: "Die Sintflut, nebst drei anderen der wichtigsten Episoden des Mahābhārata" (Berlin) 1829, p. IV s. Cf. also H. von Glasenapp: "Der Hinduismus" (Munich) 1922, pp. 91 s., 120; J. A. Dubois: "Hindu Manners" I (Oxford) 1897, p. 48; W. J. Wilkins: *Hindu Mythology: Vedic and Puranic,* Second edition (Calcutta and Simla) 1900, p. 135.

[5]Fr. Bopp, loc. cit., pp. X, XVII. A full translation of this variant of the Hindu flood myth as contained in the Mahābhārata is to be found in A. Hohenberger: "Die indische Flutsage und das Matsyapurāna" (Leipzig) 1930, pp. 6–9.

[6]Loc. cit., p. viii.

[7]Loc. cit., p. xxii.

COMPARISON BETWEEN THE BHIL AND HINDU DELUGE MYTHS

Points of Conformity or Similarity

1. Brahmā of the Hindus, insofar as he is taken to be the Supreme Being, corresponds in a measure with Bhagwān of the Bhils. Remarkable differences between the two deities will, however, be shown later.

2. In both instances it is a fish who announces the coming deluge.

3. The pious Manu has points in common with the pious, kindly girl.

4. The fish gives the advice to take seeds into the ship (or into the pumpkin).

5. The ship in the Hindu version is equivalent to the hollow pumpkin of the Bhil story.

6. Manu, the (new) progenitor of the human race, corresponds to the (washermen) brother and sister who become the first parents of post-deluge mankind.

Points of Difference

1. Both Brahmā and Bhagwān are conceived anthropomorphically; but Bhagwān has undoubtedly retained more of the character of Supreme Deity and Creator. It is he who made the brother and sister that were to survive the flood and it was he who afterwards instituted the marriage tie between them in order to ensure the propagation of the human race. In the Hindu myth Brahmā disappears from the scene and it is Manu who himself (through magic) determines the new development of humanity. In the Bhil story Bhagwān holds the reins in his hands throughout. As compared with the Hindu tendency to irrationalism we find among the Bhils a complete adherence to the demands of rational thought.

2. According to the Hindu myth the deity (Brahmā, Viṣṇu) appears in the form of a fish. In the Bhil legend the fish has no such relation to Bhagwān but is on the contrary punished by the latter.

3. Manu by means of preternatural *tapas* brings about the rise of a new humanity, of new gods, in fact of an entirely new world. This conception is typical of Hindu thought with its pantheistic and emanative trend. Of this there is no trace among the Bhils. Bhagwān creates man and then ordains marital procreation. The Bhil myth faces the problem of incest and by solving it in the forcible manner recorded above

shows that at least an effort has been made to get over the worst difficulty.[8] In the Hindu myth the question need not be raised because Manu repeoples the earth by magic. When however the problem of incest is introduced into the Hindu version (which is not the case here) then it is of a much nastier and more dangerous nature, for the simple reason that Manu is obliged to content himself with his own "daughter," the female principle which has emanated from himself, and to make her the mother of the new race. I have already elsewhere[9] called attention to this problem which is connected with a later pantheistic trend in religious thought.

It may be pertinent to recall here that the Vedic Aryans (like the ancient Iranians) recognized Yama and Yami as the first human beings. (Rgveda X, 10.) In this case also the problem of incest offers great difficulties, as is generally known. Yama does not comply with the desire of his sister Yami and accordingly the incestuous union is not consummated.[10] I hope to give a more detailed account elsewhere of how this myth survives as the conscious, or more frequently unconscious, mental background to the Indian festival of Rākhi.

4. According to Bopp, the Hindu myth at least suggests the punitive character of the deluge.[11] The Bhil myth recognizes nothing of the kind.

5. In the Hindu myth the fish, which with its horn guides the ship silently and safely over the waters, plays a prominent role. (One is

[8]Also among the Baigas the first couple, Nanga Baiga and Nanga Baigin, are reckoned as brother and sister and become finally united in marriage. (Elwin, loc. cit., p. 313.) This the Baiga accept, but today they abhor all incest, especially kin incest. Clan incest is not taken so seriously. Earthquakes are regarded as the direct result of incest and "Bhagwān could never give a child as the result of such a union" (Elwin, loc. cit., p. 189).

[9]W. Koppers: "Pferdeopfer und Pferdekult der Indogermanen" in *Wiener Beiträge zur Kulturgeschichte und Linguistik,* IV, 1936, p. 323. H. W. Schomerus: "Ist die Bibel von Indien abhängig?" (Munich) 1932, pp. 143–144, gives us a variant on the Indian myth of the deluge for which he refers us to A. Hohenberger: "Die indische Flutsage" (Leipzig) 1930. According to this variant, Manu, after his rescue, made for himself a daughter out of a sacrificial mixture of fat, butter, sour milk, cream, and curd. Singing and chastising his body, he lived with this daughter and begot offspring. But that this variant represents the oldest version of the Indian myth of the deluge must appear extremely doubtful. As Schomerus himself puts it, it is "perhaps the oldest version." It is possible that we have here the oldest draft recorded in writing. (It occurs in the Śatapathabrahmana I. 8, 1; 1–10.) With its typically Hindu coloring this version certainly gives an impression which is anything rather than convincingly archaic.

[10]Cf. A. Christensen: "Le premier homme et le premier roi dans l'histoire légendaire des Iraniens," IIme partie (Leide) 1934, pp. 3ff. M. Winternitz: "Geschichte der indischen Literatur" I (Leipzig) 1909, pp. 91ff.

[11]This view is shared by M. Winternitz: "Die Flutsagen des Altertums und der Naturvölker" in *Mitteilungen der Anthropologischen Gesellschaft Wien,* XXXI, 1901, 305–333. Cf. p. 315.

naturally reminded of the horned moon sailing through the heavens.) In the Bhil version the fish does not guide and draw the ship.

6. Above, we came to the conclusion that the Bhil legend of the deluge had probably taken certain elements from myths dealing with the creation of the world. These elements are of course lacking in the Hindu version because the religious and philosophical outlook of the Hindus eliminates the idea of creation as such.

All things taken together, we must unquestionably recognize in the Bhil story traces of an older conception, modified however by Hindu influences. It is interesting that one of our most capable interpreters, old Master Ivo, once declared quite spontaneously that the episode of the fish must have come into the Bhil myth through the Hindus while on the other hand the Hindus were unaware of the story of the deluge as told by the Bhils. The gulf of difference that still exists is therefore felt by the Bhils themselves.

As regards possible connections between the Hindu myth of the deluge and similar stories among the other peoples of antiquity—Persians, Babylonians, Greeks—I can only refer the reader to the previously mentioned study by M. Winternitz.

The Tamil Flood Myths and the Cankam Legend

DAVID SHULMAN

The student of the flood myth cannot possibly master all of the world's languages in which versions of the narrative are related. For this reason, flood myth scholars must depend upon the contributions of experts who possess the requisite linguistic skills. In India, for example, are to be found many diverse language and literary traditions. One of these traditions belongs to the Tamil of southern India. The knowledge necessary to penetrate the rich Tamil legacy of flood myths is staggering, and for this reason flood myth scholars are greatly indebted to David Shulman, Professor of Indian Studies and Comparative Religion at Hebrew University in Jerusalem, who has so ably surveyed the available Tamil data.

For additional accounts of the flood myth in India, see Franz Bopp, Die Sündflut nebst drei anderen der wichtigsten Episoden des Maha-Bharata *(Berlin, 1829); Félix Nève, "De l'origine de la tradition indienne du Déluge,"* Annales de philosophie chrétienne *38/39 (1849): 265–279, 325–344; Félix Nève, "La tradition indienne du Déluge dans sa forme la plus ancienne,"* Annales de philosophie chrétienne *52 (1851): 47–63, 98–115, 185–201, 256–273; A. S. Vaidyanatha Ayyar, "The Flood Legends of the East,"* Journal of the Bombay Historical Society *2 (1929): 1–14; A. Hohenberger,* Die indische Flutsage und das Matsyapurāṇa: Ein Beitrag zur Geschichte der Viṣṇuverehrung *(Leipzig, 1930); Surya Kanta,* The Flood Legend in Sanskrit Literature *(Delhi, 1950). See also Daniel F. Polish, "The Flood Myth in the Traditions of Israel and India," unpublished doctoral dissertation in religion (Harvard University, 1974); J. Gonda,* De Indische Zondvloed-Mythe, *Mededelingen der Koninklijke Nederlandse Akademie van Wetenschappen, afd. Letterkunde, Niuwe Reeks, Deel 41, No. 2 (Amsterdam, 1978); J. C. Heesterman, "The Flood Story in Vedic Ritual," in Peter Slater and Donald Wiebe, eds.,* Traditions in Contact and Change: Selected Proceedings of the XIVth Congress of the International Association for the History of Religions *(Waterloo, Canada, 1983), pp. 25–38, 671–673.*

Reprinted from *Journal of Tamil Studies* 14 (1978):10–31.

Tamil tradition has long been famous for an origin myth based on the idea of a destructive flood. The story first appears in the commentary attributed to Nakkīrar on the *Iṟaiyaṉār akappŏrul.*[1] There we learn that the ancient Pāṇṭiya kings established three kinds (*mūvakaippaṭṭa-*) of Caṅkam or literary "academies" to judge the compositions of the early Tamil poets. The first Caṅkam, in which the gods Śiva and Murukaṉ were included, sat for 4,440 years in "the Maturai which was flooded by the sea" (*kaṭal kŏḷḷa ppaṭṭa maturai*). The second (*iṭaiccaṅkam*) sat for 3,700 years in Kapāṭapuram, and "it seems that at that time the sea flooded the Pāṇṭiya land" (*akkālattu ppolum pāṇṭiyanāṭṭai kkaṭal kŏṇṭatu*). The third Caṅkam studied Tamil for 1,850 years in Upper Maturai (*uttara maturai*). This tradition is repeated with some elaboration in the commentary by Aṭiyārkkunallār on *Cil.* 8.1–2. Aṭiyārkkunallār informs us that the sea swallowed up forty-nine provinces (*nāṭu*) of the old Pāṇṭiya land from the Paḫṟuḷi River to the north bank of the Kumari River. In other words, the medieval tradition of the commentators regards the ancient, antediluvian Tamil land as stretching far to the south of the present southern border at Cape Comorin.[2] The story of the three Caṅkam as it appears in our sources is suspect on many counts,[3] and there is no geological evidence of any deluge affecting the

[1] *Iṟaiyaṉār Akappŏruḷ* (Madras, 1953), aphorism 1.

[2] The commentators always define the southern boundary as the *Kumari* River; see, for example, the ancient commentary on Puṟanāṉūṟu 6.1–2; 17.1; 67.6. Cf. the discussion by S. B. Bharati, "The Pre-deluge Pandinad and Her Southern Frontier," *Journal of Annamalai University* 5 (1935):64–88; M. A. Thiagarajah, "Cēranāṭu During the Caṅkam and the Post Caṅkam Period," unpublished Ph.D. dissertation, University of London, 1953, pp. 8–9, 12–13, 81–82. This tradition conflicts with Iḷaṅko's description of the southern border as *tŏṭiyol pauvam* "the sea of the maiden" (*Cilappatikāram* [hereafter *Cil.*] 8.1–2); hence *Aṭiyārkkunallār*'s lengthy gloss, which explains that the great flood which devastated the old Pāṇṭiya land happened long before Iḷaṅko's time, so that it was natural for the poet to describe the present, postdiluvian border. This ingenious explanation conveniently fits all references to the sea as the southern border and leaves intact the story of the old capitals swallowed by the flood.

[3] *Aṭiyārkkunallār*'s description of the 49 lost provinces (*nāṭu*) of the old Pāṇṭiya land shows the weak points of the tradition. The provinces are listed in groups of seven which appear to reflect a formalization akin to the conventional division of the Tamil land in *akam* poetry: there were 7 coconut provinces, 7 *Maturai* provinces, two groups of *pālai* provinces, 7 hill provinces, 7 *kārai* provinces of the east, and 7 *kuṟumpaṉai* provinces. (The last group appears in *Pērāciriyar*'s commentary to *Tŏlkāppiyam Pŏruḷ*. 649 as "palmyra province.") With the exception of the "*Maturai* provinces," the only names which look like authentic place names in *Aṭiyārkkunallār*'s description of the lost homeland follow immediately on the above list: "*Kumari, Kŏllam*, and many other mountain provinces, forests, rivers and towns." It is noteworthy that the first of these names is shared by the *historical* southern boundary of the Tamil land, while *Kŏllam* exists today as Quilon! That the present-day *Kŏllam* was not unrelated to the "lost" Kŏllam was recognized by the medieval commentators: see M. A. Dorai Rangaswamy, *The Religion and Philosophy of Tēvāram* (Madras, 1958), vol. I, p. 131. Note also that the number of prov-

area in historical times.[4] Nevertheless, the Caṅkam legend is by no means the only instance of the flood motif in Tamil literature: the epic *Maṇimekalai* describes the destruction of the ancient Cōḻa port city Pukār (Kāvirippūmpaṭṭiṉam) by a flood[5]—although Pukār exists today as a village by the seashore, near the spot where the Kāviri pours into the Bay of Bengal. And, as we shall see, nearly every Tamil shrine claims to have survived the *pralaya,* the cosmic flood that puts an end to the created universe.

All of these flood myths may well go back to a single archetype. Already in the story of the three Caṅkam we may detect the conflation of two basic elements—the idea of a complete destruction (of the ancient cities of Maturai and Kapāṭapuram), out of which a new creation emerges; and the belief that something (here the Caṅkam, the institution that symbolizes the beginning of Tamil culture) survives the deluge. These ideas are, of course, somewhat similar, for even the notion of rebirth out of a total destruction implies a degree of continuity. I will argue below that it is this concept—the renewed creation that follows upon the deluge—that underlies both the Caṅkam legend and the corpus of flood myths attached to the shrines. Tamil mythology depicts the creation of the world as a recurrent moment in the cosmic cycle, a moment that arrives after the universal deluge, and is always linked to the shrine as the center of the cosmos, hence the proper site from which to create; the connection between this conception and the Caṅkam story emerges in the local tradition of Maturai, the probable source of the Caṅkam legend, and the home of the third, possibly historical Caṅkam.[6]

Before we turn to the Maturai flood myths, let us survey the two broad categories of Tamil flood myths, which correspond to the two basic ideas isolated above—myths of creation and myths of survival. We begin with the latter category, which seems at first glance to be

---

inces in *Aṭiyārkkunallār*'s list—49—is a formulaic number which appears again in the *Caṅkam* story: 48 of the 51 characters which make up the body of *Sarasvatī* became the poets of the *Caṅkam;* their number was completed when they were joined by Śiva, who inheres in the world as the vowel *a* inheres in syllables (*Tiruviḷaiyāṭaṟpurāṇam* of *Parañcotimuṉivar*—hereinafter referred to as *Tiruviḷai;* Madras, 1965, 51.1–39). All this casts doubt on the account of *Aṭiyārkkunallār.*

[4] See P. Joseph, *The Dravidian Problem and the South Indian Culture Complex* (Madras, 1972), pp. 3–4.

[5] *Maṇimekalai* (Madras, 1951), 24.27–74, 25.178–200.

[6] On the question of the historical *Caṅkam,* see Kamil V. Zvelebil, "The Earliest Account of the Tamil Academies," *Indo-Iranian Journal* 15 (1973):109–135; J. R. Marr, "The Eight Tamil Anthologies with special reference to Puṟanāṉūṟu and Patiṟṟuppattu," unpublished Ph.D. dissertation, University of London, 1958, pp. 2–15.

more prevalent in Tamil. Most Tamil purāṇas contain a myth describing the shrine's survival of the cosmic flood. The idea of surviving the deluge may go back to the earliest flood myth in India, in which Manu, the progenitor of the human race, is saved from the flood by a fish:

> A fish warned Manu of an impending flood. Manu built a ship and, when the waters began to rise, tied it with a rope to the horn of the fish. The fish carried him over the northern mountain and instructed him to bind the ship to a tree. The waters gradually abated. Manu offered ghee, sour milk, whey, and curds into the water, and, in a year, a woman was born. She came to Manu and told him to use her in a sacrifice, and by her he had offspring.[7]

This myth has been much discussed, often in the light of the well-known Middle Eastern parallels; the possibility of borrowing cannot be ruled out.[8] Eventually this myth becomes the background to Viṣṇu's fish-avatar.[9] It is interesting to note that two purāṇas place the beginning of the story in south India: the *Matsyapurāṇa* begins with Manu practicing *tapas* on Mount Malaya,[10] and the *Bhāgavata* gives the role of Manu to Satyavrata, lord of Draviḍa.[11] Perhaps these identifications reflect an awareness of the hypertrophy of the motif in south Indian mythology; or they may indicate no more than the provenance of these particular versions. In the version quoted above, as well as later purāṇic texts, Manu's survival is a key element, for the flood is the reason for a *repetition* of the creation story, a second creation similar to the first (note the appearance here of the incest theme), and also to some extent dependent upon it. The same pattern appears in many tribal flood myths in India: no sooner is creation accomplished than it is threatened with disaster.[12] Note the idea of sacrifice in the text quoted

[7] *Satapathabrāhmana* of the White Yajurveda, Bibliotheca Indica (Calcutta, 1903–1910), 1.8.1–10.

[8] See Suryakanta Shastri, *The Flood Legend in Sanskrit Literature* (Delhi, 1950), *passim;* Paul Regnaud, *Comment naissent les mythes* (Paris, 1897), pp. 59–151; Gustav Oppert, *On the Original Inhabitants of Bharatavarṣa or India* (Westminster, 1893), pp. 311–328. In Iran the flood theme and the survival of man attaches to Yima—whose Indian counterpart is in this case not Yama but Yama's half-brother, Manu! Dumézil is oddly silent on this point, surely relevant to the comparison of Yima and Yama: see G. Dumézil, *Mythe et épopée,* vol. II (Paris, 1971), pp. 246–249; *idem,* "La Sabhā de Yama," *Journal Asiatique* 253 (1965):161–165.

[9] See Wendy Doniger O'Flaherty, *Hindu Myths* (Harmondsworth, 1975), pp. 179–181; and cf. *Ṛgveda* 7.88.3; F. B. J. Kuiper, "Cosmogony and Conception: A Query," *History of Religions* 10 (1970):104.

[10] *Matsyapurāṇa,* Ānandāśrama Sanskrit Series no. 54 (Poona, 1909), 1.11–12.

[11] *Bhāgavatapurāṇa* (Bombay, 1905), 8.24.13.

[12] Verrier Elwin, *Myths of Middle India* (Madras, 1949), pp. 20–26, 30–32, 37, 41, 46–48 (1976).

above: the post-diluvian creation is connected with a sacrificial rite; the horn of the fish that saves Manu may be a multiform of the *yūpa,* the sacrificial post.[13] A deep level of meaning may be hinted at here: the universe is created anew out of the havoc of the deluge, just as new life is attained through the violent act of sacrifice.[14]

Other Sanskrit accounts of the flood include among the survivors the Seven Sages with the seeds of creatures,[15] Brahmā, the sage Mārkaṇḍeya, the Narmadā River, Bhava (Rudra), the fish-Viṣṇu, and the Vedas, purāṇas, and sciences.[16] The *Matsyapurāṇa* mentions a "boat of the Vedas" in which the survivors escape; this motif is developed in an important Tamil flood myth, in which the survival of Manu and the others is replaced by two related elements—the escape of Śiva and Umā in a boat fashioned from the *praṇava* (the syllable *Om*), and the continued existence of the shrine:

> All creatures except Śiva, who is the First Principle, perished in the deluge that covered the universe. In order to create the worlds anew by the power of his grace (*aruḷ valiyāṉ*), Śiva, clothed only in the sixty-four arts, without his serpent ornaments, his crescent moon, his garland (of *kŏṉṟai* flowers), or his tiger skin, made the *praṇava* which is the sound of the Vedas into a boat (*toṇi*). With the name Pĕriyanāyakaṉ ("the great lord"), together with Umā he entered the boat and sailed through the waters. They found a shrine standing firm as *dharma,* undestroyed by the flood. "This shrine is the 'root' of the universe (*mūlātārakettiram* = Skt. *mūlādhārakṣetra*)," cried Śiva in joy, and he remained there in the boat. The guardians of the quarters found him there and said, "He has dried up the waters with his third eye!" Varuṇa, the lord of the sea, came there and worshiped the god who saves those without egoism from the sea (of rebirth).[17]

This story provides the explanation for one of the names of Cīkāḻi—"Toṇipuram," city of the boat. The shrine is not destroyed by the flood because it is the center of the world, the "root" or base of the spine of the cosmic man whose body symbolizes the created universe.[18] Śiva

[13] See Michael Defourny, "Note sur le symbolisme de la corne dans le *Mahābhārata* et la mythologie brahmanique classique," *Indo-Iranian Journal* 18 (1976):17–23.

[14] See D. Shulman, "Murukan, the Mango, and Ekāmbareśvara-Śiva: Fragments of a Tamil Creation Myth?" *Indo-Iranian Journal* 21 (1979):27–40.

[15] *Mahābhārata* (Bori), 3.185.29–30, 34.

[16] *Matsyapurāṇa* 2.10–12.

[17] *Cīkāḻittalapurāṇam* of Aruṇācalakkavirāyar (Madras, 1887), 2.15–41. In the interests of economy, I have summarized rather than translated myths throughout.

[18] For this symbolism, see K. Zvelebil, *The Poets of the Powers* (London, 1973), p. 42. The same image, expressing the shrine's identification as the center of the universe, occurs in *Śrīnāgeśakṣetramāhātmya* (Madras, 1935), 1.4–6 (with reference to Tiruppātāḷīccaram) and in *Tiruvārūrppurāṇam* of Campantamuṉivar (Madras, 1894), 5.17.

arrives at this spot with his bride, without his usual attributes, in a boat made from the sound of the Vedas; the indestructible shrine becomes the god's refuge from the flood, and the spot from which he can begin the work of creation once more. The sound of the Vedas will guide the god in this work, for sound (*śabda*) is traditionally an important instrument of creation.[19] The first step in this process is taken when Śiva burns up the waters with the fire of his third eye. Water must give way to land, so that creation can take place; elsewhere, however, Śiva's third eye creates not land but the flood—in the form of ten rivers—from the sweat of Pārvatī's hands when the goddess covers his eyes.[20]

The myth from Cīkāḻi clearly reveals the link between the shrine's survival and its role as the site of the new creation. The progression is not, however, always so clear; many texts content themselves with the first notion, and say nothing of the cosmogony. The shrine is eternal and has never been destroyed (hence the use of such common epithets as *maṉṉum ūr,*[21] *mūtūr,*[22] *paḻaiyapati,*[23] *nirantarapuri,*[24] and so on, all indicative of the shrine's antiquity and indestructibility). All the holy places near Maturai disappeared during the deluge except that worshiped by Kubera at Uttaravālavāy.[25] Gaṇeśa at Tiruppuṟampayam is known as Piraḷayam kātta vināyakar because he saved the world from the flood.[26] A folk etymology explains the name of a shrine mentioned in the *Tevāram*, Paravaiyuṇmaṇṭaḷi, as the temple (*maṇṭaḷi*) that swallowed (*uṇ*) the sea (*paravai*) sent by Varuṇa.[27] The Nāgagiri at Tiruccĕṅkoṭu is never destroyed during the deluge,[28] and the inhabitants of Tiruvāñciyam need not fear the end of the world—for all the worlds come to Tiruvāñciyam and enter into the goddess there.[29] Similarly, the

[19] This idea is said to be symbolized by the drum (*ḍamaru*) carried by Naṭarāja-Śiva in his upper right hand. See H. Zimmer, *Myths and Symbols in Indian Art and Civilization* (Princeton, 1972), p. 152.

[20] *Kantapurāṇam* of Kacciyappacivācāriyar (Madras, 1907), 6.3. 364–370.

[21] *Kāñcippurāṇam* of Civañāṉayokikaḷ (Kāñcipuram, 1937), 58.37; cf. *Tiruviḷai.* 13.4.

[22] *Cil.* 15.6; *Tirukkūvappurāṇam* of Turaimaṅkalam Civappirakācacuvāmikaḷ (Madras, 1908), 2.53.

[23] *Paḻanittalapurāṇam* of Pālacuppiramaṇiya kkavirāyar (Madras, 1903), 13.48; cf. *Tiruccĕṅkoṭṭuppurāṇam* of Tĕṉkāci Kavirājapaṇṭitar (Tiruccĕṅkoṭu, 1932), 1.1.2.

[24] *Tiruvŏṟṟiyūrpurāṇam* of *Tiruvŏṟṟiyūr Ñāṉappirakācar* (Madras, 1869), 2.37.

[25] *Tiruviḷai.,* 56.27.

[26] P. V. Jagadisa Ayyar, *South Indian Shrines* (Madras, 1920), p. 75.

[27] Dorai Rangaswamy, vol. I, p. 6; cf. *Cuntaramūrtti, Tevāram* 96.

[28] *Tiruccĕṅkoṭṭuppurāṇam* 1.2.6.

[29] *Tiruvāñciyakṣettirapurāṇam* (Kumpakoṇam, 1939), 14 (p. 55).

Vedas and other holy scriptures enter into the *liṅga* at Vetāraṇiyam at the time of the universal destruction, for that *liṅga* is never destroyed.[30] Śiva surrounded Tiruttеṅkūr with a great rampart so that the waters of the flood could not overwhelm it.[31] The motif is known in other literatures, as well: Palestine is higher than other lands and was therefore not submerged by the flood.[32]

An unusual development of the motif of surviving the flood is found in the story of the sand-*liṅga* at Kāñcipuram, which is one of the most popular of all Tamil myths:

> The goddess Umā came to earth to expiate the sin of hiding the eyes of her husband Śiva. She worshiped the god of Kāñci in the form of a *liṅga*, and he, in order to test her, gathered all the waters of the world into the river Kampai, which flooded the town of Kāñci. Umā embraced the *liṅga* to save it from the flood, and the *liṅga* grew soft in her embrace. Śiva arrested the flood, and ever since the *liṅga* at Kāñci bears the marks of Umā's breasts and the bracelets she wore on her arms.[33]

Here the flood motif is put to the service of the myth of Śiva's marriage to the goddess at Kāñcipuram. Other versions state that the *liṅga* was fashioned by Pārvatī from sand on the bank of the river,[34] and this idea brings us even closer to one of the possible sources of the myth, the mention in the *Cilappatikāram* of a woman who embraced a sand image of her husband on the bank of the Kāviri to protect it from the flood.[35] V. R. Ramachandra Dikshitar notes in this connection that "even today it is a custom among some classes for the chaste wife to go to the river bank, make an image of her husband in sand and after making offerings to it, to cast off the clothes she was wearing and to put on new ones."[36] The *Pĕriya purāṇam* expressly states that the image embraced by the goddess became the wedding form of the god (*maṇavāḷa naṟ kolam*), although Pārvatī leaves the imprint of her breasts and bracelets not upon sand but upon stone, which is melted by her love.[37]

In one variant of this myth, Devī at Kāñcipuram is aided by Durgā,

[30] *Vedāraṇyamāhātmya* (Kumpakoṇam, 1912), 2.65–67.

[31] *Tiruttеṅkūr talapurāṇam* (Cikāḷi, 1914), 2.1–13.

[32] *Bereshit Rabbah* (Tel Aviv, 1956), 33.6.

[33] *Pĕriyapurāṇam* of *Cekkiḷār* (Madras, 1916), 4.5.62–70; *Kāñcippurāṇam* 63.364–401.

[34] *Skandapurāṇa* (Calcutta, 1959), 1.3.1.4.21–36 (part of the *Aruṇācalamāhātmya* on Tiruvaṇṇāmalai).

[35] *Cil.* 21.6–10.

[36] V. R. Ramachandra Dikshitar, *The Cilappadikāram* (Madras, 1939), p. 251, n. 4.

[37] *Pĕriyapurāṇam* 4.5.67. For the motif of *bhakti* melting stone, see *Tiruvaiyāṟṟuppurāṇam* of *Ñāṉakkūttar* (Madras, 1930), 3.18–19.

who wins the name Pralayabandhinī, "she who holds back the *pralaya,*" by forcing the flooding river into a skull (*kapāla*).[38] The goddess is associated with the flood in other sites as well:

> The gods praised the goddess Kanyākumārī after her defeat of Bāṇāsura; they asked her to remain forever at the site of the battle, on the shore of the sea. They wanted fresh water, not salt water, to pour over her image, so the goddess split the earth with her spear, and a great flood welled up from the seven Pātālas and covered the earth. Alarmed, the gods prayed for help, and the goddess made the water remain in the cleft of the earth: that is the Mūlagaṅgā at the shrine of Kanyākumārī.[39]

Devī first creates and then controls the flood. Note that the Mūlagaṅgā at this shrine emerges from the nether world, the zone of chaos. The raging river is then contained within the borders of the shrine by the goddess, just as Durgā swallows up the flood at Kāñci. The goddess creates order from the materials of chaos, through the imposition of limits; at Kāñci she herself braves the flood in order to save the image of the god. In these myths we see again the importance of Devī as a source of *pratiṣṭhā,* the firm ground in which the deity and the shrine built around him are anchored.

The idea that the shrine must survive the flood found its way into the post-epic versions of the story of Dvārakā, the city carved out of the sea by Kṛṣṇa. According to the *Harivaṃśa,* Kṛṣṇa—who is known in another context as an enemy of the sea[40]—requested the sea to recede in order to make room for the building of Dvārakā ("the Gate"—to the nether world?).[41] After the Bhārata war and the deaths of Balarāma and Kṛṣṇa, Dvārakā was submerged by the sea.[42] But the *Viṣṇupurāṇa* explicitly excepts the shrine (*gṛha*) of Kṛṣṇa from the destruction: "On the day Hari (Kṛṣṇa) left the earth, strong black-bodied Kali came down (*avatīrṇo 'yaṃ kālakāyo balī kaliḥ*). The ocean covered the whole of Dvārakā except for the temple of Vāsudeva. The sea has not been able to violate (*atikrāntum*) it; Keśava (Viṣṇu) dwells there always."[43]

[38] *Kāmākṣīvilāsa* (Bangalore, 1968), 8.55–70.

[39] *Kanyākṣetramāhātmya,* India Office Library, London, Burnell Manuscripts, IO.B 468, 6. Cf. *Cĕvvantippurāṇam* of *Caiva Ĕllappanāvalar* (Tiruccirāppaḷḷi, 1927), 5.1–18.

[40] *Harivaṃśa* (Vārāṇasī, 1964), 2.133.12–68. Cf. J. Gonda, *Aspects of Early Viṣṇuism* (Delhi, 1969), p. 155. In this, as in other ways, Krishna is strongly reminiscent of *Skanda-Murukaṉ:* see below at notes 121–124.

[41] *Harivaṃśa* 2.59.31–38. Cf. *Visnupurāṇa* (Bombay, 1866), 5.23.13. We will return to the motif of the city reclaimed from the sea. On *Dvārakā* as the gate to the nether world, see F. B. J. Kuiper, "The Bliss of Aša," *Indo-Iranian Journal* 8 (1964): p. 113.

[42] *Mahābhārata* 16.8.40–41.

[43] *Visṇupurāṇa* 5.38.8–10.

The *Bhāgavata* repeats this statement: "The sea submerged in a moment Dvārakā, which was abandoned by Hari, except for the temple (*ālayam*) of the lord; Madhusūdana (Viṣṇu) is always present there."[44] Kṛṣṇa's death is thus the prelude to the destruction of his city and to the beginning of the Kali Age, the corrupt, unhappy period that is our present moment in time; but the god remains even now in his shrine, which no doubt offers its pilgrims an immediate salvation. Dvārakā, of course, is said to exist still today in Gujarat.[45]

There seems little reason to believe that the idea of the shrine's survival belongs to the earliest layer of the Dvārakā story; more probably, it was simply introduced by the purāṇas into the older legend. In the *MBh*, the destruction of Dvārakā is complete; indeed, this episode in the epic seems to revolve around the idea of a total devastation—it follows immediately the story of the Yādavas' fratricidal massacre—and raises the question of the god's responsibility for the existence of death.[46] This version of the story has a parallel in Tamil tradition in the myth of the flooding of Pukār:

> King Nĕṭumuṭikkiḷḷi fell in love with a girl he saw one day in a garden. She lived with him for a month and then disappeared. The king learned from a messenger that the girl was Pīlivaḷai, daughter of the Nāga king Vaḷaivāṇaṉ, and that she was to bear a son to a king of the solar dynasty. When Pīlivaḷai had given birth, she sent her son to his father on a merchant's ship, but the ship foundered and the baby was lost. In his grief the king forgot to celebrate the festival of Indra, and as a result the goddess Maṇimekalai destroyed the city by a flood.[47]

As in the *MBh* version of the Dvārakā story, the destruction of the city is complete, although Pukār, like Dvārakā, is still pointed out today. In this myth the flood is attached to the important theme of the king's marriage to a Nāga princess; ultimately it is the king's love for the Nāginī that brings ruin to the city. Union with the Nāga serpent deities, who represent the indigenous possessors of the earth, may legitimize a dynasty, but it is very often a source of danger as well: a Kashmiri legend tells of a king who burns a Nāginī in an oven in order to free himself from her magic control.[48] The basic pattern of the Pukār myth

[44] *Bhāgavatapurāṇa* 11.31.23–24.

[45] H. H. Wilson, *The Vishnu Purana: A System of Hindu Mythology and Tradition* (1840; reprinted Calcutta, 1972), p. 482, n. 4.

[46] See Vyāsa's speech to Arjuna in the sequel to the myth: *Mahābhārata* 16.9.25–36. And cf. Wendy Doniger O'Flaherty, *The Origins of Evil in Hindu Mythology* (Berkeley, 1976), pp. 260–271.

[47] *Maṇimekalai* 24.27–74, 25.178–200.

[48] Veronica Ions, *Myths and Legends of India* (London, 1970), pp. 77–83.

survives in a number of popular variants from northern Tamilnāṭu, especially the Tŏṇṭai region: for example, the purāṇic tradition of Mahābalipuram near Madras describes the destruction of the site through a flood sent by Indra, who becomes jealous of the splendor of this city of men.[49] In the Mahābalipuram tradition, the role of the serpent temptress is given to a celestial *apsaras*—the usual accomplice of the gods in their attempts to corrupt powerful mortals.[50] Another variant from this region retains the Nāginī and reverses the whole force of the myth: the Tŏṇṭai ruler Tiraiyaṉ is said to have been born from the union of a Cola king with a serpent maiden, who tied a *tŏṇṭai* creeper to her son as a sign of his lineage and sent him on the waves (*tirai*) to receive his kingdom.[51] This attempt to explain the name Iḷan-tiraiyaṉ retains the Cola hero of the Pukār myth, and thus hints at the provenance of the story; but here the infant prince is carried safely by the water, and there is no violent deluge. Other variants support the positive role of the water, which now brings a ruler instead of destruction.[52] The king rises from the ocean like the goddess Śrī from the ocean of milk,[53] and like the daughter of Manu after the flood recedes; the appearance of the dynasty may replace the motif of the *city* won from the sea. Order, in the person of the king, replaces the inchoate powers of the ocean, and the flood provides the background to the dynastic foundation—or, in other words, to a renewed creation. Again we are led back to the theme of creation from the water. We must now examine in more detail the Tamil cosmogonic myths, which begin at the moment of the universal deluge.

[49] William Chambers, "Some Account of the Sculptures and Ruins at Mavalipuram, a Place a Few Miles North of Sadras, and Known to Seamen by the Name of the Seven Pagodas," in M.W. Carr, ed., *Descriptive and Historical Papers Relating to the Seven Pagodas on the Coromandel Coast* (Madras, 1869), pp. 13–15. See summary and discussion of the myth in O'Flaherty, *The Origins of Evil in Hindu Mythology*, pp. 270–271.

[50] See Wendy Doniger O'Flaherty, *Asceticism and Eroticism in the Mythology of Śiva* (Oxford, 1973), pp. 87–89. At Mahābalipuram the king falls in love with an *apsaras* who smuggles him into heaven; upon returning to earth, he constructs his city in imitation of the splendors of heaven; this excites Indra's jealousy and leads to the city's destruction.

[51] *Nacciṉārkkiṉiyar* on *Pĕrumpāṇāṟṟuppaṭai* 30–37 (pp. 213–214 in *pattuppāṭṭu*, ed. U. Ve. Cāminātaiyar, Tiruvāṉmiyūr, 1974).

[52] Oppert, pp. 250–252; cf. *Tiruvŏṟṟiyūrpurāṇam* 12.2. One wonders if the famous relief of "Arjuna's Penance" at Mahābalipuram, with the serpent figures issuing from its central crevice, is not in part connected to this story of dynastic origins (*tŏṇṭai* presumably giving us the Sanskrit dynastic title "Pallava").

[53] *Mahābhārata* 1.16. Recall the birth of Aphrodite from the sea.

THE CREATIVE FLOOD: THE KĀVIRI AND THE LORD OF THE POT

For a typical example of a shrine's picture of creation, we may turn to the tradition of Tiruvŏṟṟiyūr:

> Brahmā was born on a lotus growing from the navel of Viṣṇu during the universal flood. The lotus swayed under his weight, and he fell into the water. He prayed to Śiva and Devī, and the goddess interceded on his behalf with Śiva. The lord agreed to his request not to be reborn, and then disappeared with the goddess.
>
> Left alone, full of sadness, Brahmā performed yoga to burn his body with his inner fire (*mūlattiṉ kaṉal*). This fire burnt the world and dried up the flood, and by the grace of Śiva the waters gathered in a heap. To grant Brahmā release, Śiva appeared as a square painted plank (*caturac-ciṟpam ākiya palakam*) in the midst of the fire, and he dwells in that form to this day at that spot, which is known as Ātipuri, since the lord came there at the beginning (*ātiyil*). The waters of the deluge became a deep lake to the northeast of the *liṅga*.[54]

The beginning (*ādi,* Tam. *āti*) celebrated in this myth is the start of creation, the reemergence of the world after the flood is burned away. This is a process that must involve the shrine: Brahmā dries up the waters with his internal fire, thus causing the shrine, the site of creation, to be revealed through the appearance of the *liṅga*/plank. Ironically, Brahmā, who traditionally performs the actual work of creation, here initiates the creative process while seeking release from existence and from the sorrows of having a body! Brahmā is, in fact, said to have gained his wish: Śiva appears to grant him release. In this case, however, release seems to be identified with the divine epiphany itself; once again, it is not the old goal of *mukti* that is praised, but the "release" that comes from worshiping the god in his local home, in this very real world. Brahmā thus attains his desire without ceasing to exist, in his present incarnation; the salvation he achieves in the shrine on earth presumably obviates any future births, so that Śiva can promise that he will not be reborn. The same immediate salvation is, of course, offered to all who come to worship at Tiruvŏṟṟiyūr. In the eyes of the Tamil author, creation is thus a positive, beneficent process leading to the possibility of happiness in the circumstances of our life on earth.[55] The waters of the flood out of which the world is created

[54] *Tiruvŏṟṟiyūrpurāṇam* 2.1.36. Cf. *Bhāgavatapurāṇa* 3.8.10–33.

[55] This is also the view of Śaiva Siddhānta: see *ciṟṟurai* of *Civañāṉacuvāmikal* on *Civañāṉapotam* (Aṇṇāmalainakar, 1953), cu. 1, 1 (pp. 8–10).

persist in a controlled, circumscribed form near the central image of the shrine—an eternal reminder of the creative act that has taken place at this spot.

Somewhat more complex is the cosmogonic myth at Kumpakoṇam, where Śiva is Ādikumbheśvara, "lord of the pot":

> When the time of the universal deluge drew near, Brahmā came to Śiva and said, "Once the world has been destroyed, how will I be able to create it anew?" Śiva instructed him to mix earth with *amṛta,* fashion a golden pot (*kumpam,* Skt. *kumbha*), and put the Vedas and other scriptures into the pot along with the Seed of Creation (*ciruṣṭipījam*). Brahmā made the pot and decorated it with leaves, and, when the flood began to rise, he put the pot in a net bag (*uṟi*) and sent it off on the waters. Pushed by the wind and the waves, the pot floated southwards; the leaves fell off and became holy shrines, and the pot came to rest at a spot proclaimed sacred by a heavenly voice. Lord Aiyaṉār tried to break the pot with an arrow, but his arrow missed. Śiva took the form of a hunter and shot an arrow, which hit the pot and let loose a flood of *amṛta.* When the waters of the deluge receded, Brahmā fashioned a *liṅga* from earth mixed with *amṛta,* and Śiva merged into the *liṅga* in the presence of the gods.[56]

Once again Śiva's appearance at a shrine after the cosmic flood marks the start of a renewed creation. The god frees the seed from its container and thus allows the world to be formed afresh. Note that Śiva's action is a violent one: the hunter god shatters Brahmā's pot with his arrow. The basic images of this myth—in particular, that of the creative seed carried in a pot—are drawn from well-known Sanskrit myths. In one version of Prajāpati's creation, Dawn appears before the gods in the form of an *apsaras*; they shed their seed at the sight of her, and Prajāpati fashions a sacrificial vessel out of gold in which he places the seed, from which Rudra is born.[57] In one of the classic myths of the creative sacrifice, Prajāpati, who is identified with the sacrificial victim, lusts for his daughter; to punish him, the gods create Rudra from their most fearful forms, and Rudra pierces Prajāpati with an arrow. The seed of Prajāpati pours out and becomes a lake.[58] In later versions Brahmā spills his seed "like water from a broken pot."[59] Rudra, the

[56] *Kumpakoṇam kṣettirapurāṇam* (Kumpakoṇam, 1933), pp. 35–38; cf. *Kumpakoṇappurāṇam* of Cŏkkappappulavar (Tañcāvūr, 1971), verse 106; *Kumbhaghoṇamāhātmya* (Kumpakoṇam, 1913), 1.70–77; *Tirukkuṭantaippurāṇam* of Tiricirapuram Mīṉāṭcicuntaram Piḷḷai (Madras, 1883), 7–8.

[57] *Kauṣitakibrāhmaṇa* (Wiesbaden, 1968), 6.1–2.

[58] *Aitareyabrāhmana,* Bibliotheca Indica (Calcutta, 1895–1896), 3.33. Cf. *Matsyapurāṇa* 158.35–38.

[59] *Saurapurāṇa,* Ānandāśrama Sanskrit Series no. 18 (Poona, 1889), 59.54–55.

archer and sacrificial butcher, has become the hunter Śiva at Kumpakoṇam; the pot that holds the seed is, in the Tamil myth as well as in the Sanskrit sources, a symbol of the womb.[60] This conjunction of seed and the pot/womb is implicit in the *kumbhābhiṣeka* ritual of consecration, in which a shrine is bathed in water from a pot. Kumpakoṇam, of course, derives its name from the pot (*kumbha*). Śiva is also known as Kumbheśvara in Nepal, where he is said to have been established by Agastya, the sage whom we have seen to be prominent in traditions about the origin of Tamil culture;[61] Agastya is himself called Kumbhayoni, "born from a pot," because of the following myth: Mitra and Varuṇa saw Urvaśī at a sacrificial session; they spilled their seed, and it fell into a jar containing water that stood overnight. Agastya was born from the seed in the jar.[62] As we shall see in a moment, Tamil tradition connects Agastya with another pot, and one Tamil myth explains his title Kumbhayoni not by the above story but by the "survival" motif: Agastya was given this epithet because he escaped from a pot during the universal flood.[63]

In the myth from Kumpakoṇam, the seed that Brahmā places in the pot may be understood in two ways—either as the actual seed of the creator (and thus a multiform of the *amṛta* that is used in fashioning the pot), or as the creative sound (the "seed-*mantra*") that helps give form to the universe, like the *praṇava* in the myth from Cīkāḻi cited above. The sound of the Vedas becomes the boat that carries Śiva and Umā to Cīkāḻi; in the myth from Kumpakoṇam, the Vedas and other scriptures are carried with the seed in the pot. When the pot is broken, a stream of *amṛta* pours forth, so that we have in effect a second, creative flood that contrasts with the destructive *pralaya* covering the earth. This motif is developed further in a popular myth about the origin of the Kāviri River:

> When Śiva sent Agastya to the south, he gave him at his request the river Pŏṉṉi so that he could have water for his ablutions. The river protested that it was not right for her, a woman, to follow a man, but Śiva assured her that the sage was in complete control of his senses. Agastya put the river in his water pot (*kuṇṭikai*) and headed south.

[60] See D. D. Kosambi, *Myth and Reality: Studies in the Formation of Indian Culture* (Bombay, 1962), pp. 72–74. For other examples of the motif, see J. J. Meyer, *Sexual Life in Ancient India* (London, 1930), vol. I, pp. 262–263. For a *tīrtha* formed from the water in Brahmā's pot, see *Tiruvaiyāṟṟuppurāṇam* 7.1.

[61] Pratapaditya Pal, *The Arts of Nepal* (Leiden, 1974), p. 48.

[62] *Bṛhaddevatā* attributed to *Śaunaka*, Harvard Oriental Series no. 5 (Cambridge, Mass., 1904), 5.148–153.

[63] Jagadisa Ayyar, p. 103.

> Indra, who was hiding from the demon Śūrapadma and his brothers, had taken the form of a bamboo in a pleasure-garden he had created for the worship of Śiva at Cīkāḻi. Śūrapadma's spies were unable to find him, so the demon king sent a drought to devastate the world. The garden at Cīkāḻi shrivelled up in the blazing heat of the sun. Indra, distressed at the loss of flowers for worship, was advised by Nārada to worship Vināyaka, who would bring the waters of the Pŏṉṉi to Cīkāḻi.
>
> Indra worshiped the elephant-headed god, and Vināyaka took the form of a crow and perched on Agastya's water pot. The sage raised his arm to drive the bird away, and the crow upset the pot. The Pŏṉṉi poured onto the earth with tremendous force, shaking the worlds.
>
> Vināyaka took the form of a Brahmin lad and fled from the enraged sage, but at length he revealed to him his true form. The sage asked forgiveness, but complained that he was now without water for his worship. The god took some water in his trunk and poured it into the pot, which immediately overflowed again. Agastya thanked Vināyaka and proceeded southwards, and the Pŏṉṉi flowed toward Cīkāḻi, where it revived Indra's garden.[64]

This story bears a superficial resemblance to that of the descent of the Ganges from heaven to earth; Indra's worship of Vināyaka-Gaṇeśa ultimately brings the river to earth to revive his garden, as Bhagīratha's worship of Brahmā and Śiva brings the Ganges to cover the ashes of the sons of Sagara and gain them entrance to heaven.[65] A further connection is the episode of the sage Jahnu who, seeing the Ganges sweep over his sacrificial site, drank up the water of the river, just as Agastya, the central figure of the Tamil myth, is said to have drunk the waters of the ocean.[66] There is, however, an important difference between the stories of the two rivers: Bhagīratha must persuade Śiva to sustain the Ganges in its descent, since the earth could not bear its violent force; but although the Kāviri descends violently, shaking the worlds, the sacred ground of the Tamil land can bear it. The text makes this point by recalling the flood at Kāñcipuram, which we discussed above: "The Pŏṉṉi fell to earth in a flood like the Kampai, which our lord called to Kāñci to demonstrate the love of the Lady who gave birth to the world";[67] by implication, the earth can survive, as did Kāñcipuram.

[64] *Kantapurāṇam* 2.23.17–28, 2.27.9–66, 2.29.1–27. For other versions of the descent of the Kāviri (Pŏṉṉi), see *Tulākāverimāṉmiyam* of Ma. Ti. Pāṉukavi (Madras, 1917), 5–6; *Kāverippurāṇam* of *Tiruccirrampalamuṉivar* (Madras, 1871), 4.1–49; *Tiruvaiyaṟṟuppurāṇam* 4.1–25; Stanley Rice, *Occasional Essays on Native South Indian Life* (London, 1901), pp. 153–161.

[65] *Rāmāyaṇa* of Vālmīki (Baroda, 1960–), 1.42–44.

[66] *Mahābhārata* 3.102.16–23, 3.103.1–29. The story of Jahnu appears in verses added by some mss. after *Rām.* 1.42.25 of the Baroda edition.

[67] *Kantaurpurāṇam* 2.27.37. See above at n. 33.

The Kāviri myth has, however, borrowed more significantly from other sources. Its basic image is once again that of the creative seed/flood carried in a pot. Agastya's appearance in the myth is natural for at least two reasons: first, Agastya is himself born from a pot (Kumbhayoni); and second, this sage is the major figure in the Tamil myth of cultural origins, and thus belongs by right in other myths of creation—especially creation from a flood. Both the Caṅkam and Kāviri myths seem to belong to this category, as we shall see. Agastya figures already in a much older version of the Kāviri myth: at the request of Kāntamaṉ the Cōḻaṉ, Agastya tipped over his pot (*karakam*), and Lady Kāviri flowed eastwards to the sea; she joined the sea at the spot where the ancient goddess Campāpati was performing *tapas*, and the goddess declared that the city would be known thereafter by the name of the river (Kāvirippūmpaṭṭiṉam).[68] Here the Śaiva veneer of the *Kantapurāṇam* is lacking, and Indra's catalytic role is fulfilled by the Cōḻa king; yet both Agastya and the origin of the river in the water pot are mentioned. They might be said to be the primary constituents of the story, and to suggest in themselves the identification of the river with the divine seed. This identification is strengthened in the *Kantapurāṇam* by the addition of several elements drawn from the myth of Skanda's birth. There, too, the seed (of Śiva or Agni) is often put into a pot (or pit);[69] or it is placed in the Ganges,[70] or in a golden lake,[71] or in a clump of reeds.[72] In the Tamil myth the clump of reeds appears as the bamboo in which Indra hides[73] until Cīkāḻi is flooded by the river. The bamboo and other trees of Indra's garden are burned—not by the fiery seed of Śiva, which burns any vehicle or receptacle in which it is placed, but by the sun, which consumes them "as the Triple City was once burned by Śiva."[74] Indra instigates the descent of the river, just as he interferes with Śiva's *tapas* to seek the birth of Śiva's child. The very name of the river that appears most often in this account—Pŏṉṉi, the Golden, "the Kauvery river, as having golden sands"[75]—recalls the constant recurrence of gold in the Skanda birth myth: the seed itself is

[68] *Maṇimēkalai, patikam,* 1–31.

[69] *Mahābhārata* 3.214.12; *Skandapurāṇa* 1.2.29.106; *Śivapurāṇa, Dharmasaṃhitā* (Bombay, 1884), 11.30.

[70] *Mahābhārata* 13.84.52–54; *Rām.* 1.36.12–17; *Vāyupurāṇa,* Ānandāśrama Sanskrit Series no. 49 (Poona, 1905), 72.28–31; *Skandapurāṇa* 1.2.29.88; *Brahmāṇḍapurāṇa* (Delhi, 1973), 2.3.10.30–34.

[71] *Kantapurāṇam* 1.11.89–91; *Kāñcippurāṇam* 25.44; cf. *Matsyapurāṇa* 158.28.

[72] *Skandapurāṇa* 1.2.29.104–106; 6.70.65; *Vāyupurāṇa* 72.32–33.

[73] Cf. *Śatapathabrāhmaṇa* 6.3.1.26 and 31; *Mahābhārata* 5.16.11.

[74] *Kantapurāṇam* 2.27.29.

[75] J. P. Fabricius, *Tamil and English Dictionary,* 4th ed. (Tranquebar, 1972), s.v. *pŏṉ*.

golden[76] (an inheritance from the Vedic Hiraṇyagarbha), as are the pot,[77] the mountain on which it is placed,[78] the reed forest or lake (with trees or lotuses),[79] the twins born by Agni's wife Svāhā,[80] the cup with which Pārvatī nurses the infant Skanda,[81] and all that the brilliant seed illuminates (grass, creepers, shrubs, mountains, and forests).[82] Moreover, the Pŏṉṉi is compared to "*amṛta* drunk by starving men";[83] *amṛta* or Soma is a common equivalent for seed in Śiva symbolism,[84] and let us recall that the Seed of Creation flows from the broken pot at Kumpakoṇam as a river of *amṛta*.

Gaṇeśa's appearance in the myth, first as a crow and then as a Brahmin boy, also has important precedents. The first image goes back to the ancient concept of the fire-bird carrying ambrosia;[85] the conjunction of birds and seed is common in Hindu mythology.[86] Birds are usually present in the Skanda myth: Agni takes the form of a parrot,[87] turtle-dove (*pārāvata*),[88] or goose[89] to interrupt Śiva and Pārvatī in their love making; Kāma comes in form of a *cakravāka* to wound Śiva;[90] and Svāhā as a Garuḍī bird carries the fiery seed to the mountain peak.[91] In the Kāviri myth, the crow-Gaṇeśa liberates the seed/river from the pot.

[76] *Mahābhārata* 13.84.68; *Rām.* 1.36.18; *Vāmanapurāṇa* (Vārāṇasī, 1967), 31.9–10, *Liṅgapurāṇa* (Bombay, 1906), 1.20.80–82.

[77] See n. 69 above.

[78] *Śivapurāṇa* (Bombay, 1953), 2.4.22.39; *Mahābhārata* 9.43.14; *Skandapurāṇa* 1.1.27.63; *Saurapurāṇa* 62.19.

[79] *Matsyapurāṇa* 158.28–29; *Padmapurāna;* Ānandāśrama Sanskrit Series no. 131 (Poona, 1894), 5.41.112; *Mahābhārata* 9.43.18; *Vāmanapurāṇa* 31.15–19; *Skandapurāṇa* 3.3.29.23.

[80] *Brahmapurāṇa,* Ānandāśrama Sanskrit Series no. 29 (Poona, 1895), 128.24–27.

[81] *Kantapurāṇam,* 1.13.23 and 31; cf. *Raghuvaṃśa* of *Kālidāsa* (Bombay, 1891), 2.36; *Pĕriyapurāṇam* 6.1.68.

[82] *Rām.* 1.36.21–22 and the line added by many mss. after verse 22; *Mahābhārata* 13.84.70.

[83] *Kantapurāṇam* 2.29.12.

[84] See O'Flaherty, *Asceticism and Eroticism in the Mythology of Śiva,* pp. 277–278.

[85] Ibid., p. 277.

[86] See, for example, *Mahābhārata* 1.57.39–46; *Manasākāvya* of *Manakar,* cited by Pradyot Kumar Maity, *Historical Studies in the Cult of the Goddess Manasā* (Calcutta, 1966), p. 120. For another instance of the crow upsetting the pot (which in this case contains milk, another multiform of the divine seed), see *Tiruvāṭpokkippurāṇam* of *Kamalainakar Vaittiṉātatēcikar* (Madras, 1911), 12.1–17.

[87] *Brahmapurāṇa* 128.16–23; *Matsyapurāṇa* 158.24–26.

[88] *Skandapurāṇa* 1.2.29.83.

[89] *Vāmanapurāṇa* 28.41.

[90] *Brahmapurāṇa* 38.1–5.

[91] *Mahābhārata* 3.213–214; *Skandapurāṇa* 1.2.29.104.

Gaṇeśa then takes the form of a young Brahmin and flees from Agastya; this element in the myth may be related to the following, somewhat unusual account of Gaṇeśa's birth:

> Viṣṇu in the form of a Brahmin ascetic, tortured by thirst, interrupted Śiva and Pārvatī when they were making love. Śiva spilled his seed on the bed. Śiva and Pārvatī offered the Brahmin food and drink, but he took the form of a child and went to the bed, where he became mingled with Śiva's seed. Seeing a baby lying on the bed and looking up at the roof, Pārvatī nursed him as her son (and he was named Gaṇeśa).[92]

The interruption of Śiva and Pārvatī's love making, which is basic to the Skanda birth myth, here produces their other child, Gaṇeśa. Gaṇeśa, instead of taking the form of a young Brahmin, is here born *from* the Brahmin, whose thirst is quenched not by water but by Śiva's seed, just as the river/seed restores the parched plants of Indra's garden in the Tamil myth.

The creative force of the Kāviri flood becomes clear at the conclusion of the myth: Cīkāḻi, which has been desiccated by the drought sent by Indra's demon adversaries, is revived by the river. We have here, in effect, a reversal of the other flood myth from Cīkāḻi, in which Śiva, who has escaped to this shrine in a boat, begins creating the world at this spot by first drying up the waters of the flood. Both myths, however, contain the same basic idea of a new creation proceeding from a flood. In the Kāviri myth, the flood is itself an equivalent of the divine seed carried in a pot; in the more conventional cosmogonies, such as the myth from Tiruvŏṟṟiyūr, the creation follows the great flood and opposes it as land is opposed to water, order to chaos. Nevertheless, the destruction of the deluge is the necessary prelude to the rebirth of the world; the violent flood holds within it the seed of a new creation. This idea is clearly conveyed by the Kumpakoṇam story, in which the creative seed is carried over the waters in a pot, just as the sound of the Vedas, Śiva's guide to creation, brings the creator god to Cīkāḻi. It now remains for us to study the relevance of these symbols for an understanding of the myths of Maturai and the Tamil Caṅkam.

[92] *Brahmavaivartapurāṇa*, Ānandāśrama Sanskrit Series no. 102 (Poona, 1935), 3.8.17–43, 83–89; 3.9.1–37.

THE MATURAI FLOOD MYTHS AND THE CAṄKAM STORY

Of all Tamil shrines, Maturai can claim the greatest number of flood myths. There are two major myths of a flood in the Maturai purāṇas;[93] in addition, we have a story about the rediscovery of the boundaries of the city after the *pralaya;*[94] a related story in which the Vedas, newly emerged from the *praṇava* after a universal destruction, are expounded to the sages of the Naimiṣa Forest in Maturai;[95] the arrival of the seven seas in Maturai for Kañcanai's ablutions;[96] the myth of the Kubera-*liṅga,* which never perishes in the flood;[97] the flooding of the Vaikai River;[98] and three examples of the closely related theme of surviving not a flood but its opposite, a drought.[99] The flood myths relating to the first two Caṅkam also belong here, as we shall see. Let us begin with the first of the flood myths in Pĕrumpaṟṟappuliyūrnampi's *Tiruvālavā-yuṭaiyār tiruviḷaiyāṭaṟpurāṇam:*

> Varuṇa, the lord of the sea, wished to test the greatness of Śiva, so he ordered the ocean to flood the world. The gods, men, Nāgas, and others took refuge with the lord of Ālavāy (Maturai), to whom the panic-stricken Indra called for help. Śiva sent the doomsday clouds (Puṣkalāvarta and three others) to drink up the waters of the ocean. Varuṇa was incensed at this action, so he sent his own clouds to destroy the city with their rain. Śiva made the doomsday clouds into buildings and sent them to protect Maturai from the rain. They towered over the city until Varuṇa's clouds dried up, and they then remained in Maturai as four buildings (*māṭam*). Hence Maturai is known as Nāṉmāṭakkūṭal ("the junction of four buildings").[100]

This story is in explanation of one of the old names of the city, Nāṉ-māṭakkūṭal, which probably dervies from four ancient temples (to Kaṉṉi, Kariyamāl, Kāḷi, and Ālavāy) in the town. The name appears in

[93] *Tiruviḷai.* 13.18–19; *Tiruvālavāyutāiyārtiruiḷaiyāṭaṟpurāṇam* of *Pĕrumpaṟṟappuliyūr-nampi* (hereafter cited as *Tiruvāl.*), ed. U. Ve. Cāminātaiyar (Madras, 1906), 21, 12.

[94] *Tiruviḷai.* 49; *Tiruvāl.* 47.

[95] *Tiruviḷai.* 16; *Tiruvāl.* 64.

[96] *Tiruviḷai.* 9; *Tiruvāl.* 8.

[97] *Tiruviḷai.* 56; *Tiruvāl.* 20.

[98] *Tiruviḷai.* 61; *Tiruvāl.* 30.

[99] *Tiruviḷai.* 14, 15, 31; *Tiruvāl.* 44, 61, 40.

[100] *Tiruvāl.* 12.

the classical sources,[101] and the identifications of the four temples given by Nacciṉārkkiṉiyar (in *Kalittŏkai* 92.65) survive in the names of the protecting divinities cited in the introduction to Pĕrumpaṟṟap-puliyūrnampi's text.[102] This, then, is an origin myth: the four great temples of Maturai were the doomsday clouds sent by Śiva to defend the city from the flood. The doomsday clouds, which are said to have been born from the seed shed by Brahmā at the wedding of Śiva and Satī,[103] connect this story with that of the Pāṇṭiyaṉ, who imprisoned the four doomsday clouds in response to a drought caused by Indra.[104] In our myth, the flood is checked by the doomsday clouds, which then protect the city from the flood of rain sent by the angry Varuṇa; here the clouds are analogous to the mountain (Govardhana) that Kṛṣṇa holds up to protect Gokula from the torrential rains of Indra.[105] In the slightly expanded version of the flood myth in the *Tiruviḷai.* of Parañ-coti, Indra is also the instigator of the flood at Maturai:

> Once when Indra came to worship in the temple at Maturai, he found Apiṭekapāṇṭiyaṉ engaged in worship there. Indra had to wait to offer his devotion. When he returned to heaven, Varuṇa came to visit and found him feeling sad because his prayers had been delayed. When Varuṇa saw how devoted Indra was to Cŏkkaliṅkam (Śiva at Maturai), he asked if the god of Maturai could cure the pain in his stomach. "Try him and see for yourself," said Indra, so Varuṇa sent the sea to destroy Maturai. The Pāṇṭiyaṉ sought the help of Śiva, and Śiva sent four clouds from his matted locks to dry up the sea. Furious at this check and unable to understand the amusement of the lord of Maturai, Varuṇa sent seven clouds to destroy the city with rain. Rain fell in streams like crystal pillars, and the inhabitants of Maturai thought the end of the world had come. To remove their distress Śiva commanded the four clouds to cover the four corners of the ancient city in the form of four buildings. The clouds of Varuṇa exhausted their rain on these buildings, and Varuṇa became

[101] *Kalittŏkai* (Madras, 1938), 92.65; *Cil.* 21.39; *Paripāṭal* (Pondicherry, 1968), fragment 1.3 and fragment 7.4.

[102] *Tiruvāl., tirunakaraccirappu* 12–15. On the name "Nāṉmāṭakkuṭal" for *Maturai,* see F. Gros, *Le Paripāṭal* (Pondicherry, 1968), pp. xxvii–xxviii; and cf. Tiruñāṉacampantar, *Tevāram* (Tarumapuram, 1953), 7.5 with commentary. "Kūṭal," "junction," may well be the original title.

[103] *Śivapurāṇa* 2.2.20.21–24.

[104] *Tiruviḷai.* 14.41; *Tiruvāl.* 44.36–37; *Cil.* 11.26–29. The same motif of imprisoning the clouds is used in the battle between *Sūrapadma* and *Vīrabāhu* in *Kantapurāṇam* 4.6.52–67.

[105] *Viṣṇupurāṇa* 5.11.1–25.

ashamed. He worshiped the lord of Maturai, and the pain in his stomach disappeared.[106]

Here it is specifically Maturai rather than the world as a whole (*ñālam*) that the sea attacks. Note that the stock idea of the rivalry between Indra and a virtuous mortal (king or sage) is transferred to a competition in devotion to Śiva: Indra must wait until the king finishes his prayer. Moreover, as in the earlier version, the idea of testing the devotee is reversed, and Varuṇa tests the god. Indra's inspiration of the test might be seen as an interesting extension of his role in opposing Śiva in other myths, for example by sending Kāma to disturb the god's meditation—an action that, like Varuṇa's trial by water, is ultimately benevolent in intent. There is also an echo of the myth of churning the ocean, which in any case shares several motifs with the cosmogonic flood (such as the emergence of *amṛta,* a multiform of the divine seed, from the waters): there Śiva neutralizes the poison that rises from the depths of the sea, as at Maturai he heals the pain in the sea-god's stomach.[107] The idea that *bhakti* can cure stomach pains is a common motif in Śaiva hagiographies.[108]

The second flood story is a multiform of the first:

> Once the sea rose against the ancient city of Maturai. The gods were alarmed and, seeing this, Śiva appeared to Ukkirapāṇṭiyaṉ in a dream and told him to throw the lance which he (as his father, Cuntarapāṇṭiyaṉ) had given him against the fearsome sea (*nām aḷitta velaiy aṟa nām aḷitta velaiy ĕṟi*). The Pāṇṭiyaṉ awoke and, after being urged again by the god, threw his spear at the sea, which became calm and lapped at his feet. Tamiḻccŏkkaṉ (Śiva) appeared, erected a *maṇḍapa,* and said, "This will be the site of the first and second Caṅkam; the third will be on the bank of the Ganges."[109]

Aravamuthan has shown that the notion of the sea lapping the feet of the king became a cliché of the commentators.[110] The bank of the Ganges is taken to be a reference to the Pŏṟṟāmarai Tank at Maturai.[111]

[106] *Tiruviḷai.* 18.1–9, 19.1–26.

[107] For the myth of churning the ocean, see *Mahābhārata* 1.15–17; *Rām.* 1.45. This myth is also linked to the *Maturai* tradition through another story: *Tiruviḷai.* 28.1–23; see D. Shulman, "The Murderous Bride: Tamil Versions of the Myth of Devī and the Buffalo-Demon," *History of Religions* 16 (1976):141–142; idem, "The Serpent and the Sacrifice: An Anthill Myth from Tiruvārūr," *History of Religions* 18 (1978):107–137.

[108] For example, the case of Appar: *Periyapurāṇam* 5.1.49–71.

[109] *Tiruvāl.* 21.1–9.

[110] T. G. Aravamuthan, "The Maturai Chronicles and the Tamil Academies," *Journal of Oriental Research, Madras* 6 (1932):291–292.

The *Tiruviḷai.* adds a pretext for the flood: Indra became jealous of the Pāṇṭiyaṉ, who was ruling virtuously and had performed ninety-six horse sacrifices, so he told the lord of the sea to flood Maturai as if it were the time of the universal deluge.[112] Instead of the god's building a *maṇḍapa* for the Caṅkam, the *Tiruviḷai.* has the king consecrate to Śiva all the area of fields and villages between the walled ancient city of Maturai and the retreating sea (verse 20).

It is this last element, the consecration of the land given up by the sea, which is the myth's focal point. Not only does the city *survive* the flood; it is in part (fields and villages or, in *Tiruvāl.*, the site of the Caṅkam) created from the flood by the casting of the spear. The same motif occurs in other myths. Aravamuthan has suggested that the idea of throwing a spear at the sea goes back to Agastya's drinking the ocean[113] or, more convincingly, to Kārtavīrya's showering arrows at the ocean[114] and Skanda's hurling his lance at Mount Krauñca.[115] There is also the tale of Bhīṣma, who dries up the Ganges by shooting arrows at it.[116] But the idea of a creative attack on the ocean is perhaps most clear in another origin myth in south India: Paraśurāma created the land from Gokarṇam to Kanyākumārī by throwing his axe at the ocean.[117] The prototype of this tradition appears in the *MBh:*

> Paraśurāma cleared the earth of Kṣatriyas and gave it to Kaśyapa as a sacrificial fee. Kaśyapa said to him, "Go to the shore of the southern ocean; you must not dwell in my territory." The sea measured out for Paraśurāma a country called Śūrpāraka. Kaśyapa made the earth an abode of Brahmins and entered the forest.[118]

[111] See the note by Cāminātaiyar on *Tiruvāl.* 21.9; the possibility that the Ganges is actually intended can be ruled out.

[112] *Tiruviḷai.* 13.1–20; cf. *Cuntarapāntiyam* of *Aṉatāri* (Madras, 1955), 3.6.11–12. Compare Indra's theft of the sacrificial horse of Sagara (sometimes by a wave of the ocean) in the myth of the descent of the Ganges and the filling of the sea: *Mahābhārata* 3.104–108. Wendy Doniger O'Flaherty, "The Submarine Mare in the Mythology of Siva," *Journal of the Royal Asiatic Society* (1971) 1:19–20.

[113] *Mahābhārata* 3.102.16–23, 3.103.1–28.

[114] Ibid., 3.116.29; 14.29.1.7.

[115] Ibid., 3.214.31. See Aravamuthan, op. cit.

[116] *Mahābhārata* 1.94.23–24.

[117] K. A. Nilakanta Sastri, *History of South India,* 3rd ed. (Bombay, 1966), pp. 71–74; K. P. Padmanabha Menon, *History of Kerala* (Ernakulam, 1924–1933), vol. I, pp. 17–20; *Raghuvaṃśa* 4.53 and 58; *Keraḷateca varalāṟu,* Madras Government Oriental Manuscript Series no. 56 (Madras, 1960), pp. 33, 41; *Kaṉṉiyākumarittalapurāṇam* of Caṅkaranāvalar (Maturai, n.d.), 18.66–75; *Pĕriyapurāṇam* 2.6.1; *Skandapurāṇa* 6.68.6–16; for the version of the *Keralōtpatti,* see Thiagarajah, pp. 120–121.

[118] *Mahābhārata* 12.49.53–60; on *Śūrpāraka* see Pargiter's note on *Mārkaṇḍeyapurāṇa*

The Kŏṅku and Tuḷuva regions have a similar myth of origins.[119] We may recall here Kṛṣṇa's war against the ocean and his building of Dvārakā on land relinquished by the sea.[120]

Another variation on this theme is the myth of the bridge at Irāmeccuram: Rāma asked the sea to help him cross to Laṅkā; when the ocean did not appear in answer to his appeal and three days had passed, Rāma began to shoot arrows at the sea. The sea came up from Pātāla and sought refuge with Rāma, begged not to be forced to transgress the laws of creation by drying up its waters, and suggested that instead the monkey Nala build a causeway.[121] Like Paraśurāma, Rāmacandra attacks the sea; and, although the sea does not recede, it provides the means of crossing over it by land.

Perhaps the most important parallel is found in the Tamil myths of Murukaṉ. Ukkirapāṇṭiyaṉ, who casts his spear against the sea in the Maturai flood myth, is himself an incarnation of Skanda/Murukaṉ, for he is the son of Śiva/Cuntarapāṇṭiyaṉ and Pārvatī/Mīnākṣī.[122] In Tamil mythology, Murukaṉ casts his spear twice—once against Mount Krauñca, as in the Sanskrit sources, and once more against the demon Cūr (Śūrapadma), who has taken the form of a huge mango tree in the midst of the sea. It is this latter episode that is particularly celebrated in Tamil literature: "We praise the wielder of the spear that killed the mango (demon) in the ocean."[123] Moreover, Murukaṉ's war against Cūr may be part of an ancient myth of creation: the spear dries up the waters of the ocean as it flies toward the mango, and the destruction of the mango creates space for the world and liberates the sun from the darkness of chaos.[124] In casting his spear in the ocean, the god thus overcomes the forces of disorder and uncontrolled violence, just as the king of Maturai subdues the threatening sea with his spear.

(translation), Bibliotheca Indica (Calcutta, 1904), p. 338; Kuiper (1964), p. 113. Elsewhere Paraśurāma is said to have retreated to Mount Mahendra. Cf. *Mahābhārata* 3.117.14; Wilson, p. 323, n. 21.

[119] Nilakanta Sastri, p. 74; Bhasker Anand Saletore, *Ancient Karnāṭaka*, I. *History of Tuḷuva* (Poona, 1936), pp. 9–38. In Assam Paraśurāma creates not land but a flood by cutting a channel for the Brahmaputra River: *Kālikāpurāṇa* (Bombay, 1891), 84–86.

[120] See above at notes 40–41.

[121] *Skandapurāṇa* 3.1.2.54–96 (from the *Setumāhātmya*); *Cetupurāṇam* of *Nirampavalakiyatecikar* (Madras, 1932), 5.27–41.

[122] See *Tiruviḷai.* 11.19, which plays on this identification.

[123] *Cil.* 24, *pāṭṭumaṭai* 6. Cf. *Tirumurukāṟṟuppaṭai* 45–46, 59–61; *Kalittŏkai* 104.13–14. The battle with the sea and the casting of the spear against *Krauñca* combine in a myth about the worship of the spear: *Coḷarājentirapuram eṉṉum iḷaiyanār velūrppurāṇam* (Madras, 1921), 6.2–8.

[124] I have discussed this myth at length in the article cited in note 14 above.

There is another set of references in ancient Tamil literature to throwing back the sea. The hero of the fifth decade of *Patiṟṟuppattu* is Cĕṅkuṭṭuvaṉ "who drove back the sea" (*kaṭal piṟakk' oṭṭiya cĕṅkuṭṭuvaṉ*). He too is said to have lifted his spear (*vel*) against the sea,[125] but the old commentary takes this to mean he fought against people whose stronghold was the sea (*taṉṉul vāḻvārkku araṇ ākiya kaṭal*). Probably the verses refer to pirates, although this is not stated explicitly.[126] There remains a strong possibility that the epithet *kaṭal piṟakk' oṭṭiya-* contributed to the later flood myths from Maturai.

Let us return to the Maturai myths. We have seen that both *Tiruviḷai.* end the second flood myth with an act of creation after the deluge, and *Tiruvāl.* (the earlier of the two) connects this with the story of the Caṅkam. Aravamuthan has argued that the last verse of *Tiruvāl.* 21, which tells us that the site established by the god served as the home of the first two Caṅkam, is spurious.[127] Certainly the verse presents difficulties if one is to attempt to put together a chronology based on the *Tiruvāl.*; this, in effect, is what Parañcoti (or rather his probable source, the Sanskrit *Hālāsyamāhātmya*) has done,[128] and it is perhaps significant that he speaks throughout of only one Caṅkam. However, the *Hālāsyamāhātmya* follows the earlier tradition in this case, and mentions three "academies," the first two in the city saved from the flood, and the third on the bank of the Ganges.[129] Evidently Parañcoti has replaced this tradition with a more consistent scheme, based on the existence of a single Caṅkam. Perhaps he was closer to the original Caṅkam legend than he knew.

The first complete account of the three Caṅkam and the two destructive floods appears, as we saw earlier, in the commentary ascribed to Nakkīrar on *Iṟaiyaṉār akappŏruḷ*. But there are still older allusions to an ancient flood in the Pāṇṭiya land. *Kalittŏkai* 104 tells us that when the sea rose and took his land, the Pāṇṭiya king (*tĕṉṉavaṉ*) carved new lands for himself from the territories of his enemies, removing the (Coḻa) tiger and the (Cera) bow, and substituting the (Pāṇṭiya) emblem of the fish.[130] Does this not confront us again with the familiar motif of land created in opposition to water? Perhaps not. The *Cilappatikāram*, which also knows the flood legend in relation to the Pāṇṭiyas, reverses

[125] *Patiṟṟuppattu* (Madras, 1957), fifth decade, 46.11–13; cf. 41.21–23; 48.3–4; *Akanāṉūru* (Madras, 1965), 127.3–5; 347.3–5; 212.15–20.

[126] Marr, p. 308.

[127] Aravamuthan, *Journal of Oriental Research, Madras* 5 (1931), pp. 203–205.

[128] Ibid., pp. 209–214; (1932), pp. 97–103.

[129] *Hālāsyamāhātmya* (Maturai, 1870), 17.46–47.

[130] *Kalittŏkai* 104.1–4.

the usual order: "May the *tĕṉṉavaṉ* prosper who ruled the South and took the Ganges and the Himālaya of the North when once the sea, refusing to bear the prowess he demonstrated to other kings by throwing against it his sharp spear, swallowed the Kumarikkoṭu together with the Pahṟuḷi River and several nearby mountains."[131] According to the old, anonymous commentary (Arumpatavurai), Kumarikkoṭu refers to the bank of the Kumari River, while Aṭiyārkkunallār takes it to mean a mountain peak. This text is unique in explaining the flood as revenge for the casting of the spear rather than its occasion, although it also implies that the Pāṇṭiyaṉ conquered new lands because of the flood. Aṭiyārkkunallār supports this: the *tĕṉṉavaṉ* ruled Muttūrkkūṟṟam in the Coḻanāṭu and Kuṇṭūrkkūṟṟam in the Ceramānāṭu in exchange for the lands he had lost in the flood.[132]

What, then, is one to conclude about the legend of the three Caṅkam and the lost lands of the Pāṇṭiyas? We have seen that the *Tiruvāl.* connects the origin of the Caṅkam with the flood, while the references in *Cilappatikāram* and *Kalittŏkai* suggest that the flood is used, as in much later purāṇic myths, to explain the origin of the present boundaries of the Pāṇṭiya land. The commentators' information on the lands that were allegedly lost in the deluge hardly inspires confidence, and early references in the literature[133] know only one Caṅkam, that which is said to have been situated in present-day Maturai. Given the prevalence of the flood motif in south Indian mythology, its particular prominence in Maturai, its association with the idea of creation, and the absence of any geological evidence of a real flood, it would seem that the story of the *first two* Caṅkam is an expansion of an early origin myth centered in Maturai.[134] Like other Tamil shrines, Maturai sees itself as the indestructible center of the universe, the site of creation, the survivor of the *pralaya;* to these notions Maturai has added its claim to be the ancient home of Tamil poetry and the site of the "academy" linked by a persistent tradition to the first flowering of Tamil culture. Literary

[131] *Cil.* 11.17–22.

[132] *Aṭiyārkkunallār* on *Cil.* 11.17–22.

[133] For example, *Tiruñānacampantar, Tevāram* 1.7.2; cf. K. Zvelebil, *The Smile of Murugan, on Tamil Literature of South India* (Leiden, 1973), p. 45, n. 1.

[134] This seems to have been recognized by Filliozat, Dessigane, and Pattabiramin in their introduction to the *Tiruviḷai.* : La légende des jeux de Çiva á Madurai d'apres les textes et les peintures (Pondicherry, 1960), p. xi. They note that the flood at Maturai was the *pralaya,* not a "cataclysme local." Was the expansion of the story assisted by the existence of the name "Southern *Maturai*" (*tĕṉmaturai*), as in *Tiruvāl., kaṭavul vāḻttu* 14; or *daksiṇā mathurā,* as in *Bhāgavatapurāṇa* (10.79.15), presumably to distinguish the present city of *Maturai* from the northern town of Mathurā? Cf. *Vatamaturai* for Mathurā: *Tiruppāvai* of Āṇṭāḷ (Pondicherry, 1972), 5.1.

origins have been described in terms borrowed from the cosmogonic myth; the flood that precedes the creation of the world has been used as the background to the establishment of the Caṅkam, as well. But creation in India is not a unique event at the beginning of time, but an ever-recurring moment, a repetition of something already known; and thus the academy of poets in historical Maturai is not, in the view of the tradition, the first of its kind, but rather a rebirth of an earlier model after a cataclysmic flood.

The institution which symbolizes the crystallization of an ancient, classical Tamil civilization inevitably emerges from the background of inchoate and violent forces which are, in the Hindu view, implicated in *any* act of creation—be it the construction of the ordered universe in which we live, or the limited holocaust of the sacrificial ritual out of which the victim is reborn. Poetry, like life itself, is won from disorder and death.

To summarize: the Tamil flood myths are essentially myths of creation. At the end of each cycle of time, a flood destroys the world—except for the shrine situated at the world's center and linked directly to the transcendent worlds above and below. At this spot God creates the universe once more by throwing back the waters of the flood, or by substituting for them a creative flood of seed or *amṛta*. The cosmogony implies the institution of order in the face of primeval chaos; hence the close connection between the Tamil flood myths and the legend of the birth of Tamil poetry and culture. Civilization and order oppose the forces of chaos out of which they emerge. Yet these forces are never wholly conquered; the violent flood will one day return to destroy the world, and it may survive inside the shrine in a limited, bounded form as part of the idealized, ordered microcosm at the center of the universe.

Noah and the Flood in Jewish Legend

LOUIS GINZBERG

One sometimes gets the impression that there is the *Judeo-Christian flood story as told in Genesis plus a host of "other" flood narratives reported in various parts of the world. The implication is that there is just the one, more or less official, fixed biblical text in contrast to the multitudinous variety of diverse flood accounts elsewhere. This view is incorrect. The flood story which was undoubtedly in oral tradition before being recorded in what we now know as the Bible has remained in oral tradition. So in addition to the oral flood narratives found in non-Western cultures, there are abundant oral flood stories circulating in Western contexts.*

An illustration is provided by a fascinating Jewish tradition consisting of different legends and glosses relating to events described in the Old Testament. In these apocryphal materials, one obtains quite a different picture of these events. The story of Noah is no exception. The composite account painstakingly assembled by Louis Ginzberg (1873–1953) as part of his valuable seven-volume compilation of Jewish legends offers delightful details not contained in Genesis. Although the sources of this elaborated story line are all presumably postbiblical, it is at least within the realm of possibility that some of the elements may be of considerable antiquity. Remember that even the Genesis account is a composite of at least two separate oral versions, which suggests that there may well have been many more which coexisted with the two combined there.

Ginzberg specifically observed that his account of "the Bible as mirrored by Jewish imagination and phantasy" was "intended for the general reader and not for the scholar." Nevertheless, in Volume 5 of The Legends of the Jews, *published some years after the initial volume in the series had appeared, Ginzberg does provide some ninety-one copious footnotes giving his sources and including commentary on various details. These notes have not been reproduced here. The interested reader should consult Volume 5 (Philadelphia, 1925), pp. 167–206. For a more modern but considerably abridged summary of much of the same Jewish legendary material, see Robert Graves and Raphael Patai,* Hebrew Myths: The Book of Genesis *(Garden City, 1963), pp. 100–124.*

Reprinted from *The Legends of the Jews,* vol. 1 (Philadelphia: Jewish Publication Society of America, 1909), pp. 145–169.

See also the section entitled "The Rabbinic Noah," in Jack P. Lewis, A Study of the Interpretation of Noah and the Flood in Jewish and Christian Literature *(Leiden, 1968), pp. 121–155. For a discussion of the representation of Noah in folk art, see folklorist Lutz Röhrich's essay "Noah und die Arche in der Volkskunst," in Klaus Beitl, ed.,* Volkskunde: Fakten und Analysen: Festgabe für Leopold Schmidt zum 60. Geburtstag *(Wien, 1972), pp. 433–442. For a comparative perspective, see Jack P. Lewis, "Noah and the Flood in Jewish, Christian, and Muslim Tradition,"* Biblical Archaeologist *47 (1984): 224–239.*

THE BIRTH OF NOAH

Methuselah took a wife for his son Lamech, and she bore him a man child. The body of the babe was white as snow and red as a blooming rose, and the hair of his head and his long locks were white as wool, and his eyes like the rays of the sun. When he opened his eyes, he lighted up the whole house, like the sun, and the whole house was very full of light. And when he was taken from the hand of the midwife, he opened his mouth and praised the Lord of righteousness. His father Lamech was afraid of him, and fled, and came to his own father Methuselah. And he said to him: "I have begotten a strange son; he is not like a human being, but resembles the children of the angels of heaven, and his nature is different, and he is not like us, and his eyes are as the rays of the sun, and his countenance is glorious. And it seems to me that he is not sprung from me, but from the angels, and I fear that in his days a wonder may be wrought on the earth. And now, my father, I am here to petition thee and implore thee, that thou mayest go to Enoch, our father, and learn from him the truth, for his dwelling-place is among the angels."

And when Methuselah heard the words of his son, he went to Enoch, to the ends of the earth, and he cried aloud, and Enoch heard his voice, and appeared before him, and asked him the reason of his coming. Methuselah told him the cause of his anxiety, and requested him to make the truth known to him. Enoch answered, and said: "The Lord will do a new thing in the earth. There will come a great destruction on the earth, and a deluge for one year. This son who is born unto thee will be left on the earth, and his three children will be saved with him, when all mankind that are on the earth shall die. And there will be a great punishment on the earth, and the earth will be cleansed from all impurity. And now make known to thy son Lamech that he who was born is in truth his son, and call his name Noah, for he will be left to you, and he and his children will be saved from the destruction which will come upon the earth." When Methuselah had heard the words of his father, who showed him all the secret things, he returned home, and he called the child Noah, for he would cause the earth to rejoice in compensation for all destruction.

By the name Noah he was called only by his grandfather Methuselah; his father and all others called him Menahem. His generation was addicted to sorcery, and Methuselah apprehended that his grandson might be bewitched if his true name were known, wherefore he kept it a secret. Menahem, Comforter, suited him as well as Noah; it indicated that he would be a consoler, if but the evil-doers of his time would repent of their misdeeds. At his very birth it was felt that he would bring consolation and deliverance. When the Lord said to Adam, "Cursed is the ground for thy sake," he asked, "For how long a time?" and the answer made by God was, "Until a man child shall be born whose conformation is such that the rite of circumcision need not be practiced upon him." This was fulfilled in Noah, he was circumcised from his mother's womb.

Noah had scarcely come into the world when a marked change was noticeable. Since the curse brought upon the earth by the sin of Adam, it happened that wheat being sown, yet oats would sprout and grow. This ceased with the appearance of Noah: the earth bore the products planted in it. And it was Noah who, when he was grown to manhood, invented the plough, the scythe, the hoe, and other implements for cultivating the ground. Before him men had worked the land with their bare hands.

There was another token to indicate that the child born unto Lamech was appointed for an extraordinary destiny. When God created Adam, He gave him dominion over all things: the cow obeyed the ploughman, and the furrow was willing to be drawn. But after the fall of Adam all things rebelled against him: the cow refused obedience to the ploughman, and also the furrow was refractory. Noah was born, and all returned to its state preceding the fall of man.

Before the birth of Noah, the sea was in the habit of transgressing its bounds twice daily, morning and evening, and flooding the land up to the graves. After his birth it kept within its confines. And the famine that afflicted the world in the time of Lamech, the second of the ten great famines appointed to come upon it, ceased its ravages with the birth of Noah.

THE PUNISHMENT OF THE FALLEN ANGELS

Grown to manhood, Noah followed in the ways of his grandfather Methuselah, while all other men of the time rose up against this pious king. So far from observing his precepts, they pursued the evil inclination of their hearts, and perpetrated all sorts of abominable deeds. Chiefly the fallen angels and their giant posterity caused the depravity of mankind. The blood spilled by the giants cried unto heaven from the ground, and the four archangels accused the fallen angels and their sons before God, whereupon he gave the following orders to them: Uriel was sent to Noah to announce to him that the earth would be destroyed by a flood, and to teach him how to save his own life. Raphael was told to put the fallen angel Azazel into chains, cast him into a pit of sharp and pointed stones in the desert Dudael, and cover him with darkness, and so was he to remain until the great day of judgment, when he would be thrown into the fiery pit of hell, and the earth would be healed of the corruption he had contrived upon it. Gabriel was charged to proceed against the bastards and the reprobates, the sons of the angels begotten with the daughters of men, and plunge them into deadly conflicts with one another. Shemḥazai's ilk were handed over to Michael, who first caused them to witness the death of their children in their bloody combat with each other, and then he bound them and pinned them under the hills of the earth, where they will remain for seventy generations, until the day of judgment, to be carried thence to the fiery pit of hell.

The fall of Azazel and Shemḥazai came about in this way. When the generation of the deluge began to practice idolatry, God was deeply grieved. The two angels Shemḥazai and Azazel arose, and said: "O Lord of the world! It has happened, that which we foretold at the creation of the world and of man, saying, 'What is man, that Thou art mindful of him?'" And God said, "And what will become of the world now without man?" Whereupon the angels: "We will occupy ourselves with it." Then said God: "I am well aware of it, and I know that if you inhabit the earth, the evil inclination will overpower you, and you will be more iniquitous than ever men." The angels pleaded, "Grant us but permission to dwell among men, and Thou shalt see how we will sanctify Thy Name." God yielded to their wish, saying, "Descend and sojourn among men!"

When the angels came to earth, and beheld the daughters of men in all their grace and beauty, they could not restrain their passion. Shemḥazai saw a maiden named Istehar, and he lost his heart to her. She promised to surrender herself to him, if first he taught her the Ineffable Name, by means of which he raised himself to heaven. He assented to her condition. But once she knew it, she pronounced the Name, and herself ascended to heaven, without fulfilling her promise to the angel. God said, "Because she kept herself aloof from sin, we will place her among the seven stars, that men may never forget her," and she was put in the constellation of the Pleiades.

Shemḥazai and Azazel, however, were not deterred from entering into alliances with the daughters of men, and to the first two sons were born. Azazel began to devise the finery and the ornaments by means of which women allure men. Thereupon God sent Metatron to tell Shemḥazai that He had resolved to destroy the world and bring on a deluge. The fallen angel began to weep and grieve over the fate of the world and the fate of his two sons. If the world went under, what would they have to eat, they who needed daily a thousand camels, a thousand horses, and a thousand steers?

These two sons of Shemḥazai, Hiwwa and Hiyya by name, dreamed dreams. The one saw a great stone which covered the earth, and the earth was marked all over with lines upon lines of writing. An angel came, and with a knife obliterated all the lines, leaving but four letters upon the stone. The other son saw a large pleasure grove planted with all sorts of trees. But angels approached bearing axes, and they felled the trees, sparing a single one with three of its branches.

When Hiwwa and Hiyya awoke, they repaired to their father, who interpreted the dreams for them, saying, "God will bring a deluge, and none will escape with his life, excepting only Noah and his sons." When they heard this, the two began to cry and scream, but their father consoled them: "Soft, soft! Do not grieve. As often as men cut or haul stones, or launch vessels, they shall invoke your names, Hiwwa! Hiyya!" This prophecy soothed them.

Shemḥazai then did penance. He suspended himself between heaven and earth, and in this position of a penitent sinner he hangs to this day. But Azazel persisted obdurately in his sin of leading mankind astray by means of sensual allurements. For this reason two he-goats were sacrificed in the Temple on the Day of Atonement, the one for God, that He pardon the sins of Israel, the other for Azazel, that he bear the sins of Israel.

Unlike Istehar, the pious maiden, Naamah, the lovely sister of Tubal-cain, led the angels astray with her beauty, and from her union with Shamdon sprang the devil Asmodeus. She was as shameless as all the other descendants of Cain, and as prone to bestial indulgences. Cainite women and Cainite men alike were in the habit of walking abroad naked, and they gave themselves up to every conceivable manner of lewd practices. Of such were the women whose beauty and sensual charms tempted the angels from the path of virtue. The angels, on the other hand, no sooner had they rebelled against God and descended to earth than they lost their transcendental qualities, and were invested with sublunary bodies, so that a union with the daughters of men became possible. The offspring of these alliances between the angels and the Cainite women were the giants, known for their strength and their sinfulness; as their very name, the Emim, indicates, they inspired fear. They have many other names. Sometimes they go by the name Rephaim, because one glance at them made one's heart grow weak; or by the name Gibborim, simply giants, because their size was so enormous that their thigh measured eighteen ells; or by the name Zamzummim, because they were great masters in war; or by the name Anakim, because they touched the sun with their neck; or by the name Ivvim, because, like the snake, they could judge of the qualities of the soil; or finally, by the name Nephilim, because, bringing the world to its fall, they themselves fell.

THE GENERATION OF THE DELUGE

While the descendants of Cain resembled their father in his sinfulness and depravity, the descendants of Seth led a pious, well-regulated life, and the difference between the conduct of the two stocks was reflected in their habitations. The family of Seth was settled upon the mountains in the vicinity of Paradise, while the family of Cain resided in the field of Damascus, the spot whereon Abel was slain by Cain.

Unfortunately, at the time of Methuselah, following the death of Adam, the family of Seth became corrupted after the manner of the Cainites. The two strains united with each other to execute all kinds of iniquitous deeds. The result of the marriages between them were the Nephilim, whose sins brought the deluge upon the world. In their arrogance they claimed the same pedigree as the posterity of Seth, and they compared themselves with princes and men of noble descent.

The wantonness of this generation was in a measure due to the ideal conditions under which mankind lived before the flood. They knew neither toil nor care, and as a consequence of their extraordinary prosperity they grew insolent. In their arrogance they rose up against God. A single sowing bore a harvest sufficient for the needs of forty years, and by means of magic arts they could compel the very sun and moon to stand ready to do their service. The raising of children gave them no trouble. They were born after a few days' pregnancy, and immediately after birth they could walk and talk; they themselves aided the mother in severing the navel string. Not even demons could do them harm. Once a new-born babe, running to fetch a light whereby his mother might cut the navel string, met the chief of the demons, and a combat ensued between the two. Suddenly the crowing of a cock was heard, and the demon made off, crying out to the child, "Go and report unto thy mother, if it had not been for the crowing of the cock, I had killed thee!" Whereupon the child retorted, "Go and report unto thy mother, if it had not been for my uncut navel string, I had killed thee!"

It was their carefree life that gave them space and leisure for their infamies. For a time God, in His long-suffering kindness, passed by the iniquities of men, but His forbearance ceased when once they began to lead unchaste lives, for "God is patient with all sins save only an immoral life."

The other sin that hastened the end of the iniquitous generation was their rapacity. So cunningly were their depredations planned that the law could not touch them. If a countryman brought a basket of vegetables to market, they would edge up to it, one after the other, and abstract a bit, each in itself of petty value, but in a little while the dealer would have none left to sell.

Even after God had resolved upon the destruction of the sinners, He still permitted His mercy to prevail, in that He sent Noah unto them, who exhorted them for one hundred and twenty years to amend their ways, always holding the flood over them as a threat. As for them, they but derided him. When they saw him occupying himself with the building of the ark, they asked, "Wherefore this ark?"

Noah: "God will bring a flood upon you."

The sinners: "What sort of flood? If He sends a fire flood, against that we know how to protect ourselves. If it is a flood of waters, then, if the waters bubble up from the earth, we will cover them with iron rods, and if they descend from above, we know a remedy against that, too."

Noah: "The waters will ooze out from under your feet, and you will not be able to ward them off."

Partly they persisted in their obduracy of heart because Noah had made known to them that the flood would not descend so long as the pious Methuselah sojourned among them. The period of one hundred and twenty years which God had appointed as the term of their probation having expired, Methuselah died, but out of regard for the memory of this pious man God gave them another week's respite, the week of mourning for him. During this time of grace, the laws of nature were suspended, the sun rose in the west and set in the east. To the sinners God gave the dainties that await man in the future world, for the purpose of showing them what they were forfeiting. But all this proved unavailing, and, Methuselah and the other pious men of the generation having departed this life, God brought the deluge upon the earth.

THE HOLY BOOK

Great wisdom was needed for building the ark, which was to have space for all beings on earth, even the spirits. Only the fishes did not have to be provided for. Noah acquired the necessary wisdom from the book given to Adam by the angel Raziel, in which all celestial and all earthly knowledge is recorded.

While the first human pair were still in Paradise, it once happened that Samael, accompanied by a lad, approached Eve and requested her to keep a watchful eye upon his little son until he should return. Eve gave him the promise. When Adam came back from a walk in Paradise, he found a howling, screaming child with Eve, who, in reply to his question, told him it was Samael's. Adam was annoyed, and his annoyance grew as the boy cried and screamed more and more violently. In his vexation he dealt the little one a blow that killed him. But the corpse did not cease to wail and weep, nor did it cease when Adam cut it up into bits. To rid himself of the plague, Adam cooked the remains, and he and Eve ate them. Scarcely had they finished, when Samael appeared and demanded his son. The two malefactors tried to deny everything; they pretended they had no knowledge of his son. But Samael said to them: "What! You dare tell lies, and God in times to come will give Israel the Torah in which it is said, 'Keep thee far from a false word'?"

While they were speaking thus, suddenly the voice of the slain lad was heard proceeding from the heart of Adam and Eve, and it addressed these words to Samael: "Go hence! I have penetrated to the heart of Adam and the heart of Eve, and never again shall I quit their hearts, nor the hearts of their children, or their children's children, unto the end of all generations."

Samael departed, but Adam was sore grieved, and he put on sackcloth and ashes, and he fasted many, many days, until God appeared unto him, and said: "My son, have no fear of Samael. I will give thee a remedy that will help thee against him, for it was at My instance that he went to thee." Adam asked, "And what is this remedy?" God: "The Torah." Adam: "And where is the Torah?" God then gave him the book of the angel Raziel, which he studied day and night. After some time had passed, the angels visited Adam, and envious of the wisdom he had drawn from the book, they sought to destroy him cunningly by calling him a god and prostrating themselves before him, in spite of his remonstrance, "Do not prostrate yourselves before me, but magnify the Lord with me, and let us exalt His Name together." However, the envy of the angels was so great that they stole the book God had given Adam from him, and threw it in the sea. Adam searched for it everywhere in vain, and the loss distressed him sorely. Again he fasted many days, until God appeared unto him, and said: "Fear not! I will give the book back to thee," and He called Rahab, the Angel of the Sea, and ordered him to recover the book from the sea and restore it to Adam. And so he did.

Upon the death of Adam, the holy book disappeared, but later the cave in which it was hidden was revealed to Enoch in a dream. It was from this book that Enoch drew his knowledge of nature, of the earth and of the heavens, and he became so wise through it that his wisdom exceeded the wisdom of Adam. Once he had committed it to memory, Enoch hid the book again.

Now, when God resolved upon bringing the flood on the earth, He sent the archangel Raphael to Noah, as the bearer of the following message: "I give thee herewith the holy book, that all the secrets and mysteries written therein may be made manifest unto thee, and that thou mayest know how to fulfil its injunction in holiness, purity, modesty, and humbleness. Thou wilt learn from it how to build an ark of the wood of the gopher tree, wherein thou, and thy sons, and thy wife shall find protection."

Noah took the book, and when he studied it, the holy spirit came upon him, and he knew all things needful for the building of the ark and the gathering together of the animals. The book, which was made of sapphires, he took with him into the ark, having first enclosed it in a golden casket. All the time he spent in the ark it served him as a timepiece, to distinguish night from day. Before his death, he entrusted it to Shem, and he in turn to Abraham. From Abraham it descended through Jacob, Levi, Moses, and Joshua to Solomon, who learnt all his wisdom from it, and his skill in the healing art, and also his mastery over the demons.

THE INMATES OF THE ARK

The ark was completed according to the instructions laid down in the Book of Raziel. Noah's next task was gathering in the animals. No less than thirty-two species of birds and three hundred and sixty-five of reptiles he had to take along with him. But God ordered the animals to repair to the ark, and they trooped thither, and Noah did not have to do so much as stretch out a finger. Indeed, more appeared than were required to come, and God instructed him to sit at the door of the ark and note which of the animals lay down as they reached the entrance and which stood. The former belonged in the ark, but not the latter. Taking up his post as he had been commanded, Noah observed a lioness with her two cubs. All three beasts crouched. But the two young ones began to struggle with the mother, and she arose and stood up next to them. Then Noah led the two cubs into the ark. The wild beasts, and the cattle, and the birds which were not accepted remained standing about the ark all of seven days, for the assembling of the animals happened one week before the flood began to descend. On the day whereon they came to the ark, the sun was darkened, and the foundations of the earth trembled, and lightning flashed, and the thunder boomed, as never before. And yet the sinners remained impenitent. In naught did they change their wicked doings during those last seven days.

When finally the flood broke loose, seven hundred thousand of the children of men gathered around the ark, and implored Noah to grant them protection. With a loud voice he replied, and said: "Are ye not those who were rebellious toward God, saying, 'There is no God'? Therefore He has brought ruin upon you, to annihilate you and destroy you from the face of the earth. Have I not been prophesying this unto you these hundred and twenty years, and you would not give heed unto the voice of God? Yet now you desire to be kept alive!" Then the sinners cried out: "So be it! We all are ready now to turn back to God, if only thou wilt open the door of thy ark to receive us, that we may live and not die." Noah made answer, and said: "That ye do now, when your need presses hard upon you. Why did you not turn to God during all the hundred and twenty years which the Lord appointed unto you as the term of repentance? Now do ye come, and ye speak thus, because distress besets your lives. Therefore God will not hearken unto you and give you ear; naught will you accomplish!"

The crowd of sinners tried to take the entrance to the ark by storm, but the wild beasts keeping watch around the ark set upon them, and many were slain, while the rest escaped, only to meet death in the waters of the flood. The water alone could not have made an end of them, for they were giants in stature and strength. When Noah threatened them with the scourge of God, they would make reply: "If the waters of the flood come from above, they will never reach up to our necks; and if they come from below, the soles of our feet are large enough to dam up the springs." But God bade each drop pass through Gehenna before it fell to earth, and the hot rain scalded the skin of the sinners. The punishment that overtook them was befitting their crime. As their sensual desires had made them hot, and inflamed them to immoral excesses, so they were chastised by means of heated water.

Not even in the hour of the death struggle could the sinners suppress their vile instincts. When the water began to stream up out of the springs, they threw their little children into them, to choke the flood.

It was by the grace of God, not on account of his merits, that Noah found shelter in the ark before the overwhelming force of the waters. Although he was better than his contemporaries, he was yet not worthy of having wonders done for his sake. He had so little faith that he did not enter the ark until the waters had risen to his knees. With him his pious wife Naamah, the daughter of Enosh, escaped the peril, and his three sons, and the wives of his three sons.

Noah had not married until he was four hundred and ninety-eight years old. Then the Lord had bidden him to take a wife unto himself. He had not desired to bring children into the world, seeing that they would all have to perish in the flood, and he had only three sons, born unto him shortly before the deluge came. God had given him so small a number of offspring that he might be spared the necessity of building the ark on an overlarge scale in case they turned out to be pious. And if not, if they, too, were depraved like the rest of their generation, sorrow over their destruction would but be increased in proportion to their number.

As Noah and his family were the only ones not to have a share in the corruptness of the age, so the animals received into the ark were such as had led a natural life. For the animals of the time were as immoral as the men: the dog united with the wolf, the cock with the pea-fowl, and many others paid no heed to sexual purity. Those that were saved were such as had kept themselves untainted.

Before the flood the number of unclean animals had been greater than the number of the clean. Afterward the ratio was reversed, because while seven pairs of clean animals were preserved in the ark, but two pairs of the unclean were preserved.

One animal, the reëm, Noah could not take into the ark. On account of its huge size it could not find room therein. Noah therefore tied it to the ark, and it ran on behind. Also, he could not make space for the giant Og, the king of Bashan. He sat on top of the ark securely, and in this way escaped the flood of waters. Noah doled out his food to him daily, through a hole, because Og had promised that he and his descendants would serve him as slaves in perpetuity.

Two creatures of a most peculiar kind also found refuge in the ark. Among the beings that came to Noah there was Falsehood asking for shelter. He was denied admission, because he had no companion, and Noah was taking in the animals only by pairs. Falsehood went off to seek a partner, and he met Misfortune, whom he associated with himself on the condition that she might appropriate what Falsehood earned. The pair were then accepted in the ark. When they left it, Falsehood noticed that whatever he gathered together disappeared at once, and he betook himself to his companion to seek an explanation, which she gave him in the following words, "Did we not agree to the condition that I might take what you earn?" and Falsehood had to depart empty-handed.

THE FLOOD

The assembling of the animals in the ark was but the smaller part of the task imposed upon Noah. His chief difficulty was to provide food for a year and accommodations for them. Long afterward Shem, the son of Noah, related to Eliezer, the servant of Abraham, the tale of their experiences with the animals in the ark. This is what he said: "We had sore troubles in the ark. The day animals had to be fed by day, and the night animals by night. My father knew not what food to give to the little ziḳta. Once he cut a pomegranate in half, and a worm dropped out of the fruit, and was devoured by the ziḳta. Thenceforth my father would knead bran, and let it stand until it bred worms, which were fed to the animal. The lion suffered with a fever all the time, and therefore he did not annoy the others, because he did not relish dry food. The animal urshana my father found sleeping in a corner of the vessel, and he asked him whether he needed nothing to eat. He answered, and said: 'I saw thou wast very busy, and I did not wish to add to thy cares.' Whereupon my father said, 'May it be the will of the Lord to keep thee alive forever,' and the blessing was realized."

The difficulties were increased when the flood began to toss the ark from side to side. All inside of it were shaken up like lentils in a pot. The lions began to roar, the oxen lowed, the wolves howled, and all the animals gave vent to their agony, each through the sounds it had the power to utter.

Also Noah and his sons, thinking that death was nigh, broke into tears. Noah prayed to God: "O Lord, help us, for we are not able to bear the evil that encompasses us. The billows surge about us, the streams of destruction make us afraid, and death stares us in the face. O hear our prayer, deliver us, incline Thyself unto us, and be gracious unto us! Redeem us and save us!"

The flood was produced by a union of the male waters, which are above the firmament, and the female waters issuing from the earth. The upper waters rushed through the space left when God removed two stars out of the constellation Pleiades. Afterward, to put a stop to the flood, God had to transfer two stars from the constellation of the Bear to the constellation of the Pleiades. That is why the Bear runs after the Pleiades. She wants her two children back, but they will be restored to her only in the future world.

There were other changes among the celestial spheres during the year of the flood. All the time it lasted, the sun and the moon shed no light, whence Noah was called by his name, "the resting one," for in his life the sun and the moon rested. The ark was illuminated by a precious stone, the light of which was more brilliant by night than by day, so enabling Noah to distinguish between day and night.

The duration of the flood was a whole year. It began on the seventeenth day of Ḥeshwan, and the rain continued for forty days, until the twenty-seventh of Kislew. The punishment corresponded to the crime of the sinful generation. They had led immoral lives, and begotten bastard children, whose embryonic state lasts forty days. From the twenty-seventh of Kislew until the first of Siwan, a period of one hundred and fifty days, the water stood at one and the same height, fifteen ells above the earth. During that time all the wicked were destroyed, each one receiving the punishment due to him. Cain was among those that perished, and thus the death of Abel was avenged. So powerful were the waters in working havoc that the corpse of Adam was not spared in its grave.

On the first of Siwan the waters began to abate, a quarter of an ell a day, and at the end of sixty days, on the tenth day of Ab, the summits of the mountains showed themselves. But many days before, on the tenth of Tammuz, Noah had sent forth the raven, and a week later the dove, on the first of her three sallies, repeated at intervals of a week. It took from the first of Ab until the first of Tishri for the waters to subside wholly from the face of the earth. Even then the soil was so miry that the dwellers in the ark had to remain within until the twenty-seventh day of Ḥeshwan, completing a full sun year, consisting of twelve moons and eleven days.

Noah had experienced difficulty all along in ascertaining the state of the waters. When he desired to dispatch the raven, the bird said: "The Lord, thy Master, hates me, and thou dost hate me, too. Thy Master hates me, for He bade thee take seven pairs of the clean animals into the ark, and but two pairs of the unclean animals, to which I belong. Thou hatest me, for thou dost not choose, as a messenger, a bird of one of the kinds of which there are seven pairs in the ark, but thou sendest me, and of my kind there is but one pair. Suppose, now, I should perish by reason of heat or cold, would not the world be the poorer by a whole species of animals? Or can it be that thou hast cast a lustful eye upon my mate, and desirest to rid thyself of me?" Whereunto Noah made answer, and said: "Wretch! I must live apart from my own wife in the ark. How much less would such thoughts occur to my mind as thou imputest to me!"

The raven's errand had no success, for when he saw the body of a dead man, he set to work to devour it, and did not execute the orders given to him by Noah. Thereupon the dove was sent out. Toward evening she returned with an olive leaf in her bill, plucked upon the Mount of Olives at Jerusalem, for the Holy Land had not been ravaged by the deluge. As she plucked it, she said to God: "O Lord of the world, let my food be as bitter as the olive, but do Thou give it to me from Thy hand, rather than it should be sweet, and I be delivered into the power of men."

NOAH LEAVES THE ARK

Though the earth assumed its old form at the end of the year of punishment, Noah did not abandon the ark until he received the command of God to leave it. He said to himself, "As I entered the ark at the bidding of God, so I will leave it only at His bidding." Yet, when God bade Noah go out of the ark, he refused, because he feared that after he had lived upon the dry land for some time, and begotten children, God would bring another flood. He therefore would not leave the ark until God swore he would never visit the earth with a flood again.

When he stepped out from the ark into the open, he began to weep bitterly at sight of the enormous ravages wrought by the flood, and he said to God: "O Lord of the world! Thou art called the Merciful, and Thou shouldst have had mercy upon Thy creatures." God answered, and said: "O thou foolish shepherd, now thou speakest to Me. Thou didst not so when I addressed kind words to thee, saying: 'I saw thee as a righteous man and perfect in thy generation, and I will bring the flood upon the earth to destroy all flesh. Make an ark for thyself of gopher wood.' Thus spake I to thee, telling thee all these circumstances, that thou mightest entreat mercy for the earth. But thou, as soon as thou didst hear that thou wouldst be rescued in the ark, thou didst not concern thyself about the ruin that would strike the earth. Thou didst but build an ark for thyself, in which thou wast saved. Now that the earth is wasted, thou openest thy mouth to supplicate and pray."

Noah realized that he had been guilty of folly. To propitiate God and acknowledge his sin, he brought a sacrifice. God accepted the offering with favor, whence he is called by his name Noah. The sacrifice was not offered by Noah with his own hands; the priestly services connected with it were performed by his son Shem. There was a reason for this. One day in the ark Noah forgot to give his ration to the lion, and the hungry beast struck him so violent a blow with his paw that he was lame forever after, and, having a bodily defect, he was not permitted to do the offices of a priest.

The sacrifices consisted of an ox, a sheep, a goat, two turtle doves, and two young pigeons. Noah had chosen these kinds because he supposed they were appointed for sacrifices, seeing that God had commanded him to take seven pairs of them into the ark with him. The altar was erected in the same place on which Adam and Cain and Abel had brought their sacrifices, and on which later the altar was to be in the sanctuary in Jerusalem.

After the sacrifice was completed, God blessed Noah and his sons. He made them to be rulers of the world as Adam had been, and He gave them a command, saying, "Be fruitful and multiply upon the earth," for during their sojourn in the ark, the two sexes, of men and animals alike, had lived apart from each other, because while a public calamity rages continence is becoming even to those who are left unscathed. This law of conduct had been violated by none in the ark except by Ham, by the dog, and by the raven. They all received a punishment. Ham's was that his descendants were men of dark-hued skin.

As a token that He would destroy the earth no more, God set His bow in the cloud. Even if men should be steeped in sin again, the bow proclaims to them that their sins will cause no harm to the world. Times came in the course of the ages when men were pious enough not to have to live in dread of punishment. In such times the bow was not visible.

God accorded permission to Noah and his descendants to use the flesh of animals for food, which had been forbidden from the time of Adam until then. But they were to abstain from the use of blood. He ordained the seven Noachian laws, the observance of which is incumbent upon all men, not upon Israel alone. God enjoined particularly the command against the shedding of human blood. Whoso would shed man's blood, his blood would be shed. Even if human judges let the guilty man go free, his punishment would overtake him. He would die an unnatural death, such as he had inflicted upon his fellow-man. Yea, even beasts that slew men, even of them would the life of men be required.

THE CURSE OF DRUNKENNESS

Noah lost his epithet "the pious" when he began to occupy himself with the growing of the vine. He became a "man of the ground," and this first attempt to produce wine at the same time produced the first to drink to excess, the first to utter curses upon his associates, and the first to introduce slavery. This is the way it all came about. Noah found the vine which Adam had taken with him from Paradise, when he was driven forth. He tasted the grapes upon it, and, finding them palatable, he resolved to plant the vine and tend it. On the selfsame day on which he planted it, it bore fruit, he put it in the wine-press, drew off the juice, drank it, became drunken, and was dishonored—all on one day. His assistant in the work of cultivating the vine was Satan, who had happened along at the very moment when he was engaged in planting the slip he had found. Satan asked him: "What is it thou art planting here?"

Noah: "A vineyard."

Satan: "And what may be the qualities of what it produces?"

Noah: "The fruit it bears is sweet, be it dry or moist. It yields wine that rejoiceth the heart of man."

Satan: "Let us go into partnership in this business of planting a vineyard."

Noah: "Agreed!"

Satan thereupon slaughtered a lamb, and then, in succession, a lion, a pig, and a monkey. The blood of each as it was killed he made to flow under the vine. Thus he conveyed to Noah what the qualities of wine are: before man drinks of it, he is innocent as a lamb; if he drinks of it moderately, he feels as strong as a lion; if he drinks more of it than he can bear, he resembles the pig; and if he drinks to the point of intoxication, then he behaves like a monkey, he dances around, sings, talks obscenely, and knows not what he is doing.

This deterred Noah no more than did the example of Adam, whose fall had also been due to wine, for the forbidden fruit had been the grape, with which he had made himself drunk.

In his drunken condition Noah betook himself to the tent of his wife. His son Ham saw him there, and he told his brothers what he had noticed, and said: "The first man had but two sons, and one slew the other; this man Noah has three sons, yet he desires to beget a fourth besides." Nor did Ham rest satisfied with these disrespectful words against his father. He added to this sin of irreverence the still greater outrage of attempting to perform an operation upon his father designed to prevent procreation.

When Noah awoke from his wine and became sober, he pronounced a curse upon Ham in the person of his youngest son Canaan. To Ham himself he could do no harm, for God had conferred a blessing upon Noah and his three sons as they departed from the ark. Therefore he put the curse upon the last-born son of the son that had prevented him from begetting a younger son than the three he had.

The Devil in the Ark (AaTh 825)

FRANCIS LEE UTLEY

There is no doubt that the flood story is told in some form in many parts of the world. Throughout South, Central, and North America and in Asia, we find countless versions of the story. It seems to be a narrative with currency even in the twentieth century. But is the Noachian deluge still recounted in modern times? Or is it merely a matter of churchgoers learning the story in compulsory Bible classes during their youth? The question can be rephrased: to what extent, if any, is the flood story still to be found in oral tradition in Europe?

To answer this question, we may turn to a study of a folktale, "The Devil in the Ark," which has been assigned number 825 in the international Aarne-Thompson tale type system (which indexes Indo-European folktales). Francis Lee Utley (1907–1974), folklorist and medievalist for many years at Ohio State University, devoted considerable time and energy to tracking down versions of this tale. Although he did not live to complete the comprehensive monograph he had hoped to write, he did deliver a paper at the 1959 congress of the International Society for Folk Narrative Research summarizing his findings. This paper, reprinted here, succeeds in surveying the general traits of some two hundred and seventy-five versions of the tale. The essay also gives some idea of how folklorists study a tale type comparatively. One has to admire the polyglot skills required even to translate versions from an incredible array of languages and cultures. Nor is it an easy task to write an essay based upon two hundred and seventy-five different versions of the same narrative and still convey specific differentiation in detail.

It should be stressed that we are dealing here with a folktale, not a myth. Nevertheless, the plot is definitely derivative from the flood myth, specifically the version of that myth in Genesis. One can conclude that the story evidently continues to fascinate taletellers and listeners whether or not they have any religious convictions.

The serious study of Aarne-Thompson tale type 825 involving the devil and Noah's wife appears to have begun with Oskar Dähnhardt's "Beiträge zur vergleichenden Sagenforschung," Zeitschrift für Volkskunde *16 (1906): 369–396.*

Reprinted from *Internationaler Kongress der Volkserzählungsforscher in Kiel und Kopenhagen* (Berlin: Walter De Gruyter, 1961), pp. 446–463.

See also Eugene S. McCartney, "Noah's Ark and the Flood: A Study in Patristic Literature and Modern Folklore," Papers of the Michigan Academy of Science, Arts and Letters *18 (1932): 71–100. For more of Utley's thoughts on the tale, see his "Noah, His Wife, and the Devil," in Raphael Patai, Francis Lee Utley, and Dov Noy, eds.,* Studies in Biblical and Jewish Folklore *(Bloomington, 1960), pp. 59–91. For information about the refined form of the comparative method employed by folklorists studying folktales, see Kaarle Krohn,* Folklore Methodology *(Austin, 1971); for example, for the linguistic classification technique to identify individual versions (SB = Slavic Bulgarian, FE = Finno-Ugric Estonian, GE = Germanic English, etc.) see pp. 50–54. For an overview of the achievements of the methodology, see Christine Goldberg, "The Historic-Geographic Method: Past and Future,"* Journal of Folklore Research *21 (1984): 1–18.*

This paper represents the first results of a complete census and classification of AaTh 825. It is based on over twenty years of collection,[1] beginning with Oskar Dähnhardt's *Natursagen*[2] and other tales in print, and confirming them with extensive material from folklore archives. About 275 variants have now been classified and compared, over four-fifths of them from authentic oral tradition, the other fifth literary.

What then is tale type 825? There has been some question about its proper place among the *Märchen*. It has a starred rival, "The Land Where No One Dies," in Aarne-Thompson, and in the French and French Canadian Indexes the number 825 is applied to the rival tale.[3] Balys classifies it as No. 3100, a "conglomeration of motifs," under the broad heading of Creation of Animals and Plants.[4] Finnish, Estonian, Swedish and Rumanian indexes tend to break it into a number of separate *Ursprungssagen* and the Hungarian index apparently does the

[1]In the original essay, Professor Utley singled out more than a dozen international folklorist-colleagues to thank them for their cooperation in calling his attention to fugitive additional sources. This acknowledgment has been omitted in the present reprinting.—Ed. Note.

[2]Oskar Dähnhardt, *Natursagen,* Leipzig, 1907–1912, I, pp. 257–294.

[3]This was ascertained when Stith Thompson, in the course of his revision of the *Type-Index,* informed me that Luc Lacourcière of the Ottowa archives had four examples of type 825. I was suspicious because of the absence of fully developed French versions in my own collections. Lacourcière informed me he was using the Delarue number, and Mme. Marie-Louise Tenèze, who is completing the publication of the Delarue index, assures me that 825*, bearing the asterisk, is the "Land Where No One Dies" (see Antti Aarne, *The Types of the Folk-Tale,* transl. and enlarged by Stith Thompson, Helsinki, 1928, Type 825*).

[4]Johan Balys, *Lietuviu Pasakajamosios Motyvu Katalogas* (Tautosakos Darbai II), Kaunas, 1936, Type 3100.

same.[5] The story lives in oral lore both in its full form and as independent floating motifs or fragments.

Before we discuss the stability of the tale and its right to be classed as a *Märchen,* we should list its major components. This listing depends on close analysis of a group of newly assembled texts, and hence there are some places where motif-numbers from Thompson's *Motif-Index*[6] cannot be assigned with complete assurance (though some fifty Thompson numbers apply, closely or remotely, to elements in the various versions of the tale). The task of the special student of a tale-complex should be to note clear omissions in or divergences from the *Index.* Any other process would be mechanical and slavish and productive of results similar to those of early scholars, like W. A. Clouston, for instance, who seriously confused motif and type, and hence created catenae of overlapping types which defeat the purpose of classification and serious study. In other words, folklore science demands continued constructive adaptation of even the accepted Thompson and Aarne-Thompson treasuries, rather than mere typing and "motifying." I shall therefore supply the motif-numbers in the text when they seem clearly to apply, and in footnotes offer loose analogous motifs, or, where possible, suggest an additional number for the Thompson *Index.*

If we conflate all the versions in hand, the major components are as follows:[7]

1. God or His angel instructs Noah to build the Ark in secret.[8]
2. The secrecy is aided by a miracle—Noah's hammer is noiseless,

[5] It is therefore absent from Dr. János Berze Nagy, *Magyar Népmesetipusok,* Pécs, 1957, and apparently also from the Czech index Vaclav Tille, *Verzeichnis der böhmischen Märchen,* Helsinki, 1921 (FFC 34) and the Slovak index Jiri Polivka, *Súpis slovenských rozprávok,* 5 vols., V. Turčianskom Sv. Martine 1923–1932. The tale is of course common in Hungary, as the discussion will show.

[6] Stith Thompson, *Motif-Index of Folk-literature,* 6 vols. Copenhagen, 1955–1958.

[7] Julian Krzyżanowski has been kind enough to send me copies of tales now included in the analysis from the third volume, now in preparation, of his Index (J. Krzyżanowski, *Polska bajka Ludowa,* 2 vols. Warszawa, 1947). His list of components deserves presentation here (translation generously provided by Charles Morley):

(a) The devil, wishing to find out what Noah, who is building the ark, is doing, suborns his wife to draw out his secret.
(b) Noah, becoming drunk on vodka which the devil supplied his wife, reveals his secret.
(c) Returning to work he notices that the lumber which formerly shortened or lengthened itself now requires an ax.
(d) The devil enters the ark with the assistance of Noah's wife,
(e) or assumes the figure of a mouse which gnaws through the side of the ark,
(f) or pursued by a cat, hides in the cat's eyes.

[8] No exact parallel in the *Motif-Index.* Compare Mot. A1015 (flood caused by gods), A1021 (deluge: escape in boat); K2213.4.2 (Noah's secret betrayed by wife). For this motif I suggest either *A1021.3* or *K2213.4.2.1.

or his ax, though used on a stone chopping-block, never gets dull. In Ireland this motif is reversed and the sound is heard everywhere (the origin of the echo); it is meant to call men to repentance (probably Mot. H 1199.13).[9]

3. The Devil seduces Noah's Wife, sometimes in a quite amorous manner, and instructs her to give Noah an intoxicating drink which will loosen his tongue. This is often the origin of brandy, *kvas, raki, gorilka,* wine or beer (Mot. K 2213.4.2).[10]

4. Noah tells his secret, and the Devil destroys the Ark, which Noah has taken from seven days to three hundred years to build. Occasionally Noah's Wife, who in some versions already knows the secret, tells it through simple feminine frailty, or she may worm the secret out of Noah by sheer persistence rather than by schnapps. The noiseless ax becomes a very noisy tool (Mot. K 2213.4.2 and H 1199.13).[11]

5. Finding the Ark destroyed, Noah weeps, and an angel instructs him how to overcome the Devil's work. Here the details vary greatly: Noah is taught to ritually wash himself (often in urine because his wife has hidden the washing water),[12] or he is asked to return to the first tree he has cut down and use the wood for a *toaca* or *bilo* or gong, which calls the scattered boards of the Ark together.[13] Or, in some

[9] The H number is a Task: squaring the lumber on a stone without blunting the ax. Woman is purposely sent to distract him. Thompson gives Lithuanian examples. This is very close in various points to the Noah motif, though it has not previously been so identified. The addition of characters like Noah, his Wife and the Devil do not violate the universality of the motif, and its appearance in the geographical area is significant. Remotely related motifs are H 1161.1 (task: cutting firewood from rocks with brass axe) and F 837 (extraordinary battle-axe).

[10] It will be observed that this motif applies generally to all of the first five components here listed, but more specifically only to components 4 and 5. Another broad rubric applying to this and other components is Mot. G 303.23 (the Devil and the Ark). Compare Mot. A 1427.1 (devil teaches how to burn brandy) and A 1426–1428, A 1456 (various numbers relating to the origin of the different kinds of alcoholic beverages).

[11] In Thompson's two motifs a necessary sequel to components 2 and 3. Compare Mot. K 2213.4, the general betrayal by a wife of her husband's secret, and Mot. G 303.14.1 (devil destroys by night what is built by day) with the subclass—Mot. G 303.14.1.1 (the same—especially applied to Adam, Noah's close relative).

[12] No close parallel. But compare Mot. D 766.1 (disenchantment by bathing in water), D 1500.1.18 (magic healing water), H 1321 (quest for marvellous water), E 29.6 (resuscitation by urine), D 1002.1 (magic urine). I suggest Mot. *D 1500.1.18.7 (magic water used for ritual washing in building of Ark) and *D 1002.1.1 (magic urine substituted for water in ritual washing in building of Ark).

[13] No close parallel. Compare Mot. D 1213 and D 1213.1 (magic bell or gong), D 838.11 (stolen magic gong), G 283.1.2.5 (witch raises wind to break up enemy's lumber pound), F 671.1 (rapid boat-builder), H 1022.8 (task: making boat from splinters of a spindle and a shuttle, significantly from Kalevala, Runo 8). I suggest Mot. *D 1213.2 (magic gong used to assemble boards for Noah's Ark and to call animals together).

cases, by the angel's help, the cut boards stretch out or diminish to fit their places by a miracle recalling the infant Jesus the Carpenter.[14]

6. The gong often turns up again at the entrance to the Ark episode as a means for assembling the animals—a proper function, since it is the instrument which still calls eastern monks to prayer.[15]

7. Certain creatures are barred from entrance to the Ark: the noxious serpent (Mot. A 2145.2) and stinging insects (Mot. A 2021.2), the massive Re'em or unicorn (Mot. A 2214.3), the griffin (Mot. A 2232.4), the giant men of before the flood (Mot. A 531.5.9), or even Noah's Wife. Barred above all is the Devil, who has asked Noah's Wife to hesitate upon entering. He hides in her bosom, her sewing-box, or merely her shadow; Noah impatiently calls her three times, the third time with some expression like "Come in, you devil," and the Old Judas, Satan, Iblis, Nicipercea, the Horned One or the Unclean One comes on board (Mot. K 485.13.5.1).[16] In Mohammedan analogues the ass takes the place of Noah's Wife and Iblis hides under its tail (or a fourth son, Canaan, refuses to come on board and hence is drowned).

8. Once on board the Devil either bores a hole in the Ark himself[17] or turns into a mouse and gnaws a hole (Mot. A 1853.1 and G 303.3.2.4).[18] Or the hole may be a nail-hole or knot-hole left in the Ark by Noah or his workmen.[19]

9. Sometimes the story omits the hole, but speaks of a plague of mice. Mohammedan versions say that the Ark was filled with the dung of men and animals, and the unclean pig taken from the elephant's

[14] There is surprisingly no entry in the *Motif-Index*, though the motif is very popular. See, for instance, Dähnhardt, a.a.O., I, 269; W. S. Kirby, *Kalevala*, London, 1907, I, pp. 166–172, 199 (Runo 16); C. Grant Loomis, *White Magic*, Cambridge (Mass.), 1948, pp. 13, 89; M. R. James, *The Apocryphal New Testament*, Oxford, 1924, pp. 52–53, 57, 63, 73, 82. Compare Mot. A2755.4 (origin of knots in wood) and A2738 (Christ puts knots in wood) and V211.1.8 (the Infant Jesus), and also AaTh 1244 = Mot. J1964.1 (trying to stretch the beam). I suggest Mot. *V211.1.8 (Infant Jesus aids Joseph the carpenter by stretching and shortening beams of wood) and *J1964.2 (beam shortened and stretched by Christ or by Noah).

[15] No parallel. See note 12 for suggestion and broader analogues, and compare also Mot. D1446.1 (saint's bell keeps cattle from straying).

[16] Compare also Mot. C10 (tabu against profanely calling up spirit), A2210 (changing of animal characteristics) and A2291 (animal characteristics obtained during deluge).

[17] No exact parallel. Mot. A1853.1 as mentioned in note 18 is too specific. I suggest another entry under Mot. G303.23 (the devil and the ark): *G303.23.2 (devil bores hole in ark).

[18] The A item refers to creation of mouse by devil on ark and the G item to the devil as mouse. Compare Mot. A2210 and A2291 under note 12, and A1751–55 (devil's animals and God's).

[19] No exact parallel. Compare Mot. A2738 and A2755.4 (knots in wood). I suggest Mot. *A2738.1 (devil puts knots in wood of Noah's Ark).

trunk in order to eat the dung. The pig now sneezes a mouse, and the lion sneezes a cat to pursue it (Mot. A 1811.2). But this pig-mouse-lion-cat story is much rarer in Europe than another, in which God, the Virgin Mary or Noah throws a glove, which turns into the therapeutic cat.[20]

10. In most versions the hole remains a constant feature and the serpent is called to stop it with his long tail. Occasionally the plug for the leak is the dog's nose, Mrs. Noah's elbow, Noah's *Sitzplatz,* or variably the mouse, the lizard, the toad, the turtle, the hare, or the Devil himself, who gets stuck in the hole as he tries to escape (Mot. B 527.2).[21]

11. The serpent who stops the hole obtains various rewards—his long and slender body, his place as a house-snake, his tailless body (if he is a viper), his gift of venom and a tabu on killing him (Mot. B 527.2 and A 2291).

12. One reward to the serpent deserves special treatment. In some stories the serpent demands, or God promises, that he will be rewarded by the sweetest blood, or by the blood of one man per day. This promise is partly evaded after the Flood in one of two ways:

(a) Noah casts the serpent into the sacrificial fire and his ashes, spread by the wind, turn into fleas, lice, gnats or mosquitoes, which still obtain the blood, statistically speaking, of one man per day.[22]

(b) Or the serpent sends out a mosquito or other insect to find out which is the sweetest blood. The insect, returning with the news that it is man's blood, tells the swallow, who bites off the insect's tongue and reports to Noah or God that frog's blood is the sweetest. Since then snakes eat frogs, mosquitoes or gnats and cannot talk but only say "zss, zss!", and swallows nest in men's houses (Mot. A 2426.3.2, A 244.2.1, 2236.1).[23] Usually the angry serpent also bites the swallow and produces his forked swallow-tail (Mot. A 2214.1, A 2378.5.1).

This summary misses many ingeniously variable details, but it will serve for a working formula. Many of these twelve elements may exist separately, with or without the Ark as scene—swallow's tail and sweetest blood, the origin of the enmity of cat and mouse, the invention of

[20] No exact parallel. Compare Mot. G303.16.1–2 (devil and Virgin Mary) and D444.10.2 (transformation: mitten to dog); compare also Mot. A2281 and A2494.1.1 (enmity of cat and mouse).

[21] The rubric "Helpful animal stops leak in Noah's Ark" is broad enough to cover all the variant versions. An interesting related motif of Moslem origin is Mot. A2236.2 (serpent carries the devil into Paradise).

[22] Mot. A2001 and A2034.2 (insects from body of slain monster) are perhaps close enough. The motifs are very common in Siberian and American Indian folklore, like other elements in the apocryphal Flood story. Compare Mot. A2034 (origin of mosquitoes) and A2000–2099 (creation of insects).

[23] These refer to the origin of the buzz of gnat and mosquito.

alcoholic liquor by the Devil, or word-play which calls up the Devil without meaning to do so. This no doubt explains why indexers have been skeptical about the stability of the tale type. In Finland, for instance, with its 39 examples, the full story rarely exists. Earlier collectors were probably unable to demonstrate the international nature of the type with any systematic body of evidence, and the strong aetiological element led to an assumption that the type was merely a group of origin stories.

We may simplify our approach to the problem of stability by reducing these twelve component elements to three major episodes:

I. The Secret Building of the Ark and the Devil's Attempt to Destroy It.
II. The Devil's Entrance to the Ark with the Aid of Noah's Wife and Noah's Curse.
III. The Hole in the Ark and Its Remedy.

Of our corpus of 275 tales 39 are Finnish, 33 Rumanian, 19 Hungarian, 18 Irish, 17 Estonian, 17 Great Russian, 16 Osman Turk, 15 Ukrainian, 11 Lithuanian, and 11 Swedish. Fewer than ten tales turn up among the following ethnic groups: Arabs, Serbo-Croats, English and Americans (this number will grow when some twenty or thirty versions of the Hole in the Ark are included), Polish, French, Greeks, Germans, Jews, Voguls and Ostyaks, Buriats, Kurds, Bulgarians, Iranians, Berbers, Livonians, Letts, Gypsies, Altai, Tatars, Bretons, Czechs, White Russians, Votyaks, Georgians, Armenians and Annamese. The bulk of the material is Celtic, Germanic, Finno-Ugric, and above all Slavic. There are 37 Romance examples, but 33 of them are Rumanian, which culturally deserves to be classed in the Slavic sphere. The center of the material is Eastern Europe—the Balkans, European Russia, Hungary, Estonia and Finland—but there are striking offshoots in Sweden, England and Ireland, as well as among Turks and Arabs. The tale is notably absent in aboriginal America, Australia, Oceania, the Far East, most of Africa, and Southern and Western Europe. These data would seem to demonstrate that we have an integral tale-transmission of some kind, based on strong oral evidence and a fairly stable group of motifs and episodes. The type is therefore complex and international—major conditions of the true *Märchen.*

But since the tale is often reduced to a fragment or an independent motif, we must look at the problem of the whole tale for a moment. The three major episodes, as I have said, are the Secret and Destruction of the Ark, the Devil's Entrance, and the Hole. A combination of all three is found in 58 out of the 275 tales, about one-fifth of the corpus. Most of the full versions are found in the geographic center, with the exception of Finland, which usually retains episodes II and III only. There are also a number of full versions in outlying areas like Sweden, England, Ireland, Siberia, and Turkey. A combination of Secret and Entrance is found in 32 versions, of Entrance and Hole in 91, of Secret and Hole in 8; Secret exists alone in 38 versions, Entrance in 13, and Hole in 30.

We may assume, therefore, an integral tale type, composed of Secret, Entrance and Hole. Type 825 is, in a sense, derived from a literary source, the Bible itself. But the Bible is a different kind of literary source than the Egyptian Tale of "Two Brothers," an Arthurian romance, or Perrault's *Little Red Riding Hood.* For the Bible is not only written down or printed, it is always present also orally, especially in non-literate societies, where Bible tales are primarily broadcast through the mouths of priest, rabbi, or mullah. It represents a strongly believed basic skeleton for the fictions of tale type 825. Were we to believe that the test of a folktale lies in its origin, we might impugn type 825, but most of us today are content with a test of oral transmission, since origins are difficult or impossible to use as anything but subjective or elaborately inferential tests.

But are we to wholly abandon the epic laws, the structural unities apart from the Biblical skeleton? I think we may keep them. The tales have a basic logic, which we could even fit into Propp's formula,[24] were there time for such a controversial procedure. But we may seek the coherence of the tale elsewhere. Though the three major episodes, Secret, Entrance, and Hole, may exist separately, they also have genuine points of juncture. In all three the Devil is a non-Biblical element: he discovers the secret by the use of brandy, he destroys the Ark, he enters the Ark and causes a hole in it, and he or his alter-ego the serpent stops up the hole. Noah's Wife betrays her husband by revealing the secret, and she also betrays him by helping the Devil to enter the Ark, where he may bore the hole and lead to the final episode. The gong which assembles the boards of the Ark after the Devil has scattered them is also the gong which assembles the animals in the entrance scene. The mouse who destroys the Ark a second time, through the hole, is either a creation of the Devil or the Devil himself. The serpent who stops the hole is often barred in the entrance scene, and is allowed to enter only because of his services—sometimes he creeps into the hole from outside unobserved and unwanted. The serpent is a helpful animal who saves the living eight men and women, but he shows his kinship with the Devil when he makes a pact with Noah to

[24] *Morphology of the Folktale,* ed. Svatava Pirkova-Jakobson, American Folklore Society Bibliographical and Special Series 9, 1958.

have the blood of a man per day after the Flood, which would, if not evaded by Noah, have destroyed mankind just as quickly and as efficaciously as if they had been drowned in the first place. Thus there is a series of variable coherencies which knit the tale together and preserve it, above and beyond the Biblical skeleton. The tale seems, then, to be both international and stable, though with nothing like the spread or stability of, say, the Cinderella story.

We must reserve the presentation of the tales and a full account of the cultural transformations of the type for a monograph now in preparation. But it is possible to speak briefly of some of the special features of the ethnic oikotypes. Great Russian variants place special emphasis on the themes of the destruction of the Ark by the Devil and the invention of kvas, on the monastic gong to assemble the animals, and on the Devil's entrance through the help of Noah's Wife. The majority of them are literary versions, from 16th or 17th century manuscripts, but perhaps going back to 12th century sources; they represent interpolations in the Byzantine-derived Revelations of Pseudo-Methodius, the expanded Historical Paleya, or the native satiric tale of the Wise Hops. Their purpose is didactic, which explains the emphasis of addiction to spirits. Adam is often the hero instead of Noah and Evga his wife, and in some forms we even have contamination with the famous circumpolar tale of Earth Diver and the dualistic creation of earth. Ukrainian tales are similarly full with regard to Secret and Entrance; they are, luckily, almost completely oral, though some of the Russian literary versions also appear in Ukrainian form. South Slavic and Polish versions tend to eliminate the Devil and concentrate on the mouse, the hole, the serpent, and the swallow's forked tail.

Oral versions are almost nonexistent in Greece, which might be taken as a natural source for the Slavic development. But there are two remarkable literary versions—one in St. Epiphanius, native of Palestine and Bishop of Cyprus (*ca.* 315–403 A.D.), in which there is attributed to the Gnostics a belief in one Noria or Pyrrha, wife of Noah, who has strange connections with the serpent and who sits on the Ark and burns it. Perhaps we may see in this story a germ of the Secret and Destruction and Entrance episodes.[25] Euthemius Zigabenus, speaking in the late 11th or early 12th centuries of the Bogomile heretics of Byzantium, connects Satanaël with the building of the Ark. Such materials, and especially the apocryphal additions to the Bible and the dualistic traces, have led Veselofskii, Gaster and Dähnhardt to assume that the tale has some connection with the Bogomiles, and may even

[25] See, for instance, Montague R. James, *The Lost Apocrypha of the Old Testament*, London, 1920, pp. 12–15.

be Bogomile in origin and transmission.[26] Such authorities would be hard to confute in toto, but the Noah apocryphal tale certainly does not follow Bogomile lines of transmission to Western Europe. It is notably absent, for instance, in the southern part of France, where Albigensians were in contact with Paulician and Bogomile.

The Finno-Ugric Estonians preserved many full examples of the type, with unusual added details—boar's froth as yeast for the intoxicating potion, the noiseless ax on the stone chopping-block, the avoidance of the Devil's name with paraphrases like Old Judas, Lutsever, Wanamust and the Evil One, and the absence of sequels to the snake's stopping of the hole. Voguls and Votyaks preserve Building and Destruction and Entrance, adapting the story to their native gods and heroes. Finland preserves Entrance and Hole episodes, but the Devil is absent, and the serpent is the banned creature who forces his way in through knot-hole or nail-hole, sticks there, and hence saves the Ark and himself. Magyars put less emphasis on the Hole story, though they have it; their major contribution to the tale seems to be a washing or fasting motif, in which the building of the Ark is hindered not through the intoxicating drink, but through Noah's failure at ceremonial purification. Instead of the Devil flies sometimes enter the Ark, but they do so likewise on the basis of a play on words.

In the Baltic sphere the Letts have only one small fragment of a Hole story, but there are eleven Lithuanian versions, all omitting the first episode and the Devil's entrance to the Ark through Noah's Wife. But Velnias or the Devil is on the Ark, usually "disguised as a mouse," which involves both the creation of the cat from the glove of God or Virgin Mary and the serpent's stopping of the hole with the swallow sequel.

Rumanian and French versions comprise the Romance group (five Catalan versions have come too late to be included in the statistics). The French examples, though individual, may be dismissed as stray fragments—once the Devil bores a hole with a center bit, and the stopper of the hole is the hare's paw or hare's tail, which explains why hares have no tail or why male hares breed without the aid of the female. The Rumanian group differ greatly from the French—no country preserves such a fine collection of complete versions, all of them oral, and at least 8 of the 33 fully integrated versions containing Secret,

[26] Moses Gaster, *Ilchester Lectures on Greeko-Slavonic Literature,* London, 1887, pp. 19, 26, 38, 164, 198; Veselovskiĭ, *Etnografičeskoe Obozrenie,* II (Moskau, 1890), pp. 32–48; and Veselovskiĭ, *Russische Revue,* XIII (1878), pp. 131–152; Dähnhardt, a.a.O., I, pp. 5, 22, 38–42, 92–93, 260–261. For more recent views on the Bogomiles, oral tales and the *Paleya* see Steven Runciman, *The Medieval Manichee,* Cambridge, 1947, pp. 85–87; Dmitri Obolensky, *The Bogomiles,* Cambridge, 1948, pp. 281–283; N. K. Gudzy, *History of Early Russian Literature,* New York, 1949, pp. 36, 43.

Entrance and Hole. The weeping of Noah after the Ark is destroyed is a constant feature which recalls the Russian literary versions; the *toaca* or gong which collects the boards of the Ark is also constant; the Devil is consistently transformed to a mouse, which involves a double element of glove-cat eating mouse and viper losing its tail in the hole. Clearly we are close to the Slavic sphere in Rumania, possible even in a country of origin.

In the main Germanic versions are literary or artistic. They have special value in dating the motifs, especially since the literary Slavic versions, which may be close to the original, have not yet been subject to critical editing, and vary from a hypothetical 12th century original to actual manuscripts of 16th and 17th century. All four versions from greater Germany are literary—they include the names of Jansen Enikel of Vienna (13th century), Hans Sachs, Martin Luther, and the 16th century Wolfgang Bütner. Enikel's version is the earliest literary document we have, unless some of the Slavic versions are older. Like all the German versions it lacks the first episode of Secret and Destruction, and incorporates a fascinating story of how Ham evaded through the Devil's help the ban on sexual intercourse in the Ark, a story which, I have shown elsewhere, must owe something to Jewish legend.[27] In England oral versions are rare, but we have two remarkable early treatments in the 14th century Queen Mary's Psalter and the 15th century mystery play on Noah's Ark.[28] An unusual English and American version, confined to the preservation of the Ark through the agency of dog, Noah's Wife, and Noah, has not yet been fully studied. Close to the pictorial treatment in Queen Mary's Psalter is a group of pictures in four 14th century Swedish churches. Art historians derive the technique of the group from the East Anglian school.[29] The tales were unconfirmed by oral sources until 1939, when C. W. von Sydow set in motion for me the Lund collectors and found a number of fragments which both testify to the presence of some form of type 825 and explain why other well-collected areas, in Germany for instance, may lack the tales, since the informants make considerable point of their belief that such tales are a Sin against the Holy Ghost. These stories are separately treated in an article which will appear next year.[30]

[27] *Germanic Review*, XVI (1941), pp. 241–249.

[28] Mill, *Publications of the Modern Language Association*, LVI (1941), pp. 613–626.

[29] See, for instance, Andreas Lindblom, *La peinture gothique en Suède et en Norvège*, Stockholm, 1916, pp. 177, 210–214, and (Lindblom) *Nordisk Tidskrift för Vetanskap, Konst och Industri* (1917), pp. 358–368.

[30] Wayland D. Hand and Gustave O. Arlt, eds., *Humaniora: Essays in Literature. Folklore. Bibliography Honoring Archer Taylor on his Seventieth Birthday* (Locust Valley, N.Y., 1960), pp. 258–279.

Another surprise is the Celtic group, above all from Eire. From the Irish archives I have 18 examples, two of them involving all three episodes, seven of them only Secret and Entrance, and four Entrance alone. Three are Hole alone. These details are significant—in Ireland, far from the geographic center, appears the most important element of Secret and Destruction in full form. One oikotypal detail, the Estonian boar's froth used to make the potion, appears clearly in Ireland as well and never elsewhere. Of special interest is the addition of the sire horse, a creature of the Devil who pulls a plug from the Ark's floor and threatens the Ark a second time with destruction. In a strangely primitive sequel Noah kills the violent stallion and is forced to carry on the breed by mating himself with the mare. One suspects a contamination from Irish myth or folktale, perhaps from the common Irish swan-maiden variant, where the mortal mates with an otherworldly horse from an Irish lake.[31] A few Irish literary versions appear in manuscripts of the 16th century or earlier, indicating a presence of the tale in that area before modern collection got under way.

Finally we must turn to the Asiatic versions. Most Siberian examples may be dismissed as mere fragments, derivative perhaps from Russian orthodox or unorthodox missionaries, and reflecting traces of Islam or of aboriginal lore. But in Turkey, Arabic circles, and Iran we have a number of versions which suggest a source for at least the last two episodes. The Arabic examples are almost wholly literary, but of recent years a number of Osmanli Turkish versions have been collected in Anatolia by Pertev Boratav. As we might expect they are close to Balkan versions. Characteristic features are the stubborn Ass who helps the Devil on board the Ark, cat from lion and mouse from swine, and the serpent stopping the hole with sweetest blood and swallow sequel. There may be a hint of the tale in the Koran (615–622 A.D.), and there is certainly plentiful evidence of the material by the time we come to collections of Moslem hadith or traditions such as are found in the chronicle of Tabari, who lived in Tabaristan or Baghdad from about 831 to 923. I have been unable to study the Old Turkish version of Rubghuzii (1310 A.D.), so brilliantly analyzed by Walter Anderson in his prize essay at the University of Kazan, but I have read H. T. Katanov's summarizing review.[32] The studies of Dähnhardt and Anderson, by the way, are the

[31] Tom Peete Cross, *Motif-Index of Early Irish Literature*, Bloomington, 1952, B181.

[32] *Učenyja Zapiski Imp. Kazanskago Universiteta (Memorabilia Universitatis Kazanensis)*, Anno 75, Kniga 12 (Kazan, 1908). The original can now be found conveniently in *Rabghuzi Narrationes de Prophetis Cod. Mus. Brit. Add. 7851* (*Reproduced in Facsimile*), ed. K. Grønbech, Copenhagen, 1948, pp. 25–30. I am still seeking a translator.

only major attempts to approach type 825 or Noah tales in general from a serious point of view before the present one.

Of transmission and history of the tale it is impossible to be final until a careful mapping of the motifs in each country has been completed. It is tempting to find the origin of at least episodes II and III in Asia Minor or Iran, as Dähnhardt did,[33] but the first episode of Secret and Destruction is almost surely European in origin. His further view that the Bogomiles had something to do with the Devil's dualistic competitions with God may be partly right, but as I have said, any theory that the Bogomiles were its sole transmittors falls down in view of the actual spread of the tale. Jewish elements are present in the larger group of apocryphal tales about Noah, some of them penetrating to non-Jewish European sources, but none of these have, as I once thought, much to do with the history of tale type 825. Perhaps we may say in highly tentative fashion that the hesitation motif and the hole in the Ark with cat, mouse and serpent crept in from Asia Minor to the Balkans and Russia, joined on the way with a Gnostic belief recorded by St. Epiphanius about the destruction of the Ark by Noah's Wife, and later met various local tales about the Devil's invention of schnapps, the gong, hammer and ax motifs, to create a full-fledged story, which later migrated in whole or in part to Finns, Estonians and Magyars, and at last in some way reached Sweden, England, Ireland and even the United States. The greatest puzzle is the close resemblance of Irish and Estonian versions.[34] Our distribution charts make slow diffusion from the Eastern European center unlikely, though we must be careful especially with this tale of the *argumentum ex silentio.* Perhaps, even before Hanseatic times, there were trade routes from the Baltic to England and Ireland which may render the hypothesis of a sea-leap possible.

For lack of time I have been forced to leave the tales in the abstract, which is a shame, since part of the charm of the type is its flavor and style and folktale logic.[35] No true folklorist will ever prefer his reconstructions to the genuine, fresh oral tale itself.

[33] Dähnhardt, a.a.O., I, pp. 260–261 (connections are even made with details in the Babylonian Gilgamesh epic).

[34] My brief discussion of such parallels, with a preview of the whole subject of Noah in folklore, science, myth, art and poetry, will appear in *Studies in Biblical and Jewish Folklore,* ed. Dov Noy, Raphael Patai and Francis L. Utley, a Memoir of the American Folklore Society, published in 1960 at the Indiana University Press.

[35] Samples of SR 10, SU 10, FM 3, FE 5, FF 11, FF 23, RR 16, RR 17, C 13, TO 10 and an American version were passed to members of the Kiel Congress. They have been since reproduced as *The Devil in the Ark Consisting of Some Sample Texts of the Noah Story,* Chillicothe: Ohio Valley Folk Research Project, 1959.

VERSIONS OF AATH 825

This list is provided primarily for the use of specialists in the various countries and archives, to whom it is assumed the extreme abbreviation will cause no trouble.

Slavic

SB 1 — A. Strausz, Die Bulgaren, 1898, p. 64 — Stojkov, Sbornik 3. 184 = Dähnhardt 1. 274
SB 2 — A. Strausz, p. 65 = Stojkov, Sbornik 7. = Dähnhardt 1. 274
SB 3 — A. Strausz, p. 70 = M. K. Tsepenhov, Sbornik 11
SC 1 — J. V. Grohmann, Aberglauben, 1864, no. 1683 = Časopis Českeho Museu 1855, p. 331
SR 1 — Afanasiev, N. R. Legendy, 1859, p. 48 no. 14
SR 2 — Afanasiev, N. R. Legendy, p. 181 no. 29 = Buslaev, Ist. Ocherki 1. 565
SR 3 — F. I. Buslaev, Istoricheskie Ocherki 1. (1861) 439 (Highminded Hops)
SR 4 — F. I. Buslaev, Istoricheskie (Count Uvarov MS) 1. 439
SR 5 — V. N. Dobrovolskii, Smolensky etn. Sbornik, 1891, p. 237 no. 18 (Zapiski IRGO 20)
SR 6 — A. Pypin, Lozhnyja in otrechennyja knigi (Kushelev-Bezboridko, Pamiatniki 3) p. 17 (1862)
SR 7 — V. A. Keltuyala, Kurs. Ist. Russ. Lit., 1906, p. 168
SR 8 — Istrin, Chteniia v Imp Obshch. Ist. i Drev. 4 p. 116 = PMLA 55 (1941). 617.
SR 9 — N. S. Tichonravov, Letopisi Russ. Lit. 1. 158 (same as SR 4?) (1859)
SR 10 — Andreii Popov, Chteniia v Imp. Obshch. Ist. i Drev. 116—117 (1881)
SR 11 — S. W. Ralston, Russian Folk-Tales, 1880 p. 334
SR 12 — P. P. Chubinsky, Trudy et-stat. exped., 1872, p. 54 = Dähnhardt 1. 275
SR 13 — A. Chekhov, The Best Known Works, 1929, pp. 433, 654
SR 14 — Chubinsky, Trudy, 1. 54 = Dähnhardt 1. 275
SR 15 — G. N. Potanin, Etnog. Zbirnik 6.1 (1864), p. 123 = Dh 1. 275
SR 16 — Tichonravov, Letopis p. 160 note (Synodal Palaia of 1477)
SR 17 — C. F. Coxwell, Siberian and other Folk-Tales, 1925, p. 819 = Afanasiev p. vii
SRW 1 — Michael Federowski, Lud Bialoruskij, 1897, 1. p. 187, no. 691 = Dh 1. 275
SS 1 — F. J. Krauss, Tausend Sagen 1914 1. 402
SS 2 — Zemaljski Musej, Sarajevo (coll V. Palavestra) — Orthodox
SS 3 — Zemaljski Musej, Sarajevo (coll V. Palavestra) — Moslem
SS 4 — Istitut za Narodnu Umjetnost, Zagreb = Srpski Etnog. Zbornik 41. (1921) 398
SS 5 — Glasnik Zemalskog Muz. u. B. i. H. 13 (1901), 151
SS 6 — N. Tordinac, Hravatske Pjesme, 1883, p. 53 no. 17
SS 7 — Bosanska Vila 5 (1890), p. 312 no. 19—20
SS 8 — F. S. Krauß, Sagen und Märchen, 1883—84, 2. 153
SU 1 — Mikhail Dragomanov, Malorusskija Narodnyja, 1876, p. 95 no. 7 = Dh 1 269
SU 2 — Mikhail Dragomanov, Sbornik za Narod. Umot. 10 (1894). 62
SU 3 — (P. B. Ivanov), Etnog. Obozrenie 17 (1893). 70 (Kupiansk)
SU 4 — (P. B. Ivanov), Etnog. Obozrenie 17 (1893). 70 (others)
SU 5 — (P. B. Ivanov), Etnog. Obozrenie 17 (1893). 70 (Marusov)
SU 6 — (P. B. Ivanov), Etnog. Obozrenie 17 (1893). 70 (Arapovka)
SU 7 — (P. B. Ivanov), Etnog. Obozrenie 17 (1893). 70 (Arapovka) (Skubak)
SU 8 — Etnog. Zbirnik 2.2 (1897?), 36
SU 9 — V. Gnatyuk, Etnog. Zbirnik 3 (1900), p. 5 = Dh 1. 269
SU 10 — V. Gnatyuk, Etnog. Zbirnik 12 (1902), 30 = Dh 1. 269, 275, 279
SU 11 — R. F. Kaindl, Die Huzulen, 1894, p. 95 = Dh 1. 277
SU 12 — Ivan Franko, Pamiatky Ukrainsko-Ruskoi Movy, 1896—1910, 3.68
SU 13 — St. Rudansky, Tvori, 1912, 1. 172 (Veletni)
SU 14 — St. Rudansky, Tvori, 1912, 1. 259 (Potop)

SU 15 — R. F. Kaindl, Die Huzulen, p. 103 = Dh l. 277
SP 1 — Zbior Wiadomosci 7 (1881—82), p. 110 no. 12 = Dh l. 258, 275
SP 2 — Zbior Wiadomosci 15 (1881—82), p. 269 no. 25 = Dh l. 277
SP 3 — Zbior Wiadomosci 5 (1881—82), p. 138 no. 9
SP 4 — Zbior Wiadomosci 5 (1881—82), p. 149 no. 46 = Dh l. 274
SP 5 — Wisła 14 (1900), 485 = Dh l. 277
SP 6 — F. Gawelek, Materialy Antropologiczno-Arch. i Etnog. 11 (1910), p. 81 no. 183
SP 7 — K. Matyas in Wisła 7 (1893), p. 108
SP 8 — E. Klich, in Materialy a. a. e. 11 (1910), p. 26 no. 25

Greek
Gre 1 — Epiphanius, Panarium ed Oehler 2.2, 170 = Migne PG 41, 331
Gre 2 — Euthymius Zigabenus, Panoplia Dogmatica = Migne PG 130, 1296, 1305 = D. Obolensky, The Bogomiles, 1948, p. 208
Gre 3 — R. M. Dawkins, Modern Greek Folktales, 1953, p. 159
Gre 4 — TO 2?
Gre 5 — Arab 2?

Finno-Ugric
FE 1 — Hurt Coll. IV 9, 243/5 (1) — Jaan Saalverk
FE 2 — Hurt Coll. III, 18, 797 — Annus Kappok
FE 3 — Hurt Coll. II, 52, 758/62 (63) — J. Poolakess
FE 4 — Hurt Coll. III, 22/347/8 (7) — Peeter Saar
FE 5 — Hurt Coll. 51, 835/6 (5) — Jaan Tamm
FE 6 — Hurt Coll. R 3, 119 — C. Allas
FE 7 — M. J. Eisen, Rahva-raamat II, 1893 — 132/3 (42) = E 4065 — J. Tamm
FE 8 — M. J. Eisen, Kọrtsi-raamat, 1896, p. 10 = E 1027 3/4 — J. Malzov
FE 9 — Hurt Coll. III, 12, 28 (6) — N. M. Eljas
FE 10 — Hurt Coll. III, 24, 113/4 (3) — J. P. Soggel
FE 11 — Hurt Coll. II, 20, 404/5 (12) — J. Reinson
FE 12 — M. J. Eisen, Miks, 1913, p. 36 (66) — Joh. Vaine
FE 13 — Hurt Coll. IV 8, 66 (32) — Joh. Vaine
FE 14 — Estonian Folklore Archives II, 194, 475/6 (12) — E. Kirss
FE 15 — AES (Univ. Grünwald) MF 183, 6/7 — Lüsa Vanker
FE 16 — Eisen Coll. 61 233 — J. Gutves
FE 17 — F. J. Wiedemann, Aus dem inneren und ausseren Leben der Ehsten, 1876, p. 440 = Dh l. 271
FF 1 — Finnish Archives — Hämeenkyro, Ahonen, S 69
FF 2 — Finnish Archives — Otto Reinikainen
FF 3 — Mannonen, Ulla 619
FF 4 — Mannonen, Ulla 612
FF 5 — N. Saarela, KRK 153. 26
FF 6 — A. Ryhänen, KRK 219. 12
FF 7 — J. Valkeinene KRK 75. 28
FF 8 — J. Tyyskä, 451
FF 9 — J. Tyyskä, a) 28
FF 10 — S. Paulaharju a) 203
FF 11 — S. Paulaharju a) 444
FF 12 — KRK 58, Enqvist p. 8
FF 13 — KRK 113, H. Pulkinnen 394
FF 14 — Fanni Aittomäki 69
FF 15 — KRK 40. L. Myllymäki 55
FF 16 — KRK 94 — E. Horttanainen 640

FF 17 — KRK 94 — E. Horttanainen 569
FF 18 — KRK 89 — Kalle Viinikainen 187
FF 19 — KRK 239 — M. Rautiainen 89
FF 20 — KRK 224 — Janne Simokoki 2434
FF 21 — KRK 216 — Fiina Palukka 59
FF 22 — K. Krohn, Suomalaisen Kansansatuja I, 1866 = Krohn Coll. 11 495 = Dh 1. 277
FF 23 — K. Krohn, Magische Ursprungsrunen der Finnen, 1924, p. 20
FF 24 — K. Teräsvuori 4. 1910
FF 25 — Jorma Partanen 59
FF 26 — J. Tyyskä a) 28 (not same as FF 9)
FF 27 — KRK 40: 55 — L. Myllimäki 55 (not same as FF 15)
FF 28 — J. Järventausta 158
FF 29 — Sulo Majala 34
FF 30 — KT 56: 50 — Hilja Soimamäki
FF 31 — KRK 58: 8 — S. Enkvist
FF 32 — KRK 113 — H. Pulkinnen 394 (differs from FF 13)
FF 33 — S. Paulaharju II H 2, 617 = Dh 1. 277
FF 34 — M. Moilanen 2308
FF 35 — KRK 224: 2434 — Janne Simojaki (differs from FF 20)
FF 36 — Johan Pirttilanti 25
FF 37 — Fanni Aittomäki 69 (differs from FF 14)
FF 38 — Fanni Mäki 24
FF 39 — J. Tyyskä 451
FM 1 — M. Dragomanov, Sbornik za Narodni Umot. 10 (1894), 62
FM 2 to 15 — A. Hermann, Globus 63, (1893), 333—336 = Kalmany, Etnographia II and III (1891—92), also in part = Kalmany, Vilagunk. See Dh 1. 258, 273, 270, 268, 279, 267, 292, 269 etc.
(FM 4 = Hermann no. 3, Dh 1. 267, 269, 278, 292, 3. 187 = Kalmany, Szeged Nepe 3, no. 36 (Mesek es bokon nemuek)
FM 16 = MS Coll. L. Kalmany, EA (Ethnographical Museum Budapest) 2771, p. 416 no. 119
FM 17 = MS Coll. L. Kalmany, EA 2771, p. 418 no. 121 = Kalmany, Vilagunk, 1893, p. 60 = Dh 1. 271
FM 18 — Linda Degh from Roka Leszlo 1947
FM 19 — Kalmany, Vilagunk, p. 58 = Dh 1. 271
FU 1 — Hermann, Globus 63, 336 = Munkacsi, Regek es enekek a vilag, 1892, I. 1 = Dh 1. 260 = Schullerus, Zs. f. Volkskunde 13, 343 = Anderson, Nordasiatische Flutsagen, p. 7 (Vogul)
FU 2 — Hermann p. 338 = (Munkacsi orally to Hermann) = Munkacsi, Regek 1, 209 f. (1902) = Dh 1. 260 = Anderson, Nordasiatische Flutsagen p. 10 (Vogul)
FU 3 — S. K. Patkanov, Die Irtysch-Ostjaken und ihre Volkspoesie I, 1897 = Holmberg, Mythology of All Races IV, 362 = Anderson, Nordasiatische Flutsagen no. 9 (Ostyaks)
FLv 1 — Kr. 229 from Estonian Archives
FLv 2 — Ti. 62 from Estonian Archives
FP 1 — Hermann, Globus 63 (1893), 338 — Munkacsi, Votjak nepkolteszeti hagyomanyok, 1887, p. 50 = Dh 1. 258 (?), 271—2 (Votyak)

Celtic

CB 1 — Lucie de V. H., Rev. des Trad. Pop. 16 (1901), 445 = Sébillot, Folklore 3.256 = Dh 1. 278
CI 1 — Bealoideas 3.485 (1932) (Carna parish)

CI 2 — Irish Folklore Commission MS 303, pp. 514—516 (Spiddal)
CI 3 — IFC 349 153 (Kinvarra)
CI 4 — An Claidheamh Soluis 11, no. 42 (1909) p. 12, and no. 43 (1910) p. 5 (Lacken)
CI 5 — Eriu 5. 49 (MS Royal Irish Acad C IV 2, f 149)
CI 6 — Ciaran Biaread = IFC? (coll July 5, 1951 in Carnmore)
CI 7 — IFC 368 65 (Claregalway)
CI 8 — IFC 2.352 (Baile an Tsleibhe)
CI 9 — IFC 560 86 (Capplewhite)
CI 10 — IFC 738. 334 (Kilcommon)
CI 11 — IFC 738. 328 (Kilcommon)
CI 12 — IFC 615. 325 (Beagh)
CI 13 — IFC MS? — S. O'D. Altnabrocai in Iorrus (Mullingar)
CI 14 — IFC MS? — Old storyteller Teelin, Co. Donegal, 1946
CI 15 — IFC 1205. 441 (Claregalway)
CI 16 — IFC 1205. 586 (Lackagh)
CI 17 — IFC 1227. 65 (Claregalway)
CI 18 — MS Egerton 1782 = Zs. für Celtische Philologie 4. 236 = Flower, Cat Irish MSS in the British Museum 2. 280

Germanic

GE (Amer) 1 — Arthur Guiterman, The Light Guitar, 1923, p. 110 — L. O. Reeves, Saturday Evening Post June 8, 1925 — Guiterman, Lyric Laughter, 1939, p. 170 „The Dog's Cold Nose"
GE (Amer) 2 — Arthur Guiterman, Song and Laughter, 1929, p. 9 = Lyric Laughter 1939 „Cold"
GE (Amer) 3 — Arthur Guiterman, The Laughing Muse, 1915, p. 100 = Lyric Laughter, 1939, p. 36 „The Best and Worst Nail in the Ark"
GE (Amer) 4 — Arthur Guiterman, The Laughing Muse, 1915, p. 168 „The First Cat"
GE 5 — Newcastle Noah's Flood, in O. Waterhouse, The Non-Cycle Mystery Plays, 1909 (EETSES 104) p. 19 = Brotanek, Anglia 21 and many other editions
GE 6 — Queen Mary's Psalter, ed Sir George Warner, 1912, p. 7
GE 7 — Mandeville's Travels, ed P. Hamelius, 1919—23 (EETS 153—4), 1.98
GE 8 — Moncure D. Conway, Demonology and Devil Lore, 1879, 1. 123
(Many more of these, not yet classified, in my notes, July 1959)
GG 1 — F. Schnorr von Carolsfeld, Archiv für Litteraturgeschichte 6 (1877), 308 = Wolfgang Bütner, Epitome Historiarum (1576) Bl 54 — Dh 1. 258
GG 2 — Philipp Strauch ed, Jansen Enikels Werke, 1900, p. 35
GG 3 — Hans Sachs, Keller-Goetze 20. 322 = A. Stiefel, Zs. d. Ver. f. Volkskunde 8 (1898), 280
GG 4 — Martin Luther tr., Verlegung des Alcoran Bruder Richardi, Wittemburg 1542, sigg D 4 v and L
GS 1 — Uppsala Landsmals — och Folkminnesarkiv 303: 170 C p. 26
GS 2 — ULMA 736, p. 113, 110
GS 3 — Lund Universitets Folkminnesarkiv M 5965. 1 and 2 (Carl Viking)
GS 4 — Lund M 5965.3 (Carl Viking)
GS 5 — Lund M 5965.4 (Carl Viking)
GS 6 — Lund M 6448.3 (Blenda Andersson)
GS 7 — Lund M 11331.2 (Svante Stahle)
GS 8 — N. M. Mandelgren, Monuments Scandinaves du Moyen Age, 1862 = Andreas Lindblom, La Peinture Gothique en Suède et en Norvège, 1916, p. 210 (Edshult church)
GS 9 — Lindblom, p. 210 (Vilberga church)

GS 10 — Lindblom, Nordisk Tidskrift för Vetenskap 1917, 358 (Örberga church)
GS 11 — Lindblom, Nordisk, p. 366 (Risinge church)

Romance

RF 1 — A. Millien, Rev. des Trad. Pop. 5 (1890). 244 = Dh, Nat. Volks. p. 49 = La Nature = Dh 1. 278
RF 2 — Paul Sébillot, Le Folklore de France, 1904—7, 3.9 = Dh 278
RF 3 — Sébillot 3. 159 = N. Guyot, Rev. des Trad. Pop. 19. 217
RF 4 — Bonaventure des Periers, Les Contes ou Les Nouvelles Récréations et Joyeaux Devis, ed Jacob and Nodier, 1841, p. 248 (Nouvelle LXVIII)
RR 1 — E. Niculita-Voronca, Datinele si Credentile pop. Roman., 1903, 1. 19 no. 1
RR 2 — E. Niculita-Voronca, no. 2
RR 3 — Marian, Insectele, 1903, 405 = Gazeta Transilvaniei 54 (1891) p. 7 no. 144 = M. Gaster, Rumanian Bird and Beast Stories, 1915 no. 71 = Dh 1. 279.
RR 4 — Pamfile, Povestea Lumei, 1913, p. 103 = Sezaroarea 2 (1893—4), 121
RR 5 — Pamfile, Povestea Lumei, p. 127 = Voronca, Datinele 1903, p. 20
RR 6 — Pamfile, Povestea Lumei, p. 131 = N. Tapu, Albina 4. 1270
RR 7 — Pamfile, Povestea Lumei, p. 134 = Voronca, p. 19?
RR 8 — Pamfile, Povestea Lumei, p. 134 = Voronca, p. 19
RR 9 — Pamfile, Povestea Lumei, p. 140 = Voronca, p. 834
RR 10 — M. Beza, Paganism in Roumanian Folklore, 1928, p. 130 (conflation?)
RR 11 — Pamfile, Povestea p. 145 = Albina 5. 334
RR 12 — C. Radulescu-Codin, Legende, Traditii si Amintiri ist, 1910, p. 2
RR 13 — Sezatoarea 2 (1893—94), 3 = Dh 1. 274
RR 14 — Gaster, Rumanian Bird and Beast Stories, p. 213
RR 15 — Sezatoarea 3 (1894—95), 105
RR 16 — Sezatoarea 9 (1905), 27
RR 17 — Sezatoarea 9 (1905), 28
RR 18 — Radulescu-Codin, Din tretecul nostru, p. 8
RR 19 — Radulescu-Codin, Din tretecul nostru, p. 11
RR 20 — Radulescu-Codin, Din tretecul nostru, p. 12
RR 21 — Radulescu-Codin, Din tretecul nostru, p. 14
RR 22 — Radulescu-Codin, Legende, traditii si amintiri ist., pp. 3, 31
RR 23 — Sezatoarea p. 15 (or Ion Creanga? — unident photostat)
RR 24 — Sezatoarea p. 15 (or Ion Creanga? — unident photostat)
RR 25 — Radulescu-Codin, Nevasta Lenesa, p. 73
RR 26 — Radulescu-Codin, Nevasta Lenesa, p. 74
RR 27 — Niculita-Voronca, p. 20 = Pamfile, Povestea, p. 143
RR 28 — Ion Creanga 2. 266
RR 29 — Ion Creanga 3. 108
RR 30 — Ion Creanga 6. 363
RR 31 — Ion Creanga 11. 16
RR 32 — Gaster, Bird and Beast Stories, p. 214 no. 68
RR 33 — Gaster, Bird and Beast Stories, p. 210

Turkic

TO 1 — V. B. de Gasparin, A Constantinople, 1867, p. 189
TO 2 — Sébillot, Rev. des Trad. Pop. 2 (1897), 369 = Dh 1. 280
TO 3 — Turkish tr. of Tabari 1. 97
TO 4 — Commentary of Hamdi Yazir, 6. 5124 (TO 3 ff. from Eberhard and Boratav correspondence)
TO 5 — Seyhi, Harname (15 cent)
TO 6 — Dede Korkut Kitabi, ed. Orhan S. Gökyay, p. 3
TO 7 — Baki Gölpinarli, coll. at Istanbul 1946

TO 8 — Baki Gölpinarli, coll. at Istanbul 1946
TO 9 — Hayrullah Örs coll. at Ankara 1946
TO 10 — P. N. Boratav coll. at Trapezunt 1946 or before
TO 11 — P. N. Boratav coll. at Trapezunt 1946 or before
TO 12 — Baki Gölpinarli coll. at Istanbul 1946
TO 13 — Hayrullah Örs coll. at Ankara 1946
TO 14 — Necati Ongay coll. at Ankara 1946
TO 15 — Frau Refet Türksal coll. at Ankara 1946
TO 16 — Rubghuzii, Ribat Ojus = H. T. Katanov review of Walter Anderson's Kazan dissertation
TT 1 — Anderson, Nordasiatische Flutsagen p. 22 = W. Radloff, Proben der Volkslitteratur der türkischen Stämme UX (1907), p. 417 no. 397 (Abaku Tartar)
TT 2 — N. F. Sumtsov, Etnografichnii Obozrenie 17. 179 = N. U. "The Borderland" 1891 no. 18 = Dh 1. 281 (Sarts)

Baltic

Let 1 — M. Boehm and F. Specht, Lettisch-Litauische Volksmärchen, 1924, p. 151 = Lerchis Putschkaitis, Latviesu tautas teikas un pasakas, 1891—1902, 1. 166 = Dh 1. 281
Let 2 — (see Gipsy, provided by Oskar Loorits, misplaced)
Lit 1 — Lietuviu pasakos, Vilnius 1905, p. 6 no. 7
Lit 2 — J. Elisonas, Dievas senelis (Musu Tautosaka 9), Kaunas 1935 p. 51 no. 118
Lit 3 — Lithuanian Folklore Archives (LTA) 141, 20 354 (Juozas Buga)
Lit 4 — Lithuanian Society of Sciences (LMD) 561 (212) (M. Slancauskas)
Lit 5 — LTA 1487 (144) (Vladas Diciunas), I, 13
Lit 6 — LTA 1487 (145) (Vladas Diciunas), I, 13
Lit 7 — S. Daukantas, Pasakas massiu, Vilnius 1932 (— Lietuvia Tauta. IV Suppl.) p. 72 no. 44
Lit 8 — M. Dowojna-Sylwestrowics, Podania zmujdzkie, Warszawa 1894 (doubtful text)
Lit 9 — LTA 670 (5) = J. Balys, Lietuviu liaudies sakmes I, Kaunas 1940, p. 76 no. 220
Lit 10 — Balys, ibid., p. 77 no. 221 = LTA 370 (42)
Lit 11 — Edmund Veckenstedt, Die Mythen, Sagen und Legenden der Zamaïten, 1883, 2. 5 no. 89 (doubtful text)

Semitic

Arab 1 — St. John D. Seymour, Tales of King Solomon, 1924, p. 66 = Salzberger, Die Salamon-Sage, p. 79?
Arab 2 — Koran, Surah xi. 25—48, xxiii. 23—30 (many translations)
Arab 3 — Demetrius Cydonius, Translatio libri Fratris Ricardi = Migne, PG 154. 1101
Arab 4 — Zotenberg ed, Chronique de ... Tabari 1. 112 = Dähnhardt 1. 266, 272 = Joseph Hammer, Rosenöl, 1813 1. 35 = Baring-Gould, Legends of Patriarchs and Prophets 1. 112 (class as Iranian?)
Arab 5 — ad-Damari, Haya al Hayawan, tr. A. S. G. Jayakar 1906, 2. 85, 495 = C. J. B. Gerard, Le Tueur de Lions, Paris 1885, p. 238 = R. Basset, Mille et un Contes 1. 27 no. 21
Arab 6 — ad-Damari, 2. 334 = Basset, 3. 23 no. 18
Arab 7 — Ibn el-Athir, Kamil, Cairo 1302 heg. 1. 31 = Basset, 1. 28 no. 22
Arab (?) 8 — al-Kisai? See E. H. Carnoy and J. Nicolaides, Traditions populaires de l'Asie Mineure, 1889, p. 227 (swallow story)
Arab 9 — J. E. Hanauer, Folk-Lore of the Holy Land, 1935, p. 13 = Joseph Meyouhas, Bible Tales in Arab Folk Lore, 1928, p. 19
Heb 1 — Ben Sira, Alphabet = Gaster, Rumanian Bird and Beast Stories, p. 362

Heb 2 — Midrash Rabbah, ed H. Freedman and M. Simon, L 1939, vol. 1 (scattered motifs)
Heb 3 — Louis Ginsberg, Legends of the Jews, 1912—38, 1. 145 ff., 5. 167 ff. (scattered motifs)

Caucasus
Georgian 1 — A. S. Khakhanov, Chteniia v Imp. Obshch. Ist. i Drev. 172—173 (1895), 168

Iranian
Iran 1 — Hamzah Ispahensis or Avendasp = Dh 1. 260 = F. Spiegel, Eranische Alterthumskunde, 1871—78, 1. 519, 521
Iran 2 — Adam Olearius, Voyages très-Curieux ... en Muscovie, Tartarie et Perse, 2 ed., Amsterdam 1727, 1. 787 = "du Paraphraste Persan de l'Alcoran" = Montesquieu, Lettres persanes, Oeuvres, 1908, 3. 23 (lettre 18)
Iran 3 = Tabari? (Arab 4)

Kurdish (Yezidi)
Kurd 1 — M. Dragomanov, Sbornik za Narod. Umot. 10 (1894), 62 = Dh 1. 280
Kurd 2 — Gertrude Forde, A Lady's Tour in Corsica, 1880, 2. 174 = A. J. Chamberlain, Am Ur-Quell, NF 4 (1893), 129 = Dh 1. 279
Kurd 3 — J. Menant, Les Yezidis, 1872, p. 85

Siberia
Altai 1 — Anderson, Nordasiatische Flutsagen 1923, p. 18 no. 13 = V. Verbickij, Vostochnoje Obozrenije 21 (1882) p. 9 no. 30 = Verbickij, Altajskije inorodcy, Moscow 1893, p. 102 no. 8
Altai 2 — the same, other versions
Buriat 1 — Skazaniya buryat, in Zapiski Vostochno-Sibirskago Otdela Russkago Geograficheskago Obshchestva 1. 2 (1890), p. 71 = Uno Holmberg, Mythology of All Races IV (1927), p. 361
Buriat 2 — the same
Buriat (Sagaiyes) 3 — the same, Holmberg p. 362 — Holmberg (Harva), FFC 125, p. 130

Africa
Berber 1 — R. Basset, Contes populaires berbères, Paris 1887, p. 25, 149 no. 12 = Dh 1. 272
Berber 2 — Belkassem ben Sedira, Cours de langue Kabyle, 1re partie no. IV, Algiers 1887, pp. ccxv, ccxlviii (see Basset)
Berber 3 — J.-B., Labat, Nouvelle Relation de l'Afrique occidentale ... Sénégal, Paris 1728, 2. 35

Asia — Annamese
Annam 1 — G. Paris, Zs. des Vereins für Volkskunde 13 (1903), 22 = Dh 1. 280

Gipsy
Zig 1 — Estonian Folklore Archives II 61, 419/20 (5) — P. Voolaine = Let 1
Zig 2 — see FF 34

Armenia
Arm 1 — Jacques Issaverdens, The Uncanonical Writings of the Old Testament, Venice 1907, p. 43 (= MS San Lazzaro, Venice, 729 by Vartan), 16—17th cent.

Science and the Universality of the Flood

DON CAMERON ALLEN

Thus far we have concentrated on the flood myth as a traditional narrative with attention to its geographical distribution and its content. Such matters are commonplace in the formal study of myth. But we must remember that the flood myth is a special case. For no other myth has been examined so meticulously from the point of view of its being reconciled with the findings of science.

In struggles between folklore and science, folklore generally is defeated. Myths are typically discarded as being "prescientific" primitive explanations of the world which may be retained as pretty metaphors to serve as ornaments or inspirations for literary flights of fancy, but which in the end must yield the higher ground to science. The difficulty in this instance, as has already been observed, is that the myth in question, the flood myth, is part of Genesis. Hence to discard the flood myth constitutes a rejection of Genesis as bona fide truth. With the principle of pars pro toto, *rejection of the part hints at rejection of the whole. Accordingly, it has increasingly fallen to defenders of the faith to sustain the historical truth of the flood myth in the face of ever more powerful science. This battle has raged unceasingly over the centuries and it is not yet over.*

For this reason, the fortunes of the flood myth have been an integral part of the history of science, especially but by no means exclusively geology. (Paleontology, for example, is also enmeshed in the debate.) Some of the issues raised in the struggle to retain the flood myth as compatible with science include the probable age of the formation of the earth, the time of mankind's first appearance on the earth, and whether the earth and man were instantaneously formed by a divine creator or whether both evolved over long periods of time into their present form. Related to these matters is the theory of uniformitarianism—the idea that scientific principles articulated or recognized now were in effect from the beginning of time. (If one were opposed to uniformitarianism, one could argue that the scientific principles empirically observable now were not in force eons ago but came into being later, after *the initial creation occurred as described in Genesis.)*

We begin our consideration of the flood versus science in the seventeenth

Reprinted from Don Cameron Allen, *The Legend of Noah: Renaissance Rationalism in Art, Science, and Letters* (Urbana: University of Illinois Press, 1963), pp. 92–112.

century in an essay by Don Cameron Allen, Sir William Osler professor of English Literature at Johns Hopkins University, who wrote an entire book on the impact of the flood myth in the Renaissance to which the interested reader may wish to refer. Most of the arguments stated in the late seventeenth century would be restated in the eighteenth and nineteenth centuries. Although science progressed and its theories became ever more sophisticated, the fundamental issues remained the same.

During the later half of the seventeenth century, the attempt to prove that the Flood was universal became an obsession of scientists, but reason, rather than supernatural revelation, was the great instrument of this attempt. Rationalism, dismayed by the perplexities that it had brought about, became repentant and strove to undo itself by demonstrating that the data of revelation were correct. The uninterrupted struggle between the mind and the heart is a rather interesting example of the dilemma of the Renaissance. As Pascal said, the heart has reasons that the reason never knows; but the late seventeenth century attempted to dissect these reasons and to show that the heart and the mind were at peace.

One of the directions taken by these exponents of reasonable unreason in their effort to place Moses on the throne of truth was governed by what we should call "comparative mythology." The fevered explorations of the bright new world were now more than a hundred years old and from them men had learned much about the traditions and legends of strange and distant peoples. We remember that the similarities between the pagan accounts of the Flood and the Hebrew account had not been unnoticed by the mediaeval chroniclers, but the new knowledge of other lands indicated that the story of the Flood was universally known. Grotius, using the travel accounts of Acosta and Herrera as his authorities, observed that the Flood legend was familiar to the natives of Cuba, Mexico, and Nicaragua.[1] Stillingfleet, who had read Martinius' reports on the Chinese, discovered that they, too, had a Flood legend,[2] a notion handsomely elaborated in John Webb's *The Antiquity of China.*[3] Patrick sums up the general attitude that we find repeated so often.

> And now it appears that the Americans have had a Tradition of it (as credible Authors, *Acosta, Herrera,* and others inform us) which saith,

[1] *De veritate religionis Christianae, Opera theologica* (London, 1679), III, 18–20.

[2] *Origines sacrae* (London, 1709), pp. 345–6.

[3] *Op. cit.* (London, 1678), pp. 60–78.

> The whole Race of Mankind was destroyed by the Deluge, except some few that escaped. They are the Words of *Augustin Corata,* concerning the *Peruvian* Tradition. And *Lupus Gomara* saith the same from those of *Mexico.* And if we can believe *Mart. Martinius's* History of *China,* there is the like among the People of that Country.[4]

The syllogism is, of course, obvious. If every race has a theory of a universal Flood, then there must have been one. But there were other arguments drawn from other fields of science which could be summoned as character witnesses to the veracity of Moses.

Several early authorities,[5] we recall, had stated that the universality of the Flood was established by the number of marine fossils found in regions far removed from the sea. This doctrine would hardly be overlooked in an age that was devoted to the collecting of such interesting natural objects. Fossils like the *Lapis Islebianus* and petrified shark's teeth (glossopetrae) are described by the sixteenth century authorities, Gesner[6] and Agricola; the latter tells even of finding fossil shells, sea hedgehogs, murex, star fish, and other calcified marine animals in the mountains near Verona.[7] Neither of these elementary paleontologists, however, seems to have realized what these objects really were. Agricola says that they are composed of earth and water, and he assumes that they developed in the earth, for at this time it was thought that minerals grew in the soil after the fashion of plants.[8] This theory persisted well into the seventeenth century, for Lachmund, who collected a great many of these petrifacts near Hildesheim, states that they were probably natural objects turned into stone in the course of time; nevertheless, he also believes that they may have been produced by the plastic powers of the earth.[9] As far as I know, Sir Matthew Hale is the first Englishman to use the evidence of fossils as arguments for the universality of the Flood.

There are only two ways, Hale writes in *The Primitive Origination of Mankind,* to explain these petrifacts. They were either left by the receding sea or they are a *lusus naturae.* In support of the second hypothesis one can say that these remains are found too far from the sea

[4] *A Commentary upon the Historical Books of the Old Testament* in *Works* (London, 1738), I, 35.

[5] Tertullian, *Liber de pallio, PL,* II, 1033–4; Pseudo-Eustatius, *Commentarius in hexameron, PG,* XVIII, 752; Michael Glyca, *Annales, PG,* CLVIII, 247.

[6] *De rerum fossilium, gemmarum, lapidum* (Zurich, 1565), pp. 162–8.

[7] *De natura fossilium, Opera* (Basel, 1558), pp. 249–52.

[8] *Op. cit.,* p. 172.

[9] Ορυκτογραφια *Hildesheimensis, sive admirandorum fossilium, quae in tractu Hildesheimensi reperiuntur descriptio* (Hildesheim, 1669), p. 39.

coast to be deposits of the sea and that the fossils found in any particular country are never comparable to the live sea animals of the nearest ocean. Scallop shells are found, for example, in the ditches of Antwerp, but live scallops are not known on the Dutch littoral. The proponents of the second theory also point out that the stone in which these objects are found is always native to that region.

> For my own part, I have seen such apparent Evidences in and near the place where I live of things of this nature, that I am satisfied that many of them are but Relicks of Fish-shells left by the Sea, and there in length of time actually Petrified; and the Instance of the great Fish-sceleton found at *Cammington* seems an undeniable Evidence thereof. And I remember in my youth, in the Lisne of a Rock at *Kingscote* in *Glocestershire,* I found at least a bushel of Petrified Cockles actually distinct one from another, each near as big as my Fist: and at *Adderly,* mentioned by Mr. *Cambden,* about 40 or 50 Years since those Configurations of great Shells in Stones were frequently found, and for their curiosity, as many as could be found were taken up by several persons and carried away since which time, for above 20 Years last past, there are none, or very few found; which nevertheless if they had been the Product of the Plastick power of the Earth, would have been Annually re-produced.[10]

Some of these shells, Hale thinks, were left by the receding sea, but others were produced by a seminal fermentation which is present in the sea and was spread over the earth by the action of the universal Deluge.

Hale's interest in marine fossils was shared by many Englishmen. In 1683, a report on a trove of fossil shells found near Hunton, Kent, was read before the Royal Society by Hatley, who believed that they grew in the soil.[11] A dozen years later, Dr. James Brewer told of finding a bed of petrified shells near Reading, Berkshire;[12] and Stephen Gray described a similar deposit near Reculver, Kent.[13] In 1700/1, Abraham de la Pryme told the Society that a great quantity of fossilized shellfish had been unearthed in a quarry near Broughton in Lincolnshire. The prelate-naturalist has an explanation of them, too.

> From all this it sufficiently appears, that there was a time when the water overflowed all our earth, which could be none but the Noachian deluge.

[10] *Op. cit.* (London, 1677), pp. 192–3. Leonardo Da Vinci did not believe that fossils were produced by nature but that they were originally living organisms that were caught in the sea mud and turned in time to stone. *The Notebooks* (Ed. MacCurdy, N.Y., 1939), pp. 311–13.

[11] *Philosophical Transactions of the Royal Society* (ed. Hutton, Shaw, Pearson, London, 1809), III, 4–5.

[12] *Ibid.,* IV, 471.

[13] *Ibid.,* IV, 549.

> And hence it happens that we find shells and shellfish, and the bones of other fish and quadrupeds, and fruits, &c petrified and lodged in stone, rocks, mountains, quarries, and pits, over the whole earth; for it was then the proper place for them to breed in, and upon, and to be found at this time. And as all countries were thus raised out of the bottom of the antediluvian sea and lakes, so that part of the country about Broughton appears manifestly to have been, in the antediluvian world, the bottom of some fresh water lake, because those are fresh water shell-fish that are found there, and the bed on which they breed, was a fine blue clay, which is the color of the stone to this day. Which bed, by the power of the subterraneous streams and effluvia, were turned by degrees into stone with all the fishes therein.[14]

We shall hear more about the fossils of marine animals as a proof of the universality of the Flood, but there were other speculations of a similar scientific nature that led to the hypothesis of Thomas Burnet, a hypothesis that begot a great controversy and focused men's attention on what was later called the "lessons of the rocks."

It was almost an intellectual pastime among a certain section of the supporters of the universal Flood theory to imagine the changes wrought by the Flood on the surface of the earth. We come on some of these notions in the Middle Ages, for we are informed in *The Mirrour of the World* that the floating Isles of Delos were created by the Flood.[15] But it is in the Renaissance that these notions truly flourish. Gonzaga de Salas, we learn from Calovius,[16] evolved a theory that the earth was completely destroyed by the Flood and all the antediluvian continents were buried in the depths of the sea. This theory, of course, is an appendage of the old Syrian heresy that a new world was created after the Flood. Kircher was also impressed by the idea that postdiluvians lived in an altered world. The earth, he observes, is regularly remolded by six major forces, and, as a result of the watery catastrophe, the power of these forces was enhanced. To illustrate his conclusions, Kircher prints a map of the world on which he indicates the alterations brought about by the wash of the Flood waters. His map suggests that there was once a solid land bridge between Brazil and Greenland and between Southern California and Chile. The Argentine and British Columbia were, he thinks, once at the bottom of the sea, and Madagascar was formerly part of Africa as the British Isles were of Europe and the East Indies of Asia.[17] This form of speculation apparently became

[14] *Ibid.*, IV, 523–4.

[15] *Op. cit.* (ed. Prior, London, 1913), EETS, CX, 94–5.

[16] *Biblia Testamenti Veteris et Novi illustrata* (Dresden and Leipzig, 1719), p. 265.

[17] *De arca Noe* (Amsterdam, 1675), pp. 187–93.

so popular that a public lecture on the subject was given in 1696 at Stockholm by Haraldus Valerius, Professor of Geometry.[18]

But there was another form of speculation about the nature of the earth before the Flood that led more directly to Burnet's theory. Some of the best thinkers of the Middle Ages had held that the earth at one time had been more of a sphere than it now is. In the *De sex dierum creatione liber* attributed to Bede, a man of the Renaissance would read that some men thought that at the beginning of things the world was flatter.[19] Alcuin also stated that there were some in his day who thought that the primordial earth was not so uneven as the present one and that the mountains of those early days were not so high as they are now.[20] Rabanus Maurus[21] and Petrus Comestor[22] echo this statement. In the *Glossa ordinaria* on Genesis 7, anyone who owned an annotated Vulgate could read: "Licet sint qui putent nec terrae qualitatem nec altitudinem montium tantam fuisse ante diluvium qualis et quanta est hodie." It is consequently not surprising to find this notion attacked by a Protestant theologian, David Pareus, who tells us of the nonsensical notion of those who say that before the Flood the earth was shaped like an apple and that the mountains were produced by the Deluge itself.[23] The same notion is possibly back of the statement of Spenser's communist giant, who declares,

> Therefore I will throw down these mountains hie,
> And make them levell with the lowly plaine:
> These towring rocks, which reach unto the skie,
> I will thrust downe into the deepest maine,
> And as they were them equalize againe.[24]

This idea became the seed of Burnet's new theory of the earth.

In 1681, Thomas Burnet, a Cambridge man, printed his *Telluris theoria sacra: orbis nostri originem et mutationes generales, quas aut jam subiit, aut olim subiturus est, complectens. Libri duo priores de diluvio*

[18] *De habitu terrae tempore diluvii,* Stockholm, 1696; Valerius says that all land bridges were broken, all volcanoes put out, etc.

[19] *Op. cit., PL,* XCIII, 222; the modern text reads *plena* for *plana.*

[20] *Interrogationes et responsiones in Genesin, PL,* C, 530.

[21] *Commentaria in Genesin, PL,* CVII, 519.

[22] *Historia scholastica, PL,* CXCVIII, 1084–5.

[23] *In Genesin Mosis* (Geneva, 1614), p. 804. Antonio de Torquemada writes in his *Jardin de flores curiosas* that some say "the whole world before the time of the flood was plaine and levell, without any hill or valley at all." V. Harris, *All Coherence Gone* (Chicago, 1949), p. 96.

[24] *F. Q.,* V. ii. 28.1–5.

et paradiso. This volume, which was issued in an edition of twenty-five copies, appeared in English in 1684 as *The Theory of the Earth: Containing an Account of the Original of the Earth and of All the Changes Which It Hath Already Undergone or Is to Undergo, Till the Consummation of All Things.* The English version is a fuller but more popular rewriting of the Latin text. In 1689, a new edition of the Latin text, appearing simultaneously in London and Amsterdam, contained two new books, a "De conflagratione mundi" and a "De novis coelis et nova terra." The four books were turned into English and were printed with the author's *A Review of the Theory of the Earth* and with his answers to Erasmus Warren's attack on his theory in 1680. The book was reissued many times during the eighteenth century and the appendix of replies to opponents grew. The last edition appeared in 1826, and we know that even at this late date Burnet had an ardent reader in William Wordsworth and S. T. Coleridge.

Burnet thinks of his theory as a great rational contribution to the history of man and his earth; he takes undeniable pleasure in this fruit of his own intellectual effort.

> For there is no sort of joy more grateful to the mind of man, than that which ariseth from the invention of Truth; especially when 'tis hard to come by. Every man hath a delight suited to his Genius, and as there is pleasure in the right exercise of any faculty, so especially in that of Right-reasoning; which is still the greater by how much the consequences are more clear, and the chains of them more long: There is no Chase so pleasant, methinks, as to drive a Thought, by good conduct, from one end of the World to the other; and never to lose sight of it till it fall into Eternity, where all things are lost as to our knowledge.[25]

Talking something like Hooker, who had said that reason was man's first guide and after reason the church, Burnet announces that reason "is to be our first Guide; and where that falls short, or any other just occasion offers itself, we may receive further light and confirmation from the Sacred writings." This is the shape of the new Christian rationalism; the community of saints, we see, had cut across country since the time of Bernard. Having announced his basic principles, Burnet now plunges into the ancient and wearying problem of how sufficient water for the Flood might have been provided by purely natural means.

It would take eight oceans, according to Burnet's calculations, to

[25] *Op. cit.* (London, 1684), p. 6. I follow the English text, but I give the parallel references, when they occur, in the Latin.

cover the world to the depths mentioned by Moses.[26] Now this weight of water could not have been obtained by forty days of rain, for in a typical steady downpour the precipitation never exceeds two inches an hour. In forty days of rain, this maximum rate would yield only 160 feet of water.[27] The supposed overflow of the seas would add nothing to this quantity, because it would simply be like emptying one vessel into another. The vessel of the sea would be emptied by evaporation and would have to be filled with something.[28] The idea that the waters above the firmament were used to make up the required amount is absurd. If the firmament is solid, water could not pass through it; if it is not solid, it could not retain water. But even if the necessary eight oceans of water could be assembled to produce a Flood, how could they be eventually drained away? All of these so-called scientific explanations of the Flood, Burnet thinks, have done no more than make the Biblical account incredible. He proposes to give a reasonable explanation that will "silence the Cavils of Atheists, satisfie the inquisitive, and recommend them to the belief and acceptance of all reasonable persons."[29]

Now there are people who would "cut the Knot when we cannot loose it"; they say that God simply created a miracle of water. In saying this, they oppose the views of Augustine, Moses, and St. Peter, all of whom have said that the Flood was achieved by natural means. They commit the error of making God create after Creation.[30] The most ingenious explanation of the Flood so far, Burnet feels, is the theory that the air was condensed into water, but this theory stands on very feeble legs. The whole problem, he writes, has resulted in the growing belief that the Flood was a purely local affair and was limited to the land of Judaea. He cannot subscribe to this doctrine for several reasons. In the sixteen generations prior to the Flood (assuming that the patriarchs multiplied at a normal rate) 10,737,418,240 people would have been born; hence it stands to reason that a great part of the world must have been populated by sinners. If the Flood had been limited to Palestine, many men could have escaped it by simply crossing the border and there would have been no need for Noah to build an Ark. Then, too, the fact that the rainbow is a universal phenomenon and the fact that all

[26] *Ibid.,* p. 11; *Telluris theoria* (London, 1681), pp. 10–11.

[27] *Ibid.,* p. 13; *Telluris,* pp. 12–13.

[28] *Ibid.,* p. 15.

[29] *Ibid.,* p. 17; *Telluris,* pp. 13–14.

[30] *Ibid.,* pp. 19–20.

peoples have an account of the Flood proves that the catastrophe was worldwide.[31]

Burnet is positive that by these arguments he has disposed of the theory of a limited Flood, yet he admits that "the excessive quantity of water is the great difficulty, and the removal of it afterward." The required eight oceans of water, he writes, preyed on his mind; then it suddenly came to him that the world might have had a different form in antediluvian times. In earlier works he had come on the notion that the earth once had more "plainness and equality" than it now has, and this suggestion had been enforced by what he had lately read in Sir Matthew Hale's book.[32] On second thought, however, he perceived that this early "smoothness" of the earth was not enough to account for the Deluge and the present condition of the earth.[33] So after ardent speculation, he came on the truth.

The antediluvian world, he thinks, "was smooth, regular, uniform; without Mountains, and without Sea."[34] But can this basic axiom be proved? The demonstration is really simple. When the earth rose out of chaos (and Burnet imagines chaos to be a spherical mass of unassorted elements), the heaviest elements went to the center and formed a hard core. The water being the next heaviest made a solid sphere about this core. The air which was about this revolving mass was impregnated with fine particles that were in themselves lighter than water, and in time they separated from the air and fell like a snow on the oily face of the watery sphere. Alighting on the water, these particles coalesced, hardened, and formed an outer crust that contained the waters as a wine skin contains the wine. It is to this process that the Scriptures refer when they say, "God hath founded the earth upon the seas," or "To Him that extended the earth above the waters," or "He shut up the water of the Sea as in bags and laid up the Abyss as in storehouses."[35]

[31] *Ibid.*, pp. 22–8.

[32] Burnet refers to the following passage in *The Primitive Origination:* For first, although I take this Flood to be somewhat more than Natural, and a thing instituted by the Will of God, yet do I not esteem it a thing purely Supernatural or Miraculous, neither do I suppose those Waters created *de novo,* nor sent out of the Orbs of Heaven to drown the Earth: I do not think the Face of the Earth and Waters were altogether the same before the Universal Deluge, and after; but possibly the Face of the Earth was more even than now it is, the Seas possibly more dilate and extended, and not so deep as now; the Waters possibly more than now (p. 187).

[33] *Ibid.*, pp. 34–51.

[34] *Ibid.*, p. 52; *Telluris*, pp. 31–3.

[35] *Ibid.*, pp. 51–62.

Once it has been assumed that the original earth had a hard core surrounded by concentric layers of water and earthy crust, the mechanics of the Deluge become, according to Burnet, easy to explain. If the outer crust is ruptured and huge pieces of it fall into the watery layer, Archimedes' principle produces the Deluge. But how did the rupture come about? Burnet assumes that in the antediluvian world the procession of seasons did not occur, and so in time the heat of a constant sun not only turned much of the subterranean water into vapor, creating thereby an intense pressure, but also dried and cracked the external crust. When the crust split, the waters oozed forth and spread over the world; and as the fragments of the crust fell into the sphere of water, volumes of displaced water surged over the earth. Since the surface of the earth was as smooth as a ball, a not very great volume of water was required to create a deluge fifteen cubits deep.[36]

Burnet then collates his theory with the Mosaic account and with other scriptural passages that seem to him to illustrate his conclusions.[37] He argues that the first creation, in keeping with the perfect nature of God, must have been symmetrical, and he asks his readers to tell him how antediluvian man could have settled the whole earth if it was then as rugged and as watery as it is now.[38] He invites his readers to look at the globe of the world, not at a flat map, so that they will see the great diluvian cracks that are now the Atlantic and Pacific Oceans and the Mediterranean Sea.[39] He conceives of the mountains as the crumpled ruins of the former crust of the earth,[40] and he thinks of earthquakes as great modern proofs that the old top crust is still breaking off and sliding into the abyss.[41] But he does not stop in this sublunary sphere, for he imagines that the same natural process has taken place in every planet except Jupiter.[42]

This theory of Burnet's is the most ingenious attempt to explain the mechanics of the Deluge that I have seen, but even the author seems to realize that his theory cannot be scientifically established; hence, he retreats into a sort of intuitive barricade that would have been worthy of the most ardent enthusiast.

[36] *Ibid.*, pp. 66–77; *Telluris*, pp. 48–57.

[37] *Ibid.*, pp. 78–94.

[38] *Ibid.*, p. 129.

[39] *Ibid.*, pp. 130–9.

[40] *Ibid.*, pp. 139–45; *Telluris*, pp. 82–98.

[41] *Ibid.*, p. 121.

[42] *Ibid.*, p. 168.

> But how fully or easily soever these things may answer Nature, you will say, it may be, that all this is but an *Hypothesis;* that is, a kind of fiction or supposition that things were so and so at first, and by the coherence and agreement of the Effects with such a supposition, you would argue and prove that they were really so. This I confess is true, this is the method, and if we would know any thing in Nature further than our senses go, we can know it no otherwise than by an Hypothesis. When things are either too little for our senses, or too remote and inaccessible, we have no way to know the inward Nature, and the causes of their sensible properties, but by reasoning upon an *Hypothesis.* If you would know, for example, of what parts Water, or any other Liquor consists, they are too little to be discern'd by the Eye, you must therefore take a supposition concerning their invisible figure and form, and if that agrees and gives the reason of all their sensible qualities, you understand the nature of Water. In like manner, if you would know the nature of a Comet, or of what matter the Sun consists, which are things inaccessible to us, you can do this no otherwise than by an *Hypothesis;* and if that *Hypothesis* be easie and intelligible, and answers all the *Phaenomena* of those two bodies, you have done as much as a *Philosopher* or as *Humane reason* can do.[43]

If Burnet had doubts about his hypothesis, there were many others who had them too.

Almost as soon as the Latin text of Burnet's theory reached the continent, it produced a reply of German origin, the *Animadversiones in T. Burnetii Telluris theoriam sacram* by C. Wagner printed at Leipzig in 1683. A similar attack by Bishop Herbert Croft was issued at London in 1685 with the title *Some Animadversions upon a Book Intituled The Theory of the Earth.* The first substantial rejoinder, however, was Erasmus Warren's *Geologia: Or a Discourse Concerning the Earth Before the Deluge* which was published at London in 1690. In his preface to the reader, Warren explains that he had originally intended only to write a letter to the learned Mr. Burnet, but his "pen growing warm" a book resulted. He also observes that the chief fault of Burnet's book is that it strikes against the roots of religion, and it is to safeguard those roots that he has written the *Geologia.*

Warren first indicates how much philosophy has come up in the world since the Middle Ages and admits that it is useful in proving the existence of God and telling man about His nature. It also can help in overcoming idolatry, in vindicating the Gospels, and in teaching the immortality of the soul, the resurrection of the body, the punishment

[43] *Ibid.,* p. 149.

of the damned, and the final fiery consumption of the world. One should not, consequently, condemn philosophy or undervalue it; nevertheless, one should not esteem it so much as Mr. Burnet has done.[44] Warren now proceeds to argue that Burnet's theory of the evolution of the earth from chaos would have taken more time than the six days mentioned in Genesis.[45] The story of the creation, he insists, is to be understood literally, not mystically;[46] and so he offers theological, scientific, and philosophical exceptions to Burnet's thesis. Then, in the fifteenth chapter, he parades his own theory.

Warren's notion is that the Flood was fifteen cubits higher than the average level of the earth, but not fifteen cubits higher than the highest mountain. If the waters rose to a height of fifteen cubits in Switzerland, they would be four or five times higher in other lower European lands. The "common surface" of the earth (by which he means an average of the highest nonmountainous surfaces) was, according to Warren, submerged everywhere by fifteen cubits. This, he thinks, is what Moses meant when he said "fifteen cubits upward the waters did prevail." By "the great deeps," Warren assumes, are meant the caverns in the high rocks from which the waters ran down, reservoirs, as it were, in which vast pockets of water had been stored since the beginning of things. With this hypothesis before us, Warren contends that it is no longer necessary to believe in Burnet's theory, or to admit supercelestial waters, the creation of new water, the condensation of air into water, or any of the other outrageous notions that have been advanced to explain the Flood. The heretical doctrine that the Deluge was limited to Palestine is also expunged by this new theory. Warren further points out that his idea agrees with 2 Peter 3:5–6, where one reads: "The Heavens were of old, and the Earth standing out of the Water and in the Water, whereby the World that then was, being overflowed with Water, perished." Finally, this doctrine makes it easier to understand how the world was quickly inhabited after the Flood, since there was not so much water to be drained away; it also avoids all those theories about the altered surface of the earth, "which Geography hitherto never dreamt of."[47] Such, in brief, is the nature of Warren's attack and his substitute theory, but the trouble did not end here.

One of the most important results of this early discussion of Bur-

[44] *Op. cit.*, pp. 2–44.

[45] *Ibid.*, pp. 46–58.

[46] *Ibid.*, p. 71.

[47] *Ibid.*, pp. 299–333. Burnet responded in 1690 in *An Answer to the Late Exceptions Made by Mr. Erasmus Warren Against The Theory of the Earth.*

net's hypothesis was that it induced the eminent naturalist John Ray to publish his *Miscellaneous Discourses Concerning the Dissolution and Changes of the World* (1692). This work, which was dedicated to Tillotson, was so popular that it was reissued in 1693 as Three Physico-theological Discourses, Concerning I. The Primitive Chaos and Creation of the World. II. The General Deluge, Its Causes and Effects. III. The Dissolution of the World and Future Conflagration. This second enlarged version of the *Discourses* is essentially an attempt to speculate about the problems that Burnet's theory had introduced to the world.

Ray believed in a universal Deluge, but he did not know how to prove that one had occurred. In a brief introductory chapter, he summarizes the historical arguments for the universal notion, but it is rather clear that his heart is not made quiet by these proofs. He then tries to explain how the Deluge could have been produced, and he sets out to find the eight oceans of water that theologians and scientists had thought necessary for the drowning of the world. Ray assumes that all the waters of the earth are connected by underground channels into a great circulatory system not unlike that of the human animal. The seas and lakes without outlets are drained into the oceans by these subterranean aqueducts; and it is by this vast interconnecting series of moist passages that the watery equilibrium of the world is maintained. In one day the average rainfall of the earth amounts to half an ocean, and this water slips down the declivities of the globe to the seas. Should this ration of water increase, the water content of the world rises uniformly everywhere. Now if it would rain all day for forty days, eighty additional oceans of water would be produced. Ray thinks this surplus would destroy the balance and cause a great flood.[48] He offers this idea as a tentative hypothesis; he will not stake his scientific reputation on it. He does not find, for instance, that Warren's theory of average levels is completely untenable;[49] he is willing to grant that perhaps America, being uninhabited, was not submerged;[50] and he thinks that Burnet's arguments against the notion of a local Flood are sound.[51] Nevertheless, if either of these other ideas is correct, his own thesis, he says, is more probable. But he is far more interested in the paleontological proofs of the universality of the Flood than in theories about the sources of sufficient water.

Ray began to collect fossils as early as 1661 and to report on his

[48] *Three Physico-theological Discourses* (London, 1693), pp. 75–118.

[49] *Ibid.*, p. 119.

[50] *Ibid.*, pp. 122–3.

[51] *Ibid.*, p. 73.

findings to the Royal Society. In that year we know that he visited Whitby and gathered some specimens of what was then called "the serpent stone" or "cornua ammonis." In 1662 he went to Alderly in Gloucestershire, "where we found plenty of the cockle-shells and scallop stones but no cornua ammonis," and to Keynsham where he saw "the serpent stones and star stones found there." Shortly after this he departed for the continent, and he tells us in his *Observations Topographical, Moral and Physiological, Made in a Journey Through Part of the Low-countries, Germany, Italy and France; with a Catalogue of Plants Not Native of England* (1673) of the fossil remains that he saw in these countries.[52] Upon his return to England, Ray seems to have read all the authorities on this subject with great care;[53] hence we are not surprised to find a large section of the *Discourses* devoted to the subject of fossils.

In 1684 Ray wrote to his friend Tancred Robinson about his own theory of the origin of fossils. This theory, illustrated by three plates, and elaborately reworked and augmented with additional information, is found in the *Discourses* under the title "Of formed stones." Ray first summarizes the orthodox notion that these petrifacts were shaped in the earth by the plastic powers of nature. He objects to this idea because it contradicts a still older one that Nature designs everything to an efficiently determined end. Then, too, one often finds unpetrified shells in strata of pure sand at a great distance from the sea, indicating either that they were not growths of Nature or that Nature produces useless objects. Teeth and fish bones are likewise found in the strata; moreover, "Mr. Doody has in his custody a petrify'd lump of Fishes, on some of which the Scales themselves still remain." These objects cannot be the results of the plastic forces, for according to Ray's way of thinking Nature never produced a tooth without a jaw. But if she did, why are not other objects resembling other animal parts found? The best argument against this, Ray thinks, is the explanation its proponents offer of the means by which these objects are created, for they say that the shaping force is a sort of crystallization. This explanation

[52] For an excellent account of Ray's interest in fossils see C. E. Raven, *John Ray, Naturalist: His Life and Works* (Cambridge, 1942), pp. 419–51.

[53] Ray read the epoch-making *De solido intra solidum naturaliter contento* of Nicholas Steno, the *Micrographia* of Hooke, and the *Mundus subterraneus* of Kircher. In the Amsterdam issue of 1678 of the latter work, the section on fossils is found in II, 40–69. He also read the early papers of Lister that were incorporated in the famous *Historia conchyliorum* and Agricola's *De natura fossilium,* Becanus' *Origines Antwerpianae;* Boetius de Boot's *Gemmarum et lapidum historia,* Bauhin's *Historia fontis Bollensis,* Scaliger's *Exercitationes,* Palissy's *Discours admirable de la nature des eaux,* and Laetius' *De Gemmis et lapidibus.*

is absurd, Ray reasons, because all natural crystals are simple, because it is impossible to imagine a crystallization that would result in a shell with two valves and a joint, because there are more varieties of petrefacts than there are crystals, and because such forms have never been produced in laboratory experiments with crystallization. But if they are not the result of Nature's plastic powers, how did fossils occur?

The pat answer in the past to this question had been the Flood, but Ray is too much of a scientist to grasp at this straw. If the originals of the fossils had been laid down during the Deluge, they would be scattered thinly over the whole surface of the earth. Unfortunately, fossils are always found in clumps and in deep stratifications that could not possibly have been deposited by a Deluge that lasted something short of a year. Secondly, though Noah was urged to preserve specimens of every creature, some of the fossils that Ray has seen have no modern counterpart. There is nothing like the cornua ammonis known to modern man, and other petrified shellfish that he has seen are much larger than their seventeenth century counterparts. This troubles Ray very much, for if these fossils were really deposited by the Flood, then some links have been lost from the great chain of being, a notion abhorrent to him and to all other men of his time. He concludes then that fossils do not prove the universality of the Flood and contends that their similars are still to be found in the vast oceanic deeps. The rush of waters through the great underground caverns drags them from their briny perches and casts them forth on distant spots of the earth during periods when the great aqueous balance is upset by unprecedented rainfall. Undoubtedly something of this sort occurred during the Noachian Flood, but it must also have happened during floods before that time and it has probably occurred since.[54]

For Ray the fossils are no proof of the universality of the Flood; they are rather something disturbing, something impossible to explain. In a special appendix to this section, he describes the dreadful philosophic and theological consequences of the theory that the fossils are *lusus naturae* and of the suggestion that some species of marine life "have been lost out of the world."[55] Were it not for his burning desire to believe in the Scriptures and the opinions of theologians, Ray might have made a great name for himself in the annals of human progress. The key was in his hand, but he refused to look for the lock. He was perplexed by the series of strata that he had seen in pits and in uptilted sections of mountains and wondered how long it had taken

[54] *Ibid.,* pp. 127–62.

[55] *Ibid.,* pp. 162 a–162 d.

for these layers to be deposited. He had also seen the lost cornua ammonis and other specimens of ancient life that were wanting in the modern zoologies. As early as 1673 he questioned momentarily the accuracy of the theological guess at the earth's age,[56] but he never went beyond this. Faith put a blindfold on the scientist and the key fell from his hands. But the search for a better explanation of the nature of the earth and the causes of the Deluge did not end with him.

In the same year that the second issue of Ray's *Discourses* was printed, John Beaumont brought out his *Considerations on The Theory of the Earth,* which was followed in the next year by *A Postscript to a Book . . . Entituled Considerations on Dr. Burnet's Theory of the Earth.* Both of these tracts are simply seriatim confutations of Burnet's hypothesis and add no truly new matter to the controversy. Beaumont argues, for example, that the elements did not arrange themselves according to their weight when the earth rose from chaos because a pure element is a "pure Chimaera."[57] He likewise thinks that it would be impossible for the constant heat of the sun to dry and crack the crust of the antediluvian earth, because a thermometer placed in a subterranean grotto does not show a variation between the hottest day in summer and the coldest day in winter.[58] A far more ingenious refutation and resolution of the problem than Beaumont's was offered by John Woodward, Professor of Physics in Gresham College and the founder of the Woodwardian Collection.

Woodward faces the problem of the fossils and the strata with which Ray had wrestled a few years earlier in *An Essay Toward a Natural History of the Earth and Terrestrial Bodies Especially Minerals as Also of the Sea, Rivers, and Springs. With an Account of the Universal Deluge and of the Effects That It Had upon the Earth.* Woodward says that all his observations have been made in England, where he has inspected "Grotto's, or other Natural Caverns, or Mines, Quarries, Colepits" and has jotted down observations in his journal. But this provinciality has not contented him, for he has checked his data against findings in France, Flanders, Holland, Spain, Italy, Germany, Denmark, Norway, Sweden, Barbary, Egypt, Guinea, Arabia, Syria, Persia, Malabar, China, Jamaica, Barbadoes, Virginia, New England, Brazil, and Peru. He has

[56] In the *Observations* (London, 1673), pp. 6–8, Ray says in connection with his description of a bed of cockle shells found at the depth of one hundred feet by Varenius "that of old time the bottom of the sea lay so deep and that hundred foot thickness of earth arose from the sediments of those great rivers which there emptied themselves into the sea . . . which yet is a strange thing considering the novity of the world, the age whereof, according to the usual account, is not yet 5600 years."

[57] *Op. cit.* (London, 1693), p. 28.

[58] *Ibid.*, p. 25 (33).

added to his information by studying the various strata, the fissures, and the fossils of all parts of England.[59] This sounds about as thoroughly scientific as one could ask, but it is really an evidence of Woodward's magisterial arrogance of which Ray complained to Lhwyd[60] and which eventually occasioned Woodward's expulsion from the Royal Society.[61]

Woodward begins his treatise by proving that the fossil shells are really petrified shells; they have the same specific gravity as real shells and the same chemical properties. He has shown his own collection of several hundred fossil shells to men of learning and none of them went away "dissatisfied or doubting whether these are really the very *Exuviae* of Sea-fishes or not."[62] Some of these fossils can be compared with modern shells, but others cannot for they have probably "their abode at main-sea, and which therefore are now never flung up upon the Shores."[63] But how does one account for their presence on land?

Some scientists think that these shells were brought by early inhabitants from the sea and discarded inland; others assume either that they were cast up by great tidal waves or that the earth has changed its bed and left them behind; still others suppose they were deposited by the universal Deluge. Because these reasons conflict, Woodward writes, most men thought that fossils were sports of nature.[64] He stands ready to deny that they were brought to their present sites by men, by watters passing from the sea to the heads of rivers through subterranean channels, by later and lesser floods like Deucalion's, by the separation of the waters at Creation, by the elevation of sea bottom, by the alteration or removal of seas, by the forming of river deltas, and by violent expulsion from the seas.[65] Having denied all previous theories of the origin of fossils, Woodward is now prepared to offer his own explanation, and he goes at it in the roundabout fashion so proper to a seventeenth-century thinker.

The main difficulty about all modern theories concerning the origin of fossils is that they are based, says Woodward, on ancient notions.

> Those ancient Pagan Writers were indeed very much excusable as to this matter. Philosophy was then again in its Infancy: There remaining

[59] *Op. cit.* (London, 1695), pp. 3–6.

[60] John Ray, *Further Correspondence* (ed. Gunther, London, 1928), p. 256.

[61] C. R. Weld, *A History of the Royal Society* (London, 1848), I, 352–5.

[62] *Op. cit.*, pp. 22–4.

[63] *Ibid.*, p. 25.

[64] *Ibid.*, pp. 35–8.

[65] *Ibid.*, pp. 41–3.

> but few marks of the old *Tradition,* and those much obliterated and defaced by Time; so that *they* had only dark and faint Ideas, narrow and scanty Conceptions, of Providence: and were ignorant of its Intentions, and of the *methods* of its Conduct in the Government and Preservation of the Natural World. They wanted a longer Experience of *these things:* a larger stock of Observations, and Records of the state of the Earth before their times; having, as things then stood, nothing to assist them in their Enquiries besides their own Guesses and Fancy.[66]

He does not agree with many of his contemporaries that there was an immediate written tradition after the Flood; the survivors simply drew pictures or made hieroglyphics to indicate their ideas. When the ancients found fossils, they did not understand them, because they had forgotten about the Flood and had no records of it. As a consequence of this ignorance, they invented hypotheses, which moderns unfortunately have been too ready to accept.[67] He now tells what really occurred.

When the Flood was on the earth, Woodward believes, all solid substance was dissolved into its constituent corpuscles. "I say all these were assumed up promiscuously into the Water, and sustained in it, in such manner that the Water, and Bodies in it, together made up one common confused Mass." After the Flood, everything settled towards the center according to its specific gravity. The shells of periwinkles and scallops being heaviest went down with the other substances that concreted into marble. In the lighter chalk layers were deposited the shells of the echini. The still lighter objects like the carapaces of lobsters were deposited in the upper layers with the remnants of trees and shrubs, and here they rotted and formed the fertile humus of the earth. All of this was laid down in parallels, "plain, eaven, and regular." The surface of the earth was spherical and smooth, and the water lay above it as a fluid sphere. In time, because of a thermal agent in the earth, some strata were elevated and others depressed. Caverns are breaches in the strata; mountains are elevations of strata; valleys are depressions in the strata; and islands are submerged strata.[68] This belief, one notices, is not unlike Burnet's, except that Woodward assumes that the perfect earth appeared after the Deluge and Burnet thought that it existed before.

Woodward realizes, however, that the inquiring reader will have many questions to ask. He will want to know how the solid matter of

[66] *Ibid.,* p. 55.

[67] *Ibid.,* pp. 56–8, 68–70.

[68] *Ibid.,* pp. 74–80.

the earth was dissolved when the shells and trees were not; he will wonder where the water of the Deluge was stored, how it was released, how it was removed, how the marble solidified first, how the mountains and islands were formed. All of this Woodward proposed to answer in a much larger and more technical work he was composing.[69] This larger book was also to explain all the other questions about the Deluge with which theologians and scientists had been struggling, and it was to account for the settlement of America and the postdiluvian migrations of men.[70] Unfortunately, this larger work was never printed, and so we have to console ourselves with only Woodward's assurance that he had the facts.

Woodward's book, which is an amazing diorama of wonders, concludes with an attack on Burnet,[71] whose thesis was having hard going in these years and was attacked again in 1696 by William Whiston, Newton's successor as Lucasian Professor at Cambridge. Before he printed *A New Theory of the Earth from Its Original to the Consummation of All Things,* Whiston submitted his manuscript to Newton, Wren, and Bentley for criticism. Its reception upon publication was uneven. Ray, who had been caustic in his remarks about Woodward's theory, wrote to Lhwyd: "the new theory seems to me pretty odd and extravagant and it is borrowed of Mr. Newton in great part."[72] Locke, on the other hand, went overboard for the Whistonian theory in a letter to Molyneux.

> You desire to know, what the opinion of the ingenious is, concerning Mr. Whiston's book. I have not heard any one of my acquaintance speak of it, but with great commendation, as I think it deserves. And truly, I think he is more to be admired, that he has laid down an hypothesis, whereby he has explained so many wonderful, and, before, inexplicable things in the great changes of this globe, than some of them should not go easily down with some men, when the whole was entirely new to all. He is one of those sort of writers, that I always fancy should be most esteemed and encouraged. I am always for the builders, who bring some addition to our knowledge, or at least some new thing to our thoughts. The finders of faults, the confuters and pullers down, do not only erect a barren and useless triumph upon human ignorance, but advance us nothing in the acquisition of truth.[73]

[69] *Ibid.,* pp. 107–14.

[70] *Ibid.,* pp. 162–70.

[71] *Ibid.,* pp. 246–8.

[72] Ray, *Further Correspondence,* pp. 227, 301.

[73] *The Works* (London, 1751), III, 534.

But what was this new hypothesis that so attracted the critical Mr. Locke?

The first part of Whiston's *A New Theory of the Earth* is a consideration of the nature and style of the Pentateuch. It is in the vein of Boyle's essay on that subject, but it also clearly shows that the rational considerations of Spinoza and Simon had weighed heavily on Whiston's mind. The style and nature of the Scriptures, Whiston declares, have been the cause of much confusion. Some have preferred "the common and vulgar, tho' less rational Exposition"; others have been so aware of "the wildness and unreasonableness" of that exposition that they have relegated the Scriptures to the realm of fable.[74] The whole theory of creation, Whiston points out, has depended on the dead philosophies of Aristotle and Ptolemy, who assumed that there was only one inhabited world and that the whole universe circled about it. Now we know differently.[75] The difficulty has not been helped much by the expositors of the Bible.

> And if the Reader will pardon a short Digression, and give me leave to speak a great Truth on this occasion, I cannot but observe That 'tis not the genuine Contents of the Holy Books themselves, but such unwary Interpretations of them as these, which have mainly contributed to their contempt, and been but too Instrumental to make 'em appear Absurd and Irrational to the Free Reason of Mankind. For when Men found that the Scriptures, according to the Universal Sense of Expositors, ascribed such things to God, as their plainest reason could not think compatible to a Wise Man, much less to the All-wise God; they were under a shrewd Temptation of thinking very meanly of the Bible it self, and by degrees of rejecting it, and therewith all Divine Revelation to the Sons of Men. How fatally this Malady hath spread, of late especially, I need not say; and though I fully believe the main stroke or step, as to the generality, be Vicious Dispositions and a Debauched Temper, yet how far such Ill-contriv'd, Unskilful and Unphilosophical Interpretations, or rather Misrepresentations of Scripture, particularly relating to the Material World of which we are now speaking, may have contributed to so fatal and pernicious an effect, deserves the most serious and sober consideration.[76]

Woodward would have his readers avoid all difficulties by realizing that the Genesis account of Creation refers just to this world and to no others. The other planets, he is quite ready to admit, may each have had a creation week.[77] It is on this misunderstanding that Burnet, "a

[74] *Op. cit.* (London, 1696), pp. 1–2.

[75] *Ibid.,* pp. 58–60.

[76] *Ibid.,* p. 61.

[77] *Ibid.,* pp. 68–9.

great and good man," came to grief.[78] He is now ready to state his theories and he uses the lemmata as his method of presentation.

In the antediluvian earth, Whiston states, men enjoyed a perpetual equinox, for the ecliptic and the equator were one.[79] The ecliptic intersected the present Tropic of Cancer at Paradise, "or at least at its meridian."[80] The original orbits of the planets and of the earth were perfect circles; this, he points out, is in the ancient tradition and it is true of the moons of Jupiter.[81] The Deluge was caused by a comet that descended in the plain of the ecliptic towards its perihelion on the seventeenth day of the second month after the autumnal equinox.[82] The actual passage of this comet before our earth can be proved.

Before the comet descended, the orbit of the earth was circular, and the sun, which is now in the focus nearest the place of the earth where the Deluge began, was in the center of the earth's orbit.[83] The passage of the comet can also be established by chronology. The year before the Flood was ten days, one hour, and thirty minutes shorter than it is now. The Antediluvians reckoned 355 days in the year; and since the orbit of the moon was isochronic with that of the earth, a lunar month and a solar month were the same. After the Flood, men were baffled by the change but clung to the tradition; hence, the Hebrew and Greek accounts of the Flood seem to have chronological variants. By tracing the sun and moon back on Flamsteed's tables, Whiston shows that there is no confusion between scientific findings and the Genesis account.[84] So far, so good; but Whiston has still to account for the water.

All the old attempts to explain the source of the water, Whiston thinks, are useless now that we know all about comets and their habits.

> For if we consider that a Comet is no other than a *Chaos;* including the very same Bodies, and Parts, of which our own Earth is compos'd; that the outward Regions of its *Atmosphere* are plain Vapors, or such a sort of Mist as we frequently see with us; and the Tail a column of the same Vapors, rarefied and expanded to a greater degree, as the Vapors which in the clearest Days or Nights our Air contains at present, are; and that withal such a Comet is capable of passing so close by the Body of the Earth as to involve it in its *Atmosphere* and *Tail* a considerable time, and leave prodigious quantities of the same Condensed and Expanded Va-

[78] *Ibid.,* p. 76.
[79] *Ibid.,* p. 79.
[80] *Ibid.,* p. 106.
[81] *Ibid.,* p. 110.
[82] *Ibid.,* pp. 123–6.
[83] *Ibid.,* p. 133.
[84] *Ibid.,* pp. 134–147.

> pors upon its Surface; we shall easily see that a Deluge of Waters is by no means an impossible thing; and in particular that such an individual Deluge as to the Time, Quantity, and Circumstances which *Moses* describes, is no more so, but fully accountable, that it *might* be, nay almost demonstrable that it really *was*.[85]

So the diluvian comet not only produced great tides in the seas, but almost single-handedly overwhelmed the earth with the vast quantities of water in its head and tail. But the Scriptures say that Noah entered the Ark on the day that the rains began; hence Whiston has to explain how the patriarch avoided being swept away in the vast celestial cloudburst. This difficulty is easy to explain. The comet, we remember, descended close to the terrestrial paradise, but the Ark was situated slightly to the east of this point; consequently Noah had almost twenty-four hours of reasonably fair weather before the diurnal motion brought him into the full rage of the comet. Then, too, the first burst of rain was from the head of the comet; and fifty to fifty-five days later, another rain was produced by the tail sweeping past the earth. When Whiston calculates the amount of water supplied by the abyss and the comet, he discovers that the earth was covered to an average depth of 10,821 feet. If one allows for the area occupied by the mountains, this mass of water would make for a general depth of three miles, which would be sufficient to cover the top of Mt. Caucasus, the highest peak in the ancient world.[86]

The anxious Bible student of the seventeenth century now had three theories to poultice his doubts. He could select Burnet's hypothesis of the smooth earth and the falling crust, or Woodward's doctrine on the dissolved and solidifying earth, or Whiston's on the great comet. But men were not willing to let him make a choice. In 1696 Archibald Lovell ran tilting at Burnet in *A Summary of Material Heads Which May Be Enlarged and Improved into a Compleat Answer to Dr. Burnet's Theory of the Earth*. Burnet, he thinks, is a freethinker and doubter of Moses,[87] but he is chiefly appalled by the attraction that Burnet's theory had for "young Philosophers."[88] Others shared his opinion, for the surmises of Burnet are challenged by continentals like Bussingius[89] and Leydekker;[90] there are acid references to it in many

[85] *Ibid.*, pp. 300–1.

[86] *Ibid.*, pp. 303–18.

[87] *Op. cit.* (London, 1696), p. 19.

[88] *Ibid.*, p. 21.

[89] *De situ telluris paradisiacae et chiliasticae Burnetiano ad eclipticam recto, quem T. Burnetius in sua theoria sacra telluris proposuit dissertatio mathematica*, Hamburg, 1695.

[90] *Archaelogia sacra*, in *De republica Hebraeorum* (Amsterdam, 1704), I, appendix.

books;[91] and it even gets a drubbing in the footnotes of works dealing with quite unrelated subjects.[92] Woodward fared little better. Several men attacked his views in letters,[93] but the longest criticism came from John Arbuthnot, whose *An Examination of Dr. Woodward's Account of the Deluge* was published at London in 1697. Arbuthnot asked many embarrassing questions. He argued that if all solids were reduced to their essential elements, we should not know what these elements are. He also claimed to have disproved Woodward's theory by laboratory tests, for he had thrown an oyster shell and an equal weight of metal powder into the water and the oyster shell was the first to sink.[94] He urged Woodward to support his contentions with fact;[95] in other words, Arbuthnot, like the rest of us, would have been delighted to see the great work that was never printed. But Woodward did not lack disciples, and in 1697 John Harris brought out his *Remarks on Some Late Papers Relating to the Universal Deluge,* in which he defended the master against the strictures of Ray and Arbuthnot. But in the following year the most important criticisms of these new theories came from the pen of the eminent mathematician John Keill.

Because of its unpromising title, Keill's *An Examination of Dr. Burnet's Theory of the Earth: with Some Remarks on Mr. Whiston's New Theory of the Earth* has been overlooked by historians of British philosophy; and yet it seems to me an important document in the great campaign against the mechanistic philosophy. Keill had little regard for the findings of speculative philosophy because it seemed to him that the cosmological systems of ancient thinkers like Anaxagoras, Anaximenes, and Thales were in reality more imaginative than the wildest fantasies of the poets. These loose flutterings of speculation were, he thinks, too characteristic of all philosophers for a rational man to endure. The modern theories brought forward by Spinoza, Hobbes, More, Malebranch, and Descartes were likewise more poetic than much that passes for poetry. Keill consequently pushed for a philosophy of science, years before philosophers came around to his view. But what bothers him most is the "presumptive pride" of the modern rationalists, for it is this pride and its attending positivism that have won so many recruits for these new doctrines among the learned. Keill then proceeds to demolish, on the basis of mathematics, Des-

[91] See the attack on Burnet and Whiston in T. Baker, *Reflections on Learning* (London, 1708), pp. 101–2.

[92] See, for example, סדר עולם רבא (ed. Meyer, Amsterdam, 1699), p. 13.

[93] Raven, *op. cit.,* p. 450.

[94] *Op. cit.* (London, 1697), pp. 21–2.

[95] *Ibid.,* p. 62.

cartes' doctrine of vortices and to level his fire against the whole of the mechanistic school.[96] This leads him to Burnet and his poetical, but not empirical, theory of the universe.

Keill is a fair critic. He does not strike at Burnet at once, but pauses to point out the fallacies in Warren's critique of Burnet. This logical review of "one of my Associates" gives the reader confidence in Keill and respect for his learning and logic. He is also ready to acknowledge Burnet's gifts as a stylist; there has never been a philosophical work "written with a more plausible stile than it is." It is, however, the style, he thinks, not the reasoning that has betrayed so many incautious readers.[97] Keill's attack on Burnet is highly technical; his mathematical knowledge enables him to defeat his opponent at almost every turn. He recognizes, to begin with, that Burnet's doctrine of the evolution of the world from chaos is simply a modification of Descartes' theories; but even Descartes did not venture so far.[98] He discovers four weak spots in Burnet's hypothesis: the mechanics of the formation of the external crust, the doctrine of the perpendicular axis, the theory of the antediluvian rivers, and the concept of the evolution of mountains. The finest authorities in science—Kepler, Boyle, Newton, and others—are used by Keill to show the utter impossibility of Burnet's notions. The Burnetian explanation of the formation of the external crust is attacked by arguing, with a fine display of mathematics, that whereas small flakes of dust might float on the sphere of waters, masses of dust would sink as soon as they coagulated into clods. It is also pointed out that the velocity at which the particle fell would have a great deal to do with whether it floated or sank. Keill also asks his readers to realize that since the antediluvians had iron implements, the crust must have been impregnated with mineral masses which would hardly float. Burnet's original earth, he concludes, would not have a crust of fine dirt, but would be little more than a watery mass peopled by fish.[99] The same sort of coldly critical analysis is bestowed on Burnet's other ideas, and then Keill puts Whiston's conjectures under the knife.

Keill praises Whiston, because he thinks his theory of the Deluge is the most intelligent and scientific explanation yet devised. Actually, he believes that a scientific discussion of the Flood is impossible although he is ready to accept the Flood as a theological fact. He subjects Whiston's theories to rigid scrutiny and proves that the passing of a comet

[96] *Op. cit.* (London, 1734), pp. 1–21. The first edition is 1698.

[97] *Ibid.,* p. 22.

[98] *Ibid.,* p. 31.

[99] *Ibid.,* pp. 32–6.

would have no effect on the waters of the abyss even though it created immense tides in the oceans. He also finds it impossible to believe Whiston's hypothesis that the rain was produced by the aqueous matter of the comet's head and tail. It is known that the substance of a comet is very fine, and Keill cannot see where in the cosmos the atmospheric pressure necessary to convert it into rain could be obtained.[100] Keill, for all his scientific learning and his will to believe, is always aware of the utter futility of supporting Genesis by laboratory data. He preferred, like Sir Thomas Browne, to erect a concrete wall in his mind, placing science on one side of it and theology on the other. It is simply the mediaeval way of facing the old trouble; it was merely a restatement of the old maxim that the things of reason be given unto reason and those of faith unto faith.

To Keill's attack on Burnet and Whiston there were rejoinders and surrejoinders, and the scientific considerations of the causes of the Flood continued well into the nineteenth century. Burnet, however, was always highly regarded by men of infinite discernment. Both he and Woodward are mentioned lovingly by Catcott, whose *A Treatise on the Deluge* was printed in 1761. The great Addison immortalized Burnet in a Latin ode which began,

> Turbae loquaces Te fidium sonant
> Burnette, musis pectus amabile
> Cui nomen inclarescit omnem
> (Materiam calami) per orbem.[101]

Richard Steele was sobered by his reading of the theory, whose author he compares to Cicero and from whose poetic prose he quotes liberally.[102] By the end of the eighteenth century, it was the prose rather than the reasonableness of the hypothesis that took the fancy of men. Warton says of Burnet that "he has displayed an imagination very nearly equal to that of Milton";[103] and Wordsworth, after he had written the opening lines of the third book of *The Excursion,* was so delighted to find a reflection of his own ideas in Mr. Burnet's theory that he could not restrain himself from quoting a long passage from the Latin version as a commentary on his own lines.

[100] *Ibid.,* pp. 140–77. Thomas Beverly replied to Keill in *Reflections upon the Theory of the Earth Occasion'd by a Late Examination of It,* London, 1699. Beverly supports most of Burnet's contentions, but he is mainly directed by his own belief that other planets are inhabited.

[101] *Miscellaneous Works* (ed. Gutkelch, London, 1914), I, 284–9.

[102] *The Spectator* (ed. Morley, London, 1891), I, 503–5.

[103] *Essay on the Genius and Writings of Pope* (London, 1806), I, 266.

In spite of the charm of Burnet and the industry of his friends and opponents, all of these attempts to prove the universality of the Flood or to account scientifically for the source of the necessary water failed. Men were no closer to an absolute proof of the Genesis legend at the end of the seventeenth century than they were at the beginning. But there was another problem. If the Flood was universal, the whole world had to be populated at the time of Noah. Could such a condition be proved? Then, too, if all men were destroyed by the Flood, how was the earth repeopled? If an incentive to geological and paleontological investigations can be found in the theories of Burnet, Ray, Woodward, and Whiston, a similar stimulus to the modern sciences of archaeology and ethnology may be found in this other seventeenth-century controversy.

Geology and Orthodoxy: The Case of Noah's Flood in Eighteenth-Century Thought

RHODA RAPPAPORT

In this essay written by Professor Rhoda Rappaport of the Department of History at Vassar College, the battleground has shifted to eighteenth-century France. The relative consistency of the intellectual positions remains, however, despite the new strategies in attacking or defending the veracity of the flood myth.

For a sample of the considerable number of books, monographs, and articles devoted to the flood in French scholarship, see Jean d'Estienne, "Les théories du Déluge," Revue des questions scientifiques *9 (1881): 415–449; 10 (1881): 148–185, 474–518. For a fascinating discussion of Swiss naturalist Johann Jacob Scheuchzer (1672–1733), who unearthed a skeleton that he believed to be* Homo diluvii testis, *the Man who Witnessed the Flood, and who published a treatise proclaiming this in 1726, see Melvin E. Jahn, "Some Notes on Dr. Scheuchzer and on* Homo diluvii testis," *in Cecil J. Schneer, ed.,* Toward A History of Geology *(Cambridge, Mass., 1969), pp. 193–213.*

The view that religious orthodoxy stifled geological progress has had many distinguished exponents, one of the earliest being Georges Cuvier. To Cuvier, however, efforts to combine Genesis with geology ended before the middle of the eighteenth century, and opened the way not for progress but for wild speculation. We may admire the genius of Leibniz and Buffon, he declared, but this should not lead us to confuse system-building with geology as "une science positive."[1] While Cuvier's

Reprinted from the *British Journal for the History of Science* 11 (1978):1–18.

[1] Report by Cuvier *et al.*, 1806, in N. André, *Théorie de la surface actuelle de la terre*, Paris, 1806, pp. 320–1, 326. See also Cuvier, 'Discours préliminaire,' *Recherches sur les ossemens fossiles des quadrupèdes*, 4 vols., Paris, 1812, i, 26–35, and William Coleman, *Georges Cuvier, Zoologist*, Cambridge, Mass., 1964, p. 113.

younger contemporary, Charles Lyell, agreed that "extravagant systems" had retarded progress, he insisted that "scriptural authority" had had a similar effect until late in the eighteenth century.[2]

In his interpretation of history, as in much else, Lyell has for a long time prevailed over Cuvier. Although modern scholars have rejected or modified many of Lyell's historical judgements, it is still possible to find the eighteenth century described in Lyellian terms:

> [By 1785] many geological observations had been made and recorded in the literature; but previous attempts to synthesize these observations into a general "theory of the earth" were unscientific and had not proved acceptable. The issue had been confused and progress retarded by a literal belief in the biblical account of the creation and the universal flood.[3]

It has even been said that geologists—many of them clerics—were appalled by their own observations, and, fearing to be heterodox or fearing punishment for heterodoxy, "scurried off in strange directions, or returned to earlier [i.e., more orthodox] positions."[4]

To scholars outside the history of geology, the idea that the eighteenth century was a period of "scurrying off in strange directions" to avoid heterodoxy will rightly seem bizarre. For the physical sciences, the condemnation of Galileo had proved to be a victory for the condemned, and Catholic apologists were reaching the Galilean conclusion that the Bible could not be used as a source of physics or astronomy. Scientists themselves had become self-consciously empirical and determined to seek explanations in terms of natural causes and uniform laws. Nor is much scurrying to be detected even among the genuinely heterodox philosophers, who found numerous ways to get their subversive views into print. Furthermore, to discuss heterodoxy at all assumes the existence of a well-defined orthodoxy, and to discuss religious scruples or timidity implies the existence of well-oiled machinery for intimidation and censorship. But historians who deal with these aspects of eighteenth-century life often stress the secularism of the clergy itself, have uncovered doctrinal conflicts even in state churches with hierarchies capable of defining dogma, and continue to argue about the efficiency of the machinery for repression.

[2] Charles Lyell, *Principles of Geology*, 3 vols., London, 1830–3, i, 29–30. M. J. S. Rudwick, "The Strategy of Lyell's *Principles of Geology*," *Isis*, 1970, *61*, especially 8–11.

[3] V. A. Eyles, "Hutton," in *Dictionary of Scientific Biography*, New York, 1972, vi, 580. The same view is to be found in many discussions of Hutton and Lyell, primarily to explain the resistance encountered by their theories. For a recent sample of revisionist literature on Lyell, see the "Lyell Centenary Issue," *The British Journal for the History of Science*, 1976, *9*, especially the articles by Porter and Ospovat, pp. 91–103, 190–8.

[4] Francis C. Haber, *The Age of the World*, Baltimore, 1959, pp. 112–13.

Although our general picture of eighteenth-century intellectual life differs somewhat from that often suggested by historians of geology, Lyell's interpretation does have some basis in fact. One undeniable fact is that some geologists—those usually cited are British writers of the first and last decades of the century—explicitly sought to defend Genesis. It is undeniable, too, that virtually all geologists discussed the biblical flood and that many of them attributed to the flood some role in the history of the earth's crust. To say this much, however, should not necessarily imply that geologists felt constrained to demonstrate their orthodoxy; mere use of the flood tells us nothing about religious convictions or geological competence unless we ask such questions as: Why and how did geologists treat the flood? To what extent did geological observation—and Lyell did not query the observational skills of his predecessors—support the notion that such a catastrophe had occurred?

The examination of these questions requires some preliminary discussion of what might be called "the status of Genesis" in the eighteenth century: was there an "orthodox" interpretation? Rather than attempt an impossible survey of all religious denominations, my emphasis will be on Catholic France. Not only was France—more accurately, Paris—the acknowledged intellectual capital of Europe, but there were also to be found in France all those conditions needed for the suppression of philosophical speculation: a vigilant, conservative Faculty of Theology at the University of Paris, elaborate machinery for censorship, and an established church with hierarchically imposed dogma and discipline.

For the geologists, the two relevant biblical texts are the narratives of the creation and the flood. I have chosen to deal with the flood because, while many geologists avoided cosmogony, few could avoid discussing the deluge and its possible effects upon the earth's crust. To what extent did geologists accept the historicity of the biblical account? Why was the flood, sent to punish mankind, often considered a natural event with geological consequences? What geological effects, in fact, was the flood supposed to have had?

This article does not pretend to survey all the geological literature of the period. An effort has been made to select works ranging in date and in country of origin, and written by men with some international reputation. The latter criterion dictated the neglect of some writers (Raspe, for instance) and the use of others who were widely read but not as widely admired for their scientific expertise (Buffon being the obvious example). Some of the writers discussed—Linnaeus is one—earned their reputations not as geologists but as botanists or chemists.

Unlike these older disciplines, however, geology was not a well-defined specialty in the eighteenth century, and so it seems worthwhile here to include those writers whose ideas carried the stamp of authority even when they ventured from their specialties into the amorphous field of natural history, of which geology was one branch. Finally, no attempt has here been made to give pride of place to such figures as Werner and Hutton, since the object of this article is not to determine which general theory excited most controversy or convinced most thinkers; instead, because the flood was discussed in connection with virtually every theory, it has seemed more relevant to focus on this issue as it was treated by an international community of scientists.

In *The Legend of Noah,* Don Cameron Allen provided a classic account of sixteenth- and seventeenth-century attempts to fill in the gaps, explain away the anomalies, and supply scientific details to substantiate the story of the flood. To the modern reader, the questions asked by these rationalists are both delightful and startling: Could one design an ark sufficient to house all the refugees from the flood? Could fish survive in the flood, or did they, too, have to be passengers in the ark? Were peculiarly American species in the ark, or had the flood not reached the western hemisphere? More significant for this article is Allen's contention that rationalist analyses produced so much confusion and disagreement and sheer doubt about the literal accuracy of Genesis, that the flood had either to remain a miracle, or be reduced to the status of one of many ancient legends. Allen argued, too, that rational explication was primarily a Protestant concern, Protestants seeking to understand "the plain words of Scripture" while Catholics more readily resorted to miracle or allegory.[5] Allen to the contrary notwithstanding, Catholic clergy in eighteenth-century France shared some of the concerns of the earlier rationalists and had not reached a miracle-or-legend consensus about the flood. Nor, in fact, had they arrived at a generally accepted mode of interpretation of Genesis.

The old tradition of literal interpretation is often said to have been dominant during this period in France, and its representatives included men as different as the Oratorian Richard Simon, the Benedictine Augustin Calmet, and the doctors of the Sorbonne. Generally considered most "typical" is Dom Calmet, whose verse-by-verse commentary aims at a more precise understanding of the Bible on the basis of philology and ancient history. When treating the flood in 1707,

[5] Don Cameron Allen, *The Legend of Noah,* Urbana, Ill., 1963, especially pp. 68, 84–5, 181.

Calmet was with obvious reluctance drawn into a brief discussion of problems raised by earlier rationalists, but he preferred to consider the event a miracle. Too much analysis, he believed, would destroy the unity and integrity of the Pentateuch.[6]

Calmet's older contemporary, Simon, also considered himself a literal expositor, and he believed that the obscurities, repetitions, and contradictions in Genesis could be explained as the historical result of compilation from older sources. Simon's scholarly efforts in the 1680s to show that the Pentateuch is a compilation rather than wholly the work of Moses aroused the wrath of censors, Jansenists, Oratorians, and Bishop Bossuet.[7] If this kind of literalism provoked a charge of "impiety and libertinism" in the late seventeenth century, the same cannot be said of the mid-eighteenth. One of Simon's few followers, the Montpellier physician Jean Astruc, created no such storm in 1753, and reviewers of his work expressed opinions ranging from praise, to reservation of judgement, to the denial that his arguments were conclusive.[8] That the Sorbonne ignored Astruc is worth noting, since it is often said that the theologians had only recently been roused to extreme vigilance by the scandalous thesis of the abbé de Prades. If the Faculty's silence about Astruc cannot be explained, one may at least suggest that the doctors were less vigilant and less united doctrinally than is usually alleged.[9]

Although the literal tradition was strong, it was neither united nor unrivalled in France, and the rationalist tradition continued to be an important rival. One member of this school, the abbé Pluche, was the author of the widely read *Le spectacle de la nature* (1732), a derivative

[6]Calmet, *Commentaire littéral sur tous les livres de l'Ancien et du Nouveau Testament,* 23 vols., Paris, 1707–16, i, 176–9, 186. Also, F. Dinago (ed.), *Publication des oeuvres inédites de Dom A. Calmet,* 2 vols., St-Dié, 1877–8, ii. 39–67.

[7]Richard Simon, *Histoire critique du Vieux Testament,* nouv. éd., Rotterdam, 1685, especially p. 33 for the flood. Discussion with long quotations can be found in Edward M. Gray, *Old Testament Criticism,* London and New York, 1923, chapter IX. Also H. Margival, *Essai sur Richard Simon,* Paris, 1900, chapter V, and J. Steinmann, *Richard Simon et les origines de l'exégèse biblique,* Paris, 1960, pp. 100–16, 124–30.

[8][Jean Astruc], *Conjectures sur les memoires originaux dont il paroit que Moyse s'est servi pour composer le Livre de la Genese,* Brussels, 1753, pp. 3–18. Also, Gray, op. cit. (7), chapter XII. Reviewers are cited at length in A. Lods, *Jean Astruc et la critique biblique au XVIIIe siècle,* Strasbourg, 1924, pp. 62–71.

[9]For changes in the Sorbonne, see R. R. Palmer, *Catholics and Unbelievers in Eighteenth-Century France,* Princeton, 1939, pp. 40–1, 51, 123, 129. Palmer considers the Sorbonne to have become more rigid and vigilant after the Prades affair (1751–3), but his book shows a continuing variety of thought in orthodox circles. An example of the Sorbonne's naive literalism is in its response to Buffon's two great works, in 1751 and after 1778, respectively; see J. Piveteau (ed.), *Oeuvres philosophiques de Buffon,* Paris, 1954, pp. 106–9, and P. Flourens, *Des manuscrits de Buffon,* Paris, 1860, pp. 254–80.

work of natural theology.[10] More interesting than Pluche were other rationalists who, like Simon and Calmet, realized that variant texts of Genesis resulted in different systems of chronology; some were aware, too, that all existing chronologies might be undermined by historical and scientific evidence. The abbé LeMascrier, for example, declared that in some of these matters the Bible is not "our sole and unique guide," and he was willing at least to countenance the theory that the earth might be millions of years old.[11] The abbé Grosier similarly found no fault in interpreting the six days of creation as six epochs should the scientific evidence so warrant—but he did not think the available evidence conclusive.[12] LeMascrier and Grosier, it should be added, were dealing with three of the most "subversive" chronologies of their day: De Maillet's *Telliamed* (1748), Mirabaud's *Le monde* (1751), and Buffon's *Les époques de la nature* (1778).

These few examples clearly suggest that, in France at least, there was no single, established, approach to Genesis. If anything united the "orthodox," this was the belief that God had revealed Himself to man and that the fact of revelation was the basis of the authority of the Catholic Church.[13] The implication of such belief for the story of Noah was simply that the flood had been sent to punish mankind. Whether the flood was universal or confined to regions inhabited by man; whether it was a miracle or produced by natural causes; whether it had appreciably changed the surface of the earth; whether the earth had had a long antediluvian history—all these matters remained subject to debate.

Diversity of opinion among the clergy is all the more noteworthy in a period when believing Christians might have been expected to close ranks against the radical French philosophers. The views of Voltaire *et al.* are too well known to require discussion here, although it seems appropriate to rehearse briefly some direct and indirect attacks upon the early chapters of Genesis. A good many philosophers were pro-

[10] Noël-Antoine Pluche, *Le spectacle de la nature,* Paris, 1756, iii. especially 515–36. For the popularity of Pluche, see D. Mornet, *Les sciences de la nature en France, au XVIII*[e] *siècle,* Paris, 1911, pp. 248–9. Also, abbé Mallet, "Arche de Noé," in Diderot and d'Alembert, *Encyclopédie,* Paris, 1751, i. 606–9.

[11] [J.-B. LeMascrier], "Essai sur la chronologie," in [J.-B. Mirabaud], *Le monde, son origine, et son antiquité,* 2nd ed., London, 1778, ii. 163–5, and the same writer in Benoît de Maillet, *Telliamed* (ed. and tr. by A. V. Carozzi), Urbana, Ill., 1968, p. 381, nn. 52, 54. Carozzi insists that LeMascrier held to the "orthodox" view of 6,000 years as the age of the earth; pp. 30 and 380, n. 50. LeMascrier was less flexible about the flood, in fact, than about the age of the earth; see below, note 24.

[12] *Journal de littérature, des sciences et des arts,* 1779, 3, 412–15.

[13] Palmer, op. cit. (9), p. 221. The whole of Palmer's book shows a range of belief on such vital matters as sin, grace, and the nature of man.

ducing wholly nonbiblical accounts of the history of primitive man, the origin of language, and the evolution of civilizations, but few would have gone as far as Rousseau did in 1755 in explicitly pointing out their divergence from Genesis:

> Religion commands us to believe that since God Himself took men out of the state of nature immediately after the creation, they are unequal because He wanted them to be so; but it does not forbid us to form conjectures, drawn solely from the nature of man and the beings surrounding him, about what the human race might have become if it had remained abandoned to itself.[14]

Rousseau's version of what "religion commands" is in itself controversial, since theologians disagreed about what constituted a "state of nature" and whether such a state was descriptive of conditions before or after the fall. Philosophers, too, failed to agree about whether the state of nature had been brutish or blissful, but their reconstruction of origins had little in common with the Mosaic account of the creation of Adam, the fall, the special status of Hebrew as the language of revelation, and the story of the tower of Babel. Boulanger might use the flood in his *Antiquité dévoilée* (1766), but his account of the disaster and of its effects on mankind shows no resemblance to Genesis.[15]

However difficult it is to define orthodoxy among theologians, much of the work by French men of letters was clearly heterodox, by any standard. In a country possessing an elaborate system of censorship, heterodoxy developed an equally elaborate system of evasion of the law, and historians of the Enlightenment know much about such techniques as anonymity, false attribution of authorship, false imprints, the smuggling of tracts from Holland or England, the clandestine circulation of manuscripts, and the pious disclaimer attached to the subversive book. In addition, evasion was helped because the will to censor was subject to variation and because the system itself was as anarchic as it was arbitrary. The royal corps of censors, the Sorbonne, and the Parlement of Paris all behaved erratically for a variety of reasons, not least among them the fact that these bodies contained individuals who sympathized with some of the radical ideas propounded by the men of letters.

While historians agree that the system was cumbersome and ineffi-

[14] Rousseau, "Discourse on the Origin and Foundations of Inequality Among Men," 1755, in Roger D. Masters (ed.), *The First and Second Discourses*, New York, 1964, p. 103.

[15] For Boulanger, see Frank Manuel, *The Eighteenth Century Confronts the Gods*, New York, 1967, pp. 214–19. Manuel's book is rich in examples of nonbiblical searches for origins, but see especially pp. 132–4. Theological conflict about the state of nature is treated by Palmer, op. cit. (9), chapter II.

cient, there remains some divergence of opinion about the effects of censorship. Should one emphasize the philosophers' fear of persecution or the fact that their writings did get into print? Certainly, it is the easier course to stress the famous cases of imprisonment, suppression, confiscation, and condemnation. The very nature of the problem should make us wary, however, since we obviously know more about the reasons behind condemnation than we do about the reasons behind the failures to molest. In the context of this article, the example of Buffon is instructive: although the Sorbonne condemned parts of his *Theory of the Earth* (1749), and although we know that the learned doctors took issue with his *Epochs of Nature* (1778), why Buffon was not censured after 1778 remains a matter for conjecture.[16]

The preceding pages are intended to cast doubt on the view that French naturalists had to contend with a well-defined orthodoxy, enforced by religious and civil authorities. A similar analysis for England or Prussia or certain Italian states would probably also yield varying tones of gray rather than sharp definitions. In England, for example, the established church was so "comprehensive," so latitudinarian, that orthodoxy would be hard to define in any but the broadest terms.[17] For Prussia, it is gross simplification to claim that heterodoxy was limited "mainly" to "anticlerical jokes," especially in a period when members of the Berlin Academy were being permitted to publish speculation as subversive as Rousseau's.[18] For all countries, including France, analysis is further complicated by changes in policy and practice during the course of the century. In France, royal censors became more erratic after 1750, while they became more vigilant in Prussia after the death

[16]The harshness of censorship is emphasized by Peter Gay, *The Enlightenment, an Interpretation,* 2 vols., New York, 1967–9, ii. 70–9; less extreme views are to be found in Palmer, op. cit. (9), pp. 16–17, and in Jacques Roger, "Introduction," in Buffon, *Les époques de la nature* (ed. by J. Roger), *Mémoires du Muséum national d'histoire naturelle,* Série C, Tome X, Paris, 1962, p. cxii. The only searching discussion of the failure of the Sorbonne to condemn Buffon after 1778 is in Roger, pp. cxxxii–vi; his conclusions are tentative because he has had to rely on Paris gossip in the absence of "harder" information.

[17]One of the many useful treatments of liberal Anglicanism is Roland N. Stromberg, *Religious Liberalism in Eighteenth-Century England,* London, 1954, especially chapter IV. See also Charles R. Gillett, *Burned Books: Neglected Chapters in British History and Literature,* 2 vols., New York, 1932, ii. chapters XXVII–VIII. Gillett has discovered virtually no "heterodox" books condemned after 1720; "virtual" is necessary because of unsubstantiated reports that there may have been two.

[18]The quotation is from Gay, op. cit. (16), p. 71. The Berlin Academy was under far greater royal control than its Paris counterpart, but it awarded its prize in 1772 to Herder's nonbiblical account of the origin of language, and it boasted Maupertuis as its President for a time. Maupertuis published several heterodox works during this period; see Bentley Glass, "Maupertuis," in *Dictionary of Scientific Biography,* New York, 1974, ix. 186–9.

of Frederick II in 1786. After 1789, the revolution in France affected writers and censors everywhere, arousing both admiration of France and fear of French materialism. Problems such as these suggest that it would be unwise to assume that there existed widespread, well-defined, long-lived constraints upon naturalists in particular. If most naturalists discussed the biblical flood, their reasons for doing so should be sought elsewhere than in coercion or timidity in the face of authority.

For the purposes of this article, the story of Noah, interpreted literally, has three salient features: the flood was universal, covering even the tops of the highest mountains; there were forty days during which the waters increased, pouring out upon the earth from the "great deep" as well as from the heavens; and the whole duration of the flood was less than one year. On the universality of the flood, there is a large literature by scientists and laymen (i.e., nonscientists, whether clerical or lay). The turbulence and duration of the event were of special concern to scientists.

The universality of the flood had been the subject of ancient debate, revived with vigor in the eighteenth century. Scientists and laymen all were aware of the existence of flood legends in many civilizations; but were these legends all memories of the biblical deluge, or were all, including the story of Noah, memories of purely local disasters? With rare exceptions, the naturalists tended to use flood legends as evidence for a once-universal catastrophe. Among nonscientists, many influential writers used the same evidence to suggest that there had never been a universal flood. The former harmonized with ancient Christian tradition (and, as I hope to show, with some geological evidence), while the latter view was shared by people ranging from an Anglican bishop to Voltaire.

Robert Clayton, Bishop of Clogher, was the author of more than one tract in defense of biblical chronology and related subjects. While much of his evidence was based on the conformities between sacred and pagan histories, he was also a spiritual descendant of those rationalists who had wondered whether uniquely American fauna had been passengers in the ark. He concluded that the flood need not have been universal, as long as it was sufficient to destroy all mankind but for the family of Noah.[19] No such pious intent can be detected in the

[19]Clayton's arguments are summarized by one of his critics, Alexander Catcott, *A Treatise on the Deluge*, 2nd ed., London, 1768, pp. 11–12. Also, K. B. Collier, *Cosmogonies of our Fathers*, New York, 1934, pp. 229, 234. At the time of his death, Clayton was in imminent danger of being charged with heresy for his Arian views; but this was so unusual

work of several philosophers who also denied the universality of the flood. A good example of their reasoning comes from J.-B. Mirabaud, Secretary of the *Académie française*, in his explanation of the psychology underlying the Greek legend of the flood of Deucalion:

> In those rude days (*temps grossiers*), men . . . knew only those parts of the world surrounding them and judged the rest by their surroundings. Thus it is that the first inhabitants of Greece told themselves that a flood which had affected them had demolished the whole human race; and it is probably in the same way that Noah, protected in his ark, . . . borne by the waves to a normally uninhabited region, or to where the inhabitants had died during the same catastrophe, thought that everyone not with him had been swallowed up by the waters.[20]

Variants of Mirabaud's message were being spread by Voltaire and the encyclopaedists. In the *Philosophical Dictionary*, Voltaire summed up Genesis as a collection of folk tales not unique to the Hebrews, and went on to state that a universal flood was a scientific impossibility. We should, he added, accept the deluge as a miracle, but some pages later shrugged off miracles which always, suspiciously, originate among illiterate peoples.[21] In 1754 in the *Encyclopédie*, Boulanger implied comparable conclusions, weighing both the legends of floods and the scientific evidence for and against a universal flood.[22] The most competent scientist among the philosophers, the Baron d'Holbach, repeatedly denied that geological phenomena could be explained by the flood; in his polemical *System of Nature* (1770), he went on to question the flood's universality.[23]

The few naturalists to argue that the flood had been a local disaster included De Maillet, Buffon, J.-C. de Lamétherie, J. G. Sulzer, and J. F. Blumenbach. All considered a universal flood to be a scientific impos-

that I suspect the problem stemmed from his being a bishop rather than a lesser cleric or a layman. See A. R. Winnett, in Derek Baker (ed.), *Schism, Heresy and Religious Protest*, Cambridge, 1972, pp. 311–21.

[20] Mirabaud, op. cit. (11), i. 95–6. See *Telliamed*, op. cit. (11), pp. 298–9, and its editor's comments, p. 300, n. *c*.

[21] Voltaire, *Philosophical Dictionary* (tr. by Peter Gay), New York, 1962, pp. 284–97, 327–8, 394: articles *Genèse, Inondation, Miracles*. For Buffon's objections to miracles, see Roger, op. cit. (16), pp. lxxxv, xlviii.

[22] Boulanger, "Déluge," in *Encyclopédie*, op. cit. (10), 1754, iv. 795–803.

[23] D'Holbach's transparent compromises with Genesis can be found in his translations of J. F. Henckel, *Pyritologie*, 2 vols., Paris, 1760, i. 122n, 123n, 131n; and J. G. Lehmann, *Traités de physique, d'histoire naturelle, de mineralogie et de métallurgie*, 3 vols., Paris, 1759, iii. pp. v–x, 83n, 192n. See also his article, "Terre, couches de la," in *Encyclopédie*, op. cit. (10), 1765, xvi. 170; Collier, op. cit. (19), p. 283; and Manuel, op. cit. (15), pp. 234, 238.

sibility—their reasons show some variation in detail—and all but Blumenbach felt obliged to discuss and reinterpret ancient flood legends, much in the fashion of Mirabaud. This did not prevent the three Frenchmen from espousing a theory (to be discussed below) of a universal ocean different from the flood, or Blumenbach from suggesting that the earth had undergone two worldwide catastrophes, and such theories were held by other geologists who often continued to believe that there had been a universal flood. In other words, one may fairly say about four of these five naturalists that they were willing to grapple with problematical concepts of worldwide change, but they objected to the particular kind of worldwide event described in Genesis.[24] In this they were not alone, for, as we shall see, those naturalists who made use of the flood often departed considerably from the biblical text.

Most naturalists did accept the historicity of the universal flood and turned their attention to what was, for them, the more immediate issue: had the flood had any geological effects? In particular, since geological strata had once had to be "soft" in order for fossils to become embedded in them, was the flood responsible for the dissolution of large parts of the earth's crust and the deposition of marine fossils? The problem of marine fossils divided naturalists into three camps: those who considered them to be relics of the flood, those who allowed some lesser role to the flood, and those who denied to the flood any such geological role.

Parenthetically, it should be noted that the fossil problem often highlighted but was not always an integral part of discussions of the flood. The two issues were closely linked early in the eighteenth century, especially in the writings of natural theologians, and again late in the century when explanations were sought for the burial of large mammals. Fossil specimens of the latter sort were, of course, known much earlier, but they were rare enough—and often so poorly identified—that they could be safely ignored or explained away as the victims of some purely local disaster. But additional specimens found in several parts of the world made the problem an urgent one after about

[24] Buffon, *Epoques*, op. cit. (16), pp. 182–4. *Telliamed*, op. cit. (11), compare pp. 213–15 with pp. 297–300. Lamétherie, *Théorie de la terre*, 3 vols., Paris, 1795, iii. 189–224, 258–84, and *Leçons de géologie*, 3 vols., Paris, 1816, especially ii. 325–34; also, K. L. Taylor, "Lamétherie," in *Dictionary of Scientific Biography*, New York, 1973, vii. 602–4. J. F. Blumenbach, *Beyträge zur Naturgeschichte*, 2nd ed., 1806, i. in *The Anthropological Treatises of J. F. Blumenbach* (tr. by T. Bendyshe), London, 1865, pp. 285–6 and 286, n. 2. J. G. Sulzer, "Conjecture physique sur quelques changemens arrivés dans la surface du globe terrestre," *Histoire de l'Académie royale des sciences et belles-lettres*, Berlin, 1762 (1769), pp. 90–8. Sulzer developed a theory of local eruptions of lakes, which, he believed, could have given rise to flood legends; this theory apparently attracted little attention in the eighteenth century.

1770. As the following pages will show, debaters often did ignore fossils and concentrated instead on whether sediments of some thickness could have been deposited by the flood or whether significant nonconformities in the strata might be explained as the result of such a cataclysm. Nonetheless, since debate about the flood was at first linked with the fossil record, it is appropriate to begin with the issues then posed.

Among those who considered fossils to be relics of the deluge were the Swiss naturalist J. J. Scheuchzer and the French author of a widely read guide to fossils, Dezallier d'Argenville. Scheuchzer had been converted to diluvialism by the English geologist and natural theologian John Woodward, and he was to remark in 1731 that the aim of all his scientific work had been to find natural evidence for the truths of Scripture.[25] Writing later, Argenville was well aware that there were serious objections to the Woodwardian theory, but he believed alternative explanations to be even more problematical and "hypothetical." By mid-century, in fact, Woodward's views had been so severely undermined that they could no longer be accepted even by those naturalists who considered the flood to have played a major role in sedimentation.[26]

One anti-Woodwardian argument repeatedly raised was that the strata of the earth's crust are not arranged in order of their specific gravity, as they ought to be if all were deposited in a universal flood; and, as a later writer put it, "the whole of Dr Woodwards [*sic*] theory of the Earth hangs on this affirmation."[27] Just as fundamental was the objection that the flood must have been turbulent, and sedimentary strata show every sign of having been laid down under tranquil conditions. In 1720 a third argument joined these two, when Réaumur presented to the Paris Academy of Sciences a memoir with the innocuous title, "Remarks on the Fossil Shells of Some Parts of Touraine." The memoir records his observations of tertiary faluns of gigantic dimen-

[25] Melvin E. Jahn, in C. J. Schneer (ed.), *Toward a History of Geology*, Cambridge, Mass., 1969, pp. 198, 200. Also, Henckel, op. cit. (23), i. 110–11, 123, 131, and Louis Bourguet, *Traité des pétrifications*, 2 vols., Paris, 1742, i. 53–94. Henckel's work first appeared in 1725.

[26] [Dezallier d'Argenville], *L'histoire naturelle éclaircie dans deux de ses parties principales, la lithologie et la conchyliologie*, Paris, 1742, pp. 156–60; and additional remarks on the deluge in the 1757 edition of this work, pp. xix, 58, 66–71. Early critiques of Woodward are mentioned by Rudwick, *The Meaning of Fossils*, London & New York, 1971, pp. 82–3, 93; others were produced before 1750 by such writers as Vallisneri, Moro, and Buffon. Later naturalists who gave the flood a sedimentary role were Lehmann and Wallerius, discussed below; see notes 42, 45.

[27] John Walker, *Lectures on Geology* (ed. by Harold W. Scott), Chicago & London, 1966, p. 181. The lectures seem to date from about 1780.

sions: more than 30,000 square meters in area and about 7 meters in thickness. No flood of short duration could have produced such fossiliferous deposits, he declared, and we must therefore conclude that this region was formerly at the bottom of the sea.[28]

These arguments convinced most naturalists that it was necessary to find a more acceptable explanation for the accumulation of fossiliferous sediments. Any such explanation would have to satisfy the corollaries of arguments used by the critics: deposition during a time span longer than a year, under tranquil conditions, and with some interruptions to account for the problem of specific gravity. Two theories soon became widespread. One group adopted the view that the present landmasses had long been at the bottom of the sea, while another thought the surface of the earth had undergone a series of "revolutions." For the first group, the flood played a variety of roles or none at all; for the second, the flood could be described as simply one of several revolutions.

The theory of a "long sojourn of the sea" was advocated by such men as Buffon, d'Holbach, Lamétherie, Réaumur, Soulavie, Valmont de Bomare, Bergman, Linnaeus, and Whitehurst. Of these, only the latter three clearly indicate their belief in the historicity of the universal flood, but they differed in assessing its geological effects. Linnaeus, indeed, remarked that he had looked long but without success for any geological traces of the deluge. Bergman had the same difficulty, but concluded that the violence and short duration of the flood probably meant that it had merely shifted some loose, superficial deposits. For Whitehurst, the flood followed a long period of sedimentation; the earth's crust ruptured, permitting uplift and the draining of water from the surface of the present continents.[29]

The views of Linnaeus and Whitehurst deserve closer examination, since the former's piety pervades much of his work while the latter's magnum opus—in its first chapters, at least—bears a strong resemblance to the cosmogonies of earlier natural theologians. Neither had any doubt that the Mosaic account of creation and flood was essentially true, but the ways in which they treat these two events suggest that in geology, if perhaps not in cosmogony, observational data might be used to reinterpret the Bible, but not vice versa.

[28] Réaumur, in *Mémoires de l'Académie royale des sciences,* 1720 (1722), pp. 400–16. References to Réaumur and the Touraine are frequent throughout the century.

[29] A. G. Nathorst, "Carl von Linné as a Geologist," *Annual Report of the Board of Regents of the Smithsonian Institution,* 1908, pp. 713, 721; Haber, op. cit. (4), p. 160; and Desmarest, "Linné," *Encyclopédie méthodique: géographie physique,* Paris, 1795, i. 304. For Bergman, see Hollis Hedberg, in Schneer, op. cit. (25), p. 189. John Whitehurst, *An Inquiry into the Original State and Formation of the Earth,* 2nd ed., London, 1786, pp. 58–9, 118–22.

Both men argue that the earth must have had a beginning—Linnaeus using, among other things, the traditional logic in favor of the existence of a first cause, and Whitehurst suggesting that only a once-fluid mass could have assumed the shape of an oblate spheroid—and thence they proceed to reconstruct the earth's early history on the basis of those sciences with which they were most familiar. Linnaeus' expertise led him to a discussion of how species of plants and animals, originating in one locality, could achieve wide geographical distribution. Whitehurst, in contrast, provides a discussion of the "separation of chaos" by the operations of the laws of gravity and elective attraction. Both realized full well that their accounts were pious, scientifically plausible, and unproven, but based on the most up-to-date information as well as on what was commonly considered to be the oldest written document. Indeed, their technique of reconstruction was common to all cosmogonists, including those who did not rely on Genesis—one need only recall the systems of Descartes and Buffon.[30]

When Linnaeus and Whitehurst move from cosmogony to geology, their emphasis undergoes some change, since they no longer need to speculate about the most remote, primordial, past. They do not lose sight of Genesis, but, after all, the flood had not occurred at some "chaotic" time, but when the earth was fully formed and inhabited; in other words, the flood interrupted some sort of recognizably normal history. One ought, therefore, to be able to find antediluvian, diluvian, and postdiluvian geological formations. Just what Linnaeus looked for in the strata seems to be unknown, but he admitted his inability to find traces of the deluge. What he did find was a succession of strata formed during "a long and gradual lapse of ages," and, in addition, he had reliable evidence that the Baltic Sea was measurably lower than it once had been. The Baltic was thus a remnant of a universal sea which had progressively retreated from the continents, leaving behind it the observed accumulation of sediments. To equate this universal sea with the flood was impossible, the flood having been both brief and turbulent.[31]

Much the same considerations troubled Whitehurst, who took pains to show that the earth's sedimentary crust had been formed in successive stages. What, then, had the flood done? His ingenious answer

[30] In addition to works cited in the preceding note, see Linnaeus, "On the Increase of the Habitable Earth," in *Select Dissertations from the Amoenitates Academicae*, tr. F. J. Brand, 2 vols., London, 1781, i. 71–127. The allusion is to Descartes' *Le monde*, available in many editions and translations, and to several features of Buffon's cosmogony, e.g., his experiments to measure the rate of cooling of an incandescent globe.

[31] See notes 29, 30, 34. The phrase by Linnaeus is quoted in F. C. Haber, "Fossils and the Idea of a Process of Time in Natural History," in B. Glass, O. Temkin, and W. L. Straus (eds.), *Forerunners of Darwin: 1745–1859*, Baltimore, 1968, p. 242.

was that the flood was not really a universal inundation, but a figurative description of orogenesis and a resultant shift in sea basins. Subterranean forces had elevated the antediluvian ocean floor, producing the present continents and mountain ranges (with marine fossils at high elevations) and turning antediluvian continents into the present ocean floor. If Linnaeus perhaps sought literal confirmation of Genesis, Whitehurst found that a geological disturbance could be reconciled with Genesis, provided only that one did not interpret Moses literally.[32] One may conclude, then, that the Bible posed a historical problem to which these men offered different solutions, while they agreed in thinking that sedimentary formations must be the work of an ocean different from the flood.

The theory of the long sojourn of the sea was said in 1767 to be "held by all philosophers, ancient and modern."[33] Although this assessment is far from true, the theory did have much to recommend it. Not only did it provide sufficient tranquillity and time for deposition, but it also could explain the occurrence of thick, uninterrupted series of strata containing marine organisms. Furthermore, since this ocean was believed to have steadily retreated from the continents, the theory seemed to receive confirmation when Scandinavian scientists reported that the level of the Baltic was falling at a measurable rate.[34]

Serious objections to this theory were to be heard through much of the century from naturalists who themselves reached no agreement about a more satisfactory alternative. One common argument was based on the discovery by Robert Boyle that the bottom of the sea remains calm even when the surface is agitated by storms; such excessive tranquillity clearly meant that little sediment could be built up on the ocean floor.[35] Another argument resembled that used against the flood: in a universal ocean, however long its duration, deposits ought

[32] Whitehurst, op. cit. (29), especially p. 131.

[33] J.-C. Valmont de Bomare, *Dictionnaire raisonné universel d'histoire naturelle*, nouv. éd., 6 vols., Paris, 1767–8, ii. 708, article "Fossiles." The articles "Déluge" in the 1764 and 1767 editions recount the views of those who think marine fossils relics of the flood; discussion of evidence is reserved for articles "Falun," "Fossiles," and "Terre," which deal with the universal ocean and the concept of successive revolutions.

[34] Details of this research and the different interpretations of results are in Desmarest, "Ferner," *Encyclopédie méthodique*, op. cit. (29), i. 133–50. Cf. Wegmann, in Schneer, op. cit. (25), pp. 386–94, who believes that these issues had little impact outside Scandinavia during the eighteenth century.

[35] Boyle's little tract, *De fundo maris* (*Relations About the Bottom of the Sea*), was first published in English and Latin in 1670. Allusions to this work are numerous, some perhaps based on the summary in the better known study by L. F. Marsigli, *Histoire physique de la mer*, Amsterdam, 1725, pp. 1, 48. Marsigli could reach no conclusion about bottom currents, later discussed in *Telliamed*, op. cit. (11), especially pp. 60–9.

to have been laid down in order of their specific gravity. One naturalist also recalled the flood when he protested that one would have to account for the amount of water needed to produce such an ocean; if the flood could be called a miracle, the idea of a universal ocean required a natural explanation.[36] These objections received a substantial addition when Elie Bertrand asked how the sea could have deposited thick accumulations of fossils when modern seas are far less densely populated. Summarizing these and other arguments, Bertrand declared it evasive to say that no one has ever seen what lives on the ocean floor. Nor was it legitimate to invoke long periods of time to solve these dilemmas. As Bertrand put it, the oldest historical accounts show that there has been little change in the position of sea basins, and why should we suppose that major changes took place in prehistoric, "fabulous" ages, and not within historical time?[37]

Seemingly insoluble problems in the theory of a universal ocean help to explain why many naturalists instead adopted the view that the earth had undergone a succession of "revolutions." The word "revolution" was synonymous with "change," and it was applied not only to violent events like earthquakes but also to marine incursions, whether universal or local, short or long in duration.[38] This type of explanation was common for more than a century, in "theories of the earth," in monographs, and in scientific handbooks. In so long a line of thinkers from Leibniz to Cuvier, it is hardly to be expected that they should agree on the nature of these revolutions or on the effects of the flood.

A philosophical defense of the concept of revolutions was provided early in the century by Antonio Vallisneri. There is, he declared, no need to have recourse to extraordinary events when the world—repeatedly called a "machine" by this good Cartesian—follows "the ordinary laws of nature." We ought in fact to be able to explain the phenomena of nature "without violence, without fictions, without hypotheses, without miracles." To Vallisneri, therefore, the explanation

[36] A. L. Moro, *De' crostacei e degli altri marini corpi che si truovano su' monti,* Venice, 1740, pp. 15–23, 142–55. Also, J. G. Wallerius, *Mineralogie* (tr. by d'Holbach), 2 vols., Paris, 1753, i. 139.

[37] Elie Bertrand, *Memoires sur la structure interieure de la terre,* Zurich, 1752, pp. 23–31, 50–1, 56–7, 64–6.

[38] For an early use of "revolutions" in this nonastronomical sense, see Fontenelle, in *Histoire de l'Académie royale des sciences,* 1718 (1719), p. 5. Also, Roger, op. cit. (16), p. 270, n. 10, and "Révolutions de la terre," *Encyclopédie,* op. cit. (10), 1765, xiv. 237–8. I am indebted to Professor Henry Guerlac for calling the last to my attention. "Revolution" was used primarily in English and French; the corresponding terms then common in other languages have no violent connotations: *Veränderung, mutatio, mutazione.*

that was "more likely, simpler, and more natural" than the flood was a series of "many local floods," occurring over "many centuries in succession."[39] Like Vallisneri, other naturalists saw no philosophical inconsistency in emphasizing the uniformity of nature's laws and in utilizing a series of unpredictable geological upheavals. Indeed, it was commonly said that a normal part of nature, in the past as in the present, is the occurrence of such events as floods, earthquakes, landslips, and volcanic eruptions. Nor did it seem philosophically inconsistent to suggest that cataclysms in the past might have been more violent than at present; not only was this said to be plausible in the epochs when parts of the earth's crust had not yet consolidated, but it was also argued that such upheavals, however great and unpredictable, could be explained by using the known laws of physics and chemistry.[40]

Revolutions proved to be a most flexible, versatile, explanatory device. How else, if not by some revolution, could one account for the burial of elephant-like bones in Siberia and North America? In the same vein, some writers attributed to a revolution the transport to Europe of fossil genera now found only in the Indian Ocean or the Caribbean. And the occurrence of erratic boulders was commonly said to be the result of some upheaval. Late in the century, it was the theory of A. G. Werner that turned out to be the most flexible of this genre, since Werner combined revolutions with the theory of a universal ocean. By positing alternate periods of turbulence and tranquillity, Werner could account for evidence of disturbance in the strata as well as for the occurrence of horizontal sediments.[41]

Naturalists who employed revolutions disagreed sharply about the role of the flood: was the flood one of these upheavals, and, if so, what geological effects could be attributed to it? For Lehmann and Wallerius the flood was unique in its universality and in its having deposited much of the sedimentary crust; but earlier and later revolutions had also played some role in producing the present arrangement of the strata.[42] In the 1770s Arduino and Pallas, on the other hand, seem to

[39] Vallisneri, *De' corpi marini, che su' monti si trovano,* 2nd ed., Venice, 1728, pp. 34, 35, 41, 47, 73.

[40] R. Hooykaas, *Natural Law and Divine Miracle: The Principle of Uniformity in Geology, Biology and Theology,* Leiden, 1963, pp. 4–17. See also Desmarest, in *Encyclopédie méthodique,* op. cit. (29), i. 417, and iii. 197, where he distinguishes between disorderly *bouleversements* and orderly *révolutions* produced by known causes.

[41] A. G. Werner, *Short Classification and Description of the Various Rocks* (tr. with introduction and notes by A. Ospovat), New York, 1971, pp. 17–24.

[42] Lehmann, op. cit. (23), especially iii. 192–8, and John C. Greene, *The Death of Adam,* New York, 1961, pp. 67–72. Wallerius, op. cit. (36), ii. 123.

have been uncertain that the flood had had identifiable effects; if Pallas was tempted to use the flood to explain the burial of large mammals, he and Arduino nevertheless preferred to say that the present state of the earth resulted from "the successive effects of volcanoes and of other subterranean forces, plus the effects of a flood or of several incursions (*débordements*) of the sea."[43] Vallisneri, Moro, and Desmarest were critics of all diluvial theories, preferred to consider the flood a miracle, and developed their own theories of local revolutions.[44]

In this range of views, one feature is in fact common to all descriptions of the flood: departures from a literal interpretation of Genesis. Even Wallerius and Lehmann—unusual in attributing to the flood a large role in producing sedimentary strata—felt obliged to point out that periods of violence and of calm during the deluge had doubtless had different effects, and Wallerius suggests that "perhaps several centuries" were needed to achieve the retreat of the waters.[45] Their theories, indeed, are reminiscent of Werner's later version of a nondiluvial, gradually diminishing universal ocean. More common, however, was the use of the flood to explain the extinction of terrestrial forms and the transport of exotic genera, marine and terrestrial, to regions which they had not inhabited during their lifetimes. Particularly in the case of the great mammals, it was argued that they must have been catastrophically annihilated because only rapid burial could have preserved them from decay, and only sudden disaster could have prevented them from migrating to escape from local upheavals or uncongenial changes in climate. If the case for the extinction of marine forms remained unclear, there could be less doubt about terrestrial ones, even when the identification of species often lacked precision; when the latter problem was tackled by Cuvier, he, like his older contemporaries, recognized at once the crucial importance of this subject for geological theory.[46]

[43] The quotation is from P. S. Pallas, *Observations sur la formation des montagnes et les changemens arrivés au globe*, St. Petersburg, 1777, pp. 35–6. See Greene, op. cit. (42), pp. 80–1. G. Arduino, "Saggio fisico-mineralogico di lythogonia, e orognosia," *Atti dell' Accademia delle scienze di Siena*, 1774, *5*, 254. Reprinted in Arduino, *Raccolta di memorie*, Venice, 1775, which was translated into German in 1778.

[44] Vallisneri, op. cit. (39), pp. 49, 76, 83–4; Moro, op. cit. (36), pp. 426–32; and Desmarest, in *Encyclopédie méthodique*, op. cit. (29), iii. 197–8, 606–15, 618–32.

[45] Lehmann, op. cit. (23), iii. 284–92, 297 ff., 314–15. Wallerius, *De l'origine du monde et de la terre en particulier*, Warsaw, 1780, pp. 354–7.

[46] Cf. Cuvier's early statement in "Notice sur le squelette d'une très-grande espèce de quadrupède inconnue jusqu'à présent, trouvé au Paraguay," *Magasin encylopédique*, 1796, *1*, 310; and Rudwick, op. cit. (26), chapter III. The case for marine invertebrates was complicated by problems of identification and classification, but it was also argued that apparently extinct forms might still be alive in unexplored ocean depths. One of the rare

As noted earlier, Pallas was one of the several naturalists who believed that the flood might have been responsible for the transport and burial of (for example) the Siberian mammoth, since the flood possessed the requisite characteristics of having been sudden, violent, and recent. Other writers were less certain, but, as one of them remarked, the suitable explanation was surely the flood or a very similar catastrophe.[47]

From this array of oceans, floods, and upheavals, one may safely draw several conclusions. First, the flood was being reduced in status, not to a legend but to one of a series of natural upheavals. Those writers who doubted or dismissed the possible effects of the flood usually did not deny its historicity, while those who stressed local upheavals usually did not reduce the flood to a local disaster. In short, the universal flood was generally accepted as historical fact, but the scientific evidence permitted no consensus about the geological significance of the event. Furthermore, descriptions of the flood and its effects—the possible centuries of Wallerius, Whitehurst's orogenesis, Bergman's shifting of loose soil, Kirwan's transport of exotics—indicate how far geologists had abandoned the original tale of the animals two-by-two.

At this point, one may well wonder why the flood was used at all. Why resort to the Bible in a period when the physical sciences no longer did so? Why not be content—as only few geologists were—with Vallisneri's argument in favor of using explanations "more likely, simpler, and more natural"? If to use Genesis necessitated modifying the meaning of the text, would it not have been sensible to abandon the attempt?

A number of answers might be suggested to these questions, but one possible answer must be discarded, namely, the idea that geolo-

efforts to gather together evidence on this subject is F. X. Burtin, "Response a la question physique, proposée par la Société de Teyler, sur les revolutions generales, qu'a subies la surface de la terre, et sur l'ancienneté de notre globe," *Verhandelingen, uitgegeeven door Teyler's tweede genootschap,* Haarlem, 1790, viii. He concludes that the great number of extinct invertebrates demonstrates that at least one catastrophe did occur. See also Blumenbach, op. cit. (24), pp. 283–6, his *Manuel d'histoire naturelle,* tr. Soulange Artaud, 2 vols., Metz, 1803, ii.148–9, and the synopsis of one of his works by Héron de Villefosse, in *Journal des mines,* 1804, *16,* 5–36.

[47] J. F. Esper, *Description des zoolithes nouvellement decouvertes d'animaux quadrupedes inconnus et des cavernes qui les renferment,* tr. J. G. Isenflamm, Nuremberg, 1774, especially p. 81. For Pallas, see above, note 43. An excellent discussion of the problem of extinction, with emphasis on the great quadrupeds, is in Greene, op. cit. (42), chapter IV. Further examples of scientists who questioned whether the recent catastrophe should be identified with the flood are given by Leroy Page, in Schneer, op. cit. (25), p. 267 and *passim.*

gists were constrained to be orthodox. Indeed, the variety of geological interpretations of the flood provides additional evidence that there was no standard biblical exegesis to which the scientists had to adhere. On the affirmative side of the problem, it is worth remembering the old common assumption that religious and scientific truths cannot be in conflict. As Galileo had long since argued, the study of nature furnishes us with "hard" information, while the Bible is notoriously difficult to understand; the two sources will be found to harmonize, however, if we reinterpret the Bible on the basis of scientific fact.[48] Except for those few naturalists who set the flood aside as a miracle, most writers seem to have shared this Galilean belief. When so many theories are all said to be in harmony with Scripture, it is more than likely that theories were based primarily on geological evidence, and the Bible then reinterpreted suitably.

Probably more important than this general desire to reconcile Genesis with geology was the methodological principle enunciated by Richard Kirwan:

> In effect, past geological facts being of an historical nature, all attempts to deduce a complete knowledge of them merely from their still subsisting consequences, to the exclusion of unexceptionable testimony, must be deemed as absurd as that of deducing the history of ancient Rome solely from the medals or other monuments . . . , to the exclusion of a Livy, a Sallust, or a Tacitus.[49]

The testimony Kirwan had in mind was that of Moses, confirmed by other ancient traditions. However staunch a defender of Genesis in the face of the "immorality and infidelity" rampant during the French Revolution, Kirwan depicts Moses as neither prophet nor scientist, but *historian.* Not only was the interpretation of ancient traditions a subject of lively interest in the eighteenth century, but Kirwan's insistence that "monuments" alone provide incomplete knowledge was also a topic debated for some decades. Both points merit further discussion, which can only be undertaken here all too briefly.

Quite early in the century, professional historians had tackled the question of the credibility of ancient legends and oral traditions. They had concluded that tradition could transmit accurately—in outline, if not in detail—any event that was large, dramatic, and public; and when essentially the same event entered into apparently independent

[48] Galileo, "Letter to the Grand Duchess Christina," in *Discoveries and Opinions of Galileo* (tr. with introduction and notes by Stillman Drake), New York, 1957, pp. 175–216.

[49] Kirwan, *Geological Essays,* London, 1799, p. 5; also, pp. 5–6, 54–86.

traditions among many peoples, a mere historical probability became a virtual certainty.[50] Such critical precepts applied in all their force to the flood. When geologists assiduously compared ancient flood legends, discarding some details and reinterpreting others, they were being very "modern" indeed. Furthermore, they were in the enviable position of being able to combine with the ancient texts the testimony of nature.

Early in the century, too, professional historians had debated the degrees of confidence one could repose in ancient texts as compared with the "medals or other monuments" referred to by Kirwan, and the faction that considered "monuments" to be more reliable than texts won at least a temporary victory. To be sure, "monuments" should ideally be correlated with other (written) evidence, but what if no texts existed? While Fontenelle could grandly announce that geologists had available "histories written by the hand of nature itself," geologists often felt reassured when "nature itself" could be supplemented by the evidence of human witnesses.[51] Lehmann, for example, hesitated to comment on the nature and extent of antediluvian geological changes for which "we lack historical monuments." Desmarest considered it quite understandable that in seeking to interpret the rocks, geologists should "have recourse to the greatest, most universal catastrophe mentioned in history." And as one writer put it, if we do not use the flood to account for the burial of mammals, we would be in the position of having to suppose another such catastrophe "without being able to base ourselves on history."[52]

For the geologist, then, there were three options: one could use historical texts when these existed, or one could construct those "hypotheses" so roundly condemned by Newton, or one could, like Blumenbach or Cuvier, make an effort to distinguish between speculation and geology as "une science positive."

[50] See articles by Pouilly and Fréret, in *Memoires de litterature tirez des registres de l'Academie royale des inscriptions et belles lettres,* Paris, 1729, *6,* especially 153, 156, 71–114. Also, Manuel, op. cit. (15), *passim;* Lionel Gossman, *Medievalism and the Ideologies of the Enlightenment: The World and Work of La Curne de Sainte-Palaye,* Baltimore, 1968, pp. 153–7; and Rénee Simon, "Nicolas Fréret, académicien," *Studies on Voltaire and the Eighteenth Century,* 1961, *17,* 120–30.

[51] Fontenelle, in *Histoire de l'Académie royale des sciences,* 1722 (1724), p. 4. On the question of "monuments," see the crucial article by Arnaldo Momigliano, "Ancient History and the Antiquarian," *Journal of the Warburg and Courtauld Institutes,* 1950, *13,* 285–315; reprinted in two collections of Momigliano's articles: *Studies in Historiography,* New York, 1966, pp. 1–39, and *Contributo alla storia degli studi classici,* Rome, 1955, pp. 67–106.

[52] Esper, op. cit. (47), p. 81. Lehmann, op. cit. (23), iii. 192. Desmarest, in *Encyclopédie méthodique,* op. cit. (29), iii. 606.

Charles Lyell and the Noachian Deluge

JAMES R. MOORE

The scene shifts to nineteenth-century England and centers on the debate inspired by the pioneering figure of geologist Charles Lyell. Sir Charles Lyell (1797–1875) was one of the founders of modern geology and was largely responsible for the classificatory nomenclature of Eocene, Miocene, and Pliocene, a stratigraphical distinction based upon the proportion of recent to extinct species of shells.

There seems little doubt that geologists with religious convictions were—and for that matter some still are—genuinely troubled by the difficulties in accepting Genesis and the results of geological research as equally valid. Can one keep one's religious beliefs separate from one's scientific hypotheses? Or must one choose one over the other? Or can they be successfully reconciled? For those adhering to Fundamentalist readings of the Bible (as absolute literal truth), these continue to be nagging questions. Usually, if their faith is especially strong, science is simply dismissed as a series of unproved hypotheses. Evolution, in such a perspective, is but an alternative theory, not a demonstrated fact. Biologists and paleontologists, for the most part, cannot accept this position, as they claim to have documented the evolutionary process for dozens and dozens of organisms. At the end of this essay by James R. Moore, Lecturer in History of Science and Technology at the Open University in England, we find numerous references to works published in the twentieth century and we realize that the flood continues to be a critical issue in this ongoing centuries-long controversy.

For another account of the struggle between the Neptunists—that is, those who believed in the primary effect of water *on geological conditions (those advocating a literal, historical flood)—and the Vulcanists—who, in contrast, believed that the critical factor was not water but* fire *or volcanic activity—see Colin Russell, "Noah's Flood: Noah and the Neptunists,"* Faith and Thought *100 (1972–1973): 143–158. Perhaps the most comprehensive review of the debate is Charles Coulston Gillispie,* Genesis and Geology: A Study in the Relations of Scientific Thought, Natural Theology, and Social Opinion in Great Britain, 1790–1850 *(New York, 1959).*

Reprinted from the *Evangelical Quarterly* 45 (1973):141–160 by permission of the Paternoster Press, Exeter, England.

Scientists and theologians who are Christians too often neglect history to their own intellectual condemnation. What appear to them to be major modern issues on which turns the perspicuous truth of biblical revelation are often problems which were long ago laid to rest. They realize too late that their labored polemics and hastily written tracts are little more than exuberant rehashes of what was once conclusively argued or contravened. This is unforgivable. They should have known that, without historical sense, it is not only possible but inevitable that men repeat the very errors which once discredited their forbears. Since "all have sinned," even twentieth-century evangelicals are likely to follow in this ignoble tradition unless they maintain a clear-minded historical perspective on contemporary relations between science and theology. Moreover, without this perspective they will surely have no access to important contributions which have been made by way of solution to controversies which still engage them.

This study attempts to present the great "high-priest of uniformitarianism," the flood-furor his work induced in theological circles, and the harmonizing efforts of nineteenth-century theological scholarship. The lessons it affords are at least two in number. In view of the "ignoble tradition," I consider the drama of dogmatic theology attacking learned science well worth pondering in order to recognize repeat performances and treat them remedially. Also, because the Genesis Flood and the philosophy of uniformitarianism have recently been so much in debate among certain evangelicals, I think an understanding of the seminal work of Charles Lyell in relation to its harmonizers with biblical teaching may possibly illuminate the technical side of this somewhat dated controversy.

SETTING THE STAGE

During the seventeenth and eighteenth centuries the problems connected with the Noachian Deluge did not so much concern its historicity as they did its universality. One problem arose from the absence in America of some Old World animals and by the presence of new varieties (viz., how did they find their way from Mount Ararat?). Together with the obstacle of insufficient water for a universal Deluge, such complications compelled some scholars to put forth a "local flood" theory.[1] In response, those who held the universal view ad-

[1]Edward Stillingfleet, *Origines Sacrae: or a Rational Account of the Grounds of Natural and Reveal'd Religion* (London: 1697); and Bishop Robert Clayton, *A Vindication of the Histories of the Old and New Testament in Answer to the Objections of the Late Lord Bolingbroke* (Dublin: 1752). Earlier interpretations of the Flood are discussed with thor-

vanced theories of the earth to explain its composition and to account for the waters of the Deluge without invoking a miraculous creation of water. Patrick Cockburn's *An Enquiry into the Truth and Certainty of the Mosaic Deluge* and Alexander Catcott's *A Treatise on the Deluge,* together with the theories of Burnet, Whiston and Woodward,[2] were "so far successful as to establish for many decades the orthodoxy of the doctrine that the Noachian deluge was universal rather than limited in extent."[3] In fact, that doctrine outlived the rather peculiar theories which purported to account for the waters of the Deluge and the constitution of the earth.[4]

By the turn of the nineteenth century a new enthusiasm for the Flood theory of geology had swept Europe. Fossils, the rock strata in which they were found, and the major geologic formations of the earth were considered to be the result of the worldwide Deluge.[5] But in its increasing sophistication the science of geology was beginning to replace armchair theories of the globe; geologists frankly suspected that the Genesis Flood was being overworked. It seemed to them incredible that the year-long inundation could have done the earth-moving task to which it had been assigned.

In the process of second-guessing the mechanisms of geological formation a heated controversy developed. The Neptunists, led by Abraham Gottlob Werner, and the Vulcanists (or Plutonists), the followers of James Hutton, were struggling to account for geological phenomena apart from the Flood.[6] The former held that all rock formations were precipitated from a primeval, mineral-laden ocean which, when it receded, revealed the continents as they are today. But the theory was formulated in a day when "indoor discussion of theories was

---

ough documentation in Jack P. Lewis, *A Study of the Interpretation of Noah and the Flood in Jewish and Christian Literature* (Leiden: E. J. Brill, 1968), and in D. C. Allen, *The Legend of Noah* (Urbana, Illinois: University of Illinois Press, 1949), which cover, respectively, the literature from the Old Testament Apocrypha and Pseudepigrapha through the church fathers, and the literature of the Middle Ages.

[2]Thomas Burnet, *A Sacred Theory of the Earth* (2 vols.; London: 1722); William Whiston, *A New Theory of the Earth* (Cambridge: 1708); and John Woodward, *An Essay Toward a Natural History of the Earth* (London: 1695).

[3]Katharine Brownell Collier, *Cosmogonies of Our Fathers* (New York: Columbia University Press, 1934), p. 241.

[4]*Ibid.,* pp. 229–30, 241.

[5]Henry M. Morris and John C. Whitcomb, Jr., *The Genesis Flood* (Grand Rapids, Michigan: Baker Book House, 1966), p. 91.

[6]Chester R. Longwell, "Geology," in *The Development of the Sciences,* ed. L. L. Woodruff (New Haven, Connecticut: Yale University Press, 1941), pp. 158–63. More detail is available in Frank Dawson Adams, *The Birth and Development of the Geological Sciences* (reprint ed.; New York: Dover Publications, 1954), pp. 238ff.

far more popular than field study."[7] Werner himself based his conclusions on a woefully inadequate foundation of induction which stemmed only from observations made in his immediate German neighborhood. He left much to the imagination in moving from the very particular to the general.

In contrast James Hutton published his *Theory of the Earth* in 1795, when he was nearly seventy years old, a mature work based on a lifetime of wide-ranging field observations. Instead of diluvialism or mineral precipitation, Hutton advanced a reasonable though unorthodox interpretation of geological phenomena.

> He contended that dynamic forces in the crust of the earth created tensions and stresses which, in the course of time, elevated new lands from the ocean bed even as other exposed surfaces were in the process of erosion. There had never been a universal flood. There was observable in the buried shell beds of the continents, which had long been taken as evidence of the Deluge, only the signs of subsidence and renewed uplift which were part of the eternal youth of the world.[8]

The key word here is "time." Hutton contended that the forces of nature he observed, in shaping the crust of the earth at the rates he observed, could only have produced the observed geologic formations by operating for many millennia.

Hutton's friend, John Playfair, considered that the book would not sell because of its ponderous, abstruse style. In 1802 he took it upon himself to elucidate Hutton's prose in a popular edition titled *Illustrations of the Huttonian Theory.* Thornbury highlights these volumes in his 1954 publication, *Principles of Geomorphology:*

> *Concept 1* The same physical processes and laws that operate today operated throughout geologic time, although not necessarily with the same intensity as now.
>
> This is the great underlying principle of modern geology and is known as the principle of uniformitarianism. It was first enunciated by Hutton in 1785, beautifully restated by Playfair in 1802, and popularized by Lyell in the numerous editions of his *Principles of Geology.*
>
> Without the principle of uniformitarianism there could hardly be a science of geology that was more than pure description.[9]

[7] Longwell, *ibid.,* p. 161.

[8] Loren Eisley, *Darwin's Century,* Anchor Books (Garden City, New York: Doubleday & Company, 1958), p. 71. Cf. Stephen Toulmin and June Goodfield, *The Discovery of Time* (London: Hutchison, 1965), *passim.*

[9] William Thornbury, *Principles of Geomorphology* (New York: John Wiley & Sons, 1954), pp. 16–17.

Hutton's postulation of excessive time rankled the religiously orthodox. If anything was certain in their minds, it was that the earth could not be more than about 6000 years old. Bishop Ussher's "received chronology" must be inspired, since it was, they thought, unerringly deduced from Scripture. But thanks to Baron Cuvier, they were able to advance what seemed for the time being unanswerable criticisms of Hutton's uniformitarian time scale. Cuvier posited a series of aqueous catastrophes to account for the major rock strata. The last of these, the Noachian Deluge, was held to account for the superficial deposits of fossils in upper strata.[10] Theologians easily found time for Cuvier's catastrophes between the original creation of the cosmos in Genesis 1:1 and the restoration described in the six-day account. Or, in another view, the days of creation were understood to be ages of organic development interrupted by Cuvier's catastrophes (an opinion generally considered to be heterodox, however). These theories found wide acclaim, especially among the leading English geologists, Sedgwick, Murchison, and Buckland.

William Buckland, Professor of Geology at Oxford, was a distinguished teacher, a committed Christian, and the foremost English geologist prior to Charles Lyell. Buckland literally uncovered many important geological facts which were considered to fit perfectly into the framework of Cuvier's multiple catastrophism. With Cuvier he maintained that the major rock strata and virtually all fossils owe their existence to a series of catastrophes that occurred in antiquity. He gave the name "alluvium" to the superficial beds of bone and rock deposited by streams in recent years. The title "diluvium" was reserved, for example, for the bones of elephants, tigers and other uncommon tropical animals he found jumbled together in a Yorkshire cave. This diluvium he took to be direct and irrefutable evidence of a universal Flood.

Buckland announced the theory in his inaugural lecture at Oxford and, in 1823, secured his fame by publishing it in his *Reliquiae Diluvianae.* "The treatise was of such a high scientific caliber, in spite of its fallacious premises, that it firmly implanted the actuality of the Deluge in the minds of geologists as well as nongeologists, not only in Britain but throughout Europe and America."[11] In France Cuvier happily adopted Buckland's conclusions and in 1826 wrote that they "now

[10]Morris and Whitcomb, *The Genesis Flood,* p. 92. For Cuvier's position in his own words see Charles C. Gillespie's translation of *Recherches sur les Ossemens Fossiles,* I, 8–9, in *Genesis and Geology* (Cambridge, Massachusetts: Harvard University Press, 1951), pp. 99–100.

[11]Francis H. Haber, *The Age of the World: Moses to Darwin* (Baltimore, Maryland: The Johns Hopkins Press, 1959), p. 211.

form, in the eyes of all geologists, the fullest proof to the senses, of that immense inundation (the Noachian flood) which came last in the catastrophes of our globe."[12] Theologians regarded *Reliquiae Diluvianae* as a great, scholarly victory for the testimony of Moses, and belief in a universal Deluge was more firmly established than ever before.

THE PROTAGONIST

There is considerable truth in Thomas Huxley's wry recollection of the twenties and thirties of his century:

> At that time, geologists and biologists could hardly follow to the end any path of inquiry without finding the way blocked by Noah and his ark . . . and it was a serious matter, in this country at any rate, for a man to be suspected of doubting the literal truth of the Diluvial or any other Pentateuchal history.[13]

Into this rather stultifying atmosphere came the inquiring mind of Charles Lyell. Lyell had grown up with an unusual interest in nature; from the day he read *Bakewell's Geology* he was marked for geological study. It thus seemed inevitable that he should later in life leave law school and the promise of a lucrative profession to study with William Buckland and to pore over James Hutton. During his geological education he travelled extensively in England and on the continent, everywhere collecting rocks and fossils and making detailed notes on formations. At length Lyell, "with full knowledge of what had been said on both sides, became a convinced Uniformitarian."[14] In 1829, six months before the first of his epoch-making three volumes, *Principles of Geology*, was published, he outlined his ideas in a letter to a friend:

> My work is in part written, and all planned. It will not pretend to give even an abstract of all that is known in geology, but it will endeavor to establish the *principle of reasoning* in the science; and all my geology

[12] Georges Cuvier, *Discours sur les Révolutions de la Surface du Globe* (3rd ed.: Paris, 1836), p. 133, cited by Morris and Whitcomb, *The Genesis Flood*, p. 94.

[13] "The Lights of the Church and the Light of Science," *Nineteenth Century*, July, 1890, p. 5. Gillespie observes that this article is "a highly colored account of the influence of the flood and of theological obscurantism in general after 1830" (*Genesis and Geology*, p. 234). It is however invaluable for its viewpoint and for the many sources it cites.

[14] Sir Edward Battersby Bailey, *Charles Lyell* (Garden City, New York: Doubleday & Co., 1963), p. 85.

> will come in as illustration of my views of those principles, and as evidence strengthening the system necessarily arising out of the admission of such principles, which, as you know, are neither more nor less than that *no causes whatever* have from the earliest time to which we can look back, to the present, ever acted, but those *now acting,* and that they never acted with different degrees of energy from that which they now exert.[15]

The substance of Lyell's great work is summed up in its subtitle: "Being an attempt to explain the former changes in the earth's surface by reference to causes now in operation."

It must however be pointed out in passing that Lyell was a child of his time. The doctrinaire naturalism which then pervaded scientific thought was fully evidenced and endorsed in his *Principles of Geology.* He asserted that "the enigmas of the moral and spiritual world . . . are found to depend on fixed and invariable laws" and that "the philosopher at last becomes convinced of the undeviating uniformity of secondary causes, and . . . determines that probability of accounts transmitted to him of former occurrences, and often rejects the fabulous tales of former ages, on the ground of their being irreconcilable with the experience of more enlightened ages."[16] Moreover, as an anti-Darwinian (in his formative years) there was as yet no compelling reason to forsake religion in the face of such a world-view. Thomas Bonney points out that Lyell was a member of the Church of England, though one more enamored with its music and architecture than with its doctrine. He thus failed to understand why scientific inquiry should elicit ecclesiastical censure.

> His mind was essentially undogmatic; feeling that certainty was impossible in questions where the ordinary means of verification could not be employed, he abstained from speculation . . . he was content, however, to believe where he could not prove . . . he worked on in calm confidence that the honest seeker after truth would never go astray.[17]

[15] Mrs. [Katharine Murray] Lyell, *Life, Letters and Journals of Sir Charles Lyell* (2 vols.; London: John Murray, 1881), I, 234.

[16] *Principles of Geology* (3 vols.; London: John Murray, 1830–34), I, 76. Note the marked similarity between this view and that of David Hume in his *Enquiry Concerning Human Understanding,* sec. x, pt. 1. Gillespie concludes: "Uniformitarian presuppositions, then, were simply those of optimistic materialism. . . . Gratuitous Lyell's assumption may have been, but it opened the way for scientific progress" (*Genesis and Geology,* p. 135).

[17] *Charles Lyell and Modern Geology* (New York: Cassell and Co., 1895), p. 212. Cf. A. P. Stanley's "Funeral Sermon on Sir Charles Lyell" in *Religious Controversies of the Nineteenth Century,* ed. A. O. J. Cockshut (Lincoln, Neb.: University of Nebraska Press, 1966), reprinted from Stanley's *Sermons on Special Occasions.*

Lyell's writings epitomized his intellectual and spiritual outlook. Anyone who has read his *Principles* will agree with Andrew Dickson White who said that "nothing could have been more cautious." It merely gave a well-documented account of the main discoveries which he and others had made up to that time. Then from his legal training he imported clear and convincing logic to tie the facts together in illustration of the uniformitarian principle.[18]

Since Lyell must have been painfully aware that the Noachian Deluge was a major barrier to the promulgation and acceptance of his ideas, "he impugned the deluge explicitly in only one passage. . . . Generally he preferred the method of draining the flood of its influence incidentally to the development of his larger interpretation."[19] Said he,

> For our own part, we have always considered the flood, if we are to admit its universality in the strictest sense of the term, as a preternatural event far beyond the reach of philosophical inquiry, whether as to the secondary causes employed to produce it or the effects most likely to result from it.[20]

With characteristic reservation, Lyell instead advanced an interpretation of the Flood diametrically opposed to that of catastrophist geology:

> It is the opinion of some writers, that the earth's surface underwent no great modification in the era of the Mosaic deluge, and that the strictest interpretation of the scriptural narrative does not warrant us in expecting to find *any geological monuments of the catastrophe.*[21]

While it appears that Lyell gave first of all a philosophical reason for his view of the Flood, we cannot easily agree that the view was merely "incidental" to the development of his "larger [uniformitarian] interpretation." With *his* doctrine of uniformitarianism, he *must* have found it

[18] *A History of the Warfare of Science with Theology in Christendom* (2 vols., reprint ed.; New York: Dover Publications, 1960), I, 232, hereafter cited as *Warfare of Science with Theology.* Gordon H. Clark, however, neatly raps White's naked prejudices in his essay, "The Nature of the Physical Universe," in *Christian Faith and Modern Theology,* ed. Carl F. H. Henry (New York: Channel Press, 1964).

[19] Gillespie, *Genesis and Geology,* p. 129.

[20] *Principles of Geology,* III, 273. Cf. n. 29 below.

[21] *Ibid.,* p. 274 (emphasis mine). Though Lyell evidently objected to a catastrophic flood on philosophical and biblical grounds, he was also rather discontented with catastrophist system builders. He objected that it is unreasonable "to call the Deity capriciously upon the stage, and to make him work miracles, for the sake of confirming our preconceived hypotheses . . . systems built with their foundations in the air, and cannot be propped up without a miracle" (p. 45).

geologically necessary to minimize the effect of the Flood. Indeed "draining the flood of its influence" meant for him that the universal Flood must have been far too tranquil a phenomenon to leave any observable geologic effects. Lyell even took pains to show that Scripture itself permitted this interpretation: he maintained that "in the narrative of Moses there are no terms employed that indicate the impetuous rushing of the waters, either as they rose or when they retreated, upon the restraining of the rain and the passing of a wind over the earth." And with a touch of irony he signalized "so remarkable a fact as that the olive remained standing while the waters were abating."[22] The "tranquil theory," as it came to be known, gained vogue with many geologists soon after Lyell's work appeared.[23]

Sir Charles Lyell was by no means a villain. He was rather an honest, nominally religious seeker after scientific truth who had no desire to agitate the Christian community. While viewing miraculous intervention in the course of nature with a distinctly sceptical eye, his naturalistic uniformitarianism (unlike that of Hutton) did not prevent him from accepting the historicity of the Noachian Deluge.

AGGRAVATION AND ALTERCATION

Lyell's work was immensely popular and widely read both by professional geologists and, surprisingly, "by the cultivated public whose curiosity about the secrets of the earth was growing."[24] However, as one might expect, laymen were confused by his relatively technical and irregular interpretation of the Deluge. Since orthodoxy apparently held the upper hand in theological circles at the time laymen expected a refutation of Lyell's tranquil, uniformitarian interpretation from their Christian leaders. But much to their consternation the Archbishop of Canterbury, the Bishop of London and the Bishop of Llandaff in 1831 instead suggested Charles Lyell be professor of geology at King's College. In a letter Lyell related their attitude toward his work:

[22] Lyell, *Principles of Geology,* III, 271–73. That the latter quotation may constitute a misinterpretation of the biblical record is suggested by Morris and Whitcomb (*The Genesis Flood,* pp. 104–106).

[23] Morris and Whitcomb, *The Genesis Flood,* p. 97. In reality this theory was proposed by the botanist Carolus Linnaeus and was introduced into England in 1826. However after Lyell's *Principles* was in circulation, many scholars came to hold that the tranquil theory was one device able to harmonize geology and Scripture. See below at text corresponding to n. 68.

[24] Eiseley, *Darwin's Century,* p. 99. For reaction to the *Principles* in scientific circles, see Robert H. Murray, *Science and Scientists in the Nineteenth Century* (New York: Sheldon Press, 1925), pp. 51–65.

> They considered some of my doctrines startling enough, but could not find that they were come by otherwise than in a straightforward manner, and (as I appeared to think) logically deducible from the facts . . . there was no reason to infer that I had made my theory from any hostile feeling toward revelation.[25]

This seemed outrageous to the orthodox. Thus Lyell's perceptive friend, Poulett Scrope, quipped:

> If the news be true, and your opinions are to be taken at once into the bosom of the Church, instead of contending against that party for half a century, then, indeed, shall we make a step at once of fifty years in the science—in such a miracle will I believe when I see it performed.[26]

Another factor which induced a flood-furor among the biblically orthodox was the humble recantation of William Buckland. In the sixth of the series of "Bridgewater Treatises," delivered in 1836, Buckland repudiated his earlier conviction that his "diluvium" may be accounted for by the Noachian Flood. He rejected Ussher's chronology and agreed with Lyell's tranquil interpretation, asserting that the waters of the Deluge "produced comparatively little change on the surface of the country they overflowed."[27] The orthodox were confused and irritated by the defection of their Flood-Champion. Bishop Shuttleworth memorialized the occasion:

> Some doubts were once expressed about the Flood;
> Buckland arose, and all was clear as mud.[28]

But at the bottom of the mud was Charles Lyell. It was his work which popularized and ultimately established the uniformitarian interpretation of geological phenomena.

War was declared. The ideological struggle to harmonize geology and Genesis began almost immediately after the publication of the third volume of Lyell's *Principles* in 1834. One author observed that "attempts [at harmonization] have been variously classified, but the fact regarding them all is that each mixes up more or less of science with more or less of Scripture, and produces a result more or less ab-

[25] Mrs. Lyell, *Life, Letters and Journals of Sir Charles Lyell,* I, 317. Lyell assured Bishop Copleston of Llandaff "that there was 'no objection to his drowning as many people as he pleased on such parts as can be shown to be inhabited in the days of Noah'" (Gillespie, *Genesis and Geology,* pp. 140–41).

[26] Mrs. Lyell, *Life, Letters and Journals of Sir Charles Lyell,* I, 317.

[27] Morris and Whitcomb, *The Genesis Flood,* pp. 98–99.

[28] White, *Warfare of Science with Theology,* p. 232.

surd."[29] While the supposition of the absurdity of mingling science and Scripture may be itself absurd, many of the concoctions which boiled on the back burners of "fundamentalist" brains were in fact served up at an absurd temperature, too hot to swallow even if they had been palatable.[30]

Robert Bakewell wrote to the famous American geologist Benjamin Silliman that "geology is in a rather strange state in England at present; the rich clergy begin to tremble for their incomes, and seek to avert their fate by a revived zeal for orthodoxy, and are making a great clamor against geology as opposed to Genesis."[31] It seems however of little consequence for our purposes whether clergymen were motivated financially or spiritually. The fact is that they often violated the canons of social decency, to say nothing of Christian propriety, in denigrating geology and geologists. When it was found that Lyell did not attribute the fossil remains to the Deluge, and when it was shown by him that the earth is older than six millennia, "orthodox indignation burst forth violently; eminent dignitaries of the Church attacked him without mercy."[32] In reflecting on his final public address given before the Geological Club in 1875, Huxley recounted that Lyell "spoke with his wonted clearness and vigor of the social ostracism which pursued him after the publication of the *Principles of Geology*, in 1830."[33]

[29] *Ibid.*, p. 234. This baleful conclusion mars J. R. Van de Fliert's otherwise superlative analysis of uniformitarianism and *The Genesis Flood* ("Fundamentalism and the Fundamentals of Geology," *Journal of the American Scientific Affiliation*, XXI [September, 1969], 69–81). Note likewise Lyell's relation to this viewpoint in the text corresponding to nn. 20 and 21, and in Shields' observation that "Sir Charles Lyell himself, who always treats the Scriptures with respect, indicates his sense of their scientific value by studiously excluding them from his 'Principles of Geology,' even from his learned chapter on oriental cosmogony" (Charles Woodruff Shields, *The Final Philosophy* [New York: Scribner, Armstrong & Co., 1877], p. 132).

[30] The sense in which "fundamentalist" is used here—that distinguished by E. J. Carnell—aptly describes theological reaction to Lyell. Carnell said that fundamentalism is a religious mentality which "draws its distinctiveness from its attempt to maintain status by negation. . . . It is a highly ideological attitude. It is intransigent and inflexible; it expects conformity; it fears academic liberty. It makes no allowance for the inconsistent, and thus partially valid, elements in other positions" ("Fundamentalism," in *A Handbook of Christian Theology*, ed. by Martin Halverson and Arthur A. Cohen, Meridian Books [New York: The World Publishing Company, 1958], p. 142).

[31] John F. Fulton and Elizabeth H. Thomson, *Benjamin Silliman, 1779–1864, Pathfinder in American Science* (New York: 1947), p. 135, cited by Haber, *The Age of the World: Moses to Darwin*, p. 220.

[32] White, *Warfare of Science with Theology*, p. 233.

[33] "The Lights of the Church and the Light of Science," p. 12. Bonney made a remarkable observation with reference to this issue: "A large number of persons—among whom are the great mass of amateur theologians, together with some experts—are always very prone to assume the meaning of certain fundamental terms to be exactly that which they desire, and then to proceed deductively to a conclusion as if their questionable

Some clergy were motivated by more noble ends than financial gain. They took up the literary sword in defense of Scripture against the perverters of Divine Truth and published volume upon laborious volume of ignorant pseudo-science.[34] While few of these books are now extant, the response to them still throws as much light on the controversy as the works themselves. Hugh Miller, for example, a prominent and popular nineteenth-century geologist, wrote concerning "The Geology of the Anti-Geologists" in his book, *The Testimony of the Rocks.* There he relates a striking example of obscurantist reaction to Lyellian uniformitarianism.[35] On the supposition that all geologic processes in the past proceeded at the present observed rates Lyell calculated the erosion taking place at Niagara Falls and concluded that 10,000 years ago the falls were located as far downstream as the present location of Queenston. This elicited from a Scottish minister a fulmination typical of orthodox reaction to many of Lyell's doctrines. After denouncing the calculation as a "stab at the Christian religion" in that Lyell alleged "the Falls were actually at Queenston four thousand years before the creation of the world according to Moses," the anti-geologist exultingly exclaimed:

> It is on grounds such as these that the most learned and voluminous among English geologists disputes the Mosaic history of the Creation and Deluge, a strong proof that even men of argument on other subjects often reason in the most childish and ridiculous manner, and on grounds totally false, when they undertake to deny the truth of the Holy Scriptures.[36]

---

postulates were axiomatic truths. They further assume, very commonly, that the possession of theological knowledge—scanty and superficial though it may be—enables them to dispense with any study of science, and to pronounce authoritatively on the value of evidence which they are incapable of weighing, and of conclusions which they are too ignorant to test. Being thus, in their own opinion, infallible, a freedom of expression is, for them, more than permissible, which, in most other matters, would be generally held to transgress the limits of courtesy and to trespass on those of vituperation" (*Charles Lyell and Modern Geology,* pp. 48–49).

[34] Edward Hitchcock correctly reflected that Christian men of good character have examined geological writings, not to understand but for the purpose of finding contradictions and untenable positions. "The next step has been to write a book against geology, abounding, as we might expect from men of warm temperament, of such prejudices, and without a practical knowledge of geology, with striking misapprehensions of facts and opinions, with positive and dogmatic assertions, with severe personal insinuations, great ignorance of correct reasoning in geology, and the substitution of wild and extravagant hypotheses for geological theories" (*The Religion of Geology and Its Connected Sciences* [London: J. Blackwood, 1862?], pp. 26–27, hereafter cited as *Religion of Geology*).

[35] Hugh Miller, *The Testimony of the Rocks* (9th ed.; New York: John B. Alden, 1892), pp. 412–23.

[36] From the *Scottish Christian Herald,* III (1838), 766, cited by Miller, *ibid.,* p. 422.

In 1838, two years after Buckland's recantation, L. Vernon Harcourt published a book dedicated to his father, the Archbishop of York. *On the Doctrine of the Deluge,* a "grave book" according to Huxley, was an attempt to reply to Buckland and Lyell. Though it apparently succeeded at one or two points,[37] Huxley refused to reproduce several of the arguments on the ground that it would be cruel to do so. He quotes Harcourt as impugning the scholarship of Buckland and Lyell by insisting that they merely dodged the scriptural account of the Flood.[38] In the same year the Reverend George Young, D.D. (author of *A Geological Survey of the Yorkshire Coast*), published his *Scriptural Geology,* a work "devoted principally to an attack upon the rising uniformitarian and evolutionary theories of geology." Advocating full-blown Flood geology, Dr. Young "vigorously attacked the works of Lyell," especially in regard to their "unwarranted [*sic*] assumptions" regarding uniformitarianism.[39]

Of the scores of books published in the nineteenth century attempting to harmonize geology and Genesis, one stands in stark contrast to all others. Though it cannot quite be classified with anti-geology works, one cannot resist using it to bridge the gap between the rancorous and the responsible reactions to Lyellian uniformitarianism. In *Omphalos* Philip Henry Gosse thought he had developed the panacea for all geological problems related to the age of the world and the effects of the Noachian Deluge. "Never was a book cast upon the waters with greater anticipation of success than was this curious, this obstinate, this fanatical volume," wrote the younger Gosse in his book *Father and Son.*[40] Gosse believed the life of the universe follows a cyclical pattern and that it was brought into existence by Divine fiat at a particular point in its cycle. The appearances of development in matter at the moment of its creation he called *prochronic* because time was not an element in them. The changes of appearance which have taken place in the life

[37] Morris and Whitcomb, *The Genesis Flood,* pp. 105–106.

[38] "The Lights of the Church and the Light of Science," p. 12, quoting L. Vernon Harcourt, *On the Doctrine of the Deluge* (London: Longman, *et al.,* 1838), pp. 8–9.

[39] Byron Nelson, *The Deluge Story in Stone* (reprint ed.; Minneapolis, Minnesota: Bethany Fellowship, 1968), pp. 105–106. The fact that Nelson calls Young's book "excellent" is one of those unforgivable mistakes mentioned earlier which those who refuse to learn from history commit, to their own intellectual condemnation. Nelson's conclusion betokens this: "Flood geology, based on faith in God's Word and the supernatural, was not the type of thing the world wanted [*sic*], and henceforth it was ignored or ridiculed" (p. 110).

[40] Quoted by Martin Gardner, *Fads and Fallacies in the Name of Science* (formerly *In the Name of Science*) (reprinted; New York: Dover Publications, 1957), p. 126.

cycle of the universe since the time matter was created he called *diachronic.*

> Admit for a moment, as a hypothesis, that the Creator had before his mind a projection of the whole life-history of the globe, commencing with any point which the geologist may imagine to have been a fitting commencing point, and ending with some unimaginable acme in the indefinitely distant future. He determines to call this idea into actual existence, not at the supposed commencing point, but at some stage or other of its course. It is clear, then, that at the selected stage it appears, exactly as it would have appeared at that moment of its history, if all the preceding eras of its history had been real.[41]

In this simple way Gosse attempted to explain away geology, uniformitarianism, and its attending controversies. What he did not realize was that his "apparent-age thesis" was compatible with an infinite number of parallel assertions to the effect, "the universe was created *n* number of years (days, hours, or minutes) ago with built-in history." Gosse's son wrote, "Atheists and Christians alike looked at it and laughed, and threw it away." Yet for those who reflected on the one "enormous and superfluous lie" which God had perpetrated (inevitably recalling Descartes' "evil genius"), he added, "a gloom, cold and dismal, descended upon our morning tea cups."[42]

DÉNOUEMENT

With other more or less reactionary sentiments better left unexamined[43] we move on to consider the first and foremost responsible harmony of geology and the Deluge produced in the nineteenth century.

[41] Philip Henry Gosse, *Omphalos: An Attempt to Untie the Geological Knot* (London: J. Van Voorst, 1857), p. 351. Chateaubriand first gave birth to this idea in the eighteenth century (*Oeuvres complètes de Chateaubriand,* II, 83) and Gosse nursed it back to health in 1857. The notion died with *Omphalos* and, apparently, without a careful reading of history, Morris and Whitcomb have disinterred this philosophical corpse in their "apparent-age" thesis. Cf. *The Genesis Flood,* pp. 232–43, 345–69.

[42] From the younger Gosse's work, *Father and Son,* quoted by Gardner, *Fads and Fallacies in the Name of Science,* p. 127.

[43] See: *A Brief and Complete Refutation of the Anti-Scriptural Theory of Geologists,* by a Clergyman of the Church of England; *Exposure of the Principles of Modern Geology,* by P. M. M'Farlane; *Popular Geology Subversive of Divine Revelation,* by Reverend Henry Cole; and *Strictures on Geology and Astronomy,* by Reverend R. Wilson. The mere mention of their titles serves the purposes of the present study. And what was Lyell's reaction to all this clamor? He "very seldom spoke of the Biblical geologists, yet evidently relished the peculiar irony which had made Burnet's 'Sacred Theory of the Earth' a favorite at the Court of Charles II and pointed Butler's jest in Hudibras:

In 1840 John Pye Smith, Principal of London's Homerton Divinity College, published *On the Relation Between the Holy Scriptures and Some Parts of Geological Science,* an edited compilation of lectures, prepared and delivered by appointment of the Committee of the Congregational Lecture. It represented a total shift of emphasis in the harmonizing movement, for Smith generalized the Mosaic history of creation and the Deluge without attempting to find exact parallels between the geological and biblical records.[44]

Smith began by explaining his point of view as a spokesman for the Christian community and by outlining his level-headed approach to scientific and biblical truth. In science and Christianity, he averred: "Truth . . . is our object"; "all truth must be consistent"; and "the criterion of truth is evidence."[45] He argued cogently for unlavished miracles in the sense of events "which, supposing a given connection of time, place, and persons, would not have come to pass in the ordinary course of things; but for the instrumental causality of which *the divine plan* had fixed the provision."[46] Smith also held to the infallible truth of Scripture when taken in "its own genuine sense," that is, with rules of interpretation derived from the text itself through careful grammatical and philological analysis.[47]

From this point Smith "went straight down the geological line, arguing forcibly the Lyellian position, and in effect conceding all the points that his theological partners had expected him to refute. Instead of defending traditional theology, Smith called for a new interpretation of it."[48] Indeed, his unabashed acceptance of uniformitarianism is evi-

---

'He knew the seat of Paradise,
Could tell in what degree it lies;
And as he was disposed, could prove it,
Below the moon or else above it'"

(Shields, *The Final Philosophy,* pp. 62–63). Also, significantly, Lyell later advised a young man named Charles Darwin "never to get entangled in a controversy, as it rarely did any good and caused a miserable loss of time and temper" (Francis Darwin, ed., *Charles Darwin: His Life Told in an Autobiographical Chapter and in a Selected Series of His Published Letters* [new ed.; London: John Murray, 1902], p. 43).

[44] Haber, *The Age of the World: Moses to Darwin,* p. 236.

[45] John Pye Smith, *On the Relation Between the Holy Scriptures and Some Parts of Geological Science* (New York: D. Appleton & Co., 1840), pp. 26–28, hereafter cited as *Geology and Scripture.*

[46] *Ibid.,* p. 82.

[47] Smith's explanation of the Genesis revelation as written in terms of "analogical representation," that is, "representative to the senses, chiefly that of sight and in words descriptive of those representations," is a highly tenable phenomenological interpretation of the Creation and Flood accounts.

[48] Haber, *The Age of the World: Moses to Darwin,* p. 234.

dent throughout the work. He said of Lyell's *Principles* that it "stands forth among the books of our day, very signally distinguished,"[49] and in an appendix to the volume he recommended highly the volumes as "an admirable collection of facts, and which carefully separates facts from hypotheses. Mr. L. makes you acquainted with the former, without urging your assent to the latter."[50]

What was Smith's "new interpretation?" After carefully reviewing past blunders in interpreting the Deluge vis-à-vis geology, Smith gave new currency and intellectual weight to what is known as the "partial-deluge theory." He examined meticulously the physical and geological problems connected with a universal Deluge. The origin of the water, the effect of the water on the earth's orbit and diurnal rotation, the size of the ark, the animals, rock strata, fossil remains, and a host of other objections, problems, and proposed solutions were reviewed and found to be best resolved by limiting the Flood to a small region on the earth's surface. While Smith, in accord with Genesis, understood the Flood to have been geographically local, he believed it had also been anthropologically universal in order to fulfil the purpose for which it was ordained by God.[51]

Smith's work is still considered the basic text on the partial-deluge interpretation.[52] In his day he was roundly criticized, not for faulty scholarship, but for iconoclasm. Nevertheless he stood firm in his commitment both to Lyellian geology and to Genesis, and in so doing his concerned, scholarly honesty commands our respect today. Said Smith:

> It is a painful position in which I stand. I seem to be taking the part of an enemy, adducing materials for skepticism. . . . The apparent discrepancies between the facts of science and the words of Scripture, must be *understood,* before we can make any attempt at their removal.[53]

He was however fully convinced that an apparent discrepancy "vanishes before careful and sincere examination."[54]

If Cuvier's multiple catastrophism distinguished attempts to harmonize geology and the Noachian Deluge prior to the time of Lyell, it

[49] Smith, *Geology and Scripture,* p. 195.

[50] *Ibid.,* p. 299.

[51] *Ibid.,* pp. 242–52.

[52] See Bernard Ramm's citations in *The Christian View of Science and Scripture* (Exeter, Devon: Paternoster Press, 1964), *passim,* and Morris and Whitcomb, *The Genesis Flood,* pp. 107–109.

[53] Smith, *Geology and Scripture,* p. 139.

[54] *Ibid.,* p. 20.

may be safely said that Smith's partial-deluge theory keynoted theological thought on the subject after the *Principles of Geology* had been in circulation for a decade. Most extant works from about 1850 to the turn of the century which evidence a significant degree of scholarship in dealing with the Deluge problem are at once in favor of Smith's theory and hospitable to Lyell.[55]

Three of these are noteworthy.

The Genesis of the Earth and Man, an anonymous work by a Protestant author, focuses on the problems connected with the antiquity of the earth and ancient ethnology. Its author wrote with the conviction that God's natural and revealed truths are one, and that "we have not sufficiently emancipated our minds if we cannot accept the revelations of science as well as those of the Bible and avail ourselves of the former to explain the *ambiguities* in the latter."[56] Likewise in *Geology and Revelation,* a first-rate, scholarly account of geological findings, Professor Molloy of the Royal College of St. Patrick wrote from a Roman Catholic perspective that "truth cannot be at variance with truth. If God has recorded the history of our Globe, as geologists maintain, on imperishable monuments within the Crust of the Earth, we may be quite sure that He has not contradicted that Record in His Written Word."[57] Both books are marked by a high respect for the work of Lyell. The first author speaks of his "characteristic comprehensiveness and perspicuity" and, in the same context, argues for a Deluge limited both geographically and anthropologically.[58] Molloy disparages catastrophist geology as the "old theory which has gradually given way," a fact for which, he says, "we are mainly indebted to the unwearied researches and great ability of Sir Charles Lyell."[59]

The Testimony of the Rocks was Hugh Miller's major contribution to the Deluge discussion. Miller, a capable field geologist and one of the

[55]But see: *Facts and Fossils Adduced to Prove the Deluge of Noah and to Modify the Transmutation System of Darwin* (1868), by George Twemlow (major-general in the British army); *Geology and the Flood* (1877), by German Jesuit scholar Athanasius Bosizio; and Henry H. Howorth's *The Mammoth and the Flood* (1887), which attempted to melt the ice ages. However it must be significant that Howorth only is mentioned in George McCready Price's *New Geology* and in Morris and Whitcomb's *Genesis Flood.* White's *Warfare of Science with Theology* mentions Bosizio only, and then simply to illustrate foreign reluctance to part with the Flood as the universal solvent for geological problems. Nowhere have I found reference made to Twemlow except in Nelson's *Deluge Story in Stone* (pp. 113–14).

[56][Edward William Lane], *The Genesis of the Earth and Man,* ed. by Reginald Stuart Poole (Edinburgh: Adam & Charles Black, 1856?), p. 51.

[57]Gerald Molloy, *Geology and Revelation* (New York: G.P. Putnam & Sons, 1870), pp. 26–27.

[58][Lane], *The Genesis of the Earth and Man,* pp. 50–51.

[59]Molloy, *Geology and Revelation,* pp. 220–21.

greatest harmonizers of Genesis and geology that Christendom has ever known,[60] observed that "in every instance in which they [plain men] have sought to deduce from it [Scripture] what it was *not* intended to teach, the truths of physical science, they have fallen into extravagant error."[61] Miller, following Smith, advanced vigorous arguments against the universal Deluge. He believed that "the deluge was but coextensive with the moral purpose which it served": namely, local destruction of men who fell under God's judgment.[62]

Likewise writers followed Smith and Lyell in religious encyclopaedias, dictionaries and Bible commentaries. Baden Powell, Savilian Professor of Geometry at Oxford, found support for his divorce of natural and supernatural theology (science and revelation) in Lyell's tranquil theory.[63] If one thinks that the Flood was a miraculous, universal catastrophe, then, said Powell, he "must also suppose that it was not only miraculously terminated also, but every trace and mark of it supernaturally effaced and destroyed."[64] In Kitto's *Cyclopaedia* he rejected catastrophism, refused to posit miracles to support a universal Flood, and, without reaching a definite conclusion in his synoptic article, leaned heavily toward the partial-deluge theory.[65] In the 1863 *Dictionary of the Bible,* John Perowne, Examining Chaplain to the Bishop of Norwich, gave up the universal Deluge altogether. Of this article Huxley permitted himself to hope "that a long criticism . . . I supplied him, may have in some degree contributed toward this happy result."[66] The article thus clearly evidences Lyellian influence in both its interpretations and citations.[67] In 1871 *The Bible Commentary,* written by the Bishops and Clergy of the Anglican Church, espoused the partial-deluge theory unreservedly. The writer on Genesis added that even if the Deluge extended to great regions, the rise and subsidence of the waters would not have disturbed the geologic formations.[68]

[60] Ramm, *The Christian View of Science and Scripture,* p. 173.

[61] Miller, *The Testimony of the Rocks,* p. 306.

[62] *Ibid.,* p. 353.

[63] Haber, *The Age of the World: Moses to Darwin,* pp. 241–42.

[64] Baden Powell, "Deluge," *A Cyclopaedia of Biblical Literature,* I, 545.

[65] *Ibid.,* pp. 544–45.

[66] Huxley, "The Lights of the Church and the Light of Science," p. 13.

[67] Rev. John James Stewart Perowne, "Noah," *A Dictionary of the Bible,* II, 570 ff. [Tradition has it that Perowne (later Bishop of Worcester) originally wrote his article for the entry "Deluge" in Volume I of Sir William Smith's *Dictionary of the Bible,* and that it was because the article was sent back to him for repeated revision that readers were faced with "DELUGE: See FLOOD" and then "FLOOD: See NOAH." ED.]

[68] Bishop of Ely, "Commentary on Genesis," *The Bible Commentary,* I, 77–78.

Lyell's theological effects in America were at first less dramatic. In a book of informal lectures for young men, James Munson Olmstead took pleasure in referring to Lyell's work.[69] He agreed with Lyell that there was little or no geological evidence for a violent Flood since its effects had been obliterated in the course of time.[70] Smith's arguments were considered in detail, but with the hope that young men would, after carefully examining them, arrive at his universalist position.[71] Writing in 1854, Olmstead was still quite removed from the mainstream of British thought where, as we have seen, the intellectual waters of the partial deluge were far from tranquil.

In Edward Hitchcock one finds America's outstanding uniformitarian apologist. Serving Amherst College both as President and as Professor of Geology and Natural Theology, Hitchcock was also a scholar of international renown. His *Religion of Geology and Its Connected Sciences* was written "to exhibit all the religious bearings of geology."[72] After a thorough historical survey of Flood theories, which served to point out various exegetical excesses and problems in biblical interpretation, he signalized Smith as the foremost of all writers on the subject, declaring that "no modern writer has treated this subject with so much candor and ability . . . he is accurately acquainted with all branches of the subject . . . fully possessed of all the facts in geology and natural history."[73] Since Hitchcock thought that there were good reasons for considering the Deluge to be local, both in natural history and in Scripture,[74] he followed his evaluation of Smith with extensive quotations from his book. While there does not appear to be a direct endorsement of Lyell's work in *The Religion of Geology,* it should be obvious even to the casual reader that Hitchcock concurs with its conclusions.[75]

Hitchcock filled his volume with sane and sobering observations on the relation between geology and theology.[76] At the end of his careful review of the Deluge dilemma, and with far more penetrating hindsight than this writer's limited historical and scientific perspective can muster, he asserted:

[69] *Noah and His Times* (Boston: Gould and Lincoln, 1854), pp. 136–37.

[70] *Ibid.,* p. 102.

[71] *Ibid.,* pp. 174, 196–97.

[72] Hitchcock, *Religion of Geology,* p. v.

[73] *Ibid.,* p. 96.

[74] *Ibid.,* p. 90.

[75] E.g., see *ibid.,* pp. 87–90, 165–66.

[76] E.g., see n. 34.

> From the facts that have now been detailed, it appears that on no subject of science connected with religion have men been more positive and dogmatical than in respect to Noah's deluge, and that on no subject has there been greater change of opinion. From a belief in the complete destruction and dissolution of the globe by that event, those best qualified to judge now doubt whether it be possible to identify one mark of that event in nature.[77]

He nevertheless emerged from his study in possession of a high doctrine of Scripture. He was convinced that the genuine facts of science and the results of careful analysis of the biblical text will always blend in harmony. With clear insight he astutely observed that whenever "geology teaches us how to interpret . . . passages respecting the age of the world, and the extent of the deluge, it is illustration and not collision."[78]

Hitchcock thus expressed the new attitude assumed by nineteenth century Christian scholarship in relation to Charles Lyell and the Noachian Deluge. Following John Pye Smith, theologians were prepared to take Lyell more seriously and to reevaluate interpretations they had often imposed upon the text of Scripture. After considering the extremes of diluvialists Granville Penn and George Fairholme, Cunningham Geikie wrote in 1886 that "thoughtful men of all shades of religious opinion have . . . come to the opposite conclusion; that the Noachian Deluge was a local one, though sufficiently extensive in its area to destroy all the then existing race of men."[79] In Bernard Ramm's words, this trend was indicative of that "noble tradition of the great and learned evangelical Christians who have been patient, genuine, and kind and who have taken great care to learn the facts of science and Scripture."

Unfortunately Ramm could not avoid the painful fact that the noble tradition "which was in ascendance in the closing years of the nineteenth century has not been the major tradition in evangelicalism in the twentieth century."[80] In particular it has been American fundamentalism, as J. I. Packer is at pains to point out, which "did not in every respect adorn its doctrine."[81] Those who have had closer contact

[77] Hitchcock, *Religion of Geology*, p. 87.

[78] *Ibid.*, p. 311.

[79] *Hours with the Bible* (6 vols.; New York: John B. Alden, 1886), I, 169. Cf. Walter S. Olson's recent conclusion that "of all events of pre-history, the Flood appears best supported by tradition and now by scientific evidence" in his article presenting a limited Flood interpretation, "Has Science Dated the Biblical Flood?" (*Zygon: Journal of Religion and Science*, II [September 1967], 272–78).

[80] Ramm, *The Christian View of Science and Scripture*, pp. 8–9.

[81] *"Fundamentalism" and the Word of God* (Grand Rapids, Michigan: Wm. B. Eerdmans, 1958), p. 31.

with the atmosphere of the last century, and have thus likely learned some important lessons from its conflict between geology and theology, must witness with dismay the regular and frequent diluvialist publications in American evangelical circles: George F. Wright's *Scientific Confirmation of Old Testament History* (1906); George McCready Price's *Fundamentals of Geology* (1913), *The New Geology* (1923), *Evolutionary Geology and the New Catastrophism* (1926), *The Geological Ages Hoax* (1931), and *The Modern Flood Theory of Geology* (1935); Byron Nelson's *The Deluge Story in Stone* (1931); Harry Rimmer's *The Harmony of Science and Scripture* (3rd ed.; 1936); Harold W. Clark's *The New Diluvialism* (1946); A. M. Rehwinkel's *The Flood in the Light of the Bible, Geology and Archaeology* (1951); Henry M. Morris and John C. Whitcomb, Jr.'s *The Genesis Flood* (1961); and at last one must mention Donald W. Patten's aberrant catastrophism in *The Biblical Flood and the Ice Epoch* (1966). Indeed, historic evangelicalism in general has good cause for feeling uncomfortable with an appellation which has been applied to this diverse (and by no means complete) array.

The primary purpose here is neither to bring wholesale condemnation on biblical catastrophism nor to whitewash Lyellian geology. Rather I shall be satisfied if I have fulfilled the noble calling outlined by Herbert Butterfield:

> Taking things retrospectively and recollecting in tranquility, the historian works over the past to cover the conflicts with understanding, and explains the unlikenesses between men and makes us sensible to their terrible predicaments; until at the finish . . . we are able at last perhaps to be a little sorry for everybody.

But let me suggest that we not stop with pity. If modern evangelicals find their heritage in some of the scientific and theological attitudes elucidated in this study, they must not content themselves with licking their ancestors' wounds. With Butterfield let us concur that "all the moral verdicts that we may pass on human history are only valid in their application as self-judgments, only useful in so far as we bring them home to ourselves."[82]

[82] *Christianity and History* (New York: Charles Scribner's Sons, 1950), pp. 92, 62, respectively.

Creationism: Genesis Vs. Geology

STEPHEN JAY GOULD

One of the principal characteristics of myth is that although it is set in the remote past, it continues to influence the thought and behavior of people living in the present time. A sacred charter for belief is how anthropologist Bronislaw Malinowski defined myth. To the extent that the flood myth continues to be a vital force in twentieth-century life, it remains a viable myth.

Intellectuals always imagine that the age in which they live is a relatively enlightened one. In reviewing the history of centuries past, they cannot help but be amused by the apparent foolishness of some of the issues their predecessors deemed worthy of debate. Some may condescendingly urge tolerance in looking back at bygone days since individuals living then did not have the advantage of all the information available to us moderns. In this context, it may come as a bit of a surprise to learn that the question of the scientific plausibility of the flood account in Genesis remains very much in the public eye and has been the repeated subject of legislation and courtroom wrangling.

In the middle of the twentieth century, the defenders of the faith are called "creationists" as they argue that creation, as delineated in Genesis, ought to be taught in schools—in biology classes, for example—as a legitimate alternative to evolution. In this updated form of the endless debate, the flood myth has continued to be a crucial bone of contention.

Professor Stephen Jay Gould of Harvard University, a distinguished and articulate voice for the natural sciences, tells of his experience testifying as a witness for the prosecution in a courtroom in Little Rock, Arkansas, challenging a state law which required creationism to be taught as a full-fledged alternative to evolutionary theory.

For more on the creationists' views of the flood myth, see John C. Whitcomb, Jr., and Henry M. Morris, The Genesis Flood: The Biblical Record and Its Scientific Implications *(Grand Rapids, Mich., 1961). Whitcomb is a professor of Old Testament and Morris is a professor of hydraulic engineering. They have jointly written a lengthy defense of the truth of the Genesis account, but they have drawn fire even from geologists with strong*

Reprinted from the *Atlantic* 250 (3) (September 1982):10, 12–14, 16–17.

religious convictions. See, for example, J. R. Van de Fliert, "Fundamentalism and the Fundamentals of Geology," Journal of the American Scientific Affiliation *21 (1969): 69–81.*

It should be noted that the published attempts to validate the Genesis flood account scientifically are simply too numerous to list. Many are to be found in various popular religious periodicals. Representative are: J. S. Stuart-Glennie, "The Traditional Deluge and Its Geological Identification," The Babylonian and Oriental Record *4 (1889–1890): 209–212; Philip J. Le Riche, "Scientific Proofs of a Universal Deluge,"* Journal of the Transactions of the Victoria Institute *61 (1929): 86–117; L. M. Davies, "Scientific Discoveries and Their Bearing on the Biblical Account of the Noachian Deluge,"* Journal of the Transactions of the Victoria Institute *62 (1930): 62–95; E. T. Brewster, "Genesis and Flood Theories in the Light of Their History,"* Bibliotheca Sacra *90 (1933): 220–227; Dudley Joseph Whitney, "The Problem of the Flood,"* Bibliotheca Sacra *90 (1933): 469–478; Raymond de Girard, "Les déluges: étude géologique,"* Le globe *81 (1942): 75–107; Fred Kramer, "The Biblical Account of the Flood," in Paul A. Zimmerman, ed.,* Rock Strata and the Bible Record *(St. Louis, 1970), pp. 180–192; Paul C. Tychsen, "Geology and the Flood," in Zimmerman, pp. 193–200; Frederick A. Filby, "Noah's Flood: Approaches to Reconciliation,"* Faith and Thought *100 (1972–1973): 159–173, or his longer work* The Flood Reconsidered: A Review of the Evidences of Geology, Archaeology, Ancient Literature, and the Bible *(London, 1970); and Arthur C. Custance,* The Flood: Local or Global*? (Grand Rapids, Mich., 1979), pp. 1–106. Also of interest is Davis A. Young,* Creation and the Flood: An Alternative to Flood Geology and Theistic Evolution *(Grand Rapids, Mich., 1977).*

For more about the Arkansas court case, see Langdon Bilkey, "Creationism: The Roots of the Conflict," in Roland Mushat Frye, ed., Is God a Creationist: The Religious Case Against Creation-Science *(New York, 1983), pp. 56–67, and Dorothy Nelkin's chapter "Legislating Science in Arkansas," in her useful overview* The Creation Controversy: Science or Scripture in the Schools *(Boston, 1982), pp. 137–147. (For a convenient transcript of the U.S. District Court decision in the Arkansas case, see Nelkin's "Appendix 1," pp. 199–228.) See also Marcel Chotkowski La Follette, ed.,* Creationism, Science, and the Law: The Arkansas Case *(Cambridge, 1983).*

For more of the rapidly burgeoning literature devoted to the creationism controversy, see Philip Kitcher, Abusing Science: The Case Against Creationism *(Cambridge, Mass., 1982); Laurie R. Godfrey, ed.,* Scientists Confront Creationism *(New York, 1983); Christopher McGowan,* In the Beginning: A Scientist Shows Why the Creationists Are Wrong *(Buffalo, 1984); Ashley Montagu, ed.,* Science and Creationism *(Oxford, 1984); and Ronald L. Numbers, "The Creationists," in David C. Lindberg and Ronald L. Numbers, eds.,* God & Nature: Historical Essays on the Encounter Between Christianity and Science *(Berkeley, 1986), pp. 391–423.*

G. K. Chesterton once mused over Noah's dinnertime conversations during those long nights on a vast and tempestuous sea:

> And Noah he often said to his wife
> when he sat down to dine,
> "I don't care where the water goes if
> it doesn't get into the wine."

Noah's insouciance has not been matched by defenders of his famous flood. For centuries, fundamentalists have tried very hard to find a place for the subsiding torrents. They have struggled even more valiantly to devise a source for all that water. Our modern oceans, extensive as they are, will not override Mt. Everest. One seventeenth-century searcher said: "I can as soon believe that a man would be drowned in his own spittle as that the world should be deluged by the water in it."

With the advent of creationism, a solution to this old dilemma has been put forward. In *The Genesis Flood* (1961), the founding document of the creationist movement, John Whitcomb and Henry Morris seek guidance from Genesis 1:6–7, which states that God created the firmament and then slid it into place amidst the waters, thus dividing "the waters which were under the firmament from the waters which were above the firmament: and it was so." The waters under the firmament include seas and interior fluid that may rise in volcanic eruptions. But what are the waters above the firmament? Whitcomb and Morris reason that Moses cannot refer here to transient rain clouds, because he also tells us (Genesis 2:5) that "the Lord God had not caused it to rain upon the earth." The authors therefore imagine that the earth, in those palmy days, was surrounded by a gigantic canopy of water vapor (which, being invisible, did not obscure the light of Genesis 1:3). "These upper waters," Whitcomb and Morris write, "were therefore placed in that position by divine creativity, not by the normal processes of the hydrological cycle of the present day." Upwelling from the depths together with the liquefaction, puncturing, and descent of the celestial canopy produced more than enough water for Noah's worldwide flood.

Fanciful solutions often generate a cascade of additional difficulties. In this case, Morris, a hydraulic engineer by training, and Whitcomb invoke a divine assist to gather the waters into their canopy, but then can't find a natural way to get them down. So they invoke a miracle: God put the water there in the first place; let him then release it.

> The simple fact of the matter is that one cannot have *any* kind of a Genesis Flood without acknowledging the presence of supernatural ele-

> ments. . . . It is obvious that the opening of the "windows of heaven" in order to allow "the waters which were above the firmament" to fall upon the earth, and the breaking up of "all the fountains of the great deep" were supernatural acts of God.

Since we usually define science, at least in part, as a system of explanation that relies upon invariant natural laws, this charmingly direct invocation of miracles (suspensions of natural law) would seem to negate the central claims of the modern creationist movement—that creationism is not religion but a scientific alternative to evolution; that creationism has been disregarded by scientists because they are a fanatical and dogmatic lot who cannot appreciate new advances; and that creationists must therefore seek legislative redress in their attempts to force a "balanced treatment" for both creationism and evolution in the science classrooms of our public schools.

Legislative history has driven creationists to this strategy of claiming scientific status for their religious view. The older laws, which banned the teaching of evolution outright and led to John Scopes's conviction in 1925, were overturned by the Supreme Court in 1968, but not before they had exerted a chilling effect upon teaching for forty years. (Evolution is the indispensable organizing principle of the life sciences, but I did not hear the word in my 1956 high school biology class. New York City, to be sure, suffered no restrictive ordinances, but publishers, following the principle of the "least common denominator" as a sales strategy, tailored the national editions of their textbooks to the few states that considered it criminal to place an ape on the family escutcheon.) A second attempt to mandate equal time for frankly religious views of life's history passed the Tennessee state legislature in the 1970s but failed a constitutional challenge in the court. This judicial blocking left only one legislative path open—the claim that creationism is a science.

The third strategy had some initial success, and "balanced treatment" acts to equate "evolution science" and "creation science" in classrooms passed the Arkansas and Louisiana legislatures in 1981. The ACLU has sued for a federal-court ruling on the Louisiana law's constitutionality, and a trial is likely this year. The Arkansas law was challenged by the ACLU in 1981, on behalf of local plaintiffs (including twelve practicing theologians who felt more threatened by the bill than many scientists did). Federal Judge William R. Overton heard the Arkansas case in Little Rock last December. I spent the better part of a day on the stand, a witness for the prosecution, testifying primarily about how the fossil record refutes "flood geology" and supports evolution.

On January 5, Judge Overton delivered his eloquent opinion, declaring the Arkansas act unconstitutional because so-called "creation science" is only a version of Genesis read literally—a partisan (and narrowly sectarian) religious view, barred from public-school classrooms by the First Amendment. Legal language is often incomprehensible, but sometimes it is charming, and I enjoyed the wording of Overton's decision: ". . . judgment is hereby entered in favor of the plaintiffs and against the defendants. The relief prayed for is granted."

Support for Overton's equation of "creation science" with strident and sectarian fundamentalism comes from two sources. First, the leading creationists themselves released some frank private documents in response to plaintiffs' subpoenas. Overton's long list of citations seems to brand the claim for scientific creationism as simple hypocrisy. For example, Paul Ellwanger, the tireless advocate and drafter of the "model bill" that became Arkansas Act 590 of 1981, the law challenged by the ACLU, says in a letter to a state legislator that "I view this whole battle as one between God and anti-God forces, though I know there are a large number of evolutionists who believe in God. . . . It behooves Satan to do all he can to thwart our efforts." In another letter, he refers to "the idea of killing evolution instead of playing these debating games that we've been playing for nigh over a decade already"—a reasonably clear statement of the creationists' ultimate aims, and an identification of their appeals for "equal time," "the American way of fairness," and "presenting them both and letting the kids decide" as just so much rhetoric.

The second source of evidence of the bill's unconstitutionality lies in the logic and character of creationist arguments themselves. The flood story is central to all creationist systems. It also has elicited the only specific and testable theory the creationists have offered; for the rest, they have only railed against evolutionary claims. The flood story was explicitly cited as one of the six defining characteristics of "creation science" in Arkansas Act 590: "explanation of the earth's geology by catastrophism, including the occurrence of a worldwide flood."

Creationism reveals its nonscientific character in two ways: its central tenets cannot be tested and its peripheral claims, which can be tested, have been proven false. At its core, the creationist account rests on "singularities"—that is to say, on miracles. The creationist God is not the noble clockwinder of Newton and Boyle, who set the laws of nature properly at the beginning of time and then released direct control in full confidence that his initial decisions would require no revision. He is, instead, a constant presence, who suspends his own laws when necessary to make the new or destroy the old. Since science can treat only natural phenomena occurring in a context of invariant natural law, the constant invocation of miracles places creationism in another realm.

We have already seen how Whitcomb and Morris remove a divine finger from the dike of heaven to flood the earth from their vapor canopy. But the miracles surrounding Noah's flood do not stop there; two other supernatural assists are required. First, God acted "to gather the animals into the Ark." (The Bible tells us [Genesis 6:20] that they found their own way.) Second, God intervened to keep the animals "under control during the year of the Flood." Whitcomb and Morris provide a long disquisition on hibernation and suspect that some divinely ordained state of suspended animation relieved Noah's small and aged crew of most responsibility for feeding and cleaning (poor Noah himself was 600 years old at the time).

In candid moments, leading creationists will admit that the miraculous character of origin and destruction precludes a scientific understanding. Morris writes (and Judge Overton quotes): "God was there when it happened. We were not there. . . . Therefore, we are completely limited to what God has seen fit to tell us, and this information is in His written Word." Duane Gish, the leading creationist author, says: "We do not know how the Creator created, what processes He used, for He used processes which are not now operating anywhere in the natural universe. . . . We cannot discover by scientific investigation anything about the creative processes used by God." When pressed about these quotes, creationists tend to admit that they are purveying religion after all, but then claim that evolution is equally religious. Gish also says: "Creationists have repeatedly stated that neither creation nor evolution is a scientific theory (and each is equally religious)." But as Judge Overton reasoned, if creationists are merely complaining that evolution is religion, then they should be trying to eliminate it from the schools, not struggling to get their own brand of religion into science classrooms as well. And if, instead, they are asserting the validity of their own version of natural history, they must be able to prove, according to the demands of science, that creationism is scientific.

Scientific claims must be testable; we must, in principle, be able to envision a set of observations that would render them false. Miracles cannot be judged by this criterion, as Whitcomb and Morris have admitted. But is all creationist writing merely about untestable singularities? Are arguments never made in proper scientific form? Creationists do offer some testable statements, and these are amenable to scientific analysis. Why, then, do I continue to claim that creationism isn't science? Simply because these relatively few statements have been tested and conclusively refuted. Dogmatic assent to disproved claims is not scientific behavior. Scientists are as stubborn as the rest of us, but they must be able to change their minds.

In "flood geology," we find our richest source of testable creationist claims. Creationists have been forced into this uncharacteristically vulnerable stance by a troubling fact too well known to be denied: namely, that the geological record of fossils follows a single, invariant order throughout the world. The oldest rocks contain only single-celled creatures; invertebrates dominate later strata, followed by the first fishes, then dinosaurs, and finally large mammals. One might be tempted to take a "liberal," or allegorical, view of Scripture and identify this sequence with the order of creation in Genesis 1, allowing millions or billions of years for the "days" of Moses. But creationists will admit no such reconciliation. Their fundamentalism is absolute and uncompromising. If Moses said "days," he meant periods of twenty-four hours, to the second. (Creationist literature is often less charitable to liberal theology than to evolution. As a subject for wrath, nothing matches the enemy within.)

Since God created with such alacrity, all creatures once must have lived simultaneously on the earth. How, then, did their fossil remains get sorted into an invariable order in the earth's strata? To resolve this particularly knotty dilemma, creationists invoke Noah's flood: all creatures were churned together in the great flood and their fossilized succession reflects the order of their settling as the waters receded. But what natural processes would produce such a predictable order from a singular chaos? The testable proposals of "flood geology" have been advanced to explain the causes of this sorting.

Whitcomb and Morris offer three suggestions. The first—hydrological—holds that denser and more streamlined objects would have descended more rapidly and should populate the bottom strata (in conventional geology, the oldest strata). The second—ecological—envisions a sorting responsive to environment. Denizens of the ocean bottom were overcome by the flood waters first, and should lie in the lower strata; inhabitants of mountaintops postponed their inevitable demise, and now adorn our upper strata. The third—anatomical or functional—argues that certain animals, by their high intelligence or superior mobility, might have struggled successfully for a time, and ended up at the top.

All three proposals have been proven false. The lower strata abound in delicate, floating creatures, as well as spherical globs. Many oceanic creatures—whales and teleost fishes in particular—appear only in upper strata, well above hordes of terrestrial forms. Clumsy sloths (not to mention hundreds of species of marine invertebrates) are restricted to strata lying well above others that serve as exclusive homes for scores of lithe and nimble small dinosaurs and pterosaurs.

The very invariance of the universal fossil sequence is the strongest argument against its production in a single gulp. Could exceptionless order possibly arise from a contemporaneous mixture by such dubious processes of sorting? Surely, somewhere, at least one courageous trilobite would have paddled on valiantly (as its colleagues succumbed) and won a place in the upper strata. Surely, on some primordial beach, a man would have suffered a heart attack and been washed into the lower strata before intelligence had a chance to plot temporary escape. But if the strata represent vast stretches of sequential time, then invariant order is an expectation, not a problem. No trilobite lies in the upper strata because they all perished 225 million years ago. No man keeps lithified company with a dinosaur, because we were still 60 million years in the future when the last dinosaur perished.

True science and religion are not in conflict. The history of approaches to Noah's flood by scientists who were also professional theologians provides an excellent example of this important truth—and also illustrates just how long ago "flood geology" was conclusively laid to rest by religious scientists. I have argued that direct invocation of miracles and unwillingness to abandon a false doctrine deprive modern creationists of their self-proclaimed status as scientists. When we examine how the great scientist-theologians of past centuries treated the flood, we note that their work is distinguished by both a conscious refusal to admit miraculous events into their explanatory schemes and a willingness to abandon preferred hypotheses in the face of geological evidence. They were scientists *and* religious leaders—and they show us why modern creationists are not scientists.

On the subject of miracles, the Reverend Thomas Burnet published his century's most famous geological treatise in the 1680s, *Telluris theoria sacra* (*The Sacred Theory of the Earth*). Burnet accepted the Bible's truth, and set out to construct a geological history that would be in accord with the events of Genesis. But he believed something else even more strongly: that, as a scientist, he must follow natural law and scrupulously avoid miracles. His story is fanciful by modern standards: the earth originally was devoid of topography, but was drying and cracking; the cracks served as escape vents for internal fluids, but rain sealed the cracks, and the earth, transformed into a gigantic pressure cooker, ruptured its surface skin; surging internal waters inundated the earth, producing Noah's flood. Bizarre, to be sure, but bizarre precisely because Burnet would not abandon natural law. It is not easy to force a preconceived story into the strictures of physical causality. Over and over again, Burnet acknowledges that his task would be much simpler if only he could invoke a miracle. Why weave such a complex tale to find water for the flood in a physically acceptable manner, when God might simply have made new water for his cataclysmic purification? Many of Burnet's colleagues urged such a course, but he rejected it as inconsistent with the methods of "natural philosophy" (the word "science" had not yet entered English usage):

> They say in short that God Almighty created waters on purpose to make the Deluge. . . . And this, in a few words, is the whole account of the business. This is to cut the knot when we cannot loose it.

Burnet's God, like the deity of Newton and Boyle, was a clockwinder, not a bungler who continually perturbed his own system with later corrections.

> We think him a better Artist that makes a Clock that strikes regularly at every hour from the Springs and Wheels which he puts in the work, than he that hath so made his Clock that he must put his finger to it every hour to make it strike: And if one should contrive a piece of Clockwork so that it should beat all the hours, and make all its motions regularly for such a time, and that time being come, upon a signal given, or a Spring toucht, it should of its own accord fall all to pieces; would not this be look'd upon as a piece of greater Art, than if the Workman came at that time prefixt, and with a great Hammer beat it into pieces?

Flood geology was considered and tested by early-nineteenth-century geologists. They never believed that a single flood had produced all fossil-bearing strata, but they did accept and then disprove a claim that the uppermost strata contained evidence for a single, catastrophic, worldwide inundation. The science of geology arose in nations that were glaciated during the great ice ages, and glacial deposits are similar to the products of floods. During the 1820s, British geologists carried out an extensive empirical program to test whether these deposits represented the action of a single flood. The work was led by two ministers, the Reverend Adam Sedgwick (who taught Darwin his geology) and the Reverend William Buckland. Buckland initially decided that all the "superficial gravels" (as these deposits were called) represented a single event, and he published his *Reliquiae diluvianae* (Relics of the Flood) in 1824. However, Buckland's subsequent field work proved that the superficial gravels were not contemporaneous but represented several different events (multiple ice ages, as we now know). Geology proclaimed no worldwide flood but rather a long sequence of local events. In one of the great statements in the history of science, Sedgwick, who was Buckland's close colleague in both science and theology, publicly abandoned flood geology—and upheld empirical science—in his presidential address to the Geological Society of London in 1831.

> Having been myself a believer, and, to the best of my power, a propagator of what I now regard as a philosophic heresy, and having more than once been quoted for opinions I do not now maintain, I think it right, as one of my last acts before I quit this Chair, thus publicly to read my recantation. . . .
>
> There is, I think, one great negative conclusion now incontestably established—that the vast masses of diluvial gravel, scattered almost over the surface of the earth, do not belong to one violent and transitory period. . . .
>
> We ought, indeed, to have paused before we first adopted the diluvian theory, and referred all our old superficial gravel to the action of the Mosaic flood. . . . In classing together distant unknown formations under one name; in giving them a simultaneous origin, and in determining their date, not by the organic remains we had discovered, but by those we expected hypothetically hereafter to discover, in them; we have given one more example of the passion with which the mind fastens upon general conclusions, and of the readiness with which it leaves the consideration of unconnected truths.

As I prepared to leave Little Rock last December, I went to my hotel room to gather my belongings and found a man sitting backward on my commode, pulling it apart with a plumber's wrench. He explained to me that a leak in the room below had caused part of the ceiling to collapse and he was seeking the source of the water. My commode, located just above, was the obvious candidate, but his hypothesis had failed, for my equipment was working perfectly. The plumber then proceeded to give me a fascinating disquisition on how a professional traces the pathways of water through hotel pipes and walls. The account was perfectly logical and mechanistic: it can come only from here, here, or there, flow this way or that way, and end up there, there, or here. I then asked him what he thought of the trial across the street, and he confessed his staunch creationism, including his firm belief in the miracle of Noah's flood.

As a professional, this man never doubted that water has a physical source and a mechanically constrained path of motion—and that he could use the principles of his trade to identify causes. It would be a poor (and unemployed) plumber indeed who suspected that the laws of engineering had been suspended whenever a puddle and cracked plaster bewildered him. Why should we approach the physical history of our earth any differently?

Suggestions for Further Reading on the Flood Myth

Allen, Don Cameron

1963 *The Legend of Noah.* Urbana: University of Illinois Press. 221 pp. A most scholarly treatment of the debate between religion and science concerning the flood with special reference to the Renaissance. One chapter from this outstanding study has been included in the present volume.

Anderson, Walter

1923 *Nordasiatische Flutsagen.* Acta et Commentationes Universitatis Dorpatensis B. Humaniora 4:1–44. Twenty-one texts of North Asian myths are presented to refute claims by earlier scholars such as Andree, Winternitz, and Frazer that the flood myth was absent from this part of the world. The nine myth traits proposed by Winternitz are utilized and critiqued.

Andree, Richard

1891 *Die Flutsagen: Ethnographisch betrachtet.* Braunschweig: Friedrich Vieweg. 152 pp. One of the first truly comprehensive compilations of flood myths worldwide.

Baumann, Hermann

1936 *Schöpfung und Urzeit des Menschen im Mythus der afrikanischen Völker.* Berlin: Verlag von Dietrich Riemer. 435 pp. The discussion of "Der Grosse Flut" in Africa (pp. 307–319) seeks to disprove the allegation repeated by most flood myth researchers (e.g., Andree, Usener, Frazer, Riem) that the myth is not reported in Africa. However, the scanty total of a bare two dozen texts which the author maps for the African continent actually supports the idea that the myth is relatively rare among the peoples of this area.

Berge, François

1951 "Les légendes de Déluge." In *Histoire generale des religions,* vol. 5. Paris: Librairie Aristide Quillet. Pp. 59–101. One of the finest, most scholarly, and succinct surveys of flood material. Includes a substantial treatment of the various interpretations proposed to explain the myth's content (pp. 93–101).

Böklen, Ernst

1903 "Die Sintflutsage: Versuch einer neuen Erklarung." *Archiv für Religionswissenschaft* 6:1–61, 97–150. The author, an advocate of lunar mythological interpretation, applies this theory to the flood myth. For example, the ark is the moon (p. 12); the black raven is the dark of the moon (p. 110); Noah's sons are phases of the moon with Ham being the dark of the moon (p. 140).

Buttmann, Philipp

1828 "Über den Mythos der Sündflut." *Mythologus.* Berlin: In der Mylius'schen Buchhandlung. Pp. 180–214. In this essay, first presented in 1812, the author compares the biblical flood with the classical Greek account of Deucalion among others.

Casalis, Matthieu

1976 "The Dry and the Wet: A Semiological Analysis of Creation and Flood Myths." *Semiotica* 17:35–67. An application of semiotics, including the binary oppositional paradigms of Claude Lévi-Strauss, to the J and P creation accounts in Genesis with special emphasis upon the contrast between dryness and wetness.

Charencey, H. de

1865 "Le Déluge, d'après les traditions indiennes de l'Amerique du Nord." *Revue americane,* 2nd series, 2:88–98, 310–320. One of the earliest serious attempts to review flood myths in the Americas.

Custance, Arthur C.

1979 *The Flood: Local or Global?* Grand Rapids, Mich.: Zondervan Publishing House. 307 pp. Only the first third of this book (pp. 7–105) treats the flood, including "the extent of the flood" and "flood traditions of the world." The author contends that although the flood was universal, mankind was originally confined to a small geographical area and thus it was essentially local—a novel solution to the global-local debate. Aware of the scientific critique of the biblical account of the age of the earth, the author wistfully hopes (pp. 44, 57) for "some little discovery" which will disprove the modern methods of dating the past.

Dalton, W. J.

1957–1958 "The Background and Meaning of the Biblical Flood Narrative." *Australasian Catholic Record* 34:292–304; 35:23–39. A valuable review of the Near Eastern analogues of the flood account in Genesis with a careful comparison of the P and J strands of the latter.

Filby, Frederick A.

1970 *The Flood Reconsidered: A Review of the Evidences of Geology, Archaeology, Ancient Literature, and the Bible.* London: Pickering & Inglis. 148 pp. A good example of a "believer's" attempt to document the historicity of the deluge. After reviewing data from a variety of disciplines, the author concludes (p. 124): "Thus from the first statement about the Flood to the last in the book of Genesis every verse that can be questioned, examined and tried has stood the test. . . . Not one sentence of the Biblical account, carefully interpreted in its context, can be shown to be incorrect or second-hand or even to be unrealistic or unlikely. It is the recorded, reliable account of an eye-witness."

Fischer, Hanns
1925 *Weltwenden: Die grossen Fluten in Sage und Wirklichkeit.* 2nd ed. Leipzig: R. Voigtländers Verlag. 230 pp. A rather extreme example of the literal-historical approach to the flood insofar as a strange admixture of astronomical and geological conjectures is invoked to prove that the flood myth represents a vestigial memory of actual ice-age and earlier catastrophic events. The problem of how humans are supposed to "remember" things that took place during a period when dinosaurs roamed the earth is not seen as an obstacle.

Frazer, James George
1916 "Ancient Stories of a Great Flood." *Journal of the Royal Anthropological Institute* 46:231–283. This Huxley Memorial Lecture for 1916 began an extensive comparative investigation of the flood myth which culminated in Frazer's treatment of the same topic in the first of three volumes of *Folk-Lore in the Old Testament.* In his revision of the 1916 paper, Frazer gives the most comprehensive survey in English of flood myths worldwide. See "The Great Flood" in *Folk-Lore in the Old Testament,* vol. 1 (London: Macmillan, 1918), pp. 104–361. A brief selection from this elaborate essay has been included in this volume.

Gillispie, Charles Coulston
1959 *Genesis and Geology: A Study in the Relations of Scientific Thought, Natural Theology, and Social Opinion in Great Britain, 1790–1850.* New York: Harper & Row, 306 pp. This work, first published in 1951, is a masterful historical overview of the early geologists' attempts to wrestle with the question of the historicity of the biblical flood.

Gittée, Auguste
1899 "Les légendes du Déluge devant l'ethnographie et l'histoire." *Revue de Belgique* 27:250–265, 350–362. A survey of classical, Indic, and "primitive" flood myths.

Hwei, Li
1955 "The Deluge Legend of the Sibling-mating Type in Aboriginal Formosa and Southeast Asia." *Bulletin of the Ethnological Society of China* 1:171–206. A survey in Chinese of some fifty-one flood myths from Southeast Asia and southern China which involve brother–sister incest. Much of the same material is covered in Walk's 1949 essay.

Kamma, Freerk C.
1978 *Religious Texts of the Oral Tradition from Western New-Guinea (Irian Jaya).* Part B, Religious Texts Translation Series NISABA, Vol. 8. Lei-

den: E. J. Brill. 196 pp. Twenty substantial flood myths (pp. 1–86) document the deluge tradition in Western New Guinea.

Lambert, G.

1955 "Il n'y aura plus jamais de Déluge (Genèse IX, 11)." *Nouvelle revue théologique* 77:581–601, 693–724. The first part of this essay consists of a detailed comparison of the P and J flood accounts in Genesis while the second part reviews the Near Eastern cognate myths and archaeological data with respect to their relevance to the Genesis flood.

Lenormant, François

1879 "The Deluge: Its Traditions in Ancient Nations." *Contemporary Review* 36:465–500. One of the most erudite of the earlier comparative surveys of flood myths. The author concludes that "the Biblical Deluge is a real and historical fact" and that it must arise "from the reminiscence of a real and terrible event, so powerfully impressing the imagination of the first ancestors of our race, as never to have been forgotten by their descendants." This event, he argues (p. 500), must have occurred "before the dispersion of the families from which the principal races were to spring."

Lewis, Jack P.

1968 *A Study of the Interpretation of Noah and the Flood in Jewish and Christian Literature.* Leiden: E. J. Brill. 199 pp. A detailed account of apocryphal and postbiblical Jewish and Christian writings on the flood with such chapters as "The Flood in Hellenistic-Jewish Writers" (pp. 42–81); "Early Christian Interpretations of the Flood" (pp. 101–120); and "The Flood and Later Christian Spiritual Exegesis (pp. 156–182).

Montgomery, John Warwick

1974 *The Quest for Noah's Ark.* Minneapolis: Dimension Books. 384 pp. One of the more comprehensive popular accounts of the numerous expeditions during the past several centuries seeking traces of the ark on Mount Ararat. It includes a substantial bibliography (pp. 360–371).

Parrot, André

1955 *The Flood and Noah's Ark.* London: SCM Press. 76 pp. This translation of a 1953 book by a distinguished French archaeologist ably reviews the Near Eastern flood texts and the archaeological data. He considers the flood as a historical event.

Peake, Harold

1930 *The Flood: New Light on an Old Story.* London: Kegan Paul, Trench, Trubner & Co. 124 pp. A survey of the evidence for a Near Eastern flood as a historical occurrence from an archaeological perspective, ending with a chapter on Leonard Woolley's "discoveries" at Ur (pp. 83–112).

Pessoa, Marialice Moura

1950 "The Deluge Myth in the Americas." *Revista do Museu Paulista,* N.S. 4:7–48. This summary essay, written in Portuguese but with accompanying English translation, includes a classification of the principal elements of the deluge story. Based upon texts from North, Central, and South America, these elements include (1) deluge is foretold, (2) causes of the deluge, (3) the physical element that produced the flood, such as rain, tears, blood, urine, and hot liquid, (4) means by which the people were saved from the flood, and (5) people saved.

Rehwinkel, Alfred M.

1951 *The Flood in the Light of the Bible, Geology, and Archaeology.* St. Louis: Concordia Publishing House. 372 pp. The author, who believes that "the flood is the greatest single event in the history of the earth since the days of Creation," argues that it was a "prototype of the Final Judgment, which will make a sudden and fearful end of the second world" (pp. 343, xix).

Riem, Johannes

1925 *Die Sintflut in Sage und Wissenschaft.* Hamburg: Rauhen Haus. 194 pp. This comparative overview, based upon some 303 texts (as opposed to the 88 amassed by Andree in his 1891 study), differs from others in its effort to provide accurate statistical counts of details. Among the 268 reports—as distinguished from 35 allusions to the myth—we find 77 simple floods, 80 instances of inundation, 3 cases of snowfall, 58 examples of excessive rain, etc.

Rooth, Anna Birgitta

1962 *The Raven and the Carcass: An Investigation of a Motif in the Deluge Myth in Europe, Asia, and North America.* FF Communications no. 186. Helsinki: Academia Scientiarum Fennica. 268 pp. A detailed study of the motif of the raven or crow which stops to eat carrion in contrast to the dove who returns with the olive branch. Rooth divides flood myths into fourteen traits: (1) cause of the fall of man, (2) the exception of one man, (3) man's explanation, (4) the size and building of the ship, (5) the loading of the boat, (6) the storm and the deluge, (7) the storm ceases, (8) stranded on a mountain, (9) sending out birds, (10) alighting from the ark, (11) the offerings, (12) the divine promise, the covenant, (13) deification, and (14) criterion of the flood's historicity (remains of the ark are still to be seen or found, for example). Concentrating on trait 9, Rooth concludes that the raven and the carcass motif which occurs in Gilgamesh and in native North America was originally an oriental motif which partly via Greek-Roman and partly via Jewish-Christian tradition spread in medieval Europe. The Amerind occurrences are said (p. 251) to be Christian borrowings presumably introduced by missionaries.

Teeple, Howard M.

1978 *The Noah's Ark Nonsense.* Evanston, Ill.: Religion and Ethics Institute. 156 pp. An eminently readable and informed account of flood myth scholarship arguing that literal belief in the Noachian flood and the purported discovery of an actual ark—as recounted in the film *In Search of Noah's Ark,* for example—does a disservice to enlightened belief in the Bible and Christianity. "If we accept the Flood story as 'true,' then we have a religion with a God who is a mass murderer!" (p. 76).

Usener, Hermann

1899 *Die Sintfluthsagen.* Bonn: Verlag von Friedrich Cohen. 279 pp. A serious attempt to apply the tenets of solar mythology to the flood myth.

1901 "Zu den Sintfluthsagen." *Rheinisches Museum für Philologie* 56: 481–496. A continuation of the solar mythological interpretation of the flood.

Utley, Francis Lee

1960 "Noah, His Wife, and the Devil." In Raphael Patai, Francis Lee Utley, and Dov Noy, eds., *Studies in Biblical and Jewish Folklore.* Bloomington: Indiana University Press. Pp. 59–91. An urbane, humanistic overview of the Noah story's impact on science, the history of ideas, fine arts, folklore, and literature.

Van De Fliert, J. R.

1969 "Fundamentalism and the Fundamentals of Geology." *Journal of the American Scientific Affiliation* 21:69–81. A Dutch geologist with religious convictions writes an intentionally devastating critique of *The Genesis Flood* by Whitcomb and Morris. Opposing Fundamentalism, he concludes (p. 80): "The reliability of the Word of God spoken in this world through His prophets and apostles is beyond the reach of scientific control, because the Bible is not a scientific book. As such, it is not vulnerable to the results of science."

Vitaliano, Dorothy B.

1973 "The Deluge." In *Legends of the Earth: Their Geologic Origins.* Bloomington: Indiana University Press. Pp. 142–178. Flood stories are "recollections—vastly distorted and exaggerated . . . of real local disasters." The author contends "there is not *one* deluge legend, but rather a collection of traditions which are so diverse that they can be explained neither by one general catastrophe alone, nor by the dissemination of one local tradition alone." She concludes: "Flood traditions are nearly universal . . . mainly because floods *in the plural* are the most nearly universal of all geologic catastrophes" (p. 178).

Walk, Leopold

1931 "Die Sintfluttradition der Völker." *Österreichische Leo-Gesellschaft Jahrbuch,* pp. 60–81. A sophisticated and succint review of the major theoretical issues involved in flood myth scholarship.

1949 "Das Flut-Geschwisterpaar als Ur- und Stammelternpaar der Menschheit: Ein Beitrag zur Mythengeschicte Süd- und Südostasiens." Mitteilungen der Österreichischen Gesellschaft für Anthropologie, Ethnologie und Prähistorie 78/79:60–115. A remarkably meticulous and massive assemblage of South and Southeast Asian flood myths involving sibling incest.

Whitcomb, John C., Jr.
1973 *The World That Perished.* Grand Rapids, Mich.: Baker Book House. 155 pp. A sequel to the 1961 work by Whitcomb and Morris seeking to rebut criticisms of that book.

Whitcomb, John C., Jr., and Henry M. Morris
1961 *The Genesis Flood: The Biblical Record and Its Scientific Implications.* Grand Rapids, Mich.: Baker Book House. 518 pp. A professor of Old Testament and a professor of hydraulic engineering teamed up to write a comprehensive but doctrinaire attempt to bring scientific evidence to argue for the historicity of a universal flood.

Winternitz, M.
1901 "Die Flutsagen des Alterthums und der Naturvölker." *Mitteilungen der Anthropologischen Gesellschaft in Wien* 31:305–333. One of the most detailed and influential comparative studies of the flood myth in which some seventy-three versions (many taken from Andree) are broken down into traits such as (1) cause of the flood, (2) the flood, (3) the spread of the flood, (4) the hero of the flood, (5) the rescue, (6) the prophecy, (7) the taking along of the "seed of life" (forms of plant and animal life), (8) the duration of the flood, (9) the end of the flood, and (10) the fate of the hero and mankind after the flood. The author further distinguishes (p. 325) what he terms *very* characteristic features such as the enclosed ark, taking along the seed of life, the sending out of birds, the sacrifice, and the rainbow. These are differentiated from such features as the ethical motive, the rescue of a hero, the prophecy, and the renewal of mankind.

Index

Designer:	Rick Chafian
Compositor:	G&S Typesetters, Inc.
Text:	10/12 Zapf Book Light
Display:	Zapf Book Demi Bold
Printer:	Maple-Vail
Binder:	Maple-Vail

DATE DUE